advanced programmer's

GUIDE

featuring
dBASE III™ and
dBASE II®

Luis Castro, Jay Hanson and Tom Rettig

Editor: Monet Thomson
Managing Editor: Robert Hoffman
Text Editor: Brenda Johnson
Production Manager: Teresa Sullivan
Text Design: Thomas Clark
Cover Design: Laurie Stern

Published by Ashton-Tate
10150 W. Jefferson Blvd.
Culver City, CA 90230

ISBN 0-912677-05-8

The software, computer, and product names mentioned in the *Advanced Programmer's Guide* are manufacturer and publisher trademarks, and are used only for the purpose of identification.

Data and Information
    The Hardware
        - The Central Processing Unit
        - Memory
        - Peripherals
    Computing Speed

    CP/M
    MS-DOS and PC-DOS
    Other Operating Systems

    Machine Language
    Assembly Language
    High-Level Languages
        - Compilers
        - Interpreters
    Procedural vs Nonprocedural Languages
    Applications

    Programming Definition
    Defining the Problem
    Designing a Solution
    Coding
    Writing Documentation
    Testing and Debugging

    Elements of Structured Programming
        - Top Down Design
        - Modular Programming

TABLE OF CONTENTS

To Wayne Ratliff and Jeb Long, who gave it life; in memory of George Tate, who gave it to the world; and to dBASE programmers everywhere, who continue to give it meaning, purpose, and direction.

ACKNOWLEDGEMENTS

Although our names appear on the cover and we wrote most of this book, we couldn't have done it without help from a lot of other people whose names appear below. Their contributions range from several pages of text and code to a simple conversation that sparked an idea. We're very grateful to everyone who freely shared their dBASE experiences and knowledge with us.

ASHTON-TATE CONTRIBUTORS

Software Support Center

Thanks especially to the technicians who picked up the telephone load when we were off doing something else.

The people whose names appear below have each spent time in Software Support. Some have moved on, most are still here, and all have contributed to dBASE and to this guide.

Kevin Armstrong	David McLoughlin
Stanley Ballenger	Kelly Mc Tiernan
Mark Boutilier	Laurie Miller
Betty Carlton	Debby Moody
Steve Crivello	Roy Moore
David Dodson	John Mortensen
Robert Doolittle	Brett Oliver
Bert Durant	Joe Pitz
Mike Fiore	Karen Robinson
Dale Foord	Jon Rognerud
Tom Gallant	Kevin Shepherd
John Gillen	Steve Silverwood
Kent Irwin	Joe Stegman
Errol Jackson	Gary Stucker
Rosaline Keenan	Nelson Tso
Steve Kurasch	Jim Warner
Perry Lawrence	Ron Watson
Tim Lebel	Chris White
Ray Love	

Other Departments

Our sincerest appreciation to:

- All the programmers in the Development Center who take time to answer our occasionally inane questions, particularly Jordan Brown, whose technical editing greatly contributed to the accuracy and completeness of this document.
- Everyone in Publications who made it real, especially Bill Jordan for his patience and for believing in us; Monet Thomson, whose style editing both preserved the accuracy and enhanced the quality of our manuscript; and Robert Hoffman for skillfully handling three authors with very different working styles.
- The enthusiastic team in Sales, especially Pat Cairns, for all those words of encouragement about how well this book is going to do if we ever get it done.
- Marketing Communications for permission to reprint material from dNEWS.

This book is richer for these contributions:

- Alastair Dallas in Product Development for dBASE III trigonometric functions in Trig.prg in appendix C.
- Mark Kevitt in Training for the "Curriculum for Educators."
- Virginia Lyons in Documentation for excerpts from an article on screen design used in chapter 18.
- Bob "Softlaw" Kohn, Esq. in Legal for the epopoean and pellucid notice on the copyright page.

OUTSIDE CONTRIBUTORS

This guide would be quite different, and not as complete, without the input from a number of dBASE programmers and consultants outside of Ashton-Tate. Their contributions have helped make this the dBASE book we all wanted.

Name	Company	Location
Kenneth Agle		Menlo Park, California
Merrill Anderson	Computer Software Consultants	Alpha, Ohio
Peter Backus	Software Solutions, Inc.	Honolulu, Hawaii
Robert A. Byers		La Crescenta, California
Michael H. Campbell	Savage & Campbell Associates	Chicago, Illinois
Brian Cleverly	Anzam Software D.P.	Sacramento, California
Richard Davidson		Chatsworth, California
Howard Dickler		Santa Monica, California
Jeri L. Frasier	Origin, Inc.	Richardson, Texas
Clyde H. Freeman		Bowie, Maryland
Ralph E. Freshour		Redondo Beach, California
Kelly J. Grant	Science Applications, Inc.	La Jolla, California
Dave Green	Micro Programming	Seattle, Washington
Michael A. Grumboski	U.S. Business Computing, Inc.	Southfield, Missouri
Gene Head		Corvallis, Oregon
Rennaye Johnson	J.E. Enterprises	Denver, Colorado
Pierre Kerr	Treasury Board of Canada	Ottawa, Ontario, Canada
Hugh LaRiviere, Ph.D.	Tekonomie, Inc.	Brossard, Quebec, Canada
Bob Larzelere		San Francisco, California

Name	Company	Location
Richard S. Locus		Eugene, Oregon
Shahab Manavi	Compute A Car	Los Angeles, California
Steve Manes	Roxy Recorders	New York, New York
Stephen Montgomery		Chicago, Illinois
Steven L. Nelson	Nelson Radio Communications	Farmington, Minnesota
Patrick Ontko	Longridge Computer	Los Gatos, California
Charles C. Pace		Buda, Texas
James T. Perry, Ph.D.	San Diego State University	San Diego, California
Russ Schomig	Midland Pipe and Supply Company	Cicero, Illinois
Lila Self	Data Application Research Technology	Mesa, Arizona
John W. Sheetz	The Applications Group, Inc.	Belmont, Massachusetts
Bob Simpson	Infosoft	Baltimore, Maryland
Keith B. Smith	A.W. Champion, Ltd.	Surrey, England
Jack Smothers	Libby Laboratories, Inc.	Berkeley, California
Brad Stark	Peoplesmith	N. Scituate, Massachusetts
Raymond Weisling		Solo, Jawa Tengah, Indonesia
Hal Wyman		Seattle, Washington
David Zarder	"1d" Software Development	Stevens Point, Wisconsin

AUTHORS' PERSONAL SUPPORT

When the writing got tough, and we didn't know whether we'd ever finish, knowing we had their unconditional support helped us keep going.

Luis: My parents, who taught me enthusiasm and diligence, and professors John Motil and Dr. Gerald Smith, who gave me an abundance of computer science knowledge and personal attention.

Jay: My parents, who pointed me in the right direction and gave me freedom to learn for myself, and my wife, Janet, who corrected many drafts and kept the tea and cookies flowing late at night.

Tom: My sons, Tom and Deane, who believed in me when I was down; my buddy, Lynne Bertram, who taught me the meaning of support; and my friend, Harry Knobel, who turned me on to dBASE.

FOREWORD

The best description of *Advanced Programmer's Guide* by Messrs. Castro, Hanson, and Rettig is a "collection of wisdom in the area of dBASE programming." The authors have worked for years as technical support for Ashton-Tate and have answered innumerable questions and solved hosts of problems from dBASE users. This is an extraordinarily difficult job since callers are generally anxious and afraid that they won't get an answer to their problems. The technical support staff must not only understand the workings of the dBASE program, but must also be part psychologist as well as expert communicators in order to solve human and computer problems over the phone. These talents coupled with years of experience have enabled the authors to set down a book that answers the needs of people who have basically learned dBASE but now have questions that are increasingly subjective, like "What is the best way to design a dBASE program?"

There are a number of fine books on the care and feeding of dBASE and users of dBASE. Most of these focus on the new dBASE user (and frequently on people who are relatively new to computers). This class of books is extremely important and necessary, since the average computer user today probably has less than a year or two of computer experience. This book, however, is intended for people who are comfortable with dBASE and with computers and want to advance to the next phase, people who want a deeper understanding of what they have been doing all along, or people whose needs and questions are not answered in the dBASE documentation.

The authors of this book have carefully laid out a methodology that will yield quality programs (reliable, robust, maintainable, and well documented). They cover system design, program design and implementation, documentation, testing, and database design. In each of these areas they explain techniques that yield success. For example, they emphasize thinking out a system before starting the coding. They explain the concept of coupling between the program modules of a system as well as the pitfalls of excessive coupling. They describe the rules for designing a database and decomposing it into distinct database files in such a way as to allow the maximum utilization of the data itself. They discuss the benefits of building a library of useful program modules. My only caution in the use of this book is that one should be rather experienced and careful before attempting the assembly language subroutines in appendix D.

In a time when it is fashionable to show disdain for programming because of its difficulty, the authors have presented a "divide and conquer" approach that will let new programmers write magnificent programs.

C. Wayne Ratliff

PREFACE

The *Advanced Programmer's Guide* is neither a tutorial nor a book for the beginning dBASE user. It is intended for people who have already achieved a basic level of competence in working with dBASE III or dBASE II and are now interested in programming. It is for people who aspire to the level of "advanced" programmer, regardless of their current programming skill level. Whether you teach programming, are just learning, or simply want to implement your own dBASE application, you will find the *Advanced Programmer's Guide* comprehensive, understandable, and easy to use.

The *Advanced Programmer's Guide* is a joint project of the technicians, programmers, analysts, and consultants in Ashton-Tate's Software Support Center. Handling hundreds of dBASE calls and letters daily since 1981, the Support Center has become *the* clearinghouse for technical information about dBASE. For those of us who are fortunate enough to work here, the Support Center provides the richest dBASE learning environment anywhere, and has molded some top-notch programmers. This guide represents the current state of our knowledge, abilities, and experiences with dBASE. The purpose of this guide is to communicate what we have learned and to provide the most accurate, complete, and useful programming book available on dBASE.

The material in this guide was born of methods that have stood the test of time, brief though that test may be for a language as young as dBASE. When a method worked better than one we were using, it was adopted and remained in place until a better one came along. Many of these approaches have come to us from people outside of Ashton-Tate, many were developed here, and all have evolved through repeated testing in the toughest of situations.

The techniques discussed herein are those of the authors and contributors, and do not necessarily represent methods and features officially supported by Ashton-Tate. Every effort has been made to ensure the reliability of these contents, but we must disclaim them completely in order to keep the shirts on our backs. So, here is a book of programs which is guaranteed to do nothing but keep you busy. If you have problems with anything in this book, write us a descriptive letter and we'll be happy to help if we can (they don't call us the Support Center for nothing).

If you have not already done so, please put aside any feeling that "real programmers don't read documentation," and read "How To Use This Guide" on page one.

HOW TO USE THIS GUIDE

The main body of the *Advanced Programmer's Guide* is in three sections:

    I.   Fundamentals (basic working knowledge)
   II.   System Design (purpose and planning)
 III.   Implementation (hands-on actualizing)

Each section covers a particular subject in as much depth as is appropriate to that section. Sections are designed to be read individually, and to be used together. For example, when covering unfamiliar territory in the Design section, referring to the same subject area in Fundamentals can assist your understanding. When working in the Implementation section, refer to both Fundamentals and Design. A bibliography appears at the end of each chapter where applicable.

Fundamentals

The Fundamentals section defines key concepts and describes most of the common hardware configurations and operating systems with which dBASE is used. It is desirable to have a complete understanding of fundamental concepts before moving on to more advanced material. However, in the real world, people without this education are writing their own complex applications in easy-to-learn dBASE. This section has been included to provide a foundation for those who do not already have one.

System Design

The System Design section presents the key concepts needed to design a database-application system. The topics include: the design of information flow through the system; the design of the database; the design of the documentation for the system; and security, recovery, and backup procedures. The purpose of mastering these concepts is to decrease the amount of time needed to develop a system, and to increase its efficiency and reliability.

Implementation

The Implementation section is divided into functional groups in the same way that a programmer looks at implementing an application in dBASE. Each functional group, or "process," is either a separate chapter or subchapter. Chapters and subchapters have the structure: details, vocabulary, and algorithms.

Details. A description of the process and how to implement it in dBASE.

Vocabulary. The dBASE language used to implement the process. Language components are listed in this order:

Operators
Functions
SET Parameters
Commands
Other Resources (macro, delimiters, and so on)

The structure of each language component is:

Specific command line syntax (except functions)
Availability in dBASE III, dBASE II, or both
Use, or purpose

Command syntax is almost completely void of square bracketed [optional] items. Most commands are listed separately by their specific syntax, rather than by the command *format* as it appears in the dBASE manuals. Because functions can be used in such a variety of syntactic situations, they appear alone with the syntax of their argument rather than in actual command-line syntax.

Algorithms. The techniques used to solve particular situations that occur in the implementation of a specific process. These are useful examples. Don't hesitate to try new ways as they occur to you. Running, or "executing," the code is the *only* way to really know if an idea will work.

Definitions

With any technical subject, it is necessary to understand the special terms comprising its nomenclature in order to understand the subject itself. Therefore, we define most key terms in the text as they are introduced. If you encounter a word that is new to you, take time to study its definition. It often helps to make up a few sentences using the word until you fully grasp the concept. This investment will pay off, because your ultimate grasp of any subject is based upon your understanding the words describing the concepts and actions of the subject. We encourage you to use a dictionary and the Glossary whenever a passage seems confusing or "fuzzy." This fuzziness nearly always traces back to a word or several words that were not fully understood, and will clear up when the words are defined.

Most jargon, or "computerese," is in the Glossary. Metalanguage variables, or "metavariables," are self-descriptive substitutes for actual items that you will choose. For example, the metavariable <command filename> is replaced in the command line syntax with the literal name of a command file. Where a metavariable is not self-descriptive, such as <database parameter>, it is defined the first time it is used and again in appendix E.

We refer to "mode" in a couple of contexts: command execution and terminal input/output (I/O). Within each of these contexts, any situation in which the operator can enter anything from the keyboard is considered an interactive mode because the operator is interacting with the computer.

There are two modes of command execution:

1. Command-file or program mode. Commands are executed from a file.
2. Dot-prompt or interactive mode. Commands are entered by the operator from the keyboard.

The dBASE interpreter does not distinguish between these modes. Any command will operate in the same way when entered from the keyboard or from a command file *if all the surrounding conditions are identical.*

There are two modes of terminal (screen) output:

1. Unformatted. The output begins at the current cursor position.
2. Formatted. The output is placed where the programmer specifies.

There are two modes of terminal (keyboard) input, both interactive:

1. Command-line. The operator is restricted to one command line or less of input, and cannot move around on the screen. Similar to entry from the dot prompt.
2. Full-screen. The operator is placed where the programmer specifies. However, the operator can move around from place to place on the screen and in the file unless restricted by the programmer.

Symbols and conventions are used throughout this book. Some are the same as those in the dBASE manuals, and others reflect programming standards which have come from other languages. The conventions we use are:

Symbol	Name	Use
*	Asterisk	Indicates a comment line in dBASE code.
::=	Definition	Indicates a definition or explanation of a metavariable or language component. For example: * ::= comment. Pronounced "is defined to be."
...	Ellipsis	Indicates missing related components. For example: DO WHILE...ENDDO. Used at the end of comment lines to indicate that they refer to the code that follows.
;	Semicolon	Used at the end of a dBASE command line to indicate that it is continued on the next line.
< >	Angle Brackets	Used in command syntax to describe items that are to be filled in by the programmer. These are called metavariables. For example: <command filename>.
[ ]	Square Brackets	Used in command syntax to enclose parameters that are optional. For example: LIST [TO PRINT]. Used in code to delimit literal character strings the same way matching single (') and double (") quotation marks are used.
{ }	Meta Brackets or "Braces"	Used to enclose items in command syntax that optionally may be repeated. For example: SET INDEX TO <filename> { , <filename>} The allowable number of repetitions are mentioned in the associated text.
|	Bar	Used to separate optional items where one *or* another must be used. For example: <switch> ::= ON | OFF. Pronounced "or."
^	Circumflex	Used in text to indicate a "control" character or key. For example, ^S ::= Ctrl-S. Used in code to indicate an exponent. For example, 3^2 ::= three raised to a power of two (which equals nine).
K	Kilobyte	Represents a unit of 1,024 bytes.

Just as a musician must be able to "say it before she or he can play it," the programmer should learn the correct pronounciation of operators, functions, and symbols in order to be able to speak the code aloud.

Latest Versions

Obviously, new versions of dBASE are likely to keep coming. We plan to revise this guide when appropriate, but there may be a period of time when there are versions of dBASE on the market that are not covered herein. The versions covered in this edition are:

dBASE II: 2.3, 2.3A, 2.3B, 2.3D, 2.4, 2.41, 2.42
dBASE III: 1.00

Note: In II, 2.42 is the international version of 2.41. The difference is that 2.42 has sixteen digits of numeric accuracy instead of ten. This slows it down a bit during most operations.

We refer to groups of versions with an "x" after the version number. For example, 2.4x refers to all versions of 2.4 (which are 2.4, 2.41, and 2.42 at the time of this writing). Other versions which have had extremely limited exposure and are not covered are 2.02, 2.3C, and 2.4E. 2.02 was a very early release which was replaced by 2.3, the first widespread distribution of dBASE II. 2.3C was intended to replace 2.3B, but was withdrawn from distribution almost immediately. 2.4E could be called dBASE II and a half. Developed for AT&T's UNIX environment, 2.4E is the predecessor of dBASE III.

Programs Available on Disk

The programs, subroutines, and longer algorithms in this book are available in source code on disk in two formats only:

1. IBM, 5-1/4 inch, PC-DOS, 8 sector, double-sided. One disk.
2. IBM 3740, Standard 8 inch, CP/M-80, single sided, 128 bytes per sector. Two disks.

Other formats are not available from us. However, your computer dealer or manufacturer should be able to suggest where you can have one of these popular formats copied to theirs. These disks are *not* copy-protected in any way. (Please see the title page for information about what you may and may not do with the disk).

There is nothing on the disk that is not in this book. We make it available only as a convenience for programmers who do not want to key in these routines themselves. To order, send $25.00 in U.S. funds along with your name, address, and desired format to:

Advanced Programmer's Disk
Ashton-Tate Software Support Center
10150 W. Jefferson Boulevard
Culver City, California, 90230
USA

$25.00 includes sales tax and first-class postage in the U.S. and Canada. Orders from other countries are $35.00 and are sent via international air (customs or import charges are not included and may have to be paid on receipt). VISA and MasterCard are accepted (include card type, account number, expiration date, and signature). Orders paid by personal or business check are not sent until the check clears (make payable to Software Support Center). Please print clearly.

Your Feedback

This Guide was made possible by our communication with dBASE programmers like yourself. If you would like to contribute to future editions with your feedback on this edition and/or with algorithms, programs, work-arounds, or whatever, please write us. We do not pay for contributions because we could not possibly pay what they're worth. However, appropriate acknowledgement is always given. For submissions longer than a few lines of code and text, we appreciate a disk (any format) as well as hard copy. All submissions *must* include source code and will not be returned. Please direct your correspondence to the authors at:

Ashton-Tate Software Support Center
10150 West Jefferson Boulevard
Culver City, California 90230
USA

```
* REMEMBER.PRG
* Sometimes we forget...
*
USE Yourself
SET TALK OFF
CLEAR
*
DO WHILE Alive
    STORE "love" TO heart
    STORE "health" TO body
    STORE "peace" TO mind
    STORE "compassion" TO others
    STORE "esteem" TO self
    STORE "trust" TO humanity
    STORE "faith" TO God
    REPLACE Negative WITH Positive,;
            Judgment WITH Acceptance,;
            Resentment WITH Forgiveness
    REPLACE Hopelessness WITH Choice,;
            Confusion WITH Clarity,;
            Procrastination WITH Participation
    REPLACE Separation WITH Connection,;
            Lack WITH Abundance,;
            Sorrow WITH Celebration
    @ all, times SAY your_truth
    IF its_time
        EXIT
    ENDIF
ENDDO
*
SAVE TO Always
CLEAR ALL
RETURN
*
* EOF: Remember.prg
```

SECTION ONE

FUNDAMENTALS

CHAPTER ONE

FUNDAMENTAL CONCEPTS

Y ou may be wondering why we have included a section on fundamentals in an advanced programmer's guide. There are several reasons for this. First, it is necessary to have a complete understanding of fundamental concepts before moving on to more advanced topics. This section on fundamentals defines key concepts and describes the common hardware configurations and operating systems with which dBASE is used. We want to provide at least an overview of these concepts so that the material is available for those who may not have studied the areas before or feel they could use a review of these topics.

dBASE is easy to learn and even a novice can begin writing dBASE programs in short order. However, to successfully design and write larger programs or systems requires a knowledge of programming techniques and data structures. In "Fundamental Concepts" we present information which will be useful to a dBASE programmer writing small programs or larger systems. The topics covered are broad, and we present those points that are most applicable to programming with dBASE on a microcomputer. Since it is impossible to cover each of the topics comprehensively in this book, a list of recommended references is provided at the end of each chapter. In addition, in the back of the book, there is a glossary which defines many technical terms.

DATA AND INFORMATION

A ll digital computers, whether large or small, operate on the same fundamental principles. You might think that the hardware and software of an IBM mainframe would be quite different than that found in the IBM personal computer that sits on your desk. However, in both systems the same component parts are present and fulfill the basic functions necessary to any computer system.

Though personal computers have a relatively brief history, in a short span of time they have advanced rapidly. These small computers are currently capable of executing sophisticated computing tasks which, until recently, required machines costing millions of dollars and filling entire rooms. As the personal computer has evolved, numerous different hardware designs have been developed. In addition to variations in hardware, many operating systems and languages have become available for small computers. The working environment any computer system provides is determined by its hardware and operating system. This section defines some basic concepts and describes the most common types of hardware and operating systems available in the personal computer marketplace at the time of this writing.

A computer is an information or data processing system. By this we mean that a computer accepts information or data (input), performs a set of operations on the data (processes the data), and then presents you with the results (output). *Data* is defined in computer science as *the symbols used to represent information to be processed by the computer*. Data is a collection of symbols or information which is put into a computer. The fact that data is recognized by a computer does not necessarily mean it will contain meaning for people. It could be a set of apparently random numbers which have no meaning, or a phone number

that would be understandable. It could be a string of words which may or may not make sense. In contrast to data, *information* is defined as *knowledge, especially as it provides people with new facts about the real world.*[1] In other words, information is comprehensible by people and contains meaning, whereas data *may or may not* make sense when read. Some examples of data and information are given below.

Data	**Information**
0E1FC90834FF	Joe's Phone #: 456-8765
jfhd870i jfkdk	Turn right at the stop sign.
hello world	PI = 3.1416

The purpose of a computer system, when used for data processing, is to provide us with *useful information* to help increase our understanding of things and phenomena. When viewed in this way, the computer can be seen to be a powerful tool enabling us to expand the horizons of our knowledge. It allows us to process large volumes of data or complex patterns of information that would otherwise be difficult to organize and understand. In addition, it allows us to easily manipulate or "play" with the data in order to look at it in different ways and make it more meaningful. dBASE is particularly useful for manipulating data. Of course a computer can also be used for other purposes, such as playing games, controlling machines, or sending and receiving information through communication devices.

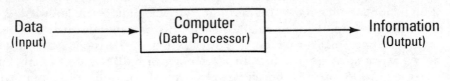

Figure 1-1
Processing information

When writing software, it is important to decide what the inputs are and what outputs are desired. Properly understanding and selecting the inputs and outputs of a system will avoid much trouble in data processing systems.

DATA REPRESENTATION

All digital computers represent data in binary digits. These are usually called bits, since the word "bit" is a contraction of "BInary digiT." A bit is the smallest unit of information a digital computer recognizes. It is always in one of two states, commonly represented as 1 or 0, on or off, or true or false. These representations are just different symbols used to describe the same concept. The bit can be represented by any bistable device, that is, any device that can occupy one of two states. A light switch is an example: it is either on or off. Any device that can be "on" or "off" can create a signal representing a zero in one state and a one in the other state. While information can be stored and manipulated at the bit level, it is more common to use a slightly larger unit, the byte, to represent information. A byte is composed of eight bits. Two hundred and fifty-six different combinations can be represented by these eight bits (two raised to the eighth power is 256).

There have been different standards adopted for character representation, but the one that is universally used for personal computers is ASCII (American Standard Code for Information Interchange, pronounced "ass-key"). Using this method, all commonly used symbols, including the alphabet and numbers, can be represented. Figure 1-2 shows how some letters and numbers are represented by different combinations of bits in the standard ASCII format. Included are the decimal (base 10) and hexadecimal (base 16) values for the ASCII codes as well as the binary values. A complete ASCII table can be found in appendix E.

ASCII Character	Decimal	Hexadecimal	Binary
A	65	41	10000001
B	66	42	10000010
C	67	43	10000011
0	48	30	00110000
1	49	31	00110001
2	50	32	00110010
?	63	3F	00111111
=	61	3D	00111101

Figure 1-2
Some examples of ASCII values

THE HARDWARE

A computer system is made up of several hardware components. These can be conveniently thought of in terms of the function they perform in the system and how they interact with the other components. The principle elements of a computer system are:

- Central Processing Unit (CPU)
- Main Memory (RAM)
- Secondary Storage Devices (disk drives, magnetic tape, etc.)
- Input/Output Devices (terminals, printers, etc.)

A more comprehensive description of these components follows in the text, but for now, briefly:

The CPU does the actual computing. It is capable of simple arithmetic and logical operations such as addition and data comparison, which it carries out at exceedingly high speed. The power of a computer stems directly from the speed and accuracy with which the CPU can carry out computations and move information around. The main memory in a computer system is usually referred to as *Random Access Memory* or *RAM*. This part of the computer contains the programs and information that are currently being processed by the CPU. Secondary storage devices such as magnetic disks, magnetic tapes, and optical disks are capable of reliably holding large amounts of data. Programs and data are normally stored on these secondary devices until needed. They are then loaded into main memory and executed. The results of the processing can then be written onto the secondary storage device or sent to an output device such as a display terminal or printer. Peripheral devices or Input/Output (I/O) devices allow people either to put data into a computer or to receive output from a computer. A terminal is a peripheral which contains both a keyboard for input and a video monitor for output. Other peripherals include printers and plotters (used to draw graphs and diagrams). Figure 1-3 shows a diagram of the key components in a personal computer.

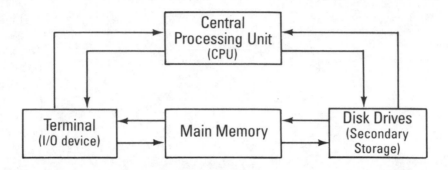

Figure 1-3
Functional diagram of a computer system

THE CENTRAL PROCESSING UNIT

All computers must have at least one central processing unit, or CPU. The CPU in a microcomputer is typically packaged with two rows of pins, called a Dual Inline Package, or DIP. It is housed in a rugged container approximately two inches long, one inch wide, and one eighth of an inch thick. It directs and handles all actual data manipulations within the computer. It can perform simple arithmetic and logical operations such as addition, subtraction, and data comparison.

The information residing in a computer system can be divided into two categories: programs (instructions) and data. Instructions which direct the activity of the CPU are stored in memory along with the data that is to be processed by the CPU. A *program* consists of a set of related instructions which are designed to accomplish some task. The instructions are placed in a logical order so that when the CPU reads them, they result in a sequence of processing actions designed to produce the intended result. Any information that is not composed of CPU instructions is classified as *data*. Data has no direct effect on the operation of the CPU; it is what is processed by the computer.

Each CPU has a unique set of instructions which it recognizes as valid, usually referred to as the *instruction set* of the processor. Each operation the CPU can perform corresponds to a unique code known as an *operation code* or *instruction code*. For the Intel 8080 CPU, an 8 bit processor, these codes are one byte (eight bits) in length, which yields 256 possible instruction codes.

Since the memory also contains the data to be processed, the data and instructions must be organized so that the CPU does not read data and mistake it for an operation code. Normally, memory is partitioned into separate areas for data and code so that these two types of information remain distinct. The CPU can access the data in memory very rapidly, but if the memory is not large enough to contain all the data needed for a particular application, the data must be read into memory from a secondary storage device such as a disk before it can be processed by the CPU. When you see the light on your disk drive activate, it means that information is being written to or read from the disk.

A CPU typically contains the following functional elements: registers, an arithmetic and logic unit (ALU), and a control unit (CU).

Registers

Registers are temporary storage locations within the CPU where data fetched from memory can be held. There is often a special register called the *Accumulator* containing the results of operations the CPU has executed. For example, the result of adding two numbers together would be stored in the accumulator. Another register, the *Instruction Register*, stores the CPU instruction to be executed.

The instructions that make up a program reside in memory. Each location in memory is numbered with a unique *address* which distinguishes it from all other memory locations. These addresses are similar to the unique addresses used to number houses on a street. In a simple case, the program is stored in sequential memory locations.

The *Program Counter (PC)* is a CPU register containing the address of the next instruction to be executed. When the program begins, the program counter contains the address of the first instruction. The CPU then fetchs the first instruction from memory and places it into the instruction register. It updates the program counter by incrementing it (by one or more) so that it now contains the address of the second instruction to be performed. The first instruction is decoded and executed, then the second instruction is fetched from memory to the instruction register. This process continues until all the processing instructions in the program have been executed.

The Arithmetic and Logic Unit (ALU)

The arithmetic and logic unit is usually referred to as the ALU. It contains the necessary internally coded logic and circuitry to perform binary addition. From this basic capability, routines can be constructed to perform subtraction, multiplication, and division. ALUs also provide functions such as logical operations, data comparisons, and bit shifting capabilities. All actual data manipulations are handled by the ALU.

The Control Unit (CU)

The control unit (CU) is that part of the CPU responsible for decoding the contents of the instruction register. The bit pattern (instruction) in the instruction register results in the CU sending appropriate control signals to accomplish the correct processing action. The CU sends the proper data through the ALU logic modules, using the clock inputs to ensure proper timing and synchronization. The CU also responds to external signals requesting the CPU to interrupt its processing and/or wait for some external event to complete before it continues processing.

MEMORY

The main memory in a computer is called random access memory, or RAM. Random accessibility means that each individual bit in the entire memory space is immediately accessible. RAM is also known as read/write memory. It can be considered to be a set of temporary storage locations in which data can be written, stored, and then read back again. This type of memory is like a blank page; whatever you write on it can be read back again at a later time.

In order for a program to run, it must be loaded from the disk into main memory and then executed. When the power is turned off or interrupted, the information in memory is lost. Thus, this type of storage is termed "volatile." If the power disappears, so does the information. Another type of storage, called "non-volatile," does not depend on a continuous source of power to maintain information.

ROM (Read Only Memory) is an example of non-volatile storage. Once information has been written to a ROM, it will remain recorded, independent of any external power source. This type of memory has a predetermined set of information written to it which can only be read. A ROM is not designed to be written

to; it has been filled with data or programs which remain embedded and unchangeable. These programs are usually key control programs necessary to the operation of the computer and are called upon to do such things as boot the system, execute system diagnostics, send data to the monitor, or control disk drives.

Another type of non-volatile storage is *bubble memory*. This is a type of read/write memory. It has one key advantage over others: it doesn't require a power source to maintain the information it stores. Bubble memory stores data as moveable magnetic zones, or "domains." These domains resemble tiny bubbles when viewed with a microscope and so became known as *bubbles*. The domains move about under the influence of an external magnetic field and exist on a thin film of magnetic material which is divided into microscopically small magnets.[2] There is no mechanical movement; only the magnetic field is moving. Because of its nonmechanical nature, bubble memory is very reliable compared to mechanical storage media such as floppy disks. Bubble memory is still relatively expensive compared to other types of storage, and so is not widely used at the time of this writing. However, as its price comes down, its popularity will increase due to its non-volatility and reliablity.

The performance and capability of a computer system is always influenced by the size of its main memory. Since programs and data must be loaded into memory before they can be processed, a larger memory space allows more programs or data to be loaded and processed at a single time. Machines with smaller memories will be slower at processing large amounts of data or running large programs, simply because they require the data or programs to be loaded in smaller pieces before processing.

The maximum memory size that can be effectively used is determined by the characteristics of the CPU in the system. Eight-bit CPUs can typically "address" 64K (65,536 bytes or characters) of memory. The most common family of 16-bit CPUs currently used in personal computers is the Intel 8086 family. This includes the 8088 used in the IBM PC, and 8086 CPUs. These CPUs can address up to one megabyte (1,048,576 bytes) of memory. To give you an idea of how big a megabyte is, if each memory location in the computer was represented by a one-inch-square postage stamp, lining up a megabyte's worth would stretch more than sixteen miles.

PERIPHERALS

The word peripheral comes from the Greek "*peripherein*—to carry around." A peripheral is any external device which attaches to the main computer. Examples are disk drives, terminals, printers, or modems.

Disk Drives

Flexible Disks.   The most common type of disk drive used in personal computers today is the flexible, or "floppy," disk. These disks come in three sizes: 8 inch, 5 1/4 inch, or 3 1/2 inch. They are thin circular plastic sheets coated with iron oxide so that they can retain the magnetic patterns recorded on them. The surface is similar to magnetic tape used to record music. The disk is contained in a square cardboard envelope in which it spins. The 3 1/2 inch disks, which have recently become popular, are contained in a hard plastic case with a metal shutter to protect the disk. A floppy disk can store from 80 kilobytes (one kilobyte = 1024 bytes) to 1.2 megabytes of data. This wide range in capacity is due to different methods of recording the data onto the disk. Floppy disk systems are slower and have less storage capacity than hard disk systems, but their lower cost makes them a popular choice for personal computers.

Hard Disks.   A hard disk is made of metal, and can either be removable or non-removable. The most common type of hard disk found in personal computers today is non-removable. These disks typically hold from five to 150 megabytes of information. Each megabyte is equivalent to 1,048,576 characters of information, or roughly 300 single-spaced typewritten pages. You can see that this is a very efficient way to store large volumes of information. An example of a computer with a built-in nonremovable hard disk is the IBM XT personal computer. It contains one drive for flexible disks and one 10 megabyte hard disk. A hard disk spins at approximately 3,600 revolutions per minute, whereas a floppy disk rotates at only 320 RPM. This enables hard disk systems to read and write data many times faster than floppy systems. The removable hard disk functions similarly to a nonremovable disk except that it can be taken out of the computer. Many removable hard disk systems also contain a nonremovable disk. This allows you to run programs on the fixed disk and also make a backup copy of the information onto the removable disk to store in a secure place.

Data safety is a very important issue when you are considering disk systems that hold large amounts of valuable data. Many people have learned this lesson the hard way. Only after their disk crashes and the information on it is lost do they realize that they should have made a backup copy of the data. A *backup copy* is a copy of the original data, often on magnetic tape or floppy disk, which serves as a "safety copy" in case the original data is lost or damaged. If you are designing a system which will be handling large volumes of important data, be sure to consider how you will back up the data.

How Data is Organized on Disks

In order to read and write data efficiently onto a disk, a coordinate system (similar to a grid on a map) must be generated on the disk so that locations can be easily referenced. The pattern used to create this "grid" is composed of *tracks* and *sectors*. Tracks are concentric rings which are numbered from the outer edge of the recording surface inward. The number of tracks ranges from forty tracks (on low capacity 5 1/4 inch floppy disks) to several hundred tracks on hard disk systems. Sectors are wedge-shaped slices which can vary from eight to fifty in number, depending on the format being used. Each block of data can be located by specifying its track and sector identification code. This code is recorded on the disk in a specific pattern.

A *soft sectored* format occurs when the sector pattern is determined by software and can vary from machine to machine. When a disk is manufactured, it contains neither track nor sector identification codes. These must be recorded onto the disk before it can be used. The process of *initializing* or *formatting* a disk involves writing a specific sector format onto the disk. Formatting a disk uses up some of the disk surface for sector identification codes, so a disk that has been formatted will have less space available for data storage.

Some floppy disks use a separate index hole to identify the location of each sector instead of writing a software pattern. Light passing through each hole triggers a photo sensor as the disk spins. With this method, sectoring is determined by the hardware. Formats which use this method are called *hard sectored* formats. The sectoring is "hard," that is, cannot be changed.

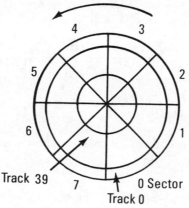

Figure 1-4
Tracks and sectors on a floppy disk

Monitors and Terminals

A monitor is the screen or video display peripheral which is the main output device on a personal computer. It is used to display text and graphics information and is available in a variety of sizes and types. When it is combined with a keyboard used for data input, it is called a *video terminal*.

Monitors can be divided into two broad groups: those designed to display text information and those designed to display graphics information, such as charts or pictures. Within the graphics group, there are color or monochrome (single color) displays. A high-quality graphics monochrome display is capable of showing a considerable range of high resolution patterns and may be quite satisfactory for purposes that do not require color. This type of display can be found in the Apple Macintosh and Lisa computers.

Monitors can vary widely in price and quality and should be chosen to match the particular purpose for which they will be used. If you will be doing primarily text processing and have no real need for graphics capability, we recommend a high-quality monochrome character display system. This provides crisp, easy to read characters that minimize eye fatigue. Green or amber displays are usually considered to be easier on the eyes than white. The IBM PC monochrome system is an example of such a high resolution character display.

One convention used to allow software control of characters on a video screen is to establish a set of "control codes" which allow a programmer to control the display. These are specific codes used to clear the screen, position the cursor at a given row and column, turn video attributes (special visual effects) on or off, and perform other display operations. For example, the Televideo 925, a common terminal, uses the following terminal codes to clear the screen and position the cursor (values are in decimal):

Clear the Screen:	27,42
Position cursor at Row,Column:	27,61,R+32,C+32

The "32" in the cursor positioning sequence is called the *offset*. This means that thirty-two is added to the row and column position before the coordinates are sent to the screen. Thirty-two is a common value for cursor offset, though other values are also used and some terminals use no offset. The hardware manual for your terminal should contain a table of its video codes. Using the CHR() function, dBASE can send any decimal code within the range 0-255 to most video screens. This allows you to directly control the screen from dBASE using appropriate control codes. For example, to perform the display operations of clearing the screen and saying "Hi," beginning at a location ten rows from the top and five columns from the left, the following sequence could be used:

```
* Clear the screen
?? CHR(27)+CHR(42)
* Position the cursor at 10,5 and output "H" then "i"
?? CHR(27)+CHR(61)+CHR(32+10)+CHR(32+5)+CHR(72)+CHR(105)
|-----------------------------------| |-----| |------|

        position cursor at 10,5              "H"      "i"
```

Of course, if you have installed your copy of dBASE to match your terminal's characteristics, it is easier to say:

```
ERASE
@ 10,5 SAY "Hi"
```

In dBASE II, the command to clear the screen is ERASE. In dBASE III, the command is CLEAR. The @ <coordinates> SAY command displays the characters in quotes at specified coordinates. This is a handy way to display messages wherever you want on the screen. The purpose of the dBASE INSTALL program is to provide dBASE with the proper terminal codes so that it will know which codes are used to send information to the screen. If dBASE is not displaying information properly, chances are that it has not been installed correctly for that terminal.

Another common method of displaying information on a screen is called "memory mapping." Memory mapped video uses a section of RAM (read/write memory) to store the information displayed on the screen. RAM used for this purpose is often called video RAM. The screen mimics whatever information currently exists in that portion of memory. To send information to the screen, simply write it to the correct memory locations. This allows the CPU to change the image on the screen by writing directly to video RAM. The screen can be changed very rapidly, since updates to the video RAM are immediately seen on the screen in the next refresh cycle. Once an image is created on the screen, it is periodically *refreshed* to reinforce the glow caused by electrons striking the phosphorescent screen. This is usually done sixty times per second, a rate that is fast enough to avoid flicker.

Printers

Another common peripheral found in personal computer systems is the printer. Two common types of printers are *dot matrix* printers and *daisy wheel* or *thimble* printers. The *dot matrix* printer produces its image by printing a group of dots that form the image of a character or symbol. The matrix used to create one printed character can vary in size, but is typically five to nine dots wide and seven to twelve dots high. An Epson MX-80 printer uses a matrix of five by nine dots. This type of printer can usually also be used to print high resolution (120 dots/inch) images and graphics, as well as different type styles, fonts, and international character sets. The various type styles and character sets are usually contained in a ROM. A single ROM can contain several international character sets or type styles, resulting in a very versatile printer.

There are several methods used to create the patterns of dots, and the most common are impact, thermal, and ink-jet technologies. The impact dot matrix printers use a print head composed of an array of wires, usually one or two columns wide. These wires are selectively extended to form a pattern, the head is then thrust against the ribbon, and an image is formed on the paper behind the ribbon corresponding to the wire's pattern. Most impact dot matrix printers do not use print heads composed of the full array of wires, that is, five by nine. They may only have a single column of wires (one by nine). In this case, each time the head strikes the paper a single column of dots is printed. Five columns would be printed to form a single character. Despite the fact that only one or two columns of dots are printed at a time, these printers are quite fast. They can commonly print 200 characters per second as well as print bi-directionally (in two directions). Their main shortcoming is that they do not produce "letter quality" output. Letter quality is the clean, crisp print produced by, for instance, an IBM Selectric typewriter. This type of output is usually required for word processing applications.

Thermal printers contain a dot-matrix head which is electrically heated. This pattern of heated wires activates a heat sensitive dye embedded in the paper–resulting in the final image. This type of printer requires special paper, and the images produced are usually not as stable as inked images and may fade over time.

Ink-Jet printers spray droplets of ink directly onto the paper forming dot matrix characters. With this method, as with thermal printers, there is no mechanical impact against the paper, thus they cannot be used to make carbon copies. However, they are quiet in comparison with impact type printers.

The second principal type of printer found in personal computer systems is the *daisy wheel* printer. This is an impact type printer which produces fully formed characters of typewritten quality. A daisy wheel printer contains a print head which is mounted on a rotating disk. It is composed of flexible "petals," each of which contains a character on its outer end. The wheel spins and is struck by a hammer when the correct character is lined up. The image is produced by an inked ribbon on the paper. A thimble print head is similar to a daisy wheel except that the arms are turned up, forming a thimble shape. This thimble spins as it moves horizontally across the paper. A hammer strikes the correct petal creating an impact against the

ribbon to form an image on the paper. These printers are slower than dot-matrix printers and usually print at fifteen to fifty characters per second. They are primarily used for word processing applications.

COMPUTING SPEED

A 16-bit CPU can theoretically process data faster than an 8-bit CPU since whenever it performs an action, it operates on twice as much data as an 8-bit processor. In actual practice, however, the overall speed with which a computer system operates is determined by the type of task it is performing, the speed of the secondary storage devices (usually disk drives) and I/O (Input/Output) devices, as well as how many instructions per second the CPU can execute.

The speed that a CPU runs is governed by a device called a "clock." An increased clock speed will result in faster processing. All CPUs have an upper limit to the speed with which they can operate reliably. The second important factor in determining the speed of a system is the rate at which data can be read from and written to the secondary storage devices. The IBM personal computer is available with several options for secondary storage. In ascending order of speed, these are a cassette tape drive, floppy disk drives, or a hard disk. One way to speed up a program that is I/O bound (CPU waiting for I/O) is to use a RAM disk. This strategy utilizes a section of memory as if it were a "disk drive." The computer thinks that it is talking to a disk drive but it is actually reading and writing information to memory. Since there are only electronic transfers and no mechanical operations, the data transfer rate can be tremendously increased. One drawback to this technique is that if a power failure occurs, all data on the RAM drive will be lost. When using a RAM drive, it is a good idea to write important data to a permanent storage device frequently.

The third factor which may have an important bearing on the speed of a system is the rate at which data can be sent to and received from peripherals. If you are using a computer for word processing and your printer will print a maximum of eighty characters per second, the computer will be limited by the printer's speed when printing a large document. If you are only dealing with small amounts of data, the speed of secondary storage and I/O devices will have less impact on the overall speed of the system. However, for most applications, the speed of the disks and I/O devices are a major limiting factor in determining the overall speed of a system.

Microcomputer hardware continues to advance at an amazing rate. Machines that were considered "state of the art" only two or three years ago are now outdated. New technologies continue to make existing hardware obsolete and allow increasingly sophisticated software to be designed and written. The concepts covered in this chapter apply to any digital computer system. Understanding these concepts will enable you to write better software and utilize your computer more fully. In the next chapter we will discuss the operating system, another area of knowledge that can aid your programming.

END NOTES

1. Anthony Ralson, *Encyclopedia of Computer Science* (New York: Van Nostrand Reinhold, 1976).
2. Intel Corporation, "A Primer on Magnetic Bubble Memory."

BIBLIOGRAPHY

Hohenstein, C. Louis. *Computer Peripherals For Minicomputers, Microprocessors And Personal Computers*. New York: McGraw-Hill, 1980.

Intel Corporation. "A Primer on Magnetic Bubble Memory."

Libes, Sol and Mark Garetz. *Interfacing to S-100/IEEE 696 Microcomputers*. Berkeley, CA: Osborne/McGraw-Hill, 1981.

Norton, Peter. *Inside the IBM PC*. Bowie, MD: Robert J. Brady Co., 1983.

Osborne, Adam. *An Introduction to Microcomputers: Volume I*. Berkeley, CA: Osborne/McGraw-Hill, 1980.

Ralson, Anthony. *Encyclopedia of Computer Science*. New York: Van Nostrand Reinhold, 1976.

Short, Kenneth L. *Microprocessors and Programmed Logic*. Englewood Cliffs, NJ: Prentice-Hall, 1981.

CHAPTER TWO

OPERATING SYSTEMS

An operating system is a set of control programs which manage the computer's resources and create a well-defined software environment for computer applications. Computer hardware by itself can perform little useful work. It requires software to bring the computer to life and make it capable of communicating with people and doing useful work. The first "layer" of software in a computer system is the operating system. This is what starts, or "boots up," the machine—helps it pull itself up by its own bootstraps—and establishes a predetermined set of conditions so that applications can be run. When you turn on your computer or hit the reset switch, control is passed to a set of programs usually found in a ROM, often called a "Boot ROM." These programs perform several tasks: they often first check the hardware to ensure that it is functioning correctly, then load a set of control programs (part of the operating system) from the disk into memory, and finally pass control to a routine which will accept your input. At this point, the operating system is loaded and you can execute an application program such as dBASE, Framework, or WordStar.

An operating system can be simple, offering a limited set of commands and functions, or it can be sophisticated, offering a large number of complex functions and utilities. Early microcomputer systems possessed primitive operating systems comprised of a set of routines occupying perhaps 2K of ROM, which only allowed users to load or dump memory. Today, operating systems such as MS-DOS or CP/M contain many useful utilities and provide a rich set of functions, which simplify the programmer's job of writing applications and controlling the hardware.

An operating system can be considered to have two levels of functionality. One is the level seen by a user running applications and utilizing system commands and utilities. At this level, each operating system has its own set of commands used to accomplish frequently performed tasks. Operations such as copying files, renaming files, and formatting disks fall into this category. Another example is the system command DIR. In both MS-DOS and CP/M, this command is used to display a directory of disk files. Normally, frequently used functions are included in the operating system as system commands.

The second level of functionality provided by an operating system is at the programming, or system, level. All operating systems contain a set of pre-packaged routines which perform the primitive functions necessary in nearly all applications. Such actions as sending a character to the screen, reading and writing information from a disk file, and accepting input from the keyboard are common to nearly all programs. The operating system gives the programmer a set of standardized routines to perform these tasks. The programmer is not forced to use the operating system functions to communicate to the hardware, but the wise programmer will use these functions unless there is a very good reason not to. There are several reasons to use the operating system to talk to the hardware. The routines are already written and tested, and they are easy to use. An application which adheres to the conventions within a given operating system will be "portable." This means that if you write a program on a CompuPro computer using CP/M, it will probably also run on the many other types of CP/M machines in existence. Portability is a key

concern when writing commercial software. It may not be as important if you are writing a program to be used privately or only on a small number of systems.

dBASE began life as an 8-bit application running under CP/M. It has since become available on several other operating systems: eight, sixteen, and thirty-two bit. In the following sections we give an overview of two of these, CP/M-80 and PC-DOS. CP/M is the most popular operating system in the 8-bit world, and dBASE II can run on nearly every CP/M machine. PC-DOS (MS-DOS) is the most popular 16-bit operating system and dBASE runs on most 16-bit machines, as well. dBASE can also run under several other operating systems, which are summarized at the end of this chapter.

CP/M-80 VERSION 2.2

CP/M-80, often simply called CP/M, is an 8-bit, single user disk operating system. It is manufactured by Digital Research, a microcomputer software publishing company in Pacific Grove, California, that develops and publishes operating systems and languages. CP/M stands for "Control Program for Microcomputers." It was developed in 1973 by Gary Kildall, which makes it one of the earliest microcomputer operating systems. CP/M currently runs on the Intel 8080 family of microprocessors. It was originally designed for the Intel 8080A, but since the 8085 and Z-80 can both run 8080 programs, CP/M will run on any computer with the above CPUs. CP/M allows files up to eight megabytes in size, and will support up to sixteen disk drives. CP/M enjoys an installed base of approximately two million users, which means there are more microcomputers running CP/M than any other 8-bit operating system.

Description of CP/M-80 Commands

CP/M has two classes of commands. The first type resides in memory and are called *intrinsic*, or "built-in," commands because they do not need to be loaded from a disk file to run. The second type are called *transient* commands. Transient commands reside as disk files and must be loaded into memory before executing. The transient commands provided with CP/M are also called *system utilities*.

CP/M-80 Built-in Commands

DIR	Display a directory of the files on a disk.
ERA	Erase a file.
REN	Rename a file.
SAVE	Save a section of memory to a disk file.
TYPE	Display the contents of a text file on the screen.

CP/M-80 Transient Commands

ASM	This is the CP/M assembler. It translates an 8080 assembly language program into Intel hex format, which can in turn be translated to an executable file.
DDT	"Dynamic Debugging Tool," used to debug programs at the assembly language level.
DUMP	This will dump (display on the screen) the contents of a file in hex format.
ED	The CP/M text editor. Used to create and edit text files.
LOAD	This utility produces an executable file (of type COM) from an Intel hex file.

MOVCPM   Generates a CP/M system corresponding to a particular memory size. If you had a 48K system and added another 16K of memory MOVCPM would allow you to "resize" CP/M so that it utilized the additional memory.

PIP   "Peripheral Interchange Program," used to transfer files between peripherals. Commonly used to copy files between drives.

STAT   Lists number of bytes remaining on disk, as well as statistical information about files. STAT can also be used to display and alter physical to logical device assignments.

SUBMIT   This is CP/M's batch file utility. It is used to run a sequence of programs or commands.

SYSGEN   This program is used to transfer an image of the operating system to a designated disk thus making the disk "bootable."

Table 2-1

CP/M is a compact operating system occupying between 6K and 8K within the 64K space addressable by the CPU. The operating system can be divided into four distinct parts:

BIOS   Basic Input Output System
BDOS   Basic Disk Operating System
CCP   Console Command Processor
TPA   Transient Program Area

The Basic Input/Output System

The BIOS is the section of CP/M which is hardware dependent and must be customized for each individual machine. The functions performed by the BIOS are those that CP/M uses to communicate directly with the hardware, such as reading and writing characters to the various hardware devices in the system: the console, printer, disk drives, etc. A specific routine must be written in the BIOS for each of the basic operations needed to perform system input and output (I/O). These routines can then be called upon to execute the standard I/O functions. Without a BIOS, CP/M would not be able to control the peripheral devices or communicate with them.

The Basic Disk Operating System

The BDOS consists of a number of routines used for file handling and accessing the disk drives. There are also BDOS routines which perform input and output functions to other peripherals attached to the system. The BDOS remains constant from machine to machine. It provides the link between an application program and the BIOS, which talks directly to the hardware. Since the BDOS is constant from machine to machine, it provides applications with a uniform interface to the hardware. The BDOS routines are called (accessed) using a set of standard conventions so that an application program using BDOS calls will be portable and run on a variety of CP/M computers. Some applications access the BIOS directly and thus may not be portable, since the customized BIOS on one machine is different than the BIOS customized for another machine. To give you an idea of what can be performed using the BDOS, a few of the thirty-seven BDOS functions are listed below.

Some Examples of CP/M-80 BDOS Functions

Function number	Function	Description
0	System Reset	Passes control to CP/M.
1	Console Input	Reads the next character from the console.
2	Console Output	Sends a character to the console.
9	Print String	Sends a string of characters to the console.
15	Open File	Opens a file in the directory for access.
16	Close File	Closes a file which is currently open.

Table 2-2

Console Command Processor

The Console Command Processor interprets the command typed at the system prompt, A>. When a command is typed in, the CCP checks to see if it is one of the built-in commands, and if so, it executes the command. If a transient command is entered, such as DBASE, the CCP searches the disk directory for a COM-type file which matches the command typed in. In the case of DBASE, it would search for the existence of DBASE.COM. If it finds the file, the program is loaded into memory and control is passed to that program, which then runs.

Transient Program Area

The Transient Program Area is the area in memory where transient programs (applications) are loaded and run. The exact size of this area can vary and will depend upon how much memory your computer has and the size of the BIOS and BDOS sections in your version of CP/M. dBASE 2.4 (8 bit) and earlier versions require at least 48K of memory and 42K of TPA to run. dBASE 2.41 (8 bit) requires a TPA of 43K. Figure 2-1 shows a typical map of a CP/M system with 64K of memory.

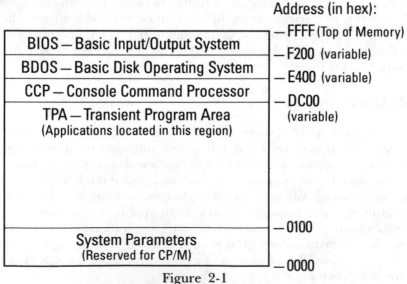

Figure 2-1
CP/M-80 memory map

CP/M 3 or CP/M-Plus

Version 3 of CP/M is upward-compatible with CP/M 2.2, which means that if an application such as dBASE runs on CP/M 2.2, it usually will also run on CP/M 3. Though CP/M 3 offers improved performance and a number of additional features over earlier versions of CP/M, at the time of this writing it is not yet widely available.

MS-DOS (PC-DOS)

MS-DOS or PC-DOS is currently the most popular 16-bit operating system for microcomputers. Often MS-DOS and PC-DOS are simply referred to as DOS. DOS is the acronym for *Disk Operating System*. MS-DOS began life in 1979, when Tim Patterson of Seattle Computer Products wrote 86-DOS for Intel's 8086 microprocessor. At that time, CP/M was the dominant microcomputer operating system; so 86-DOS was modeled after CP/M in many respects. However, since the 8086 was considerably more powerful than the 8-bit CPUs running CP/M, it was possible to develop a more sophisticated operating system for the 8086, which is what Patterson did. Microsoft of Bellevue, Washington, one of the early companies writing software for micros, acquired the rights to 86-DOS, which became MS-DOS. When IBM went looking for an operating system for its PC, it settled on MS-DOS. IBM PC sales took off and PC-DOS became the *de facto* standard operating system for 16-bit micros.

Every operating system must be customized, or "ported," to the specific hardware on which it runs. Since each computer is unique, and the operating system must be able to send and receive data from the disk drives, console, and other devices in the computer, the operating system must contain routines specifically tailored to work with that hardware. This customized section of the operating system is usually called the BIOS (Basic Input Output System). PC-DOS is MS-DOS which has been customized for the IBM PC.

There have been several versions of MS-DOS and PC-DOS since they were originally introduced. The table below shows the released versions of MS-DOS and the equivalent PC-DOS version.

MS-DOS Version	PC-DOS Version	Notable Changes
1.1	1.0	Initial Release, single sided drives only.
1.25	1.1	Worked with double sided drives.
2.0	2.0	Allowed sub-directories and other UNIX-like features.
2.1	2.1	Allowed use of international character set, and new device interface.

Table 2-3

DOS has been implemented on many machines which use the 8086, 8088, 80186, or 80188. All these chips are designed to be software compatible so that they will execute the same object code. Due to its popularity, DOS will probably also be available on other families of CPUs, such as the Motorola 68000, by early 1985.

Description of DOS Commands

DOS, like CP/M, has both intrinsic (built-in) commands and transient commands (commands which must be loaded from a disk file before execution). The table below is a summary of the internal commands. These are always available and are usually present in memory ready for instant use. This table gives a brief description of each command. Consult your DOS manual for a complete discussion of these commands.

DOS 2.1 Internal Commands

COPY	Copy disk files
CHDIR	Change current directory
CLS	Clear the screen
CTTY	Change standard input and standard output device
DATE	Display the system date and allow date to be set
DIR	Display a directory of files on disk
DEL	Erase disk file(s)
ERASE	Erase disk file(s) (same as DEL)
MKDIR	Create a subdirectory
PATH	Set search path for commands or batch files
RENAME	Rename a disk file
RMDIR	Remove a subdirectory
SET	Inserts strings into the command processor's environment
TIME	Display the system time and allow time to be set
TYPE	Display the contents of a text file on the screen
VER	Display DOS version number
VERIFY	Verify data in copy operations
VOL	Display disk volume identification

Table 2-4

In addition to these internal commands, DOS has a rich set of utilities, many of which came from the UNIX operating system. To give you an idea of what is available, the most commonly used utilities are listed below. Refer to your DOS User's Guide for a complete description of all the DOS utilities.

Some DOS Utilities

CHKDSK	Shows statistics on disk contents and memory. Fixes some types of disk errors.
COMP	Compares two sets of files to see if they are identical.
DEBUG	Debugging utility used to monitor and control program execution while debugging programs.
DISKCOPY	Does a track by track copy of a disk. This produces a duplicate of the source disk.
EDLIN	A line editor. Allows editing of text.
FIND	Finds a specified string in a list of text files.
FORMAT	Formats a new disk so that it can be used by DOS.

LINK	Links separately produced object modules. Object modules are created with an assembler or compiler. LINK creates an executable file of type EXE.
MASM	8086 Macro Assembler. Translates assembly language source files into object files.
MODE	Sets options for printer or color display. Initializes serial ports and allows re-direction of printer output.
PRINT	Prints a sequence of text files from a print queue. Allows other tasks to continue while printing takes place.
RECOVER	Recovers a file from a disk that has developed a bad sector.

Table 2-5

DOS INTERNAL ARCHITECTURE

PC-DOS is the most popular implementation of MS-DOS by a wide margin. In this section, we give a short description of PC-DOS. If you wish to better understand this operating system, the references listed at the end of this chapter cover it in more detail. The key parts of PC-DOS are: the ROM BIOS; the BOOT RECORD; the files IBMBIO.COM, IBMDOS.COM, and COMMAND.COM; and the DOS UTILITIES. Other MS-DOS systems have the same functional parts, however they will have slightly different names.

The BIOS (Basic Input/Output System) section of DOS performs the same set of functions that was described for the CP/M BIOS, that is, providing low level I/O routines to control and communicate with the hardware specific devices (keyboard, display, disk drives, etc.) in the computer. In DOS, the BIOS is divided into two parts, the ROM BIOS and IBMBIO.COM.

The ROM BIOS

On the IBM PC, the ROM BIOS is located in Read Only Memory at the top of addressable memory. It contains all the I/O support routines for the standard IBM PC hardware devices. It also contains the instructions to perform the initial self-test when the computer is first turned on, and the code to begin the booting process which loads the rest of DOS. Since all these routines are stored in ROM, they cannot be changed. When the PC is turned on, it runs the self-test and, if everything checks out, it reads the boot record which is the first record (side 0, track 0, sector 1) on the disk in drive A:. The ROM BIOS routines were written by IBM and are an integral part of the IBM PC. PC-DOS uses these routines as does any other operating system running on the IBM PC.

The Boot Record

The *boot record* is a short program whose sole purpose is to load the IBMBIO.COM and IBMDOS.COM files. This action occurs whenever the computer is re-booted by pressing the <Ctrl-Alt-Del> keys, or cold-booted by turning the power on.

IBMBIO.COM

IBMBIO.COM contains DOS-specific I/O routines. These I/O routines are in addition to the general routines found in the ROM BIOS. It can override the ROM BIOS if it needs to fix an error present in the ROM, and it allows extensions to the BIOS to be added for additional peripherals. These extensions are called "device drivers" and provide the necessary communication and control for hard disks, plotters, special printers, or other additional devices connected to the computer. This makes it easy to extend the operating system's control to new devices as they are added.

IBMDOS.COM

IBMDOS.COM can be thought of as the next layer of DOS above the BIOS portion. It is a "higher level" in that it does not deal directly with the hardware itself, but provides a means for application programs to access the DOS functions, similar to CP/M's BDOS. This is done using a specific protocol, and it gives application programs access to a wide range of operations. If a program uses these standard DOS service routines, it will be relatively portable and will run on other machines that use DOS. A program which uses its own customized method of controlling or communicating with the hardware instead of the standard DOS functions, will often only work on the single machine it was designed for. A "well-behaved" program will use the operating system to talk to the hardware. Some examples are listed below to give you an idea of the types of functions DOS makes available. The *DOS Technical Reference* gives a full description of all the DOS functions.

Some Examples of DOS Functions

Function number	Function	Description
0	Program terminate	Gracefully terminates a program
1	Keyboard input	Reads a character from keyboard and echoes it to display
2	Display output	Sends a character to display
5	Printer output	Sends a character to printer
16	Create a file	Create a new disk file

Table 2-6

COMMAND.COM

COMMAND.COM is the part of DOS which puts the system prompt, A>, onto the display and interprets commands that are issued from the keyboard in a manner similar to CP/M's Console Command Processor. When a command is typed in at the system prompt, COMMAND.COM first searches a table of internal commands. These are listed in Table 2-4. If the command doesn't match one of these, COMMAND.COM assumes it is an external command and begins to search the disk directory for the command. It searches for three types of commands in this order: .COM, .EXE, and .BAT. If it finds a disk file matching the command typed, it loads that file and passes control to it. If it doesn't find a match it gives an error message.

Besides interpreting commands, COMMAND.COM handles critical errors such as disk read or write errors. It gives an error message and allows options for recovery from the error. There are two parts to COMMAND.COM: one stays resident in low memory and the other is in high memory and can be overwritten by an application program (see Figure 2-2). When called, the resident portion checks to see if the transient portion is present. If it isn't, it will be reloaded from the disk. This gives an application program more available memory since it can use the space occupied by COMMAND.COM in high memory.

DOS Utilities

DOS contains a healthy set of utilities. Many of these are application programs for functions necessary to the operation of the computer such as formatting and copying disks. Others, such as SORT (which sorts text data) are quite useful but not necessary. Table 2-5 describes some of these utilities.

Figure 2-2 shows a map of memory after DOS has been loaded. This is a picture of where the various parts of DOS reside in memory and where an application program is located. Notice how the transient portion of COMMAND.COM is at the top of memory which allows it to be overwritten by the application should the application need the memory. If this occurs, DOS re-loads this portion of COMMAND.COM when needed.

Transient portion of COMMAND.COM (command interpreter, internal commands, batch processor, external command loader)	— Top of RAM High Memory
User Stack for .COM files (256 bytes)	
APPLICATION PROGRAM	
Resident portion of COMMAND.COM	
DOS buffers & installed device drivers	
IBMDOS.COM (DOS service routines)	
IBMBIO.COM (Input/Output routines)	
DOS Communication Area	— 0050:0000 Low
ROM Communication Area	— 0040:0000 Memory
Interrupt Vector Table	— 0000:0000

Figure 2-2
PC-DOS memory map

DOS FEATURES

DOS has several notable features not found in earlier microcomputer operating systems. These are discussed below. We anticipate many future enhancements and refinements to DOS as it evolves.

Hierarchical Directories

Hierarchical comes from the word "hierarchy," which means to organize or classify according to rank or authority. A directory is a list, or catalog, of the files on a disk. You are probably familiar with the process of typing the DIR command and watching the disk directory scroll past as you look for a file. This system works fine on a floppy disk with limited storage; however, on a hard disk capable of containing hundreds or thousands of files, it can be difficult to locate one file out of many unless the files are organized in some logical fashion. Beginning with DOS version 2.0, it is possible to organize a directory by creating a system of subdirectories. This feature was borrowed from the UNIX operating system developed at Bell Labs, which has been in operation on minicomputers for years.

The number of files each subdirectory can contain is limited only by the space available on the disk. All the files in a single subdirectory are usually related in some fashion. For instance, if you have word processing files, dBASE files, and general utility files, three subdirectories could be created which would contain only the files related to each purpose. This makes it easy to organize and make use of a large number of files. A subdirectory is actually a file and can contain other subdirectories below it. A system of subdirectories organized in this fashion can be viewed as a tree. The top directory is called the ROOT directory. Figure 2-3 shows an example of using subdirectories to organize several types of files on a single hard disk. All the word processing files are found in either the LETTERS or MEMOS subdirectory. Both of these fall under the WPROC sudirectory. If LETTERS or MEMOS starts to accumulate many entries they could be further subdivided, or a new type of word processing subdirectory could be created. This type of organization is a necessity when dealing with a large number of files.

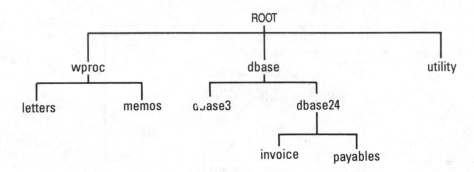

Figure 2-3
Subdirectories

I/O Redirection and Piping

I/O Redirection and Piping are two more concepts borrowed from UNIX. DOS assumes that the STANDARD INPUT device is the keyboard and that the STANDARD OUTPUT device is the display screen. I/O redirection allows a program to receive its input from a source other than the keyboard, such as a file. It also allows the output from a program to be directed to a file rather than the display screen. For example, *DIR > Diskdir* would send the output of the DIR command to a file called *Diskdir* instead of the display screen. Output could be directed to the printer by *DIR > PRN*. In addition to redirecting output, the input to a program can be redirected. *PROGRAM < File* results in PROGRAM taking its input from FILE rather than the keyboard. As you can see, I/O redirection directs the data flow either TO or FROM a FILE. I/O redirection can also direct a data flow to or from another peripheral device such as a printer or terminal.

Piping allows the screen output of one program to be used as the keyboard input of another program. The symbol | indicates piping in DOS. This makes it easy to combine several operations into a single command line. For example, to obtain an alphabetically sorted directory, the following command line could be used.

```
DIR | SORT
```

Here, the output of DIR is fed into SORT, which sorts the directory entries and then sends a sorted output to the screen. This sorted directory could be captured in a file by redirecting its output as in:

```
DIR | SORT > Diskdir
```

If you were writing some documentation for an accounting package written in dBASE, you would want to include a list of each command file and its purpose. To quickly get a sorted list of all the PRG files the following command line could be used.

```
DIR | FIND "PRG" | SORT > Prgfiles
```

This will pipe the output of the DIR command to the FIND utility which will find all lines in the directory that contain the string "PRG." The output of FIND will be piped to SORT which will then sort the list and write its output to the text file Prgfiles. This text file could easily be inserted into your documentation to provide a sorted list of all program files. The best way to become familiar with piping and I/O redirection is to practice with it. Refer to your DOS manual for a more detailed discussion of these features.

OTHER OPERATING SYSTEMS

From this brief overview of CP/M and DOS, you can see many similarities between the two operating systems: both contain a BIOS section interfacing with the hardware, an I/O function section providing routines for application programs with which to access the hardware, a command processor section, and an assortment of utilities. You can also see that DOS is the more sophisticated operating system of the two with its hierarchical directory structure, piping, and I/O redirection.

dBASE is compatible with several operating systems. Table 2-7 gives a summary of these operating systems and the version(s) of dBASE that run on them.

dBASE Compatibility With Operating Systems

O/S Name	O/S Type	dBASE version(s)
CP/M-80	8-Bit Single User	2.3b,2.4,2.41
CP/M-86	16-Bit Single User	2.3d,2.4,2.41
Concurrent CP/M	16-Bit Single User	2.3d,2.4,2.41
Concurrent DOS	16-Bit Single User	2.3d,2.4,2.41
PC-DOS	16-Bit Single User	2.3d,2.4,2.41, dBASE III
MS-DOS	16-Bit Single User	2.3d,2.4,2.41, dBASE III
TurboDOS	8-Bit Multi-user	2.3b,2.4,2.41 (Single User)
MP/M-II	8-Bit Multi-user	2.3b,2.4 (Single User)
MP/M-86	16-Bit Multi-user	2.3d,2.4,2.41, Single User
DPC/OS	8/16-Bit Multi-user	2.3b,2.4,2.41 (Single User)
MMOST	8-Bit Multi-user	2.3b,2.4,2.41 (Single User)
3-COM Ethernet	16-Bit Multi-user	2.3d,2.4,2.41, Multi-user
PC-NET	16-Bit Multi-user	2.3d,2.4,2.41, (Single User)
UNIX System V on AT&T 3Bx computers	32-Bit Multi-user	2.4e, dBASE III

Table 2-7

Our purpose in this chapter has been to introduce the fundamental principles of operating systems, since they are a key part of any computing environment. Many excellent books have been written on the subject of operating systems. Some recommended references are provided in the following bibliography if you are interested in further reading.

BIBLIOGRAPHY

Cortesi, David I. *Inside CP/M: A Guide for Users and Programmers.* New York, NY: Holt, Rinehart, and Winston, 1982.

Dahmke, Mark. *Microcomputer Operating Systems.* Peterborough, NH: Byte Books, 1982.

Hogan, Thom. *Osborne CP/M User Guide.* Berkeley, CA: Osborne/McGraw-Hill, 1981.

Microsoft Corp. *Disk Operating System Technical Reference.* Boca Raton, FL: IBM, 1983.

Norton, Peter. *MS-DOS and PC-DOS User's Guide.* Bowie, MD: Robert J. Brady Co., 1984.

CHAPTER THREE

LANGUAGES

The hardware and operating system of a computer provide the environment in which application programs can run. An application program is any program which is executed after the operating system has been loaded. Some examples of application programs are accounting software, word processors, electronic spreadsheets, languages, and even games. Computer languages make it possible to write applications. Today, there are thousands of applications available for microcomputers. This book is about only one of those applications, dBASE. dBASE contains a language as part of its functionality and this gives it a great deal of flexibility. With the dBASE language, you can write database applications tailored to your specific needs, whether it's keeping track of a coin collection or a fully integrated accounting package. Computer languages provide the fundamental structures and rules for constructing software and provide a means for transforming the programmer's concepts into a form understandable by the computer. In this chapter we will give an overview of the different types of languages and how they relate to each other.

MACHINE LANGUAGE

Any computer language contains similarities to spoken languages such as English, German, or Chinese. Language is essential to communication. A language provides a set of agreed-upon symbols (words) and rules of syntax (specific ways of combining words with punctuation) to allow you to convey a concept, idea, or message. As noted in chapter 1, every CPU is designed to recognize a specific group of basic instructions, called an *instruction set.* The instruction set precisely defines the language which directs the operation of the processor. Since it is an electronic digital device, a computer can recognize only digital electronic signals, represented by either on or off states. The lowest level of programming would be to send instructions to the computer with codes which correspond to these electronic signals. Such instructions would be in *machine language.* Early programming was done in machine language, because there was no other choice. This meant that the computer was sent instructions that were binary or hexadecimal, such as the pattern 10000011 or its hexadecimal equivalent, 83. Programming with the numeric codes of machine language is a tedious and error-prone process simply because these codes are not easy to remember and are difficult to think with conceptually.

The next step in the evolution of languages was the creation of a set of English-like symbols to substitute for the machine's numeric instructions. For example, ADD was used instead of 10000011 to represent the Add operation. These symbols are called instruction *mnemonics,* and each mnemonic directly represents a machine language instruction. (The word "mnemonic" means "assisting or designed to assist the memory.") The language made up of these mnemonics is called *assembly language.* Because these higher level symbols are much easier to work with than numeric codes, they improved the quality of programs tremendously. Larger, more complex programs were developed quickly and with fewer mistakes. Naturally, a program written with English-like symbols needed to be translated into machine language before it could be recognized by the computer. A program which translates assembly language to machine language is called an *assembler*.

ASSEMBLY LANGUAGE

There are both advantages and disadvantages to programming in assembly language. The advantages are that it allows you to write programs which take full advantage of the hardware features of a machine. In addition, assembly language can produce programs which are very fast and compact. Often, large programs written in higher level languages are optimized (made to run faster) by re-writing in assembly language those specific portions of the program where the processor spends most of its time. If a BASIC program spent 90% of its time executing a loop which took two seconds and this particular loop was rewritten in assembler so that it took only a tenth of a second, a seven-fold increase in program speed would be realized.

Along with these advantages come disadvantages. In order to use assembly language well, you must be intimately familiar with the technical details of the hardware, especially the CPU. When writing programs in assembler, you must concern yourself with many details of the computer's operation that can be ignored when working in a higher level language such as BASIC. Simply reading information from a file could involve hundreds of assembly language instructions and detailed interactions with the operating system. The same operation could be accomplished by one or two commands in dBASE. Such programs are naturally more complex to write and more difficult to debug. Today's computers have faster processors and more memory, and as the software becomes more complex and sophisticated it makes less sense to do software projects in assembly language. The trend today is toward higher level languages such as Pascal or C. With these languages, large software projects can be designed, written, and debugged faster than if the project were done in assembly language.

Learning assembly language, however, will give you a deeper understanding of how the computer works, and allow you to do things that cannot be done with some higher level languages. In appendix D we have included a section on assembly language subroutines that can be called from dBASE II. These allow you to do things from within dBASE II that dBASE II cannot do by itself.

HIGH-LEVEL LANGUAGES

High-level computer languages allow you to communicate concepts to the computer using words and phrases which are closer to natural language. This section gives an overview of the types of high-level languages commonly in use.

Any high-level language allows algorithms and data structures to be represented using a set of well-defined rules, commands, and constructs. In this sense, a language is a *formalism*. Separate from the language is its *implementation*. An implementation is the method used to interpret the language on the computer. Any implementation can be thought of as a translator, transforming a high level language into the machine language which is ultimately run by the computer. Language implementations can be divided into two types: batch-oriented, usually referred to as *compilers*, and interactive implementations, usually referred to as *interpreters*. The speed and efficiency with which a program runs is determined by the implementation, not the language. An implementation which produces compact, efficient machine code will produce programs which run fast. A different implementation using the same high level language might produce inefficient machine code resulting in a program which runs slowly.

Compiled Languages

Compilers have been written for all of the most commonly used computer languages such as BASIC, FORTRAN, COBOL, C, and Pascal. Compilers operate in a batch mode, that is, they translate an entire program during one batch operation from source code to *object code*, a term often used to mean machine code. The process of producing an executable module, one that will stand alone and run without further modification, actually requires several steps. The first step is to compile the source, written in a high level language, into an object module (machine code). Next, a program called a *linker* is used to attach the main object module and any additional sub-programs (also object modules) or support routines used by the main program. A particular set of support routines is often called the *runtime system*. A program usually uses I/O devices on the system such as the screen, printer, or disk drives, and these devices are normally reached via the operating system. The runtime support is a set of routines that perform functions such as input/output processing, mathematical operations, and interfacing with the operating system during program execution. For example, when the compiled program sends a character to the screen, a routine in the runtime system lets the operating system know this, and sends the character to the screen via the operating system. This process of compiling and then linking results in an executable module needing no further modification.

Compilers are designed to produce object code for a specific processor and a good compiler produces compact, fast-running object code optimized for that processor. Again, both advantages and disadvantages are incurred in this process. An obvious advantage is that the resulting program will stand alone and execute quickly. A disadvantage is that the batch process of a compiling and linking is sometimes slow. The programmer may take a coffee break while the compiler is chewing on the latest modifications to the source code, only to return and find an error message on the screen because of a forgotten semicolon on line 2973. After correcting the error, the source code must be compiled and linked again—possibly only to find another error. This process of locating and correcting compile-time errors can be time consuming, particularly if you are learning the language and making many mistakes. Of course, if you make very few errors in your code and it compiles on the first or second pass, you won't find compile time to be particularly tedious.

Figure 3-1 illustrates the steps to generate an application with a compiled high-level language.

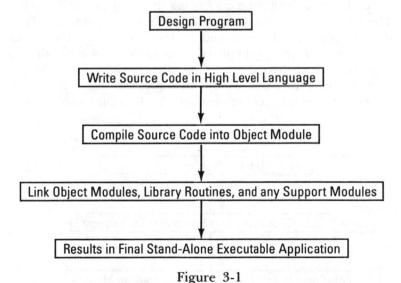

Figure 3-1
Development steps using a compiler

Interpreted Languages

dBASE is an interpreted language. BASIC, another common language, and LISP are also available as interpreters. To interpret means "to translate orally." Interpreters are used at international meetings to translate from one language to another as a speaker is talking. This translation occurs with only a slight time lag to allow for "processing" by the interpreter. A strict interpretive computer language works much the same way. It scans a source line typed in by the programmer and analyzes it, immediately reporting any error it may find. This immediate error detection makes coding much less painful. The error can be corrected on the spot while the programmer's attention is still on that section of code. The lesson learned can prevent similar errors later. This is an ideal way to learn a language and is one reason that dBASE is popular. dBASE allows people without formal training in computer science to learn a programming language with which they can write useful programs. An interpreter will either execute a single line and give the result or run a program which is comprised of many lines stored as a text file.

Although interpreters are more "friendly" than compilers, they also have a few drawbacks. Code that is executed by an interpreter runs considerably slower than the same source code which has been compiled and is then run as object code. There are several reasons for this slowdown, the main one being that during interpretation, the analysis and decoding process occurs as the program is running. With a compiler, this process has already been completed before runtime. Another drawback is that the interpreter must be present at runtime (when the application is running) in addition to the application. This means that the application is not a stand-alone package, since an additional file must also be included which will interpret (run) the application. Depending on the particular application, these may or may not be severe disadvantages.

An ideal development process would be to develop programs with an interpreter and then after they are complete and debugged, compile them into fast running, stand-alone modules. BASIC is one language that has been implemented this way.

Pseudo Compilers and Interpreters

A pseudo compiler or interpreter is a cross between a compiler and an interpreter. CBASIC, UCSD Pascal, and dBASE RunTime are examples of this type of language. For example, with dBASE RunTime, coding and testing can be done with the dBASE interpreter and when the code is complete, it can be partially compiled into *tokens*. Tokens result from translating the source code into a form that can be more efficiently interpreted. The tokens are then interpreted by a runtime program. The partial compilation process translates the source code into the intermediate form of tokens that are interpreted with less overhead since some of the analysis and preliminary translation steps have already been done.

The major benefit is greater speed than a normal interpreter. The increase in speed depends on how much translation has occurred during the partial compilation process. Both CBASIC and UCSD Pascal run considerably faster than interpreted languages, whereas dBASE RunTime may not show much increase in speed over dBASE itself.

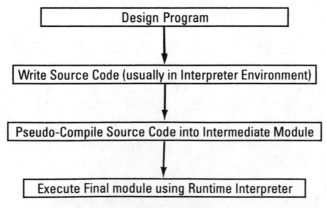

Figure 3-2
Steps in pseudo-compiler operation

PROCEDURAL VS. NONPROCEDURAL LANGUAGES

The high-level languages we have looked at so far are procedural or procedure-oriented languages. This means that the programmer specifies in a step-by-step fashion exactly *how* the program will go together in order to produce the desired result. Traditional high-level languages such as COBOL, FORTRAN, and PL/I are examples of procedural languages. With a nonprocedural language, a programmer describes *what* is wanted as output and the language takes care of many details required to produce the desired output. dBASE is procedural since it contains commands and programming constructs which allow a programmer to specify detailed program steps describing exactly how the program should run. However, dBASE also contains nonprocedural statements such as CREATE and REPORT that execute many high-level operations and produce output specified by the user's brief description of what is wanted.

The following two dBASE command lines allow a dBASE III user to create a report and then print it. The report can contain page headers, page numbers, selected subtotals, page length, page width, and other options. The process of creating a report in dBASE is done by selecting options and filling out a blank form on the screen. No programming is needed in the traditional sense. This allows non-programmers to prepare reports which would have taken several pages of code if written in a procedural language.

```
CREATE REPORT <report filename>
REPORT FORM <report filename> TO PRINT
```

One disadvantage of nonprocedural commands is that they lack flexibility since they are designed to satisfy a specific set of conditions. Since dBASE contains a procedural language, it gets around this limitation. For example, in addition to the REPORT command, the dBASE language allows a programmer complete freedom to create custom reports in which nearly any type of output can be generated for special circumstances.

An example comparing procedural to nonprocedural commands is shown below. On the left is the Pascal code (procedural) necessary to create a datafile (with one field called "names") and allow the operator to input names. The righthand side shows the single dBASE command (nonprocedural) which will do the same thing. dBASE will prompt the operator for the size of the name field, automatically create an appropriate file and then present a data input screen.

PASCAL	dBASE
	CREATE Names

```
program names;
(* sets up a record structure for
one name field and allows data input. *)

type
   names =
      record
      Name: string[15];
   end; (* names *)
Const
   blank = '                  ';
Var
   NamesFile: file of Names;
   NamesRec: names;
begin
   Assign(NamesFile, 'NAMES.DBF');
   Rewrite(NamesFile);
   with NamesRec do
   begin
      repeat
         Name := blank; (* initialize name *)
         Write('Name: ');
         ReadIn(Name);
         ClrScr; (* clear screen for next name *)
         Write(NamesFile,NamesRec);
      Until Length(Name) = 0;
   end;
   Close(NamesFile);
end.
```

Example 3-1

In sum, nonprocedural languages allow a wide variety of people who are not programmers to quickly create useful applications which they can use in their businesses. The future is very bright for nonprocedural languages. There are several, such as NOMAD, MAPPER, and RAMIS, which have been in wide use on mainframes for years. As microcomputers get faster CPUs and larger memories, we will see these types of languages showing up at microcomputer retail stores.

BIBLIOGRAPHY

Brown, P.J. *Writing Interactive Compilers and Interpreters*. New York: John Wiley & Sons, 1979.

Leventhal, Lance A. and Winthrop Saville. *8080/8085 Assembly Language Subroutines*. Berkeley, CA: Osborne/McGraw-Hill, 1983.

Purdum, Jack. *C Programming Guide*. Indianapolis, IN: Que Corp, 1983.

Scanlon, Leo. *IBM PC Assembly Language*. Bowie, MD: Robert J. Brady Co., 1983.

Zaks, Rodnay. *Introduction to Pascal*. Berkeley, CA: Sybex, 1981.

Zarrella, John. *Language Translators*. Suisun City, CA: Microcomputer Applications, 1982.

CHAPTER FOUR

PROGRAMMING CONCEPTS

After several years of experience in Ashton-Tate's Software Support Center talking and working with a variety of dBASE programmers, we have found the source of many problems to be poor programming practices in general rather than a specific lack of dBASE knowledge. This chapter gives an overview of the fundamentals of good programming. Important points are expanded upon in the chapters that follow. Since programming is a broad area, we present here the key elements which are of practical use in actual dBASE programming projects. Most of the principles discussed are applicable to any high-level language, although our focus is on dBASE applications. The discipline of programming, like any intellectual skill, takes some effort to master and can always be improved upon. Many experts have written books on these topics, and some of these are listed at the end of this section. We recommend that you read them. Time spent on improving your programming skills will be repaid in many ways. Your code will have fewer bugs, it will be concise, easier to maintain and modify, it will run faster, it will be more easily understood by others, and you will more fully enjoy the process of creating software.

WHAT IS PROGRAMMING?

Programming, coding, hacking, bit twiddling, and software engineering all refer to the same activity: designing and writing a series of instructions to be executed by a computer. Programming results in software. A software project can range in complexity from a simple one-line program which prints "hello" on the screen to exceedingly large projects such as the one described by Frederick Brooks in *The Mythical Man-month,* the development of an operating system for the IBM System/360 which took 5,000 people-years and involved more than 1,000 people. [1] The larger the project, the more important it is to follow good programming procedures. However, even with small projects you should write concise, well-documented code rather than slap it together in a slipshod fashion. So you can clearly see how to approach the activity of programming, we will break it into a sequence of logical steps:

    Problem definition
    Designing a solution
    Coding
    Documentation
    Testing
    Debugging

PROBLEM DEFINITION

Before turning on your computer, first make sure you completely understand the problem to be solved. This will often require careful study and examination. If you are writing the program for someone else, have the person write down exactly what the program is to accomplish. The following guidelines are useful when defining the problem.

What is the purpose of this program?   Try to keep this to a single sentence. Boil it down to a clean statement of what the program will do. If it is a large program with many functions, divide it into its component parts and state the purpose of each module.

What are the inputs?   Describe the types of data and any relationships they may have. Do this for each module. A module is a stand-alone routine which usually performs a specific function, such as print a report or accept data input.

What are the outputs?   Clearly show what output is wanted and describe what format it should be in. This should also be done for each module.

What are the operations involved?   Describe what operations are necessary to transform the inputs into the desired results. Diagrams are often helpful during this step to define clearly the transformations involved.

DESIGNING A SOLUTION

Doing a good job defining the problem will open the door to its solution. In fact, if you find yourself having trouble formulating a solution, go back and develop a more detailed and specific problem definition. Large programs should be divided into separate logical parts and each of these solved individually. Logical parts are sections which act as stand-alone units or perform single functions or operations. In this sense, a *function* can be defined as the action taken by the module, or the change produced by the module. When the module is executed, it performs an action or transformation on the input to produce an output, and this describes its function. A module should be limited to a single function and not try to perform many. Functions such as data input, data lookup, and reports can be thought of as separate modules of an overall system.

One of the most important parts of solution planning is to select the proper algorithms for use in your program. An *algorithm* is a recipe, or a set of clearly defined steps, which describes how to do something. For example, to find the average value for a list of ten numbers:

1.   Add up the ten numbers.
2.   Divide the sum by ten (the number of elements).

This two-step algorithm will result in the average. Algorithms specify what actions and operations a program will take. Since there can be a wide variation in the efficiencies of algorithms which accomplish the same result, it pays to select your algorithms carefully. Here are some tips on how to go about constructing algorithms.

1.   Clearly define the relationships between the variables and constants in the problem. If possible, state these relationships in an algebraic form.

2.   Work from the top down in describing the algorithm. You will hear the phrase "top down" frequently. It simply means to start from the important aspects or generalized view of a problem and work down to the more detailed or subordinate aspects. This technique is covered in more detail in chapter 5, "Structured Programming." Looking from the top or most general statement of the problem, describe the key steps of the algorithm in brief English-like statements. Don't get too detailed at first. Limit this first description to no more than ten or twelve steps. Next, begin at the top step and expand each one into a more detailed

description of the operations involved. Continue this process of refining your descriptions of each step until the entire process has been completely described. This process is called *stepwise refinement*. The result is a precise description which can be transformed into a computer language.

3.   Strive for simplicity. Whenever there is a choice, select the simplest method for accomplishing an operation.

4.   Don't re-invent the wheel. Many times the problem you are working on has already been solved. It is nearly always worth the effort to check the literature for existing algorithms. Published algorithms have usually been tested or proven to be correct, so, besides saving time, you get a solution you can have confidence in. We suggest the following references for a start: *The Art of Computer Programming*, Vols. 1-3 by Donald Knuth, *The Design and Analysis of Computer Algorithms* by Alfred Aho et al., *Algorithms* by Robert Sedgewick, *Algorithms + Data Structures = Programs* by Niklaus Wirth, and *Collected Algorithms from the CACM* (Association for Computing Machinery).

In addition to selecting the correct algorithms, selecting the best data structures for an application is critical. Each language offers a specific number of ways to represent data such as character strings, integers, real numbers, or Boolean data. Several factors enter into selecting the optimum data representations. You should first be familiar with the different data types available in a given language. (Data types and structures are covered in chapters 6 and 7.) Next, you should consider factors such as what linkages and transformations will occur between the data, how to avoid unnecessarily complex data relationships, and how to accommodate possible changes to the data structure. These topics are covered in chapter 9, "Database Design."

One final decision in the solution phase is to select the proper language for your application. There is no one language that does it all. Some (such as PL/I and Ada) have tried, but these large languages are cumbersome to work with. At the time of this writing, only subsets of PL/I and Ada are available on microcomputers. dBASE is somewhat specialized since it is built around the relational database model, which represents data in tables allowing relations to be established between data items. Since dBASE is specifically designed for database applications, it would be inappropriate to try to write a word processor with dBASE.

CODING

The solution step merges with the coding step of the process. Before actually beginning to write dBASE code you should clearly describe the logic of your program with *pseudo-code*. Pseudo-code is English-like statements that show the logic of your programs in an easily readable fashion. There is no specific format required but it should be consistent. If several programmers are working on a project, it is a good idea to adopt conventions for pseudo-code that everyone will follow. Some people like pseudo-code which uses formal structures similar to the language itself (such as IF. . .ELSE. . .ENDIF or DO WHILE), while others prefer a looser form of pseudo-code such as "Set up a loop to process all records in the file."

Example of pseudo-code for a program to print a list of customers from California:

```
Open customer database.
Set up a loop to process all records.
If Customer is in CA print the record as follows:
Last Name, First Name
Address
Skip to next record
If Customer is not in CA, skip to the next record.
```

Here is another style of pseudo-code for the same program.

```
Open Customer database.
Do While not End of File
     If State = CA
          Print
                    Last Name, First Name
                    Address
     Endif
     Skip to next record
Enddo
```

Use a style that you feel comfortable with. Remember, the purpose of pseudo-code is to show the logic of your programs in an easily readable format. Pseudo-code fits in naturally at the end of the stepwise refinement process. It is the final English-like description of your code before beginning the actual coding process. It also can provide many of the comment lines you will use to clarify and describe your code.

By now you may be itching to begin actual coding. Here are some guidelines to follow. We will go into more detail later.

1. Start coding from the top down. For example, if you have a program which performs several functions, first code the main routine which calls (temporarily transfers control to) the subordinate routines. If the main routine requires a subroutine in order to run, rather than code the entire subroutine, write a dummy module which provides the data needed by the main routine in a simple form. This way, the main routine can be coded and debugged. Any major errors can be removed before adding the complexity of many subordinate modules.

2. Use library routines when possible. As you program with any language, it is a good idea to build up a library of general purpose modules which can be used over and over. After these have been tested, they can be quickly implemented, sometimes requiring only minor changes. Routines which print formatted reports, display menus, or request data for input can be used over and over again.

3. Keep modules fairly short. Very long modules are difficult to understand and are thus difficult to debug, maintain, and modify. Divide long modules into shorter ones.

4. Keep modules independent from one another. Think of each routine as a stand-alone black box. It takes input in a given form and produces output in a given form. A routine should not depend upon code outside of itself to function properly. Modules which are dependent upon each other are said to be *coupled*. Coupling leads to a situation where a small change in module A can cause modules D, E, and F to malfunction. These concepts are discussed in detail in *Reliable Software through Composite Design* by Glenford Meyers.

5. Use procedures in dBASE III. dBASE III allows you to put up to thirty-two procedures in a single file. Each procedure is a separate module that can be accessed quickly since the main file is opened only once. This means you can break your program into modules and not worry about it slowing down. dBASE II does not allow procedures. Whenever a separate command file is called in dBASE II, it must be located on the disk and read into memory before running. This process slows down the execution speed of the overall program.

DOCUMENTATION

Documentation can be divided into two broad categories. The first is documenting the program itself so that it can be understood six months later. The second type of documentation is an explanation of the program for the people who will use it. Both types are very important. The reason is simple: programs are to be understood and used by humans. This is sometimes overlooked or forgotten, and the documentation (and the user) suffers. Since this section is an overview of programming practices, we summarize program documentation here. Program documentation is thoroughly covered in chapter 13. User documentation is covered in chapter 10.

Good documentation is particularly important on larger systems because they are more complex and thus more difficult to understand. You should begin documenting at the design stage. As you go through the problem definition and solution design steps, you should begin to define the architecture of the system, the various modules in the system and their relationships. You make decisions on what data representations to use and how they interrelate. As you proceed with stepwise refinement, the logic of each module is designed and the system takes shape on a detailed level. The pseudo-code for a module provides an excellent description of the logic and program flow. All of this information is very useful to anyone trying to understand the code and so should be incorporated into the system documentation. If you wait until the system is finished before starting the documentation, it will almost always be incomplete.

The code itself should also be documented in several ways. As changes are made in the program, the documentation must be updated to reflect them. A frequently used method to document program changes is to have a *change log* at the top of each program. This log is a running record of what changes have been made, who made them, and the date of the change. In addition to a change log, a *preamble* should be included at the top of each module. The preamble states the function of the module, its inputs, its outputs, what modules call it, what modules it calls, a list of important variables, any special operating requirements, descriptions of key algorithms used, and any other important information necessary to understand what the module does and how it works. The program itself should contain comments within it which explain any code that is not obvious in itself. Important branches and loops should be commented to explain what is being done and why.

The content of the comment is important. It should not mimic the code, but should explain the logic or purpose of the code. Assume that whoever is reading the code is familiar with the programming language. For example,

```
; Subtract 80H from x      (comment)
x - 80H                     (code)
```

The comment above is not informative, since it simply repeats what is already stated by the code. The comment below explains what is being done and why.

```
; If a byte has a value greater than 7F hex (top of  ASCII),
; convert it to ASCII by stripping off the high order bit.
; If this is not done,  some  non-ASCII bytes will be sent
; to printer and may cause problems.
x - 80H
```

Comments should be written as the coding is being done, not after it is complete. When you are coding, the section in progress is fresh in your mind and you can easily describe what it does.

The code itself will be much easier to read if it is properly structured and indented. Indentations should clearly show where control structures such as loops and branches begin and end. Which of the examples below is easier to read, the one with or without indentations?

```
DO WHILE nextdate <= enddate
   mday = substr((CDOW(nextdate)),1,3)
   mdate = DTOC(nextdate)
   DO CASE
     CASE mday="Fri" .OR. mday="Sun" .OR. mday="Tue"
        exercise = "RUNNING"
     CASE mday="Wed" .OR. mday="Sat"
        exercise = "WEIGHTS"
     CASE mday = "Mon" .OR. mday="Thu"
        exercise = "REST    "
   ENDCASE
   nextdate = nextdate +1
ENDDO


DO WHILE nextdate <= enddate
mday = substr((CDOW(nextdate)),1,3)
mdate = DTOC(nextdate)
DO CASE
CASE mday="Fri" .OR. mday="Sun" .OR. mday="Tue"
exercise = "RUNNING"
CASE mday="Wed" .OR. mday="Sat"
exercise = "WEIGHTS"
CASE mday = "Mon" .OR. mday="Thu"
exercise = "REST    "
ENDCASE
nextdate = nextdate +1
ENDDO
```

A final important point which will make your code understandable is to select variable names and field names which have meaning. Both dBASE II and III allow field names and variable names up to ten characters in length. Some suggested style guidelines for naming are given in chapter 13.

VOLUME = LENGTH * WIDTH * HEIGHT

is much more descriptive than

X = L * Q * R.

The following is a summary of important documentation points:

1. Start the documentation during the design process.
2. Use a preamble at the top of each program module to summarize the key information concerning that module.
3. Keep an up-to-date change log for each module.
4. Use comments within the code to explain what is being done whenever this is not obvious from the code itself.
5. Use indentation to clearly show the beginning and end of control structures.
6. Select variable names which describe the quantities they represent.

It may appear that we have gone overboard on documentation and that what we recommend is too elaborate. It isn't. It does take a certain amount of discipline to do a good job documenting your code, but it will pay off in the long run. If you come back to the code a year later to make a modification, good documentation will enable you to understand the code quickly. Many programs are written with the thought that they will be short-lived and then discarded so "there is no need to document," but we have found that "short-lived" utilities often wind up being used for a long time and must be maintained. After you follow these guidelines for a while, you will find that good documentation becomes part of your coding process and actually helps you do a better job in organizing and planning. Chapter 13, "Program Documentation," gives some suggested conventions to use in documenting dBASE programs.

TESTING AND DEBUGGING

All programs of any size are likely to contain bugs. Some bugs have been very expensive. On July 22, 1962, the U.S. Mariner I rocket was launched on a mission to explore Venus. This was the first U.S. attempt to explore the planets. The rocket veered off course and had to be destroyed. An investigation revealed that a software error was responsible for the problem. Despite extensive testing and debugging, the omission of a single hyphen from one of the program statements had been overlooked. This bug caused the entire mission to fail at a cost of $18.5 million.[2]

Debugging is the process of correcting errors which have been found by testing. This is usually the final step of software development, and the time needed to accomplish the process is often underestimated. Programmers tend to be optimistic about their creations and think there are few if any errors present. Yet it is not uncommon to spend more than 50% of a project's programming time on debugging. In this section we give an overview of common types of errors and the debugging process. A more detailed discussion of debugging dBASE programs can be found in chapter 24.

Debugging cannot occur unless you are aware of a program error. Errors are located by testing. The process of testing and debugging are entirely separate. At Ashton-Tate we have an entire department, Software Test, which is responsible for testing all of the software produced by the company. The people in Software Test systematically test the software to see if it performs according to specification. Whenever an error is encountered, it is fully documented in an "error report" and sent to the programmers in the development group who then correct the error. The Software Test department is not directly involved in the activity of debugging.

The process of testing could be considered more important than debugging because, if errors are not uncovered, they cannot be fixed. Inadequate testing leaves errors lurking in the software which are likely to manifest after the program is in use. If the resources are available, it is a good idea to have the testing done by a separate group from the programmers who are doing the debugging. The programmers who write the software are often too close to it to be able to find errors efficiently. The better the two groups work as a team, the faster the entire process will be accomplished.

It is practically impossible to prove that a program is correct by exhaustive testing. The number of unique paths in a system increases exponentially as branches and loops are added. This, combined with the fact that the number of unique inputs can be astronomical, makes it nearly impossible to test all combinations. A test plan should be designed carefully. Here are some rules of thumb for software testing.

1. Do *unit testing* first. This means testing each module independently from the total program. Provide the module with inputs which systematically check as many paths as possible and verify that the output from each module is correct. It is also important to test border cases. Border cases are tested by using inputs near and at the designed input limits for the module. If for example, a payroll input routine is designed to take values between 5,000 and 50,000, both 5,000 and 50,000 should be tested, as well as 4,999.99 etc. Studies have shown that 50% to 65% of the bugs available can be found by thorough unit testing. Unit tests should be designed by someone familiar with the code being tested.

2.   Develop and maintain a library of standard test routines. These can then be used over and over as the software is debugged. Often, correcting one error results in introducing other errors. As the testing and debugging process continues, the test library can be run on the latest version of the software. As new tests are developed, they are added to the test library.

3.   Test how error conditions are handled. Intentionally create error conditions using wrong inputs and see if these are handled correctly. Input a number when the program is looking for a character string, divide by zero, give it input outside acceptable ranges, and subject data to other such situations to test how input errors are handled.

4.   Do functional testing. Functional testing treats the program as a black box and checks to see if it performs according to specification. This means that you have a specification describing precisely how the program should perform. Functional testing does not concern itself with the internal structure of the program. These tests should be incorporated into your test library and should be done after the unit testing is complete.

Software testing is a very challenging field and has developed a considerable body of technology in the past few years. It is an important topic which is often overlooked in a software project. We have listed several books on software testing at the end of this chapter if you wish to pursue this topic further.

Types of Errors

Errors can occur during every phase of the software development process. Errors during the problem definition and solution design steps are particularly expensive to correct late in a project's development since these types of errors often require a re-design and re-coding of major modules. Studies in large corporations that use data processing facilities heavily have shown that over 50% of the bugs are in the problem definition stage of development. Worse yet, more than 80% of the effort needed to fix bugs is devoted to those errors generated during the problem definition stage.[3] Many of these fundamental errors occurred as a result of communication breakdown between program was being written for and the programmers. This should alert you to be very careful whenever you decide to write a program for another party. Make certain that both parties understand exactly what is wanted. When possible, it is a good idea to produce a prototype and let the user try it out. It is natural for users to come up with new requests for the system based on their experience using the system.

The next serious place to make an error is during the solution design step. During this step the problem is analysed stepwise and divided into its functional parts. Algorithms are selected to carry out each function efficiently and pseudo-code is written to specify the details of the program flow. If an error is made in any of these steps, it results in incorrect code. After the design error has been corrected, the code may need to be rewritten from scratch. Sometimes an algorithm is selected which turns out to be too slow or to yield an incorrect answer. *Flowcharts* are often helpful in showing up errors during the design process. Above all, don't hurry this phase of development. Many programmers are eager to begin coding and skimp on the design phase which can result in serious problems later on.

After the solution has been formulated, the coding process begins. Several specific types of errors which can occur here are summarized below. Chapter 24, "Debugging," contains a more complete discussion of these errors and gives suggestions on how to locate and fix them in dBASE programs.

Syntax Errors.   All languages have precise rules of syntax which must be followed when coding. Syntax errors are such things as misspelled words, incorrect symbols, omitted punctuation, or unmatched parentheses.

Logic Errors.   These errors can occur during coding as well as during the design phase. Failing to specify a looping criteria correctly will cause the loop to execute either too many or too few times. Incorrect branching criteria will cause a wrong path to be taken at an IF...ELSE...ENDIF juncture. Branching decisions are based on the outcome of statements which evaluate to either true or false. These expressions must be correct.

Misunderstanding.   Major errors can occur if the program design is misunderstood, and such errors will require that the module be re-written.

These are the most common classes of errors that can occur during coding. dBASE will catch many of these errors and issue appropriate error messages. However, logic errors will often not be flagged. No programming language can know what a correct logic path is for your program; so, these errors must be located and removed by the programmer. Chapter 24 as well as some of the references in the bibliography give a detailed discussion of debugging methods for dBASE programs.

The activity of programming can be viewed from many perspectives. In this chapter, we have divided it into six distinct phases which build upon one another.

Defining the problem
Designing a solution
Coding
Documentation
Software testing
Debugging

If you follow these procedures, and do a systematic job at each step, you will find that the quality of your programs will improve considerably. The philosophy embodied in this systematic approach to programming comes from what is called *structured programming*. Structured programming has gained wide acceptance, and stresses the importance of program design and modular, understandable code. It is the topic of our next chapter.

END NOTES

1.   Frederick P. Brooks Jr., *The Mythical Man-month* (Reading, MA: Addison-Wesley, 1975).
2.   B. Wallace, D. Wallenchinsky, A. Wallace, and S. Wallace, *The Book of Lists #2* (New York: William Morrow & Co. Inc., 1980), p. 486.
3.   James Martin and Carma McClure, *Software Maintenance* (Englewood Cliffs, NJ: Prentice-Hall, 1983).

BIBLIOGRAPHY

Aho, Alfred et al. *The Design and Analysis of Computer Algorithms.* Reading, MA: Addison-Wesley, 1974.
Beizer, Boris. *Software Testing Techniques.* New York: Van Nostrand Reinhold, 1983.
Brooks, Frederick P. Jr. *The Mythical Man-month.* Reading, MA: Addison-Wesley, 1975.
Collected Algorithms from the CACM, Association for Computing Machinery.
Knuth, Donald. *The Art of Computer Programming: Vol. 1-3.* Reading, MA: Addison-Wesley, 1969.
Lewis, William E. *Problem-Solving Principles For Programmers: Applied Logic, Psychology, and Grit.* Rochelle Park, NJ: Hayden Book
      Co., 1980.
Linz, Peter. *Programming Concepts and Problem Solving.* Menlo Park, CA: Benjamin-Cummings Publishing Co., 1983.
Martin, James, and McClure, Carma. *Software Maintenance.* Englewood Cliffs, NJ: Prentice-Hall, 1983.
Myers, Glenford J. *The Art of Software Testing.* New York: John Wiley & Sons, 1979.
Myers, Glenford J. *Reliable Software Through Composite Design.* New York: Van Nostrand Reinhold, 1975.
Sedgewick, Robert. *Algorithms.* Reading, MA: Addison-Wesley, 1983.

Van Tassel, Dennie. *Program Style, Design, Efficiency, Debugging, and Testing*. Englewood Cliffs, NJ: Prentice-Hall, 1978.

Wallace, B., Wallenchinsky, D., Wallace, A., and Wallace, S. *The Book of Lists #2*. New York: William Morrow & Co. Inc., 1980.

Wirth, Niklaus. *Algorithms + Data Structures = Programs*. Englewood, NJ: Prentice-Hall, 1976.

CHAPTER FIVE

STRUCTURED PROGRAMMING

The technology of software engineering has evolved in parallel with computer hardware technology. Chapter 3 described the evolution of languages from machine language to the high-level languages in use today. As the capability of computers and software systems grew, languages were called upon to solve increasingly complex tasks and to manage ever larger databases. A major hurdle in the evolution of software has been developing methods that enable us to create large, complex software systems which are both reliable and easy to maintain. Structured Programming is a body of techniques which makes the process of programming easier to accomplish. The techniques are general enough so that they can be applied to virtually any size project and used with any language.

Edsger Dijkstra started the ball rolling toward structured techniques when, in 1968, he wrote a letter to the editor of *Communications of the ACM* (Association for Computing Machinery). The letter was titled "Go To Statement Considered Harmful" and observed that the quality of programmers decreased as a function of the number of GOTO statements used in their programs.[1] He went on to describe how GOTO statements tend to create convoluted logic paths which obscure program clarity. He recommended that the GOTO statement be abolished from all high-level languages.

This recommendation had been made before but had not been widely accepted. Prior to Dijkstra's letter, in 1966, Giuseppe Jacopini and Corrado Bohm had shown that *any* proper program could be written without GOTO statements using only three programming structures.[2] These structures are *sequence, choice* (if...then...else), and *repetition* (do...while). A proper program is one which has only one entrance and one exit point and no endless loops or portions of code that are unreachable. If programs are written using these structures they will be easier to understand, debug, and maintain. The acceptance of what is now known as structured programming took several years. These principles are now in wide use and taught by many schools.

The GOTO statement is present in many languages and, when executed, causes unconditional branching to another location in the program. Unconditional means there is no choice: the program just branches, that is, goes to the label or line number specified in the GOTO statement. A program with many GOTO statements sprinkled throughout is difficult to understand because the program flow is disjointed and jumps back and forth. People tend to think in a forward direction and can only hold a limited number of related facts in the mind at once. Most programmers can trace a program through approximately seven levels of branching before getting confused. A program that jumps back and forth is difficult to understand, much more likely to contain errors, and certainly more difficult to test and debug. Dividing a program into small, easy to understand modules using the three structured constructs (sequence, choice, repetition) results in programs that are easier to understand and that contain fewer errors.

dBASE does not contain a GOTO statement in the sense described here. dBASE does contain a GOTO command, but it is used to move the record pointer in a data file to a specific record. For example: *GOTO 267* would cause dBASE to move its record pointer to record number 267 in a data file. This is entirely different from a GOTO which causes program control to jump to a different place in the program.

dBASE does contain the three structured constructs mentioned above which encourage the use of structured programming methods.

ELEMENTS OF STRUCTURED PROGRAMMING

Structured programming contains four important elements:

1. Top-down design with stepwise refinement
2. Modular program structures
   –designed in a hierarchical fashion with one function per module
   –designed to be understandable
3. All programs and modules are proper
   –contain a single entrance and exit point
   –contain no endless loops
   –contain no unreachable sections of code
4. Programs are written in a structured fashion
   –using structured constructs
   –well commented and designed to be readable

Structured programming allows you to organize the process of design and coding in such a way as to avoid errors in logic.

We introduced the top-down approach to designing a solution in chapter 4. As you saw, a solution should first be approached from the "top" or most general view. This method is not necessarily intuitive. Programmers often have a tendency to work from the bottom up for several reasons. Because programmers are oriented toward writing code (bottom activity) and are often under time pressure, the following type of thinking often occurs: "Design is OK if it doesn't take too much time"; "The computer doesn't care how well the program was designed or how difficult the program is for humans to understand"; and "If the program results in the desired output then it has accomplished its purpose and is correct." This type of thinking results in coding before an adequate design has been formulated.

Consider a simple program which allows a company to manage its customer list. Here are some typical functions that might be performed:

Entry of data
Finding data by customer name
Editing data
Reports, labels, billing

A bottom-up approach begins coding each module separately and then, after the individual modules are complete, "ties them all together." In contrast to this, a top-down approach first designs a solution by dividing the program into its functions and placing them into a hierarchy according to how they relate to one another.

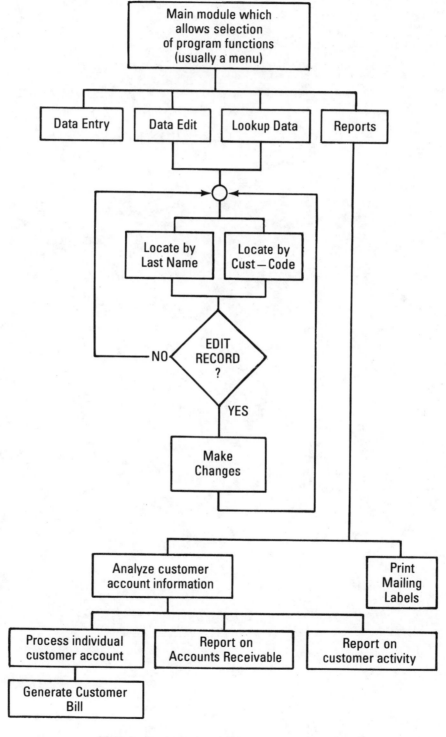

Modules in a customer data management system

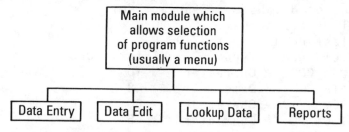

Figure 5-1
Customer data management system divided into four functions

These four functions can be further subdivided (stepwise refinement) into smaller modules which would define the system at a more detailed level and show the flow of control between modules.

Creating a hierarchy is important when diagramming a modular system; it shows the flow of control in a program. Thus, a module is called by the one above it and can call those below it but not those above it. Another rule is that a module returns to the one which invoked it after it has finished performing its function. Limiting the flow of control to clearly specified paths has several advantages. It reduces the interaction between modules so that if a change is made in one module it will only affect the module which is directly above it. A large program that exists as a monolithic chunk is very difficult to modify because a change in one section of the program can have unpredictable effects on other parts of the program. Like a bowl of Chinese noodles, everything is intertwined. If you pull a noodle on one side, something on the other side of the bowl moves. Even if the program is divided into modules, trouble can occur if many modules invoke each other and there is not a well defined hierarchy of control. Dividing your program into modules and then specifying a hierarchy of program control that minimizes module interaction produces a program which is easier to understand and modify.

After specifying program flow, the programmer should define the data structures. It is important to use efficient data structures which do not contain unnecessary duplication. It is useful to list what data is input to and output from each module. This step will show clearly what data is passed between modules. Often only a few fields need to be passed instead of an entire record. A complete understanding of the data flows in a program allows efficient data structure design. Figure 5-2 shows two dBASE data structures which could be used in our customer database. The first one, Customer.dbf, contains the basic information for each customer, including a unique customer code, Cust_code. The second structure contains the information for a transaction and is tied, or related, to a customer by the customer code. The two structures share a single common field, Cust_code. This allows us to have many transactions for each customer and not enter all the customer data for each transaction, which saves space on the disk as well as data entry and updating time.

```
Structure for database : Customer.dbf
Number of data records :      1
Date of last update    : 07/06/84
Field  Field name  Type        Width    Dec
    1  COMPANY     Character      25
    2  CUST_NAME   Character      25
    3  ADDRESS     Character      30
    4  CITY        Character      25
    5  STATE       Character       2
    6  ZIP_CODE    Character       5
    7  CUST_CODE   Character      10
    8  CREDIT_LIM  Numeric        10      2
** Total **                      133
```

```
Structure for database : Transact.dbf
Number of data records :      0
Date of last update    : 07/06/84
Field  Field name   Type       Width    Dec
    1  CUST_CODE    Character     10
    2  DATE         Date           8
    3  ITEM         Character     50
    4  STOCK_NO     Character      5
    5  QUANTITY     Numeric        4
    6  PRICE        Numeric        6       2
    7  TAX          Numeric        4       2
    8  SHIPPING     Numeric        4       2
    9  TOTAL_COST   Numeric        8       2
** Total **                      100
```

Figure 5-2
Data structures for customer database

Using structured programming techniques does not guarantee a good design. A good design is usually not your first design. It pays to take several passes at the design phase with the intention of simplifying both structures and module interactions during each pass. Problems vary widely in complexity and in how precisely they are defined. In general, the complexity of a solution is proportional to the complexity of the problem. Sometimes you will discover a relationship in the system which will greatly simplify the solution. This type of breakthrough leads to an improved design, but such discoveries usually only come after studying the problem carefully. Research has shown that more than 50% of software errors are introduced at the design phase which means that time spent on improving a design is well worth it. [3] A design error discovered late in a project may be expensive to fix and can mean scrapping work and doing parts of the program over from scratch. In the next section, we discuss program control structures which allow you to write programs that are easier to follow and contain fewer errors.

PROGRAMMING CONTROL STRUCTURES

In addition to the structured design process outlined above, structured programming involves the use of three programming control structures (sometimes called constructs): sequence, choice, and repetition. These three control structures allow any proper program to be written in a structured fashion. The example below shows the programming constructs provided by dBASE II and dBASE III.

dBASE II
Sequence
Choice (branching)

- IF. . .ELSE. . .ENDIF
- DO CASE. . .ENDCASE

Repetition (looping)
- DO WHILE. . .ENDDO

Subroutine
- DO <command file>

dBASE III
Sequence
Choice (branching)

- IF. . .ELSE. . .ENDIF
- DO CASE. . .ENDCASE

Repetition (looping)
- DO WHILE. . .ENDDO

Subroutine
- DO <command file>
Procedures
- DO <procedure>

In order to show pictorially how these structures work, we use three standard flow chart symbols.

Process Symbol

This symbol shows one entrance and one exit and means that an operation will be performed. The operation can be a single statement or several structures.

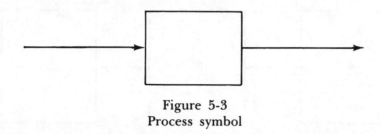

Figure 5-3
Process symbol

Decision Symbol

This symbol has one control path in and two possible paths out. Control is transferred to one (not both) of the two paths based on whether the expression P evaluates as true or false. This symbol represents a choice or decision. P stands for predicate and represents the test for true or false.

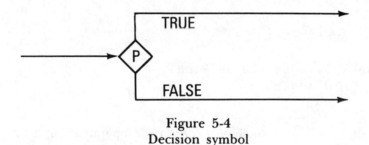

Figure 5-4
Decision symbol

Collector Symbol

This symbol has two inputs and a single output. It represents no operation being performed but means that two control paths converge and a single path results.

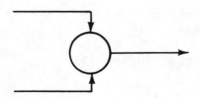

Figure 5-5
Collector symbol

dBASE PROGRAMMING STRUCTURES

Sequence

Sequence, or series, structures are sets of commands which are performed one after another in a linear fashion. The natural flow of a dBASE command file is sequential until a branching, repeating, or procedural command is encountered. The diagram below illustrates this type of program flow.

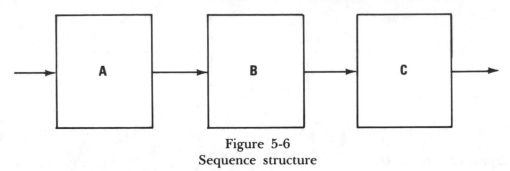

Figure 5-6
Sequence structure

All dBASE commands can be used in series. The order in which the commands are written dictates the order dBASE will follow in executing them. The sequence in which commands are executed can be quite important in some instances and meaningless in others. For example, the following code can be executed in any order with the same results and in the same amount of time:

```
USE File1
STORE 0.00 TO amount
SET BELL OFF
INPUT "Enter Bank Balance" TO bank:bal
STORE " / / " TO mdate
SET EXACT ON
```

Of course, it makes more sense to combine related code operations into modules for readability, understanding, and commenting. It is also a good practice not to open *any* file before it is absolutely necessary:

```
* Establish working environment.
SET BELL OFF
SET EXACT ON
*
* Initialize memvars, and get current balance from operator.
STORE " / / " TO mdate
STORE 0.00 TO amount
INPUT "Enter Bank Balance" TO bank:bal
*
* Open the file.
USE File1
```

In the following example, using the SET LINKAGE ON flag, the order of execution is quite important.

```
* The following method will NOT link the files.
USE File1
SELECT SECONDARY
USE File2
SET LINKAGE ON

* This is the proper way to link files.
SET LINKAGE ON
USE File1
SELECT SECONDARY
USE File2
```

Branching Structures (Choice)

A branching (conditional) structure allows the selection of one or more alternatives to the logical program flow. This branching involves the "detouring" of the path of command execution. At the start of the branch, a logical expression is evaluated for its truth or falsehood. If the expression is evaluated as true, the commands immediately following the expression are executed. These commands are "in the branch." If the expression is evaluated as false, the commands in the branch are not executed. Whether these branch commands are executed or not, program flow continues with the command immediately following the end of the conditional structure.

dBASE contains two branching structures, IF...ELSE...ENDIF and DO CASE...ENDCASE. The IF...ELSE...ENDIF construct is used when a single test is to be made and one of two alternative paths taken based on the result of the test. This structure can be nested to provide multiple decision points. There is no limit to the number of IF...ELSE...ENDIFs which may be nested. However, when IF...ELSE...ENDIF commands are nested too deeply, the resulting code can be difficult to read. When possible the DO CASE...ENDCASE construct should be used instead of deeply nested If...ELSE...ENDIF structures. Figure 5-7 shows the IF...ELSE...ENDIF structure.

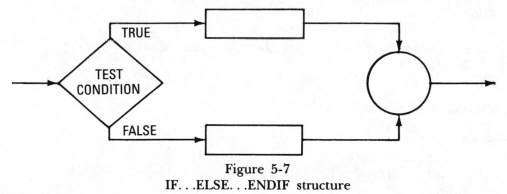

Figure 5-7
IF...ELSE...ENDIF structure

The CASE structure, DO CASE...ENDCASE, is a multi-branch construct used to select one of several options. The CASE structure is not one of the primary constructs of structured programming because it can be duplicated with several nested IF...ELSE...ENDIF statements. It is used because in multi-branch situations, it executes faster than nested IF...ELSE...ENDIF statements and it reduces complexity—thus making the program flow easier to follow.

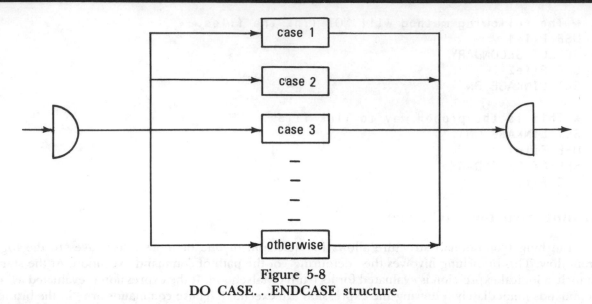

Figure 5-8
DO CASE. . .ENDCASE structure

A key point to remember when using the IF. . .ELSE. . .ENDIF structure is that you must properly construct the logical expression to be tested. This determines which branch will be taken. Sometimes these expressions are complex and must be formed carefully. The subject of how logical expressions are evaluated is covered in chapter 6. Here are three examples of IF. . .ELSE. . .ENDIF. The second one contains a more complex logical expression to be tested, the third shows nested IFs.

```
IF mselect = "Y"
    DO Paybills
ELSE
    RELEASE ALL
ENDIF

IF Part=mPart .AND. (Qty < Reorder .OR. Date < mDate)
    Do Update
ENDIF

IF mselect = "Y"
    DO Program1
ELSE
    IF mdate = Date
        DO Program2
    ELSE
        IF Quantity < 10
            DO Program3
        ENDIF   (Quantity)
    ENDIF   (mdate)
ENDIF   (mselect)
```

Every IF must have a corresponding ENDIF and only one ELSE branch is allowed per IF statement. In the example above, the ENDIFs have comments showing to which IF they correspond. dBASE does not read the text on the same line following an ENDIF and therefore allows comments to be placed there.

Here is an example of a CASE statement and the same code written with IF...ELSE...ENDIF statements. Notice how much easier it is to read the CASE statement. The CASE statement will also execute faster.

```
* Execute one of three options          * Execute one of three
* or return                             * options or return
DO CASE                                 IF option=0
   CASE option=0                           RETURN
      RETURN                            ELSE
   CASE option=1                           IF option=1
      DO Program1                             DO Program1
   CASE option=2                           ELSE
      DO Program2                             IF option=2
   CASE option=3                                DO Program2
      DO Program3                             ELSE
ENDCASE                                         IF option=3
                                                   DO Program 3
                                                ENDIF (option=3)
                                             ENDIF (option=2)
                                          ENDIF (option=1)
                                       ENDIF (option=0)
```

The dBASE CASE structure also contains an OTHERWISE clause which can be placed *after* the CASE options. Only one OTHERWISE clause is allowed per CASE statement. dBASE will execute the code which follows the OTHERWISE if all the CASE options are false. If no OTHERWISE statement is present and all of the CASE statements are false, the program will then exit from the DO CASE...ENDCASE structure without executing any of the CASE statements. Here is an example of a CASE structure using OTHERWISE.

```
DO CASE
   CASE your_age < my_age
      ? "You are younger than I"
   CASE your_age > my_age
      ? "You are older than I"
   OTHERWISE
      ? "We are the same age"
ENDCASE
```

Repetition (Looping)

dBASE has only one structure for repetition or looping, and that is the DO WHILE...ENDDO statement. The DO WHILE evaluates a logical expression and if the expression is true, the commands between the DO WHILE and ENDDO are executed. These commands are called *the body of the loop*. Each time the ENDDO is reached, the logical expression at the DO WHILE is evaluated again and if it is still true, the body of the loop continues to be executed. When the expression evaluates to false, the program jumps to the matching ENDDO and continues executing with the statement following the ENDDO. Figure 5-9 shows a DO WHILE...ENDDO loop.

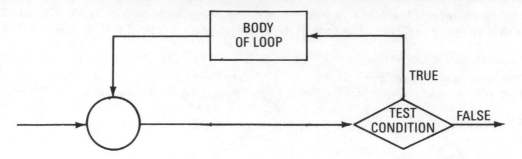

Figure 5-9
DO WHILE...ENDDO structure

The following is an example of a DO WHILE loop which initializes memory variables. In this example the logical expression *number <= 5* is evaluated and while this expression is true, the body of the loop continues to be executed. The first statement in the loop body, *STORE STR(number,1) to stringnum* converts the numeric value of *number* to a character and stores it to the variable *stringnum*. The next line concatenates two strings "string"+ *the value of stringnum* to create a variable which "dummy value" is stored to. Notice that the third statement in the loop's body, *STORE number + 1 TO number,* increments the value of number by one each time the loop is executed. After five repetitions the value of *number* is 6 and the expression *number <= 5* becomes false—thereby terminating the loop. If the expression evaluated by the DO WHILE is always true, you will have an "endless loop," which means the program will loop "forever."

```
* Generate five string memory variables
SET TALK OFF
STORE 1 TO number
DO WHILE number <= 5
    STORE STR(number,1) TO stringnum
    STORE "dummy value" TO string&stringnum
    STORE number + 1 TO number
ENDDO
DISPLAY MEMORY
```

Here is the output from the above loop showing the memory variables created.

```
NUMBER        priv  N            6  (           6.00000000)
STRINGNUM     priv  C   "5"
STRING1       priv  C   "dummy value"
STRING2       priv  C   "dummy value"
STRING3       priv  C   "dummy value"
STRING4       priv  C   "dummy value"
STRING5       priv  C   "dummy value"
     7 variables defined,        77 bytes used
   249 variables available,    5923 bytes available
```

In order to avoid an endless loop, the body of the loop must provide some way for the loop to terminate:

1. A command with the potential to change the value of the logical expression evaluated by the DO WHILE.
2. A conditional branch containing a command that will exit the loop such as EXIT or RETURN.

SUBPROGRAMS AND PROCEDURES

Any program can be written with the structures we have described so far. However, because it is advantageous to divide larger programs into smaller programs or subprograms, most languages have facilities that allow this. Both dBASE II and III allow subprograms to be used. However, only dBASE III has a specific procedure structure. Procedures are a special type of subprogram. A subprogram is usually called to perform a specific operation. dBASE allows you to write separate command files which can be invoked by the command DO <command filename>. This command causes the named command file to be executed. When the subprogram has completed its sequence of commands or a RETURN is encountered, control is passed back to the calling module at the command just after the DO <command filename> command. Figure 5-10 shows a flowchart of how subprograms operate.

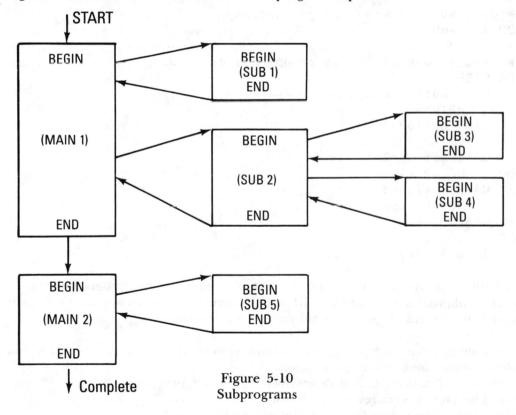

Figure 5-10
Subprograms

In the example below, the program AP_main.prg calls several subprograms which perform all the work. After each subprogram is finished, it returns to AP_main. The choice that the user makes in AP_menu sets the memory variable *option* to 0,1,2, or 3, and control is returned to AP_main. Next, the appropriate option is selected from the DO CASE selections. This shows that in dBASE II, all memory variables are global; that is, all variables are available to all command files. When the subprogram AP_menu changed the value of *option*, the new value was recognized by the CASE statement in AP_main.

Global variables can sometimes cause problems. For example, if Program1 changes a variable used by Program2 in a way that was not intended by Program2, Program2 will give a wrong answer because one of its variables was unexpectedly altered by Program1. In dBASE III, this type of problem is avoided, since variables are local (private) to the program they exist in, unless you specifically declare them as global (public).

dBASE III variables are only available to the file that created them and any other files that are called by the original file:

```
* Program.: AP_main.prg   (dBASE II)
* Notes...: An example of a modularized command file.
*
* Set flags and initialize memory variables
DO AP_init
*
DO WHILE T
   *
   * Display main menu and get option.
   DO AP_menu
   *
   * Execute one of the three options or return.
   DO CASE
      CASE option=0
         RETURN
      CASE option=1
         DO AP_add
      CASE option=2
         DO AP_view
      CASE option=3
         DO AP_repo
   ENDCASE
ENDDO
* EOF AP_main.prg
```

dBASE III allows procedures. The word "procedure" can refer to a subprogram itself or to a file which contains several subprograms. In dBASE III a procedure file can contain up to thirty-two separate procedures or subprograms. Procedures fall into four categories:

1. Those that stand alone and perform a function without input from another program.
    Example: A stand-alone report procedure.
2. Those that accept data from and return data to another program.
    Example: The Stat procedures shown below.
3. Those that only accept data from another program.
    Example: A routine that prints a report header.
4. Those that only return data to another program.
    Example: A routine that returns the current time.

A procedure that performs a function independent of program variables external to that procedure can stand alone. Examples of this type of procedure would be displaying a screen layout, printing a report header, or initializing a set of known variables. Here is an example of a stand-alone procedure that prints a custom report.

```
* PROGRAM.: Example.prg (dBASE III)
* NOTES...: Example of calling stand-alone procedure.
*
SET PROCEDURE TO REPORT
DO WHILE .T.
   SET PRINT ON
   DO Header
   DO Report1
   DO Report2
   SET PRINT OFF
   ACCEPT "Do you want to print another report?" TO again
   IF UPPER(again) = "N"
      EXIT
   ENDIF
ENDDO
* EOF Example.prg


* Program.: Report.prg (dBASE III)
* Notes...: Example of stand-alone procedures
*
PROCEDURE HEADER
   * Prints Report Header
   ? " ++++++   JONES COMPANY - 1984 SALES REPORT   ++++++++"
   ?
   ?
RETURN

PROCEDURE REPORT1
   * Prints Report # 1
   *
   * <Commands for custom report # 1>
   *
RETURN

PROCEDURE REPORT2
   * Prints Report # 2
   *
   * <Commands for custom report  # 2>
   *
RETURN
* EOF Report.prg
```

Another type of procedure takes values passed to it from the calling program, performs operations on the data, and then passes back values to the calling program. This passing of information between programs is called *parameter passing*. The example given below shows two command files, Statcall.prg and Stat.prg and illustrates parameter passing. Stat computes the mean, median, and standard deviation of all the records for any numeric field in the specified database. Statcall is the main program which asks for the user to input the filename and fieldname to be used. In this example, the field must be numeric. After the filename and fieldname are entered, the database is opened and the first procedure, *mean*, is called. Notice that the variables *mfield* and *answer* are passed to *mean* which computes the mean value for the specified field by averaging all the records in the database. This value is passed back to Statcall as the variable *answer* and then displayed on the screen. Two other procedures are then called in a similar fashion. Each of these answers is then passed back to Statcall and displayed. The lines which are involved in parameter passing are in boldface because this concept is important.

```
* Program.: Statcall.prg   (dBASE III)
* Notes...: Control module which calls statistic procedures
*
SET PROCEDURE TO STAT
answer = 0
DO WHILE .T.
   ACCEPT "Enter filename to check " TO mfile
   IF LEN(mfile) = 0
      CLOSE PROCEDURE
      EXIT
   ENDIF
   ACCEPT "Enter fieldname to check " TO mfield
   USE &mfile
   DO Mean WITH mfield,answer
   ? "Mean= ",answer
   DO Median WITH mfield,answer
   ? "Median= ",answer
   DO Stan_dev WITH mfield,answer
   ? "Standard Deviation= ",answer
ENDDO
* EOF Statcall.prog

* Program.: Stat.prg
* Notes...: Example of procedures in dBASE III
*
PROCEDURE MEAN
   * Computes mean value
   PARAMETERS fieldname,mean
   AVERAGE &fieldname TO mean
RETURN
```

```
PROCEDURE MEDIAN
   * Computes median value
   PARAMETERS fieldname,median
   SORT ON &fieldname to Temp
   USE TEMP
   COUNT TO N
   IF (N/2)-INT(N/2) > 0
      * Odd number of elements
      GOTO ROUND((N+1)/2,0)
      median = &fieldname
   ELSE
      * Even number of elements
      GOTO (N/2)
      lower = &fieldname
      SKIP
      upper = &fieldname
      median = lower + (upper - lower)/2
   ENDIF
   USE &mfile
   DELETE FILE Temp.dbf
RETURN

PROCEDURE STAN_DEV
   * Computes standard deviation
   PARAMETERS fieldname,stand_dev
   SUM &fieldname,0 TO mtotal,squares
   stotal = mtotal*mtotal
   GO TOP
   DO WHILE .NOT. EOF()
      squares = squares + (&fieldname)*(&fieldname)
      SKIP
   ENDDO
   N = RECNO()-1
   stand_dev = SQRT(((N*squares)-(stotal))/(N*(N-1)))
RETURN
* EOF Stat.prg
```

This introduction to structured techniques will allow you to get started with a structured approach to programming. As with any skill, it will take time and practice to become proficient. We recommend that you use the references listed at the end of this chapter as you study this subject further.

END NOTES

1. E. Dijkstra, "Go To Statement Considered Harmful," *Communications of the ACM*, March, 1968.
2. C. Bohm and G. Jacopini, "Flow Diagrams, Turing Machines and Languages with Only Two Formation Rules," *Communications of the ACM*, May, 1966.
3. Dennie Van Tassel, *Program Style, Design, Efficiency, Debugging, and Testing*, Englewood Cliffs, NJ: Prentice-Hall 1978.

BIBLIOGRAPHY

Bennett, William R. Jr. *Scientific And Engineering Problem-solving With The Computer*. Englewood Cliffs, NJ: Prentice-Hall, 1976.

Bohm, C., and G. Jacopini. "Flow Diagrams, Turing Machines and Languages with Only Two Formation Rules." *Communications of the ACM*, May, 1966.

Dijkstra, Edsger. "Go To Statement Considered Harmful." *Communications of the ACM*, March, 1968.

Ejiogu, Lem O. *Effective Structured Programming*. New York: Petrocelli Books, 1983.

Hughes, Joan K. *PL/I Structured Programming*. New York: John Wiley & Sons, 1979.

Kernighan, Brian W., and P.J. Plauger. *The Elements of Programming Style*. New York: McGraw-Hill, 1978.

Linger, Richard C., Harlan D. Mills, and Bernard I. Witt. *Structured Programming: Theory and Practice*. Reading, MA.: Addison-Wesley, 1979.

Martin, James, and Carma McClure. *Software Maintenance*. Englewood Cliffs, NJ: Prentice-Hall, 1983.

Meyers, Glenford J. *Reliable Software Through Composite Design*. New York: Van Nostrand Reinhold Co., 1975.

Pressman, Roger. *Software Engineering: A Practitioner's Approach*. New York: McGraw-Hill, 1982.

Shneiderman, Ben. *Software Psychology*. Cambridge, MA: Withrop Publishers, 1980.

Van Tassel, Dennie. *Program Style, Design, Efficiency, Debugging, and Testing*. Englewood Cliffs, NJ: Prentice-Hall, 1978.

Wirth, Niklaus. *Algorithms + Data Structures = Programs*. Englewood Cliffs, NJ: Prentice-Hall, 1976.

CHAPTER SIX
DATA TYPES

Data is defined as *something known or assumed; facts from which conclusions can be inferred.* Data usually represents some aspect of the physical world around us, such as a list of names and addresses, the temperature of the room, today's date and time, a musical score, the composition and structure of a molecule, or a bank statement.

Information can be represented in many different ways. The way that makes data manipulation easiest and most convenient is usually the best. Numbers, for example, can be represented using decimal, hexadecimal, binary, or Roman numeral notation. Chapter 1 showed how computers represent data in a binary fashion. Although binary representation may be natural for computers, it is not for people. For most people, remembering their phone numbers as decimal numbers is easier than as binary numbers.

213-204-5570   decimal phone number
11010101-11001100-1010111000010   binary phone number

People think with natural language concepts and symbols. Often the concepts and symbols with which we solve problems are imprecise and must be converted into a more precise form to be used by the computer. If someone says "this room is hot," a specific meaning may be conveyed to another person, but since the adjective "hot" is subjective and relative to other temperatures, it is not precise. This type of information must be translated into a form suitable for a computer.

There is a hierarchy in data representation. This is analogous to the hierarchy of machine language (binary) to high-level languages discussed in chapter 3. *A data type is a high level representation of data as seen by the user which has a corresponding internal binary form understood by the computer.* Data types allow people to write programs using data representations with which they are comfortable. The high level representation is maintained internally as a binary format processed by the computer.

Each language provides a limited number of elementary data types. Complex data structures can be constructed from the elementary types. Here are the data types that dBASE provides:

dBASE II	**dBASE III**
Character	Character
Numeric	Numeric
Logical	Logical
	Date

Using these data types, complex data structures useful in representing a multitude of real world situations can be constructed. These data types are discussed in detail in the following sections.

CHARACTER DATA TYPE

Character data is used to represent letters of the alphabet, numbers, and special characters. In both dBASE II and III, the character type is made up of the set of all ASCII characters. A complete table of ASCII characters can be found in appendix E. A *character string*, often just called a *string*, is any sequence of ASCII symbols. When a number is represented as character type data, it must first be converted to numeric data before calculations can be performed with it. It is often convenient to use the character data type for numbers such as telephone numbers, addresses, and inventory stock numbers which will not be used in calculations. Some of the more common operations performed on strings are:

Concatenating strings (linking them together)
Splitting up strings into "substrings"
Testing strings for equality
Finding substrings (string patterns)

dBASE contains operators and functions which allow all of the above processes.

Operator	Description	Examples
+	concatenation	A + B
–	concatenation with blank move	A – B
$	substring comparison	A $ B

Figure 6-1

Here is an example of the concatenation operators.

```
. STORE "TOM       "+"JONES" TO nameplus
TOM       JONES

. STORE "TOM       "-"JONES" TO nameminus
TOMJONES

. ? nameplus
TOM       JONES          (spaces trailing first name remain)

. ? nameminus
TOMJONES                 (spaces trailing first name trimmed
                          before strings are concatenated)
```

Example 6-1

The substring operator tests to see whether a character string, *String1*, matches a substring (portion of the total string) within *String2* and returns a logical value of either TRUE or FALSE.

Here is an example of the substring comparison operator:

```
. STORE "TOM" TO firstname
TOM

. STORE "TOM JONES" TO fullname
TOM JONES

. ? firstname $ fullname
.T.

. ? fullname $ firstname
.F.
```

Example 6-2

dBASE contains a number of other functions to perform string operations. These are discussed in chapter 16.

dBASE character variables are represented in memory in the following manner:

dBASE II

Byte	Contents	Meaning
0	8 bit no.	number of chars in string
1−n	bytes	data bytes 1 $\langle$= n $\langle$= 255

dBASE III

Byte	Contents	Meaning
0−n	bytes	data bytes 0 $\langle$= n $\langle$= 254
n + 1	NUL (00H)	terminator

Figure 6-2

For example,

dBASE II "ABC" =

03H	41H "A"	42H "B"	43H "C"

dBASE III "ABC" =

41H "A"	42H "B"	43H "C"	00H NUL

Figure 6-3

Since dBASE internally represents characters as numbers, it allows the use of relational operators to compare strings. The order of precedence among characters is determined by their relative position in the ASCII chart. Here are some examples:

Character	ASCII value (decimal)
a	97
b	98
c	99
A	65
B	66
C	67

a) . ? "ABC" = "ABC"
   .T.

d) . ? "ABCD" < "AbCD"
   .T.

b) . ? "ABCD" > "ABC"
   .F.

e) . ? "ABCD" > "abc"
   .F.

c) . ? "ABC" > "ABCD"
   .F.

f) . ? "a" > "A"
   .T.

Example 6-3

Lowercase letters are represented by a higher ASCII value and are therefore "greater than" the corresponding uppercase letters. In the example above, "A" has an ASCII value of 65 (decimal), and "a" has a value of 97. This property is used when ordering a set of strings as well as comparing strings. When comparing strings, dBASE compares the character in each position of the first string to the character in the corresponding position in the second string. When using > or <, if two strings differ in length, the characters in the longer string which come after the corresponding position of the last character in the shorter string have no weight in the comparison. This can be seen in (b) and (c) of Example 6-3 where both expressions evaluate to false.

NUMERIC DATA TYPE

Numeric data is used to represent integers or decimal quantities that will undergo computations. dBASE allows a wide range of numbers and has adequate precision for most business and scientific applications. The numeric limits on dBASE III are significantly larger than on dBASE II. dBASE II maintains an internal precision of ten digits; dBASE III, of fifteen or sixteen digits, depending on the size of the number. This allows dBASE III to be accurate on calculations with fairly large numbers without error from rounding off (see Example 6-4). Internally, dBASE III uses the IEEE floating point standard to represent numbers and this is compatible with the 8087 numeric coprocessor. However, at the time of this writing, dBASE III does not use the 8087. The number of places to the right of the decimal point can be controlled when displaying a number using the SET DECIMALS and SET FIXED ON commands. When dealing with dollar values, for example, the decimal point can be set two digits from the right by entering the following commands.

```
SET DECIMALS TO 2
SET FIXED ON
```

Owing to the nature of its internal representation, dBASE II has the following limits on numeric size and precision:

Largest number :	1.8X10^63 approx.
Smallest positive number:	1 X10^-63 approx.
Numeric accuracy:	10 digits

dBASE III has the following limits on numeric size and precision.

Largest number:	1 X 10^308
Smallest positive number:	1 X 10^-307
Numeric accuracy:	15-16 digits (decimal point not included as a digit)

In general, dBASE III will maintain sixteen digits accurately. In the case of large numbers (greater than approximately 8,589,934,591.xxxxxx),dBASE III will maintain fifteen digits. In the example below, when x is incremented by one, the result is accurate to sixteen places, but when x is incremented by two, precision is maintained to fifteen places.

```
. x = 8589934590.123456
8589934590.123456        (16 digit precision)

. limit = x+1
8589934591.123456        (16 digit precision)

. limit = x+2
8589934592.123457        (15 digit precision)

. DISPLAY MEMORY

X          pub   N   8589934590.123456   (8589934590.12345600)
LIMIT      pub   N   8589934592.123457   (8589934592.12345695)
2 variables defined,        18 bytes used
254 variables available,    5982 bytes available
```

Example 6-4

The arithmetic operators are:

Operator	Description	Examples	Version
** or ^	exponentiation	A ^ B	dBASE III
*	multiplication	A * B	dBASE II, III
/	division	A / B	dBASE II, III
+	addition	A + B	dBASE II, III
−	subtraction	A − B	dBASE II, III

Figure 6-4

In addition to these arithmetic operators, dBASE III contains the following mathematical functions (see chapter 16):

Symbol	Description	Example
EXP( )	Exponential (e∧x)	EXP(10) --⟩ 22026.5
INT( )	Integer	INT(123.45) --⟩ 123
LOG( )	Logarithm	LOG(10) --⟩ 2.30
ROUND( )	Round Off	ROUND(2.36,1) --⟩ 2.40
SQRT( )	Square Root	SQRT(2) --⟩ 1.41

Figure 6-5

dBASE II numeric variables are represented in memory in the following manner:

Byte	Contents	Meaning
0	1 bit 7 bits	sign bit, 1 = negative exponent biased by 40H
1-n	packed decimal	mantissa, n = 5

Figure 6-6

Some examples:

Number	Memory Image
0	00 00 00 00 00 00
1	40 10 00 00 00 00
-1	C0 10 00 00 00 00
.1	3F 10 00 00 00 00
123	42 12 30 00 00 00

Figure 6-7

A dBASE programmer need not be concerned with the internal numeric representation dBASE III uses. However, we include a brief description here for those who are curious.

dBASE III represents numbers with the IEEE long real (64-bit) binary floating point representation.[1] This format is compatible with the long real representation used by the 8087. A binary floating point representation is the computer's equivalent to scientific notation. Each number contains three parts: the *sign*, either + or –, the *significand* which represents the significant digits of the number, and the *exponent* which multiplies the significand by the appropriate power to yield the correct binary point position in the final result. The binary point is the binary equivalent of the decimal point. *Mantissa* is another term for the significand.

Examples:

Number	Scientific Notation	Sign	Significand	Exponent
127	1.27×10^2	+	1.27	^{2}
-.67	-6.7×10^{-1}	-	6.7	$^{-1}$
6,925	6.925×10^3	+	6.925	^{3}

Each number is represented internally by a string of sixty four bits (eight bytes). Since there is no way to easily represent the *binary point*, it is positioned implicitly and always at the same location. It is assumed to be immediately to the right of the most significant bit of the significand (See Figure 6-8).

Binary floating point numbers are stored in a *normalized* format. This format is compact and follows certain rules. The leading bit of the significand is always one. This maintains the maximum number of significant digits for the significand. The significand is shifted left or right and the exponent changed appropriately in order to preserve this format. The integer bit (leading significand bit) is implicit and is not actually stored. Using this method, all normalized numbers fall between one and two.

The exponent field determines the actual binary point. A *biased exponent* is used rather than positive or negative exponents which would require a sign bit. The biased exponent is generated by adding a constant, or bias, to the true exponent. The value of this constant is 1023 (3FFH). This forces the biased exponent to a positive value. If, for example, the true exponent is minus three, the biased exponent would be 1020. Zero is represented by all bits in the exponent and significand fields set to zero.

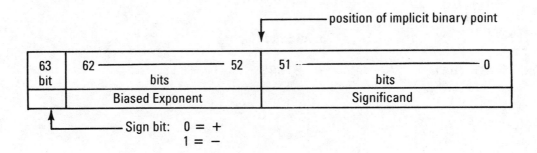

Figure 6-8

Examples:

Number	Memory Image
10	00 00 00 00 00 00 24 40
100	00 00 00 00 00 00 59 40
−127	00 00 00 00 00 C0 5F C0

Figure 6-9

A complete discussion of how to handle numeric data and dBASE numeric functions is given in chapter 16.

LOGICAL DATA TYPE AND BOOLEAN OPERATORS

Implementing Decisions with dBASE

dBASE—like all languages—has the ability to implement decisions. There are several programming structures that have a conditional test built in as part of their execution: DO WHILE...ENDDO, IF...ELSE...ENDIF, DO CASE...CASE...ENDCASE. Each of these structures performs one or more conditional tests during execution and the outcome results in appropriate branching. All such conditional tests must evaluate to either a TRUE or FALSE result. Data or expressions which are either true or false are said to be *Boolean* expressions. They are named after George Boole, an English mathematician who developed an algebra based on true/false logic. The terms *logical* and *Boolean*, as adjectives, are used interchangeably in this discussion. It is important to understand how Boolean operations and logical data behave in order to properly use decision-making structures in dBASE.

Logical Type Data

dBASE allows you to create fields of a type called *logical*. In both dBASE II and dBASE III, a logical field is always one byte long and can only contain a value of true or false. If you list or display logical fields, they are shown as *.T.* or *.F.*. Memory variables can also be logical, either true or false, but dBASE II uses a slightly different symbol than dBASE III to represent logical memory variables. dBASE II represents logical constants or literals with either a *T* or *Y* for true and *F* or *N* for false (periods omitted), whereas dBASE III represents logical constants or literals with *.T.* or *.Y.* for true and *.F.* or *.N.* for false. Lowercase letters may also be used.

Example:

dBASE II

```
. STORE T TO test
```

dBASE III

```
. STORE .T. TO test
```
or
```
. test = .T.
```

Logical fields or memory variables are used to represent types of data when there are only two choices for any element, such as male/female, positive/negative, yes/no, dead/alive. dBASE can perform conditional tests which depend on the value of a logical field or memory variable. The example below would print out "The power is on" since the memory variable *is_on* has been assigned a value of true.

```
is_on = .T.
IF is_on                         (conditional test: is it True or False?)
   ? "The power is on"
ELSE
   ? "The power is off"
ENDIF
```

Relational Operators

In addition to logical fields and memory variables, dBASE has a full set of relational operators that allow logical expressions to be created. *Relational* comes from the word "relation" which means "a logical or natural association between two or more things." dBASE allows you to use relational operators to compare character strings, numbers, or dates, but not logical values or memo fields. The relational expression must compare two values of the *same data type*. Dates must be compared to dates, and numbers compared to numbers. A number cannot be compared to a character or a date. If you want to compare a number to a character, first convert the number to a character with the STR() function or convert the character to a number with the VAL() function, and then make the comparison. dBASE has many conversion functions which make it easy to convert data of one type to another. These functions are summarized in appendix E.

The result of a relational expression is always TRUE or FALSE. This result is used to determine the path in a branching decision such as in an IF. . .ENDIF construct. The six relational operators are listed in Table 6-1 along with the six arithmetic operators. Arithmetic operators are often used in relational expressions involving numeric quantities, and it is often necessary to know the order of precedence for these operations when evaluating an arithmetic expression.

Relational Operators (all have equal precedence)

=	Equal to
<> or #	Not equal to
<	Less than
>	Greater than
<=	Less than or equal to
>=	Greater than or equal to

Arithmetic Operators (in order of precedence)

()	Parentheses for grouping
** or ^	Exponentiation
*, /	Multiplication, Division
+, -	Addition, Subtraction

Table 6-1

How Relational Expressions Are Evaluated

A relational expression is evaluated by first evaluating the expressions on both sides of the relational symbol, then comparing these values. Expressions can contain variables which change value as the program runs, and this provides the power and flexibility of conditional evaluation. An algorithm can test the value of a variable or combination of variables at any point and decide which branch to take depending on the outcome of the test.

For example:

```
IF name = "Joe"
   ? "Hello Joe!"
ENDIF
```

```
IF age >= 65
    ? "You get the Senior Citizen Discount"
ELSE
    ? "You pay Full Boat"
ENDIF
```

The following example uses relational expressions along with the DO CASE construct to determine what type of roots a quadratic equation has. The roots are calculated after the type of root has been identified. dBASE gives an error message on the square root of a negative number; so, in this routine, complex roots are not calculated. Notice how the arithmetic expressions take precedence over the relational expressions.

```
* Program.: Root.prog (dBASE III)
* Notes...: Finds quadratic roots
*
? "Finds roots for ax^2 + bx + c = 0"
INPUT "a= " TO a
INPUT "b= " TO b
INPUT "c= " TO c
discrim = (b^2)-4*a*c
DO CASE
    CASE discrim = 0
        ? "TWO EQUAL ROOTS"
    CASE discrim > 0
        ? "TWO REAL ROOTS"
    CASE discrim < 0
        ? "PAIR OF COMPLEX CONJUGATE ROOTS"
ENDCASE
? "ROOT1 =", (-b + SQRT(discrim))/2*a
? "Root2 =", (-b - SQRT(discrim))/2*a
```

When using complex arithmetic expressions, always use parentheses to group subexpressions—making it easier to see how they relate to each other and in what order operations are performed. Parentheses may also be used to override the order in which operations are performed.

Logical Operators

Another way to compose Boolean expressions is to use the logical operators. A logical operator is one which acts on logical (Boolean) values and gives a result based on simple rules. dBASE provides three fundamental logical operators: AND, OR, NOT. There are others, and they can be created from these three, but these are the most common and can be made to serve in all circumstances. The rules defining the actions of these operators are listed in Table 6-2. NOT is a *unary* operator; that is, it acts only on a single value. It negates the truth value of the logical variable or expression which follows it. dBASE uses a period on each side of the operator to show that it is acting as a logical operator in the command line. The table below shows the results of each logical operator on all possible combinations of true and false. The value of A and B is given on the left side of the table and is either TRUE or FALSE. The result of the operation is given in each column.

Logical Operators

A	B	A .AND. B	A .OR. B
TRUE	TRUE	TRUE	TRUE
TRUE	FALSE	FALSE	TRUE
FALSE	TRUE	FALSE	TRUE
FALSE	FALSE	FALSE	FALSE

.NOT. TRUE   = FALSE
.NOT. FALSE   = TRUE

Table 6-2

Logical operators .AND. and .OR. are used to combine two or more logical expressions, variables, or constants according to the rules defined above.

Let's say a used car dealer wanted to find a 1975 Ford Pinto. Assume the dealer has a database of available cars containing the fields *Year, Manuf, Model*. The following expression would search through the database and locate all records matching these criteria.

```
LOCATE FOR Year = '1975' .AND. Manuf = 'Ford' .AND. Model = 'Pinto'
```

Here are the separate relational subexpressions. Each one evaluates to either TRUE or FALSE.

Year = '1975'
Manuf = 'Ford'
Model = 'Pinto'

Because the logical operator connecting each of these is .AND., all of the individual subexpressions must be true for the entire expression to be true. A 1973 Ford Pinto would not be listed even though it matched two of the three criteria.

Order of Precedence in Operators

If an expression contains several operators, its value can be ambiguous and depend on the order in which the operations are performed. As you may have guessed, there are rules which resolve these situations to give a consistent result. Such rules create an *order of precedence* among operators. The word precedence means "the right of preceding or priority." With some operators it doesn't matter in which order they are performed. These operations are said to be *commutative* if there are two elements and *associative* if there are three or more elements. Addition and multiplication are examples of associative operations. In the example below, the same result is obtained if you start from either end, or anywhere in between, and perform the additions.

2+3+4+5 = 5+4+3+2 = 3+2+4+5 = 14

Subtraction is not associative and the result depends on the order in which the operations are performed. One rule dBASE follows is that when operators have the same order of precedence, they are evaluated from *left to right*. Using parentheses, we can force right to left evaluation to obtain a different result as shown in the example below.

Normal left to right evaluation: 10-3-2-4 = 1
Right to left evaluation: 10-(3-(2-4)) = 5

If adjacent operators do not have the same precedence, the one with higher precedence is applied first. Since multiplication has precedence over addition, the following example is evaluated as follows

2+3*4 = 14

We can force the addition to be done first with parentheses:

(2+3)*= 20

Summary of Precedence Rules

1. Parentheses take precedence over all operators.
2. When two adjacent operators have unequal precedence, the one of higher precedence is applied first.
3. Operators of equal precedence are evaluated left to right.
4. The order of precedence among logical operators for both dBASE II and dBASE III is .NOT..AND..OR..

Mixed Operators

What happens when types of operators are mixed? The precedence rules shown here are for dBASE II and III with mixed operators. Other languages may not have the same rules. Remember that by using parentheses, you can make your own rules by overriding the rules of precedence.

1. Arithmetic operators are evaluated before relational operators. Thus, this type of syntax will work:

```
IF y/z > t+6              IF SQRT(x)/37 = t-y
   <do this code>            <do this code>
ENDIF                     ENDIF
```

2. Relational operators are evaluated before logical operators. This means that in dBASE the following expressions make sense:

```
IF x=y .AND. y<z          IF .NOT. y=z
   <do this code>            <do this code>
ENDIF                     ENDIF
```

Combining the two rules above allows us to create expressions of the following form:

```
IF y+x/3 < t+z .AND. t-76 <= 400/x
 <do this code>
ENDIF
```

The above expression contains arithmetic, relational, and logical operators. dBASE first does the arithmetic, then evaluates the relational expressions which yield true or false results for the final logical operations. When you are developing expressions such as these, you will find that processing mixed expressions in this order makes sense. If you don't like it, you can force a different order by using parentheses.

Keep It Simple

As you can imagine, some very complex expressions can be concocted by combining these operators. Whenever you have a complex situation or set of decision paths to write code for, draw it out on a piece of paper and divide it into its components. Instead of writing a large complex expression, write several simpler ones. Straightforward code is easier to read and to debug later. Always document key expressions in your code by describing what the variables represent, the purpose of the expression, and where the branches go. Such useful comments can save hours if the code must be understood at a later date. Simplicity is the heart of elegance.

DATE DATA TYPE (dBASE III ONLY)

The Date data type, available in dBASE III, is designed specifically to hold dates in the following formats:

American :: = mm/dd/yy
European :: = dd/mm/yy

The date is stored internally as the number of days since a base date. This representation is very useful in accounting applications since it is easy to do date arithmetic such as:

<date1> - <date2> = number of days between date1 and date2

Each date occupies eight bytes of space and can be manipulated with seven different date functions. A complete discussion of how to use the Date data type can be found in chapter 16 in the section on Date data handling.

MEMO FIELDS (dBASE III ONLY)

dBASE III makes available a special type of character field used to store blocks of ASCII data. This is not a different data type since it uses character data. It deserves mention here because it allows the manipulation of large blocks of text as single units. This representation is a unique data structure and differs from the other data representations available in dBASE. At the time of this writing, dBASE III's internal editor has a file size limit which limits the size of Memo fields to 5,000 bytes. However, if an external word processor such as WordStar is used, the size of the Memo field is limited only by the word processor or operating system. The text is stored in 512 byte blocks in a separate file with the same filename as the database but with a .DBT extension. Memo fields make it easy to enter and edit several pages of text at a time. For a more complete discussion of Memo fields and how to use them see chapter 19.

This chapter has introduced you to the concept of a data type and the elementary data types available in dBASE: Character, Numeric, Logical, and Date. Selecting the proper data type to represent the information in a programming problem is often a central factor in devising an efficient solution. In order to accurately represent the involved patterns of data existing in everyday situations, more complex data structures are created. Such complex data structures can be built up from these primary data types. This is the subject of our next chapter.

END NOTES

1. J. Coonan, W. Kahan, J. Palmer, T. Pittman, and D. Stevensen, "A Proposed Standard for Binary Floating Point Arithmetic," *ACM SINNUM* Newsletter (October, 1979).

BIBLIOGRAPHY

Comer, D. *The Ubiquitous B-tree*. ACM Computing Surveys 11, No. 2, June 1979.

Coonan, J., W. Kahan, J. Palmer, T. Pittman, and D. Stevensen, "A Proposed Standard for Binary Floating Point Arithmetic," *ACM SINNUM* Newsletter, October, 1979.

Date, C. J. *An Introduction to Database Systems , Volume I*. Reading, MA: Addison-Wesley, 1981.

Date, C. J. *Database: A Primer*. Reading, MA: Addison-Wesley, 1983.

Kruglinski, David. *Data Base Management Systems*. Berkeley, CA: Osborne/McGraw-Hill, 1983.

Martin, James and Carma McClure. *Software Maintenance*. Englewood Cliffs, NJ: Prentice-Hall, 1983.

Meyers, Glenford J. *Reliable Software Through Composite Design*. NY: Van Nostrand Reinhold Co., 1975.

Wirth, Niklaus. *Algorithms + Data Structures = Programs*. Englewood Cliffs, NJ: Prentice-Hall, 1976.

CHAPTER SEVEN

DATA STRUCTURES

The data types discussed in chapter 6 are sometimes referred to as "primitive" since they are the building blocks used to construct more complex data structures. dBASE contains powerful high level commands which allow you to create and manipulate sophisticated data structures easily.

There are several common models used to represent data structures. dBASE uses the *relational* model: the data is represented in flat (two-dimensional) tables composed of rows and columns. The relational model was developed by E.F. Codd working at IBM and was first published widely in 1976.[1] In the jargon of relational databases, a two-dimensional table is known as a "relation," and operations on these tables can be described with mathematical precision.[2] There are other models used to represent data, and these are touched on at the end of this chapter. However, the relational model is very powerful and *all other common data models can be represented using two-dimensional (relational) tables*.[3]

There are two structured data types in dBASE: the data file (static structured type) and the index file (dynamic structured type).

The CREATE command is used to create a data file structure matching the body of data that it is intended to represent. This structure can store data as individual records and the data can then be easily accessed and manipulated. Below is an example of a data file containing names and addresses in which the structure was created, five records were entered, and the records were displayed. The individual records are listed below the structure of the data file:

```
Structure for database : Nad.dbf
Number of data records :        5
Field  Field name  Type        Width    Dec
    1   NAME        Character      15
    2   ADDRESS     Character      15
    3   CITY        Character      15
    4   STATE       Character       2
    5   ZIP_CODE    Character       5
** Total **                        53
```

Record#	NAME	ADDRESS	CITY	STATE	ZIP_CODE
1	John Jones	1234 Hop St.	Los Angeles	CA	90765
2	Susan Smith	345 Lake Ave.	San Rafael	CA	98776
3	Charlie Stokes	8673 Sea Dr.	Uptown	NY	09876
4	Alice Trover	32 North St.	Bull City	CO	45397
5	Charlie Brown	23 Stove St.	Bakersfield	CA	97433

THE DATA FILE STRUCTURE

The dBASE data file can be seen as a two-dimensional table containing the following properties:

1. All items in a column are of the same data type; that is, the data file is column-homogenous. A column in dBASE is a *field*.
2. Each column (or field) must have a distinct fieldname. No duplicate fieldnames are allowed.
3. Each row is a *record* and is assigned a number. The record number assigned is relative to the record's position in the data file.

A conceptual view of a dBASE data file is:

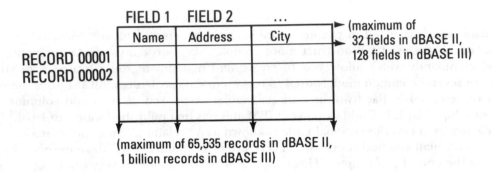

Figure 7-1

The limitations on dBASE data files are:

File limits (maximum sizes)	dBASE II	dBASE III
Number of records/file	65,535	1 billion
Record size (bytes)	1000	4000 bytes in .DBF file
Number of fields/record	32	128

Field limits		
Character fields	254 bytes	254 bytes
Logical fields	1 byte	1 byte
Numeric fields	254 bytes (2.3-2.41)	19 bytes
	63 bytes (2.42)	
Date fields	N/A	8 bytes
Memo fields	N/A	10 bytes in .DBF file
		.DBT file size limit only by
		operating system, hardware
		or word processor used.

dBASE II Data File Internal Structure

The internal structure of a dBASE II data file is composed of a header and data records. The header is a block of data which contains information about the structure of the data file, such as how many records it contains, and the date it was last updated. The tables below show how this information is stored.

dBASE II DATA FILE HEADER:

BYTE	CONTENTS	MEANING
0	02H	denotes dBASE II database file
1-2	16 bit no.	number of records in data file
3-5	3 bytes	date of last update (MM DD YY)
6-7	16 bit no.	size of the record
8-519	32x16 byte array	Field descriptors terminated by a carriage return (0DH)
520	1 byte	0DH if all 32 fields present, otherwise a hex zero

EACH FIELD DESCRIPTOR:

BYTE	CONTENTS	MEANING
0-10	11 bytes	field name in ASCII, zero-filled
11	1 byte	field type in ASCII (C N or L)
12	1 byte	field length
13-14	16 bit number	field data address (address is set in memory)
15	1 byte	field decimal count

Figure 7-2

The data records are laid out as follows:

1. Data records are preceded by one byte that is a space (20H) if the record is not deleted and an asterisk (2AH) if it is deleted.
2. Data fields are packed into records without separators or record terminators.
3. Data types are stored in ASCII format as follows:

Data Type	Data Record Storage
Character	(ASCII characters)
Numeric	- . 0 1 2 3 4 5 6 7 8 9
Logical	Y y N n T t F f (20H when not initialized)

dBASE III Data File Structure

The structure of a dBASE III data file is composed of a header and data records. The layout is given below.

dBASE III DATA FILE HEADER:

BYTE	CONTENTS	MEANING
0	1 byte	dBASE III version number (03H without a .DBT file) (83H with a .DBT file)
1-3	3 bytes	date of last update (YY MM DD)
4-7	32 bit number	number of records in data file
8-9	16 bit number	length of header structure
10-11	16 bit number	length of the record
12-31	20 bytes	reserved bytes (version 1.00)
32-n	32 bytes each	field descriptor array (see below)
n+1	1 byte	0DH as the field terminator

A FIELD DESCRIPTOR:

BYTE	CONTENTS	MEANING
0-10	11 bytes	field name in ASCII, zero-filled
11	1 byte	field type in ASCII (C N L D or M)
12-15	32 bit number	field data address (address is set in memory)
16	1 byte	field length
17	1 byte	field decimal count
18-31	14 bytes	reserved bytes (version 1.00)

Figure 7-3

The data records are laid out as follows:

1. Data records are preceded by one byte that is a space (20H) if the record is not deleted and an asterisk (2AH) if it is deleted.
2. Data fields are packed into records with no field separators or record terminators.
3. Data types are stored in ASCII format as follows:

Data Type	Data Record Storage
Character	(ASCII characters)
Numeric	- . 0 1 2 3 4 5 6 7 8 9
Logical	? Y y N n T t F f (? when not initialized)
Memo	(10 digits representing a .DBT block number)
Date	(8 digits in YYYYMMDD format, such as 19841231 for December 31, 1984)

INDEXING

One of the most important features of any database system is the ability to find a specific data item from among many items quickly. There are several ways to locate a specific record in a data file. The most obvious is to search sequentially from the beginning to the end of the file. This works well for small data files but can be very slow if the file is large. Searching an index instead can shorten long sequential search times to only a couple of seconds.

The concept of an index is quite common. For example, if you wanted to find the various places in this book that discuss the CREATE command, you would probably turn to the index in the back. The index would give a list of page numbers where CREATE is discussed, allowing you to go directly to the desired page. This would be much faster than sequentially searching every page in the book. Libraries have card catalogs which are a type of index. Most libraries have two types of catalogs: one is an index by title, and the other is an index by author. This allows you to look up a book either by its title or author. In this example, the title or author is the *key* for the index. Each card gives the location in the library where a particular book may be found. Each element in an index contains two parts: a *key*, which is an identifying tag for the information you're searching for, and a *pointer*, which gives the location of the actual data sought. Thus, an index is an ordered (sorted) set of keys with pointers to data records.

When the INDEX ON <key> command is issued in dBASE, a separate index file is created based on the key expression specified in the command line. The following two commands create an index file called *Custname* for a *Customer* data file using the field *Names* as the key.

```
. USE Customer              (Select data file)
. INDEX ON Names TO Custname  (Generate index)
```

This index will allow rapid searches of the *Customer* database by *Name*. Any record could be found in two seconds or less with the FIND or SEEK command.

BINARY TREES

Any search has only two possible outcomes: success or failure. Because an index is in sorted order, it can be rapidly searched using the following approach. Suppose you wanted to search an index (alphabetical list) of names for the name "Arwin." One fast way to do this is to start at the midpoint and compare "Arwin" to the value of the middle key. If it is identical, your search is successful and ends. If it is greater than the middle key, we know that all keys less than the middle key can be ignored. The next operation is to compare "Arwin" to the middle key of the upper half of the index. This process is repeated, each time comparing to the midpoint of the appropriate half of the remaining keys. The search will eventually yield either a successful comparison or failure.

One way to visualize this type of search path is to think of a tree-like structure. The tree is composed of *nodes*, each of which contains a key value and its associated pointer. This structure is usually represented as an upside-down "tree" having the "root node" at the top and "leaf nodes" at the bottom. Each tree has only a single root node. One type of tree, called a "binary tree" (because each "parent node" has two "child nodes") is shown in Figure 7-4. Each parent has two child nodes, left and right children. Each node is connected to those above and below it by "branches" and the "height" of the tree is the maximum number of branches (longest path) between the root node and a leaf node.

A *binary search* begins at the root node and progresses according to the following rules.

1. If the key is equal to the node value, the search is successful.
2. If the key is greater than the node value, move to the right.
3. If the key is less than the node value, move to the left.

Using this strategy, ten comparisons allow us to search 1,024 (2^10) keys, twenty comparisons allow a search of 1,048,576 (2^20) keys. In general, after at most $\log_2 N$ comparisons, the target key will have been found or we will know it is not present.

When a record is added or deleted from the main data file, the index must also reflect this change. After many additions or deletions the tree can become "unbalanced"; that is, the height at one point of the tree becomes much larger than the height at another point. If this happens, the search path for some keys becomes much longer than the search path for other keys and the search begins to degenerate into a sequential operation rather than a binary search. It is important to keep trees "balanced" so that the search time for any record is similar to the search time for other records. A commonly accepted definition for a balanced tree is that *the height of the right subtree of every node never differs by more than one from the height of its left subtree.* Figure 7-4 is a balanced binary tree. There are several algorithms for balancing trees, and they are covered well in *The Art of Computer Programming, Volume 3/Sorting and Searching.*[4]

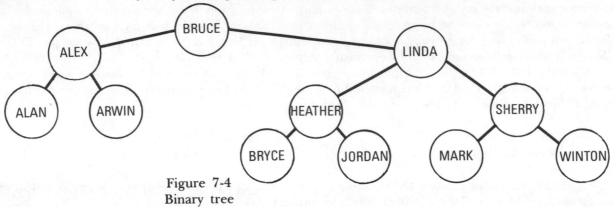

Figure 7-4
Binary tree

B-Trees

Binary search techniques work well when operating on a file residing in memory. However, the method slows down considerably when applied to larger files stored on disk because of the high number of disk accesses needed to complete a search. Disk accesses are very slow compared to internal processing speeds. An improved method for searching disk files was published in 1972 by Bayer and McCreight.[5] This method was based on a new data structure similar to a binary tree, called a "B-tree." A B-tree contains several keys per node rather than a single key per node. This reduces the height of the tree and allows the search process to proceed with fewer disk accesses. Figure 7-5 shows an example of a B-tree. Though B-trees perform excellently when randomly looking for entries, it is often necessary to do a sequential scan of records after a particular record has been found. Unfortunately, B-trees do not perform well in sequential searches since locating "the next record" may involve searching through several nodes before finding the next key. As we shall see, this problem was solved with the B+ tree.

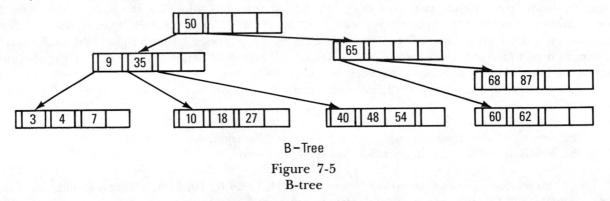

B–Tree

Figure 7-5
B-tree

B+ Trees

dBASE uses a structure called a B+ tree, which is similar to a B-tree in that it contains many keys per node but differs in the following respect. Every key in a B-tree contains a pointer to its associated data record in the data file. Thus, whenever a match occurs in the index, the associated data record is immediately available. In a B+ tree, only the leaf nodes contain pointers to data records. The upper nodes contain only key values and pointers to the appropriate lower level node in the tree. This means that the tree must be traversed to a leaf node before the pointer to a data record is available. This has an advantage because the leaf nodes form a sequential list pointing to all records in the database. This allows easy sequential access to the records as well as indexed access. One can locate a particular record via the index and then easily list the next ten in order by simply "skipping" along the leaves at the bottom of the tree. Figure 7-6 shows an example of a B+ tree.

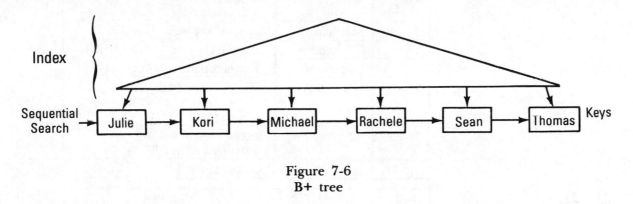

Figure 7-6
B+ tree

dBASE II Index File Structure

A dBASE II index file uses the B+ tree structure. The number of keys per node is given in the formula below and depends on the key size. Each node of the tree is a fixed size of 512 bytes. The first node is the *anchor node*, which contains information on the key expression, root node, next available node, and maximum number of keys per node. All the other nodes are composed of key values and pointers to lower nodes. The leaf level pointers have a value of zero because they are at the lowest level. The leaf nodes contain the record number of the associated record in the data file. A conceptual view of an index file is given in Figure 7-7.

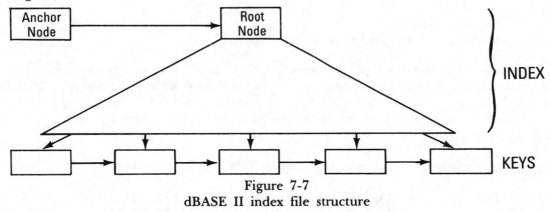

Figure 7-7
dBASE II index file structure

The structure of the index file nodes in dBASE II is given below:

ANCHOR NODE (NODE ZERO):

BYTE	CONTENTS	MEANING
0-1	2 bytes	Reserved
2-3	16 bit no.	Node number of root node
4-5	16 bit number	Node number of next available node
6	8 bit number	length of key (KEY—LENGTH)
7	8 bit number	size of a key entry (KEY—ENTRY)
8	8 bit number	maximum number of keys per node
9	1 byte flag	TRUE if numeric key (0 if character, non-0 if numeric)
10-109	100 byte string	key expression in ASCII (terminated by 00H)
110-511	bytes	unused bytes

ALL OTHER NODES:

BYTE	CONTENTS	MEANING
0	8 bit number	number of keys in this node
1-511	array	array of key entries

A KEY ENTRY:

pointer to lower level (2 bytes)	record number (2 bytes)	key expression value in ASCII (n bytes)
	KEY—LENGTH	
KEY—ENTRY		

Figure 7-8

Estimating the Size of an Index File in dBASE

An index file is a dynamic structure that "grows" and "shrinks" as record values are added and edited. Pointer relationships are constantly changing and rotating in the index structure, and as nodes fill up, they split to maintain the tree's balance. Since each 512-byte index record (node) may or may not contain the maximum number of allowable keys at any given time, only approximate index file sizes can be computed. The computation is given below.

1. Determine the number of keys plus key pointers that will fit in an index node:

```
KEY_ENTRY        = (key value length) + 8   (dBASE III)
KEY_ENTRY        = (key value length) + 4   (dBASE II)
ENTRIES_PER_NODE = INT( 509 / KEY_ENTRY )
```

2. Next, compute the number of nodes the index file will contain, based on the number of records in the data file.

```
TOTAL_RECS  = (number of records in the data file)
TOTAL_NODES = INT( TOTAL_RECS / ENTRIES_PER_NODE ) + 1
```

3. Now, compute the minimum and maximum sizes (in bytes) the index file will have with the given number of records.

```
MIN_SIZE = ( 512 * TOTAL_NODES )
MAX_SIZE = 2 * ( 512 * TOTAL_NODES )
```

MIN_SIZE represents the most compact size the index file will have with the given number of records. In this case, every node is filled to capacity with key entries. MAX_SIZE represents the most expanded size the index file will have given the number of records and the most unlikely balancing condition in which every node in the index file "splits" because of an insertion. Newly created index files will usually be closest to MAX_SIZE.

The index file nodes are maintained in a balanced condition; that is, the difference in height between branch nodes from any given node varies at most by one level of branching. This balanced condition provides the best searching environment possible for a tree index. To keep the index balanced, a set of routines involving "node splitting" and "rotation" are used. The simplest operation is a search through the index on a particular key. The search algorithm is given below.

dBASE II Index Search Algorithm

1. The anchor node resides in memory and indicates what node to fetch as the root node.
2. The root node is fetched and sequentially scanned until a higher or equal key value is obtained. This key value points to the node in the next level.
3. The second level node is fetched and sequentially scanned in the same manner as the root node. This process of scanning and branching to lower level nodes continues until a leaf node is encountered, which is when the pointer to the lower level node has a value of zero. If the key value is equal at the leaf level, then the search has been successful and the record number of the key is returned. If the key value is not equal, then a record number of zero is returned.

dBASE uses one of the most efficient index structures available today. In the Support Center we have been using dBASE to search a database which contains over 50,000 records. This is an 8-bit system with a four megahertz clock running under CP/M. CP/M has a size limit of eight megabytes per file, and so, the records are located in two 7.8 megabyte files. Both data files are indexed, and we are able to find any record within three seconds.

COMPLEX STRUCTURED DATA TYPES

The representation of more complex data structures such as trees and networks can be reduced to dBASE data files (two-dimensional tables) by allowing a certain amount of redundancy in the data.[6]

Tree Data Structure

A tree data structure is sometimes referred to as a *hierarchical structure* because a tree is composed of a hierarchy of nodes. In a tree-structure database, every node has only one node related to it at a higher level. Figure 7-9 illustrates this structure. The following manager–employee example shows how a tree data structure can be reduced to a relational structure.

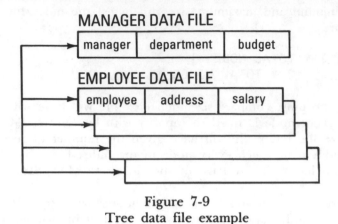

Figure 7-9
Tree data file example

Each manager may have several employees, but each employee has only one manager. The tree structure above might have been represented with two dBASE data files containing the following structures:

MANAGER DATA FILE   EMPLOYEE DATA FILE

FIELD NAME   FIELD NAME

MANAGER   **EMPLOYEE**
DEPARTMENT   ADDRESS
BUDGET   SALARY

However, deciding which employees went with which manager is impossible with the above structures since there is no way of referencing a record in the employee data file from a record in the manager data file.

What is needed is a referencing method in which each employee can be linked with a manager. The best referencing method is to add the identifying key in the upper data file to the lower data file. In this example, the manager field is added to the employee data file. The reworked data file follows. It allows records in the manager data file to be referenced from the employee data file.

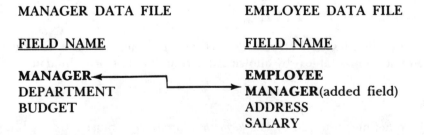

MANAGER DATA FILE   EMPLOYEE DATA FILE

FIELD NAME   FIELD NAME

MANAGER   **EMPLOYEE**
DEPARTMENT   **MANAGER**(added field)
BUDGET   ADDRESS
                                           SALARY

Network Data Structure

A network data structure occurs when each data item has more than one "parent" associated with it. Network structures allow any item to be linked to any other item. Figure 7-10 shows some examples of network structures.

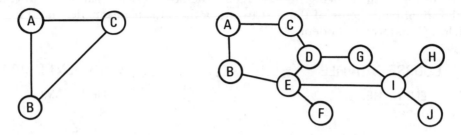

Figure 7-10
Network data structures

A network data structure can be illustrated with the course-student relationship given below.

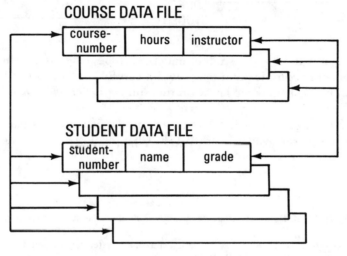

Figure 7-11
A network data file example

Each course has a course number and several students enrolled in that course. At the same time, each student in a course has signed up for several other courses. This networking relationship can be represented with two dBASE data files containing the following structures:

COURSE DATA FILE	STUDENT DATA FILE
FIELD NAME	FIELD NAME
COURSE	**STUDENT**
HOURS	NAME
INSTRUCTOR	GRADE

Determining which course number contains which students and which student has selected which course number is impossible with the above structures since there is no way of referencing a student record in one file from a course record in the other.

The approach to follow in reducing network data structures to relational files is to create a third data file containing the identifying fields of the first two data files. In this example, the third data file would contain both fields Course and Student.

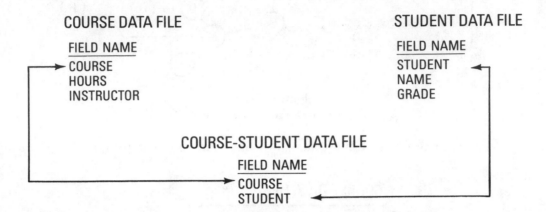

COURSE DATA FILE

FIELD NAME
COURSE
HOURS
INSTRUCTOR

STUDENT DATA FILE

FIELD NAME
STUDENT
NAME
GRADE

COURSE-STUDENT DATA FILE

FIELD NAME
COURSE
STUDENT

Using these three files, any field in the student data file can be linked to any field in the course data file. Network structures can become complex and may require careful study in order to reduce them to dBASE files, but it can be done. The best book we know on this subject is *Computer Data-base Organization* by James Martin.

By now, you should have a grasp of what data types and data strutures are as well as an idea of how to represent data using the structures available in dBASE. Chapter 9 provides a more detailed discussion of how to design database structures.

END NOTES

1.   E.F. Codd, "A Relational Model of Data for Large Shared Data Banks," *Communications of the ACM*, 13, No. 6, June, 1979.
2.   E.F. Codd, *Relational Completeness of Data Base Sublanguages*. Data Base Systems, Courant Computer Science Symposia Series, (Vol. 6), (Englewood Cliffs, NJ: Prentice-Hall, 1972).
3.   James Martin, *Computer Data-Base Organization* (Englewood Cliffs, NJ: Prentice-Hall, 1977), 202-214.
4.   Donald E. Knuth, *The Art of Computer Programming, Vol. 3/Sorting and Searching* (Reading, MA: Addison-Wesley, 1973), 451-471.
5.   R. Bayer and E. McCreight, "Organization and Maintenance of Large Ordered Indexes," *Acta Informatica*, 1, No. 4, 1972.
6.   James Martin, *Computer Data-Base Organization* (Englewood Cliffs, NJ: Prentice-Hall, 1977), 202-214.

BIBLIOGRAPHY

Bayer, R. and E. McCreight. "Organization and Maintenance of Large Ordered Indexes,"*Acta Informatica* 1, No. 4 1972.
Codd, E.F. *Relational Completeness of Data Base Sublanguages*. Data Base Systems, Courant Computer Science Symposia Series, Volume 6. Englewood Cliffs, NJ: Prentice-Hall, 1972.
Codd, E.F. "A Relational Model of Data For Large Shared Data Banks." *Communications of the ACM* 13, No. 6 (June, 1976).
Knuth, Donald E. *The Art of Computer Programming, Volume 3/Sorting and Searching*. Reading, MA: Addison-Wesley, 1973.
Martin, James. *Computer Data-Base Organization*. Englewood Cliffs, NJ: Prentice-Hall, 1977.

SECTION TWO

SYSTEM DESIGN

CHAPTER EIGHT

INFORMATION SYSTEMS DESIGN

This chapter gives an overview of the following information systems design topics:

- Systems Analysis

- Management Information Systems

- Accounting Information Systems

The Systems Analysis section discusses the methods and tools the developer will need to learn about a system. In the Management Information Systems section, we present illustrations that show the importance of evaluating the information needs of an organization at each management level. Lastly, the Accounting Information Systems section gives an overview of the resource-allocation reporting and analysis conducted in every profit-making business.

This chapter offers a general overview of a complex subject. It is also geared toward the needs of profit-making business organizations (although other business organizations, such as non-profit and government entities, will benefit from our discussion). This was done to simplify the presentation of the material and to meet the needs of those who typically use dBASE, that is, the business community. If you are interested in more information on this subject, consider the references listed at the end of this chapter.

It is critical to the success of a business organization that its information system be adequately designed. When an organization's information systems complement its business objectives, the business can operate efficiently and reliably, and its managers can respond effectively to changes in the marketplace.

SYSTEM DEFINED

A system may be defined as a set of objects with relationships between the objects. This is a general definition and is helpful in explaining the seemingly unrelated uses of the word (solar system, school system, digestive system, political system, and so on). Systems can be conveniently classified in the following ways:

Class	Examples
Physical	material, organic, and energy systems
Abstract	organizational, theoretical, and philosophical systems
Natural	systems occurring in nature
Man-made	systems designed by man
Adaptive	systems able to adapt to changes in the environment
Nonadaptive	systems not able to adapt to the environment

Class	Examples
Open	systems with inputs and outputs (practically all systems are open systems)
Closed	systems without inputs and outputs
Subsystem	a system within a system
Supersystem	very large, complex systems

Information Systems

In the computer science field, a system is like a black box with inputs and outputs:

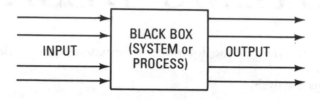

Figure 8-1

An information system is viewed in the same way—the inputs are the adding and editing of data, the process is the computing of data, and the outputs are the retrieval and reporting of data. An information system safeguards the data by providing constraints and integrity logic throughout the process (the chapter on Security and Recovery gives more details on the design of constraints and integrity logic for a system).

SYSTEMS ANALYSIS

Systems analysis can be defined as the study of a system. It determines the effective ways of planning and allocating resources to achieve the desired goals. In the business realm, the systems analyst uses business rules and economic concepts for analytical tools.

There are two approaches to systems analysis: process analysis and final outcome analysis. *Process analysis* studies the system by looking at its structure through the analysis of its subsystems, but *final outcome analysis* studies the system by viewing its inputs and outputs and their relationship to the system. Both methods may be used in the study of a system.

Process Analysis

The process analysis approach can best be described through the use of a business example. In a business organization, a top-down view of the structure will first yield the departments in the organization. A business organization may have the following departments:

THE BUSINESS ORGANIZATION
    Accounting
    Personnel
    Production
    Sales
    Finance

A deeper look into the organization's structure may reveal the operations performed by each of the departments. For the Production department this may consist of:

PRODUCTION DEPARTMENT
    Inventory control
    Purchasing
    Receiving
    Machine maintenance
    Assembly and Warehousing

The final step in the analysis is the recording of the procedures followed by each of the operations. For instance, for the purchasing function in the Production department, the operations might consist of:

PRODUCTION DEPARTMENT'S PURCHASING FUNCTION
    Create requisition
    Select supplier
        Supplier information inquiry
        Supplier performance analysis
    Create purchase order
    Follow up delivery
        Check with receiving
    Create information for Accounts Payable

At this point the developer is ready to prepare the system structure, and to develop or recommend the software that will be needed.

Final Outcome Analysis

In final outcome analysis, the input and output relationships to the system are studied in decision-making situations where there is *certainty*, *risk*, and *uncertainty*.

Certainty: In situations where there is certainty, the outputs of the system can be directly derived from its inputs. Each input results in only one output. Examples of analytical tools used to study these types of system inputs and outputs are:

Analytical Tools	Examples
forecasting tools	moving average, exponential smoothing
linear programming	graphical method, simplex method
matrix modeling	material requirements planning
financial formulas	interest formulas, economic life
inventory planning	economic lot size, quantity discounts

Risk: In situations where there is risk, each input may result in a number of possible outputs. The outputs of the system have probability values associated with them or these values can be estimated. Examples of analytical tools used to study these types of system inputs and outputs are:

Analytical Tools	Examples
probability concepts	decision trees, distribution curves
project planning	critical path method, PERT
inventory planning	for perishable products, variations in demand, variations in lead time with opportunity costs
waiting line analysis	arrival and service time distributions, single channel-single phase modeling

Uncertainty: In situations where there is uncertainty, each input may result in a number of possible outputs, but, unlike risk situations, the probability values for each output cannot be determined. Examples of analytical tools used to study these types of system inputs and outputs are:

Analytical Tools	Examples
game theory	two-person zero-sum games
procedures for noncompetitive situations	maximin, maximax, Hurwicz criteria

For more information on the analytical tools discussed in this section, refer to *Systems Analysis for Managerial Decisions* by P. Ramalingam.

MANAGEMENT INFORMATION SYSTEMS (MIS)

In the management information systems discipline, a business organization is viewed as having a three-level hierarchy of information needs—on planning, administrative, and operations levels. Management responsibilities are related to the gathering of information at each of the three levels. Executive management typically handles the planning level, middle management maintains the administrative level, and line management manages the operations level. Figure 8-2 illustrates the flow of information between the three levels, and Figure 8-3 suggests the software that can be used at each of these three levels.

Figure 8-2
MIS information flow

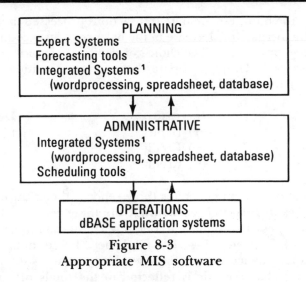

Figure 8-3
Appropriate MIS software

ACCOUNTING INFORMATION SYSTEMS

In the accounting information systems field, the type of information systems developed depends on the type of business the organization is in. In a service or merchandising business, most of the time is devoted to the buying and selling of goods. In a manufacturing business, most of the time is devoted to manufacturing goods in addition to buying raw materials and selling finished goods. These differences are accounted for in different ways. In the discussion that follows, we outline the design of an accounting information system for a service or merchandising organization. The topics include the transaction network, the three primary accounting reports, and the accounting cycle. An accounting glossary is provided at the end of this chapter to help the reader understand the accounting terms used in this section.

A view of the network of accounts and transactions for a service or merchandising business is provided in Figure 8-4.

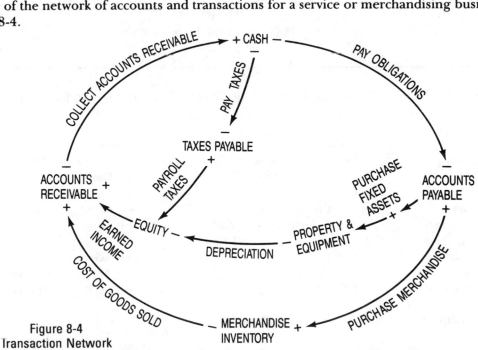

Figure 8-4
Transaction Network

This network describes the minute-by-minute transactions processed in the business. The plus (+) and minus (–) signs represent the increase or decrease in the balance of an account. The increase or decrease of the balance is termed *debiting* or *crediting*. The choice of debiting or crediting an account depends on the type of account being processed. The appropriate debiting and crediting of each of the three types of business accounts are given in the following:

Account Type	Increase	Decrease
Assets	(+) Debit	(–) Credit
Liabilities	(+) Credit	(–) Debit
Equities	(+) Credit	(–) Debit

The accounting information system generates three reports: the balance sheet, the income statement, and the statement of changes in financial position. Of the three reports, the balance sheet is especially designed to group the three types of accounts into one report. An example of a balance sheet derived from the above transaction network is given below. The fundamental accounting model, Assets = Liabilities + Equities, requires that the total balance amount for assets be equal to the total balance amount for liabilities plus equities. This balancing characteristic is reflected in the totals of our example balance sheet.

BALANCE SHEET
At December 31, 1984

ASSETS (DB +)		LIABILITIES (CR +)	
Cash	$ 5,000	Accounts Payable	$ 4,000
Accounts Receivable	4,000	Taxes Payable	1,000
Merchandise Inventory	6,000		
Property & Equipment	20,000		
		EQUITIES (CR +)	
		Owner's Equity	30,000
Total Assets	$35,000	Total Liabilities and Equities	$35,000

With the aid of the balance sheet and the transaction network, we can derive all of the transactions shown below.

Transaction	Debit	Credit
Purchase fixed assets	(+) Fixed Assets	(+) Accounts Payable
Pay taxes	(–) Taxes Payable	(–) Cash
Payroll taxes	(–) Equity	(+) Taxes Payable
Depreciation expense	(–) Equity	(–) Fixed Assets
Earned income (Income Summary Account)	(+) Accounts Receivable	(+) Equity
Purchase merchandise	(+) Inventory	(+) Accounts Payable
Cost of goods sold	(+) Inventory	(–) Accounts Receivable
Collect accounts receivable (cashin)	(+) Cash	(–) Accounts Receivable
Pay obligations (cashout)	(–) Accounts Payable	(–) Cash

The other two primary reports generated by the accounting information system are the income statement (which reports the total revenues and expenses processed during a given period) and the statement of changes in financial position (which reports the inflows and outflows of working capital). Examples of these are given below.

INCOME STATEMENT
For Period Ended November 30, 1984

Net Sales	$80,000
Cost of Goods Sold	
Beginning Inventory Less:	
Ending Inventory	
Cost of Goods Sold	50,000
Gross Margin on Sale	30,000
Operating Expenses:	
Selling Expenses	
Administrative Expenses	
Income Tax Expense	
Total Expenses	20,000
NET INCOME	$10,000

STATEMENT OF CHANGES IN FINANCIAL POSITION
For the Year Ended December 31, 1984

Resources provided by:	
Operations:	
Net Income	$10,000
Other Sources:	
Stock Issued	
Loan - note payable	
Total from other sources	30,000
Total resources provided	40,000
Resources applied to:	
Purchase office equipment	
Purchase land	
Total resources applied	25,000
Increase in working capital	$15,000

These three reports are obtained via the journalizing, posting, and trial balancing of all transactions processed in a given period. This accounting cycle followed in an accounting information system is given in Figure 8-5:

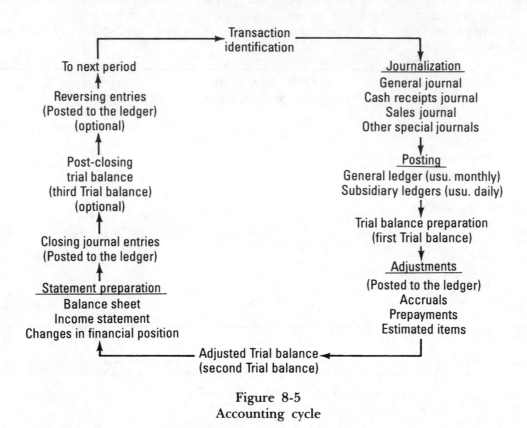

Figure 8-5
Accounting cycle

OPERATIONAL BUSINESS INFORMATION MODEL

The operational model of a business organization describes the interaction between the different subsystems in the organization. Typically, these subsystems are the departments in the organization. These subsystems process not only the monetary aspects of the organization but also the non-monetary aspects, such as personnel records, customer credit histories, routing schedules, and inventory stock levels. An example of an operational business information model is given in Figure 8-6.

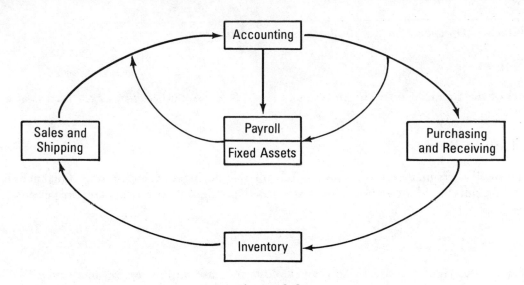

Figure 8-6
Operational business information model

ACCOUNTING GLOSSARY

Account

A record of the effects of transactions on the *assets*, *liabilities*, and *equities* of a business. This record has two sides: the left, or *debit*, side and the right, or *credit*, side.

Accounting

The measuring and reporting of the financial activities of a business. The information obtained from this process is used in decision making, evaluating performance, and reporting to investors, creditors, and regulatory agencies.

Accounts Payable

An account of amounts owed to others. This account reflects the time lag between the receiving of goods and their payment.

Accounts Receivable

An account of amounts due from others. It is restricted to the amounts due from the sale of goods and services during normal business operations. The more descriptive designation "Receivables from trade customers" is often used.

Assets

The resources owned by a business. These include land, buildings, equipment, and intangibles (characterized by legal claims or rights).

Balance

The difference between an account's total *debits* and *credits*.

Balance Sheet

A report of the financial position (in terms of *assets*, *liabilities*, and *equities*) of a business at a particular point in time.

Cost Of Goods Sold

The sum of all costs incurred to prepare goods for sale during a period in time. This includes the cost of the materials purchased, transportation costs when purchased, receiving and inspection costs, and storage costs.

Credit

An entry on the right side of an account. Credits increase *liability*, *equity*, and *revenue* accounts, and decrease *asset* and *expense* accounts.

Debit

An entry on the left side of an account. Debits increase *asset* and *expense* accounts, and decrease *liability*, *equity*, and *revenue* accounts.

Depreciation

The decline in value of a *fixed asset*. This decline in value is measured on a periodic basis and treated as a cost to the normal operations of the business.

Earned Income

The excess of business *revenues* over *expenses* for a given period.

Equity

The interest or claims in the *assets* of the business remaining after the *liabilities* are deducted.

Expenses

The outflow of resources used by a business to earn *revenues*.

Fixed Assets

An account of goods held for operating the business. These goods include land, buildings, equipment, and furniture. The account is a measure of the cost of the goods when first purchased.

Income Statement

A report of the profit performance (in terms of *revenues* and *expenses*) of a business for a specific period of time.

Journal

The record in which the *transactions* of a business are first recorded.

Ledger

A collection of accounts. A *general ledger* contains all the *asset, liability, equity, revenue,* and *expense* accounts of the business. A *subsidiary ledger* contains a group of accounts that constitute a single general ledger account.

Liabilities

The obligations (or debts) of a business to other entities.

Merchandise Inventory

An account of merchandise held for resale in the ordinary course of business. The account is a measure of the cost of the merchandise when first purchased.

Net Sales

A subtotal on an *Income Statement* representing total sales *revenue* reduced by sales returns and allowances, and sales discounts.

Posting

The process of transferring the transaction information in a *journal* to *accounts* in a *ledger*.

Revenues

The inflow of resources in the form of cash and accounts receivable from the sale of goods and services.

Statement of Changes in Financial Position

A report of the business sources and use of cash for a specific period of time.

Transaction

An event that changes the financial position of a business in terms of *assets, liabilities,* and *equities.*

Trial Balance

A list of all accounts with their respective *debit* or *credit* balances.

END NOTES

1. *Framework*, an Ashton-Tate product, is an excellent integrated software product that can be used for MIS support. *Framework* efficiently couples word processing, spreadsheet, graphics, and database operations.

BIBLIOGRAPHY

Kieso, Donald E. and Jerry J. Weygrandt. *Intermediate Accounting*. New York: John Wiley & Sons, 1980. New York: John Wiley & Sons, 1980.
Martin, James. *Managing the Data-Base Environment*. Englewood Cliffs, NJ: Prentice-Hall, 1983.
Merrett, T.H. *Relational Information Systems*. Reston, VA: Reston Publishing Company, Inc., 1984.
Ramalingam, P. *Systems Analysis for Managerial Decisions*. New York: John Wiley & Sons, Inc., 1976.

CHAPTER NINE

DATABASE DESIGN

This chapter covers three aspects of the database design process:

- Data File Design
  remove all repeating fields
  correct for partial dependence
  correct for transitive dependence

- Linkage Among Data Files
  tree and network linkages
  cyclical linkages
  naturally inherent and business rule linkages
  adjustments to compensate for machine performance

- Future Changes
  hidden keys
  addition of dependent fields
  high-usage of secondary key

Database design is covered in great depth by other authors (see the references at the end of this chapter). As in the previous chapter, we intend to give only a summary treatment of the subject.

Properly designing a database minimizes future database restructuring and application program rewriting. Another outstanding benefit is that proper design minimizes the amount of redundant data in the system, leading to better data integrity and better data searching times.

THE DATABASE DEFINED

A database is a collection of data files that are logically linked, independent of application software. This is the definition of a database in its ideal form. "Logically linked" refers to referencing with key expressions without the need of pointers or other underlying software referencing techniques. "Independent of application software" means the database reflects the inherent structure of the data, requiring no application interpretation or support. However, independence from application software is not possible in every case. It is sometimes necessary to structure a database so as to meet specific application needs. A database of this kind is referred to as an application-database. An application-database in a database environment is acceptable as long as it can be isolated from other database and application activity.

A database designed independent of application software takes longer to develop. It requires a number of iterations of modeling and remodeling and considerable knowledge of the inherent properties of the data. The minimized need for future database restructuring makes such a database well worth the extra design effort. A database designed in this way is known as a subject-database. Examples of subject-databases found in the business environment are: customers, suppliers, parts, products, personnel, orders, and accounts.

DATA FILE DESIGN

Three rules should be followed when designing a data file. These rules are progressive refinements in the design process, where rule one precedes rule two and rule two precedes rule three. A data file passing the third rule is in the proper form to be added to a database. In existing literature, these rules are referred to as first, second, and third "normal forms." They are basic to the design of a database data file and should be thoroughly understood.

- *The First Rule: Remove all repeating fields*

A repeating field is one in which there are several possible occurrences or values for a field in a given record. An example of a repeating field is given in the DEPARTMENT data file illustrated below.

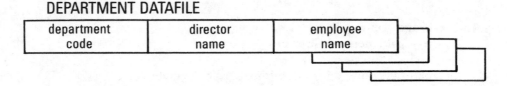

DEPARTMENT DATAFILE

department code	director name	employee name

Figure 9-1

The repeating field in this data file is the employee name, where several employees can be under one department. The proper techniques to remove repeating fields are discussed in "Data Types" and "Data Structures." In the above case, the data file would need to be split into two files, as shown below:

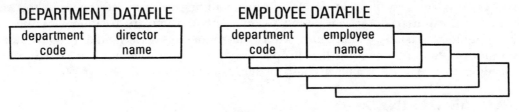

DEPARTMENT DATAFILE

department code	director name

EMPLOYEE DATAFILE

department code	employee name

Figure 9-2

- *The Second Rule: The dependent fields in the record must be dependent on the entire key expression.*

This rule refers to key expressions that consist of more than one field. The key expression must fully identify each of the dependent fields in the record. The dependent fields must be derivable from the entire key and not a portion of it.

Example of Partial Dependence

The following ORDER-CUSTOMER data file contains the key expression of order-number and customer-number. The dependent field, customer-name, is only dependent on customer-number and therefore is not dependent on the entire key expression.

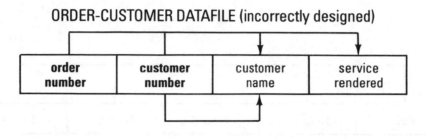

ORDER-CUSTOMER DATAFILE (incorrectly designed)

| order number | customer number | customer name | service rendered |

Figure 9-3

Potential problems with partial dependence include:

Problems that arise when the customer name has to be edited. Given that the ORDER-CUSTOMER data file might contain several orders per customer, the entire file might have to be scanned to update every occurrence of the customer name.

Problems that arise when a customer address and phone number needs to be added. This would require the adding of these fields to the existing ORDER-CUSTOMER data file or would require the creating of a separate CUSTOMER data file to receive this information. Problems would occur with whichever method chosen. In the case where the fields are added to the ORDER-CUSTOMER, the problem arises in the need to update every record containing the customer's information. If a separate CUSTOMER data file is created, then any changes to the customer name or deletion of the customer record would also have to be made to every matching record in the ORDER-CUSTOMER data file. In either case the redundant data would make the updating process difficult.

Correcting Partial Dependence

To correct for partial dependence in the above example, the data file should be divided into two data files. The customer-name field is removed from the ORDER-CUSTOMER data file and added to a new CUSTOMER data file. Any updating of the ORDER-CUSTOMER data file or adding of customer information to the CUSTOMER data file can then be done without generating redundant data.

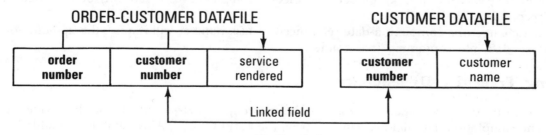

ORDER-CUSTOMER DATAFILE   CUSTOMER DATAFILE

| order number | customer number | service rendered | | customer number | customer name |

Linked field

Figure 9-4

● *The Third Rule: There should not be dependence among the dependent fields.*

The dependent fields must not be dependent upon each other, but only on the key expression. Following this rule leads to a simple, direct relationship between the key expression and the dependent fields, as shown below.

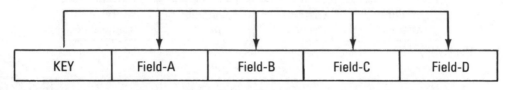

KEY	Field-A	Field-B	Field-C	Field-D

Figure 9-5

Example of Transitive Dependence

The term "transitive dependence" is used for undesirable dependence among dependent fields. The following EMPLOYEE-TASK data file contains a completion date field that is transitively dependent on task number, where task number is also a dependent field.

EMPLOYEE-TASK DATAFILE (incorrectly designed)

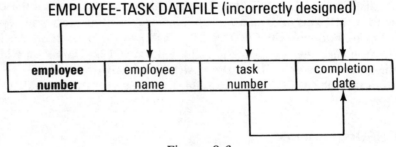

employee number	employee name	task number	completion date

Figure 9-6

Potential problems with transitive dependence may occur:

In deletions. Deletion of an employee record will also cause the loss of the "task number" referencing the "completion date."

In appends. The fact that a task number references a completion-date can only be recorded when an employee record is added.

In edits. A change in a completion-date referenced by task-number will require the updating of all the records in the data file containing that condition.

Correcting Transitive Dependence

To correct the transitive dependence in the above example, the data file should be divided into two data files. The completion-date field is removed from the EMPLOYEE-TASK data file and added to a new TASK data file.

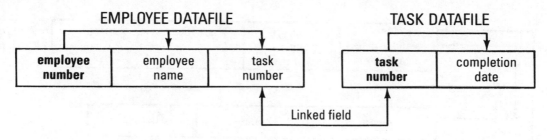

Figure 9-7

LINKAGE AMONG DATA FILES

Logical linkage among data files is done through key expression references, rather than through pointers or other underlying software referencing techniques. There are four areas to be considered in the design of proper "implied" linkage among the data files: tree and network linkages, cyclical linkages, naturally inherent and business rule linkages, and adjustments to compensate for machine performance.

Tree and Network Linkages

The techniques used to construct tree and network linkages are discussed in the chapters on "Data Types" and "Data Structures." These techniques can be summarized as follows:

1. For tree linkage, make a duplicate field in the lower-level data file.
2. For network, treat the networked field(s) as a solitary key on a separate data file.

The following diagram illustrates how linkages would appear in a purchasing-inventory business application. Lines with double arrows at one end represent one-to-many relationships, or tree and network linkages. Notice that the data files used in this illustration were designed by following the three rules under data file design.

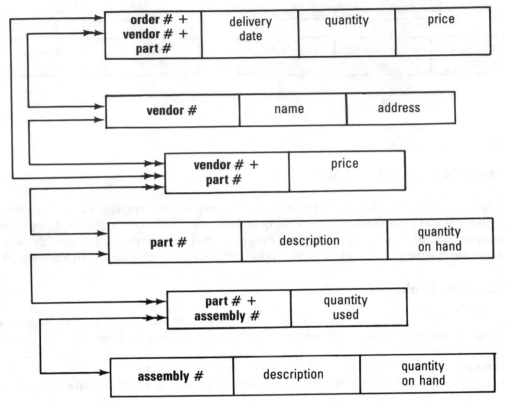

Figure 9-8
Purchasing-Inventory Database Model

Cyclical Linkages

Cyclical linkages should be reduced to a minimum. In the example below, the student-textbook linkage may be removed because the textbook field can be referenced through the teacher field.

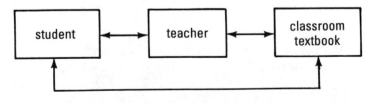

Figure 9-9

However, there are cases where the extra cyclical linkage is needed. It may provide quicker access to the information or a unique relationship among the fields that would be lost if removed. An example of this is given in Figure 9-10. The employee may have a direct relationship with the chairman—such as being the chairman's personal pilot—that would be lost if the linkage were not there.

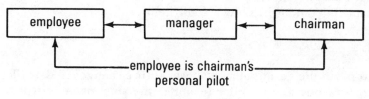

Figure 9-10

Naturally Inherent and Business Rule Linkages

Naturally inherent linkages are those that reflect properties inherent to the data. Examples include a school course with many students, a department head with many employees, and a part number with one description. Linkages guided by business rules, however, are subject to change when the business rules change. Such linkages therefore need to be identified and studied so as to arrange the best possible data file structure and linkage. An example of a business rule linkage would be an insurance policy based on age grouping alone, in contrast to insurance policy based on age grouping, cigarette smoking habits, and medical history.

Adjustments to Compensate for Machine Performance

It is sometimes necessary to sacrifice data file design or linkage in order to improve machine performance. This requires the adding or removing of fields from the data files where machine performance will be a factor.

The additional information needed to make a decision in this area is as follows:

1. With a one-to-many linkage, determine what is the occurrence ratio between the records. In the example below, there are at most seven part number records to every assembly number record. If the occurrence ratio is great (that is, there are a large number of part number records to a single assembly number record), then the part number field would be a candidate for inclusion in the assembly number data file structure. This would eliminate the need to access a large number of records in a separate data file, and would, therefore, reduce the number of searching operations on the disk.

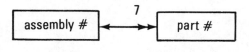

Figure 9-11

2. Determine how often certain linkages will be performed. This helps in deciding whether certain data files will need to be modified or whether certain linkages will need to be redesigned. For example, there are cases where a dependent field in the data file may act as a key field. This is especially true with the generation of reports sequenced on a particular dependent field. The question to ask in this case is whether this "secondary-key" may have higher usage at a later time. If higher usage is expected, then the data file should be designed initially as two separate data files.

3.   Determine whether the activities on the data files will be performed interactively or in batch form. If the process is interactive, what time responses would be tolerable? If quick responses are required, it might be necessary to combine data files and set aside certain fields.

FUTURE CHANGES

This is the last major topic in the design of a database. Future changes to data files in a database should be anticipated as much as possible in order to buffer the amount of restructuring required. Future changes encompass three areas: hidden keys, addition of dependent fields, and high-usage of a secondary key.

Hidden Keys

Each of the dependent fields in a data file should be examined to determine whether any might become key fields in the future. If they are identified, they can either be removed from the data file and added to a new data file, or left in the existing data file, as long as flexibility is provided to accommodate future key field changes.

Addition of Dependent Fields

The data file structures should have room for the addition of dependent fields. Even though this will require reloading of the records whenever new fields are added, it should not affect the application programs written.

High-Usage of Secondary Key

If you anticipate that a dependent field acting on occasion as a key field will be used more in the future, the data file structures and application programs should be designed to accommodate change. This may require the dividing of the data file into two data files at the very start, or the writing of the application programs to accept this anticipated future change.

BIBLIOGRAPHY

Kroenke, David. *DATABASE, A Professional's Primer*. Chicago: Science Research Associates, Inc., 1978.
Martin, James. *Managing the Data-base Environment* . Englewood Cliffs, NJ: Prentice-Hall, Inc., 1983.

CHAPTER TEN

SYSTEM DOCUMENTATION

The approach we recommend in the development of system documentation is to generate the documentation *before* writing the programs. It is a great temptation to leave the work of documenting the system until the end of the development cycle. By then, the developer is eager to move on to the next project, and the customer just wants to get started with the new system. Generating system documentation *before* the system is developed has several important benefits:

The Document as a Contract.   The document can serve as a contract between the developer and the end user. It can present the specifications and limitations of the system to help the end user understand what the system is able to do. The document could also be used to list program modules and system design sections as evidence of the amount of work required to complete the system or for use in placing a bid on the project. The system analysis and documentation could be billed separately from the work needed to develop the system. The bid on a project might consist of asking for a third of the proposed amount upon delivery of the documentation (and completion of the systems analysis before the software is written), a third of the amount upon completion of the software, and the final third within thirty days of the completion date.

The Document as Specifications to the Programmer.   The document could serve as the developer's specifications for the programmers. They only need to look at the documentation to see what it is they need to program. The developer could also parcel out the work among the programmers in his or her company, or sub-contract the work to outside programmers if necessary in order to complete it in the expected time.

The Document as a Teaching Aid to the End User.   The end user can begin learning how to use the system before it is finished by simply reading the documentation. This helps the developer give some of the training during the development phase and reduces the amount of time he or she will need to spend with the user after the system is completed.

This chapter can serve as a model for designing the documentation for a system. The following overview can be a guide to the sections to include in the documentation.

- STARTUP
  Purpose of the system
  Startup procedures
  Security, backup, and recovery procedures
  Brief description of the system's main options

- **SYSTEM LIMITATIONS**
  Hardware environment
  Storage requirements
  Input/Output speeds

- **LOG OF CHANGES**

- **DATA STRUCTURES**
  Data file, index file, data file linkages
  Memory files
  Data dictionaries

- **PROGRAM LOGIC**
  Command file execution outline
  Pseudo-code listing

- **REPORTS**
  Description of reports generated

The documentation would look like the following diagram:

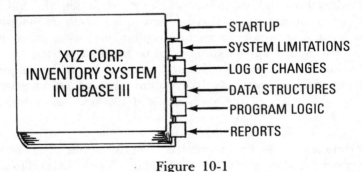

XYZ CORP.
INVENTORY SYSTEM
IN dBASE III

STARTUP
SYSTEM LIMITATIONS
LOG OF CHANGES
DATA STRUCTURES
PROGRAM LOGIC
REPORTS

Figure 10-1

STARTUP

The startup section includes the purpose of the system, startup procedures, security, backup and recovery procedures, and a brief description of the system's main options.

Purpose of the System. A paragraph or two describing the purpose of the system is enough to give readers sufficient information to decide whether it is what they are looking for. An example is:

PURPOSE. Entirely menu driven, this INventory application program is written in dBASE III, version 1.0. Entry is direct from booting via an Autoexec.bat file in MS-DOS. All INventory files are on drive E in the INV sub-directory.

Startup Procedures. A description of how to start the system. This may be as brief as:

TO START THE SYSTEM. Place disk labeled "SYSTEM DISK" in drive A and type:

```
A>dBASE START <RETURN>
```

Security, Backup, and Recovery Procedures. A description of how to use any security, backup, and recovery procedure in the system, as in the following example:

SECURITY and RECOVERY. On entry into the INventory system, the operator is prompted to enter a password. If three successive wrong entries are made, the system will prevent further attempts at access, thereby locking out the intruder and warning its owner that an unauthorized access has been tried. If the correct password is used, the operator will be prompted to enter the current date if it was not entered at the system level. This date is used to stamp all transactions with the transaction entry date. All dates are in the format MM/DD/YY. To restore the password after an unauthorized attempt, the system administrator must do the following:

1. Exit to the system prompt.
2. Type 'dBASE IN_util2'

If the operator escapes during a report or command file execution by hitting the <Esc> key, immediately close the files by typing 'QUIT'. To get back into the menu, type 'dBASE Start' at the system prompt.

To use the computer for other purposes that will not involve the use of the INventory system, select the EXIT or QUIT options on all the menus until the system prompt is seen. This is the only supported way to exit the INventory system, and other methods could lead to corruption of or loss of data. It is recommended that all interactive computer work not involving the INventory system be done on a drive other than drive C which holds the INventory files. This is because it is possible to make a mistake which could cause the loss of files from the directory.

Brief Description of the System's Main Options. This may consist of a paragraph or two describing the main options in the system. Since the main options are usually found in the main menu, a description of the menu may suffice. This information can also be added to the main menu of the system as a separate help option, which would add a convenient and easily implemented on-line help facility. An example of what could be presented in this sub-section is given below.

INVENTORY SYSTEM'S MAIN OPTIONS. The hub or center of the INventory system is its Main Menu [IN_menu.prg]. This is where the operator chooses a particular course of action.

The options available are:

          A -> Enter new purchase order.
          B -> Review/Edit purchase orders.
          C -> Enter new release.
          D -> Review/Edit releases.
          E -> Enter new customer.
          F -> Review/Edit customer file.
          G -> Enter new product.
          H -> Review/Edit product file.
          I -> Combine customers & products.
          J -> Adjust inventory amounts.
          K -> Display inventory by customer.
          L -> Print reports.
          M -> Help.
     RETURN -> Backup and exit.

SYSTEM LIMITATIONS

The system limitation section includes hardware environment, storage requirements, and input/output speeds. Explanations should be clear enough so that the developer's intentions are apparent to the reader.

Hardware Environment.   Specify what hardware the application will run on in terms of computers, printers, and hard disks. Other hardware configuration questions that may be covered are:

- How much recoding would be required to convert the application to other hardware environments?
- Is it portable to other microprocessor environments, such as the 8086 and 68000?
- Does it have assembly routines that would have to be rewritten?
- Are there video or printer codes that would have to be changed?

The following is an example of what could be said in this sub-section.

HARDWARE ENVIRONMENT. This system is designed to run under either MS-DOS or CP/M-86 on the DEC Rainbow with a DEC monochrome monitor, a 10MB hard disk, and a DEC LA50 printer. Code modifications may be required for compatibility with different computers, terminals, printers, or operating systems. One operating system will be decided upon before coding begins.

Storage Requirements.   A list of the data files and index files with the maximum number of records and storage requirements in megabytes. (The program Ndx-size.prg found in appendix C will help compute the storage values for index files.) An example is:

STORAGE REQUIREMENTS. The system is designed to run on a 10MB hard disk with the following data file and program file storage requirements (in megabytes):

	Maximum recs	Storage (in MB)
1. Program files		.250
(PRG,FMT,FRM,MEM)		
2. Data files (DBF)		
IN_PRODM	300	.020
IN_CUSTM	100	.020
IN_INVTM	1,000	.060
IN_PO	1,000	.130
IN_REL	5,000	.550
IN_ADJ	1,000	.080
3. Index files (NDX)		
IN_PM-1 (4 byte key)	300	.004 approx.
IN_CM-1 (3 byte key)	100	.002 approx.
IN_IM-1 (20 byte key)	100	.020 approx.
IN_IM-1 (7 byte key)	1,000	.020 approx.
IN_PO-1 (7 byte key)	1,000	.020 approx.
IN_RL-1 (7 byte key)	5,000	.100 approx.
IN_AJ-1 (7 byte key)	1,000	.020 approx.
		1.280
4. Backup files, sort work area		x2
		2.560

Input/Output Speeds. Provide input, update, and report generation times (or estimated times) with a given number of records. This helps the user understand what speeds to expect when entering data or generating reports.

REPORT PRINTING SPEEDS. The following report generation times are to be expected when printing on a DEC LA50 printer:

REPORT NAME	KEY	RECS	TIME
1) Customer Activity	Customer	300	10 min.
2) Release Report (creates an index)	Prod:code	300	15 min.
3) PO History	Customer	1000	30 min.
4) Open PO Report	Customer	500	15 min.

LOG OF CHANGES

During the lifetime of an installed application, much time will be spent in making changes to the system. It is recommended that these changes be logged in a separate section of the documentation. Any changes to the other sections can be made by crossing out the older version of the documentation and referring to the Log of Changes section. This helps keep the information in a central location and chronological order. When the number of changes or type of changes demands it, the document can be rewritten to include the new changes. The Log of Changes can also serve as a measure of the amount of maintenance work provided to the system. An example of a Log of Changes section containing a minimum of author, date, and description information is given below.

```
            XYZ CORP. INVENTORY SYSTEM
                LOG OF CHANGES

Tom Rettig, 10/5/84.  Revised three programs to enhance
existing customer reports:

    IN_RPT01.PRG  =  Customer Activity Report
    IN_RPT03.PRG  =  PO History by Customer
    IN_RPT05.PRG  =  Open PO Report by Customer

Jay Hanson, 10/11/84.  Revised IN_ENPOR.PRG to include
record locking.

Luis Castro, 10/16/84.  Added IN_RVPRD.PRG to
review/edit master product file.
```

DATA STRUCTURES

The data structures section includes information on the data files, index files, data file linkages, and information on memory files and generated data dictionaries.

Data File, Index File, Data File Linkages. The data file structures, index file key expressions, and data file linkages can be listed using the PRINTDOC utility found in appendix C. The index file expressions and data file linkages are placed below the data file structures they are associated with. An example of how this could be presented is given below.

```
Customer File:
   STRUCTURE FOR FILE:  IN_CUSTM.DBF
   NUMBER OF RECORDS:   100 aprox. (899 max.)
   FLD        NAME       TYPE WIDTH    PICTURE
   001        CUST:CODE   C    003     '###'
   002        CUST:NAME   C    020     'XXX...'
   003        ADDRESS     C    030     'XXX...'
   004        CITY        C    020     'AAA...'
   005        STATE       C    002     'AA'
   006        ZIP         C    010     '#####-####'
   007        PHONE       C    013     '(###)###-####'
   008        CONTACT     C    020     'XXX...'
   009        SHIP:PNT1   C    010     'XXX...'
   010        SHIP:PNT2   C    010     'XXX...'
   ** TOTAL **               00139

Indexes:
IN_cm-1 = Cust:code
IN_cm-2 = Cust:name

Linkages:
<-->> IN_po  = Cust:code
<-->> IN_rel = Cust:name
```

Memory Files.   dBASE II memory files can be listed using the PRINTDOC utility found in appendix C. An example dBASE II memory file listing is given below. (A listing of a dBASE III memory file is given in chapter 17.)

```
MEMORY FILE LISTING:

MEMORY.MEM

EXTENSION     (C)   .PRG
Y:N           (C)   N
MWIDTH        (C)   VAL($(option11,1,2))
DATA FILE     (C)   NAMES
LMARGIN       (C)   1
PAGELEN       (C)   56
PAGEWIDTH     (C)   80
PAGEHDG       (C)   NAMES REPORT HEADING
STRING        (C)   CITY
IS:TOTAL      (L)   .F.
ITEM          (N)      12
OPTION11      (C)   20,NAME
PROMPT        (C)    4. Width,Contents.
HEADING11     (C)   NAME
** TOTAL **       14 VARIABLES USED   00132 BYTES USED
```

Data Dictionaries. A data dictionary documents the use of all the field names in the system. This helps determine duplicate or similar-sounding field names so that the differences can be documented. A data dictionary also helps determine the impact (at the systems level) of changing or adding a field name to a data file. There are two types of data dictionaries that can be constructed, database and command file. A *database data dictionary* can be generated by using the PRINTDOC utility found in appendix C.

```
DATABASE DATA DICTIONARY

FIELD NAME        DATA FILE OCCURRENCES

ADDRESS      ACCOUNTS   INVENT
CITY         NAMES      ACCOUNTS   AR/MEN2
COMPANY      NAMES      ACCOUNTS
NAME         NAMES      DATA FILE  AP/INVE
QUANTITY     INVENT     AP/INVE
STATE        INVENT     ACCOUNTS
ZIP          NAMES      DATA FILE
```

A *command file data dictionary* can be generated with the CROSSREF utility found in appendix C.

```
COMMAND FILE DATA DICTIONARY

FIELD NAME    PROGRAM      OCCURRENCES (line numbers)

ADDRESS       AP/REPL      14,   19,   33
CITY          AP/EDIT      11,   21,   24
NAME          AP/SELE       2,    5,   10,   31,   60
              AP/EDIT      10,   22,   25
ZIP           AP/REPL      12,   18,   32
```

PROGRAM LOGIC

This section includes a command file execution outline and pseudo-code listing for a system.

Command File Execution Outline. A command file execution outline of a system helps determine the program-flow relationships between command files. An example of how this can be documented is,

```
IN_MENU
     START
     IN_ENPOR
          IN_RVPOR
          IN_ENREL
               IN_RVREL
               IN_ADJWH
          IN_ADJCS
     IN_ENCUS
          IN_RVCUS
               IN_COMBN
          IN_RVPRD
```

```
     IN_RPMNU
          IN_RPTO1
          IN_RPTO2
          IN_RPTO3
          IN_RPTO4
     IN_BCKUP
```

Pseudo-Code Listing. The program logic of a system can be documented with a pseudo-code listing. The benefit of pseudo-code over regular program listings is that pseudo-code captures the essence of the program logic without getting into details. Pseudo-coding (or some form of pseudo-coding) is usually done before any programming is begun. The pseudo-code, therefore, can be added to the system documentation long before any of the programs are written. The pseudo-code listings can provide the interested reader with an understanding of the program logic. If a question arises about any of the methods followed, it can be handled before the expensive process of coding is begun. An example of a pseudo-code listing for an order entry system is given below.

```
ORDER-ENTRY SYSTEM

LEGEND

[ ]  =  Procedure
[ ].<filename>  =  Data file used in a procedure
<>  =  Condition

[Enter an order]
DO WHILE <There is an order>
   [Print order header].Order

   DO WHILE <There is an order-line-item>
      [Check for valid product].Product

      IF <It is a valid product>
         [Check product quantity].Product

         IF <Quantity is in stock>
            [Print order-line-item].Order.Product
            [Record update].Product
         ELSE
            [Backorder].()
         ENDIF

      ELSE
         [Error].()
      ENDIF

   ENDDO <There is an order-line-item>

   [Print order trailer].Order
   [Record update].Order
ENDDO <There is an order>
```

Command File Listings

Command file listings are not included as part of the system documentation for at least three reasons:

1. They are time-consuming to update. Small changes are always being made to the programs. These are mostly of a superficial nature and do not affect the program logic.
2. The bulkiness of program listings would place a misleading emphasis on their value in the documentation. Other essential information would go unnoticed.
3. Command file listings make uninteresting reading for non-programmers.

For debugging purposes however, command file listings are a must. There are several ways to print them, as shown below.

-   The PIP utility on CP/M-80 and CP/M-86 operating systems allows you to print command files. The following example will print the IN-menu.cmd command file to the LST: device and paginate at 60 lines per page.

    ```
    A>PIP LST:=IN-menu.cmd[P60]
    ```

-   The COPY command or PRINT utility on the MS-DOS operating systems allows you to print command files:

    ```
    A>COPY IN-menu.prg PRN:
    ```

    or

    ```
    A>PRINT IN-menu.prg
    ```

-   The TYPE command in dBASE III, MS-DOS, CP/M-80, and CP/M-86 also allows the printing of command files:

    ```
    A>TYPE IN-menu.prg <control-P>
    A><control-P>
    ```

    or

    ```
    . * ---In dBASE III only:
    . TYPE IN_menu.prg TO PRINT
    ```

REPORTS

The report section describes the reports a system generates. An example of how to describe the reports generated by the system follows:

Report Descriptions. The operator is presented with the Report Menu. Its options are:

1. Customer Activity Report
2. Release Report by Product Code
3. PO History by Customer
4. PO History by Product Code
5. Open PO Report by Customer
6. Master Customer List (including their products)
7. Master Product List (including their customers)
8. Inventory Report
9. Die Inventory
10. Adjustment Report (by product or customer)

For all reports *except* 6 and 7, the operator is prompted to enter a starting date and ending date. The report is generated for the period between those two dates. Reports are designed to go to the printer only—not the screen.

1. Customer Activity Report by Customer:
    Product code number
    Product description
    Quantity released
    Date released
    Plant location
    Monthly usage
    Year-to-date usage
    Warehouse inventory balance—total
    Work "in process"
    Date due of each current "in process"
2. Release Report by Product Code
    (same data as 1 - for inhouse use)
3. PO History by Customer
    Product code number
    Product description
    Produce die number
    Customer PO number
    XYZ PO number
    Quantity ordered
    Date placed
    Final ready date
    Year-to-date total complete (closed)
    Year-to-date total "in process" (open)
4. PO History by Product Code
    (same as 3—for inhouse use)

CHAPTER ELEVEN

SECURITY, RECOVERY, AND BACKUP

This chapter covers the following topics:

- SYSTEM SECURITY
  user logon sequence
  access level codes
  user log
  program control

- SYSTEM RECOVERY
  system crash
  crash recovery

- SYSTEM BACKUP

System security is discussed from the standpoint of protecting the data from unauthorized viewing and editing. Other security topics such as data encryption and guarding against unauthorized destruction of equipment are not presented. The techniques discussed in this section do not give a complete protection scheme but provide the necessary first steps in developing such a system. The section on system recovery gives the common causes of system crashes as well as recovery methods and ways of preventing system crashes in the first place. Finally, the system backup section provides guidelines to follow in setting up a backup procedure for a system.

SYSTEM SECURITY

To guard against unauthorized viewing and editing of data, the system must have at least two features in place: a user logon sequence (to identify the user positively), and an access level structure (to restrict unauthorized access to the data).

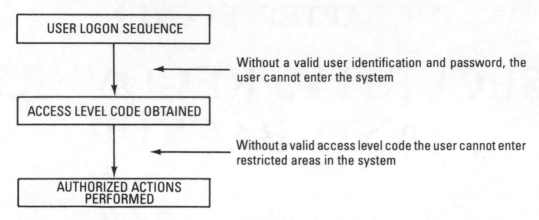

Figure 11-1

User Logon Sequence

The logon sequence has the user enter his or her identification code and password. The identification code can simply be the user's first name. The password, however, is the user's personal software key into the system. It should be an unpublished and unique sequence of characters. A software password cannot be kept secret forever—other users will eventually learn it. We recommend, therefore, that user passwords be changed on a periodic basis—once a month or once a quarter depending on the need. To prevent others from viewing the password on the screen as it is being entered, the screen may be disabled during entry as in the following examples:

```
* ---Enter password.
* ---Assumes TALK and ESCAPE flags are OFF.
@ 6,0 SAY "Enter password :"
SET CONSOLE OFF
ACCEPT TO password
SET CONSOLE ON
```

or

```
* ---Enter password.
* ---This will work on dBASE II version 2.4
* ---for the IBM PC using PC-DOS.
STORE "          " TO password
SET COLOR TO 0,0
@ 6,0 SAY "Enter password " GET password
READ
SET COLOR TO 112,7
```

Access Level Codes

An access level code is designed to restrict several types of access and several classes of users from viewing or editing the data in the system. The several types of access and classes of users are given below.

Access Type	Examples
programs	payroll, order entry, end-of-period
data classes	secret, confidential
transactions	posting, reversing entries
time and day	8:00 am to 5:00 pm, Monday thru Friday

Access Class	Restrictions
master	none
management	some programs and transaction types
users	some programs, transaction, data, and time/day types

The user identification, password, and access codes can be stored in a data file as shown in the table below. The first two digits of the access code can represent the access class, and the last two digits can represent the access type.

User ID	Password	Access Code
GEORGE	LA204-55	00/00
HARVEY	GLEN-517	01/05
ROD	213+EURO	01/02
SUSAN	RT*COMM	02/03
MIKE	MGT&MKTG	02/00
NORMA	EDU&FRAM	02/02

User Log

A data file containing information on when users have entered and exited the system can provide an additional security item. A user log monitors the duration and frequency of system use by different users. In the event of a system malfunction or security violation, the user log can be investigated to determine who was using the system last and what can be done to retrace the steps toward the malfunction or violation. A user log, however, represents an additional execution overhead to the system. The data file may be laid out in the following manner:

User ID	Status	Date	Time
SUSAN	IN	12/07/84	08:23
MIKE	IN	12/07/84	09:54
SUSAN	OUT	12/07/84	12:45
SUSAN	IN	12/07/84	14:02
MIKE	OUT	12/07/84	17:54
SUSAN	OUT	12/07/84	18:07

The pseudo-code for a security system including all of the features mentioned is given below.

```
SECURITY LOGON
[Enter user identification]
[Open data file or memory file to obtain
     user password and access level code].Security
*
[Get the system date and time of day]
```

```
IF <user is not allowed at this date or time>
    [Error("Illegal user")]
ENDIF
*
[Enter user password]
IF <An invalid password>
    [Give the user another chance]
    IF <Still an invalid password>
        [Error("Illegal user")]
    ENDIF
ENDIF
*
[Close security data file or memory file].Security
[Update user status file].Status
*
[Perform programs according to the access level code]
```

PROGRAM CONTROL

Providing restricted access to programs and data in the system can be implemented in a number of ways. The ones discussed here assume two access types (programs and day/time), three access classes (master, management, and users), and the following menu structure:

MASTER MENU
1. Order Entry {sales department users}
    ORDER ENTRY (sub-menu)
        1. Enter Orders
        2. View/Complete Orders
        3. Print Orders
        4. Sales Reports department manager
2. Accounts Receivable {accounting department users}
    ACCOUNTS RECEIVABLE (sub-menu)
        1. Enter Old Invoices
        2. Enter Cash Receipts
        3. Adjustment Entries
        4. Daily Journal Reports
        5. Monthly Reports {department manager}
        6. Credit History
3. System Maintenance {managers}
    SYSTEM MAINTENANCE (sub-menu)
        1. Startup & Shutdown Procedures
        2. Backup Procedures
        3. Program Documentation
        4. Security Password Maintenance {master}

The simplest approach to program control is to allow all the users to view all of the menu options. The program logic would then only allow authorized users to execute the selected programs. The following dBASE program segment illustrates how this can be done.

```
* ---Execution portion of MAIN MENU.
DO CASE
   CASE selection = 1
   * ---Order Entry.
      * ---Access to master, managers, and Sales department.
      IF access = "00/00" .OR. $(access,1,2) = "01" .OR.;
         $(access,4,2) = "01"
         DO Orders
      ENDIF
   CASE selection = 2
   * ---Accounts Receivable.
      * ---Access to master, managers, and Acctg department.
      IF access = "00/00" .OR. $(access,1,2) = "01" .OR.;
         $(access,4,2) = "02"
         DO Acctrec
      ENDIF
   CASE selection = 3
   * ---System Maintenance.
      * ---Access to master and managers.
      IF access = "00/00" .OR. $(access,1,2) = "01"
         DO Sysmaint
      ENDIF
ENDCASE
```

The best approach to program control is to provide separate menus for the different classes of users. This approach prevents the users from knowing which programs they are not allowed to run and also eliminates the obvious temptation to learn how to use the unauthorized programs. There are at least two ways of implementing this approach: one is building separate menu programs for each class of use; the other is running a table-driven menu system.

Though building separate menu programs is the simplest method, it requires additional program maintenance. To implement the given menu structure, we need a total of nine menu programs. The following table example shows how this can be determined.

Menu Options Available for Each Access Class

Menu name	Menu options	Access class
MASTER	1-3	MASTER, MANAGEMENT
	1	USER (Sales Department)
	2	USER (Accounting Department)
ORDER ENTRY	1-4	MASTER, Sales Manager
	1-3	MANAGEMENT, USER (Sales Dept.)
ACCOUNTS	1-6	MASTER, Accounting Manager
RECEIVABLE	1-4, 6	MANAGEMENT, USER (Accounting Department)
SYSTEM	1-4	MASTER
MAINTENANCE	1-3	MANAGEMENT

The second method for providing separate menus for different classes of users is with a table-driven menu system. A program control table is built with a file structure similar to the following:

```
STRUCTURE FOR FILE:  IN_TABLE.DBF
FLD          NAME      TYPE WIDTH
001     MENU_NAME      C    008  <---| KEY
002     ACCESS_NUM     C    003  <---|
003     DESCRIPTN      C    025
004     PRG2EXEC       C    008
** TOTAL **                00045
```

The table-driven menu system can be implemented using program logic similar to the following pseudo-code listing.

```
* ---To execute MAIN MENU.
[Open program control table].IN_TABLE
STORE <menu:name memvar> + <access:num memvar> TO mkey
FIND &mkey
[Display all menu items equal to mkey]
[Get menu selection]
[Get name of program to execute <Prg2exec>]
IF <exit menu>
    RETURN
ELSE
    DO &<Prg2exec memvar>
ENDIF
```

SYSTEM CRASHES

Another area of concern to the system developer is the building of reliability into the system. A system is reliable when it always does what it's supposed to do. In the event of a system failure, or "crash," reliability cannot always be guaranteed. System crashes interrupt the processing of data, and with any sophisticated application it is often difficult to determine which data files have been affected and where to resume operations.

System crashes and malfunctions can be minimized with adequate precautions and maintenance procedures. If you understand the possible causes of system crashes, you can design appropriate preventive measures. The most common causes of system crashes are power pollutants and equipment malfunctions.

Power Pollutants

Blackouts and Brownouts.　A blackout is a power outage—a total shutting off of power—generally lasting fewer than ten seconds. Fortunately, only a small percentage of users (less than 5%) experience blackouts during any given year. A brownout is a reduction in the voltage received. Power utilities commonly reduce voltage when power demands exceed generating capacity. When operating in a brownout condition, computer equipment is more susceptible to the effects of other power pollutants. An uninterruptible power supply is the only safeguard against blackouts and brownouts.

Voltage Transients.　These are voltage spikes and sags that are above or below normal levels. Voltage spikes and sags commonly occur with the turning on and off of other electrical equipment. The more damaging of the two is the voltage spike—a voltage spike of several thousand volts (for example, during lightning storms) can wreak havoc on semiconductor-based equipment. Voltage transient suppressors are the most common and inexpensive devices used to protect computer hardware from voltage transients.

Electrical Noise.   Electrical noise comes in the form of electromagnetic interference and radio-frequency interference. Digital electronic equipment is the most common source of this power pollutant. Electrical noise going into and out of computer equipment can be controlled with the use of power-line filters.

Equipment Malfunctions

Disk Damage.   System Read/Write errors or Bad Sector errors can occur with a worn or damaged disk, a misaligned disk drive, or a head crash on a hard disk. Periodic replacing of used floppy disks and cleaning and aligning disk drives are the best protection against these types of errors. With hard disks, the developer must make sure the hard disk is protected in such a way that it is never jarred. When computer facilities make it possible and the hard disk manufacturer does not indicate otherwise, leave the hard disk turned on at all times. This keeps the hard disk interior at a constant temperature and reduces the amount of stress placed on the internal parts.

Parity Errors.   A memory chip may have lost good contact on the memory board or may have become damaged. It is also possible that a memory board is not seated well on its slot or is touching the computer casing (such as may happen when a heavy monitor is placed on an IBM PC CPU box containing a memory expansion board). The simplest corrective measure to take when parity errors occur is to uncover the computer's CPU box and examine the memory expansion card (if there is any) and the installed memory chips. If all the memory chips are correctly seated, carefully press the memory chips with your fingers to make certain they are making good contact (the chips will often make a crackling noise when you are doing this). If there is an expansion memory board, re-seating the board is also worth trying. If all of this fails to eliminate parity errors, then the memory will have to be checked with diagnostic software to determine which memory chip, if any, is malfunctioning.

CRASH RECOVERY

In the event of a system crash, there are two dBASE data file structures that will require immediate attention: the data file record count and the index file structures. In a system crash, or any other form of system interruption, the correct value for the data file's record count can always be suspect. It is the last item to be updated before a data file is closed and is therefore the most vulnerable to incorrect updating. Methods for restoring the data file's record count are given in appendix F.

An index file has a dynamic structure (see the chapter on complex data structures) that is constantly undergoing change during record updates. If any data file integrity has been lost after a system crash, it is likely the index files have also been affected. We recommend, therefore, that the index files be recreated.

A crash recovery procedure should be set up in case there is ever a system crash. Let us suppose a system is in the middle of posting transactions to a ledger file when suddenly a power spike blows one of the disk drives. If the transaction data was being REPLACEd into the ledger file (known as in-place updating), there would be no way of knowing where in the updating process the system had been interrupted. It would be extremely difficult to know where to resume operations, and starting the process from the beginning would be to update incorrectly records that had been updated in the previous run. Either choice, starting from the beginning or attempting to resume from where we left off, would give incorrect results. The only recovery procedure possible would be to reload an older version of the ledger file and start the posting procedure from the very beginning.

Two Recovery Methods

There is another way, however, and that is to implement two design features into the system: updating by adding and time-stamping of records. We can discuss the first design feature by thinking of it as a rule: *never update in-place*. This rule can be satisfied in the following way: whenever a record needs to be edited, a copy of the record is appended to the end of the file, the old version of the record is marked for deletion, and the new one is edited. In the event of a system crash, the updating process can be restarted from the last record appended to the data file.

Admittedly, this method would increase file sizes in direct proportion to the number of updates made and potentially could build huge files. However, this problem can easily be handled with proper file maintenance. To keep the data files at a manageable size, the system will need to PACK (or as we prefer, COPY) frequently its data files (once a day or once a week depending on the amount of updating performed).

The second design feature is the *time-stamping of transactions*. A date-and-time field can be added to the data files involved in transactions. The time-stamp would be the last field updated to the record in an updating procedure. Thus, the field would record the sequence of updates made to the system, based on date and time. In the event of a system crash, the recovery procedure would be to restart the updating process from the last record with a valid time-stamp. The time-stamping technique has the additional benefit of putting the transactions made to the system in chronological order and serving as a trail of transactions.

These two recovery design techniques would be especially useful when updating groups of data files. In the event of a crash, the updating procedure could be restarted either with the last or next to last group of records appended to the data files, or with the last group of records with a valid time-stamp.

The method of last resort—when all other recovery procedures have failed or when it would be too time-consuming to determine what has occurred—is to reload the most recent system backup. It behooves the system administrator to make system backups regularly so that the amount of time lost will not be great.

The term "catastrophe" is used when no system recovery is possible from either a recovery procedure or a backup system. This should never happen to anyone.

BACKUP SYSTEM

When designing a backup system, you will need to consider the importance of the data and the extent of changes in the data. The importance of the data to an organization can be grouped into three types:

Scratchpad Data. If the data being used is not important (that is, there is no concern with losing the information), then a single backup copy can be made every five to ten days. In the event of a system crash, the data would not have to be completely rewritten.

Important Data. If the data is important but not critical to the organization, then a backup system using two backup copies and an archival copy would be necessary. The backup copies could be made on alternating days such as Tuesday and Thursday, and the disks (or tapes) could be labelled with the day of the week in which they are used. For example, every Tuesday the backup copy labelled "Tuesday" would be used to make a backup. Also, an archival copy would be made once a week and stored at an offsite location (such as another room in the building) so that the data could be recovered from this archival copy in the event of a catastrophe.

Critical Data. When the data is vital to the organization, daily backup copies and a weekly archival copy are necessary. If making daily backup copies is not practical, the system can be designed with a combination of internal and external backup systems. With this approach, critical data is duplicated daily on the same storage media, and backup copies are made twice a week. For example, with storage on a hard disk, the data can be transferred daily to another logical drive and tape backup copies made on Tuesday and Thursday.

Backing up to another logical drive will not safeguard the data from a system crash that damages the hard disk, but will offer recovery from most other types of system crashes. In addition, an archival copy would be made once a week and stored at an offsite location.

When considering the extent of changes in the data, if only a few data files are modified when the system is used, then only these few data files need to be backed up. The backup system can therefore be designed to copy these data files on a regular basis and the entire system only on a periodic basis. For another rotational backup system, see chapter 12.

BIBLIOGRAPHY

Ciarcia, Steve. "Keep Power-Line Pollution Out of Your Computer." *BYTE* 8, No.12, 1983, pp. 36-44.
Martin, James. *Managing the Data-Base Environment.* Englewood Cliffs, NJ: Prentice-Hall, Inc., 1983.
Merrett, T.H. *Relational Information Systems.* Reston, VA: Reston Publishing Company, Inc., 1984.

SECTION THREE

IMPLEMENTATION

CHAPTER TWELVE

PRELIMINARIES

The Implementation Section is divided into functional groups in the same way as a programmer looks at implementing an application written in dBASE. These chapters are structured, and they use conventions with which you may not be familiar. Please read "How to Use this Guide" on page one before beginning this Implementation section.

Staying Out of Trouble

Some futuristic version of dBASE will have only two commands:

```
. SET BUGS OFF
. DO WHAT I'M THINKING
```

Until that version is released, there are a couple of basic ground rules you can follow for preventive programming: make backup copies and close files.

Backup.   Always have a backup disk before you do *any* work on your files, and make additional backups periodically as the work is completed. The disk in the computer should always be just a "working copy," with no more importance than a scratchpad. Three or four disks are used in rotation so that there is always a backup copy of more than one working session. See Algorithms below and Back_up.prg in appendix C for details.

Close files.   Another very important technique that prevents a variety of difficulties is to close your files frequently. The basic rule is never to open a file before you need to, and close it immediately after accomplishing the purpose for which it was opened. A file is vulnerable to damage while it is open.

If there are repeated operations on a file and it will remain open for a long time, close and re-open it periodically to save the work to disk. Some of the changes to a database file remain in the computer's memory and are only written to disk when the file is closed. See chapter 19, "Opening and Closing."

Never exit from dBASE by powering down or resetting the computer. Always issue the QUIT command when you are through with dBASE.

Also check algorithms in the chapters that follow for more specific prevention techniques.

Necessary Files

Not all of the files supplied with dBASE are required to be present when dBASE is running. In all cases, utility files that are operated outside of dBASE, such as INSTALL and dCONVERT, may be removed from the working disk.

The files that are used while dBASE is running are of two types, either necessary or optional. Necessary files *must* be present when dBASE is running, and optional files may be removed unless the features they provide are used.

1. dBASE III, version 1.00:
   These must be present:
dBASE	.EXE	::=	Main program file
dBASE	.OVL	::=	Main overlay

   These may be removed:
HELP	.DBS	::=	On-line documentation
ASSIST	.HLP	::=	Menu-driven Assistant mode

2. dBASE II, version 2.4x:
   These must be present:
dBASE	.COM	::=	Main program file
dBASEOVR	.COM	::=	Main overlay

   This may be removed:
dBASEMSG	.TXT	::=	On-line documentation

3. dBASE II, version 2.3x:
   These must be present:
dBASE	.COM	::=	Main program file
dBASEMSG	.COM	::=	Messages
dBASEMAI	.OVR	::=	Main overlay
dBASEMSC	.OVR	::=	Miscellaneous overlay
dBASEAPP	.OVR	::=	Append command

   These may be removed:
INSTALL	.COM	::=	Installation program
dBASEBRO	.OVR	::=	Browse command
dBASEJOI	.OVR	::=	Join command
dBASEMOD	.OVR	::=	Modify command
dBASERPG	.OVR	::=	Report Form command
dBASESRT	.OVR	::=	Sort command
dBASETTL	.OVR	::=	Total command
dBASEUPD	.OVR	::=	Update command

The main program file is loaded into memory when it is first called. Therefore, it can reside on a drive or in a directory other than the current, or "default," drive/directory. To call it, the filename dBASE must be preceded by the drive designator. Or, if the operating system supports it, a *path* can be set to its location.

An overlay file is called by the dBASE main program file whenever a command whose code resides in the overlay is issued. In dBASE II, the overlay files must reside in the current drive/directory because that is the only place dBASE will look for them. In III, the overlay files may reside in a different location as long as the operating system path has been set to tell dBASE where to find them. See your operating system manual to determine whether the path concept is supported and how to use it.

In II, all other files (database, command, index, memory, etc.) can reside on another drive because dBASE II will accept a drive designator in front of the filename. They cannot, however, reside on the same drive in a different directory because dBASE II does not accept a path parameter in the filename. dBASE III does not have this limitation, and files can be located anywhere desired.

A popular convention among software publishers is an ASCII text file called *Read.me,* which is often placed on distribution disks to update the documentation. If you receive a disk with this file on it, read it before using the software.

Files in dBASE

These are the files used inside dBASE. Each is discussed in the chapter appropriate to its process.

dBASE File Type:	Default Extension:	Supported Versions:	Binary Header:	Covering Chapter:
Alternate	.TXT	III/II	No	20
Command	.PRG or .CMD	III/II	No	14
Database	.DBF	III/II	Yes	19
Database-Text	.DBT	III	Yes	19
Format	.FMT	III/II	No	18,"Output"
Index	.NDX	III/II	Yes	19,"Ordering"
Label	.LBL	III	Yes	21
Memory	.MEM	III/II	Yes	17
Procedure	.PRG	III	No	14
Report	.FRM	III/II	Yes III No II	21

The files without a binary header are standard ASCII text files without any control codes or structural information. See chapter 20, "Foreign Files."

Filenames

In most command syntax, a <filename> may optionally include:

- In II, a drive designator (letter and colon) preceding the filename. For example, B:Filename.ext.
- In III, a drive designator and/or directory list preceding the filename. For example, B:\directory\subdirectory\Filename.ext.

Installation

At the time of this writing, dBASE III comes pre-installed, but dBASE II requires that an installation program be run first on most computers. The installation program need only be run once, and its primary purpose is to assign the correct screen handling sequences for that particular computer. A few other options are also available, such as changing the symbol used for the macro (&), selecting a multi-user operating system such as MP/M, or changing the format of the date.

If the screen does not operate correctly in full-screen mode, dBASE needs to be installed for that particular hardware. Version II-2.3D is preinstalled for the IBM PC and was not shipped with an install program.

Operating System Configuration

In MS-DOS and PC-DOS, two system default values must be changed, or "configured," before dBASE III will run. This is accomplished by specifying the new system parameters in an ASCII text file called *Config.sys*. Config.sys executes automatically when DOS is booted. It executes before Autoexec.bat and must be located on the boot drive of the computer.

The parameters we want to change are the number of buffers that DOS will use and the number of files that DOS will allow to be open at one time. The Config.sys file contains:

```
Buffers = 15
Files   = 20
```

Each buffer specified increases the resident size of DOS by 528 bytes. Since this makes that much RAM unavailable to run software, it may be necessary to set fewer buffers if the hardware has a minimal memory capacity. However, if extensive use of dBASE III is anticipated, the memory capacity of the computer should be expanded to allow for fifteen buffers. Early dBASE III manuals recommend twenty-four buffers, but our tests show between ten and fifteen to be faster.

The files parameter of twenty is the maximum available in DOS, version 2.x, and each file specified over the default of eight increases DOS by thirty-nine bytes. Of those, DOS reserves five for standard input, output, error, auxiliary, and standard printer. This means that only fifteen files of any type can be open simultaneously in the entire system, including dBASE. A dBASE application can only open thirteen files because dBASE itself uses two, one for the main program file and one for the overlay.

Although dBASE II will run without this configuration, its performance (speed) is greatly improved when the buffers parameter is raised. Setting files does not affect dBASE II because it deals directly with the File Control Block (FCB) instead of using the DOS "handles" (see "Procedural Structures" in chapter 14). This allows sixteen files of any type to be open simultaneously inside dBASE II, not counting dBASE itself.

dBASE III uses all available RAM, and it is certainly possible to run it out of memory in a 256K system. Note that ten database files open with 4K records and 128 fields will each use 80K of memory.

dBASE II uses a fixed amount of RAM regardless of how much is available:

dBASE Version:	Memory Used:
II - 16-bit	128K less the operating system
II - 8-bit	64K less the operating system
II - 8-bit (Apple)	56K less the operating system

dBASE Buffers

DOS buffers act between the computer's peripheral devices (such as the disk drive and keyboard) and the software. dBASE *also* has buffers that act between the DOS buffers and dBASE.

dBASE III uses twenty buffers of 512 bytes each to place disk files into memory where they can be accessed quickly. These buffers are referred to as *hot, warm,* or *cold*. When data in a buffer has just been read in and has not been changed, we call it "cold." When the data in a buffer has been changed, we call it "hot" until it has been saved to disk. Hot buffers are written to disk when the computer is waiting for keyboard input. After a buffer has been written to disk, we call it "warm." Neither cold nor warm buffers will be written to disk.

dBASE II uses eight buffers of 512 bytes each. They are only written to disk when they are needed for another operation. Therefore, at least some of any additions or changes made will remain vulnerable in the computer's volatile memory until the file is closed.

dBASE III Configuration

An optional file called *Config.db* can be used to configure dBASE III. This is in addition to the Config.sys file which is used to configure the operating system. When dBASE III is booted, it looks for a

Config.db file anywhere in the operating system path. If one exists, dBASE will come up with the attributes specified in Config.db.

Config.db, like *Config.sys*, is an ASCII text file with each parameter on a new line.

The parameters allowed in *Config.db* are undelimited literals only and cannot contain operators or functions.

```
ALTERNATE       =    <text filename>
* Both specifies the filename, and sets it ON.
BELL            =    <switch>
BUCKET          =    <number>                ::=  Integer from 1 to 31
* This "bucket" is used to hold all limiting options on @...GETs
* such as range and picture templates (chapter 19, "Input").
* The default is 2K.
CARRY           =    <switch>
COLOR           =    <color parameter list>
* See Chapter 18, "Output" for parameters.
COMMAND         =    <command> <command parameters>
* Command to execute when dBASE is first booted.
CONFIRM         =    <switch>
CONSOLE         =    <switch>
DEBUG           =    <switch>
DECIMALS        =    <number>                ::=  Integer from 0 to 14
DEFAULT         =    <drive designator>
DELETED         =    <switch>
DELIMITERS      =    <one or two characters>
DELIMITERS      =    <switch>
DEVICE          =    SCREEN | PRINT
ECHO            =    <switch>
ESCAPE          =    <switch>
EXACT           =    <switch>
F2              =    <command list>          ::=  up to 30 characters
F3              =    <command list>          ::=  up to 30 characters
F4              =    <command list>          ::=  up to 30 characters
F5              =    <command list>          ::=  up to 30 characters
F6              =    <command list>          ::=  up to 30 characters
F7              =    <command list>          ::=  up to 30 characters
F8              =    <command list>          ::=  up to 30 characters
F9              =    <command list>          ::=  up to 30 characters
F10             =    <command list>          ::=  up to 30 characters
GETS            =                            ::=  Integer from 35 to 1023,
                                                  default is 128.
HEADINGS        =    <switch>
HELP            =    <switch>
INTENSITY       =    <switch>
MARGIN          =    <number>                ::=  Integer from 0 to 254
MAXMEM          =    <number>                ::=  Integer from 200 to 720
* Used to define the amount of memory that dBASE
* III does not release when executing an external
* program. <number> represents the top address released
```

```
*  to the system for DOS to execute an external processor.
*  Amount of memory required is MAXMEM + 17K + <size of
*  memory needed by external processor>. Default value is
*  256K. Note that there is no protection against dBASE
*  III using more memory than this, thereby placing data in
*  memory that can be trashed by RUNning an external
*  program from within dBASE.
MENUS            =        <switch>
MVARSIZ          =        <number>                    ::=  Integer from 1 to 31
*  <number> represents size of the memory variable area in
*  kilobytes.
PATH             =        <path list>
PRINT            =        <switch>
PROMPT           =        <string>                    ::=  Undelimited literal
SAFETY           =        <switch>
STEP             =        <switch>
TALK             =        <switch>
TEDIT            =        <text editor filename> (no extension)
*  <text editor> will come up when MODIFY COMMAND is
*  executed.
UNIQUE           =        <switch>
WP               =        <word processor filename> (no extension)
*  <word processor> will come up when a Memo field is
*  entered in the interactive mode.
```

- All parameters are undelimited literals.
- <switch> ::= ON | OFF.
- F2 through F10 are function key settings.
- Undefined settings are SET command parameters, see chapter 15, "The Working Environment."

Hard Disk Systems

In dBASE III, whenever an external word processor assigned to TEDIT or WP in Config.db is used, or when an external program is RUN, DOS will reload Command.com before returning to dBASE. DOS assumes that Command.com is located in the root directory of the drive from which the computer was booted. In the cases where an external hard disk is used, the computer often boots from the floppy drive A. To reload Command.com from a floppy drive takes considerably longer than from a drive on the hard disk, and requires that the boot disk remain in the drive.

The DOS command SET COMSPEC is used to tell DOS where to look for its command processor other than on the boot drive. The command is usually placed in the Autoexec.bat file, and its syntax is:

```
SET COMSPEC=<drive>:{\<subdirectory>} \Command.com
```

Please see your DOS documentation for more information.

VOCABULARY

Operators

None.

Functions

None.

SET parameters

None.

Commands

QUIT

> `QUIT`
> [III/II] To exit from dBASE to the operating system.

> `QUIT TO {<quit parameter>, <quit parameter>}`
> [II] To exit from dBASE to another program or operating system command.

Other Resources

None.

ALGORITHMS

Rotational Backup

In this scheme, the working disk is copied over the reserve disk at the end of each working session. If the disks are labeled A, B, C, and D, the rotation scheme for the first eight working sessions looks like this:

Session:	Working:	Backup to:	Reserve:	Last Used:
1	A	B		
2	B	C		A
3	C	D	A	B
4	D	A	B	C
5	A	B	C	D
6	B	C	D	A
7	C	D	A	B
8	D	A	B	C

On hard disk systems, the hard disk is always the working disk, and the rotation looks like this:

Session:	Working:	Backup to:	Reserve:	Last Used:
1	H	A		
2	H	B		A
3	H	C	A	B
4	H	A	B	C
5	H	B	C	A
6	H	C	A	B
7	H	A	B	C
8	H	B	C	A

See Back_up.prg in appendix C.

Add-On Software

We've all seen advertisements for "add-on" software that provide a variety of operations not currently available in dBASE. These include array capability, command file generators, screen generators, statistics, graphics, and a variety of others. We do not use them for a couple of reasons: we have not run into an application that required their use, and we've not found the ones that write code to save any time. If anything, it took us longer to modify and debug the code they write than to write it from scratch ourselves. However, we have not tried them all, and we encourage you to experiment. One word of advice though: there is no software at the time of this writing that will do it all for you, where you just turn it on, go to the beach, and when you return, there it is: your finished application. If you find one, please let us know immediately.

Work-Arounds

- In dBASE II, QUIT TO does not work in 16-bit versions of 2.4. Quit_to.prg in appendix C is a program that simulates the inoperable command in MS(PC)-DOS.

Related Algorithms

"Where Are We?" in chapter 16.

CHAPTER THIRTEEN

PROGRAM DOCUMENTATION

There are many reasons to write code with standardized conventions and to comment and document every command file fully. Among the top reasons are clarification of design, ease of debugging, and facilitation of future modifications. Stated simply, we don't want to rely on our memory months later when we're deeply involved in another project. The standardization of code writing conventions becomes even more important on projects where two or more programmers may be working on separate modules that will be built into one program.

The standards detailed in this chapter are the ones we have chosen to follow in the Software Support Center. They are not intended to be viewed as the final word in dBASE coding conventions, but rather as a guideline to encourage completeness and excellence in writing dBASE code.

In setting standards, we want to make sure that they are general enough to apply to all the programs we will write, and detailed enough so that we will know exactly what we did several months later and, even more importantly, why we did it. We may alter our conventions a bit for a new system that requires something we had not anticipated, and we look for a new convention that, as with any true paradigm, can encompass both the old and new requirements. Select your standards carefully, and use them faithfully.

The file documentation standards in this section are divided into five categories: filenames, alias names, field names, memory variable names, and program documentation.

Filenames

This is an expanded view of a filename example:

database system	separator	unique function	dot	extension
A G	_ or /	M E N U	.	P R G

Database System. The first one or two letters in the filename are used for the database system. In this case, AG identifies all files in the *Advanced Guide* system used to facilitate the writing of this guide. This makes it easier to identify all the files belonging to an entire system. Copying or getting directory listings of the entire system can be done with relative ease when using this method. For example:

```
A>DIR AG_*.DBF
A>BACKUP AG_*.* B:
```

Separator. Typically, we use the underscore (_) or slash (/) as the second or third letter. This serves two purposes:

1. One can easily distinguish the database system name from the unique function name.
2. It will distinguish the database system files from other system files having the same first one or two letters. For example, on a DIR of AG_*.*, the files Agent.lst or Agenda.dbf will not appear since they do not have the unique "_" as the third character and therefore are not part of the *Advanced Guide* system.

The underscore is the preferred separator in both MS(PC)-DOS and UNIX, while the slash is used only in CP/M. The slash is permitted in CP/M and forbidden in DOS, whereas the underscore is permitted in DOS and forbidden in CP/M. Although the dash (-) is permitted by both CP/M and DOS, it is frequently used in the unique function portion of the filename; so, either the slash or underscore is still the preferred separator depending on which operating system is being used.

Unique Function. The next five or six letters describe the unique function of the file. This name should be as descriptive as possible. Occasionally, the unique function will be a date or report number. The last character of this group is sometimes a number used to describe a different version of the same function.

> B_parts1.frm
> B_parts2.frm
> B_06-20.txt
> B_entry.prg

Extension. The last three characters are used for the file extension. We use the default extensions provided by dBASE for all dBASE files, although other extensions can be used if specified after the filename.

Default Extension	Description
.BAK	backup file
.CMD	command file on 8-bit computers
.DBF	database file
.DBT	database-text file (for memo fields, III only.)
.FMT	format file
.FRM	report form file
.LBL	label form file (III only.)
.MEM	memory file
.NDX	index file
.PRG	command or procedure file on 16-bit computers
.TXT	standard ASCII text file

Reserved Words. Words that have meaning to dBASE are "reserved," and we never use them for file or variable names. For example, the command file in appendix C called *Chgcase.cmd* (as in *change case*) was originally named *Case.cmd* during its development. When it came time to try it out, the command DO CASE was typed at the dot prompt. Rather than executing the command file called Case, dBASE waited for a CASE statement and would do nothing else until ENDCASE was entered. Although there are words reserved by dBASE that will not cause problems when used in names, we stay away from using them for anything other than what dBASE intends.

Capitalization. When used in command files, we capitalize the system designators (first one or two letters) of all filenames, and use lowercase for the remainder of the filename.

Alias Names

In dBASE II, the two work areas are called PRIMARY and SECONDARY. In dBASE III, each of the ten work areas may be assigned a name, called an *alias*. If no alias is specified during the USE command, the filename will become the alias name. For alias names, we use almost the same conventions that we do for filenames.

Alias names make it easier to specify or SELECT a work area. Since there are no global operations to be performed with alias names, we don't use the system designators. We use the unique function part of the filename, usually expanded, for the alias because it makes the code more understandable. For example:

```
USE AP_parts ALIAS Parts
SELECT 2
USE AP_comp  ALIAS Components
SELECT 3
USE AP_invce INDEX AP_inv-1 ALIAS Invoices
```

Now, when reading the code, it is easy to tell the relation between the files operation and the <commands>:

```
SELECT Parts
? Part_no
SELECT Invoices
? Invoice_no
SELECT Components
? Comp_no, Parts->Part_no, Invoices->Invoice_no
```

As with filenames, dBASE reserved words are not used and the first letter of the alias name is capitalized.

Field Names

In naming our fields, we prefer to be descriptive rather than cryptic. The use of a separator in the field name greatly improves readability. In II, the permissible field name separator is the colon (:). In III, it is the underscore (_).

Descriptive	Cryptic
First:name, Fname	Fn, N1
Address, Street	Add, St
Item_amt, Prod_code	Iamt, Pc
New:bal, Balance	Nbal, Bal
Is_valid, Istrue	Vld, Tr

Logical Fields. If the field is a logical type, we start the field name with the letters "Is". Since logical fields are handled differently in logical expressions than character, date, or numeric fields, this makes them stand out and improves understanding of the program logic. The use of the separator after "Is" is optional and a matter of personal preference.

Reserved Words. We never use dBASE reserved words for field names. If we wanted a field called Pack, we would name it Packs, Packed, Packing, or something similiar.

Capitalization. As with filenames, the first letter of field names is capitalized when writing command files.

Memory Variable (Memvar) Names

Our standards for memvar names are almost exactly the same as for field names, except that memvar names are all lowercase.

- Be descriptive, not cryptic.
- No dBASE reserved words.
- Start logical memvars with "is".

Unique Identifiers. When the memvar duplicates a filename, field name, or dBASE reserved word, we add an "m" as the first letter. For example, say we want a memvar called "name." We call it "name" unless there is a field called "Name" in a file within this system, in which case we call it "mname," "m:name," or "m_name." If we want a memvar called "store," we call it "mstore" because STORE is a dBASE reserved word. We call a logical memvar "mis_true" only if there is a database field called "Is_true." The memvar name separator is the colon (:) in dBASE II, and the underscore (_) in dBASE III. Do not confuse this convention with the memvar *prefix* "M->" in III or "M." in II (chapter 17).

With the enhancement started in dBASE II, version 2.4, of being able to RELEASE ALL LIKE, RELEASE ALL EXCEPT, and SAVE ALL LIKE, we saw systems develop that maximize their use. For example, all local, or "transient," variables–those that are used solely within one command file and get released at the end of that file–start with "t:". The memvar name separator, like the filename separator, allows similar groups of memvars to be manipulated. This way, the command at the end of the file can read RELEASE ALL LIKE t:* instead of RELEASE name, mstore, is:true. In III, memvars are naturally local (see chapter 17), however if there is a group of memvars that gets SAVEd during the course of the program, we might start them all with "s_" and then say SAVE ALL LIKE s_*.

A convention can be used to distinguish character and numeric memvars that both contain numbers. For example, we could call a numeric memvar *part:num* and a character memvar *part:no*.

Capitalization. In command files, memory variable names are all in lowercase letters.

Program Documentation

There are two comment commands in dBASE: * and NOTE. They are command verbs themselves and therefore must always begin the command line on which they appear. Comments in dBASE occupy a full command line and normally cannot be combined with executable commands on the same line. The exceptions to this last statement are the structured commands (see "End Structure Comments" under Algorithms below).

The asterisk is by far the more popular of these two commands for its faster execution and better readability in programs. The only time we use the NOTE command is on those rare occasions when the command will be issued from a macro-memvar in dBASE II. The asterisk does not work in this situation:

```
STORE 'NOTE ' TO memvar
&memvar This is a comment
```

Header. All of our command files begin with a heading that states the name of the program, the programmer's name, the date, the copyright notice, a brief description of what the program does, and any information necessary for the running and maintenance of the program. Optionally, the header may also contain the names of local memory variables initialized, memvars passed from previous command files, and the status of the SET functions passed from previous command files. The format is:

```
*  Program..:  <program name with extension>
*  Author...:  <your name>
*  Date.....:  <first date written>, <last date worked on>
*  Notice...:  <Copyright or other notice>
*  Version..:  <dBASE III or II, and version number>
*  Notes....:  <brief description of what program does>
*             <structure of data files used>
*             <names of command files called>
*             <files called from, if part of a system>
*             <files called, if part of a system>
*             <parameters passed>
*             <other information necessary to run the program>
*             <if applicable: transient memvars, and
*             function key status>
```

During writing, debugging, and testing, the date of the latest change is added to the Date header. Once the system is finished, and modifications are to be made, another header field called "Revised..:" is added under Date. Each revision adds another Revised field with a description of the changes and the date when they were made.

Footer. At the end of the command or procedure file, we put a line giving the end-of-file sign (EOF) and the name of the file. This way, we can always tell at a glance whether the entire file is present or whether the last portion of it has been lost.

```
*  EOF: <Filename.ext>
```

A dBASE III procedure file has an end-of-procedure footer at the end of every procedure. They have not been around long enough at the time of this writing to have established a standard. One idea is to use an end-of-procedure symbol like the end-of-file.

```
*  EOP: <Procedure name>
```

Another idea is to use a line with it to make the separation from the following procedure more visible.

```
*  EOP: <Procedure name>-------------------------------------
```

Body.   When writing a program, proper construction is necessary for ease of reading and debugging. If pseudo-code was written first, it will usually serve well as comments for code modules as they are written. A code module can be defined as a group of commands that act together to perform a similar or complementary operation. Separate the internal code modules of the program with an asterisk (*) or a blank line, and precede each module of code with a brief description of the module's purpose:

```
* dBASE II...
*
* Initialize memory variables...
STORE " " TO select
STORE $(STR(0,81),1,80) TO blank
STORE "Y" TO continue
*
* Open the database file and locate record...
USE Names
LOCATE FOR Name = "Jim"
DISPLAY
```

Note: dBASE II versions earlier than 2.4 have difficulty with blank lines in the code, and so, every line must have a command. This anomaly motivated the single asterisk method of separating groups of code.

The comments for some modules should explain the reason for using that code in addition to its purpose:

```
* dBASE III...
*
* Save the record number in order to resume at this
* record after the file has been closed and reopened...
m_recno = RECNO()
*
* Decrement last customer number if operator chose to abort
* because a new number was assigned to start the edit...
IF choice = 'A'
   cust_no = cust_no - 1
ENDIF
```

Proper indentation in the body of the command file is extremely important for ease of reading and debugging. Only command statements contained within structured programming commands are indented. The structured programming commands in dBASE are: DO WHILE...ENDDO, IF...ENDIF, and DO CASE...ENDCASE. We use three spaces as the standard for our indentation.

```
* dBASE III...
* Print only those records that match
* the city specified by the operator...
ACCEPT "Enter a city from which to print: " TO m_city
DO WHILE .NOT. EOF()
   IF City = m_city
      IF Phone = " "
         ? Name + " has no telephone."
      ELSE
         ? Name, Phone
      ENDIF
      * Skip a line between names...
      ?
   ENDIF
```

```
     * Next record...
     SKIP
 ENDDO
```

TEXT...ENDTEXT is the only structured command that is an exception to the indentation rule. It is a structured output command and does not branch or otherwise affect program flow. All text contained within this command is handled as a literal, and will display any indentation as leading spaces in the output. Therefore, indent the embedded text in this command only as much as is desirable in the output.

Capitalization. All dBASE reserved words are capitalized. This includes all commands, logical operators, functions, and fixed parameters.

Four-letter Words

The dBASE language can get kind of "rough." That is, four-letter abbreviations of all commands and functions are processed the same as the full word. Although this makes no difference to the interpreter, it makes things rough for humans who try to understand the code. We recommend against using abbreviations in the source code. However, once written and debugged, the source code can be copied to an execute-only file where indents and comments are removed, and the commands are all trimmed to four letters. This may or may not result in slightly faster processing speeds in dBASE II. Because III uses more buffers to hold command files, trimming the code results in an even smaller saving of execution time.

Command File Documentation Summary

- No dBASE reserved words used as a name.
- No four-letter abbreviations in the source code.
- Indent commands three spaces within DO CASE, DO WHILE, and IF structures only.
- Comment lines precede code modules.

Name	Method	Examples
dBASE reserved words	All capitals	ERASE, DO WHILE, APPEND FROM, LOCATE FOR
Filenames	Capitalize first letter or two	Names, AG_names, Parts, GL_start
Alias names	Capitalize first letter	Name, Expenses, Products, Amounts
Field names	Capitalize first letter	First_name, Address, Product, Amount_1
Memory variables	All lowercase	blank, string, t:row, sc_bright, counter

Memory variables in place of file, field, alias, or dBASE names	Lowercase "m" as first letter	mname, m:address, m_product, m_amount_1
Logical fields and memory variables	"is" as the leading characters	Isdigit, is:julian Is_valid, m_is_valid

Figure 13-1

VOCABULARY

Operators

None.

Functions

None.

SET parameters

ALTERNATE

    SET ALTERNATE <switch>
        [III/II] To start/stop sending screen output to a file.

    SET ALTERNATE TO
        [III/II] To close an open "alternate" file.

    SET ALTERNATE TO <text filename>
        [III/II] To create or overwrite a text file for recording what appears on the screen.

Commands

*

    * <comment>
        [III/II] For placing comments in a command, procedure, format, or Config.db file.

CLOSE

    CLOSE ALTERNATE
        [III] To close an open alternate file.

DISPLAY

   DISPLAY MEMORY
      [III/II] To display all of the active memory variables.

   DISPLAY STATUS
      [III/II] To find out the current state of the working environment.

   DISPLAY STRUCTURE
      [III/II] To review the structure of a database file.

LIST

   LIST MEMORY
      [III/II] To display all of the active memory variables.

   LIST STATUS
      [III/II] To find out the current state of the working environment.

   LIST STRUCTURE
      [III/II] To review the structure of a database file.

NOTE

   NOTE <comment>
      [III/II] For placing comments in a command, procedure, or format file.

Other Resources

None.

ALGORITHMS

Recording Details for Documentation

Occasionally, it is desirable to include the structure of a file in the notes part of a command file's header. This is easily generated with LIST STRUCTURE and recorded in a text file with SET ALTERNATE:

```
* Open the database file...
USE <database filename>
* Open the text file, and begin output...
SET ALTERNATE TO <text filename>
SET ALTERNATE ON
* Display the database file structure...
LIST STRUCTURE
* Stop output to, and close the text file..
SET ALTERNATE OFF
SET ALTERNATE TO
* Close the database file...
USE
```

If your word processor supports inserting, or "reading in," external files (as MODIFY COMMAND does in dBASE III), the alternate text file can be read into the command file. In both dBASE III's MODIFY COMMAND and WordStar, the command to read in external files is ^KR. If this feature is not available, generate the structure into a text file first, and then add the code to that file.

This method may also be used to generate a memvar listing by substituting LIST MEMORY for LIST STRUCTURE. Memvar listings are usually desired at various stages of program execution, and so, this code may be inserted anywhere in a command file to capture a list of its currently active memvars at any particular point:

```
* Open the text file, and begin output...
SET ALTERNATE TO <text filename>
SET ALTERNATE ON
* Display the memvars...
LIST MEMORY
* Stop output to, and close the text file...
SET ALTERNATE OFF
SET ALTERNATE TO
```

As with memvars, a listing of the current status may be desired at various stages of program execution, typically upon entry into or exit from a command file. The same code sequence is used, but substitute LIST STATUS for LIST MEMORY.

End Structure Comments

When constructing nested or lengthy conditional structures with DO WHILE <logical expression> and IF <logical expression>, it is useful to repeat the <logical expression> after the command that ends the structure in order to see more clearly the logic of the program flow. Some programmers place this comment in square brackets to enhance its readability as a comment.

```
IF <condition 1>
   <commands>
ELSE
   IF <condition 2>
      <commands>
      DO WHILE <condition 3>
         <commands>
         IF <condition 4>
            <commands>
         ENDIF [<condition 4>]
      ENDDO [<condition 3>]
   ENDIF [<condition 2>]
ENDIF [<condition 1>]
```

CHAPTER FOURTEEN

COMMAND FILE HANDLING

All commands, except those with a multi-line structure, may be issued either from the dot prompt (interactive mode), or from a command file or procedure (program mode). Multi-line structured commands are useful only from the program mode. Although they will execute from the dot prompt, we are not aware of any practical reason for doing so. The three *structured programming commands* in dBASE are:

```
DO CASE...ENDCASE
DO WHILE...ENDDO
IF...ENDIF
```

The other structured command, TEXT...ENDTEXT, is a structured *output* command rather than a structured *programming* command because it has no effect at all on program flow. It is simply a convenient way of outputting large amounts of unformatted literal text.

The command file is a standard ASCII text file that contains only executable dBASE commands. It may be prepared with any word processor or text editor as long as they do not insert non-printable control characters into the command file and use a carriage-return/line-feed pair for their end-of-line. For information on using MODIFY COMMAND to write command files, see chapter 25. There are no dBASE limits regarding command file size. The default command file extension is .CMD in 8-bit systems, and .PRG in 16-bit and larger systems.

Each command appears on its own line, and a command line may be up to 254 characters long. A command line may be thought of as a sentence, made up of words and grouped into paragraphs or "programs." Words in a command line must be separated by at least one blank space; a space is optional around data operators. The command line words may be categorized into the same parts of speech that identify words in the English language, and just as with any verbal language, each command verb has rules of grammar, or "syntax," which must be followed.

Each command line must have a command verb which is always the first word in the line. Depending on the command verb and the desired action, the command line may or may not contain additional words, or command "parameters." All commands are expressed in the imperative mood in which the subject is omitted and assumed to be the dBASE interpreter software. Some examples of command line grammar are:

\<verb\>	[\<adverb\>]	[\<object\>]	[\<prepositional phrase\>]
USE		Datafile	
CLOSE		DATABASES	
SET		TALK	ON
SET		ALTERNATE	TO Altfile
COPY		FIELDS Name,Address	TO Newfile FOR State = 'CA'
@	5, 10 SAY	"Hello"	USING "XXXXX"
SORT	ON Keyfield		TO Sortfile ASCENDING

The command line is broken up, or "parsed," by dBASE into individual components from left to right. Usually, the entire command line is parsed and evaluated before action is taken by the command interpreter. The parser stops immediately after encountering any syntax error without parsing the rest of the command line. In some cases, action is taken before the entire line is parsed. For example, the USE command closes an open data file even on an error.

A command line can be continued on the next line by ending the line that is to be continued with a semicolon (;). When writing command files with MODIFY COMMAND in dBASE III, lines will automatically break at the sixty-eighth column and continue on the next line. Although no semicolon is inserted, dBASE uses MODIFY COMMAND's soft carriage return in the same manner as a semicolon. Although no semicolon is necessary in this case, we recommend inserting it for readability. Soft carriage returns in other word processors may not replace the semicolon, and can result in a syntax error.

Programming Structures

There are four basic programming structures available within dBASE:

1. Sequential (series)
2. Conditional (branching)
3. Iterative (repeating)
4. Procedural (substructure)

Both the branching and conditional structures rely on the evaluation of a logical expression which a programmer will occasionally have difficulty constructing. This is due to the many possible combinations of relational and Boolean operators that can be constructed, and not knowing which combination will give the desired result. Testing the logic with an output command (interactively or program mode) before using it in the conditional command is a good way to "hack it out." Also see logical data handling in chapter 6 and chapter 16.

Sequential (series) Structures. The natural flow of a dBASE command file is sequential until a branching, repeating, or procedural command is encountered.

Conditional (branching) Structures. The two commands used for branching in dBASE are the IF. . .ELSE. . .ENDIF and the DO CASE. . .ENDCASE commands. The basic rule of thumb for choosing between IF or CASE is:

Use IF:

When there are two or fewer possible conditions:

```
                    IF <condition 1>
                        <commands>
                    ENDIF
```

or

```
                    IF <condition 1>
                        <commands>
                    ELSE
                        * This is condition 2...
                        <commands>
                    ENDIF
```

When you want to select more than one condition from among several:

```
                    IF <condition 1>
                        <commands>
                    ENDIF
                    *
                    * and...
                    IF <condition 2>
                        <commands>
                    ENDIF
                    *
                    * and...
                    IF <condition 3>
                        <commands>
                    ENDIF
```

Use CASE:

When you want to select only one condition from among more than two (there is no limit):

```
                    DO CASE
                        CASE <condition 1>
                            <commands>
                        CASE <condition 2>
                            <commands>
                        OTHERWISE
                            * This is condition 3...
                            <commands>
                    ENDCASE
```

The DO CASE command will execute faster than its equivalent in nested IFs:

```
        DO CASE
            CASE <condition 1>
                <commands>
            CASE <condition 2>
                <commands>
            CASE <condition 3>
                <commands>
            CASE <condition 4>
                <commands>
            OTHERWISE
                * This is condition 5...
                <commands>
        ENDCASE
```

is slightly faster and far more readable than:

```
        IF <condition 1>
            <commands>
        ELSE
            IF <condition 2>
                <commands>
            ELSE
                IF <condition 3>
                    <commands>
                ELSE
                    IF <condition 4>
                        <commands>
                    ELSE
                        * This is condition 5...
                        <commands>
                    ENDIF <conditions 4,5>
                ENDIF <condition 3>
            ENDIF <condition 2>
        ENDIF <condition 1>
```

Iterative (repeating) Structures.   Contained within every DO WHILE loop must be either one of:

1.   A command with the potential to change the value of the logical expression.
2.   A conditional branch containing a command that will exit the loop such as EXIT or RETURN.

If this is not done, an endless loop will result. This is a common programming error which is usually easy to spot and fix.

DO WHILE loops may be categorized by the type of their <logical expression>.

1.   <logical expression> is provided by the <relational operator> comparing two expressions of the same data type (except logical type):

```
DO WHILE <expression 1> <relational operator> <expression 2>
```

For example:

```
* [II]
* In a file indexed on State...
FIND "CA"
DO WHILE State = "CA" .AND. (.NOT. EOF)
    <commands for one record>
    * Change condition by moving to next record...
    SKIP
ENDDO
```

```
--------------
```

```
* [II]
* In operations where a counter is kept...
*
* (counting lines on a page in the printer)
STORE 0 TO counter
DO WHILE counter < 56
    <print new line>
    * Change condition by incrementing the counter...
    STORE counter + 1 TO counter
ENDDO
*
* (counting loops to pause for a moment)
? "This message will self-destruct any moment now."
counter = 0
DO WHILE counter < 40
    * Change condition by incrementing the counter...
    counter = counter + 1
ENDDO
CLEAR
```

```
--------------
```

```
* [III/II]
* Error trapping operator entry...
STORE "?" TO choice
DO WHILE .NOT. choice $ "ABC"
    STORE "?" TO choice
    @ <coordinates> GET choice PICTURE "!"
    * Change condition by operator input...
    READ
    CLEAR GETS
ENDDO
```

The loop is exited when the operator enters A, B, or C, making the relational condition true, and thus, the logical expression false.

2.   <logical expression> is the literal true:

```
        DO WHILE .T.   [III]
        DO WHILE T     [II]
```

This form is always true because the constant true is the <logical expression>. In II, the only way out of this loop is to exit the command file with RETURN, CANCEL, or QUIT. In III, the EXIT command may also be used to get out of this loop.

This loop's primary use is to have program control begin again at the top of a command file that is RETURNed to from a subprogram. While it is most often seen in menus, it is valuable to consider in any program that executes repeatedly, and particularly those that call subprograms. Many of the programs and subroutines in the Appendix demonstrate the usefulness of this loop.

There really is another way to exit a DO WHILE T loop in dBASE II, but it makes the code so difficult to understand that we strongly recommend against its use. It is mentioned here only for its value as an example of "dirty" programming. Once inside the loop, it is possible to STORE F TO T which creates a logical memvar called T with the literal F stored in it. When dBASE II next evaluates the <logical expression>, instead of seeing the literal value T, it sees the memvar T with the value F. The <logical expression> is now false, and program control passes out of the loop. dBASE III eliminated the possibility of doing this by improving the consistency of the language (logical constants are .T. and .F. instead of T and F).

3.   <logical expression> is a logical memvar:

```
        DO WHILE is:again
```

This type of DO WHILE requires that the logical memvar be initialized outside the loop, and then changes it when a apecified condition inside the loop is produced.

```
    STORE T TO is:again
    DO WHILE is:again
       <commands>
       * Change condition by evaluating a logical expression...
       STORE <logical expression> TO is:again
    ENDDO
```

4.   <logical expression> is the beginning- or end-of-file function:

```
        DO WHILE .NOT. EOF     [II]
        DO WHILE .NOT. EOF()   [III]
        DO WHILE .NOT. BOF()   [III]
```

This form is used to move through a database file until there are no more records at the beginning (TOP) or end (BOTTOM) of the file. It is often used alone:

```
USE Datafile
GO BOTTOM
DO WHILE .NOT. BOF()
   <commands for one record>
   * Next record...
   SKIP -1
ENDDO
```

It is *always* used in combination with other logical expressions that move through a database file:

```
USE Datafile INDEX Data_x1
FIND "Ashton-Tate"
DO WHILE Company = "Ashton-Tate" .AND. ( .NOT. EOF() )
   <commands for one record>
   * Next record...
   SKIP
ENDDO
```

Procedural (Substructure) Structures. The dBASE commands used to execute the commands in a programmed substructure are:

1. To transfer program control to another group of dBASE commands:

```
        DO <command filename>    [III/II]
        DO <procedure filename>  [III]
```

These are covered in this chapter.

2. To transfer program control to a binary (machine language) file:

```
        QUIT TO <executable file/command list>   [II]
        RUN <executable file/command name>       [III]
        ! <executable file/command name>         [III]
```

These are covered in chapter 22.

3. To transfer program control to a machine language routine poked into memory:

```
        CALL  [II]
```

This is covered in chapter 22.

As a structured programming language, dBASE supports subroutines in the form of additional command files or procedures, referred to as both "subprograms" and "subroutines." The 'DO <subroutine>' command is the only way to transfer program control to a subroutine written in dBASE. RETURN is used in the subroutine to transfer program control back to the calling command file or procedure. This is a convenient way of "modularizing" the program coding, or put another way, of breaking up the program into smaller, more manageable modules.

An application program, or "system," can be made up of one or more command files, each with a specific function or purpose. "Nesting" is where command file-1 calls command file-2, which then calls command file-3. This is said to be "nested two deep."

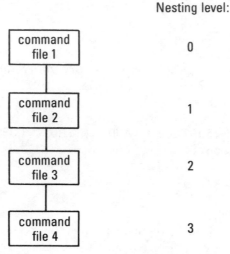

Nesting level:

command file 1	0
command file 2	1
command file 3	2
command file 4	3

Figure 14-1

There are no limits regarding the number of command files in a program. However, the nesting depth is limited by how many files are allowed by dBASE or by the operating system to be open *simultaneously*. dBASE II uses FCB (File Control Block) I/O and contains internal buffer space for sixteen FCB blocks, thus sixteen files can be open at one time. dBASE III, however, uses the UNIX type of "ASCII I/O" handles for which DOS provides the control block for each open file. At the time of this writing, MS(PC)-DOS has a limit of twenty control blocks. Of those, five are reserved DOS which leaves only fifteen available to dBASE and its applications. See Operating System Configuration in chapter 12.

A general rule of thumb is that if a group of commands will execute more than once in a program or will be used by more than one program, make that group a separate, or "sub," command file. However, when the group of commands is extremely brief, say only a line or two of code, it may be preferable to repeat it in each place where it is required. Note that this is an exception and must be used carefully, if at all. A procedure file makes it practical to have just a single line of code in a separate subroutine.

Entry into the application system is always through one point, usually a menu. This command file is called the "main" file, or "hub" of the system. Likewise, exit from the system should occur at only one point. Rather than having an exit in several "sub-files," each sub-file in the system should return program control to one central point from which exit from the system is implemented.

dBASE III adopted the procedure concept of having several subroutines in the same file. A *procedure* is made up of a group of commands the same as a command file. A *procedure file* holds up to thirty-two procedures. This saves the time spent in opening and closing a disk file each time a new group of commands is called. In large applications, it is easier to write separate command files and, when debugging is complete, combine them into a single procedure file. This text uses the term *command file* to mean both "command file" and "procedure" unless otherwise noted. Only one procedure file can be open at any time, and individual procedures can be nested to a maximum depth of eighteen. The default procedure file extension is .PRG unless otherwise specified.

A command file is opened with a DO <command filename> command. The only commands that close command files are:

RETURN
CANCEL
QUIT

If it is encountered, the actual end of the file or the end-of-file marker ^Z <Ctrl-Z> will operate the same as the RETURN command. However, we always use the RETURN command for its consistency, clarity, and readability, even when the end-of-file would work in its place. Unless ESCAPE has been SET OFF, pressing the <Esc> key from the keyboard behaves the same as executing a CANCEL command. In dBASE III, the RETURN command has a TO MASTER option that transfers program control directly to the top level command file without returning through all the command files in between.

A procedure file is opened with a SET PROCEDURE TO <procedure filename> command. The individual procedures in the file are accessed with a DO <procedure name> command. Program control travels among the procedures with a series of DO <procedure name> and RETURN commands, the same as with a group of command files in a single application system. A procedure file is closed with either CLOSE PROCEDURE or SET PROCEDURE [TO]. If a procedure in an open procedure file has the same name as a command file, the procedure has precedence and will be executed.

Data Exchange Among Command Files

Subroutines may be divided into two categories. One category simply performs an operation such as printing a report, and the other category performs a data operation and returns a result to the calling file. The exchange of information between command files is called "parameter passing." The calling command file usually passes parameters in the form of memory variables. Memory variables, or "memvars," are fully covered in chapter 17. We also cover the following points here because memvars play such an important part in the use of subroutines and in the control of program flow, or "logic."

In dBASE II, all memory variables have a *global* life, or "characteristic," to them. In dBASE III, memory variables can be broken down into three types: PRIVATE, PUBLIC, and *Hidden*. Their type affects their ability to be used by other command files in the program. A more complete description of memvar types and their characteristics is in chapter 17, and here are the rules by which they operate in command files and procedures.

1. Memory variables are automatically released at the end of the routine in which they are created. They are implicitly PRIVATE to the routine that created them, and therefore are available only to it and its subroutines.

2. Memvars may be declared PRIVATE before they are created in a subroutine in order to insure that the subroutine will not overwrite or otherwise affect higher-level memvars of the same name. Any existing higher-level memvars mentioned in the PRIVATE declaration become *Hidden* until program control returns to a higher level when the subroutine is closed.

3. Memvars may be declared PUBLIC before they are created in order to make them permanent and globally available. This is the same as creating them at the dot prompt, which is the highest level possible.

4. A memvar specifically passed with the DO. . .WITH command and received in the subroutine with the PARAMETERS command behaves the same as if it had been declared PRIVATE in the subroutine, except that any changes made in the subroutine *will* be reflected in the memvar of the higher-level routine. This

implicit private status is necessary only because havoc would result if the subroutine released the original memvar. See *Do Without* under Algorithms below.

The value of this form of parameter passing with the DO...WITH command comes when it is desirable to pass constants or expressions which initialize *local* memvars in the subroutine and are released upon return to the calling command file, or when it is desirable to use a different memvar name in the subroutine and still have the value returned to the original memvar name passed. This makes the subroutine very modular so that it can be easily called from a variety of unrelated command files. A practical example is Trig.prg in appendix B.

```
* MF_CALLR.PRG   [dBASE III]
*
* Local variables:
*         entry    (C) 1
*         is_error (L)
*         result   (C) 3-5
*
* Prompt for an entry to be calculated...
WAIT "Enter a number from 1 to 3 --> " TO entry
*
* Initialize variables used by the subroutine to
* return values back to this command file...
is_error = .T.
result   = " "
*
* Call the subprogram to do the calculation,
* and specify the parameters to be passed...
DO MF_subrt WITH entry, is_error, result
*
* Program execution resumes here after return from
* subroutine.
* Memvar values have been altered by the subroutine.
*
* Conditional branch to detect error...
IF is_error
   * Display error message...
   ? "Your entry was not a 1, 2, or 3 and did not compute."
ELSE
   * Display the result...
   ? "The result is: ", result
ENDIF
* EOF: MF_callr.prg

* MF_SUBRT.PRG
*
* Local variables:
*         entry2    (C) 1
*         is_error2 (L)
*         result2   (C) 3-5
*
```

```
* Receive parameters from calling file by
* declaring new local variables in the subprogram...
PARAMETERS entry2, is_error2, result2
*
* Branch for calculation...
DO CASE
    CASE entry2  = "1"
        result2   = "One"
        is_error2 = .F.
    CASE entry2  = "2"
        result2   = "Two"
        is_error2 = .F.
    CASE entry2  = "3"
        result2   = "Three"
        is_error2 = .F.
ENDCASE
*
* Return to MF_callr...
RETURN
* EOF: MF_subrt.prg
```

In modular programming like this, it is a good idea for the subprogram to pass a verification parameter back to the calling file. This is usually done with a logical memory variable called "is:valid" or "is_error." Because there are times when different errors can result in a wide variety of results being passed back to the calling file, checking one logical variable for an error standardizes the code.

Related Details

See Technical Support Notes 69 and 74, and Technical Reference Note 7 in appendix F.

VOCABULARY

Operators

None.

Functions

None.

SET parameters

ESCAPE

```
SET ESCAPE <switch>
```
[III/II] To enable/disable the operator's ability to interrupt a command or program with the ESCAPE key.

PROCEDURE

SET PROCEDURE TO `<procedure filename>`
[III] To open a procedure file in order to execute one of its procedures with the DO command.

SET PROCEDURE [TO]
[III] To close a procedure file.

Commands

CANCEL

CANCEL
[III/II] To exit directly to the dot prompt from the current command file or procedure without returning to any previous one. Primarily used in debugging.

CLOSE

CLOSE PROCEDURE
[III] To close a procedure file.

DO

DO `<command filename>`
[III/II] To transfer program control to another command file.

DO `<procedure name>`
[III] To transfer program control to another procedure.

DO `<subroutine>` **WITH** `<expression>` {,`<expression>`}
[III] To transfer program control to another command file or procedure while specifying certain parameters that will be given local memvar names in the new command file.

DO CASE...ENDCASE

DO CASE
 { **CASE** `<logical expression>`
 `<commands>` }
ENDCASE
[III/II] To select only one option out of many choices.

```
DO CASE
    { CASE <logical expression>
        <commands> }
    OTHERWISE
        <commands>
ENDCASE
```
[III/II] To select only one option out of many choices, with a default option if none are selected.

DO WHILE...ENDDO

```
DO WHILE <logical expression>
    <commands>
ENDDO
```
[III/II] To repeat execution of certain command groups.

EXIT

```
EXIT
```
[III] To exit from a DO WHILE loop without returning to test the <logical expression>.

IF...ENDIF

```
IF <logical expression>
    <commands>
ENDIF
```
[III/II] To execute certain commands depending on a specified condition.

```
IF <logical expression>
    <commands>
ELSE
    <commands>
ENDIF
```
[III/II] To execute a certain group of commands depending on a specified condition, or else to execute a different group of commands.

LOOP

```
DO WHILE <logical expression>
    <commands-1>
    LOOP
    <commands-2>
ENDDO
```
[III/II] To bypass lots of code in the DO WHILE loop from the current line to the ENDDO. LOOP operates exactly the same as ENDDO.

MODIFY

MODIFY COMMAND <command or procedure filename>
[III/II] To create or edit a command or procedure file.

PARAMETERS

PARAMETERS <memvar name> {,<memvar name>}
[III] To accept parameters passed from another command file or procedure with the DO...WITH command into memvars which are private to the executing subroutine.

PROCEDURE

PROCEDURE <procedure name>
[III] To identify a procedure.

RETURN

RETURN
[III/II] To exit from the current command file or procedure to the preceding one.

RETURN TO MASTER
[III] To exit from the current command file or procedure to the first one in the program.

WAIT

WAIT
[III/II] To require an acknowledgement from the operator before continuing.

WAIT <prompt>
[III] To require an acknowledgement from the operator before continuing.

<keypress>

<Escape>
[III/II] To abort command execution from the keyboard.

<^S>
[III/II] To momentarily pause command execution and screen scrolling from the keyboard.
^S or ^Q to restart.

Other Resources

&

&<character memvar name>
[III/II] To execute a dBASE command that is stored in a memory variable.

```
;
```
```
<command line> { ; <new line> <command line> }
```
[III/II] To continue a line of code on the next line in a program.

ALGORITHMS

Using Subroutines

This dBASE III example demonstrates the use of subroutines in both dBASE III and II command files.

```
* Program.: AG_MAIN.PRG  [III]
* Notes...: Example of a highly modularized command file.
*
* Subroutine to set initial flags and initialize global
* memvars...
DO AG_init
*
DO WHILE .T.
   *
   * Subroutine to display main menu and get operator's
   * selection...
   DO AG_menu
   *
   * Execute one of the three options or exit...
   DO CASE
      CASE select = 0
         QUIT
      CASE select = 1
         * Subroutine to append records...
         DO AG_add
      CASE select = 2
         * Subroutine to edit selected records...
         DO AG_edit
      CASE select = 3
         * Subroutine to print reports...
         DO AG_reprt
   ENDCASE
ENDDO [WHILE .T.]
* EOF: AG_main.prg

* AG_INIT.PRG
<commands>
RETURN
* EOF: AG_init.prg
```

```
* AG_MENU.PRG
<commands>
RETURN
* EOF: AG_menu.prg

* AG_ADD.PRG
DO WHILE <more additions>
   <commands>
ENDDO
RETURN
* EOF: AG_add.prg

* AG_EDIT.PRG
<commands>
RETURN
* EOF: AG_edit.prg

* AG_REPRT.PRG
<commands>
RETURN
* EOF: AG_reprt.prg
```

The RETURN command transfers program control back to the calling file at the line of code immediately following the DO <command filename> command. Notice the DO WHILE .T. loop so that the program restarts almost from the beginning after being RETURNed to from a subroutine.

In dBASE III, these command files could all be combined into one procedure file to save file opening time:

```
* Program.: AG_PROC.PRG
* Notes...: Example of a highly modularized procedure file.
*
* The first, or "main," procedure must have a name...
PROCEDURE AG_main
*
* Subroutine to set initial flags and initialize global
* memvars...
DO AG_init
*
DO WHILE .T.
   *
   * Subroutine to display main menu and get operator's
   * selection...
   DO AG_menu
   *
```

```
         * Execute one of the three options or exit...
      DO CASE
         CASE select = 0
            QUIT
         CASE select = 1
            * Subroutine to append records...
            DO AG_add
         CASE select = 2
            * Subroutine to edit selected records...
            DO AG_edit
         CASE select = 3
            * Subroutine to print reports...
            DO AG_reprt
      ENDCASE
   ENDDO [WHILE .T.]
   * --------------------EOP: AG_main
   *
   PROCEDURE AG_init
   <commands>
   RETURN
   * --------------------EOP: AG_init
   *
   PROCEDURE AG_menu
   <commands>
   RETURN
   * --------------------EOP: AG_menu
   *
   PROCEDURE AG_add
   DO WHILE <more addtions>
      <commands>
   ENDDO
   RETURN
   * --------------------EOP: AG_add
   *
   PROCEDURE AG_edit
   <commands>
   RETURN
   * --------------------EOP: AG_edit
   *
   PROCEDURE AG_reprt
   <commands>
   RETURN
   * --------------------EOP: AG_reprt
   *
   * EOF: AG_main
```

Although the order of individual procedures in a file does not affect the program execution, the file is more readable when the procedures are listed in some logical order such as alphabetical or according to program flow.

Recursion

"Recursion" in programming refers to the practice of calling a command file from within itself, or calling a command file that is still open. Recursion is either limited or forbidden entirely in dBASE as follows:

1. In II-2.3x, recursive command file calls are allowed until the dBASE limit of sixteen files or the operating system limit is reached, whichever comes first. The error message is: TOO MANY FILES ARE OPEN.
2. In II-2.4x, recursive command file calls are forbidden. The error message is: FILE IS CURRENTLY OPEN.
3. In III-1.00, recursive command file calls are forbidden. The error message is: *File is currently open*. Recursive procedure calls are allowed up to the point where the nesting limit of eighteen procedures is reached.

When program control transfers from a command file or procedure with a DO <subroutine> command, the calling command file or procedure remains open until program control is RETURNed to it and one of the commands is issued that will close it: RETURN, CANCEL, or QUIT. CANCEL and QUIT close all open command files and procedures regardless of the level from which they are executed.

This is the proper way to repeat <commands>:

```
* ITERATN.PRG
DO WHILE <condition>
    <commands>
ENDDO
* EOF
```

This is *not* the way to repeat <commands>:

```
* RECURSN.PRG
<commands>
* Recursive call...
DO Recursn
* EOF
```

This is the proper way to use multiple command files or procedures in a program:

```
* MF_MENU.PRG
DO WHILE .T.
   <display options>
   <prompt for choice>
   DO CASE
      CASE choice = "0"
      * Includes an option to exit.
         RETURN
         * Returns to the interactive mode.
      CASE choice = "1"
         DO MF_file1
      CASE choice = "2"
         DO MF_file2
   ENDCASE
ENDDO
* EOF


* MF_FILE1.PRG
<commands>
* Return to MF_menu...
RETURN
* EOF


* MF_FILE2.PRG
<commands>
DO MF_file3
* Return to MF_menu...
RETURN
* EOF


* MF_FILE3.PRG
<commands>
* Return to MF_file2...
RETURN
* EOF
```

This is *not* the way to use multiple command files or procedures in a program:

```
* MF_MENU.PRG
<display options>
<prompt for choice>
DO CASE
   CASE choice = "1"
      DO MF_file1
   CASE choice = "2"
      DO MF_file2
ENDCASE
* EOF
```

```
* MF_FILE1.PRG
<commands>
* Recursive call...
DO MF_menu
* EOF

* MF_FILE2.PRG
<commands>
DO MF_file3
* EOF

* MF_FILE3.PRG
<commands>
* Recursive call...
DO MF_menu
* EOF
```

Do Without [III]

When a value in a memory variable is passed to a subroutine via the DO...WITH command, any changes made in the subroutine will be reflected in the memvar of the passing routine. At times, it is desirable to avoid this, and we can do so by enclosing the memvar in parentheses.

```
* This memvar will reflect changes...
DO <subroutine name> WITH memvar
*
* This memvar will not...
DO <subroutine name> WITH ( memvar )
```

By using the parentheses, dBASE III evaluates the contents of the memvar as an expression, and therefore passes it as a literal. Although the subroutine uses it in a local memvar created with the PARAMETERS command, that memvar will be released on return to the higher level, where the "passed" memvar remains unaffected.

Routine Library

Use previously written and tested routines whenever possible. Store these separately with descriptive names in a library, either on disks or in a subdirectory. This way, a search through previous applications is not necessary. If a routine is improved in an application, remember to update the library.

RunTime

The dBASE interpreter will also execute command files that have been encrypted with dBCODE in RunTime, Ashton-Tate's program-mode-only version of dBASE. RunTime is dBASE without the dot prompt. It is used to run dBASE programs that are complete applications developed for commercial purposes by dBASE programmers. This way, the source code is not available to users.

The encryption process reduces reserved words to one symbol, thus picking up a small reduction in execution time and command file size. Each version of dBASE II has had a "sister" version of RunTime. To run coded programs in dBASE, the version of dBCODE must match the version of the dBASE interpreter.

For example, a command file crunched under version II-2.4 of RunTime will not execute by version II-2.3 of dBASE. The command look-up tables differ from version to version.

At the time of this writing, there is no RunTime available for dBASE III, although it is planned that there will be something similar in the near future.

Work-Arounds

1.   dBASE II, version 2.3x, occasionally executes the command file's backup (.BAK) instead of the edited command file. This can be prevented by specifying the command file extension (.CMD or .PRG) in the DO <command filename.ext> syntax.

2.   dBASE II, version 2.4, (on 16-bit systems only) expects to see the end-of-file (EOF) marker at the end of a 128-byte block in your command file. Many word processing programs place the EOF at the actual end of text rather than at the end of a physical block. Therefore, when executing a command file created by one of these programs, 2.4 may not read the last partial block of information. There are two work-arounds and one patch for this situation. The first work-around is to bring the command file into MODIFY COMMAND and go to the bottom of the file to make sure that the last lines of code have been read in. If the code is not there, type it in. Save the file with a <Ctrl-W>. The other work-around is to "pad" the bottom of your command file with enough bytes so that dBASE II will read all the code and anything truncated will be insignificant. We usually use asterisks for this padding, and two lines of 64 asterisks each do the job. To cure the situation permanently, use the patch in Technical Support Note 74 in appendix F.

CHAPTER FIFTEEN

THE WORKING ENVIRONMENT

The working environment is a group of conditions that affect the characteristics of certain operations as they occur. Usually, the first task of any command file is to establish the "local" working conditions in which it will operate. The definitive example is the command SET TALK OFF which appears as the first line of code in the first command file in most application systems.

In dBASE III, the default setting of most of the environmental SET parameters can be changed in the Config.db file (chapter 12). There is also a menu-driven SET option in the interactive mode (chapter 25).

Any environmental changes made by a command file are always:

1. Passed to nested sub-files which may change them as required.
2. Restored back to original setting before RETURNing from the command file that changed them.

Each environmental setting affects only a portion of the working environment. For example, SET PRINT has absolutely no effect on database handling. Neither does SET DELETED affect screen handling, nor does SET FUNCTION affect command files, and so on.

SET Parameters, Type, and Default

ALTERNATE	::=	<text file setting>	OFF
BELL	::=	<audio setting>	ON
CALL	::=	<system setting>	none
CARRY	::=	<database setting>	OFF
COLON	::=	<screen setting>	ON
COLOR	::=	<screen setting>	(chapter 18, "Output")
CONFIRM	::=	<input setting>	OFF
CONSOLE	::=	<screen setting>	ON
DATE	::=	<date setting>	"00/00/00"
DEBUG	::=	<debug setting>	OFF
DECIMALS	::=	<numeric setting>	2
DEFAULT	::=	<system setting>	<system default drive>
DELETED	::=	<database setting>	OFF
DELIMITERS	::=	<screen setting>	OFF
DEVICE	::=	<output setting>	SCREEN
ECHO	::=	<debug setting>	OFF
EJECT	::=	<report setting>	ON

ESCAPE	::=	<command file setting>	ON
EXACT	::=	<logical setting>	OFF
FILTER	::=	<database setting>	none
FIXED	::=	<numeric setting>	OFF
FORMAT	::=	<database setting>	none
FORMAT	::=	<output setting>	SCREEN
F	::=	<hardware setting>	(chapter 25)
FUNCTION	::=	<hardware setting>	(chapter 25)
HEADING	::=	<report setting>	none
HEADINGS	::=	<database setting>	ON
HELP	::=	<background setting>	ON
INDEX	::=	<database setting>	none
INTENSITY	::=	<screen setting>	ON
LINKAGE	::=	<database setting>	none
MARGIN	::=	<print setting>	0
MENUS	::=	<input setting>	OFF
PATH	::=	<system setting>	none
PRINT	::=	<print setting>	OFF
PROCEDURE	::=	<command file setting>	none
RAW	::=	<screen setting>	OFF
RELATION	::=	<database setting>	none
SCREEN	::=	<screen setting>	ON
SAFETY	::=	<background setting>	ON
SCOREBOARD	::=	<background setting>	ON
STEP	::=	<debug setting>	OFF
TALK	::=	<background setting>	ON
UNIQUE	::=	<database setting>	OFF

SET Parameters, by process affected

Global: (affects all or most processes and commands)

HELP	::=	<background setting>
SAFETY	::=	<background setting>
SCOREBOARD	::=	<background setting>
TALK	::=	<background setting>

Program Documentation:

| ALTERNATE | ::= | <text file setting> |

Command File Handling:

| ESCAPE | ::= | <command file setting> |
| PROCEDURE | ::= | <command file setting> |

Data Handling - Character:

EXACT	::=	\<logical setting\>

Data Handling - Date:

DATE	::=	\<date setting\>

Data Handling - Numeric:

DECIMALS	::=	\<numeric setting\>
FIXED	::=	\<numeric setting\>

Screen Handling - Output:

COLON	::=	\<screen setting\>
COLOR	::=	\<screen setting\>
CONSOLE	::=	\<screen setting\>
DELIMITERS	::=	\<screen setting\>
DEVICE	::=	\<screen/print command\>
FORMAT	::=	\<database setting\>
FORMAT	::=	\<screen/print command\>
INTENSITY	::=	\<screen setting\>
RAW	::=	\<screen setting\>

Screen Handling - Input:

BELL	::=	\<audio setting\>
COLON	::=	\<screen setting\>
CONFIRM	::=	\<input setting\>
DELIMITERS	::=	\<screen setting\>
FORMAT	::=	\<database setting\>
INTENSITY	::=	\<screen setting\>
MENUS	::=	\<input setting\>
SCREEN	::=	\<screen setting\>

Database - Adding data:

BELL	::=	\<audio setting\>
CARRY	::=	\<database setting\>
CONFIRM	::=	\<input setting\>
DELETED	::=	\<database setting\>
FORMAT	::=	\<database setting\>
MENUS	::=	\<input setting\>

Database - Ordering the file according to its data:

DELETED	::=	\<database setting\>
FILTER	::=	\<database setting\>

| INDEX | ::= | \<database setting\> |
| UNIQUE | ::= | \<database setting\> |

Database - Moving around and finding data in the file:

DELETED	::=	\<database setting\>
EXACT	::=	\<logical setting\>
FILTER	::=	\<database setting\>
INDEX	::=	\<database setting\>

Database - Changing the data in the file:

BELL	::=	\<audio setting\>
CONFIRM	::=	\<input setting\>
FORMAT	::=	\<database setting\>
MENUS	::=	\<input setting\>

Database - Displaying the data in the file:

DELETED	::=	\<database setting\>
FORMAT	::=	\<database setting\>
HEADINGS	::=	\<database setting\>

Database - Copying the data to another file:

| DELETED | ::= | \<database setting\> |

Database - Multiple open files:

| LINKAGE | ::= | \<database setting\> |
| RELATION | ::= | \<database setting\> |

Foreign Files:

| ALTERNATE | ::= | \<text file setting\> |

Printing and Form Generators:

DELETED	::=	\<database setting\>
DEVICE	::=	\<screen/print command\>
EJECT	::=	\<report/print setting\>
FORMAT	::=	\<screen/print command\>
HEADING	::=	\<report setting\>
MARGIN	::=	\<print setting\>
PRINT	::=	\<print setting\>

Operating System Interface:

CALL	::=	\<system setting>
DEFAULT	::=	\<system setting>
PATH	::=	\<system setting>

Debugging:

DEBUG	::=	\<debug setting>
ECHO	::=	\<debug setting>
STEP	::=	\<debug setting>
TALK	::=	\<background setting>

Interactive Mode:

CONFIRM	::=	\<input setting>
F	::=	\<hardware setting>
FUNCTION	::=	\<hardware setting>
MENUS	::=	\<input setting>

VOCABULARY

All SET parameters are included here, and repeated in the vocabulary of their appropriate process(es).

Operators

None.

Functions

None.

SET parameters

ALTERNATE

> SET ALTERNATE \<switch>
> [III/II] To start/stop sending screen output to a file.

> SET ALTERNATE TO
> [III/II] To close an open "alternate" file.

> SET ALTERNATE TO \<text filename>
> [III/II] To create or overwrite a text file for recording what appears on the screen.

BELL

> SET BELL \<switch>
> [III/II] To enable/disable output to the computer's audio tone device.

CALL

SET CALL TO
[II] To cancel a previously specified address for the CALL command.

SET CALL TO <decimal address>
[II] To specify the address of a machine language subroutine to be executed with the CALL command.

CARRY

SET CARRY <switch>
[III/II] To enable/disable the database feature that copies the previous record to a new one during interactive APPENDs.

COLON

SET COLON <switch>
[II] To enable/disable display of a colon delimiter around variables.

COLOR

SET COLOR TO <background> <delimiter> <foreground>
[II] To change the color and/or attribute of the screen display.

SET COLOR TO <command-line mode values> ;
           [,<full-screen mode values>] [,<border value>]
[III] To change the color and/or attribute of the screen display.

CONFIRM

SET CONFIRM <switch>
[III/II] To enable/disable the feature that forces the operator to press return in order to exit each input field.

CONSOLE

SET CONSOLE <switch>
[III/II] To enable/disable all output to the screen.

DATE

SET DATE TO <nn/nn/nn>
[II] To change the dBASE II system date. <n> may be any number, </> may be any character.

DEBUG

SET DEBUG <switch>
[III/II] To send the output of ECHO and STEP to the printer in order to keep the screen display intact.

DECIMALS

SET DECIMALS TO <numeric expression>
[III] To specify the number of decimal places displayed after division, SQRT(), LOG(), and EXP().

SET DECIMALS [TO]
[III] To set the number of decimal places to zero.

DEFAULT

SET DEFAULT TO <drive letter>
[III/II] To tell dBASE on which drive to perform all file operations.

DELETED

SET DELETED <switch>
[III/II] To include or exclude records that are marked for deletion from being seen by commands that reposition a database file's record pointer. In II, only commands that allow the <scope> parameter are affected.

DELIMITERS

SET DELIMITERS <switch>
[III] To enable/disable display of a specified delimiter around variables.

SET DELIMITERS TO <character expression>
[III] To select specific delimiters around full-screen variable displays. Only the first two characters in <character expression> are significant.

SET DELIMITERS TO DEFAULT
[III] To select the colon delimiter around full-screen variable displays.

DEVICE

SET DEVICE TO <device parameter>
[III] To direct formatted output from @...SAY to either the screen or printer.

ECHO

SET ECHO <switch>
[III/II] To enable/disable output of the command line just prior to execution.

EJECT

    SET EJECT <switch>
        [II] To enable/disable the initial form-feed just prior to printing report forms.

ESCAPE

    SET ESCAPE <switch>
        [III/II] To enable/disable the operator's ability to interrupt a command or program with the <Esc> key.

EXACT

    SET EXACT <switch>
        [III/II] To enable/disable the feature that forces a precise match of character strings compared with relational operators.

F

    SET F<function-key number> TO "<character string>"
        [II] To change the operation of the computer's function keys.

FILTER

    SET FILTER TO <logical expression>
        [III] To limit all database operations to records for which the expression is true.

    SET FILTER [TO]
        [III] To remove any existing FILTER.

FIXED

    SET FIXED <switch>
        [III] To enable/disable the feature that forces a specified number of decimal places in all numeric output.

FORMAT

    SET FORMAT TO
        [III/II] To close an open format file.

    SET FORMAT TO <device parameter>
        [II] To direct formatted output from @...SAY to either the screen or printer.

    SET FORMAT TO <format filename>
        [III/II] To specify a format for the database file fields during full-screen commands.

FUNCTION

> SET FUNCTION <numeric expression> TO <character expression>
> [III] To change the operation of the computer's function keys. <numeric expression> is the function-key number (from 2 to 10).

HEADING

> SET HEADING TO
> [II] To cancel a previously specified report form heading.

> SET HEADING TO <character string>
> [II] To specify a heading for dBASE report forms.

HEADINGS

> SET HEADINGS <switch>
> [III] To enable/disable the display of field names in commands that display database data.

HELP

> SET HELP <switch>
> [III] To enable/disable the help option when a syntax error occurs.

INDEX

> SET INDEX TO
> [III/II] To close index files.

> SET INDEX TO <index filename> {,<index filename>}
> [III/II] To open new index files with the already open database file.

INTENSITY

> SET INTENSITY <switch>
> [III/II] To enable/disable the enhanced video display used primarily in the full-screen interactive mode.

LINKAGE

> SET LINKAGE <switch>
> [II] To enable/disable sequential movement in one database to cause the record pointer to move accordingly in the unselected database file.

MARGIN

> SET MARGIN TO <numeric expression>
> [III/II] To specify the left margin for all output to the printer.

MENUS

SET MENUS `<switch>`
[III] To enable/disable the display of cursor control keys in full-screen commands.

PATH

SET PATH TO `<path>` {,`<path>`}
[III] To tell dBASE III where to look for files in addition to the current directory.

SET PATH [TO]
[III] To tell dBASE III to look for files in the current directory only.

PRINT

SET PRINT `<switch>`
[III/II] To enable/disable command-line mode, or "unformatted", output to the printer.

PROCEDURE

SET PROCEDURE TO `<procedure filename>`
[III] To open a procedure file in order to execute one of its procedures with the DO command.

SET PROCEDURE [TO]
[III] To close a procedure file.

RAW

SET RAW `<switch>`
[II] To enable/disable certain automatic display formatting features.

RELATION

SET RELATION INTO `<alias name>`
[III] To cause the `<alias name>` database file to continuously position its record pointer to the same record number as the currently selected database file.

SET RELATION INTO `<alias name>` **TO** `<key expression>`
[III] To cause the `<alias name>` database file, which is indexed on `<key expression>`, to continuously position its record pointer to the record that matches the `<key expression>` in the currently selected database file.

SET RELATION INTO `<alias name>` **TO** `<numeric expression>`
[III] To cause the `<alias name>` database file, which is not indexed, to position its record pointer to the record number equal to the `<numeric expression>`.

SET RELATION [TO]
[III] To cancel any previously specified relation.

SAFETY

> ### SET SAFETY <switch>
> [III] To enable/disable the feature that displays a warning and gives the operator the option to proceed or abort whenever a command is issued that will overwrite or otherwise destroy data in a file.

SCOREBOARD

> ### SET SCOREBOARD <switch>
> [III] To toggle on/off the dBASE messages on line zero.

SCREEN

> ### SET SCREEN <switch>
> [II] To enable/disable full-screen mode. Useful on machines for which dBASE II has not been installed.

STEP

> ### SET STEP <switch>
> [III/II] To pause program execution after every command.

TALK

> ### SET TALK <switch>
> [III/II] To enable/disable the display of interactive dBASE messages.

UNIQUE

> ### SET UNIQUE <switch>
> [III] To create an index file with no duplicate key expressions.

Commands

CLOSE

> ### CLOSE ALTERNATE
> [III] To close an open alternate file.

> ### CLOSE FORMAT
> [III] To close an open format file.

DISPLAY

> ### DISPLAY STATUS
> [III/II] To find out the current state of the working environment.

LIST

> LIST STATUS
> > [III/II] To find out the current state of the working environment.

SELECT

> SELECT <work area parameter>
> > [III/II] To specify the currently selected work area.

SET

> SET
> > [III] To enter the interactive SET-menu mode.

> SET <set parameter> <switch>
> > [III/II] To turn the <set parameter> on or off.

> SET <set parameter> TO <set object>
> > [III/II] To specify the <set object> to be actively assigned to the <set parameter>.

Other Resources

None.

ALGORITHMS

SET Example

This code demonstrates the management of the working environment when moving between command files or procedures with different requirements.

```
* EX_MAIN.PRG
*
* Establish working environment...
SET TALK OFF
SET DEFAULT TO B
*
<commands>
*
* Branch to subroutine...
DO EX_subrt
*
<commands>
*
```

```
* Restore environment before exiting...
SET TALK ON
SET DEFAULT TO A
RETURN
* EOF: EX_main.prg

* EX_SUBRT.PRG
*
* Expects:  DEFAULT drive B
*           TALK (OFF)
*
* Make any needed changes in the local environment...
SET BELL OFF
SET EXACT ON
*
<commands>
*
* Restore environmental changes made locally before
* exiting...
SET BELL ON
SET EXACT OFF
RETURN
* EOF: EX_subrt.prg
```

Related Algorithms

In dBASE III, most of the SET parameters can be set from the Config.db file upon booting dBASE. See chapter 12.

CHAPTER SIXTEEN

DATA HANDLING

Data can be divided into categories, or "types," according to how it is handled by the software. The data types available in dBASE are:

dBASE II	dBASE III	Description
Character	Character	All ASCII-code characters
Numeric	Numeric	Numbers used for math operations
Logical	Logical	True or false only
	Date	Calendar dates only

For a description of how data is stored by dBASE, see chapter 7.

In dBASE III, *memo* is not another data type, although it helps to think of it that way. It is actually an additional category for character type data stored in variable length fields in a database file. Memo refers only to database fields which are of a varying length and whose character type contents are stored in a database-text (.DBT) file. At the time of this writing, there are no operators or functions to manipulate character data in a memo field. Data in a memo field can be output only with the ?, LIST, and DISPLAY commands (chapter 19, subchapter "Displaying the Data"), and with the REPORT command (chapter 21). It can be input or edited only in the full-screen interactive mode (chapter 25).

Literally Variable

All types of data can be handled in two ways, *directly* or *indirectly*. *Direct* refers to using the actual, or "literal," value of the data. A literal in a command line is also called a constant because the command line cannot be changed during program execution, and therefore remains constant. *Indirect* refers to placing the data in memory with a label, or "name," that points to the memory address, and using the label name in place of the literal data value.

```
* Direct uses the literal character string...
@ 5,5 SAY "Press any key..."
*
* Indirect uses the memory variable name...
STORE "Press any key..." TO prompt
@ 5,5 SAY prompt
```

Since a name has been attached to this particular data item, the name is used in command lines throughout the program. This is called a variable because the data literal can be changed, or "varied," without rewriting the program. Even if the data item will not change *during* the program, as with screen handling codes, variables are still used to simplify coding, debugging, and future modifying of the program because they allow the data to be changed in only one place. See Memvars in chapter 17.

There are two kinds of variables in dBASE, memory and field. Data stored in a database file are kept in a structure with *fields*. When a database file is in USE, one of its *records* (a single set of fields) is active in memory. The data in those fields can then be accessed by field name. See Database Files in chapter 19.

If a database field and a memvar have the same name (not recommended), dBASE will only see the field unless the memvar prefix (M) is used.

      dBASE III: M->memvarname
      dBASE II: M.memvarname

Operators

Each data type has its own operators which perform their operations on data of that specific type only. There are four types of data operators in dBASE:

1. Numeric (or Arithmetic, or Mathematical)
        Operates on numeric data, returns numeric data.

+ and -	Signs (Unary operators)
^ and **	Exponentiation
*	Multiplication
/	Division
+	Addition
-	Subtraction

        Operates on numeric and date data, returns date data.

+	Addition
-	Subtraction

        Operates on date data, returns numeric data.

-	Subtraction

2. Character (or String)
        Operates on character data, returns character data.

+	Concatenation
-	Concatenation with blank shift

3. Relational
        Operates on character, date, and numeric data, returns logical data.

=	Equal to
# and <>	Not equal to
<	Less than
<=	Less than or equal to
>	Greater than
>=	Greater than or equal to

        Operates on character data only, returns logical data.

$	Substring found within string

4. Logical

        Operates on logical data, returns logical data.

.NOT.	Complement (negation)
.AND.	Conjunction
.OR.	Disjunction

A space is optional around operators in an expression. See examples under Expressions below.

Functions

Functions are used to evaluate data and return a result. The data type of the result does not always match the type of the function's parameters, or "arguments," as in the case of the AT() function which evaluates the location of one character string in another and returns a numeric result. This evaluation takes additional time to execute.

Functions may be nested as long as the type of data returned by the function is appropriate in relation to where the function appears. For example, the substring function returns a character type result and belongs in a <character expression>. However, two parameters *in* the substring function require a numeric type argument and may be fulfilled with a function, like AT(), that returns a numeric result.

It has become the accepted standard to categorize functions according to the data type they return. Yet, the type of data returned, particularly in higher level languages, may give no indication of the type of operation performed by the function. We categorize functions by their functionality rather than by their result. However, programmers may still correctly refer, for example, to AT() as a numeric function.

1. Character Processes

    Operates on character type data

!()	Returns uppercase characters [II]
$()	Returns substring of string [II]
@()	Returns numeric location of one string within another [II]
ASC()	Returns numeric ASCII code number [III]
AT()	Returns numeric location of one string within another [III]
LEN()	Returns numeric length of string
LOWER()	Returns lowercase characters [III]
RANK()	Returns numeric ASCII code number [II]
SUBSTR()	Returns substring of string [III]
TRIM()	Returns string without trailing blanks
UPPER()	Returns uppercase characters [III]
VAL()	Returns numeric value of character type numbers

    Operates on numeric type data

CHR()	Returns ASCII character
SPACE()	Returns string of blank spaces [III]
STR()	Returns character type numbers

2. Database Processes

    Operates on currently selected database file

#	Returns numeric current record number [II]
*	Returns logical data: is current record marked for deletion? [II]

BOF()	Returns logical data: is record pointer at beginning-of-file? [III]
DELETED()	Returns logical data: is current record marked for deletion? [III]
EOF	Returns logical data: is record pointer at end-of-file? [II]
EOF()	Returns logical data: is record pointer at end-of-file? [III]
RECNO()	Returns numeric current record number [III]

Multi-User systems only

| LOCK() | Returns logical data: was the current record available, and is now locked to me? [II] |
| LOCKNDX() | Returns logical data: was the active master index file available, and is now locked to me? [II] |

3. Date Processes
    Operates on date data [III]

CDOW()	Returns character day of week [III]
CMONTH()	Returns character month [III]
DATE()	Returns the operating system date [III]
DAY()	Returns numeric day of month [III]
DOW()	Returns numeric day of week [III]
DTOC()	Returns character calendar date [III]
MONTH()	Returns numeric month of year [III]
YEAR()	Returns numeric year [III]

    Operates on character data

| CTOD() | Returns date type calendar date [III] |
| DATE() | Returns character data: the dBASE system date [II] |

4. Numeric Processes
    Operates on numeric data

EXP()	Returns numeric e to a power [III]
INT()	Returns numeric integer
LOG()	Returns numeric natural logarithm [III]
ROUND()	Returns numeric rounded off number [III]
SQRT()	Returns numeric square root [III]
STR()	Returns character type numbers

    Operates on character data

| VAL() | Returns numeric value of character type numbers |

5. Output Processes
    Operates on printer head position

| PCOL() | Returns numeric current printer column [III] |
| PROW() | Returns numeric current printer row [III] |

Operates on screen cursor postion

COL()	Returns numeric current cursor column [III]
ROW()	Returns numeric current cursor row [III]

6. System Processes

Operates on the operating system level

DATE()	Returns date type operating system date [III]
DATE()	Returns character data: the dBASE system date [II]
TIME()	Returns character type operating system time [III]
FILE()	Returns logical data: does the named file exist?
PEEK()	Returns numeric contents of a byte in memory

7. Validation Processes:

Operates on all data types to test for validity of expression and existence of variables.

TEST()	Returns numeric symbol of data type [II]
TYPE()	Returns character symbol of data type

Other Resources

dBASE also has these other resources which are neither operators nor functions. They are more fully discussed in their appropriate chapters.

1. Command line (chapters 12 and 14):

,	The *comma* delimits items in a <list>.
;	The *semicolon* continues a command statement on next line.

2. All data types (see Expressions below):

( )	Opening and closing *parentheses* determine the order in which operations will occur, or "precedence."

3. Character data (chapter 16):

" "	Matching *quotation marks* delimit strings.
' '	Matching *apostrophes* or *single-quotes* delimit strings.
[ ]	Left and right *square brackets* delimit strings.
;	The *semicolon* divides and centers strings. [II]

4. Memory variable (chapter 17):

&	The *ampersand*, or "macro" substitution symbol, replaces a memvar name in a command line with the literal contents of the memvar.
.	The *period* terminates a macro-memvar and concatenates it to a character expression.

5. Work area (chapter 19, "Multiple Files"):

–>	The *arrow* concatenates an alias name or memvar prefix with its variable name. [III]
.	The *period* concatenates a work area initial or memvar prefix with its variable name. [II]

Expressions

An expression is part of the command statement and must be preceded by a command verb. Expressions can contain:

Literals (Constants)
Operators
Functions
Variable names: database fields and memvars
Other Resources: macro, parentheses, etc.

The size of an expression is limited only by the 254-character command line limit, which must include the command as well as the expression.

An expression always results in one data type even though it may contain different data types. Through the use of operators and functions, mismatched parts of an expression are evaluated to produce a result of a single data type. Expressions are said to be the same type as that of the data which they return.

The type of the result returned by an operator or function determines its appropriateness in an expression. That is, a character expression can only have a function that returns a character result. If a function returns a numeric result, it may be included in a character expression only after being nested in the STR() function to convert it to character type. Even though a relational operator might compare two numeric expressions, relational operators always belong in logical expressions.

Expressions are frequently used as command parameters because of the flexibility they offer the programmer. An <expression> always occurs within a command line which must begin with a command verb. A command verb plus an expression is sometimes called a "statement."

Some examples of expressions are given below. For the purpose of these examples, assume that four memory variables exist:

Memvar	Type	Contents
char	C	"ABC"
mdate	D	07/04/84
num	N	3 (3.00000000)
logic	L	.T.

<character expression>	Evaluates to
"a"	"a"
"abc" + [def] - char	"abcdefABC "
TRIM(char) + UPPER("def")	"ABCDEF"
SUBSTR('ABCD', 3, 2) + SPACE(2)	"CD "
DTOC(mdate)	"07/04/84"
STR(num,4,2)	"3.00"

<date expression>	Evaluates to
CTOD("12/10/41")	12/10/41
mdate - 366	07/04/83

<numeric expression>	Evaluates to
123	123
2 * num	6
(AT('b', 'abc') + 10) + num	15
(2^3 + INT(1.4)) / num	3
MONTH(mdate + 45)	8

<logical expression>	Evaluates to
1 = 2	.F.
1>2	.F.
1 + 2 = num	.T.
char = "ABC" .AND. num < 2	.F.
char="ABC".OR.num<2	.T.
.NOT. logic	.F.
FILE(mdate)	.F.

An expression may require multiple operations and evaluations to produce a desired result. The order of execution, or "precedence," is as follows:

1. Other resources evaluate first. The macro and semicolon have a higher order of precedence than the string delimiters.
2. Functions evaluate next. There is no order of precedence among functions other than that provided by nesting.
3. Numeric and character operators evaluate next. Numeric in this order:

    ^ and **

    Exponentiation

    + and –

    Signs (unary operators).

    * and /

    Multiplication and division

    + and –

    Addition and subtraction

    Character in this order:

    " ", ' ', and [ ]

    String delimiters

    + and -

    Concatenation

4. Relational operators evaluate next. There is no order of precedence among relational operators other than left to right evaluation.
5. Logical operators evaluate last in this order:

    .NOT.

    Complement (negation)

    .AND.

    Conjunction

    .OR.

    Disjunction

VOCABULARY

Operators

None.

Functions

TEST()

> TEST(<expression>)
> To determine whether the <expression> is valid, and if so, what type of data it contains.

TYPE()

> TYPE(<character expression>)
> [III] To determine whether an expression contained within the <character expression> is valid, and if so, what type of data it contains.

> TYPE(<expression>)
> [II] To determine the data type of a valid <expression>.

SET parameters

None.

Commands

None.

Other Resources

,

> <command> <item> { , <item> }
> [III/II] To separate items in a <parameter list>.

ALGORITHMS

Validate Expressions

TYPE() and TEST() are general data functions whose purpose is to determine the validity and data type of an expression.

Type of <expression>	TYPE() [III]	TYPE() [II]	TEST() [II]
Character	C	C	String length
Date	D	(n/a)	(n/a)
Logical	L	L	1
Numeric	N	N	-6
Undefined	U	SYNTAX ERROR	0

In dBASE III, the TYPE () function requires the <character expression> to be delimited:

```
. ? TYPE( 12/3*4 )
* Undefined because the argument must be a character
* expression containing the expression to be tested...
U
. ? TYPE( '12/3*4' )
* numeric...
N
. ? TYPE( ['12/3*4'] )
* character...
C


* Store null to memvar
. a = [ ]
. ? TYPE( 'a' )
C
. ? TYPE( 'a + a' )
C


. ? TYPE( 'DATE()' )
* date...
D
. ? TYPE( 'DTOC( DATE() )' )
C


. ? TYPE( [.T.] )
* logical...
L


* Assign result of system date function to a memvar...
. mdate = DATE()
06/30/84
* Assign result of validation to a memvar...
. mtype = TYPE( 'mdate' )
D
* The type of the validation memvar is...
. ? TYPE( 'mtype' )
C
```

In dBASE II, the TYPE() function requires only literal character strings *within* the <expression> to be delimited.

```
. ? TYPE( 12/3*4 )
N
. ? TYPE( '12/3*4' )
C
. ? TYPE( ['12/3*4'] )
C
* Test returns -6 for all numeric expressions...
. ? TEST( 12/3*4 )
  -6
. ? TEST( 3 )
  -6

* Store one blank space to a memvar...
. STORE [ ] TO a
. ? TYPE( a )
C
. ? TYPE( a - a )
C
* Test returns the string length as a positive number...
. ? TEST( a )
   1
. ? TEST( a + a )
   2

* There is no Undefined result from TYPE in II,
* so TEST must be used...
. ? TYPE( a + 3 )
*** SYNTAX ERROR ***
. ? TEST( a + 3 )
   0

. ? TYPE( DATE() )
C
. ? TEST( DATE() )
   8

* Test's downfall: can't tell a logical expression from a
* character expression with a length of one...
. ? TEST( a = " " )
   1
. ? TEST( a )
   1
. ? TYPE( a )
C
. ? TYPE( a = " " )
L
```

```
. STORE TYPE( a = " " ) TO typeresult
. STORE TEST( a = " " ) TO testresult
. ? TYPE( typeresult )
C
. ? TYPE( testresult )
N
```

In dBASE II, for the TEST() function to perform accurately when the expression is undefined, it must be the last item in a logical expression. The command line parser operates from left to right and will not continue to parse that line once it sees an undefined data type. This will *not* work:

```
IF TEST(<expression>) = 0
```

This will work:

```
IF 0 = TEST(<expression>)
```

This is the reason for the different behavior of the TYPE() function in dBASE III. Because TYPE() in dBASE II is incapable of dealing rationally with erroneous expressions, TEST() has to resort to this kind of idiosyncratic work-around, or "kludge."

Where Are We?

There is a conditional test to determine whether a program is running under dBASE III or dBASE II. Now, one would think that all programs would be designed to run under one or the other, and most programs are. However, as exemplified in the program Ndx_size. prg in appendix C, some command files can be designed to be run under both dBASE III and II with a very slight modification to a small portion of the code, which can be placed in a conditional structure using this test.

The TYPE() function is ideal for this purpose, since it returns a distinctly different result in dBASE III than it does in dBASE II for the same literal parameter. The test is a delimited digit, which returns a "C" in II and an "N" in III. It can be tested for in either of two ways:

```
IF TYPE('3') = 'C'
   * This is dBASE II...
ELSE
   * This is dBASE III...
ENDIF

IF TYPE('3') = 'N'
   * This is dBASE III...
ELSE
   * This is dBASE II...
ENDIF
```

DATA HANDLING–CHARACTER

...mmonly used data type is character. It may contain any printable character including letters,
digits, ...d symbols. It may also contain ASCII code characters that are not printable, by using the
CHR() function. Character type literals are usually surrounded, or "delimited," with matching single or
double quote marks or with left and right square brackets. The FIND and SET COLOR TO commands are
examples of when character type literals are not delimited.

Character fields and memvars are used to store numbers whenever arithmetic will not be performed on
them. Zip codes and phone numbers are two examples of numbers that are kept as character type rather
than numeric. Occasionally, numbers will be stored as character data and still require mathematical
operations (see Character Numbers under Algorithms below).

In dBASE II, there is no date data type. The system date and all date handling is done with character
type dates. The following subchapter, "Data Handling–Date," deals with both the dBASE III date type as
well as the dBASE II character type dates. Also see the date routines in appendix B for handling of
character type dates.

Substrings

A substring is a portion, or "subset," of a character string. It can be found intact within the larger
string. The function used for the manipulation of character strings is the substring function, $() in II and
SUBSTR() in III. This invaluable function is used frequently, as is the character location function, @() in II
and AT() in III. The character location, or "AT" function is often used as a parameter in the SUBSTRing
function, allowing the parsing of a character string. For example, this DO WHILE loop parses a list of
filenames which is delimited with commas:

```
* dBASE II
* Do while there is a comma in the memvar "filelist"...
DO WHILE @(",", filelist) > 0
   *
   * Output the substring from string start to the comma...
   ? $( filelist, 1, @(",",filelist)-1 )
   *
   * Store the remainder of the string to the memvar...
   STORE $( filelist, @(",",filelist)+1 ) TO filelist
ENDDO
*
* No more commas, output the last filename left in the list...
? filelist
```

Notice that the AT function is used as the <substring length> parameter in the first SUBSTRing
function, and as the <start location> in the second SUBSTRing function. Both the AT and the SUBSTRing
functions must be thoroughly understood in order to manipulate character type data.

Equal Strings

Relational operators can compare character expressions, and this comparison takes place on the ASCII
code value of the characters which, for example, places a higher value on lowercase alpha characters than
on uppercase. This comparison takes place in one of two ways, depending on the state of the SET EXACT
switch. Remember that the command line parser evaluates from left to right.

```
STORE "Tom"      TO a
STORE "Tomato"   TO b
SET EXACT OFF

? a = b
.F.
? b = a
.T.
? b > a
.F.

SET EXACT ON
? a = b
.F.
? b = a
.F.
? b > a
.T.
```

This is akin to having a key field contain "Tomato" and issuing the command FIND "Tom". It allows the key to be found unless EXACT has been SET ON. SET EXACT affects all of the relational operators' evaluation of character data, except the *found-within* ($) operator.

VOCABULARY

Operators

+

> <command> <character expression 1> + <character expression 2>
>   [III/II] To connect two character expressions together.

–

> <command> <character expression 1> – <character expression 2>
>   [III/II] To connect two character expressions together and move any trailing blanks from the first expression to the second.

=

> <command> <expression 1> = <expression 2>
>   [III/II] To determine whether one data item is identical to another.

#

> <command> <expression 1> # <expression 2>
>   [III/II] To determine whether one data item is identical to another.

`<>`

    `<command> <expression 1> <> <expression 2>`
       [III/II] To determine whether one data item is identical to another.

`<`

    `<command> <expression 1> < <expression 2>`
       [III/II] To determine whether one data item is less than another.

`<=`

    `<command> <expression 1> <= <expression 2>`
       [III/II] To determine whether one data item is less than or equal to another.

`>`

    `<command> <expression 1> > <expression 2>`
       [III/II] To determine whether one data item is greater than another.

`>=`

    `<command> <expression 1> >= <expression 2>`
       [III/II] To determine whether one data item is greater than or equal to another.

`$`

    `<command> <character expression 1> $ <character expression 2>`
       [III/II] To determine whether one character string is contained in another.

Functions

`!()`

    `!(<character expression>)`
       [II] To convert lowercase letters to uppercase.

`$()`

    `$(<character expression>,<start location>)`
       [II] To get a portion of a character string.

    `$(<character expression>,<start location>,<substring length>)`
       [II] To get a portion of a character string.

@()

`@(<character expression 1>,<character expression 2>)`
[II] To determine if <character expression 1> also occurs in <character expression 2>, and if so, what the location is where <character expression 1> begins in <character expression 2>.

ASC()

`ASC(<character expression>)`
[III] To determine the ASCII code value of a single character.

AT()

`AT(<character expression 1>,<character expression 2>)`
[III] To determine if <character expression 1> also occurs in <character expression 2>, and if so, what the location is where <character expression 1> begins in <character expression 2>.

CHR()

`CHR(<numeric expression>)`
[III/II] To enter characters for which there are no keys. To send control characters to the printer or screen.

CTOD()

`CTOD(<character expression>)`
[III] To convert a character type date to a date type date. The only way to create a date type outside of a date type database field.

DATE()

`DATE()`
[III/II] To get the usually current date.

LEN()

`LEN(<character expression>)`
[III/II] To determine the length of a character literal, variable, or expression.

LOWER()

`LOWER(<character expression>)`
[III] To convert uppercase letters to lowercase.

RANK()

RANK(<character expression>)
[II] To determine the ASCII code value of a single character.

SPACE()

SPACE(<numeric expression>)
[III] To output a specified number of blank spaces. Useful for initializing blank memvars.

SUBSTR()

SUBSTR(<character expression>,<start location>)
[III] To get a portion of a character string.

SUBSTR(<character expression>,<start location>,<substring length>)
[III] To get a portion of a character string.

TRIM()

TRIM(<character expression>)
[III/II] To remove trailing blanks from a character string.

UPPER()

UPPER(<character expression>)
[III] To convert lowercase letters to uppercase.

VAL()

VAL(<character expression>)
[III/II] To convert character type numbers to numeric type.

SET parameters

EXACT

SET EXACT <switch>
[III/II] To enable/disable the feature that forces a precise match of character strings compared with relational operators.

Commands

None.

Other Resources

&

&<character memvar name>
[III/II] To execute a dBASE command that is stored in a memory variable.

FIND "&<character memvar name>"
[II] To use the contents of a variable as the parameter in FIND. Delimiters are used when both the index key and the variable contain leading blanks. The delimiters prevent any leading blanks in the variable from being truncated.

FIND &<character memvar name>
[II] To use the contents of a variable as the parameter in FIND.

( )

<command> (<expression 1> <operator> <expression 2>)
[III/II] To specify the order in which evaluations will occur within an expression.

" "

"<character string>"
[III/II] To identify (delimit) a character type literal, or "string".

' '

'<character string>'
[III/II] To identify (delimit) a character type literal, or 'string'.

[ ]

[<character string>]
[III/II] To identify (delimit) a character type literal, or [string].

;

<command> "<text 1> ; <text 2>"
[II] To generate multi-line headings in the REPORT generator.

ALGORITHMS

Concatenation

There are two methods for connecting, or "concatenating," character strings.

1. <string-1> + <string-2>
   Straight concatenation. Attaches <string-1> to <string-2>.

```
"ABC   " + "XYZ" ::= "ABC   XYZ"
"ABC"   + "XYZ" ::= "ABCXYZ"
```

2. \<string-1\> – \<string-2\>

Blank-shift, or "squash," concatenation. Moves trailing blanks, if any, from \<string-1\> to \<string-2\>, and then attaches the strings.

```
"ABC   " – "XYZ"            ::= "ABCXYZ   "
"ABC   " – "XYZ" + "dBASE" ::= "ABCXYZ   dBASE"
"ABC   " – "XYZ" – "dBASE" ::= "ABCXYZdBASE   "
```

The string concatenating operators are associative with themselves but not with each other:

```
(a+b) + c   equals a + (b+c)
(a-b) – c   equals a – (b–c)
(a-b) + c   does not equal a – (b+c)
```

In the last example, (a–b)+c moves the spaces from the end of a to the end of b, and a–(b+c) moves the spaces from the end of a to the end of c.

Changing a Substring

There is no simple command to change a part of a string without rebuilding the whole string. The only way to do this is to use the substring function to put the string together piece by piece. Take the first part of the string up to the start of the change, add (concatenate) the change, and then add the remaining portion of the string after the change. An example is a dBASE II character field called T:date which contains the date SEPTEMBER 30, 1984. To replace the 30 with a 15, the syntax is:

```
REPLACE T:date WITH $(T:date,1,10) + "15" + $(T:date,13,6)
```

In III, the syntax is:

```
REPLACE T_date WITH SUBSTR(T_date,1,10) + "15" + ;
                    SUBSTR(T_date,13,6)
```

Justification

Left-justification. This takes spaces from the beginning of the string and places them at the end.

```
* II...
DO WHILE $(string,1,1) = " " .AND. LEN(string) > 1
   STORE $(string,2) + " " TO string
ENDDO

* III...
DO WHILE SUBSTR(string,1,1) = " " .AND. LEN(string) > 1
   string = SUBSTR(string,2) + " "
ENDDO
```

Right-justification. This takes spaces from the end of the string and places them at the beginning.

```
* II...
IF string > " "
   STORE $( STR(0,254) , 1, LEN(string)-LEN(TRIM(string)) ) +;
         TRIM(string) TO string
ENDIF

* III...
IF string > " "
   string = SUBSTR( SPACE(254) , 1,;
           LEN(string)-LEN(TRIM(string)) ) + TRIM(string)
ENDIF
```

To use either of the justification algorithms with a database field:

```
* In II, use EOF instead of EOF()...
DO WHILE .NOT. EOF()
   STORE <character field> TO string
   *
   * Insert 3-line left or right justifying
   * algorithm here...
   *
   REPLACE <character field> WITH string
   SKIP
ENDDO
```

Space Function Simulator [II]

Frequently there are times when we want to use a string of blank spaces for initializing memory variables or positioning text on the screen. Ordinarily, a programmer would do something like this:

```
STORE "                     " TO spaces20
```

In III, the space function allows this to be done more easily and accurately:

```
STORE SPACE(20) TO spaces20
```

In II, we accomplish the same thing with the string and substring functions:

```
$( STR(0,<n>+1) ,1,<n>)
```

```
<n>            ::=    The desired number of spaces.
```

For example, to create a memvar with 20 spaces:

```
STORE $( STR(0,21) ,1,20) TO spaces20
```

STR(0,21) creates a string twenty-one characters long with a zero in the twenty-first place preceded by twenty spaces. We then take the first twenty characters (spaces) with the substring function ($) by specifying a start in first position and a length of twenty.

If there are a lot of varying lengths needed and there is room in memory for more memvars, it is easier to use this formula once to STORE the maximum amount of spaces needed to a variable. Then use the substring function to select a specified number of blanks from the variable.

```
STORE $(STR(0,254),1,253) TO blank
STORE $(blank,1,20)       TO spaces20
STORE $(blank,1,231)      TO spaces231
STORE $(blank,1,3)        TO spaces3
```

Character Numbers [II]

The VAL() function converts a character type number to numeric type, unless the character type number contains other characters like commas. dBASE III allows numeric fields to be "expanded out" to include commas during data entry, dBASE II does not. A dBASE II application using large numbers may require the data to be stored as numeric and input as character.

To convert from character to numeric:

```
VAL( $( <c_number>,1,1 ) +'000000' ) +;
VAL( $( <c_number>,3,3 ) +   '000' ) +;
VAL( $( <c_number>,7,3 )             )
```

```
<c_number>    ::=    Ten byte character string with commas.
                     Format [ ,    , ] holds to "9,999,999"
```

To convert from numeric to character:

```
$( STR( <number>, 7 ) , 1, 1) + "," +;
$( STR( <number>, 7 ) , 2, 3) + "," +;
$( STR( <number>, 7 ) , 5, 3)
```

```
<number>      ::=    Integer under 10,000,000
```

Leading Zeros

Sometimes it may be desirable to create a character number with leading zeros. This algorithm produces leading zeros in front of a variable number.

```
SUBSTR( STR( <n> + <n1> , <n2> ) , 2 )
```

```
<n>    ::=    The numeric number to be displayed with leading zeros
<n1>   ::=    A numeric expression with as many trailing zeros as are desired if <n>
             has a value of one
<n2>   ::=    A numeric expression with a value of the maximum number of zeros
             plus one
```

For example, to have a maximum of six leading zeros:

```
SUBSTR( STR( <n> + 1000000 , 7 ) , 2 )
```

Incrementing a Character Variable

1. Character memvar contains a number:

    ```
    STR( VAL(<memvar>)+1, <n> )
    ```

    <n>   ::=   A numeric expression equal to the number of digits in <memvar>+1:

For example:

```
STORE "123" TO <memvar>
STORE STR( VAL(<memvar>)+1, 3 ) TO <memvar>
```

2. Character memvar contains a letter:

    ```
    SUBSTR(<string>, (AT(<memvar>,<string>)+1)- <n>* ;
    INT((AT(<memvar>,<string>)+1)/<n+1> ),1)
    ```

    <string>   ::=   A string containing all the characters in the order in which they are to be incremented.
    <n>   ::=   A numeric expression equal to the number of characters in <string>.
    <memvar>   ::=   Contains the last character output.

    ```
    * III...
    * String is "ABC", <memvar> contains 'A'
    <memvar> = SUBSTR('ABC',(AT(<memvar>, 'ABC')+1)-3* ;
               INT((AT(<memvar>,'ABC')+1)/4),1)
    * <memvar> contains 'B'

    * II...
    * String is "ABC", <memvar> contains 'C'
    STORE $('ABC',(@(<memvar>,'ABC')+1)-3* ;
         INT((@(<memvar>,'ABC')+1)/4),1) TO <memvar>
    * <memvar> contains 'A'
    ```

Semicolon Centering [II]

If there are two or more strings, each separated by a semicolon, the strings will output centered one above the other. The output is centered on both the screen and the printer, and in a text file if the SET ALTERNATE ON option is used. This is most useful in formatting output in report form headings, however it can be used in any character string.

```
? "string1;string222;string33333"
```

becomes:

```
        string1
      string222
    string33333
```

The centering is in relation to the length of the whole string. To center the above in an eighty column line, it would be necessary to add a number of spaces to bring the total length of the whole string to eighty, and place a semicolon between the last character in the string and the spaces. Any spaces between the strings and the semicolons will affect the centering. When used with memory variables, the correct syntax is:

```
? memvar1 + ";" + memvar2 + ";" + memvar3
```

Using the semicolon for centering is only possible with the report form or the question mark (line output). It cannot be used with the @...SAY command (full-screen, or "formatted," output).

The semicolon's centering function can also interfere with character data handling. If the semicolon will be used in a character string, field, or memvar, its centering function should be disabled. In version 2.4 and later, SET RAW ON disables the centering. In 2.3, a POKE sequence or patch must be used; see Technical Support Note 10 in appendix F.

Work-Arounds

1.   In dBASE II, the <length> parameter of the substring function $() must be a literal number, not a numeric variable. The macro can be used in this case with a character type memvar holding the appropriate digit(s). For example:

```
STORE "4" TO length
? $("dBASE II", 1, &length)
```

2.   The substring function treats zero and negative numbers in the <length> parameter differently from positive numbers. In dBASE II, a negative number is treated the same as a positive number, and zero causes a logical false (.F.) to be returned. In dBASE III, both a negative number and zero cause a null string to be returned.

DATA HANDLING–DATE

dBASE handles its dates in one of two ways. In dBASE III, the date has its own data type which make the handling of dates so easy and automatic that the programmer can easily construct any date algorithm by simply using the date functions. In dBASE II, the date is stored as character type and requires a variety of algorithms and substring manipulations to return the same results as the dBASE III functions.

dBASE II date handling is covered here for functional clarity, even though it is character type data. dBASE II date routines are in appendix B, and Algorithms are at the end of this chapter.

dBASE III	dBASE II	
CDOW()	Routine:	Weekday.prg
CMONTH()	Algorithm:	Character Month
DAY()	Expression:	$(DATE(), 4, 2)
DOW()	Routine:	Weekday.prg
MONTH()	Expression:	$(DATE(), 1, 2)
TIME()	Routine:	Gettime.prg
YEAR()	Expression:	$(DATE(), 7)

Date Format

There are two date formats available in dBASE:

American	::=	mm/dd/yy
European	::=	dd/mm/yy

Of course, the sequential format (yy/mm/dd) used in Japan can be used in character type variables, although this is not necessary to place the file in true sequential date order. See the True Date Order algorithm in chapter 19, "Ordering by Data."

In II-2.3, there is no provision for changing the American date format. In II-2.4, either American or European may be selected during the installation procedure. In dBASE III, database fields store the date in American format, which can be altered during input/output with the @D and @E functions in the @...SAY and @...GET commmands.

Date Calculations

dBASE III allows the following numeric operations on date types:

<date> + <numeric expression>	::=	Returns a date that will occur in the future
<date> - <numeric expression>	::=	Returns a date that occurred previously
<date 1> - <date 2>	::=	Returns number of days between <date 1> and <date 2>

This can be accomplished because dBASE III stores the date internally as a number. In II, the date must be converted to a number. See Julian Period Day under Algorithms below.

VOCABULARY

Operators

+

    `<command> <date> + <numeric expression>`
      [III] To determine a date that will occur a given number of days after the specified date.

–

    `<command> <date> – <numeric expression>`
      [III] To determine a date that occurred a given number of days before the specified date.

–

    `<command> <date 1> – <date 2>`
      [III] To determine the number of days between two dates.

=

    `<command> <expression 1> = <expression 2>`
      [III/II] To determine whether one data item is identical to another.

#

    `<command> <expression 1> # <expression 2>`
      [III/II] To determine whether one data item is identical to another.

<>

    `<command> <expression 1> <> <expression 2>`
      [III/II] To determine whether one data item is identical to another.

<

    `<command> <expression 1> < <expression 2>`
      [III/II] To determine whether one data item is less than another.

<=

    `<command> <expression 1> <= <expression 2>`
      [III/II] To determine whether one data item is less than or equal to another.

>

    `<command> <expression 1> > <expression 2>`
      [III/II] To determine whether one data item is greater than another.

>=

> `<command> <expression 1> >= <expression 2>`
> [III/II] To determine whether one data item is greater than or equal to another.

Functions

CDOW()

> `CDOW(<date expression>)`
> [III] To get the weekday name.

CMONTH()

> `CMONTH(<date expression>)`
> [III] To get the name of the month.

DATE()

> `DATE( )`
> [III/II] To get the usually current date.

DAY()

> `DAY(<date expression>)`
> [III] To get the numeric day of the month.

DOW()

> `DOW( )`
> [III] To get the number of the weekday. Sunday ::= 1.

DTOC()

> `DTOC(<date expression>)`
> [III] To convert a date type date to character.

MONTH()

> `MONTH(<date expression>)`
> [III] To get the numeric month. January ::= 01.

TIME()

> `TIME( )`
> [III] To get the operating system time.

YEAR()

```
YEAR(<date expression>)
```
   [III] To get the numeric year.

SET parameters

DATE

```
SET DATE TO <nn/nn/nn>
```
   [II] To change the dBASE II system date. <n> may be any number, </> may be any character.

Commands

None.

Other Resources

( )

```
<command> ( <expression 1> <operator> <expression 2> )
```
   [III/II] To specify the order in which evaluations will occur within an expression.

ALGORITHMS

Julian Period Day [II]

   Many applications involve the use of two dates, such as when we want to know what the calendar date will be exactly 90 days from now. This is simply handled numerically in dBASE III, whereas a Julian date conversion is necessary in dBASE II.

   In dBASE II, a "Julian" date routine is used to calculate a number representing the Julian period day. According to the 1984 *World Almanac*, the Julian period was devised in 1582 by Joseph Scaliger and named after his father Julius, not after Julius Caesar or the Julian calendar. Scaliger began the first Julian Day (JD) at noon, January 1, 4713 B.C., the most recent time that three major chronological cycles began on the same day: the twenty-eight-year solar cycle, the nineteen-year lunar cycle, and the fifteen-year indication cycle. It will take to the year 3267 to complete the period, a total of 7,980 years which is the product of twenty-eight, nineteen, and fifteen.

   The true Julian period day algorithm is in Julian.prg. A pseudo-Julian algorithm is in Weekday.prg. The difference is that Julian.prg requires a four-digit year input and works for other centuries (useful in scientific applications), and Weekday.prg accepts a two-digit year and is valid for the twentieth century only. They are both in appendix B.

Character Month [II]

   To output the month in a word rather than a number, first store the names of the months to a memory variable with equal spacing for each word:

```
STORE "January   February March     April     May       June      " +;
      "July      August   SeptemberOctober   November December "   ;
      TO date:str
```

Then when it is time to output the date, use the substring function to get the proper month word by using the month's number for the substring's <start location>. Because the month's number is in the form of a character string, it is converted to a numeric with the VAL function:

```
VAL( $( DATE() ,1,2) )
```

This number must then be multiplied by the length of the space reserved for each word, which in this case is nine. This puts the substring START pointer in column nine of the appropriate month word, and we want it in column one. So, subtract one less than the word's reserved length, in this case eight:

```
VAL( $( DATE() ,1,2) )*9 - 8
```

This formula now makes up the entire number for the <start location>. We know that the <substring length> is nine, but since the words don't all take up the full nine spaces, add the TRIM function to the substring once it has been extracted (remember that the innermost nested functions evaluate first):

```
TRIM( $(date:str, VAL( $( DATE() ,1,2) ) * 9-8, 9) )
```

This returns the month's word which is concatenated to the day and year with appropriate spaces and comma:

```
TRIM( $(date:str, VAL( $( DATE() ,1,2) ) * 9-8, 9) ) ;
 + " " + $( DATE() ,4,2 ) + ", 19" + $( DATE() ,7,2 )
```

Quick Date Trap [II]

In many applications, it is not practical to wait for a subroutine to validate a date. This algorithm may be inserted in any command file to accept a date from the operator and fully error trap it. Note that the logical expression also allows the date to be left blank. It is so close to the 254 character limit that it cannot be indented by more than two spaces. Also note the use of the system date function to format the entered date with leading zeros.

```
* Start of date entry routine...
*
@ <entry coordinates> GET m:date PICTURE [##/##/##]
READ NOUPDATE
CLEAR GETS
STORE VAL($(m:date,1,2)) TO t:month
STORE VAL($(m:date,4,2)) TO t:day
STORE VAL($(m:date,7,2)) TO t:year
DO WHILE (m:date # [  /  /  ]) .AND.;
(t:month<1 .OR. t:month>12 .OR. t:day<1 .OR.;
t:day > VAL($("312931303130313130313031" , ;
(t:month-INT((t:month-1)/12)*12) *2-1, 2)) .OR.;
(t:month=2 .AND. t:day>28 .AND. t:year/4.0>INT(t:year/4.0)))
```

```
    @ <message coordinates> SAY;
      "Not a valid date, please re-enter..."
    @ <entry coordinates> GET m:date PICTURE [##/##/##]
    READ NOUPDATE
    CLEAR GETS
    STORE VAL($(m:date,1,2)) TO t:month
    STORE VAL($(m:date,4,2)) TO t:day
    STORE VAL($(m:date,7,2)) TO t:year
    @ <message coordinates>
ENDDO
*
* Format the string if it contains a date with blank spaces...
IF " " $ m:date .AND. (.NOT. m:date = [  /  /  ])
    *
    * Right justify the characters in each subvariable...
    STORE STR(t:month,2) +"/"+ STR(t:day,2) +"/"+ STR(t:year,2);
       TO m:date
    *
    * Use the date function to add leading zeros...
       * Save the system date...
    STORE DATE() TO t:date
       * Set system date to entered date...
    SET DATE TO &m:date
       * Replace entered date with formatted system date...
    STORE DATE() TO m:date
       * Restore original system date...
    SET DATE TO &t:date
    *
    * Redisplay the formatted date...
    @ <entry coordinates> GET m:date PICTURE [##/##/##]
    CLEAR GETS
ENDIF
*
* End of date entry routine.
```

Other Centuries [III]

With one exception, all dates are entered with two digits representing the year. Using the CTOD() function, dates can be entered with two, three, four, or five digits for the year. Whenever a date is entered with two digits for the year, dBASE III assumes it is in the twentieth century. Dates entered with three, four, or five digits in the year parameter are taken literally.

```
. a = CTOD("7/4/1776")
07/04/76
. b = CTOD("7/4/76")
07/04/76
```

```
. DISPLAY MEMORY
A              pub   D  07/04/76
B              pub   D  07/04/76
* They look the same from here, but they're not.

. ? a = b
.F.
. ? YEAR(b)
 1976
. ? YEAR(a)
 1776
. ? YEAR(b) - YEAR(a)
   200
. ? b - a
     73048
* Number of days between a and b.
```

The smallest date that can be entered is 1/1/100, and the largest date is 12/31/32767. However, at the time of this writing, accuracy over this entire range is unknown.

Work-Arounds

● In dBASE III, data variables that are empty, or "blank," and are to be compared with a literal must be compared as character types rather than data types. For example:

```
. x = CTOD(" / / ")
. ? x = CTOD(" / / ")
.F.
. ? DTOC(x) = " / / "
.T.
```

Related Algorithms

● True Date Order and Descending Date Order in chapter 19, "Ordering by Data."

DATA HANDLING–LOGICAL

Logical data is always one byte with a logical, or "Boolean" value of true (.T.) or false (.F.). Logical expressions always evaluate to a Boolean true or false and are used as signals, or "flags," to control program flow. The three structured programming commands IF, CASE, and DO WHILE all use a <logical expression> as the condition for branching.

There is a difference in handling logical data that is a frequent source of confusion to new programmers. Character, date, and numeric data all require the use of a relational operator to return a <logical expression>.

```
IF State = 'CA'
CASE Amount > 1000 .OR. Amount < 100
DO WHILE Name = m_name
```

With a logical type variable, just the variable by itself is a <logical expression>:

```
IF is:state
CASE is_over .OR. is_under
DO WHILE is_found
```

A <logical expression> is also part of the <database parameter> that affects commands that move the record pointer. The <logical expression> in a <database parameter> is always preceded with FOR or WHILE.

```
DISPLAY ALL FOR State = 'CA'
COUNT WHILE Name = mname
SUM Amount FOR is_over
COPY TO Newfile WHILE is_found
```

If a <logical expression> is to be compared with another <logical expression>, one of the logical operators must be used, not a relational operator.

```
IF State = 'CA' .OR. Name = m_name
CASE is_over .AND. is_found
DO WHILE is_found .AND. .NOT. EOF()
```

Note that SET EXACT *only* affects the way character expressions are evaluated by the relational operators and database search commands. It does not affect other logical operations.

Logical literals are different in dBASE III than they are in dBASE II:

dBASE III:				**dBASE II:**			
.T.	.t.	.Y.	.y.	T	t	Y	y
.F.	.f.	.N.	.n.	F	f	N	n

VOCABULARY

Operators

.NOT.

```
<command> .NOT. <logical expression>
```
[III/II] To reverse the value of a logical expression.

.AND.

```
<command> <logical expression 1> .AND. <logical expression 2>
```
[III/II] To determine the combined value of two logical expressions.

.OR.

```
<command> <logical expression 1> .OR. <logical expression 2>
```
[III/II] To determine the value of either of two logical expressions.

Functions

None.

SET parameters

None.

Commands

None.

Other Resources

( )

```
<command> ( <expression 1> <operator> <expression 2> )
```
[III/II] To specify the order in which evaluations will occur within an expression.

ALGORITHMS

XOR

At the time of this writing, XOR is not an operator in dBASE so an algorithm must be used. XOR stands for eXclusive OR, and its purpose is to determine whether two logical expressions are the same or different, regardless of their value. In comparison to the other logical operators, it looks like this:

<x>	<y>	<x> .AND. <y>	<x> .OR. <y>	<x> <XOR> <y>
.T.	.T.	.T.	.T.	.F.
.T.	.F.	.F.	.T.	.T.
.F.	.T.	.F.	.T.	.T.
.F.	.F.	.F.	.F.	.F.

The alogorithm for implementing XOR is:

\<XOR\> ::= (\<x\> .OR. \<y\>) .AND. .NOT. (\<x\> .AND. \<y\>)

Initialize Memvar with \<logical expression\>

When first writing the program, we tend to think in terms like this:

```
IF 200 > 100
    STORE .T. TO logical
ELSE
    STORE .F. TO logical
ENDIF
```

The same result is acomplished with one line of code in less processing time with:

```
STORE 200 > 100 TO logical
```

Long Logical Expressions

There is a limit of 254 characters allowed in any one command line. This is usually more than enough until we have a very lengthy \<logical expression\> such as:

```
IF Name = mname .AND. Zip = mzip .AND. Date1 = mdate1;
   .AND. Date2 = mdate2 .AND. Id:number = mid:number;
   .AND. ( Amount > mamount .OR. Amount < new:amount );
   .AND. ( Invoice:no > last:no .OR. Invoice:no < 0 );
   .AND. ( Interest = minterest .OR. Interest > approved);
   .AND. ( Sales = msales .OR. Sales > sales:aver );
   .AND. ( Cost = mcost .OR. Cost < cost:aver );
   .AND. ( Time = mtime .OR. Time < time:aver )
```

This command line requires 404 characters if it is not indented at all (the number of spaces used to indent each line after a semicolon are included in the line's total). The spaces surrounding the relational and logical operators may be removed. Although this would pick up around 75 characters, we would still exceed the 254 character limit. In addition, removing the spaces would render the code nearly unreadable.

The logical expression can be evaluated in sections, the results stored in logical memvars, and the logical memvars used in the \<logical expression\> of the conditional command.

```
STORE Name = mname .AND. Zip = mzip .AND. Date1 = mdate1;
   .AND. Date2 = mdate2 .AND. Id:number = mid:number;
   .AND. ( Amount > mamount .OR. Amount < new:amount );
   .AND. ( Invoice:no > last:no .OR. Invoice:no < 0 );
   TO is:true1
STORE ( Interest = minterest .OR. Interest > approved);
   .AND. ( Sales = msales .OR. Sales > sales:aver );
   .AND. ( Cost = mcost .OR. Cost < cost:aver );
   .AND. ( Time = mtime .OR. Time < time:aver );
   TO is:true2
IF is:true1 .AND. is:true2
```

Of course, it is only necessary to create as many logical memvars as will allow the expression to fit in the conditional command:

```
STORE Name = mname .AND. Zip = mzip .AND. Date1 = mdate1;
      .AND. Date2 = mdate2 .AND. Id:number = mid:number;
      .AND. ( Amount > mamount .OR. Amount < new:amount );
      .AND. ( Invoice:no > last:no .OR. Invoice:no < O );
      TO is:true1
IF is:true1;
      .AND. ( Interest = minterest .OR. Interest > approved);
      .AND. ( Sales = msales .OR. Sales > sales:aver );
      .AND. ( Cost = mcost .OR. Cost < cost:aver );
      .AND. ( Time = mtime .OR. Time < time:aver )
```

DATA HANDLING–NUMERIC

The numeric data type is used for arithmetic, or mathematical operations. The numeric capacities of dBASE are:

	II 2.3 - 2.41	II 2.42	III 1.00
Numeric Accuracy (digits)	10	16	15.9[a]
Largest Number (+ or −)	1.8×10^{63}	1.8×10^{63}	1×10^{308}
Smallest Number (+ or −)	1×10^{-63}	1×10^{-63}	1×10^{-307}
Largest Numeric Field	254	63	19
Largest Numeric Memvar	63	63	40[b]

a. This is the IEEE standard. IEEE (pronounced "eye-triple-ee") is the Institute of Electrical and Electronic Engineers.
b. The first release of dBASE III, version 1.00, has this limitation with both memvars and numeric literals.

Figure 16-1

The largest number means that, in dBASE II for example, you may have a number as large as a one with sixty-three zeros after it. If all of these were digits other than zero, only the first ten digits would accurately show the actual value. The rest of the trailing digits default to zeros.

Version	Largest accurate integer	Largest accurate money
II 2.3x, 2.4, 2.41	9,999,999,999	$99,999,999.99
II 2.42	9,999,999,999,999,999	$99,999,999,999,999.99
III 1.00	999,999,999,999,999	$9,999,999,999,999.99

In III, four new math functions were added: exponent, log, round, and square root. In II, programs and algorithms are used to simulate these functions. dBASE II math routines are in appendix B, and algorithms are at the end of this chapter.

dBASE III		dBASE II
EXP()	Routine:	Exponent.prg
INT()	Function:	INT()
LOG()	Routine:	Natlog.prg
ROUND()	Algorithm:	Rounding
SQRT()	Routine:	Sqroot.prg
STR()	Function:	STR()

Asterisks are returned upon completion of any numeric operation that did not produce a valid result. This is caused by a number of things including:

1. Placing a number into a variable that is not big enough to accept it. Numbers between 0.00 and 1.00 must have enough room for the zero preceding the decimal point.
2. Dividing any numeric expression by a value of zero.
3. Creating a number larger than allowed by dBASE.
4. Exceeding the range of a function, such as LOG(-1)

In dBASE II, numeric variables will always display a zero in the absence of another value. The only way to display a zero value as blank is with a character type variable. In dBASE III, the @Z function can be used in the PICTURE clause of @...SAY (see chapter 18, "Output").

VOCABULARY

Operators

+

    `<command> +<numeric expression>`
        [III/II] To identify a number as positive.

−

    `<command> -<numeric expression>`
        [III/II] To identify a number as negative.

^

    `<command> <numeric expression 1> ^ <numeric expression 2>`
        [III] To raise a number to a power.

**

    `<command> <numeric expression 1> ** <numeric expression 2>`
        [III] To raise a number to a power.

*

    `<command> <numeric expression 1> * <numeric expression 2>`
        [III/II] To multiply.

/

    `<command> <numeric expression 1> / <numeric expression 2>`
        [III/II] To divide.

+

    `<command> <numeric expression 1> + <numeric expression 2>`
        [III/II] To add.

−

    `<command> <numeric expression 1> - <numeric expression 2>`
        [III/II] To subtract.

=

    `<command> <expression 1> = <expression 2>`
        [III/II] To determine whether one data item is identical to another.

#

    `<command> <expression 1> # <expression 2>`
        [III/II] To determine whether one data item is identical to another.

<>

    `<command> <expression 1> <> <expression 2>`
        [III/II] To determine whether one data item is identical to another.

<

    `<command> <expression 1> < <expression 2>`
        [III/II] To determine whether one data item is less than another.

<=

    `<command> <expression 1> <= <expression 2>`
        [III/II] To determine whether one data item is less than or equal to another.

>

    `<command> <expression 1> > <expression 2>`
        [III/II] To determine whether one data item is greater than another.

>=

    `<command> <expression 1> >= <expression 2>`
        [III/II] To determine whether one data item is greater than or equal to another.

Functions

EXP()

    `EXP(<numeric expression>)`
        [III] For calculating the exponential function.

INT()

    `INT(<numeric expression>)`
        [III/II] To drop the decimal portion of <numeric expression> and retain the integer only.

LOG()

LOG(<numeric expression>)
[III] To calculate the logarithm to the base e.

ROUND()

ROUND(<numeric expression>, <number of decimal places>)
[III] To round off a number to a specified number of decimal places.

SQRT()

SQRT(<numeric expression>)
[III] To get the square root of a number.

STR()

STR(<numeric expression>,<resulting string length>)
[III/II] To convert numeric type numbers to character type numbers without decimals.

STR(<numeric expression>,<resulting string length>, <decimal places>)
[III/II] To convert numeric type numbers with decimals to character type numbers with decimals.

SET parameters

DECIMALS

SET DECIMALS TO <numeric expression>
[III] To specify the number of decimal places displayed after division, SQRT(), LOG(), and EXP().

SET DECIMALS [TO]
[III] To set the number of decimal places to zero.

FIXED

SET FIXED <switch>
[III] To enable/disable the feature that forces a specified number of decimal places in all numeric output.

Commands

AVERAGE

AVERAGE <numeric expression list> [<database parameter>]
[III] To display the individual averages of specified numeric fields.

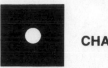

AVERAGE <numeric expression list> [<database parameter>] ;

    TO <memvar name list>
        [III] To store the individual averages of specified numeric fields to memory variables.

    AVERAGE [<database parameter>]
        [III] To display the individual averages of all numeric fields in a database file.

    AVERAGE [<database parameter>] TO <memvar name list>
        [III] To store the individual averages of all numeric fields to memory variables.

SUM

    SUM <numeric expression list> [<database parameter>]
        [III/II] To display the individual totals of specified numeric fields.

    SUM <numeric expression list> [<database parameter>];
        TO <memvar name list>
        [III/II] To store the individual totals of specified numeric fields to memory variables.

    SUM [<database parameter>]
        [III] To display the individual totals of all numeric fields in a database file.

    SUM [<database parameter>] TO <memvar name list>
        [III] To store the individual totals of all numeric fields to memory variables.

Other Resources

( )

    <command> (<expression 1> <operator> <expression 2>)
        [III/II] To specify the order in which evaluations will occur within an expression.

ALGORITHMS

Rounding [II]

In many applications, numbers need to be rounded off after a computation. The expression for accomplishing this is:

    INT(<n> * <a> + .5) / <b>

<n>	::=	The numeric expression to be rounded.
<a>	::=	Integer. A one followed by as many zeros as there are decimal places to be left in the rounded number.
<b>	::=	Decimal. A one followed by as many zeros as there are decimal places to be left in the rounded number, plus a decimal point, plus the same number of zeros repeated in the decimal portion.

For example, imagine computing six percent sales tax on an item that sells for $155.99. Take $155.99 and multiply it by .06 to return an answer of $9.3594. Adding the price and the tax returns $165.3494 which we want to look like $165.35.

```
INT(165.3494 * 100 + .5) / 100.00
```
(Number of zeros is two)

Looking at how it works, we see that 165.3494 is multiplied by 100 giving us 16534.94. Adding .5 to this gives us 16535.44, and the INTeger of this is 16535. Divide that by 100.00 to get 165.35.

Modified MODulus Function

There are some occasions when we must limit the range of a numeric expression, such as when it is used in the argument of a function. The formula for accomplishing this is called a *modulus* function. Modulus functions deal in zero-based numbers, which means that the lowest positive number can be a zero:

```
a MOD b  ::=  a - INT(a/b) * b
```

To eliminate the possibility of returning a zero, we *modify* the formula to give us one-based numbers by subtracting one from the original number and adding one to the result:

```
modified MOD  ::=  ( (a-1) - INT((a-1)/b) * b ) + 1
```

The modified form translates "a" from one-based to zero-based, does the MOD, and translates back. This simplifies to:

```
modified MOD  ::=  a - INT((a-1)/b) * b
```

So, this is the formula we use for restricting numeric expressions:

```
<a> - INT( (<a>-<c>) / <b> ) *<b>
```

<a>	::=	The numeric expression to be limited
<b>	::=	The desired upper limit of <a>
<c>	::=	The desired lower limit of <a>, zero if omitted

As an example, in the algorithm Quick Date Trap (chapter 16), the variable "t:month" is used as the <start location> parameter in a substring function. Because the string used in the substring function only has twelve places, a beyond-string error would occur if the value of t:month were greater than twelve or less than one. To prevent this, a numeric expression is used in place of the memvar name for the <start location>:

```
t:month - (INT((t:month-1)/12)*12)
```

This prevents <start location> from ever exceeding twelve or returning zero. Looking first inside the function because this is where the first computations are made, we see that one is subtracted from the month, making the lower limit one. This result is then divided by twelve, the higher limit. The resulting number of division is called the *quotient*. So, if the month is twelve or less to begin with, the quotient is less than one. If the month is over twelve, the quotient is greater than one. Because we don't care about anything to the right of the decimal point in the quotient, we take the INTeger of the quotient and multiply it by the higher limit, twelve. If the quotient is zero, the result of multiplying it by twelve will still be zero. Subtracting this from the original month leaves us with whatever we started with. If, however, the original month is from twelve to twenty-four, the quotient is one, multiplied by twelve is twelve. Subtracting twelve from the original value places the result between one and twelve. If the original month is from twenty-five to thirty-six, the quotient is two, and so on.

Notice that the parentheses surrounding the expression to be subtracted from month are not necessary for processing because the minus sign has the lowest precedence in the algorithm. However, they are included (unless restricted by lack of space on the command line) to enhance readability, recognition, and understanding of the algorithm.

Character Conversion With Decimals

Even though the VAL() function has been called the character to integer function in some dBASE manuals, the entire number (including decimals) is converted and can be obtained.

```
. STORE "123.456garbage" TO char
. STORE VAL(char) TO num
. LIST MEMORY
CHAR          pub   C   "123.456garbage"
NUM           pub   N        123  (         123.45600000)
```

As you can see in this dBASE III example, the entire number is evaluated even though VAL() only appears to return the integer. This is also true in dBASE II, although it cannot be readily observed. By adding the desired number of decimal places in zeros, we can get the complete numeric result:

```
. ? num
        123

. ? num+.000
        123.456

. ? VAL(char)+.000
        123.456
```

Related Algorithms

1. To convert dollar amounts to words, see Amt2word.prg in appendix B.
2. To eliminate display of zero amounts in numeric variables, see the algorithm Blank Zeros in chapter 21.

CHAPTER SEVENTEEN
MEMORY VARIABLES (MEMVARS)

The memory variable area is a storage area for temporary, or "working," data. The data kept here is used for controlling a variety of processes during program execution. Each data item is stored in memory and assigned a memvar name that points to it. This set of memvars is similar to having another database file always open with no particular field structure (see Literally Variable in chapter 16, and also chapter 19, "In General").

The most important uses of memvars are:

1. To hold frequently used constants, such as prompts to the operator and screen-handling codes.
2. To save communications received from the operator in order to have the program act on them.
3. As a working, or "buffer," area for data entry into database files.
4. To save evaluations or results of expressions and functions.
5. As a scratchpad for numeric equations and counters.

Memvars are created and data is assigned to them in a single line of code. All commands that assign memvar names to data are *initialization* commands, that is, if that memvar name already exists, its data will be overwritten. Memvars are the same type as their data, either character, date, logical, or numeric. These commands initialize memvars:

Command	Memvar Type
= (assignment command)	C, D, L, or N
ACCEPT TO	C
AVERAGE TO	N
COUNT TO	N
INPUT TO	C, D, L, or N
PARAMETERS	Same as the corresponding expression in the DO...WITH command
PUBLIC	L (until specifically initialized otherwise)
RESTORE FROM	C, D, L, or N
STORE TO	C, D, L, or N
SUM TO	N
WAIT TO	C

These commands release memvars:

CANCEL	[III]
CLEAR	[II]
CLEAR ALL	[III]
CLEAR MEMORY	[III]
QUIT	
RELEASE	
RETURN	[III]

There are two notes regarding these memvar commands. In dBASE II, versions 2.41 and 2.42 running under MS(PC)-DOS, QUIT TO keeps active memvars alive and returns to dBASE after running the specified programs or operating system commands. In dBASE III, CANCEL, RETURN, and RELEASE ALL only release PRIVATE memvars, not PUBLIC ones.

Size

The memory variable area has a fixed size in dBASE II, and a variable size in dBASE III. The specifications are:

dBASE III

1. Maximum of 256 memvars active simultaneously.
2. Maximum number of bytes for all active memvars is variable from 1K to 31K (default ::= 6K). See Config.db in chapter 12.

dBASE II

1. Maximum of 64 memvars active simultaneously.
2. Maximum number of bytes for all active memvars is 1.5K (1,536 bytes).

Data stored in memvars occupies a certain number of bytes according to its data type.

	Number of Bytes Used			
Data Type	II 2.3	II 2.4	III 1.00	Comment
Character	len +1	len +2	len +2	len ::= string length.
Date	n/a	n/a	9	Stored as numeric.
Logical	2	2	2	2.3 displays 0 used.
Numeric	6	7	9	2.42 uses 10.

Characteristic

In dBASE II, all memory variables have a global, or "public," characteristic to them. In other words, they exist until they are intentionally erased, or "released," by the programmer. They are available to all command files in the program regardless of which nested level of command file initializes them.

In dBASE III, memory variables can be broken down into three types according to their characteristic, which only affects their ability to be used by other command files (see chapter 14). The three types are *private*, *public*, and *hidden*.

Private: Private memvars are available only to the command file in which they are created and in its subroutines, or "lower-level" command files. All memvars initialized from a command file are created as private unless they have previously been declared to be PUBLIC. Private memvars are automatically released when program control RETURNs to a higher-level command file in the system, or to the dot prompt.

Public: public memvars are available to all command files regardless of their nesting level, and to the dot prompt. All memvars created from the dot prompt are automatically public. However, memvars created in command files must be declared PUBLIC *before* being created, or they will be released when program control RETURNs to a higher level command file, or to the dot prompt. After being declared PUBLIC, but prior to being initialized, memvars have a logical type with a value of false (.F.). Public memvars can only be deleted with RELEASE <memvar name>, CLEAR MEMORY, and CLEAR ALL.

Hidden: Existing memvars, either public or private, may be declared to be *Hidden* with the PRIVATE command. Hidden memvars become unavailable to the command file which declared them hidden, as well as to lower-level command files called by the declaring file. This allows subroutines to initialize and use memvar names that already exist in higher-level files without altering or overwriting the value of the higher level memvar. Note that the PRIVATE command does *not* change a public memvar to a private one, it just hides it. PRIVATE may not be declared from the dot prompt.

Ignoring how they are implemented, a consistent way of looking at memory variables is:

- Memvars are implicitly PRIVATE to the routine that created them, and are available to it and its children.
- Memvars may be declared PRIVATE to insure that the routine will not affect higher-level versions of the memvar.
- Memvars may be declared PUBLIC to make them globally available and immune from being released automatically.

The effect is to make them act like Pascal variables. If you view PRIVATE as a verb (which it is), then it should really be called HIDE. However, if you view it as a declaration statement (simulating other languages), then it affects not the previously created memvars, but any newly created ones. In this sense, it makes the newly created memvars PRIVATE. It is best to think of it as a declaration since it makes more sense and probably will be a declaration in future compiler implementations.

Macro Substitution

The macro (&) is used to replace a memvar name with the literal contents of the memvar in the command line. It returns the undelimited literal characters stored in the memvar, which *must* be character type to be used with the macro.

The macro is *not* a function, even though it is called one in some of the dBASE manuals. It is unique unto itself, and can perhaps best be analogized as a small DO <file>. It looks at the memvar, takes the contents, and moves them onto the command line in place of itself and the memvar name. Although the macro can be useful, we discourage its use for three reasons:

- Portability. dBASE compilers will have a difficult time with the macro.
- Understanding. The macro makes code difficult to comprehend and debug.
- Speed. The macro takes time.

The practical use of the macro is to let the programmer use the contents of a character memvar in commands where dBASE expects an undelimited literal of any type. For example:

```
. STORE "LIST MEMORY" TO command
. command
*** Unrecognized command verb
. &command
COMMAND      pub   C  "LIST MEMORY"
    1 variables defined,        13 bytes used
  255 variables available,   5987 bytes available

. STORE "*.MEM" TO files
. SAVE TO memfile
. LIST FILES LIKE files
Database files    # records     last update      size
None
. LIST FILES LIKE &files
MEMFILE.MEM
     83 bytes in      1 files.

. STORE "w+" TO sc_bright
. SET COLOR TO sc_bright
Syntax error
                   ?
SET COLOR TO sc_bright
. SET COLOR TO &sc_bright

* dBASE II only ...
. STORE "Marybeth" TO first:name
. USE Names INDEX Fname
. FIND first:name
NO FIND
. FIND &first:name
. ? Fname
Marybeth
* Use SEEK first_name in dBASE III (macro is unnecessary)
```

If there are leading spaces in the memvar string that must be retained in the command line expression, delimit the macro-memvar with quotes so that its leading spaces won't be truncated by the parser.

```
. STORE "    Ace" TO space:ace
. FIND &space:ace
NO FIND
. FIND "&space:ace"
. ? Fname
    Ace
```

A character type memvar can contain a string whose undelimited literal value would be seen as a different data type by dBASE. There is no practical reason to do this. We present it only to clarify further the operation of the macro:

```
. STORE ".T." TO char
. STORE char  TO still_char
. STORE &char TO logical
. DISPLAY MEMORY
CHAR        pub   C   ".T."
STILL_CHAR  pub   C   ".T."
LOGICAL     pub   L   .T.

. STORE "08/07/84" TO char_date
. STORE char_date  TO char_date2
. STORE &char_date TO not_a_date
. DISPLAY MEMORY
CHAR_DATE   pub   C   "08/07/84"
CHAR_DATE2  pub   C   "08/07/84"
NOT_A_DATE  pub   N          0.01 (          0.01360544)
* The literal of char_date is a numeric expression of
* division.
* Use the CTOD() function for this conversion...
```

Macro-memvars can be used together without a separator:

```
STORE "B:" TO drive
STORE "Filename" TO file
USE &drive&file
```

To use a macro-memvar as a prefix to a literal string, the memvar-terminator (.) is used to tell dBASE where the memvar name ends:

```
USE &drive.Filename
```

A macro-memvar can hold the name of another variable so that the operation will take place on the nested variable. A good example of this is in the Prompt Pad algorithm in chapter 18, "Input."

It takes experience to know just when and where to use the macro. The best way to get that experience is to try the command both with and without the macro, and see which one produces the desired results. A basic rule of thumb is *not* to use the macro if there is another algorithm that will do the job.

Precedence

If there is redundancy or ambiguity in the syntax of a command statement, dBASE handles it in this order of precedence:

1. Keyword
2. Field name
3. Memvar name
4. Literal string

If a field has the same name as a keyword (not recommended), the field may not be seen. For example, DISPLAY STATUS will not display a field called *Status*.

If a database field and a memvar have the same name (not recommended), dBASE will only see the field unless the prefix "M" is used.

```
dBASE III:   M->memvarname
dBASE II:    M.memvarname
```

However, there is no ambiguity in using a macro-memvar because the macro cannot be used with a field name, and therefore dBASE knows to use the macro-memvar.

If a memvar has the same name as a literal (not recommended), dBASE will not be able to use the literal; it only sees the memvar. This is why, for example in dBASE II, we can escape a DO WHILE T loop with the command STORE F TO T.

If a macro-memvar is used in a literal character string (not recommended), the order of precedence holds and dBASE evaluates the memvar expression before it processes the literal string. For example, in dBASE II, the macro is needed to use a memvar with some of the command prompts like:

```
ACCEPT "&file:name not found, re-enter -->" TO file:name
```

In III, those commands accept an expression, making this use of the macro unnecessary.

```
ACCEPT file_name + " not found, re-enter -->" TO file_name
```

Permanency

Memory variables are temporary unless saved in a memory file on disk with the SAVE command. Constant data such as screen handling codes, file backup flags, and other data not in the database are usually kept this way. The memvars can then be initialized by the program in a single line of code with the RESTORE command instead of several STORE commands.

With certain data that changes, such as the last check number written, it is faster to use a memvar than to search the database file for the highest number every time a check is written. In order to carry this memvar over from one working session to another, it is kept in a "constant" memory file.

Memory files are also used when the maximum number of memvars allowed by dBASE are not enough. Active memvars can always be saved until needed to make room for more. This occurs fairly frequently in dBASE II, although good memory management in the first place can usually prevent it. However, there are the occasional applications that simply require more than sixty-four memvars, and these can be implemented with the careful saving and restoring of sixty-four memvars at a time.

Memory Management

dBASE III requires the programmer to manage memvars with more awareness than dBASE II because of the global/local characteristic differences. This ultimately results in a better program and a more skillful programmer. The better programmers working in dBASE II will emulate its techniques by thinking of memvars as global or local and implementing the application the way dBASE III would require. In order to do this easily, name memvars so that they can be released and saved in groups (see chapter 13).

Null Memvar

dBASE III allows the initialization and use of a character type memvar with a length of zero. This allows the programmer to distinguish between <RETURN> or <SPACE> pressed in response to an ACCEPT or WAIT command.

VOCABULARY

Operators

None.

Functions

CTOD()

```
CTOD(<character expression>)
```
[III] To convert a character type date to a date type date. The only way to create a date type outside of a date type database field.

SET parameters

None.

Commands

=

```
<memvar name> = <expression>
```
[III] To create or overwrite a memory variable.

ACCEPT

```
ACCEPT <prompt> TO <memvar name>
```
[III/II] To get a character string from the operator in command-line mode. Delimiters are not entered by the operator.

AVERAGE

```
AVERAGE <numeric expression list> [<database parameter>] ;
        TO <memvar name list>
```
[III] To store the individual averages of specified numeric fields to memory variables.

```
AVERAGE [<database parameter>] TO <memvar name list>
```
[III] To store the individual averages of all numeric fields to memory variables.

CLEAR

CLEAR
[II] To close all open files, select the PRIMARY work area, and release all active memory variables.

CLEAR ALL
[III] To close all open files, select work area number one, and release all active memory variables.

CLEAR MEMORY
[III] To release all active memory variables.

COUNT

COUNT [<database parameter>] TO <memvar name>
[III/II] To store the result of count to a memvar.

DISPLAY

DISPLAY MEMORY
[III/II] To display all of the active memory variables.

INPUT

INPUT <prompt> TO <memvar name>
[III/II] To get an expression of any data type from the operator in command-line mode. As in all expressions, character strings must be delimited.

LIST

LIST MEMORY
[III/II] To display all of the active memory variables.

PARAMETERS

PARAMETERS <memvar name> {,<memvar name>}
[III] To accept parameters passed from another command file or procedure with the DO...WITH command into memvars which are private to the executing subroutine.

PRIVATE

PRIVATE <memvar name> {,<memvar name>}
[III] To declare that specified memvars created at this and lower levels will not interfere with higher-level memvars of the same name.

PRIVATE ALL
[III] To declare that all memvars created at this and lower levels are private and will not interfere with higher-level memvars of the same name.

PRIVATE ALL EXCEPT <memvar name skeleton>
[III] To declare that all memvars created at this and lower levels which do not share a common name key are private and will not interfere with higher-level memvars of the same name.

PRIVATE ALL LIKE <memvar name skeleton>
[III] To declare that all memvars created at this and lower levels which share a common name key, are private and will not interfere with higher-level memvars of the same name.

PUBLIC

PUBLIC <memvar name> {,<memvar name>}
[III] To declare that specified memvars will be globally available to all levels of command files and the dot prompt.

RELEASE

RELEASE <memvar name> {,<memvar name>}
[III/II] To remove currently active memory variables by name.

RELEASE ALL
[III/II] In II, to remove all currently active memory variables. In III, to remove all memvars except those declared PUBLIC or initialized in a higher level command file.

RELEASE ALL EXCEPT <memvar name skeleton>
[III/II] To release currently active memory variables which do not fit a specified name key.

RELEASE ALL LIKE <memvar name skeleton>
[III/II] To remove currently active memory variables with a common name key.

RESTORE

RESTORE FROM <memvar file name>
[III/II] To overwrite all existing memvars with those from a memory file.

RESTORE FROM <memvar file name> ADDITIVE
[III/II] To add memvars from a memory file to the currently active memvars.

SAVE TO

SAVE TO <memvar file name> ALL EXCEPT <memvar name skeleton>
[III/II] To create or overwrite a memory file with specified memvars.

SAVE TO <memvar file name> ALL LIKE <memvar name skeleton>
[III/II] To create or overwrite a memory file with specified memvars.

SAVE TO <memvar filename>
[III/II] To create or overwrite a memory file with all currently active memvars.

STORE

    STORE <expression> TO <memvar name> {,<memvar name>}
        [III/II] To create or overwrite one or more memory variables.

SUM

    SUM <numeric expression list> [<database parameter>];
        TO <memvar name list>
        [III/II] To store the individual totals of specified numeric fields to memory variables.

    SUM [<database parameter>] TO <memvar name list>
        [III] To store the individual totals of all numeric fields to memory variables.

WAIT

    WAIT <prompt> TO <memvar name>
        [III] To get a single character from the operator.

    WAIT TO <memvar name>
        [III/II] To get a single character from the operator.

Other Resources

&

    &<character memvar name>
        [III/II] To execute a dBASE command that is stored in a memory variable.

    FIND "&<character memvar name>"
        [II] To use the contents of a variable as the parameter in FIND. Delimiters are used when both the index key and the variable contain leading blanks. The delimiters prevent any leading blanks in the variable from being truncated.

    FIND &<character memvar name>
        [II] To use the contents of a variable as the parameter in FIND.

    <command> &<memvar name>.<character string>
        [III/II] To use the contents of a macro-memvar as the prefix to a string.

ALGORITHMS

Macro in a DO Loop

A loop takes time to evaluate its logical expression, and time to move back and forth between DO and ENDDO in addition to the execution time required by the DO WHILE command. Loops with complex logical expressions take a long time to execute. To speed up this process, dBASE III saves the variable pointers in the DO WHILE's <logical expression> the first time it executes the loop. Therefore, if there is a variable name inside a macro-memvar and it is changed inside the loop, the <logical expression> will no longer evaluate correctly. dBASE II can accept macro-memvars in the DO WHILE without any effect other than slowing down execution.

A Memvar of a Different Type

These functions convert from one data type to another:

STR()	::=	Numeric to Character
VAL()	::=	Character to Numeric
CTOD()	::=	Character to Date [III]
DTOC()	::=	Date to Character [III]

In dBASE II, the STR() and VAL() functions cannot be used to change the type of a memvar:

```
STORE 42 TO number
STORE STR(number,2) TO number
```

In dBASE III, that can be done, although it is not a terrific programming technique to have your variables changing types throughout a program. In this example, we wind up with a character type memvar called number. In the rare cases where this needs to be done (though I can't think of one), the dBASE II solution is to use a "scratch" memvar for the conversion and then overwrite the original one.

```
STORE 42 TO number
STORE STR(number,2) TO string
STORE string TO number
```

Pseudo Arrays

Long requested by dBASE programmers is array capability. At the time of this writing, there still isn't any, so we use a dBASE algorithm to simulate arrays.

An array is series of items arranged in a meaningful pattern. Moreover, an array used in programming terms implies the existence of an algorithm to locate data at any coordinate in the array. For example, if we have a list of items, we can store each one in a memvar with a slightly different name.

```
* AR_DEMO.PRG [III]
*
* Initialize a memvar to use as a counter...
* A character type is used because it will be
* concatenated to a memvar name to give us
* programming access to the array.
STORE '000' TO counter
*
* Set up a loop for the size of the array, twelve in this
* example.  (Remember the limit of active memory variables)
DO WHILE counter < '012'
   *
```

```
      * Increment counter by 1...
      STORE SUBSTR( STR( &counter+1001,4 ) ,2,3) TO counter
      * [In II, substitute $ for SUBSTR]
      *
      * Assign values to the array elements...
      STORE VAL(counter) TO number&counter
      STORE 'EXAMPLE ' + counter TO alpha&counter
ENDDO
```

Upon displaying the memory, we see that the array created above looks like:

```
      NUMBER001    N                1
      ALPHA001     C    "EXAMPLE 001"
      NUMBER002    N                2
      ALPHA002     C    "EXAMPLE 002"
      NUMBER003    N                3
      ALPHA003     C    "EXAMPLE 003"
      NUMBER004    N                4
      ALPHA004     C    "EXAMPLE 004"
      NUMBER005    N                5
      ALPHA005     C    "EXAMPLE 005"
      NUMBER006    N                6
      ALPHA006     C    "EXAMPLE 006"
      NUMBER007    N                7
      ALPHA007     C    "EXAMPLE 007"
      NUMBER008    N                8
      ALPHA008     C    "EXAMPLE 008"
      NUMBER009    N                9
      ALPHA009     C    "EXAMPLE 009"
      NUMBER010    N               10
      ALPHA010     C    "EXAMPLE 010"
      NUMBER011    N               11
      ALPHA011     C    "EXAMPLE 011"
      NUMBER012    N               12
      ALPHA012     C    "EXAMPLE 012"
```

Note that the counter is character type in order to be used with the macro, and that it has leading zeros in order to avoid problems when going from nine to ten and ninety-nine to one hundred as the suffix of a memvar name. The leading zeros and incrementing character string algorithms are in chapter 16, "Character."

Arrays also have dimensions. The above example is called a one-dimensional array because it operates on a single vertical axis as a simple list of twelve items. A two dimensional array adds another axis horizontally which we create by using "subvariables" within each character type memvar. For example, suppose we have a group of forty products that consists of a three-digit product number and a five-digit price as follows:

Product No.	Price
101	$275.03
102	68.07
103	214.17
104	210.00
105	197.15
106	220.00
107	117.08
108	127.56
109	152.81
110	122.63
111	152.84
112	117.63
113	95.17
114	2.50
115	5.75
116	15.82
117	18.26
118	29.28
119	42.76
120	53.26
121	305.72
122	708.60
123	714.12
124	.21
125	517.91
126	.22
127	807.11
128	657.21
129	182.51
130	362.21
131	482.51
132	367.11
133	715.90
134	52.00
135	575.00
136	285.10
137	628.10
138	929.20
139	672.40
140	623.50

Instead of using forty memory variables or creating a database file to look up the price for a given product, here's a way to do it with a combination of the substring ($) and VAL functions. In this dBASE II example, we STORE the entire list of products and prices in two memory variables and still have sixty-two memvars left for other uses.

Since our product numbers are three digits and our largest price is five digits, each product and price "cluster" requires eight characters. Each memvar has a total storage requirement of 160 characters in our array, which looks like this:

```
1 0 1 2 7 5 0 3 1 0 2 0 6 8 0 7 1 0 3 . . . 0 5 3 2 6
  \ /     \   /   \ /     \   /   \ /           \   /
 Prod-1  Price-1 Prod-2  Price-2 Prod-3   . . .  Price-20
```

This is STOREd TO the memory variable, "prodtable1." To search for a product, we must first examine position one of prodtable1 for a length of three, then position nine for a length of three, position seventeen for a length of three, and so on until we find a match or have reached the end of that memvar. If not found, we want to search the next memvar in the array, "prodtable2."

The substring function (SUBSTR() in III, $() in II) works beautifully for this. Each time we look at the next product, we must increment our starting position pointer by eight in order to skip past the three-digit product number and the three-digit price. Once we locate our product, we extract the price using the VAL function.

Notice that a price of $68.07 is stored as 06807. The reason for this is that each price field must accommodate the largest possible price, which is five digits in this example. We do not use a decimal point because it is not necessary and would waste valuable space. The decimal value is obtained by dividing the product price by 100.00.

Array.cmd shows how to search an array for a product number and extract the price. In this example, we enter a product number, search the array, and display the price if an entry is found.

```
* ARRAY.CMD [II]
*
* Initialize the array(s) with values...
STORE "101275031020680710321417104210001051971510622000"+;
      "107117081081275610915281110122631111528411211763"+;
      "113095171140025011500575116015821170182611802929"+;
      "1190427612005326" TO prodtable1
STORE "121305721227086012371412124000211255179112600022"+;
      "127807111286572112918251130362211314825113236711"+;
      "133715901340520013557500136285101376281013892920"+;
      "1396724014062350" TO prodtable2
*
* Initialize a variable for entry...
STORE "   " TO prod:nmbr
*
* Set up a loop for repetition...
DO WHILE T
   *
   * Prompt for the product number...
   @ 5,20 SAY "Enter the product number (Return to Quit)";
         GET prod:nmbr PICTURE "999"
   READ
   CLEAR GETS
   *
   * Depending on the contents of prod:nmbr, either
   * RETURN out of this program, LOOP back to DO WHILE T,
   * or select the proper table and execute the rest of
   * this program...
```

```
      DO CASE
        CASE prod:nmbr = " "
            SET TALK ON
            RETURN
        CASE prod:nmbr < "101" .OR. prod:nmbr > "140"
            @ 10,25 SAY "Incorrect product number "
            LOOP
        CASE prod:nmbr > "100" .AND. prod:nmbr < "121"
            STORE "prodtable1" TO array
        CASE prod:nmbr > "120" .AND. prod:nmbr < "141"
            STORE "prodtable2" TO array
      ENDCASE
      *
      * Search for the prod:nmbr...
      * Notice the use of the macro function to specify the array.
      STORE 1 TO pointer
      * (The macro cannot be used in a DO loop in dBASE III.)
      DO WHILE prod:nmbr # $(&array,pointer,3) .AND. pointer < 160
         STORE pointer + 8 TO pointer
      ENDDO
      *
      * Display the results...
      STORE VAL($(&array,pointer+3,5)) / 100.00 TO prod:price
      @ 10,25 SAY "   The price is:  $" + STR(prod:price,6,2)
      *
      * Housekeeping...
      STORE "   " TO prod:nmbr
ENDDO
* EOF: Array.cmd
```

In actual use, these arrays remain fairly constant and are usually initialized by a utility command file and saved to a memory file. The searching subroutine simply RESTOREs FROM the memory file which is much faster. Speaking of speed, substring searching in an incremental DO loop like this does take some time.

Work-Arounds

● When a lot of memvars are repeatedly initialized and released, the memory variable area can become *fragmented*. This reduces its usable area and can lead to a crash when an attempt is made to initialize a memvar for which there is no longer any room. If you are having trouble with memvars for no apparent reason, reconstruct the memory area by saving the existing memvars to a memory file, and then restore from that file:

```
      SAVE TO <memory filename>
      RESTORE FROM <memory filename>
```

Related Algorithms:

1. See Initializing Memvar with Logical Expression in chapter 16, "Logical."
2. See work-around number one in chapter 16, "Character."

CHAPTER EIGHTEEN

SCREEN HANDLING

Screen handling refers to the process of communication between the programmer and the operator. This communication can be broken down into two categories:

1. Output: The programmer speaks to the operator.
2. Input: The operator speaks to the programmer.

As in any one-on-one conversation, each participant has her or his own needs and preferences. The programmer may want to use numeric fields for numbers, and the operator may want to enter numbers in a character field with commas. Unlike ordinary conversations, the programmer has complete control over the conversation. The operator can only speak when the programmer allows it, and cannot ask a question like, "What is the program doing now? Is it still working?"

This places a responsibility on the programmer to consider the operator's needs first. As the programmer, it helps to think of the communication process that will occur as taking place between the operator and yourself rather than between the operator and your program. This personal involvement in the process can facilitate the writing of a program that is truly "user-friendly." That overworked term can be defined as an implementation that *contributes to the quality of a person's experience in using it.*

Of course, it takes time to design and write screens that are works of art. This is time well spent, particularly if a client or employer is paying for it. Though they may not be aware of it when the project is begun, they will want the very best screen they can get when they're using it for hours on end. In many business applications, designing and testing screens takes as much time as the entire remainder of the project.

Building Computer Screens for Easier Use

Designing visually attractive and uncluttered computer screens is a skill that you can learn. There are rules of visual aesthetics and communication that you can use to apply to your application programs. Areas where you can immediately improve your screen are:

Screen layout (format)
Menu selections
Instructions
Error messages

Screen layout is where you place the information on the screen. A menu is a list of choices from which the user selects the next operation procedure. An instruction, or "prompt," explains a program feature or operation. An error message informs the user that an incorrect response has been entered or tells the user how to get back to the program.

Visual Perception of Two-Dimensional Space

The most important thing to remember when designing a computer screen is the size of your screen. Most systems have a display of eighty characters by twenty-four or twenty-five lines.

People tend to logically see a computer screen as having a top, middle, and bottom—and a left, center, and right. Not every character space on the screen has equal importance. Western traditions of reading from left to right and top to bottom greatly determine where the user looks first.

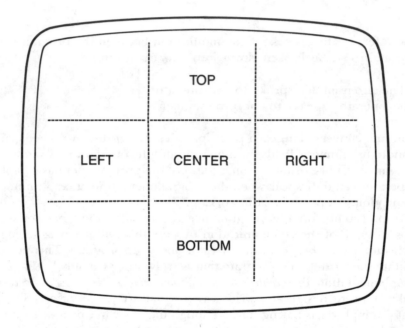

Figure 18-1

There are also aesthetic and emotional responses to placing information centered, off-center, or directly next to the screen border. Information that's centered appears stable, or "balanced." Information that's placed off center is dynamic because it creates a sense of "tension." As information moves farther from the center of the screen toward the edge, it becomes more dynamic. Consequently, the user gets the feeling of motion, crowding, and tension.

Figure 18-2

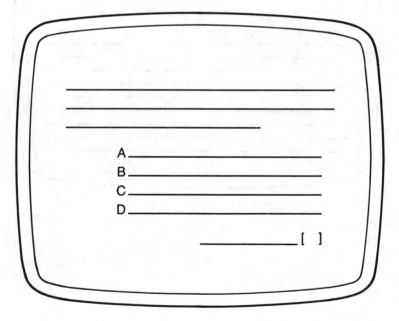

Figure 18-3

As a programmer, build upon the knowledge of how people see graphic and textual presentations. The most prominent part of the screen is the exact center. Obviously, the content of your message is the most important part of your information. So, place the content in the center of the screen.

Focusing the Reader's Attention

Too much information crowded into one area of the screen is confusing and results in an overload to sensory perception. Blank space helps the reader absorb your message by focusing her or his attention on where the important information is. Use blank space as a means of directing the user's attention. You can use margins, headings, lists, text blocks, and indentations. Be sure to leave ample space for borders, then the message won't appear crowded. A rule-of-thumb is to keep the amount of blank space equal to the amount of information.

Written information is much easier to remember when it comes in small amounts. Keep your text length between forty and sixty-five characters per line. Strive to limit the main message, be it text or a menu, to appearing between columns ten and seventy, rows six and nineteen. That leaves top and bottom borders of five lines and side borders of ten columns.

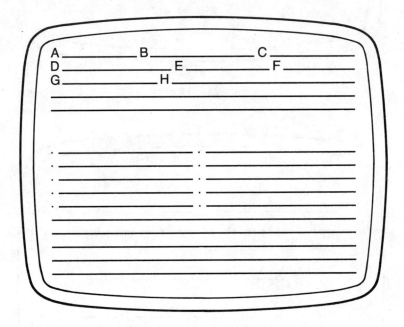

Figure 18-4

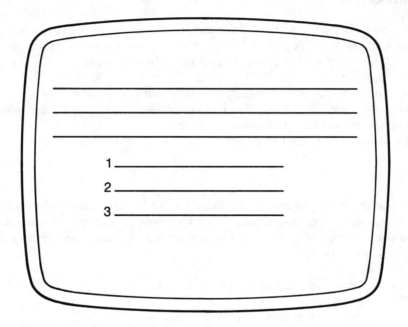

Figure 18-5

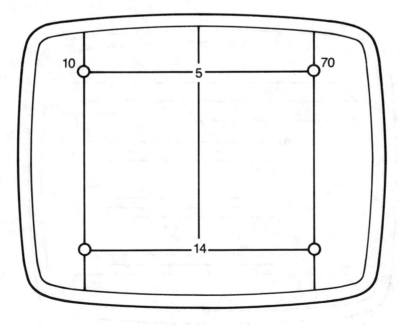

Figure 18-6

Organizing the Message

One computer screen is just enough to enclose about one paragraph. A paragraph expresses just one idea. So, don't think of a screen as a "page" in the conventional sense with three or four paragraphs, but as a single paragraph. If your screen is a paragraph, follow these rules:

- State the main thought of the paragraph in the first sentence.
- Organize the paragraph logically. Cause and effect, process sequences, and multiple examples are all logical ways to present and develop an idea.
- Keep the paragraph short and to the point.

Constructing Menus

Menus and lists are another way of presenting material. Never have a menu stand alone on the screen. Always introduce the menu with a heading or title. That way, your reader has a context for the menu items. Avoid using lists within lists. Remember that a computer screen expresses one idea; so, don't include two primary menus on the same screen.

Some good formatting rules to remember about menus are:

- Justify menu item ragged right rather than right justified.
- Whenever possible, leave a blank line between each item on the menu.
- Limit the number of menu items.
- Indent menu items about five columns.

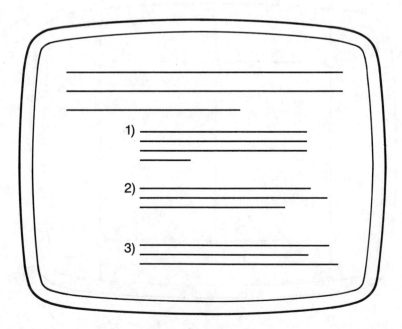

Figure 18-7

Menu Flow

Traditionally, execution of menu items takes two forms. The simplest form is where the user presses a key and execution begins. This is certainly the fastest method, but there is an obvious caution. The user has no way of changing her or his mind once the selection is made.

The alternative form of menu selection is where the user presses a key, sees that letter or number appear on the screen, and then presses a second key (usually the return key) to begin execution. This method allows users to change their minds about the selection before execution. They simply type over their first choice. However, it's a little redundant to have to press a key and then the return key for simple operations.

You may want to include more sophisticated forms of menu flow such as escape routes, choice verification, and preview of results. Leaving the user with no option but to select an operation is rather cruel.

Escape routes take several forms. You can give the user options to go back one step to a previous menu or sequence. You can also save the user lots of time by letting her or him move back several levels of menus to a main menu. You might even want to provide a method of interrupting the execution of a menu item and returning the user to some logical starting place.

Choice verification usually takes the form of yes-no (Y/N). The user presses "Y" to proceed or "N" to go back and do something else. Again, you're asking the user to choose from more than just one key. Be sure and explain specifically what you want the user to do.

Preview of results lets a user know what the result of a choice will be prior to selecting a menu item. These previews are really help screens.

Consistent Placement of Information

You can build a sense of trust in users by always placing the same type of information in the same screen location. Make menu titles, menu selections, error messages, and help screens consistently appear in the same place on the screen.

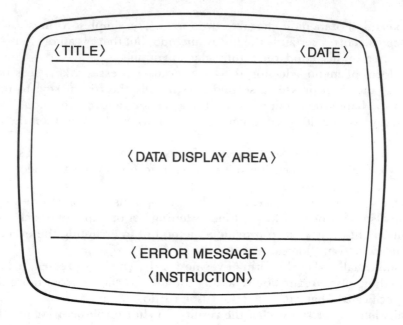

Figure 18-8

Highlighting for Emphasis

By using various forms of highlighting, you call attention to important parts of your message. You also break up boredom by creating some visual differences. Highlighting techniques include inverse video, underlining, and characters used for decorative effects.

Inverse video and flashing video are dramatic ways to highlight information. These characters are so bright that too many of them grouped together are terribly annoying and eye straining. Underlining is a more subtle way to highlight information, if your computer allows it.

Overuse of a highlight, or too many different ones, tends to detract from the effectiveness of your screen. By making everything seem important, nothing seems distinct. You end up with a cluttered and confusing look.

Graphic characters that you can use for focusing attention or decoration include characters such as

```
    +     -     =     <     >     *     |     /.
```

These characters are great for making boxes, lines, arrows, banners, and titles. For example:

```
Type your response --> here

-==**{   Main Menu   }**==-
```

Graphic characters not available on the keyboard can be displayed with the CHR() function.

Audio Prompts

Although the speaker in your computer is not a part of screen visuals, you can combine sound effects in imaginative ways. Beeps, buzzes, bells, and musical cues all reinforce what the user sees on the screen. Be careful, however, that you don't overload the program with too many "cute" sounds. Remember to keep your sound effects appropriate to the task. Unless you're writing a game or an educational program, you're better off just having some simple sounds. More involved sound effects such as whistles, screams, and musical cues are more entertaining than informative. They're great for keeping the kids involved in drill and practice exercises, but annoying in a busy office.

VOCABULARY

The screen handling vocabulary appears in the following Output and Input subchapters.

ALGORITHMS

Screen Conventions

Although different applications have different screen requirements, the programmer can adopt certain general conventions which will apply to most of the situations that arise. This makes it easier to use code modules from a library of previously written routines. One popular convention is described below and pictured in the following screen examples.

Line Number	Display	Intensity
0	Not used	
1	Left flush screen title, right flush current date	Low
2	A line across the screen	Low
3	Not used	
4 through 19	Data display area	Low for headings, High for data
20	Not used	
21	A line across the screen	Low
22	Error messages or 2-line instructions	High
23	Instructions to operator	High
24(if available)	Not used	

Example Screens

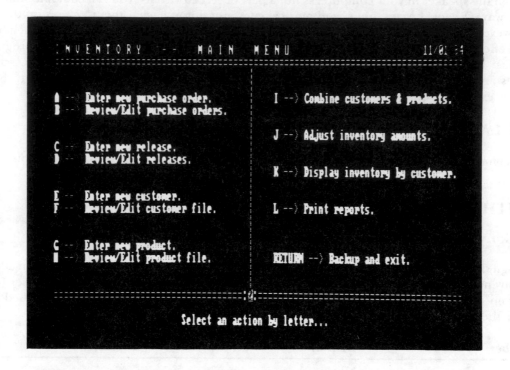

Figure 18-9
Main menu

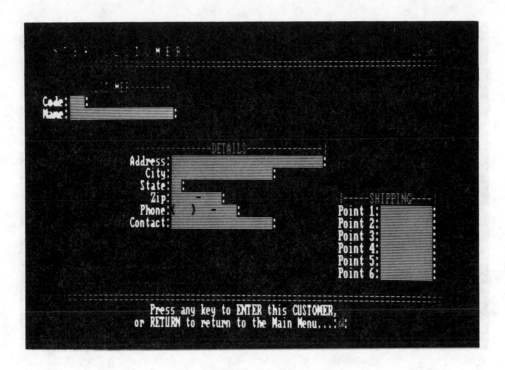

Figure 18-10
Customer entry

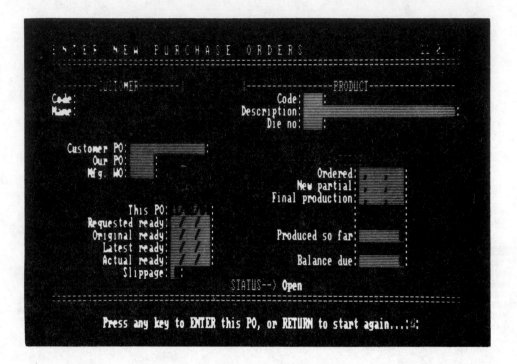

Figure 18-11
Purchase order entry

Figure 18-12
Report menu

SCREEN HANDLING—OUTPUT

Output screen handling refers to the process by which the programmer speaks to the operator. Input screen handling is the reverse of this and is covered in the next subchapter. The output commands in dBASE can be categorized according to the mode in which they work:

Formatted mode

    @...SAY

This command places its output at the screen location specified by the programmer, thus formatting the screen. In addition, it has options which allow the programmer to modify the display of its data, thus formatting its output.

Unformatted mode

   General:

                    ?
                    ??

   Specialized:

                    DIR   [III]
                    DIRECTORY   [III]
                    DISPLAY
                    LABEL   [III]
                    LIST
                    REMARK   [II]
                    REPORT
                    TEXT...ENDTEXT
                    TYPE   [III]

These commands are dependent upon the current cursor position and begin their output at that location.

Of these, the most frequently used in communicating with the operator in dBASE programming applications is the @...SAY command because of the degree of control it offers. The ? command is commonly used when precise screen placement is not an issue or when a screen scrolling effect is desired.

TEXT...ENDTEXT is a structured output command, rather than a structured programming command because it has no effect at all on program flow. It is simply a convenient way of outputting large amounts of unformatted text. The literal text must be contained within the TEXT...ENDTEXT structure, and therefore is a constant in the command file.

Formatted Screen

The <coordinates> specified in the @...SAY command control where the output will appear on the screen. The syntax and range for computers with 24 by 80 screens is:

```
@ <coordinates> SAY <expression>

    <coordinates>  ::=    <row>, <column>
           <row>   ::=    numeric expression, range 0 - 23 Also called <line>.
        <column>   ::=    numeric expression, range 0 - 79
```

Row zero is rarely used because the READ command will blank out columns eighteen through twenty-four in dBASE II, and columns forty-one through forty-five and forty-seven through fifty-two in dBASE III. If these situations are avoided, row zero can be used if desired. dBASE III also reserves row zero in its entirety for RANGE errors and other messages. However, these messages can be disabled with the SET SCOREBOARD command.

The IBM PC has a twenty-five by eighty screen, and line twenty-four (which is the twenty-fifth line) can be addressed in versions II-2.3D and in III. In all 16-bit versions of II-2.4 however, attempts to address line twenty-four will overwrite line twenty-three. See Twenty-Five Line Display under Algorithms for a way to address line twenty-four in II-2.4x.

Relative addressing refers to the use of a <numeric expression> that includes a reference to the previous or current cursor position. The cursor position reference is available in three ways:

1. dBASE III only: Functions COL() and ROW() return current cursor position.

```
@ ROW()  , COL()+2 SAY <expression>
@ ROW()+1,       0 SAY <expression>
@ ROW()-1, COL()-6 SAY <expression>
```

2. dBASE II, version 2.4x: The dollar sign ($) returns current cursor position.

```
@ $  , $+2 SAY <expression>
@ $+1,   0 SAY <expression>
```

Note that minus numbers cannot be used with this relative addressing operator. This is *not* valid syntax:

```
@ $-1, $-2 SAY <expression>
```

3. dBASE III and II: Memvar set up and maintained by programmer returns previous (prior to last output) cursor position.

```
STORE 10 TO row
STORE 10 TO col
@ row  , col-10 SAY <expression>
@ row+1, col    SAY <expression>
STORE row + 2 TO row
@ row  , col+5  SAY <expression>
```

Formatted Output

In addition to formatting the screen, we can also format the individual picture of each data item when we display it. The @...SAY command offers the programmer a variety of options for displaying data in a format different than the format in which it exists. For example, a numeric field cannot contain commas, but it can be displayed with commas when output with the @...SAY command. The syntax and formatting options are:

@ <coordinates> SAY <expression> <format option>

<format option>	::=	PICTURE "<picture template>"	[III]
		| FUNCTION "{<function>}"	[III]
		| USING "{<using symbol>}"	[II]

<picture template>	::=	@{<function>}
		| {<picture symbol>}

<picture symbol>	::=	! | A | L | X | $ | * | , | # | 9
		| <other symbol>
!	::=	Converts alpha character to uppercase (C)
A, L, X, #, 9	::=	Displays any character (C,D,L)
$	::=	Displays dollar sign instead of leading zero (N)
*	::=	Displays asterisk instead of leading zero (N)
,	::=	Displays comma only if number is large enough (N)
#	::=	Displays number (N)
9	::=	Displays number (N)

<other symbol>	::=	Overwrites the data character unless the @R function is included (C); no effect on numeric data without the @R function (N)

<function>	::=	! | A | R | D | E | (| B | C | X | Z
!	::=	Converts alpha characters to uppercase (C)
A	::=	Displays only alpha characters (C)
R	::=	Causes <other symbol> to be inserted in the display instead of overwriting it (C,N)
D	::=	mm/dd/yy (C,D)
E	::=	dd/mm/yy (C,D)
(	::=	negative number enclosed in parentheses (N)
B	::=	Left justify (N)
C	::=	Displays "CR" after a positive number (N)
X	::=	Displays "DB" after a negative number (N)
Z	::=	No display of zero value (N)

<using symbol>	::=	! | A | X | $ | * | # | 9 | <other symbol>
!	::=	Converts alpha character to uppercase (C)
A	::=	Displays any character (C)
X	::=	Displays any character (C)
$	::=	Displays dollar sign instead of leading zero (N)

*	::=	Displays asterisk instead of leading zero (N)
#	::=	Displays number (C,N)
9	::=	Displays number (C,N)

<other symbol>	::=	Overwrites the data character 2.4 (C). Is inserted without overwriting in 2.3 (C) and all (N). (C,N)

(C)	::=	Character type data only
(D)	::=	Date type data only
(L)	::=	Logical type data only
(N)	::=	Numeric type data only

Appearance

Both color and monochrome screens offer the programmer a variety of choices about the appearance of each output. Although the color environment offers a larger selection, there are screen attributes which may be used when outputting to most monochrome monitors:

Dim (normal, all attributes off)
Bright (bold)
Underscore
Reverse video (black on white)
Blinking (flashing)

Both colors and monochrome attributes can be used individually or in combination, and they greatly enhance the appearance of screens. Depending on the equipment and version of dBASE, they can be implemented in one of six ways.

1.   dBASE III only

Syntax:

```
SET COLOR TO <standard> [,<enhanced> [,<border>]]
```

Definitions:

<standard>	::=	<foreground> [/<background>]
<enhanced>	::=	<foreground> [/<background>]
<border>	::=	<number> {<attribute>}
		| <letter> {<attribute>}
		| <default>
<foreground>	::=	<number> {<attribute>}
		| <letter> {<attribute>}
		| <default>
<background>	::=	<number> {<attribute>}
		| <letter> {<attribute>}
		| <default>
<default>	::=	Black

| `<number>` | ::= | Integer value from 0 to 255 |
| | | See Color and Attribute Tables below. |

`<letter>`	::=	`<space>` | B | G | BG | R | BR | GR | W | RB | U
`<space>`	::=	Black
B	::=	Blue
G	::=	Green
BG	::=	Cyan
R	::=	Red
BR	::=	Magenta
GR	::=	Yellow
W, RB	::=	White
U	::=	Underline (monochrome only)

`<attribute>`	::=	+ | *
+	::=	High Intensity
*	::=	Blinking

In dBASE III, it is preferable to use the letters rather than the numbers for maximum portability among various machines.

2.   dBASE II, version 2.4 only

Syntax:

    SET COLOR TO [`<full-screen mode>`,] `<command-line mode>`

Definitions:

`<command-line mode>`	::=	`<numeric expression>`
`<full-screen mode>`	::=	`<numeric expression>`
`<numeric expression>`	::=	Integer value from 0 to 255
		See Color and Attribute Tables below.

3.   dBASE II, versions 2.41 and 2.42 only

Syntax:

    SET COLOR TO `<full-screen mode>`, `<command-line mode>`

Definitions:

`<command-line mode>`	::=	`<numeric expression>`
`<full-screen mode>`	::=	`<numeric expression>`
`<numeric expression>`	::=	Integer value from 0 to 255
		See Color and Attribute Tables below.

4.   This method works with any version of dBASE II and on almost any standard ANSI terminal. It must be used every time an output command is executed.

Syntax:

<output command> <ANSI escape sequence> <output expression>

Definitions:

<output command>	::=	?
		| ??
		| @...SAY
<output expression>	::=	+ <character expression>
		| –<character expression>
		| , <expression list> (not with @...SAY)
<ANSI sequence>	::=	CHR(27) + "[<n>{;<n>}m"
<n>	::=	<attribute>
		| <foreground color>
		| <background color>
<attribute>	::=	0 | 1 | 4 | 5 | 7 | 8
0	::=	All attributes off, normal white on black
1	::=	High intensity (Bold)
4	::=	Underscore (monochrome only)
5	::=	Blinking (flashing)
7	::=	Reverse video, black on white
8	::=	Invisible
<foreground color>	::=	30 | 31 | 32 | 33 | 34 | 35 | 36 | 37
30	::=	Black
31	::=	Red
32	::=	Green
33	::=	Yellow
34	::=	Blue
35	::=	Magenta
36	::=	Cyan
37	::=	White
<background color>	::=	40 | 41 | 42 | 43 | 44 | 45 | 46 | 47
40	::=	Black
41	::=	Red
42	::=	Green
43	::=	Yellow
44	::=	Blue
45	::=	Magenta
46	::=	Cyan
47	::=	White

For example:

```
? CHR(27) + "[7m",    "This is reverse video."
? CHR(27) + "[5;7m", "This is blinking reverse video."
@ 5, 5 SAY CHR(27) + "[4m"   + "This is dim  underlined."
@ 5, 5 SAY CHR(27) + "[1;4m" + "This is bright underlined."
```

5. This works only on dBASE II, all versions of 2.4 that are installed for ANSI terminals, and affects only the @...SAY and @...GET commands. The POKEd attribute remains in effect until a new value is POKEd. Only one attribute at a time can be implemented with this method.

```
POKE <address>, <ANSI attribute in ASCII>
```

\<address\>	::=	893
\<ANSI attribute in ASCII\>	::=	48 | 49 | 52 | 53 | 55 | 56
48	::=	All attributes off
49	::=	High intensity (Bold)
52	::=	Underscore (monochrome only)
53	::=	Blinking (flashing)
55	::=	Reverse video, black on white
56	::=	Invisible

For example, the syntax for high intensity is:

```
POKE 893, 49
```

6. This works only on dBASE II, versions 2.3B and 2.3D on the IBM PC, and affects only the @...SAY command. The POKEd attribute remains in effect until a new value is POKEd. Only one attribute at a time can be implemented with this method.

```
POKE <address>, <n>
```

\<address\>	::=	\<2.3B address\>
		| \<2.3D address\>
\<2.3B address\>	::=	1047
\<2.3D address\>	::=	1062
\<n\>	::=	Integer value from 0 to 255
		See Color and Attribute Tables below.

Note: All versions of dBASE after 2.3 have the SET COLOR TO command which allows the programmer to change these with relative ease. However, SET COLOR TO was implemented for different machines at different times, and may not be available in a particular programming situation.

SET COLOR TABLE

BLACK		BLUE		GREEN		CYAN		RED		MAGENTA		YELLOW		WHITE		—II only— BACKGROUND COLOR:
low	hi	low	hi	low	hi	low	hi	low	hi	low	hi	low	hi	low	hi	
0	8	1	9	2	10	3	11	4	12	5	13	6	14	7	15	—Black
16	24	17	25	18	26	19	27	20	28	21	29	22	30	23	31	—Blue
32	40	33	41	34	42	35	43	36	44	37	45	38	46	39	47	—Green
48	56	49	57	50	58	51	59	52	60	53	61	54	62	55	63	—Cyan
64	72	65	73	66	74	67	75	68	76	69	77	70	78	71	79	—Red
80	88	81	89	82	90	83	91	84	92	85	93	86	94	87	95	—Magenta
96	104	97	105	98	106	99	107	100	108	101	109	102	110	103	111	—Yellow
112	120	113	121	114	122	115	123	116	124	117	125	118	126	119	127	—White

1. Adding 128 produces blinking or flashing.
2. Adding multiples of 256 has no effect.
3. Foreground characters on a background of the same color cannot be seen.
4. In III, both foreground and background must be specified. Therefore, only the numbers 0-15 are significant although they all can be used. In II, only one number is used for both the foreground and background, so the entire table is significant.

Figure 18-13

dBASE III only:

BLACK		BLUE		GREEN		CYAN		RED		MAGENTA		YELLOW		WHITE	
low	hi	low	hi	low	hi	low	hi	low	hi	low	hi	low	hi	low	hi
⟨sp⟩	⟨sp⟩+	B	B+	G	G+	BG	BG+	R	R+	BR	BR+	GR	GR+	W	W+

1. ⟨sp⟩ ::= ⟨space⟩
2. Adding an asterisk (*) produces blinking or flashing.
3. It is preferable to use letters over numbers in dBASE III.
4. RB may be used in place of W for WHITE.
5. GR (low yellow) appears brown.

Figure 18-14

MONOCHROME ATTRIBUTE TABLE

	NORMAL low	high	UNDERLINE low	high	REVERSE low	high	INVISIBLE (blanks)
II	7	15	1	9	112	120	0
III	7	15	1	9	0/7	0+/7	0
III	W	W+	U	U+	/W	+/W	⟨space⟩
	B L I N K I N G						
II/III	135	143	129	137	240	248	
III	7*	7+*	1*	1+*	0*/7	0+*/7	
III	W*	W+*	U*	U+*	*/W	+*/W	

Figure 18-15

Whether SET COLOR or another method is used, it is a good idea to place all the screen routines in memory variables and use the memvar names throughout the program. This allows the program to be easily moved to a different computer by simply changing the screen routines in the one place where the memvars are initialized. It also allows the programmer to use meaningful names rather than cryptic numbers or letters during coding.

By way of example, this is the memvar initialization routine for using SET COLOR TO with a monochrome monitor:

```
* dBASE II...
*
STORE "112, 07" TO sc:dim
STORE "112, 15" TO sc:brt
STORE "112, 01" TO sc:dim:lin
STORE "112, 09" TO sc:brt:lin
STORE "112,135" TO sc:dim:blk
STORE "112,143" TO sc:brt:blk
STORE "112,112" TO sc:rev
STORE "  0,  0" TO sc:invis

* dBASE III...
*
sc_dim     = "W"
sc_brt     = "W+"
sc_dim_lin = "U"
sc_brt_lin = "U+"
sc_dim_blk = "W*"
sc_brt_blk = "W+*"
sc_rev     = "0/7"
sc_invis   = "0/0"
```

To use the memvars with the SET COLOR TO command, the macro must be used:

```
SET COLOR TO &sc:rev
SET COLOR TO &sc_dim
```

Using ANSI sequences in the output command requires the setup:

```
* ANSI.PRG [II]
*
STORE CHR(27) + "[0m"    TO sc:dim
STORE CHR(27) + "[1m"    TO sc:brt
STORE CHR(27) + "[0;4m"  TO sc:dim:lin
STORE CHR(27) + "[1;4m"  TO sc:brt:lin
STORE CHR(27) + "[0;5m"  TO sc:dim:blk
STORE CHR(27) + "[1;5m"  TO sc:brt:blk
STORE CHR(27) + "[7m"    TO sc:rev
STORE CHR(27) + "[8m"    TO sc:invis
*
RETURN
*
* EOF: ANSI.prg
```

Syntax examples are:

```
? sc:rev + "This is reverse video."
? sc:brt:blk + "This is blinking bold."
@ 5, 5 SAY sc:dim:lin + "This is dim underlined."
@ 5, 5 SAY sc:dim + "This is low intensity normal."
```

See Color Demo under Algorithms for a program to output all the various color combinations.

VOCABULARY

Operators

None.

Functions

CHR()

```
CHR(<numeric expression>)
```
[III/II] To enter characters for which there are no keys. To send control characters to the printer or screen.

COL()

```
COL()
```
[III] To use the current cursor position for relative addressing with @...SAY/GET.

ROW()

ROW()
[III] To use the current cursor position for relative addressing
with @...SAY/GET.

SET parameters

COLON

SET COLON <switch>
[II] To enable/disable display of a colon delimiter around variables.

COLOR

SET COLOR TO <background> <delimiter> <foreground>
[II] To change the color and/or attribute of the screen display.

SET COLOR TO <command-line mode values> ;
[,<full-screen mode values>] [,<border value>]
[III] To change the color and/or attribute of the screen display.

CONSOLE

SET CONSOLE <switch>
[III/II] To enable/disable all output to the screen.

DELIMITERS

SET DELIMITERS <switch>
[III] To enable/disable display of a specified delimiter around variables.

SET DELIMITERS TO <character expression>
[III] To select specific delimiters around full-screen variable displays. Only the first two
characters in <character expression> are significant.

SET DELIMITERS TO DEFAULT
[III] To select the colon delimiter around full-screen variable displays.

DEVICE

SET DEVICE TO <device parameter>
[III] To direct formatted output from @...SAY to either the screen or printer.

FORMAT

SET FORMAT TO
[III/II] To close an open format file.

SET FORMAT TO <device parameter>
[II] To direct formatted output from @...SAY to either the screen or printer.

SET FORMAT TO <format filename>
[III/II] To specify a format for the database file fields during full-screen commands.

INTENSITY

SET INTENSITY <switch>
[III/II] To enable/disable the enhanced video display used primarily in the full-screen interactive mode.

RAW

SET RAW <switch>
[II] To enable/disable certain automatic display formatting features.

SCOREBOARD

SET SCOREBOARD <switch>
[III] To toggle on/off the dBASE messages on line zero.

Commands

?

? <expression> {,<expression>}
[III/II] To output data in command-line, or "unformatted," mode on the next line.

??

?? <expression> {,<expression>}
[III/II] To output data in command-line, or "unformatted," mode on the current line.

@

@ <row>,<column>
[III/II] To clear or erase a portion of a single line.

@ <row>,<column> SAY <expression>
[III/II] To display an <expression> on the screen or printer.

@ <row>,<column> SAY <expression> FUNCTION "{<function>}"
[III] To display an <expression> on the screen or printer modified by the <function{s}>.

@ <row>,<column> SAY <expression> PICTURE <picture template>
[III] To display an <expression> on the screen or printer modified by the <picture template>.

@ <row>,<column> SAY <expression> USING "{<using symbol>}"
[II] To display an <expression> on the screen or printer modified by the <using symbol{s}>.

CLEAR

`@ <row>,<column> CLEAR`
[III] To clear or erase a portion of the screen.

`CLEAR`
[III] To clear or erase the entire screen.

CLOSE

`CLOSE FORMAT`
[III] To close an open format file.

DIRECTORY

`DIR [ [ON] <drive designator>] [TO PRINT]`
[III] To display a listing of the database files [on another drive] [and output to the printer].

`DIR <file directory parameter> [ [ON] <drive designator> ] [TO PRINT]`
[III] To display any files [on another drive] [and output to the printer].

`DIRECTORY [ [ON] <drive designator>] [TO PRINT]`
[III] To look at a listing of database files [on another drive] [and output to the printer].

`DIRECTORY <file directory parameter> [ [ON] <drive designator>] ;`
`          [TO PRINT]`
[III] To display a listing of any files [on another drive] [and output to the printer].

DISPLAY

`DISPLAY FILES <file directory parameter> [ON <drive designator>]`
[III/II] To display any files [on another drive].

`DISPLAY FILES [ON <drive designator>]`
[III/II] To display the database files [on another drive].

`DISPLAY MEMORY`
[III/II] To display all of the active memory variables.

`DISPLAY STATUS`
[III/II] To find out the current state of the working environment.

`DISPLAY STRUCTURE`
[III/II] To review the structure of a database file.

`DISPLAY [OFF] [<database parameter>] [<expression> {,<expression>}]`
[III/II] To display the contents of database files [without record numbers].

ERASE

`@ <row>,<column> ERASE`
[II] To clear or erase a portion of the screen (IBM PC only).

`ERASE`
[II] To clear or erase the entire screen.

LIST

`LIST FILES <file directory parameter> [ON <drive designator>]`
[III/II] To get a listing of any type of file [on another drive].

`LIST FILES [ON <drive designator>]`
[III/II] To get a list of database files [on another drive].

`LIST MEMORY`
[III/II] To display all of the active memory variables.

`LIST STATUS`
[III/II] To find out the current state of the working environment.

`LIST STRUCTURE`
[III/II] To review the structure of a database file.

`LIST [OFF] [<database parameter>] [<expression> {,<expression>}]`
[III/II] To display the contents of database files [without record numbers].

REMARK

`REMARK <character string>`
[II] To display an undelimited <character string>.

TEXT...ENDTEXT

`TEXT`
`{ <character string> <new line> }`
`ENDTEXT`
[III/II] To output multiple lines of text.

TYPE

`TYPE <text filename.ext>`
[III] To view the contents of command and other text files.

<keypress>

`<^S>`
[III/II] To momentarily pause command execution and screen scrolling from the keyboard. ^S or ^Q to restart.

Other Resources

None.

ALGORITHMS

Clearing the Screen

The entire screen is cleared, or erased, with the CLEAR command in dBASE III, or the ERASE command in dBASE II. Individual lines are cleared with individual @...SAYs used without an expression. These perform faster if they are coded sequentially rather than in a loop. For example:

```
* Fast...* Slow...
@  6,0                          row = 6
@  7,0                          DO WHILE row <= 13
@  8,0                             @ row, 0
@  9,0                                row = row + 1
@ 10,0                          ENDDO
@ 11,0
@ 12,0
@ 13,0
```

In dBASE II, an @...SAY with no expression erases the line of both SAYs and GETs. However, in the first release of dBASE III, it does not erase the GETs unless an expression is used which will overwrite them:

```
@ 14,0 SAY SPACE(80)
@ 15,0 SAY [                    ]
```

Specifying the column number in an expressionless @...SAY is the way to clear a partial line, or "to end of line." To clear a partial screen, the @...CLEAR (III) or @...ERASE (II) command is used:

```
* Clear the screen from line 10 to the bottom...
@ 10, 0 CLEAR
*
* Clear the lower right corner of the screen
* from line 10, column 15...
@ 10,15 CLEAR
```

In dBASE II, the @...ERASE command is only implemented for the IBM PC.

No Display

Occasionally, we don't want a message to appear on the screen, and dBASE doesn't appear to offer a choice. The common example here is the WAIT command in dBASE II which always outputs the message WAITING...to the screen. In these cases, we can disable the screen prior to issuing the command:

```
SET CONSOLE OFF
WAIT
SET CONSOLE ON
```

In dBASE II, there is a danger that there may be an interruption in the program while the screen is disabled (as happens when the operator presses the <Esc> key in response to the WAIT command). If this happens, the computer will appear to be dead, or "hung," because the screen is not functioning. The operator can either type SET CONSOLE ON or QUIT in this situation. We recommend QUIT in order to make sure all files are closed and the headers are updated. Resetting or rebooting the computer, as most operators will do in this situation, may cause data loss and file corruption. In dBASE III, the CONSOLE is automatically SET ON whenever program control is RETURNed to the dot prompt.

By the way, we can avoid the automatic prompt in dBASE III by using a *null* variable (character type with length of zero):

```
WAIT "" TO memvar
```

Twenty-Five Line Screen Display

This only works on the IBM PC and compatibles with dBASE II, all 16-bit versions of 2.4, to allow the @...SAY command to address the twenty-fifth line. Executing two POKE commands will accomplish this. The addresses to change are different in each version of 2.4:

2.4	2.41	2.42
POKE 1601,25	POKE 1715,25	POKE 1847,25
POKE 1605,24	POKE 1719,24	POKE 1851,24

To make the change permanent, these bytes can be patched with the DOS utility, DEBUG. See your DOS manual.

Color Demo

This program demonstrates all the possible color combinations. You might want to set the DO WHILE loops to a smaller value, or increment the counters n1 and n2 by a larger number, in order to see a good representation of combinations without sitting through 65,535 combinations.

```
* COLORS.PRG [II]
*
SET TALK OFF
ERASE
*
STORE ' VIDEO FOR "SAYS" =' TO text1
STORE ' VIDEO FOR "GETS" =' TO text2
STORE 0 TO line
STORE 1 TO n1
*
```

```
DO WHILE n1 < 255
   STORE $(text1,1,19) + STR(n1,3) + ' ' TO text1
   STORE 1 TO n2
   DO WHILE n2 < 255
      STORE $(text1,1,19) + STR(n2,3) + ' ' TO text2
      SET COLOR TO n2,n1
      IF line > 22
         ERASE
         STORE 0 TO line
      ENDIF
      @ line,12 SAY text1
      @ line,38 GET text2
      STORE line + 1 TO line
      STORE n2 + 1 TO n2
   ENDDO
   STORE n1 + 1 TO n1
ENDDO
SET TALK ON
RETURN
* EOF: Colors.prg
```

Just a Quickie

To flash a message to the operator without requiring a response, a DO WHILE loop is used with a counter to pause long enough for the message to be seen. This is considered very antisocial on time-sharing systems such as UNIX because it needlessly ties up the CPU.

```
* Display message...
@ <coordinates> SAY <message>
*
* Initialize memvars for pause loop...
STORE  0 TO counter
* Length of pause is determined by this number...
STORE 25 TO pause
*
* Pause...
DO WHILE counter < pause
   * Increment counter...
   STORE counter + 1 TO counter
ENDDO
*
* Erase message...
@ <coordinates>
```

This is only useful when it makes no difference whether the operator sees the message or not. In order to be certain that the operator sees the output, an algorithm that requires an acknowledgement is used. These are covered in the next subchapter, "Input." Also see dWAIT.prg and Timewait.prg in appendix D.

Centering Variables on the Screen

The algorithm is:

```
@ <row>, ( <width> - LEN(<variable>) ) / 2 SAY <variable>
```

<row>	::=	The screen row, or line, on which the <variable> is to be centered.
<width>	::=	The total screen width, usually 80.

For example, to center a memvar called prompt on line 10, the syntax is:

```
@ 10,(80-LEN(prompt))/2 SAY prompt
```

Graphic Characters

If your computer supports graphic characters, they can be output with the CHR() function. On the IBM PC, for example, CHR(205) produces a double line. To draw this across the entire screen of eighty columns, we initialize a memvar with 80 CHRs by starting with five and using a DO loop to double the memvar four times.

```
STORE CHR(205) + CHR(205) + CHR(205) + CHR(205) + ;
    CHR(205) TO graphic
STORE 0 TO counter
DO WHILE COUNTER < 4
    STORE graphic + graphic TO graphic
    counter = counter + 1
ENDDO
? graphic
```

Expanded Display

Once in a while, there will be an application that wants data displayed with each character separated by a space. In a heading, for example, the desired display might be:

E X P A N D E D   H E A D I N G

It can be stored that way, but that takes up twice as much space. In dBASE II, version 2.4x, the only solution *is* to store it expanded. However, in II-2.3 and III-1.00, the heading can be stored compressed and be expanded during display with the USING or PICTURE option of @...SAY. These examples both assume that the above heading is contained in a field called Head.

```
* dBASE II, 2.3x...
@ <coordinates> SAY Head USING;
            "X X X X X X X X X X X X X X X"

* dBASE III...
@ <coordinates> SAY Head PICTURE;
            "@RX X X X X X X X X X X X X X X"
```

This is only useful when there are several headings in a database file, and the same PICTURE can be used to expand them all.

ASCII Display

This little program displays all the ASCII characters and their decimal values on the screen:

```
CLEAR
* (Use ERASE instead of CLEAR in dBASE II)
SET TALK OFF
STORE 0 TO char
STORE 1 TO col
DO WHILE char < 256
    STORE 1 TO row
    DO WHILE row < 24 .AND. char < 256
        @ row, col SAY STR(char,3) +" "+ CHR(char)
        STORE char + 1 TO char
        STORE  row + 1 TO row
    ENDDO
    STORE col + 6 TO col
ENDDO
SET TALK ON
RETURN
```

Work-Arounds

1.   There are a few programming situations that will fail when a reserved word related to the program flow is the first word on a line within the TEXT...ENDTEXT output structure. For example:

```
DO CASE
    CASE choice = "Y"
        TEXT
            Case is not a command word here.
        ENDTEXT
ENDCASE
```

If the variable *choice* does not equal "Y," a syntax error will occur because dBASE tries to evaluate the next occurrence of the word CASE that begins a command line. The only place we know of where this will cause trouble is within a programming structure when the reserved word could be interpreted to be part of the structure. These words are CASE, ELSE, EXIT, LOOP, OTHERWISE, ENDDO, ENDIF, or ENDTEXT. Avoid their use as the first word in lines of text within TEXT...ENDTEXT.

2. In dBASE II, the use of the substring $() function with the @...SAY command *must* contain the optional <length> parameter or only the first character of the substring will be displayed.

Related Algorithms

1.   Multiple Screens in chapter 19, "Displaying the Data."
2.   Prompt Pad in chapter 18, "Input."

SCREEN HANDLING–INPUT

Input screen handling refers to the process by which the operator speaks to the programmer. Output screen handling is the reverse of this and is covered in the previous subchapter.

Operator input must be carefully handled. This is the time to trap *all* the possible errors so that the data in the database is always known to be accurate and good. No error trapping should ever be required when outputting data because it was thoroughly error-trapped when input. Garbage in, garbage out.

The input commands in dBASE can be categorized according to the mode in which they work.

1. Full-screen mode

```
@...GET
```

This command places a variable (field or memvar) at the screen location specified by the programmer. In addition, it has options which allow the programmer to restrict the operator's input.

```
READ [NOUPDATE]
```

This command places the cursor in variables which have been placed on the screen with @...GET. This enables the operator to enter or edit data in the variable.

```
CLEAR GETS
```

This command removes READ's ability to access previously issued GETs even though they may still be displayed on the screen. (CLEAR in III and ERASE in II also clear the active GETs, as do the full-screen database commands.)

The above commands all work in conjunction with each other and are almost always used together.

Database:

```
APPEND
BROWSE
CHANGE
EDIT
INSERT
```

Specialized:

```
CREATE
CREATE LABEL   [III]
CREATE REPORT  [III]
MODIFY COMMAND
MODIFY LABEL   [III]
MODIFY REPORT  [III]
MODIFY STRUCTURE
```

2.   Command-line mode

Memvar:

```
ACCEPT (character type)
INPUT  (date, logical, and numeric types)
WAIT   (character type, one character only)
```

Of these, the most frequently used in receiving communications from the operator is the @...GET/ READ combination because of the degree of control it offers. WAIT is often used to simply pause the program execution until the operator hits any key; the keystroke itself is frequently disregarded.

ACCEPT and INPUT are usually used for quick utility type applications where a high degree of error trapping is not a requirement, or when it is desirable to give the operator lots of flexibility, such as in programmer's utilities. ACCEPT will only accept a character type literal while INPUT will accept an expression of any data type.

The database and specialized commands all enter an interactive full-screen mode which requires the operator to be familiar with the cursor control keys, and allows the operator to do just about anything he or she wants to. These are discussed in the chapters dealing with database files, report generators, and foreign files. They are primarily used in the interactive mode; see chapter 25.

Formatted Placement and Appearance

Screen placement and appearance of @...GET are the same as for @...SAY, which are covered in the previous chapter. There is one combination form, the @...SAY...GET which places the GET <variable> on the screen immediately following the SAY <prompt>.

```
* One way...
@ 5, 0 SAY "Here it is -->"
@ 5,14 GET memvar
*
* Another way...
@ 5, 0 SAY "Here it is -->" GET memvar
```

These both produce the same results. The first form makes writing some screens easier. The second form runs faster.

Get It

When a variable is placed on the screen with @...GET, it can be entered with READ. In fact, the anticipation of a READ command is the only reason to use @...GET. When the operator is finished entering into the GET variable, program execution resumes after the READ.

1.   Access one variable.

```
@ <coordinates> GET <variable>
READ
CLEAR GETS
```

2. Access multiple variables together.

```
@ <coordinates> GET <variable-1>
@ <coordinates> GET <variable-2>
@ <coordinates> GET <variable-3>
@ <coordinates> GET <variable-4>
READ
CLEAR GETS
```

When this form is used, the screen behaves as though in full-screen interactive mode. The operator can move forward and backward through the variables with the cursor control keys.

3. Access multiple variables individually.

```
@ <coordinates> GET <variable-1>
READ
CLEAR GETS
@ <coordinates> GET <variable-2>
READ
CLEAR GETS
@ <coordinates> GET <variable-3>
@ <coordinates> GET <variable-4>
READ
CLEAR GETS
```

When this form is used, entry into each variable must be completed before the next is displayed. The operator cannot move backward to previous variables, except from four to three because they are accessed with the same READ.

We CLEAR GETS to prevent the next READ from accessing a GET with which we are finished. There are exceptions to this, as when we want to loop around and re-edit the same GETS without GETting them a second time.

```
@ <coordinates> GET <variable-1>
@ <coordinates> GET <variable-2>
@ <coordinates> GET <variable-3>
@ <coordinates> GET <variable-4>
READ
@ <coordinates> SAY "Is this correct? (Y/N)"
SET CONSOLE OFF
WAIT TO answer
SET CONSOLE ON
DO WHILE !(answer) # "Y"
    READ
ENDDO
```

At the time of this writing, it is not possible to do this in dBASE III because each READ behaves as though a CLEAR GETS follows it. No matter, because there is another, albeit slower, way of programming it in the first place. This method redisplays the variables.

```
DO WHILE .T.
    @ <coordinates> GET <variable-1>
    @ <coordinates> GET <variable-2>
    @ <coordinates> GET <variable-3>
    @ <coordinates> GET <variable-4>
    READ
    CLEAR GETS
    @ <coordinates> SAY "Is this correct? (Y/N)"
    SET CONSOLE OFF
    WAIT TO answer
    SET CONSOLE ON
    IF UPPER(answer) = "Y"
        EXIT
    ENDIF
ENDDO
```

To shorten the code in the command file, the @...GETs could be placed in a *format* file (described below), and deleted from this code. The format file is opened with the SET FORMAT TO <format filename> statement placed immediately above the DO WHILE .T. command. See Format Without Erase under Algorithms below.

There is a limit as to how many GETS can accumulate. The limit is 64 in dBASE II, and 128 in dBASE III unless it has been set otherwise in the *Config.db* file. When this limit is exceeded, it will cause a variety of problems including the error message "Insufficient memory" in dBASE III, and the possibility of hanging the computer in dBASE II.

The GET counter (III maximum 35 to 1,023; II maximum 64) is reset with these commands:

```
CLEAR GETS
CLEAR        [III]
ERASE        [II]
READ         [III]
```

Although the GET counter is also reset by many of the full-screen interactive commands like APPEND and BROWSE, we make it a rule of thumb when writing programs to always follow a READ with CLEAR GETS unless there is an ERASE in II or a CLEAR in III that would make the CLEAR GETS redundant.

The NOUPDATE option is only in dBASE II-2.4x. It tells dBASE II that the READ does not refer to a key field when there is an indexed database file open. dBASE II is not able to tell what variables, key field or simply memvar, are active with @...GET. So, when the READ is executed, dBASE traverses the index to make sure it gets properly updated *if* a key field is changed. Because this slows down the entry, use READ NOUPDATE with all GETs *except* a key field.

```
@ <coordinates> GET <memvar>
@ <coordinates> GET <non-key field>
READ NOUPDATE
CLEAR GETS
*
@ <coordinates> GET <key field>
READ
CLEAR GETS
```

NOUPDATE is also an option in II-2.4x REPLACE. In II-2.41, there is an anomaly that rearranges the current record position in the index if NOUPDATE is *not* used in non-key entries when there is an open indexed database file.

Formatted Input

The @...GET command offers the programmer a variety of options for limiting the data that the operator can enter. For example, a character type variable can be limited to accepting only numbers from the keyboard. The syntax and formatting options are:

```
@ <coordinates> GET <variable name> <format option>
```

\<variable name\>	::=	A currently active memvar	
		| A field in the currently selected database file	
\<format option\>	::=	PICTURE "\<picture template\>"	[III]
		| PICTURE "{\<picture symbol II\>}"	[II]
		| FUNCTION "{\<function\>}"	[III]
		| RANGE \<n1\>, \<n2\>	[III]
RANGE	::=	Can be used in addition to other format options with date and numeric variables only.	
\<n1\>	::=	numeric expression of lower limit	
\<n2\>	::=	numeric expression of upper limit	
\<picture template\>	::=	@{\<function\>}	
		| {\<picture symbol III\>}	
\<picture symbol III\>	::=	! | # | 9 | A | L | N | X | . | , | \<other symbol\>	
!	::=	Converts alpha character to uppercase (C)	
#	::=	Allows digits, spaces, signs, and periods (C)	
		Allows digits, spaces, and signs (N)	
9	::=	Allows digits (C)	
		Allows digits, signs, (N)	
A	::=	Allows alpha characters (C)	
L	::=	Allows T | t, Y | y, F | f, N | n (C,L)	
N	::=	Allows alpha characters and digits (C)	
X	::=	Allows any character (C)	
.	::=	Specifies location of decimal point (no entry allowed) (N)	
,	::=	Displays comma when number is large enough (N)	
\<other symbol\>	::=	Inserted into the display. Does not overwrite data and cannot be entered over (C)	
\<function\>	::=	! | A | D | E | B | Z	
!	::=	Converts alpha characters to uppercase (C)	
A	::=	Allows only alpha characters (C)	
D	::=	American format mm/dd/yy (C,D,N)	
E	::=	European format dd/mm/yy (C,D,N)	
B	::=	Left justify (N)	

Z	::=	No display of zero value (N)
<picture symbol II>	::=	! | # | 9 | A | X | <other symbol>
!	::=	Converts alpha character to uppercase (C)
#	::=	Allows digits, spaces, signs, and periods (C)
		Allows digits, spaces, and signs (N)
9	::=	Allows digits, spaces, signs, and periods (C)
		Allows digits, spaces, and signs (N)
A	::=	Allows alpha character (C)
		Also allows space in 2.41, 2.42 (C)
X	::=	Allows any character (C)
<other symbol>	::=	Overwrites the data character 2.4 (C). Is inserted without overwriting in 2.3 (C) and all (N). (CN)
(C)	::=	Character type data only
(D)	::=	Date type data only
(L)	::=	Logical type data only
(N)	::=	Numeric type data only

Format Files

Format files are like command files except that they contain only @...SAY and @...GET commands and comments. Format files allow the formatting of the screen during the full-screen interactive database commands APPEND, CHANGE (III only), EDIT, and INSERT (chapters 19 and 25). An open format file also affects the execution of the READ command by clearing the entire screen, resetting the GET counter, and redisplaying its SAYs and GETs.

dBASE II can have only one format file open at a time, and it remains in effect regardless of which work area is active, even when database files are opened and closed. dBASE III can have one format file for each of its ten work areas if this will not exceed the limit of thirteen simultaneously open files of all kinds. dBASE III also closes any open format file in the currently selected work area when a new database file is opened or any current one closed (chapter 19, "Multiple Files").

This command opens a format file:

```
SET FORMAT TO <format filename>
```

These commands close *all* open format files:

```
CLEAR            [II]
CLEAR ALL        [III]
CLOSE DATABASES  [III]
QUIT
SET FORMAT TO    [II]
```

These commands close *only* the open format file in the currently selected work area:

```
CLOSE FORMAT     [III]
SET FORMAT TO    [III]
USE              [III]
```

These commands are affected by active format files:

```
APPEND
CHANGE    [III]
EDIT
INSERT
READ
```

There are two disadvantages to using format files with the READ command. One is that the entire screen must be contained in the format file because the screen is cleared automatically. Another is that only one READ can be executed for the entire series of GETs, whereas in a command file selected groups of GETs can be accessed individually by using more than one READ command. See Format Without Erase under Algorithms below.

VOCABULARY

Operators

None.

Functions

COL()

```
COL( )
```
    [III] To use the current cursor position for relative addressing with @...SAY/GET.

ROW()

```
ROW( )
```
    [III] To use the current cursor postion for relative addressing with @...SAY/GET.

SET parameters

BELL

```
SET BELL <switch>
```
    [III/II] To enable/disable output to the computer's audio tone device.

COLON

```
SET COLON <switch>
```
    [II] To enable/disable display of a colon delimiter around variables.

CONFIRM

```
SET CONFIRM <switch>
```
    [III/II] To enable/disable the feature that forces the operator to press return in order to exit each input field.

DELIMITERS

SET DELIMITERS `<switch>`
[III] To enable/disable display of a specified delimiter around variables.

SET DELIMITERS TO `<character expression>`
[III] To select specific delimiters around full-screen variable displays. Only the first two characters in <character expression> are significant.

SET DELIMITERS TO DEFAULT
[III] To select the colon delimiter around full-screen variable displays.

EXACT

SET EXACT `<switch>`
[III/II] To enable/disable the feature that forces a precise match of character strings compared with relational operators.

FORMAT

SET FORMAT TO
[III/II] To close an open format file.

SET FORMAT TO `<format filename>`
[III/II] To specify a format for the database file fields during full-screen commands.

INTENSITY

SET INTENSITY `<switch>`
[III/II] To enable/disable the enhanced video display used primarily in the full-screen interactive mode.

MENUS

SET MENUS `<switch>`
[III] To enable/disable the display of cursor control keys in full-screen commands.

SCOREBOARD

SET SCOREBOARD `<switch>`
[III] To toggle on/off the dBASE messages on line zero.

SCREEN

SET SCREEN `<switch>`
[II] To enable/disable full-screen mode. Useful on machines for which dBASE II has not been installed.

Commands

@

@ <row>,<column> GET <date/numeric variable> RANGE <n1>,<n2>
[III] To place a <date or numeric type variable> in position to be edited with the READ command as restricted by the RANGE parameters.

@ <row>,<column> GET <variable>
[III/II] To place a <variable> in position to be edited with the READ command.

@ <row>,<column> GET <variable> FUNCTION "{< function>}"
[III] To place a <variable> in position to be edited wit h the READ command as restricted by the <function{s}>.

@ <row>,<column> GET <variable> PICTURE "<picture template>"
[III/II] To place a <variable> in position to be edited with the READ command as restricted by the <picture template>.

CLEAR

CLEAR GETS
[III/II] To prevent the READ command from accessing previously issued @...GETs. To reset the GET counter without clearing the screen.

CLOSE

CLOSE FORMAT
[III] To close an open format file.

READ

READ
[III/II] To place the cursor in variables placed on the screen with @...GET.

READ NOUPDATE
[II] To put the cursor in non-key variables placed on the screen with @...GET whenever there is an open indexed database file.

<keypress>

<^S>
[III/II] To momentarily pause command execution and screen scrolling from the keyboard. ^S or ^Q to restart.

Other Resources

None.

ALGORITHMS

Error Trapping

Much error trapping can be accomplished through the proper use of PICTURE parameters with the GET. Where additional trapping is required, a DO WHILE <not correct> loop is used.

```
STORE "?" TO sex
@ 5, 0 SAY "Enter sex as M or F"
DO WHILE .NOT. sex $ "MF"
    STORE "?" TO sex
    @ 5,19 GET sex PICTURE "!"
    READ
    CLEAR GETS
ENDDO
```

When the input will be more than one letter, the character string in the DO WHILE's <logical expression> must be delimited. For example, if we wanted the operator to enter a three-letter code for the month, we could set it up in several ways.

```
DO WHILE .NOT. month $ "JANFEBMARAPRMAYJUN"
```

This would allow "ANF", "NFE", "RAP", and others to be valid entries. Not acceptable.

```
DO WHILE .NOT. month $ "JAN FEB MAR APR MAY JUN"
```

This works in all versions except 2.41x where the picture template "AAA" allows the entry of a space and cannot prevent entries like "N F", "B M", "AR ", and others from being valid entries. In dBASE II, the DO WHILE command would use the uppercase function !(month) since "AAA" allows lowercase letters. In dBASE III, the option FUNCTION "!A" will force the entry of only uppercase letters.

```
DO WHILE .NOT. month $ "JAN!)FEB@(MAR#*APR$ ^MAY?JUN"
```

Although not completely foolproof, the operator would have a hard time entering an invalid combination accidentally.

```
STORE "JANFEBMARAPRMAYJUN" TO months
DO WHILE AT(month,months)/3 <> INT( AT(month,months)/3 )
```

The modulus function (Algorithms in chapter 16, "Numeric") can be used to restrict access to multiples of a number, in this case three.

Other foolproof alternatives are to have the operator select the three-letter month from a menu or prompt pad by entering a single letter or number, and in versions that permit it, up to nine allowable entries can be assigned to the function keys, and the operator selects one by pressing a function key.

Another common application is the trapping of the entry of any particular character. For this, we compare the result of the AT() function with zero since the presence of the specified character causes AT() to report its location numerically. (In dBASE II, it's the @() function.)

```
DO WHILE AT("<character>") > 0
```

There are applications where the entry of more than one of a particular character is undesireable. The algorithm for preventing duplicate characters is:

```
DO WHILE AT("<x>", SUBSTR(<var>, 1+AT("<x>",<var>) )) > 0
```

      <x>   ::= The character that cannot be entered twice.
     <var>   ::= The @...GET variable name being entered into.

   Note: In dBASE II, substitute $ for SUBSTR and @ for AT.

For example, in an application where the operator enters character type data that will be converted to numeric type data, this code traps data entered with more than one decimal point.

```
STORE "..          " TO amt
DO WHILE AT(".",SUBSTR(amt+" ",1+AT(".",amt))) > 0
    STORE "            " TO amt
    @ 5,5 SAY "Amount?" GET amt PICTURE "########"
    READ
    CLEAR GETS
ENDDO
```

Testing

In the process of running the program to see if it works, enter everything possible to try to make it fail, or "crash." Don't just enter what the operator is supposed to enter, because the operators will not always do so.

Don't Wait for WAIT

In dBASE II, the WAIT command is in an overlay file and takes a while to execute. In dBASE III, WAIT is in the main file and is much faster, but you may still prefer to use this method. Just initialize a one-character wide memvar and GET it. If CONFIRM is SET OFF, it behaves the same as WAIT.

```
STORE [ ] TO waiting
@ <coordinates> GET waiting
READ
CLEAR GETS
*
* If this was just a pause, you don't need the answer,
* and you are tight on memvar space...
RELEASE waiting
```

The only place this creates a problem is if you are asking the operator whether or not to enable editing with READ.

```
@ <coordinates> GET <variable-1>
@ <coordinates> GET <variable-2>
@ <coordinates> GET <variable-3>
@ <coordinates> GET <variable-4>
@ <coordinates> SAY "Press E to edit, RETURN to select another."
SET CONSOLE OFF
WAIT TO answer
SET CONSOLE ON
IF UPPER(answer) = "E"
    READ
    CLEAR GETS
ENDIF
```

Obviously an @...GET/READ could not substitute for WAIT in this situation because the READ would place the cursor in <variable-1> instead of in "answer."

Inkey Function

At the time of this writing, there is a void in the dBASE language that is desirable in many applications. That is a way to monitor the keyboard to determine whether a particular key has been pressed, such as the "INKEY" function in some versions of the BASIC language.

There are two routines in appendix D that simulate this: Inkey.cmd for CP/M-80 and Timewait.prg for MS(PC)-DOS.

Prompt Pad

The dBASE III Assistant uses this popular software concept where the user hits one key to activate a different choice, or <RETURN> to execute the currently active choice. This is particularly valuable when there is a crowded screen and you want to present a menu of selections to the operator. Each selection appears in the same place. The operator can hit the <SPACE> bar to see, or activate, the next sequential choice. Pressing the <B> key moves <B>ackward in the choice list, and <RETURN> selects the currently displayed choice for execution.

This example assumes that SET TALK OFF has been executed:

```
* Prompt-Pad Algorithm  [III]
*
* Initialize prompts in memvar array...
STORE '<prompt-1>' TO prompt_001
STORE '<prompt-2>' TO prompt_002
STORE '<prompt-3>' TO prompt_003
STORE '<prompt-4>' TO prompt_004
STORE '<prompt-5>' TO prompt_005
STORE '<prompt-6>' TO prompt_006
STORE '<prompt-7>' TO prompt_007
STORE '<prompt-8>' TO prompt_008
*
* Can have as many prompts as there are available memvars.
* (60 in II, 252 in III because this algorithm uses 4 memvars)
*
```

```
* Initialize controlling memvars with first and last numbers...
STORE '001' TO first, counter
STORE '008' TO last
*
* Display instructions to operator...
@ 23,17 SAY "Press SPACE or B to change, RETURN to enter..."
*
* Set up loop to redisplay <prompts> until one is chosen...
SET BELL OFF
STORE " " TO switch
DO WHILE switch # "?"
    *
    * Blank the previous display if there is one...
    @ 20,23
    *
    <set screen attribute that highlights the prompt>
    *
    @ 20,23 SAY prompt_&counter
    STORE "?" TO switch
    *
    <set screen to invisible in order to conceal the GET>
    *
    @ 23,77 GET switch PICTURE "!"
    READ
    CLEAR GETS
    *
    * Branch to increment counter and switch selection...
    DO CASE
        CASE switch = " " .AND. counter < last
            STORE SUBSTR( STR( &counter+1001,4 ) ,2,3) TO counter
        CASE switch = " " .AND. counter = last
            STORE first TO counter
        CASE switch = "B" .AND. counter > first
            STORE SUBSTR( STR( &counter+ 999,4 ) ,2,3) TO counter
        CASE switch = "B" .AND. counter = first
            STORE last TO counter
    ENDCASE
ENDDO
*
* Restore the environment before moving on...
<set screen back to normal>
SET BELL ON
@ 20, 0 SAY [                          ]
@ 23,17
*
```

```
* Branch to execute selection...
DO CASE
    CASE counter = '001'
        <commands>
    CASE counter = '002'
        <commands>
    CASE counter = '003'
        <commands>
    CASE counter = '004'
        <commands>
    CASE counter = '005'
        <commands>
    CASE counter = '006'
        <commands>
    CASE counter = '007'
        <commands>
    CASE counter = '008'
        <commands>
ENDCASE
*
* EOA: Prompt-Pad
```

A variation on this algorithm is used to toggle TALK on and off in Bnchmk_1.prg and Bnchmk_2.prg in appendix C.

Format Without Erase: [II]

The use of format files to hold your @...SAYs and @...GETs can cut down tremendously on the amount of code in a command file as well as eliminate duplication. The only drawback is that an open format file officiously causes the screen to be ERASEd when an activating command such as READ is executed. This means that the entire screen must be repainted and contained in the format file, even if you want to only redisplay the GETs.

By disabling the ERASE feature of dBASE II, we can use format files like *procedures* in dBASE III. This is accomplished with a POKE command that nullifies *any* instructions to clear the screen, thereby allowing the programmer to utilize a separate format file for a portion of the screen only.

```
POKE <address>, <value>
```

<address>	::=	<version 2.4, MS(PC)-DOS>
		| <version 2.41, MS(PC)-DOS>
		| <version 2.3x, 2.4x, CP/M-80>
<version 2.4, MS(PC)-DOS>	::=	1487
<version 2.41, MS(PC)-DOS>	::=	1602
<version 2.3x, 2.4x, CP/M-80>	::=	304
<value>	::=	<disable> | <enable>
<disable>	::=	0

$$<enable> \quad ::= \quad <DOS> \mid <CP/M>$$
$$<DOS> \quad ::= \quad 187$$
$$<CP/M> \quad ::= \quad 5$$

A couple of precautions are in order when using this technique. First, the CLEAR GETS command must be issued before sixty-four GETs are exceeded because the ERASE feature is disabled and unable to handle this automatically. Each @...GET command in the format file counts as one more GET *every time* the format file is accessed. Second, the ERASE feature should be re-enabled as soon as possible after it is disabled because, as with all tampering of source code, we can never be sure of what other ramifications it might have on other operations. For example, in version 2.41 running under MS(PC)-DOS:

```
* Erase and paint the screen with messages...
SET FORMAT TO <format file with SAYs>
READ
*
* Disable erase, and open format file...
POKE 1602,0
SET FORMAT TO <format file with GETs>
*
* Loop for repeated access to edit variables...
STORE "Y" TO answer
DO WHILE !(answer) = "Y"
   READ
   CLEAR GETS
   @ <coordinates> SAY "Is this correct? (Y/N)"
   SET CONSOLE OFF
   WAIT TO answer
   SET CONSOLE ON
ENDDO
*
* Enable erase...
POKE 1602,187
```

Work-Arounds

1. In II-2.4, if a logical memvar with a value of .T. is the GET <variable>, and if the operator hits the <RETURN> key without changing the value, the value of the memvar is changed to .F.. This only affects memvars, not fields. The work-around is to use a character memvar and trap the entry to "T" or "F". The result can be converted to a logical type with the macro function.

2. In II-2.3, if there are numeric variables as the object of GET, the combination of SET CONFIRM ON and SET BELL OFF will cause the rightmost digit to be dropped. The work-around is not to use this combination of SETs when there are numeric variables involved. A POKE can be used to disable the bell if you know the address for that particular computer's tone device.

3. When using SET CONSOLE OFF with WAIT in dBASE II (see No Display in the previous subchapter), it is a good idea to SET ESCAPE OFF so the operator does not escape into an inactivated environment. In II-2.3x, the operator can escape from a WAIT regardless of the state of SET ESCAPE. The work-around is to use a GET instead of WAIT (see Don't Wait for WAIT above). In dBASE III, the CONSOLE is automatically SET ON whenever control returns to the dot prompt.

4. In II-2.41, there is an anomaly that rearranges the current record position in the index if NOUPDATE is *not* used in non-key entries when there is an open indexed database file. See work-around number five in chapter 19, "Changing Data."

5. In dBASE III, at the time of this writing, access to a memo field cannot be gained through the READ command. Put the @...GET <memo field> statement in a format file, and access it with one of the full-screen interactive database commands: APPEND, CHANGE, EDIT, or INSERT.

CHAPTER NINETEEN

DATABASE FILE HANDLING

Database files are the storage facility for the application's permanent data. Their default file extension is .DBF unless otherwise specified. A database file is a set, or "structure," of variable names called *fields*. Each full set of fields is one record. The specifications of database files are:

Maximum Allowed	dBASE III	dBASE II
Number of fields	128	32
Number of records	1,000,000,000	65,535
Bytes per file	2,000,000,000	8,000,000
Bytes per record	4,000	1,000

The maximum number of bytes per file may be further limited by the operating system. For example, CP/M limits file size to eight megabytes, MS(PC)-DOS limits file size to thirty-two megabytes, and UNIX limits file size to around one gigabyte.

Each field must be the same type as the data it contains. However, all data regardless of its type is stored in the database file as ASCII characters. For example, a numeric field with a length of one occupies only one byte in the database and will hold only one digit. When dBASE uses that digit, it treats it as a numeric type with as many bytes as any numeric number (see chapter 16, "Numeric Data Handling"). The field types and maximum lengths are:

	Maximum Number of Bytes		
	II	II	III
Field Type	2.3x, 2.4, 2.41	2.42	1.00
Character	254	254	254
Date	n/a	n/a	8
Logical	1	1	1
Memo	n/a	n/a	10 (in .DBF file)
Numeric	254	63	19

Each record in the database file occupies the total number of bytes of all of its fields *plus one*. This extra byte is used to flag whether or not the record has been marked for deletion (chapter 19, "Moving Around" and "Changing Data").

In dBASE III, *memo* fields occupy only ten bytes in the database file (.DBF), regardless of their actual size. Memo fields are not another data type, but an additional field type for storing character-type data in fields whose lengths can vary in size according to their contents. The contents of all memo fields for all records in a single database file are kept in a separate *database-text* file with the same filename and a .DBT extension. The default file extension .DBT cannot be changed. The maximum size of a memo field is 5,000 bytes unless another word processor is assigned to WP in the Config.db file (chapter 12), in which case the memo field size *in each record* is only limited by the maximum file size limitation of the word processor. The entire database-text file size is limited only by the operating system.

The database file's structural information is kept in the file's "header" which is a particular number of bytes (depending on the version) that is the first part of every dBASE database file. This structure includes the number of fields, and each field's name, data type, length or width (number of bytes), and number of decimal places, if any. See Database File Structures in chapter 7. The number of fields and each one's name, data type, and size are established with CREATE, and can be changed with MODIFY STRUCTURE. The number of records is determined as they are added.

All database and associated index and format files can reside on a drive other than the one dBASE is on, because both dBASE III and II will accept a drive designator in front of the filename. In dBASE II, however, these files cannot reside on the same drive in a different directory because dBASE II does not accept a path parameter in the filename. dBASE III doesn't have this limitation, thus files can be located anywhere desired. If a dBASE III path is specified with the SET PATH TO command, existing files can reside anywhere in the <path list> without their location being specified in the command syntax.

File Creation

The file's structure is specified at the time of creation, which, unlike memvars, is a separate act from that of storing data. Files get created, then data is added. Database files are set up, or "created," in three ways.

1. Interactive mode

    ```
    CREATE
    ```

Database files are usually created interactively during the programming stage, and are already present when the finished program is run. At least one database file must be created interactively since creation under program control requires the presence of an existing database file.

2. Program mode from existing database file(s)

    ```
    COPY [STRUCTURE]
    JOIN
    SORT
    TOTAL
    ```

This only works when the desired database is to have either the same structure as existing database files or a subset of those structures.

3. Program mode from a structure-extended database file

    ```
    CREATE FROM
    ```

This offers the programmer the greatest control when creating files under program control. It requires the presence of a *structure-extended* database file. This is a file that always has the structure:

```
* dBASE III...
Field  Field name  Type        Width    Dec
    1  FIELD_NAME  Character      10
    2  FIELD_TYPE  Character       1
    3  FIELD_LEN   Numeric         3
    4  FIELD_DEC   Numeric         3
** Total **                       18

* dBASE II...
FLD       NAME        TYPE WIDTH    DEC
001       FIELD:NAME   C    010
002       FIELD:TYPE   C    001
003       FIELD:LEN    N    003
004       FIELD:DEC    N    003
** TOTAL **                00018
```

A structure-extended file can be created either interactively or under program control from the currently selected database file with the command:

```
COPY TO <new structure-extended filename> ;
        STRUCTURE EXTENDED
```

Each *record* in the structure-extended file holds the specifications of one *field* in the file to be created. The data for each desired field is added or changed by the usual data entry and edit methods (chapter 19, "Adding Data" and "Changing Data"). The new database file can then be created with:

```
CREATE <new database filename> ;
       FROM <structure-extended filename>
```

Changing the File's Structure

The structure of the file can be changed, or "modified," interactively with MODIFY STRUCTURE, or under program control with COPY STRUCTURE EXTENDED and CREATE FROM. Depending on what the intended modification entails, there may be other commands required. A backup copy of the original file should *always* be made before changing its structure.

Structural changes can be classified into four types:

1. Field name
2. Field type
3. Field size (length and decimals)
4. Position of the field in the record

This distinction of the type of change is only important when it is desirable to retain the existing data in the database and database-text files. Only certain combinations of structural changes can be executed at one time if the data is to be retained. If changes are to be made that involve more than one allowable combination, separate passes for each are required.

In dBASE III, MODIFY STRUCTURE automatically appends the data back after the modifications are complete. However, the following changes must be made separately (memo fields cannot change size or type):

Field size
Field name and type

In dBASE II, the data must be copied to a temporary file and appended back by the operator or programmer after the structural changes are made. MODIFY STRUCTURE destroys the data in the database file. These changes must be made separately:

Field size and position
Field name and type

To modify the structure and change the fields' size and/or position (may *not* change field name or type):

```
* [II] If there is not a lot of data in the database...
*
USE <database filename>
COPY TO <temporary database filename>
MODIFY STRUCTURE
APPEND FROM <temporary database filename>
USE <database filename>

* [II] If there is a lot of data in the database...
*
USE <original database filename>
COPY STRUCTURE TO <temporary database filename>
USE <temporary database filename>
MODIFY STRUCTURE
APPEND FROM <original database filename>
USE
DELETE <original database filename>
RENAME <temporary database filename> ;
       TO <original database filename>
USE <database filename>
```

To modify the structure and change the fields' name, type, and size (may *not* change any field's position in the file).

```
* [II] Regardless of size...
*
USE <database filename>
COPY TO <temporary text filename> DELIMITED
MODIFY STRUCTURE
APPEND FROM <temporary text filename> DELIMITED
USE <database filename>
```

The following program-mode methods can also be used interactively from the dot prompt. However, no full-screen interactive commands like MODIFY STRUCTURE are employed, thus allowing these methods to be used under full program control.

1. If the new structure desired is simply a subset (some of the fields) of an existing file:

    ```
    * dBASE III and II...
    *
    USE <original database filename>
    COPY TO <temporary database filename> FIELDS <field list>
    USE
    DELETE <original database filename>
    RENAME <temporary database filename> ;
           TO <original database filename>
    USE <original database filename>
    ```

    SORT and TOTAL can also be used. They are covered in chapter 19, "Copying to Another File."

2. If the desired structure is a combination of the fields in two existing files, use JOIN which is covered in chapter 19, "Copying to Another File."

3. If the desired structure cannot be entirely found in existing files, it can be entered by the operator while under program control. Data entry and edit algorithms are in chapter 19, "Adding Data" and "Changing Data."

    ```
    * dBASE III and II...
    *
    USE <original database filename>
    COPY TO <structure-extended filename> STRUCTURE EXTENDED
    USE <structure-extended filename>
    <Display current structure to the operator.>
    <Use input algorithms to get changes from the operator.>
    *
    * Close the open file, and create the new one...
    USE
    CREATE <new database filename> ;
           FROM <structure-extended filename>
    *
    * If change is to field size and position only...
    APPEND FROM <original database filename>
    *
    * If change is to field name, type, and size only...
    * (Will not work with memo fields)
    USE <original database filename>
    COPY TO <temporary text filename> DELIMITED
    USE <new database filename>
    APPEND FROM <temporary text filename> DELIMITED
    ```

Precedence

If a memvar has the same name as a field in the currently selected database file (not recommended), dBASE only sees the field unless the memvar *prefix* (M) is used (chapter 17). However, there is no ambiguity in using a macro-memvar because the macro cannot be used with a field name, and therefore dBASE knows to use the macro-memvar (still not recommended).

VOCABULARY

Operators

None.

Functions

#

    #
        [II] To determine the record number of the current record.

*

    *
        [II] To determine whether the current record is marked for deletion.

BOF()

    BOF( )
        [III] To determine whether the record pointer is at the beginning of the file.

DELETED()

    DELETED( )
        [III] To determine whether the current record is marked for deletion.

EOF

    EOF
        [II] To determine whether the record pointer is at the end of the file.

EOF()

    EOF( )
        [III] To determine whether the record pointer is at the end of the file.

RECNO()

    RECNO( )
        [III] To determine the record number of the current record.

SET parameters

None.

Commands

COPY

COPY STRUCTURE TO <database filename>
[III/II] To create an empty database file with the same structure as the currently selected database file.

COPY STRUCTURE TO <database filename> ;
                  FIELDS <field name> {,<field name>}
[III/II] To create an empty database file with a partial structure of the currently selected database file.

COPY TO <database filename> ;
       FIELDS <field name> {,<field name>} ;
       [<database parameter>]
[III/II] To create another database file with a partial structure of the currently selected database file.

COPY TO <database filename> [<database parameter>]
[III/II] To create another database file with the same structure as the currently selected database file.

COPY TO <structure-extended filename> ;
       [FIELDS <field name> {,<field name>}] ;
       STRUCTURE EXTENDED
[III/II] To modify [specified fields in] a database structure under program control.

CREATE

CREATE [<database filename>]
[III/II] To begin a new database file in the interactive mode.

CREATE [<database filename>] FROM <structure-extended filename>
[III/II] To begin a new database file in program mode.

DIRECTORY

DIRECTORY [[ON] <drive designator>] [TO PRINT]
[III] To look at a listing of database files [on another drive] [and output to the printer].

DISPLAY

DISPLAY FILES [ON <drive designator>]
[III/II] To display the database files [on another drive].

DISPLAY STRUCTURE
[III/II] To review the structure of a database file.

JOIN

JOIN TO <new filename> FOR <logical expression>
[II] To create a third database file from two others.

JOIN TO <new filename> FOR <logical expression> ;
      FIELDS <field name list>
[II] To create a database file with specified fields from two others.

JOIN WITH <alias name> TO <new filename> ;
      FOR <logical expression>
[III] To create a third database file from two others.

JOIN WITH <alias name> TO <new filename> ;
      FOR <logical expression> FIELDS <field name list>
[III] To create a third database file with specified fields from two others.

LIST

LIST FILES [ON <drive designator>]
[III/II] To get a list of database files [on another drive].

LIST STRUCTURE
[III/II] To review the structure of a database file.

MODIFY

MODIFY STRUCTURE
[III/II] To modify a database structure interactively.

SORT

SORT ON <field name> TO <new filename> [<sort parameter>]
[II] To create a new, sorted database file from the currently selected one.

SORT TO <new filename> ON <field name> [<sort parameter>] ;
                       { ,<field name> [<sort parameter>] } ;
                       [<database parameter>]
[III] To create a new, sorted database file with specified fields from the currently selected one.

TOTAL

```
TOTAL ON <key field name> TO <new filename> ;
       [<database parameter>]
```
   [III/II] To place key field sums in another database file.

```
TOTAL ON <key field name> TO <new filename> ;
       [<database parameter>] FIELDS <field name list>
```
   [III/II] To place key sums in another database file with specified fields only.

Other Resources

None.

ALGORITHMS

Damaged Files

When a file is open, it is vulnerable to damage from a variety of causes. When a database file has been damaged, the easiest and most reliable solution is to use the most recent backup file. Often, some data will have to be re-entered, and this is one reason we recommend frequent backups (chapter 12). In cases where you feel a need to attempt to save the data in the damaged file, there are several methods you can try, although it is possible that none will work. The damage can be to the file's header, body, or both.

Damage to the file's body is likely if you have a database file that says it has more records in it when you LIST FILES or LIST STRUCTURE than when you try to simply LIST the contents of that file. It probably has an end-of-file marker (^Z, 1A hex) embedded before the actual end of file. The most common cause of this is exiting from dBASE without executing a QUIT command, and therefore not closing the files that are open. The EOF marker is not removed from its prior position, and any recently entered data may be either lost or irretrievable. This happens most often when there is an inadvertent system reset during a working session, or when you change the disk without properly closing the files. *Never intentionally exit from dBASE without issuing the QUIT command.*

To recover data in a file with a misplaced EOF marker, reconstruct the file using the COPY and APPEND commands. Reminder: always have a backup copy of any file on which you are working.

```
USE <Sickfile>
*
* Copy out first part (before the EOF)...
COPY TO <Goodfile>
*
* Skip past the EOF...
GO <current record number> + 2
* <current record number> ::= RECNO() in III, # in II.
*
* Copy out last part (after the EOF)...
COPY NEXT <n> TO <Tempfile>
* <n> ::= maximum number of records in the file, or more...
*
```

```
* Use file with first part, and
* append from the file with last good part...
USE <Goodfile>
APPEND FROM <Tempfile>
*
* Close the file to save the changes...
* CLEAR in II, CLEAR ALL in III
```

The <Goodfile> can now be RENAMEd, and the bad and temporary files deleted. If there is more than one embedded EOF, you can modify this routine to copy out the data between EOFs, or change the code that skips past the EOF to GO <current record number> plus <x>, where <x> is a number large enough to get past all the embedded EOFs.

The file's header can also get corrupted, or fail to get updated. This is true when the file's header says that there are less records than you can see when you LIST the entire file. Fixes for this situation are in Technical Support Notes 16 and 36 in appendix F.

Large Files

dBASE II allows datafiles as large as eight megabytes, while dBASE III allows up to one gigabyte. In both cases, *one* of the computer's mass storage devices must be big enough to hold the entire file, or the file must be broken down into smaller files that will each fit on one disk, whether floppy or hard. See chapter 19, "Using Multiple Files and Disks."

An easy way to condense database files for backup/archival storage or data transmission is to use the DELIMITED parameter of the COPY command which trims all the trailing blanks. This can reduce file size tremendously, usually around fifty percent. This command is covered in chapters 19 and 20. Note that the compressed file is a text file. The extension .TXT is the default unless otherwise specified. This file does not contain the header and must be APPENDed back into a database file with the appropriate structure before it can be USEd by dBASE. In dBASE II, there is only one syntax regardless of which delimiter is used:

```
APPEND FROM <Filename> DELIMITED
```

In dBASE III, the delimiter *must* be specified if it is anything other than a single quotation mark ('):

```
APPEND FROM <Filename> DELIMITED WITH <delimiter>
```

Obviously, you also want to store or transmit the structure of the database file along with the text file. Create this with the COPY STRUCTURE command.

The public domain utilities SQ and USQ work very well in compressing, or "squeezing," database files, often resulting in a seventy percent reduction in size.

Periodic Files

In some applications, a new database file is desirable periodically. In this dBASE II example, the application calls for a new file every month. The operator enters the month and year of the data to be entered, and the program checks for a file with that date in the filename. If no file exists for that month, this algorithm will create one.

```
* dBASE II...
*
* Prompt for the file to use...
STORE T TO select
DO WHILE select
   STORE "   " TO t:month,t:year
   @  5, 9 SAY "Enter the month and year of the data to enter."
   @  7,17 SAY "Month " GET t:month PICTURE [##]
   @  7,31 SAY "<Ctrl-C> to return to main menu."
   @  8,17 SAY "Year  " GET t:year  PICTURE [##]
   READ
   CLEAR GETS
   @ 10,0
   *
   DO CASE
      *
      CASE t:month = "   " .AND. t:year = "   "
      * Branch to exit to main menu if there is no entry...
         RELEASE ALL LIKE t:*
         RETURN
      *
      CASE VAL(t:month) < 1  .OR. VAL(t:month) > 12 .OR.;
           VAL(t:year)  < 83 .OR. VAL(t:year)  > 98
      * Branch to trap invalid entries...
         @ 10,22 SAY "Invalid entry --please re-enter..."
         LOOP
      *
      CASE VAL(t:month) < 10
      * Branch to format leading zero in month...
         STORE "0" + STR(VAL(t:month),1) TO t:month
   ENDCASE
   *
   * Set up filename in the format PL_<mm>-<yy>
   * where <mm> ::= month, and <yy> ::= year...
   STORE "PL_" + t:month + "-" + t:year TO t:use:file
   *
   * Verify existence of file, exit loop if file exists...
   IF FILE("&t:use:file")
      STORE F TO select
   ELSE
      * Prompt to create new file or re-enter the date...
      @ 10,20 SAY "I cannot find the file " + t:use:file + ".DBF."
      @ 12, 7 SAY "Press <C> to Create this file, " + ;
                  "or any other key to re-enter..."
      STORE "?" TO t:waiting
      @ 12,69 GET t:waiting
      READ
      CLEAR GETS
      @ 10, 0
```

```
        @ 12, 0
        *
        * Branch to create a new placement file...
        IF !(t:waiting) = "C"
            @  7,31
            @ 10,15 SAY "Just a moment, while I prepare the files..."
            USE PL_place
            COPY STRUCTURE TO &t:use:file
            STORE F TO select
        ENDIF
    ENDIF
    *
ENDDO [WHILE select]
*
* Clear the used part of the screen...
@  5,0
@  7,0
@  8,0
@ 10,0
@ 12,0
*
* Open the file for processing by another routine...
USE &t:use:file
*
* EOA
```

More Fields per Record

Adhering to the design rules in chapter 9 will usually eliminate the need for more fields than dBASE allows (128 in III, 32 in II). However, there will still be applications where more fields are needed, particularly in dBASE II. There are two ways to accomplish this, subfields and additional files. Because dBASE II only allows two files open and LINKAGE between them is limited, we use subfields when necessary.

The use of subfields in a database file requires that there be additional room in bytes remaining in the record, even though the maximum number of fields are used. This technique requires that some fields, preferably character type, are combined into one field which *must* be character type. The awkwardness can be kept to a minimum if a fixed length is designated for each subfield within the field. For example, if we have a name and address database with this structure:

Field	Field name	Type	Width	Dec
1	FNAME	Character	15	
2	LNAME	Character	15	
3	ADDRESS	Character	30	
4	CITY	Character	15	
5	STATE	Character	2	
6	ZIP	Character	9	
** Total **			87	

We could combine both the first and last name into one full name, and combine the rest into one full address like this:

```
Field  Field name  Type        Width   Dec
   1   FULL_NAME   Character     30
   2   FULL_ADDR   Character     56
** Total **                      87
```

All we need to know is the number of bytes reserved for each subfield in a field, and we can both add data to the field and report on the data with the substring function (see chapter 16, "Character"). For example, this will display the *City* subfield from the *Full_address* field:

```
? TRIM( SUBSTR( Full_addr, 31, 15 ))
```

Use the TRIM() function when reporting on subfields to eliminate the trailing blanks, if any. To replace the data in a subfield, TRIM() must not be used:

```
REPLACE Full_addr WITH SUBSTR(Full_addr, 1, 30) +;
        <replacement expression> + SUBSTR(Full_addr, 46)
```

<replacement expression> ::= Character type with length of 15.

Work-Arounds

In dBASE III, the ten work areas are numbered from one through ten and have alias names from A through J. These alias initials prevent the USE of a file with the same name. For example, if you create a database file with the name A.DBF and attempt to execute the command USE A, you will get the error message "ALIAS name already in use."

Related Algorithms

1. In dBASE II, there is no way to determine the amount of space remaining on a disk. The programs Diskstat and Dos-stat in appendix D can be used for this purpose.
2. See Preallocating Disk Space under Algorithms in subchapter "Changing the Data" below.

DATABASE FILE HANDLING—
OPENING AND CLOSING

Opening a data file marks the beginning of a process which is not complete until the file is closed. Closing a data file is the most important form of restoring the environment, since the data in a database file is at risk during the entire time that the file is open. This risk can come about in several ways: an operator may remove a disk at the wrong time, or a programmer may neglect to work around a bug in dBASE, or a power failure, static electricity, or any number of other problems.

When a data file is first opened, dBASE places the header in memory so that it knows immediately the field variable names as well as the locations where each field and record begins and ends. dBASE also reads in as much of the file following the header as will fit in the buffers ("dBASE Buffers" in chapter 12). This allows the use of larger files than will fit in memory because, as more of the file is scanned, new data from the disk is brought into the buffers.

All additions and changes to a database file are being done in these temporary buffers in the computer's volatile memory. Even though dBASE II saves its buffers when it needs them and dBASE III saves its buffers during periods of inactivity, neither header gets updated until the file is closed. Therefore, at least *some* of any work done in a data file remains vulnerable in memory *until the file is closed*. The rule of thumb is to open a database file only when you must and close it just as soon as you can.

These commands open a data file in the currently selected work area, and close the one data file that is already open *in that area*:

```
CREATE [<database filename>]
USE <database filename>
```

This command closes an open data file in the currently selected work area *only*, and does not open another one:

```
USE
```

This command closes all open data files regardless of their work area location:

```
CLOSE DATABASES [III]
```

These commands close all open data files regardless of their work area location *and* release all active memory variables:

```
CLEAR          [II]
CLEAR ALL      [III]
QUIT
```

Work areas are discussed in subchapter "Multiple Files" below.

The CREATE command can be misleading in dBASE II because it closes the newly CREATEd data file when the process of creation is finished. This is the *only* time dBASE ever closes a database file automatically. At all other times, it is up to the programmer or operator to take care of this important task. The CREATE command in dBASE III is more consistent with the rest of the language in that it leaves the file open.

Whenever a data file is opened, the record pointer is positioned to the *top* record in the file (subchapter "Moving Around" below). The top record may not be record number one if the data file is opened with an index file (subchapter "Ordering the File" below).

A data file may be closed and reopened periodically in order to save new work to the disk and continue working in that file. This is highly recommended during lengthy operations in a file whether these operations are taking place from a program or the dot prompt. Simply USE the same file that is already open.

When a file is closed and reopened, the record pointer will be moved. In order to return the record pointer to a prior position, the current record number is saved before the file is closed. For example, say the file is open and positioned somewhere in the middle:

```
* dBASE III...
*
STORE RECNO() TO recn
CLOSE DATABASES
*
USE Datafile
GO recn

* dBASE II...
*
STORE # TO recn
CLEAR
*
USE Datafile
GO recn
```

This is also useful in applications using more files than are allowed to be open simultaneously (subchapter "Multiple Files" below).

VOCABULARY

Operators

None.

Functions

FILE()

```
FILE(<filename>)
```
    [III/II] To determine whether a file exists on the disk. <filename> is a character expression.

SET parameters

None.

Commands

CLEAR

CLEAR
[II] To close all open files, select the PRIMARY work area, and release all active memory variables.

CLEAR ALL
[III] To close all open files, select work area number one, and release all active memory variables.

CLOSE

CLOSE DATABASES
[III] To close all open database and their associated index and format files, and select work area number one.

CREATE

CREATE [<database filename>]
[III/II] To begin a new database file in the interactive mode.

CREATE [<database filename>] FROM <structure-extended filename>
[III/II] To begin a new database file in program mode.

USE

USE <database filename>
[III/II] To open a database file, or to save changes in the currently open database file to the disk.

USE <database filename> ALIAS <alias name>
[III/II] To open a database file, or to save changes in the currently open database file to the disk. And to specify an <alias name> other than <database filename>.

USE <database filename> INDEX <index filename> ;
                             {,<index filename>}
[III/II] To open a database file with an index, or to save changes in the currently open indexed database file to the disk.

USE <database filename> INDEX <index filename> ;
                             {,<index filename>} ;
                             ALIAS <alias name>
[III/II] To open a database file with an index, or to save changes in the currently open indexed database file to the disk. And, to specify an <alias name> other than <database filename>.

Other Resources

None.

ALGORITHMS

Periodic File Saving

Keep a counter during data entry or editing in order to close and reopen the file every so often. The number of operations that you will allow between reopenings is determined by two opposing factors:

1. How much data are you willing to lose should a catastrophe occur?
2. How often are you willing to wait for the operation of writing to the disk?

Your choice will be a balance of these, and is best determined by experimentation. This sample demonstrates a counter technique for reopening every twenty-five iterations:

```
STORE 1 TO counter
DO WHILE <condition>
    <entry or edit commands for one record>
    IF counter = 25
        USE <database filename>
        STORE 1 TO counter
    ENDIF
    STORE counter + 1 TO counter
ENDDO
```

In order to keep a running total of all the iterations instead of resetting the counter, a synthesized modulus function can be used:

```
STORE 1 TO counter
DO WHILE <condition>
    <entry or edit commands for one record>
    IF counter - INT(counter/25)*25 = 0
        USE <database filename>
    ENDIF
    STORE counter + 1 TO counter
ENDDO
```

Subroutines

Following the examples of the working environment and memory variables, open data files are usually left open when calling subroutines that use them, or when these subroutines are so brief and so infrequently called that there is little risk. This is most convenient because the data files will still be open on return from the subroutine.

If it is necessary for the subroutine to close a data file that was previously open, the record number is saved before closing. When program control is about to return to the calling routine, the environment is restored by opening the file and positioning the record pointer to the saved record number (see details of this subchapter above).

Work-Arounds

1. In dBASE II, version 2.3x, there are some conditions under which using MODIFY COMMAND while there is an open database file will cause data to be transferred to the command file. Close all data files before using MODIFY COMMAND.

2. In dBASE II, version 2.4, there are some conditions under which the use of the FILE() function while there are open data files can cause the disappearance of files from the directory. Close all data files before using the FILE() function.

3. In order to save a file by reopening it under some operating systems (like MP/M), it may be necessary to first execute a USE with no argument and then execute the USE <filename> in order to avoid a FILE IS CURRENTLY OPEN error. This is not necessary in MS- or PC-DOS.

Related Algorithms

Closing Multiple Files in subchapter "Multiple Files" below.

DATABASE FILE HANDLING–ADDING DATA

Data should always be fully error-trapped before being added to a database file in order to preserve the integrity of the file. In this way, there need never be a concern for the accuracy of data when printing reports or reviewing the file. See chapter 18, "Input."

The only way to add data to a database file from another file is with the APPEND FROM <filename> command. However, there are at least five ways to add data to a database file from the keyboard, each of which has specific advantages and disadvantages.

Interactive mode. The operator is actually in control and can move around in the data file at will:

```
APPEND
* (Can also add data with BROWSE in III)
```

This is the least desirable method in a programming situation because the operator is given almost unlimited access to the file and previously entered data. There can be no error-trapping without a format file (chapter 18, "Input"), and the integrity of the data depends completely on the operator who must learn the various control keys used in the interactive mode.

The advantage to this method is speed. It's "quick and dirty," which is to say that it takes very little code to implement and there is no waiting for error-trapping or saving the file.

Limited interactive mode. The operator enters directly into the file, but has access to one record only.

```
INSERT
```

In a programming situation, this is much better than the first method because the operator cannot get to existing data. However, there is still no error-trapping without a format file, and if the entry is incorrect and the operator fails to press <Ctrl-Q>, the bad entry will be in the data file and must be deleted. INSERTs are time consuming, and deletions pose additional problems (subchapter "Changing Data" below).

There is little, if any, advantage to using this method interactively since only one record can be added at a time. It is usually faster to APPEND and then place the file in the order desired (subchapter "Ordering by Data" below). When the data file is indexed, INSERT actually APPENDs a single record.

Program mode. The operator enters directly into the file, has access to one record only, and entries can be restricted by the programmer:

```
APPEND BLANK
{ @...GET <field name> <format option> }
READ
```

This is similar to the previous method of INSERT used with a format file in that the operator only has access to one record, which must be deleted if incorrectly entered. The additional advantage here is that by not using a format file, the entire screen is not cleared and fields can be READ individually and conditionally.

At the time of this writing, this does not work with memo fields in dBASE III. See the fifth work-around in chapter 18, "Input."

"Buffer" memory variables.   The operator enters into temporary memvars, whose contents can then be added to the data file by the programmer:

```
<initialize memvars>
{ @...GET <memvar name> <format option> }
READ
*
* If the entry is correct...
APPEND BLANK
{ REPLACE <field name> WITH <memvar name> }
```

This is perhaps the most popular method of data entry in program mode because it offers the most control and does not add the entry to the data file until it is correct. The @...GET command and its <format options> are covered in chapter 18, "Input." ACCEPT and INPUT are not usually used because they do not have options to restrict entry.

When data is entered into a memvar instead of a field, the programmer then places it in the field with the REPLACE command. However, REPLACE does *not* work on memo fields. In fact, the *only* way to add data to a memo field is to actually be in the field interactively, and read it in from an external file or key it in.

Temporary, or "buffer," file.   The operator enters into a temporary data file in one of the above ways. The contents of the buffer file can then be added to the actual data file by the programmer:

```
APPEND FROM <buffer filename>
```

There are two advantages to this method. If the operator makes an incorrect entry, it is deleted and therefore only the valid entries are APPENDed to the real file. Also, there is no waiting for index files to be updated during entry because the buffer file usually does not have to be indexed. Even with an index, the wait is shorter because the buffer index file is always significantly smaller than the real index file. Index files are covered in the subchapter "Ordering by Data" below.

The disadvantages are the additional space required for the buffer file and the time it takes to do the batch APPEND.

VOCABULARY

Operators

None.

Functions

None.

SET parameters

BELL

```
SET BELL <switch>
```
    [III/II] To enable/disable output to the computer's audio tone device.

CARRY

SET CARRY <switch>
[III/II] To enable/disable the database feature that copies the previous record to a new one during interactive APPENDs.

CONFIRM

SET CONFIRM <switch>
[III/II] To enable/disable the feature that forces the operator to press return in order to exit each input field.

FORMAT

SET FORMAT TO
[III/II] To close an open format file.

SET FORMAT TO <format filename>
[III/II] To specify a format for the database file fields during full-screen commands.

MENUS

SET MENUS <switch>
[III] To enable/disable the display of cursor control keys in full-screen commands.

Commands

APPEND

APPEND
[III/II] To add records to a database file without command file control.

APPEND BLANK
[III/II] To add records to a database file without placing the operator in full-screen editing mode.

APPEND FROM <database filename> [<condition>]
[III/II] To add records to a database file by bringing in data from another database file.

APPEND FROM <text filename> DELIMITED [<condition>]
[II] To add records to a database file by bringing in data from a delimited ASCII text file.

APPEND FROM <text filename> DELIMITED [WITH <delimiter>] ;
          [<condition>]
[III] To add records to a database file by bringing in data from a delimited ASCII text file.

APPEND FROM <text filename> SDF [<condition>]
> [III/II] To add records to a database file by bringing in data from an undelimited ASCII text file in System Data Format.

CLOSE

CLOSE FORMAT
> [III] To close an open format file.

INSERT

INSERT BLANK [BEFORE]
> [III/II] To insert a new record into an unindexed database file immediately following [or preceding] the current record, without placing the operator in full-screen editing mode.

INSERT [BEFORE]
> [III/II] To insert a new record into an unindexed database file immediately following [or preceding] the current record, and place the operator in full-screen editing mode.

READ

READ
> [III/II] To place the cursor in variables placed on the screen with @...GET.

READ NOUPDATE
> [II] To put the cursor in non-key variables placed on the screen with @...GET whenever there is an open indexed database file.

REPLACE

REPLACE <field name> WITH <expression> ;
   { ,<field name> WITH <expression> }
> [III/II] To place data in the current record of a database file in program mode.

REPLACE <field name> WITH <expression> ;
   { ,<field name> WITH <expression> } [<database parameter>]
> [III/II] To place data in specified records of a database file in program mode.

Other Resources

None.

ALGORITHMS

From Fields to Memvars

Initializing the memvars to use as buffers for data entry into the file can be done in two ways. The easiest method is to position the record pointer to a blank record (subchapter "Moving Around and

Finding Data" below) and STORE <field> TO <memvar> for each field. When a blank record is unavailable or inconvenient, memvars are initialized with literals (chapter 17).

Namegen2.prg (dBASE II) and *Namegen3.prg* (dBASE III) in appendix C create memvar names from the field names and generate the code for both types of initialization as well as the REPLACE statements.

From Memvars to Fields

Debugging is made easier by using individual REPLACE commands for each transfer from memvar to field:

```
REPLACE Name      WITH mname
REPLACE Address   WITH maddress
REPLACE City      WITH mcity
```

Once thoroughly debugged, they can be combined into one command statement which will execute faster:

```
REPLACE Name      WITH mname,;
        Address   WITH maddress,;
        City      WITH mcity
```

Be careful not to exceed the 254-character limit of the command line (including indentation). A convenient way to keep track of how close you are to the limit is that three full lines of eighty characters each total 240 characters, only fourteen shy of the limit.

Preallocating Disk Space

When records are added one by one over a period of time, the data file may be spread out over the disk rather than occupying one single, consecutive block of disk space. This increases the time required for disk access and can slow down some operations.

There are two ways to improve this situation. The data file may be periodically copied with the COPY command in dBASE or the operating system's *file* copy utility (not the *disk* copy utility). The other way is to APPEND a large number of blank records to the file at one time, and then add data by editing an existing blank record. This example preallocates space for a thousand records:

```
<create a new database file>
STORE 1000 TO limit
DO WHILE limit > 0
   APPEND BLANK
   STORE limit - 1 TO limit
ENDDO
<close the database file>
```

dBASE II does not release disk space back to the operating system once the size of a file is decreased. This behavior can be used to our advantage since we can DELETE ALL and PACK a file while still reserving the space on the disk. The advantage to doing this is that newly APPENDed records will use up the preallocated space before actually increasing the file size, and the file structure will only show as many records as are actually in the file. This is also useful in multi-user applications (chapter 23).

dBASE III does release unused space back to the operating system, thereby requiring that any preallocation technique leave the blank records in the database. They can be *marked* for deletion, but not PACKed.

Use Existing Blank Records

A single blank record in a data file is useful for initializing memvars, and can be used for additions to the file before adding more records. This is easiest to implement in a data file with an open index, which is assumed in this example:

```
* Find or create a blank current record...
FIND [                    ]
*
* dBASE III...
IF EOF()
    APPEND BLANK
ENDIF
*
* dBASE II...
IF # = 0
    APPEND BLANK
ENDIF
*
* Initialize memvars from blank record,
* or REPLACE data into it.
```

Work-Arounds

In dBASE II, version 2.3x, if a REPLACE statement exceeds the command-line limit of 254 characters, parts of the command file will be transferred to the database file. Do not exceed this limit, and always have a backup of any file on which you're working.

Related Algorithms

1. The second and fifth work-arounds in "Changing Data" below.
2. Adding data from "foreign" files (chapter 20, "Foreign and Closed Files").
3. The fifth work-around in chapter 18, "Input."

DATABASE FILE HANDLING–ORDERING BY DATA

Records are usually added to a database file with some form of the APPEND command, which results in a file ordered by the sequence in which data was entered rather than by the data itself. Latest entries are at the bottom; oldest, at the top. This is a data file's *natural order*. There are two ways to change the natural order and specify an order based on content. Data files can be INDEXed or SORTed, and both methods have their advantages and disadvantages.

SORTing

SORTing creates another database file the same size as the currently selected file. The new file is in the order specified in the SORT command.

<sort parameter>	::=	<dBASE II parameter> |/<dBASE III parameter>}
<dBASE II parameter>	::=	ASCENDING | DESCENDING
<dBASE III parameter>	::=	A | D | C
A	::=	Ascending order
D	::=	Descending order
C	::=	Case independent (ignores differences between uppercase and lowercase letters)

The advantage of having a fully SORTed database file is that the numerous sequential access commands will perform faster (subchapter "Moving Around and Finding Data" below). However, a truly sorted database file can be obtained with far greater flexibility by INDEXing and COPYing the source data file instead of SORTing.

As a technique, SORT's disadvantage is that the command does not accept an expression for its <key>, although dBASE III allows a <field list> and greater choice of options. In dBASE II, SORT is remarkably slow and overwrites the area of memory used for assembly language subroutines (chapter 22). Because we can simply INDEX and COPY with greater speed and flexibility, SORT is rarely used in dBASE II.

In dBASE III, SORT creates a temporary working file with the filename extension T44. When the SORT is complete, this file is erased, but there must be enough space on the target disk to accommodate it while SORTing. The target file is temporarily given the extension W44 until complete, at which time it is renamed to a DBF extension.

INDEXing

INDEXing creates an *index* file which is usually smaller than the currently selected data file (see Index File Size under Algorithms below). The default extension of an index file is NDX unless otherwise specified. An index file is ordered as specified in the INDEX command that creates it, and contains only the record number and <key expression> of each record in the data file.

<key expression>	::=	<dBASE III expression>
		| <dBASE II expression>
<dBASE III expression>	::=	Character type to 100 characters
		| Numeric type to largest accurate number
		| Date type, one date
<dBASE II expression>	::=	Character type to 100 characters
		| Numeric type to largest accurate number

The index <key expression> must be a fixed length, thus the TRIM() function cannot be used, and the substring function (SUBSTR() in III, $() in II) must include a consistent <length parameter> when used in the <key expression> of an INDEX.

When an index file is in use with a database file, all movement in the data file takes place according to the order of the index file. Commands that reposition the record pointer are all influenced by an open index file (subchapter "Moving Around and Finding Data" below).

The primary advantage of an INDEXed data file is the ability to position the record pointer directly to the first record whose data matches the <key expression>. This *random access* is remarkably fast (under two seconds) on even the largest data files. Another advantage is that the index file can be updated during entry and edit operations, thereby keeping the data file in order as the work is being done.

The disadvantages of using an index file are that sequential operations usually take longer unless the files are routinely maintained, and data entry takes longer because the index file must be updated. See Maintaining Order under Algorithms below.

This command creates a new index file for the currently selected database file and leaves it open:

```
INDEX ON <key expression> TO <index filename>
```

These commands open existing index files:

```
SET INDEX TO <index filename> {,<index filename>}
USE <database filename> INDEX <index filename> {,<index filename>}
```

These commands recreate open index files from scratch (not in dBASE II, version 2.3x):

```
REINDEX
PACK      (also removes records marked for deletion)
```

These commands close all open index files in all work areas:

```
CLEAR           [II]
CLEAR ALL       [III]
CLOSE DATABASES [III]
QUIT
```

These commands close any open index files in the currently selected work area only:

```
CLOSE INDEXES [III]
SET INDEX TO
USE
```

As with data files, some data written to index files will remain in RAM until the index file is closed. It is therefore advisable to close and reopen index files immediately after creating them and periodically as they are updated.

Each data file can have up to seven index files open, or "active," at one time. The first file in the <index filename list> is the "master" file which controls movement in the data file. Additional active index files have no effect on movement, and are active for the sole purpose of being automatically updated when data in their <key expression> is added or changed in the data file.

Index files are not affected, and may be closed, when data is changed in fields that are "non-key," or *not* included in the <key expression> of an index.

VOCABULARY

Operators

None.

Functions

None.

SET parameters

DELETED

> SET DELETED <switch>
> [III/II] To include or exclude records that are marked for deletion from being seen by commands that reposition a database file's record pointer. In II, only commands that allow the <scope> parameter are affected.

FILTER

> SET FILTER TO <logical expression>
> [III] To limit all database operations to records for which the expression is true.

> SET FILTER [TO]
> [III] To remove any existing FILTER.

INDEX

> SET INDEX TO
> [III/II] To close index files in the currently selected area.

> SET INDEX TO <index filename> {,<index filename>}
> [III/II] To open new index files with the already open database file.

UNIQUE

> SET UNIQUE <switch>
> [III] To create an index file with no duplicate key expressions.

Commands

CLOSE

    CLOSE DATABASES
       [III] To close all open database and their associated index and format files, and select work area number one.

    CLOSE INDEXES
       [III] To close open index files in the currently selected area.

INDEX

    INDEX
       [II] To retain the ability to FIND on the old <key expression> of a record whose <key expression> has been altered.

    INDEX ON <key expression> TO <index filename>
       [III/II] To order the database file according to its <key expression> and speed up the process of locating data.

REINDEX

    REINDEX
       [III/II] To rebuild the currently active index files.

SORT

    SORT ON <field name> TO <new filename> [<sort parameter>]
       [II] To create a new, sorted database file from the currently selected one.

    SORT TO <new filename> ON <field name> [<sort parameter>] ;
                    { ,<field name> [<sort parameter>] } ;
                    [<database parameter>]
       [III] To create a new, sorted database file with specified fields from the currently selected one.

Other Resources

None.

ALGORITHMS

Routine Maintenance

All applications using index files that add or change <key expressions> are benefitted by periodically copying the database file while the most frequently used index file is controlling the order. This creates a data file that is actually sorted in the natural order of the index <key expression>. Working with an indexed data file in the natural order of its index speeds up all sequential movements of the record pointer.

```
* Open the file with its most frequently
* used index file, and copy...
USE Oldfile INDEX Indxfile
COPY TO Tempfile
*
* Close the file, and rename both files...
USE
RENAME Oldfile  TO Holdfile
RENAME Tempfile TO Oldfile
*
* Open the new file with all of its index files,
* and create new index files from this new order...
USE Oldfile INDEX Indxfile, Indx2, Indx3, Indx4
REINDEX
* (dBASE II, version 2.3x, has no REINDEX command and
*  must therefore create the index files from scratch.)
*
* Check the new Oldfile and if it's OK, delete the Holdfile.
```

Reminder: Always have backups of all files on which you are working. When a new file is to completely replace an old one as in this example, keep a copy of the old file until the new file has been tested at least once in every routine that uses it in the "real world" of its application. Also, take the time to make a backup of the newly created data file before using it.

Case Independent Order: [II]

The SORT command in dBASE III has the /C option which ignores uppercase and lowercase differences in letters. The same result is obtained in dBASE II by INDEXing on the uppercase function !() of a character expression and COPYing to a new file.

```
* Make a backup copy of the Oldfile before doing this.
*
USE Oldfile
INDEX ON !( <character expression> ) TO Tempindx
COPY TO Newfile
USE
RENAME Oldfile TO Holdfile
RENAME Newfile TO Oldfile
*
* Check the new Oldfile.  If it's OK and there is a
* backup copy, delete the Holdfile and Tempindx files.
```

True Date Order

In dBASE III, an index file created on a date type field will naturally be in true date order:

```
INDEX ON Date_field TO Indxfile
```

In dBASE II, if dates are kept in the data file as MM/DD/YY, and the file is INDEXed or SORTed ON the date field, everything will be fine as long as there is only one year throughout the file. With more than one year, all dates with the same month will be grouped together for all years. This happens because the month is in the *most significant* position, and the year is in the *least significant* position.

True date order can be obtained by INDEXing on substrings of the date to create the index <key expression> in the order YY/MM/DD. This example assumes the name of the database field to be Datef:

```
* American date format...
INDEX ON $(Datef,7,2) +"/"+ $(Datef,1,5) TO Indxfile
*
* European date format...
INDEX ON $(Datef,7,2) +"/"+ $(Datef,4,2) +"/"+ ;
        $(Datef,1,2) TO Indxfile
```

Descending Date Order

Ordering a data file by date in descending order is handled differently in dBASE III than in dBASE II. These examples assume the name of the database field to be *Datef*:

```
* dBASE III...
* (Datef is a date type field)
INDEX ON CTOD("12/31/99") - Datef TO Indxfile
*
* dBASE II American date format...
INDEX ON STR( 99 - VAL( $(Datef,7,2) ), 2 ) +"/"+ ;
        STR( 99 - VAL( $(Datef,1,2) ), 2 ) +"/"+ ;
        STR( 99 - VAL( $(Datef,4,2) ), 2 ) TO Indxfile
*
* dBASE II European date format...
INDEX ON STR( 99 - VAL( $(Datef,7,2) ), 2 ) +"/"+ ;
        STR( 99 - VAL( $(Datef,4,2) ), 2 ) +"/"+ ;
        STR( 99 - VAL( $(Datef,1,2) ), 2 ) TO Indxfile
```

Note that FINDing in an index has to utilize the same algorithm that created the <key expression>.

Set Reverse On

Many paper filing systems are maintained by placing the most recent entry first rather than last. We commonly see this done with the contents of folders in file cabinets where the most recent dates are filed in front. Likewise, in some database applications, we often want to look at the last few entries that were made. To do this, we usually GO BOTTOM and SKIP backwards several records in order to display the latest entries. Here's another way:

```
* dBASE III...
INDEX ON -RECNO() TO <index filename>
*
* dBASE II...
INDEX ON -# TO <index filename>
```

Because the <key expression> is "minus record number," the data file appears to be turned upside down with the latest record on top and record number one on the bottom. New records appear to be APPENDed to the top of the file instead of the bottom, and whenever the file is opened with this index, the record pointer is always at the most recently added entry.

Ordering by Mixed Data Types

As with all expressions, the INDEX <key expression> must evaluate to a single data type, even though it can be made up of different types (chapter 16). This useful example results in a most significant ascending order on a character field plus a less significant descending order on a numeric field:

```
INDEX ON <character field name> + ;
     STR( <x> - <numeric field name>, <n> [,<d>] ) TO Indxfile
```

<x>	::=	The largest possible number that can fit in the <numeric field>
<n>	::=	Integer representing the total size (width) of the <numeric field>
<d>	::=	Integer representing the number of decimal places [if any] in the <numeric field>

This particular algorithm is useful in creating an alphabetical report of, for example, sales people and the multiple amounts of each one's sales listed with the highest amount first under that person's name.

Index File Size

Index files will usually be smaller than their data files. Exceptions to this occur when the <key expression> is nearly as large as an entire record, in which case the index file will be larger than the data file because index files leave room for expansion (chapter 7).

We can easily determine when there's not enough room on the disk to SORT, but how do we determine whether there is enough to create an index? This formula gives an approximate answer and serves well if you don't try to hold it literally to the byte. A full explanation is in "Estimating the Size of an Index File" in chapter 7. The program Ndx-size.prg in appendix C shows the calculation in both dBASE III and II.

```
* dBASE II...
( INT( <y> / INT( 509/(<x>+4) )+1 ) * 512 ) * 2
*
* dBASE III...
( INT( <y> / INT( 509/(<x>+8) )+1 ) * 512 ) * 2
```

<x>	::=	Integer representing the number of bytes in the <key expression>
<y>	::=	Integer representing the number of records in the data file

Work-Arounds

1. Index files opened with the SET INDEX TO command will not be synchronized with the database file unless the record pointer happens to be positioned to the record in the data file that matches the record at the top of the index file. Align the files with any command that repositions the record pointer and begins its operation at the top of the file, such as FIND, COUNT, GO TOP, LIST, etc.

2. In dBASE II, version 2.3x, index files get off to a bad start if created on an empty database file. Add a "dummy" record to create a new index.

3. dBASE II, version 2.3x, has trouble with some indexes that have a complex <key expression>. Combine the elements of the <key expression> into one additional field, and index on that field. Take, for example, a data file in which it is desirable to create this key:

```
INDEX ON Lastname + Firstname + Zipcode TO Complex
```

Add another field to the data file that is large enough to hold all elements of the <key expression>, and then:

```
REPLACE ALL Newfield WITH Lastname + Firstname + Zipcode
INDEX ON Newfield TO Simple
```

4. In dBASE II, any index created by using the substring function $() will lose the last character of the <key expression> if the optional <length> parameter is omitted. Always use the <length> parameter when INDEXing with a substring function.

Related Algorithms

1. "Estimating the Size of an Index File" in chapter 7.
2. Technical Reference Note 13 in appendix F.
3. Work-around number one in subchapter "Changing Data" below.
4. Work-around number two in subchapter "Copying To Another Data File" below.

DATABASE FILE HANDLING–
MOVING AROUND AND FINDING DATA

The current record pointer in a database file is moved in one of two ways, either sequentially or randomly. *Sequential* movement takes place one record at a time without regard to data content or record number. *Random* movement goes directly to a particular record according to its record number.

These commands produce movement of the record pointer in the currently selected database file without doing anything else, and are covered in this subchapter:

Sequential:

```
CONTINUE
LOCATE
```

Random:

```
FIND
GO
GOTO
<numeric expression>
SKIP [<numeric expression>]
SEEK   [III]
```

These commands produce movement of the record pointer in the currently selected database file while performing another process, and are covered in their appropriate subchapters:

Sequential:

```
APPEND
AVERAGE   [III]
COPY
COUNT
DISPLAY <database parameter>
INDEX
INSERT
JOIN
LIST
REPORT
SORT
SUM
TOTAL
UPDATE
```

Random:

```
EDIT <numeric expression>
```

Many of the commands that cause sequential movement of the record pointer have optional parameters in their syntax that limit the command to particular records only. These <database parameters> can be separated into two kinds, *scope* and *condition*. Some commands allow both scope and condition, some allow just one, and others allow only a subset of one or the other.

1. Scope limits the file according to its structural records.

<table>
<tr><td><scope></td><td>::=</td><td>ALL
| NEXT <n>
| RECORD <x></td></tr>
<tr><td align="right">ALL</td><td>::=</td><td>The entire database, all records.</td></tr>
<tr><td align="right">NEXT <n></td><td>::=</td><td>The next <n> records starting with the current record.</td></tr>
<tr><td align="right">RECORD <x></td><td>::=</td><td>The specified record, one only.</td></tr>
<tr><td align="right"><n></td><td>::=</td><td>In III, any positive numeric expression. In II, must be a literal or macro-memvar. The command will stop when it reaches the current record number + <n> or the end of file, whichever comes first.</td></tr>
<tr><td align="right"><x></td><td>::=</td><td>A positive numeric expression between one and the maximum number of records that are in the database file.</td></tr>
</table>

2. Condition limits the file by data content.

<table>
<tr><td><condition></td><td>::=</td><td>FOR <logical expression>
| WHILE <logical expression></td></tr>
<tr><td align="right">FOR</td><td>::=</td><td>Looks at every record from the top of the file to the bottom. Acts on those records for which the logical expression evaluates to true. As with all sequential access, this is considerably slower if the file is indexed.</td></tr>
<tr><td align="right">WHILE</td><td>::=</td><td>Looks at, and acts on, the current record and each successive record *until* the condition is no longer true. File must be indexed or sorted on a component of the <logical expression> in order for every record meeting the condition to be grouped together where they all can be acted upon.</td></tr>
</table>

ALL commands that cause movement of the record pointer, whether sequential or random, can be looked at as working in one of two ways: by data content or by physical record.

These commands move the record pointer according to data:

```
CONTINUE
LOCATE
FIND
SEEK    [III]
```

These commands move the record pointer according to record number:

```
GO
GOTO
<numeric expression>
SKIP
```

As with all character data comparisons, the SET EXACT flag will affect the outcome of FIND, LOCATE, and SEEK. See chapter 16, "Character."

Moving by Data

LOCATE starts at the top of the data file (unless NEXT <scope> is included in the syntax) and searches each successive record for the first occurrence where its <conditional expression> evaluates to true. LOCATE stops in one of three places:

1. It has found a match.

    <conditional expression> returns .T.
    EOF() returns .F.   [III]   (Not valid if <scope> was specified)
    EOF returns .F.   [II]   (Not valid if <scope> was specified)

2. It has reached the end of its specified <scope> without finding a match.

    <conditional expression> returns .F.

3. It has reached the end of the file without finding a match.

    <conditional expression> returns .F.
    EOF() returns .T. [III]
    EOF returns .T. [II]

In cases where LOCATE has found a match, it finds only the first record where the match occurs. To locate the next occurrence, the CONTINUE command is used. CONTINUE uses the same conditional test as did the most recently executed LOCATE, and behaves virtually the same except it begins its operation with the current record rather than the top of the file. The tests for a match with CONTINUE are identical to those with LOCATE. For example:

```
* dBASE III...
*
LOCATE FOR Name = mname
DO WHILE Name = mname .AND. .NOT. EOF()
   <commands for each record that meet the condition>
   CONTINUE
ENDDO

* dBASE II...
*
LOCATE FOR Name = mname
DO WHILE Name = mname .AND. .NOT. EOF
   <commands for each record that meet the condition>
   CONTINUE
ENDDO
```

Both FIND and SEEK require the existence of an active index file which they search for a match of their argument with the <key expression> in the index. If a match is found, the record pointer is moved directly (random access) to the corresponding record number in the currently selected database file. If not found, the record pointer is moved to a "dummy" record.

1. It has found a match. The record pointer is at the record number containing the match.

> EOF() returns .F. [III]
> # (record number function) returns a value greater than zero. [II]

2. It has not found a match. In dBASE II, the record pointer is at a "dummy" record number zero just before the top of the file. In dBASE III, the record pointer is at a "dummy" record just past the bottom of the file.

> EOF() returns .T. [III]
> RECNO() returns a number equal to the maximum number of records
>   in the data file plus one . [III]
> # (record number function) returns a value of zero. [II]

In cases where FIND or SEEK has found a match, only the first record where the match occurs is found. To locate the next occurrence, the SKIP command is used because all records with the same <key expression> are grouped together in the index. A conditional test must be made to see if the next record is still a match:

```
* dBASE III...
*
SEEK m_name
DO WHILE Name = m_name .AND. (.NOT. EOF())
   <commands for each record that meet the condition>
   SKIP
ENDDO

* dBASE II...
*
FIND &m:name
DO WHILE Name = m:name .AND. (.NOT. EOF)
   <commands for each record that meet the condition>
   SKIP
ENDDO
```

The only difference between FIND and SEEK is that FIND only accepts a literal character string, either delimited or undelimited, and SEEK accepts any expression: character, date, or numeric. In dBASE II where there is no SEEK, we use the macro substitution to place the contents of a memvar on the command line of the FIND statement. For example:

```
STORE "Data to be found" TO memvar
*
* dBASE III...
SEEK memvar
*
* dBASE II...
FIND &memvar
```

When data in the <key expression> could contain leading blanks, the FIND or SEEK argument must contain the same number of leading blanks and any macro-memvar must be delimited:

```
STORE "      Data to be found" TO memvar
*
* dBASE III...
SEEK memvar
*
* dBASE II...
FIND "&memvar"
*
* Both dBASE III and II literal...
FIND "      Data to be found"
```

When the <key expression> contains concatenated fields, the argument of both the FIND and SEEK commands must contain the same number of trailing blank spaces that may exist in between each of the data items in the index. This is most easily accomplished by initializing memvars to the appropriate width and using @...GETs instead of ACCEPTs to receive the operator's input of the data to be searched for. Also see Eliminate Separating Blanks under Algorithms below. For example, in a data file indexed on *Lastname + Firstname* where each field has a width of ten:

```
STORE "          " TO mfirstname, mlastname
@ <coordinates> GET mfirstname
@ <coordinates> GET mlastname
READ
CLEAR GETS
*
* dBASE III...
SEEK mlastname + mfirstname
*
* dBASE II...
FIND &mlastname&mfirstname
```

Moving by Record

If the database file has an active index or if a FILTER has been SET, the next logical record will not usually be the next sequential record number unless the data file is in the actual order of its index (see Routine Maintenance under Algorithms in subchapter "Ordering the File" above).

If the current record is the logical last, or "bottom," record in the database when SKIP is executed, the end-of-file flag will be set to true. dBASE II will continue to show the record number of the *bottom* record, while dBASE III will show the record number of the *last appended* record plus one.

The following examples assume a database file with 100 records and no index file in use:

```
USE <file>
GO BOTTOM
* dBASE III...
*    RECNO() ::= 100
*    EOF()   ::= .F.
```

```
*  dBASE II, all versions...
*     #         ::= 100
*     EOF       ::= .F.
*
*
SKIP [+<n>]
*  dBASE III...
*     RECNO() ::= 101
*     EOF()   ::= .T.
*  dBASE II, all versions...
*     #         ::= 100
*     EOF       ::= .T.
*
*
SKIP [+<n>]
*  dBASE III...
*     Error message: End of file encountered
*  dBASE II, all versions...
*     #   ::= 100
*     EOF ::= .T.
*
*
GO TOP
*  dBASE III...
*     RECNO() ::= 1
*     BOF()   ::= .F.
*  dBASE II, all versions...
*     #         ::= 1
*
*
SKIP -<n>
*  dBASE III...
*     RECNO() ::= 1
*     BOF()   ::= .T.
*  dBASE II, versions 2.3x and 2.4...
*     #         ::= 0
*  dBASE II, versions 2.41 and 2.42...
*     #         ::= 1
*
*
SKIP -<n>
*  dBASE III...
*     Error message: Beginning of file encountered
*  dBASE II, all versions...
*     #  ::= 1
```

When writing command files, we prefer to use the GO <n> form of the command for increased readability and understanding of the program. GOTO can be confusing to *Basic* programmers new to dBASE, and <n> by itself is very cryptic. The <database position> parameter of the GO command is either TOP or BOTTOM.

VOCABULARY

Operators

None.

Functions

#

> \#
> [II] To determine the record number of the current record.

*

> *
> [II] To determine whether the current record is marked for deletion.

BOF()

> BOF( )
> [III] To determine whether the record pointer is at the beginning of the file.

DELETED()

> DELETED( )
> [III] To determine whether the current record is marked for deletion.

EOF

> EOF
> [II] To determine whether the record pointer is at the end of the file.

EOF()

> EOF( )
> [III] To determine whether the record pointer is at the end of the file.

RECNO()

> RECNO( )
> [III] To determine the record number of the current record.

SET parameters

DELETED

> SET DELETED <switch>
> [III/II] To include or exclude records that are marked for deletion from being seen by commands that reposition a database file's record pointer. In II, only commands that allow the <scope> parameter are affected.

EXACT

> SET EXACT <switch>
> [III/II] To enable/disable the feature that forces a precise match of character strings compared with relational operators.

FILTER

> SET FILTER TO <logical expression>
> [III] To limit all database operations to records for which the expression is true.

> SET FILTER [TO]
> [III] To remove any existing FILTER.

Commands

CONTINUE

> CONTINUE
> [III/II] To find the next occurrence of <logical expression> in a previously issued LOCATE command.

FIND

> FIND "&<character memvar name>"
> [II] To quickly locate the contents of <character memvar name> in the <key expression> of an indexed database file when there are leading blank spaces in both the key and memvar.

> FIND "<character string>"
> [III/II] To quickly locate a <character string> with leading blanks in the <key expression> of an indexed database file.

> FIND &<character memvar name>
> [II] To quickly locate the contents of <character memvar name> in the <key expression> of an indexed database file.

> FIND <character string>
> [III/II] To quickly locate a <character string> in the <key expression> of an indexed database file.

FIND <number>
> [II] To quickly locate a <number> in the <key expression> of an database file which was indexed on a numeric key.

GO

<numeric expression>
> [III/II] To make the current record the one that has a record number of <numeric expression>.

GO <database position>
> [III/II] To make the current record the one that is at the logical beginning or end of the database file.

GO <numeric expression>
> [III/II] To make the current record the one that has a record number of <numeric expression>.

GOTO <database position>
> [III/II] To make the current record the one that is at the logical beginning or end of the database file.

GOTO <numeric expression>
> [III/II] To make the current record the one that has a record number of <numeric expression>.

LOCATE

LOCATE <database parameter>
> [III/II] To find a particular item in a database file.

SEEK

SEEK <expression>
> [III] To quickly locate an <expression> in the <key expression> of an indexed database file.

SKIP

SKIP
> [III/II] To move the record pointer forward one record.

SKIP <numeric expression>
> [III/II] To move the record pointer forward or backward a specified number of records.

Other

&

FIND "&<character memvar name>"
> [II] To use the contents of a variable as the parameter in FIND. Delimiters are used when both the index key and the variable contain leading blanks. The delimiters prevent any leading blanks in the variable from being truncated.

FIND &<character memvar name>
> [II] To use the contents of a variable as the parameter in FIND.

ALGORITHMS

For a While

When using sequential commands in an indexed data file, it is always faster to use the WHILE phrase in the <condition> instead of the FOR phrase. For example, if you have a transaction file indexed on account number and you are interested in LISTing all of the transactions for a particular account number, consider the difference between the following two methods:

```
1.    LIST FOR Acctnmbr = "7500"

2.    FIND 7500
      LIST WHILE Acctnmbr = "7500"
```

In the first example, dBASE will start at the beginning of the file and sequentially proceed through the entire file looking for entries with the account number 7500. If the data file is large, there will be noticeable periods of inaction before, during, and after the listing. In the second example, we use the FIND command to jump to the beginning of the transactions for account 7500 and then use the WHILE option to limit the operation to those transactions only.

Eliminate Separating Blanks

Particularly in the interactive mode, FINDing or SEEKing on a concatenated, or "complex," character <key expression> is made easier if the index file is created by concatenating with the minus rather than the plus operator. This shifts all separating blanks to the end (right) of the expression, thus allowing the search parameters to be keyed in one right after the other. For example, where each field has a width of ten:

```
INDEX ON Lastname + Firstname
FIND Tom        Rettig
*
INDEX ON Lastname - Firstname
FIND TomRettig
```

Because all <key expressions> must be the same width in an index file, the TRIM() function cannot be used. However, the minus concatenating operator shifts trailing blanks instead of removing them (chapter 16, "Character").

Binary Locate

A sequential search of large database files can take quite a long time with the LOCATE command as it is usually employed. However, through the use of a binary searching algorithm, this time can be shortened tremendously. In fact, this dBASE II example program will LOCATE an item of data in any size file in under eight seconds without an index file.

Why not INDEX the file and use FIND or SEEK, which takes under two seconds on any size database? Well, there are a number of instances where that is not as practical as it may seem. For instance, a file that infrequently changes the contents of a key, and is rarely added to, may be sorted once and its data accessed rapidly without the need for an index. This method also is useful in files which have an index, but occasionally need to be searched on a field for which there is no index.

There is one condition that enables this algorithm to work. The file *must* be in sequential order on the field in which you want to search. This may be accomplished by SORTing on the field to a new file, or by INDEXing on the field and then COPYing to a new file. Do not have an INDEX in use when DOing Locating.prg.

```
* LOCATING.PRG [II]
*
* A binary search to replace the LOCATE command
* when the key is in sequential order...
*
* is:found   ::=   .T. if a match occurs, current record is match.
* is:found   ::=   .F. if no match, current record varies.
*
* Establish working environment...
ERASE
SET TALK OFF
STORE F TO is:found
*
* Prompt operator for details of the search...
ACCEPT "Enter file name    -->" TO file:name
ACCEPT "Enter field name   -->" TO field:name
INPUT  "Enter data to find -->" TO search:key
* Note that the INPUT command requires
* character type data to be delimited.
*
* Open the file...
USE &file:name
*
* Branch for first or last records...
IF &field:name = search:key
   *
   * Found: it's the first record.
   STORE T TO is:found
ELSE
   * Maybe it's the last record...
   GO BOTTOM
   IF &field:name = search:key
      *
```

```
        * Found: it's the last record.
        STORE T TO is:found
    ELSE
        * Not there either, so let's search.
        * Set the top, middle, and bottom markers...
        STORE # TO high
        STORE 0 TO mid
        STORE 1 TO low
        *
        * Establish a loop for repetition...
        DO WHILE .NOT. is:found
            *
            * Branch to end search if record does not exist...
            IF mid = low + INT((high-low)/2)
                SET TALK ON
                RELEASE file:name, search:key, field:name, low, mid, high
                RETURN
            ELSE
                *
                * Set new middle marker; see where to go next...
                STORE low + INT((high-low)/2) TO mid
                GO mid
                DO CASE
                    CASE &field:name > search:key
                        *
                        * Field value is high, so set next block
                        * to lower half of existing block...
                        STORE mid TO high
                    CASE &field:name < search:key
                        *
                        * Field value is low, so set next block
                        * to upper half of existing block...
                        STORE mid TO low
                    OTHERWISE
                        *
                        * Found it...
                        STORE T TO is:found
                ENDCASE
            ENDIF [record does not exist]
        ENDDO [WHILE .NOT. found]
    ENDIF [last record]
ENDIF [first record]
RELEASE file:name, search:key, field:name, low, mid, high
RETURN
* EOF: Locating.prg
```

Note that this example has no error-trapping for an incorrectly entered filename or field name, either of which will cause an error.

Check for Duplicates

A common practice in many applications is to check new entries to see if they already exist in the database file. Duplicate trapping can be done for different purposes, each requiring its own algorithm. In some applications, duplicate entries are forbidden in order to prevent, for example, two parts from having the same part number. For example:

```
* dBASE III...
*
memvar = SPACE(6)
DO WHILE .T.
    * Prompt for an entry from the operator...
    @ <coordinates> GET memvar PICTURE [AA9999]
    READ
    CLEAR GETS
    @ <coordinates> SAY "Please be patient while I check for duplicates."
    *
    * Save the current record number in order
    * to return after searching...
    record_no = RECNO()
    *
    * Search for the entry, and test for a find...
    SEEK memvar
    IF .NOT. EOF()
        ? "This already exists, please re-enter..."
    ELSE
        *
        * Restore record pointer
        * to previous position, and exit the loop...
        GO record_no
        EXIT
        EXIT
    ENDIF
    *
    * Restore record pointer to previous position...
    GO record_no
ENDDO

* dBASE II...
*
STORE "      " TO memvar
STORE T TO condition
DO WHILE condition
    * Prompt for an entry from the operator...
    @ <coordinates> GET memvar PICTURE [AA9999]
    READ
```

```
    CLEAR GETS
    @ <coordinates> SAY "Please be patient while I check for duplicates."
    *
    * Save the current record number
    * in order to return after searching...
    STORE # TO record:no
    *
    * Search for the entry, and test for a find...
    FIND &memvar
    IF # > 0
        ? "This already exists, please re-enter..."
    ELSE
        * Change the <condition> to exit the loop...
        STORE F TO condition
    ENDIF
    *
    * Restore record pointer to previous position...
    GO record:no
ENDDO
```

In other applications, duplicate checking is done in order to display several allowable duplicates to the operator, so that the operator can select one. A practical example of this is a large mailing list indexed on *Lastname + Finitial + Zipcode*. The <key expression> structure minimizes the occurrence of duplicate entries, but the application must allow for valid duplicates because they could possibly occur. Another example is where there are multiple entries from which the operator may select one as in Multiple Screens under Algorithms in subchapter "Displaying Data" below.

Work-Arounds

1. In dBASE II, version 2.3x, the SKIP command will only skip forward when the data file is opened with an index file. It is not possible to SKIP backward in an indexed file.

2. In dBASE II, versions 2.3x and 2.4, when a NO FIND has occurred and the record number function (#) returns zero, a SKIP will position to the *bottom* of the file and a SKIP -1 to the *top*. In 2.41 and 2.42, a SKIP will position to just past the bottom record where EOF is true, and a SKIP -1 will position to the first record preceding the bottom record.

Related Algorithms

- RECORD OUT OF RANGE in appendix A, "Error Messages."

DATABASE FILE HANDLING–CHANGING DATA

Changing the data in a data file is very similar to adding data, except that a particular data item or record must first be located before it can be edited. See subchapters "Adding Data" and "Moving Around" above.

The only way to change data in a database file from data in another database file is with the UPDATE command. However, as with adding data, there are several ways to make changes from the keyboard, each of which has its own advantages and disadvantages.

Interactive mode. The operator is actually in control and can move around in the data file at will:

    BROWSE
    EDIT

As with adding data, this is the least desirable method in a programming situation because the operator is given almost unlimited access to the file and all of its data.

Limited interactive mode. The operator enters directly into the file, but access can be limited by the programmer to even just one record.

    CHANGE

In a programming situation, this is much better than the first method because the operator cannot get to existing data other than that which the programmer specifies. However, there is still no error-trapping without a format file in dBASE III, and in dBASE II, the CHANGE command is prompted and unformatted, and is therefore nearly useless in a programming situation.

Program mode. The operator enters directly into the file, has access to one record only, and entries can be restricted by the programmer:

    <position the record pointer to the desired record>
    { @...GET <field name> <format option> }
    READ

This is better, but if the operator makes an incorrect change and fails to abandon with <Ctrl-Q>, the file will have already been changed.

"Buffer" memory variables. The operator enters into temporary memvars, whose contents can then be REPLACEd into the data file by the programmer:

    <position the record pointer to the desired record>
    <initialize memvars from the current record>
    { @...GET <memvar name> <format option> }
    READ
    *
    * If the entry is correct...
    { REPLACE <field name> WITH <memvar name> }

As with adding data, this is probably the most popular method because of the degree of control it offers. The @...GET command and its <format options> are covered in chapter 18, "Input."

Temporary, or "buffer," file. This method used in adding data is rarely used for editing because the methods of getting from the buffer file to the real file are more complex, involving either the UPDATE command or an additional command file.

The *only* way to change data in a memo field is actually to be in the field interactively, and key it in or read it in from an external file.

VOCABULARY

Operators

None.

Functions

None.

SET parameters

BELL

    `SET BELL <switch>`
        [III/II] To enable/disable output to the computer's audio tone device.

CONFIRM

    `SET CONFIRM <switch>`
        [III/II] To enable/disable the feature that forces the operator to press return in order to exit each input field.

FORMAT

    `SET FORMAT TO`
        [III/II] To close an open format file.

    `SET FORMAT TO <format filename>`
        [III/II] To specify a format for the database file fields during full-screen commands.

MENUS

    `SET MENUS <switch>`
        [III] To enable/disable the display of cursor control keys in full-screen commands.

SAFETY

>   SET SAFETY <switch>
>   [III] To enable/disable the feature that displays a warning and gives the operator the option to proceed or abort whenever a command is issued that will overwrite or otherwise destroy data in a file.

Commands

APPEND

>   APPEND
>   [III/II] To add records to a database file without command file control.

BROWSE

>   BROWSE
>   [III/II] To interactively review/edit several database records at a time.
>
>   BROWSE FIELDS <field name> {,<field name>}
>   [III/II] To interactively review/edit specified fields in several database records at a time.
>
>   BROWSE [FIELDS <field name> {,<field name>}] ;
>   [LOCK <numeric expression>] [FREEZE <field name>] ;
>   [NOFOLLOW]
>   [III] To interactively review/edit [specified fields in] several database records and to establish the working environment of the BROWSE mode.

CHANGE

>   CHANGE FIELD <field name> {,<field name>} [<database parameter>]
>   [II] To review/edit selected fields in database records. Rarely used due to the awkwardness of the prompted line mode.
>
>   CHANGE FIELDS <field name> {,<field name>} [<database parameter>]
>   [III] To review/edit selected fields in database records.
>
>   CHANGE [<database parameter>]
>   [III/II] To review/edit database records. Full-screen mode in III, command-line mode in II.

CLOSE

>   CLOSE FORMAT
>   [III] To close an open format file.

DELETE

>   DELETE
>   [III/II] To mark the current record for deletion.

EDIT

EDIT
[III/II] To review/edit database records.

EDIT <numeric expression>
[III/II] To review/edit database records starting with a specified record number.

EDIT RECORD <numeric expression>
[III] To review/edit database records starting with a specified record number.

PACK

PACK
[III/II] To permanently remove records that are marked for deletion.

READ

READ
[III/II] To place the cursor in variables placed on the screen with @...GET.

READ NOUPDATE
[II] To put the cursor in non-key variables placed on the screen with @...GET whenever there is an open indexed database file.

RECALL

RECALL [<database parameter>]
[III/II] To remove the deleted flag from the database records.

REPLACE

REPLACE <field name> WITH <expression> ;
    { ,<field name> WITH <expression> }
[III/II] To place data in the current record of a database file in program mode.

REPLACE <field name> WITH <expression> ;
    { ,<field name> WITH <expression> } [<database parameter>]
[III/II] To place data in specified records of a database file in program mode.

UPDATE

UPDATE FROM <database filename> ON <key field name> ;
    REPLACE <field name> WITH <expression> ;
        { ,<field name> WITH <expression> } [RANDOM]
[III/II] To change data in the active database file from another [unindexed] file.

```
UPDATE FROM <database filename> ON <key field name> ;
ADD <field name list> [RANDOM]
```
    [II] To change data in the active database file from another [unindexed] file.

```
UPDATE FROM <database filename> ON <key field name> ;
REPLACE <field name list> [RANDOM]
```
    [II] To change data in the active database file from another [unindexed] file.

```
UPDATE FROM <database filename> ON <key field name> [RANDOM]
```
    [III/II] To change data in the active database file from another [unindexed] file.

ZAP

```
ZAP
```
    [III] To remove all records from a database file.

Other Resources

None.

ALGORITHMS

Work-Arounds

1. In dBASE II, version 2.3x, PACKing with an open index file will, on occasion, destroy most of the data in the database file. Close all index files before executing a PACK, and then recreate the index files with the INDEX command.

2. In dBASE II, all versions, the PACK command does not release any disk space back to the operating system, and files will occupy whatever number of bytes they did at their largest number of records. However, newly appended records will use up the currently unused allocated space before increasing the actual file size. COPYing the file with or without PACKing is the only way to release the space.

3. In dBASE III, PACK and ZAP will release unused disk space only after the data file has been closed. Database-text files (.DBT) will only release space if copied with the COPY command while in USE.

4. In all versions of dBASE, there is no warning or second chance when a PACK command is issued, even with SET SAFETY ON in III. Always have a backup before using PACK or any other command that permanently alters a data file, whether or not the command offers a second chance.

5. In dBASE II, versions 2.41 and 2.42, the current record is moved to the bottom of its <key expression> group in the index file when any changes are made to a variable that is not part of the <key expression>. This even occurs when the object of a READ command is a memvar and there is an index file open. Use the NOUPDATE option in all READ and REPLACE statements that operate on non-key variables. This cannot be prevented when using the interactive commands APPEND, EDIT, and INSERT with an open index file, so make any interactive changes without an index file and then SET INDEX TO and REINDEX.

6. In all versions of dBASE, any change to a key field of an indexed data file causes the record to be moved in the index. When the record pointer is then moved, it moves relative to the *new* position of the

record in the index. For this reason, any use of a <database parameter> in the syntax of the REPLACE command can produce undesirable results. When working with indexed files, REPLACE only the current record, and then reposition the record pointer. Or, close the index file, REPLACE <database parameter>, reopen the index file, and REINDEX.

Related Algorithms

1. Preallocating Disk Space in subchapter "Adding Data" above.
2. S-update.prg in appendix C is a program that simulates the UPDATE command.
3. Work-around number five in chapter 18, "Input."

DATABASE FILE HANDLING–DISPLAYING DATA

The process of displaying the data in a file usually encompasses some of the techniques discussed in chapter 18, "Output," and chapter 21, as well as other techniques in the subchapter "Moving Around" above.

These commands display data from the current record only:

```
@...SAY
?
??
DISPLAY
```

These commands display data from several records by sequentially moving the record pointer as specified in the <database parameter> of their syntax (described in subchapter "Moving Around" above).

```
DISPLAY <database parameter>
LABEL [III]
LIST
REPORT
```

The LIST and DISPLAY commands that display data as well as move the record pointer are useful in certain situations, mostly during interactive work. However, for maximum control in a programming environment, it is preferable to handle movement and display separately. For example:

```
<open data file>
<move to first record that meets a given condition>
DO WHILE <condition> .AND. .NOT. EOF()
    <display commands for one record>
    <move to next record that meets the condition>
ENDDO
<close data file>
```

In dBASE III, the display of memo fields is fixed to a width of fifty characters unless a REPORT form is used in which the width is specified otherwise. Memo fields can only be displayed with:

```
?
??
DISPLAY
LIST
REPORT
```

These commands collect, or "accumulate," data from several records. The results are displayed only when TALK is SET ON, or they can be stored in memvars for future display.

```
AVERAGE [III]
COUNT
SUM
```

VOCABULARY

Operators

None.

Functions

None.

SET parameters

DELETED

> `SET DELETED <switch>`
> [III/II] To include or exclude records that are marked for deletion from being seen by commands that reposition a database file's record pointer. In II, only commands that allow the <scope> parameter are affected.

EXACT

> `SET EXACT <switch>`
> [III/II] To enable/disable the feature that forces a precise match of character strings compared with relational operators.

FILTER

> `SET FILTER TO <logical expression>`
> [III] To limit all database operations to records for which the expression is true.

> `SET FILTER [TO]`
> [III] To remove any existing FILTER.

FORMAT

> `SET FORMAT TO`
> [III/II] To close an open format file.

> `SET FORMAT TO <format filename>`
> [III/II] To specify a format for the database file fields during full-screen commands.

HEADINGS

> `SET HEADINGS <switch>`
> [III] To enable/disable the display of field names in commands that display database data.

Commands

?

> **? <expression> {,<expression>}**
> [III/II] To output data in command-line, or "unformatted", mode on the next line.

??

> **?? <expression> {,<expression>}**
> [III/II] To output data in command-line, or "unformatted", mode on the current line.

@

> **@ <row>,<column> SAY <expression>**
> [III/II] To display an <expression> on the screen or printer.

> **@ <row>,<column> SAY <expression> FUNCTION "{<function>}"**
> [III] To display an <expression> on the screen or printer modified by the <function{s}>.

> **@ <row>,<column> SAY <expression> PICTURE <picture template>**
> [III] To display an <expression> on the screen or printer modified by the <picture template>.

> **@ <row>,<column> SAY <expression> USING "{<using symbol>}"**
> [II] To display an <expression> on the screen or printer modified by the <using symbol{s}>.

AVERAGE

> **AVERAGE <numeric expression list> [<database parameter>]**
> [III] To display the individual averages of specified numeric fields.

> **AVERAGE <numeric expression list> [<database parameter>] ;**
> **   TO <memvar name list>**
> [III] To store the individual averages of specified numeric fields to memory variables.

> **AVERAGE [<database parameter>]**
> [III] To display the individual averages of all numeric fields in a database file.

> **AVERAGE [<database parameter>] TO <memvar name list>**
> [III] To store the individual averages of all numeric fields to memory variables.

COUNT

> **COUNT [<database parameter>]**
> [III/II] To count the number of records in a database file [that meet a specified condition].

```
COUNT [<database parameter>] TO <memvar name>
```
[III/II] To store the result of count to a memvar.

DISPLAY

```
DISPLAY [OFF] [<database parameter>] [<expression> {,<expression>}]
```
[III/II] To display the contents of database files [without record numbers].

LABEL

```
LABEL FORM <label filename> [<database parameter>] ;
        [<label options>]
```
[III] To output an existing label form.

LIST

```
LIST [OFF] [<database parameter>] [<expression> {,<expression>}]
```
[III/II] To display the contents of database files [without record numbers].

REPORT

```
REPORT FORM <existing report filename> [<database parameter>] ;
          [<report options>]
```
[III/II] To output an existing report form.

SUM

```
SUM <numeric expression list> [<database parameter>]
```
[III/II] To display the individual totals of specified numeric fields.

```
SUM <numeric expression list> [<database parameter>] ;
TO <memvar name list>
```
[III/II] To store the individual totals of specified numeric fields to memory variables.

```
SUM [<database parameter>]
```
[III] To display the individual totals of all numeric fields in a database file.

```
SUM [<database parameter>] TO <memvar name list>
```
[III] To store the individual totals of all numeric fields to memory variables.

Other Resources

None.

ALGORITHMS

Interactive Display

A format file (chapter 18, "Output") with all @...SAYs and no @...GETs can be used with the usually interactive command EDIT (also CHANGE in III) to display records without allowing the operator to write to the file.

Multiple Screens

This dBASE II-2.4 example assumes that an indexed file with the fields *Key*, *Address*, and *Telephone* has been opened. All the records that match a <key expression> will be displayed on the screen, one line per record. When a screen is full (twelve records), the operator may either select one of the records on the current screen, look at another screen of more records, or return to the calling program. Displayed records are selected by a single menu letter which positions the record pointer to that record in preparation for calling another routine.

```
* Multiple screen routine [II, 2.4x]
*
DO WHILE T
   *
   * Prompt the operator for a key expression to find...
   <Do a subroutine for this entry>
   *
   * Find the first occurrence of a particular key...
   FIND &m:key
   *
   * Branch for no find...
   IF # = 0
      STORE ' ' TO t:waiting
      @ 22,23 SAY "There are no records for this key.''
      @ 23,24 SAY "Press any key to continue..." GET t:waiting
      READ NOUPDATE
      CLEAR GETS
      RETURN
   ELSE
      STORE T TO t:is:found
   ENDIF
   *
   * Display headings for the output...
   @ 6, 8 SAY "Key:"
   @ 6,30 SAY "Address:"
   @ 6,60 SAY "Phone Number:"
   *
   * Initialize memvars to control screens...
      * String of possible menu items (12 per screen)...
   STORE 'ABCDEFGHIJKL' TO t:menu:str
      * Line counter initialized for first item...
   STORE 8 TO t:line
```

```
     * Used as parameter in substring function to get
     * menu item from string of possibilities...
STORE 1 TO t:menu:num
       * Possible choices in operator entry trapping routine...
STORE ' ?' + $(t:menu:str,t:menu:num,1) TO t:selectns
         * Screen number used as macro
         * in memvar array of record numbers...
STORE '11' TO t:scrn:no
         * Number of the first record on this screen is used to
         * reposition record pointer when changing screens...
STORE # TO t:record&t:scrn:no
*
* A loop for each record on the screen...
DO WHILE t:is:found
         * Save the menu letter for this record...
     STORE $(t:menu:str,t:menu:num,1) TO t:menu:ltr
           * Save current record number in a memvar using the
           * current menu letter in the memvar name.  This is
           * used in the DO CASE structure below to position the
           * record pointer to a record selected by menu letter.
     STORE # TO t:menu:&t:menu:ltr
     *
     * Display the menu letter and pointer...
     @ t:line, 2 SAY t:menu:ltr
     @ t:line, 4 SAY "-->"
     *
     * Display data from the current record...
     @ t:line, 8 SAY Key
     @ t:line,30 SAY Address
     @ t:line,60 SAY Telephone
     *
     * Next record, and increment display line...
     SKIP
     STORE t:line + 1 TO t:line
     *
     * Branch for another menu item...
     IF .NOT. ( t:menu:num = 12 .OR. EOF .OR. (.NOT. m:key = Key))
        STORE t:menu:num + 1 TO t:menu:num
        STORE t:selectns + $(t:menu:str,t:menu:num,1) TO t:selectns
        LOOP
        *
     ELSE
     * Branch for another screen, eof, or end of this key data...
```

```
DO CASE
    *
    CASE t:scrn:no = '11' .AND. ( (m:key # Key)  .OR. EOF)
     * No more records, only one screen...
        @ 21, 0 SAY "There are NO more records for this key."
        @ 22, 0 SAY "Select a record by letter,"
        *
    CASE m:key = Key .AND. t:scrn:no = '11' ;
                    .AND. (.NOT. EOF)
     * More records, still on first screen...
        @ 21, 0 SAY "MORE records for this key on the NEXT screen."
        @ 22, 0 SAY "Select a record by letter, N = NEXT screen,"
        STORE t:selectns + 'N' TO t:selectns
        *
    CASE VAL(t:scrn:no) > 11 .AND. ((m:key # Key) .OR. EOF)
     * No more records, more than one screen...
        @ 21, 0 SAY "MORE records for this key on the PREVIOUS screen."
        @ 22, 0 SAY "Select a record by letter, P = PREVIOUS screen,"
        STORE t:selectns + 'P' TO t:selectns
        *
    CASE m:key = Key .AND. VAL(t:scrn:no) > 11 .AND. (.NOT. EOF)
     * More records, more than one screen...
        @ 21, 0 SAY "MORE records for this key " +;
                    "on both the PREVIOUS and NEXT screens."
        @ 22, 0 SAY "Select a record by letter, "+;
                    "N = NEXT screen, P = PREVIOUS screen,"
        STORE t:selectns + 'NP' TO t:selectns
ENDCASE
*
* Display the last line in the prompt...
@ 23, 0 SAY "SPACE = another customer, RETURN = Main Menu."
*
* Get the operator's selection...
STORE '\' TO t:select
DO WHILE .NOT. t:select $ t:selectns
    STORE '?' TO t:select
    @ 23,47 GET t:select PICTURE '!'
    READ NOUPDATE
    CLEAR GETS
ENDDO
*
* Branch for selection...
DO CASE
    CASE t:select = '?'
     * Restore environment and exit...
        RELEASE ALL LIKE t:*
        USE
        RETURN
```

```
        CASE t:select = ' '
      * Loop around to enter another customer...
        STORE F TO t:is:found
        LOOP
      CASE t:select $ 'ABCDEFGHIJKL'
      * View or edit a displayed record...
          *
          * Position record pointer to selected record...
          GO t:menu:&t:select
          *
          * Clear some room in memory, and do editing routine...
          RELEASE ALL LIKE t:menu:*
          <Do a subroutine to edit the record>
          *
          * Exit the inner loop to enter another key expression...
          * (This is a good example of where the EXIT command
          *   in dBASE III really speeds things up!)
          STORE F TO t:is:found
          LOOP
      CASE t:select = 'N'
      * Next screen...
          * Reset screen line counter...
          STORE  8 TO t:line
          * Increment screen number...
          STORE STR( VAL(t:scrn:no)+1 ,2) TO t:scrn:no
          * Save first record of this screen...
          STORE # TO t:record&t:scrn:no
      CASE t:select = 'P'
      * Previous screen...
          * Reset screen line counter...
          STORE  8 TO t:line
          * Decrement screen number...
          STORE STR( VAL(t:scrn:no)-1 ,2) TO t:scrn:no
          * Position to first record of previous screen...
          GO t:record&t:scrn:no
    ENDCASE
    *
    * Reset memvars for the next screen's menu...
    STORE ' ?A' TO t:selectns
    STORE 1 TO t:menu:num
    *
    * Clear the current screen leaving the header...
    @  8,0
    @  9,0
    @ 10,0
    @ 11,0
    @ 12,0
    @ 13,0
    @ 14,0
```

```
        @ 15,0
        @ 16,0
        @ 17,0
        @ 18,0
        @ 19,0
        @ 21,0
        @ 22,0
        @ 23,0
        *
      ENDIF
  ENDDO [WHILE t:is:found]
    *
    * Clear the header...
    @  6,0
ENDDO [WHILE T]
*
* End of multiple screen routine
```

Work-Arounds

● Items displayed in an <expression list> with the DISPLAY and LIST commands will behave differently in dBASE III than in dBASE II when their size varies from record to record. For example, in dBASE II, TRIM() always works regardless of where it is used. In dBASE III, it cannot be used to eliminate the separating blanks between items in an expression list.

```
    * dBASE III...
    *
    Structure for database : D:Names.dbf
    Number of data records :      3
    Field  Field name  Type       Width    Dec
        1  FNAME       Character     10
        2  LNAME       Character     15
        3  EXTENSION   Character      2
    ** Total **                      28
    *
    * Each full field appears separated by a space...
    . LIST
    Record#  FNAME     LNAME         EXTENSION
        1    Rosaline  Keenan        44
        2    Debby     Moody         20
        3    Roy       Moore         39
    *
    * Each expression in the expression list will line up
    * by disregarding variations in the expression length...
    . LIST TRIM(Fname), Lname, Extension
    Record#  TRIM(Fname)   Lname        Extension
        1    Rosaline      Keenan       44
        2    Debby         Moody        20
        3    Roy           Moore        39
```

```
*
* To eliminate this automatic separation between columns,
* concatenate items into a single expression in the list...
. LIST TRIM(Fname) +" "+ Lname, Extension
Record#  TRIM(Fname) +" "+ Lname          Extension
      1  Rosaline Keenan                  44
      2  Debby Moody                      20
      3  Roy Moore                        39


* dBASE II..
*
* (Data file has same structure as in the dBASE III example above.)
*
* Each full field appears separated by a space...
. LIST
00001   Rosaline    Keenan         44
00002   Debby       Moody          20
00003   Roy         Moore          39
*
* Variations in the expression length of one item affect
* the line up of all following items in the list...
. LIST TRIM(Fname), Lname, Extension
00001   Rosaline Keenan          44
00002   Debby Moody          20
00003   Roy Moore          39
*
* To compensate for varying length expressions, and make
* dBASE II behave like dBASE III, we use an algorithm to
* replace any removed blanks and restore the column format...
. LIST TRIM(Fname), Lname,;
      $( STR(0,80), 1, LEN(Fname) - LEN(TRIM(Fname)) ) ,;
      Extension
00001   Rosaline Keenan              44
00002   Debby Moody                  20
00003   Roy Moore                    39
```

See Space Function Simulator under Algorithms in chapter 16, "Character," for more on this algorithm.

Related Algorithms

- For a While in the subchapter "Moving Around" above.

DATABASE FILE HANDLING–
COPYING TO ANOTHER DATA FILE

All copying activity either creates a new target data file or overwrites an existing one. Data cannot be added to a file through the process of copying.

All copying commands act upon the currently selected database file only, with two exceptions: the JOIN command also uses a second open data file (subchapter "Multiple Files" below), and the COPY FILE command in dBASE III copies only closed files (chapter 20).

All copying commands that work on open data files produce movement of the record pointer according to the <database parameter> in their syntax (subchapter "Moving Around" above).

VOCABULARY

Operators

None.

Functions

FILE()

FILE(<filename>)
[III/II] To determine whether a file exists on the disk. <filename> is a character expression.

SET parameters

DELETED

SET DELETED <switch>
[III/II] To include or exclude records that are marked for deletion from being seen by commands that reposition a database file's record pointer. In II, only commands that allow the <scope> parameter are affected.

EXACT

SET EXACT <switch>
[III/II] To enable/disable the feature that forces a precise match of character strings compared with relational operators.

FILTER

SET FILTER TO <logical expression>
[III] To limit all database operations to records for which the expression is true.

SET FILTER [TO]
[III] To remove any existing FILTER.

SAFETY

> SET SAFETY <switch>
> [III] To enable/disable the feature that displays a warning and gives the operator the option to proceed or abort whenever a command is issued that will overwrite or otherwise destroy data in a file.

Commands

COPY

> COPY TO <database filename> FIELDS <field name> {,<field name>} ;
>   [<database parameter>]
> [III/II] To create another database file with a partial structure of the currently selected database file.

> COPY TO <database filename> [<database parameter>]
> [III/II] To create another database file with the same structure as the currently selected database file.

JOIN

> JOIN TO <new filename> FOR <logical expression>
> [II] To create a third database file from two others.

> JOIN TO <new filename> FOR <logical expression> ;
>   FIELDS <field name list>
> [II] To create a third database file with specified fields from two others.

> JOIN WITH <alias name> TO <new filename> ;
>   FOR <logical expression>
> [III] To create a third database file from two others.

> JOIN WITH <alias name> TO <new filename> ;
>   FOR <logical expression> FIELDS <field name list>
> [III] To create a third database file with specified fields from two others.

SORT

> SORT ON <field name> TO <new filename> [<sort parameter>]
> [II] To create a new, sorted database file from the currently selected one.

> SORT TO <new filename> ON <field name> [<sort parameter>] ;
>   { ,<field name> [<sort parameter>] } ;
>   [<database parameter>]
> [III] To create a new, sorted database file with specified fields from the currently selected one.

TOTAL

      TOTAL ON <key field name> TO <new filename> ;
            [<database parameter>]
      [III/II] To place key field sums in another database file.

      TOTAL ON <key field name> TO <new filename> ;
            [<database parameter>] FIELDS <field name list>
      [III/II] To place key sums in another database file with specified fields only.

Other Resources

None.

ALGORITHMS

Faster Copy

    Copying data files is faster with the operating system's file copy utility. In dBASE III, COPY FILE can be used, although database-text files (.DBT) have to be copied separately (chapter 20).

Work-Arounds

1. When using the TOTAL command, the fields in the currently selected file must be large enough to accommodate the full amount of the total that will be written to a *target* file. This is because the structure of the source file is used without modification to create the structure of the target file. Even though the target file can be precreated in dBASE II, there are other problems that are prevented by enlarging the numeric fields of the source file.

2. In dBASE III, the SORT command creates a temporary file which it uses during the SORT process and erases on completion. This requires additional space on the target disk drive over and above that required for the new sorted file alone. INDEX the source file and COPY. The index file does not have to be located on the target drive.

Related Algorithms

1. Copying with an open index file to create a sorted file is discussed in the subchapter "Ordering" above. Also see Routine Maintenance under Algorithms in the same subchapter and Preallocating Disk Space in subchapter "Adding Data" above.

2. Copying to non-dBASE files is covered in chapter 20, "Foreign Files."

3. The assembly language programs in appendix D, Diskstat and Dos-stat, provide a way to determine available disk space from within dBASE II.

4. S-join.prg and S-total.prg in appendix C are programs that simulate the JOIN and TOTAL commands.

DATABASE FILE HANDLING–
USING MULTIPLE FILES AND DISKS

Multiple Files

Movement and alignment of record pointers in multiple database files is a fairly simple process when the database is well designed and thought out. On the other hand, if your database looks like bouillabaisse, turn directly to Database Design (chapter 9) and start over.

Both dBASE III and dBASE II have the ability to open more than one database file at one time. dBASE III provides ten work areas, *each* of which can open one database file, one format file, and up to seven index files. dBASE II provides two work areas, each of which can open one database file and up to seven index files. Obviously, this capacity is also subject to the limits imposed by the operating system (chapter 12).

The work areas in dBASE II are named PRIMARY and SECONDARY. In dBASE III, they are called by the letters A thru J, the numbers 1 thru 10, or an <alias name> determined by the syntax of the USE command. Both dBASE III and dBASE II use the SELECT command to determine the currently selected work area:

```
SELECT <work area parameter>
```

<work area parameter>	::=	<dBASE III work area name>
		| <dBASE II work area name>
<dBASE III work area name>	::=	A | B | C | D | E
		| F | G | H | I | J
		| 1 | 2 | 3 | 4 | 5
		| 6 | 7 | 8 | 9 | 10
		| <alias name>
<alias name>	::=	<name specified in ALIAS option of USE command>
		| <filename of open database file if ALIAS not specified>
<dBASE II work area name>	::=	PRIMARY | SECONDARY

The currently selected work area defaults to PRIMARY in dBASE II and A or 1 in dBASE III whenever dBASE is first booted, and when any command that closes all database files in all areas is executed:

```
CLOSE DATABASES    [III]
CLEAR              [II]
CLEAR ALL          [III]
```

All commands that simply read from a data file can access data in files open in unselected work areas by specifying the <work area prefix> of any unselected file in their syntax:

```
@...SAY
?
??
AVERAGE [III]
```

```
COUNT
DISPLAY
LABEL    [III]
LIST
REPORT
SUM
```

<work area prefix>	::=	<dBASE III prefix>
		| <dBASE II prefix>
<dBASE III prefix>	::=	A | B | C | D | E
		| F | G | H | I | J
		| <alias name>
<dBASE II prefix>	::=	P | S
<dBASE III concatenator>	::=	->
<dBASE II concatenator>	::=	.
<dBASE III example>	::=	@ <coordinates> SAY B->Fieldname
<dBASE II example>	::=	@ <coordinates> SAY S.Fieldname

All functions, as well as commands that are able to write to a file or read its structure can access the data file in the currently selected work area only: (REPLACE can access an unselected data file only in the passive WITH phrase of its syntax.)

```
<all functions>
@...GET
APPEND
CHANGE
CREATE
DELETE
DISPLAY STRUCTURE
EDIT
INSERT
LIST STRUCTURE
MODIFY STRUCTURE
PACK
REPLACE <currently selected> WITH <unselected>
UPDATE
ZAP [III]
```

All commands that reposition the record pointer do so in the currently selected data file only:

```
AVERAGE [III]
CONTINUE
COPY
COUNT
DISPLAY <database parameter>
FIND
GO
GOTO <numeric expression>
```

```
JOIN
LABEL      [III]
LIST
LOCATE
REPORT
SEEK       [III]
SKIP
SORT
SUM
TOTAL
```

Movement in the currently selected data file can trigger corresponding movement in an unselected data file only by using the SET RELATION command in dBASE III or the SET LINKAGE command in dBASE II. In dBASE II, SET LINKAGE ON moves the record pointer in the unselected data file only during the sequential forward movement of these commands:

```
CONTINUE
COPY
COUNT
DISPLAY  <database parameter>
JOIN
LIST
LOCATE
REPORT
SORT
SUM
TOTAL
```

Keeping the record pointers aligned with SET LINKAGE in dBASE II requires that any random or backward positioning of the record pointer be done manually and separately in both files.

In dBASE III, SET RELATION is much more flexible, and any movement—sequential or random, forward or backward—in the currently selected file will produce movement in the unselected file to which a RELATION has been SET. When the unselected file is indexed, an established RELATION causes a SEEK to take place in the related file based on the specified <key expression> in the currently selected file. The usual tests for a match must still be performed on the related file (subchapter "Moving Around" above).

Multiple Disks

A single database file must fit on a single disk in both dBASE III and dBASE II. Any disk containing an open file of any type *must* remain in the machine all the while the file is open. If an application requires the use of more disks than will fit in the machine at one time, it must be designed so that files can be closed whenever the disks are changed.

In all versions of dBASE II running under CP/M, the RESET command is executed immediately *after* a disk is changed and before a new file is opened. RESET neither closes files nor alters the necessity of closing files before removing disks. RESET simply informs CP/M to expect a new disk directory, similarly to a <Ctrl-C> executed at the system prompt, but on the default drive only. Always SET DEFAULT TO the drive that is changing disks.

VOCABULARY

Operators

None.

Functions

None.

SET parameters

LINKAGE

> `SET LINKAGE <switch>`
> [II] To enable/disable sequential movement in one database to cause the record pointer to move accordingly in the unselected database file.

RELATION

> `SET RELATION INTO <alias name>`
> [III] To cause the <alias name> database file to continuously position its record pointer to the same record number as the currently selected database file.

> `SET RELATION INTO <alias name> TO <key expression>`
> [III] To cause the <alias name> database file, which is indexed on <key expression>, to continuously position its record pointer to the record that matches the <key expression> in the currently selected database file.

> `SET RELATION INTO <alias name> TO <numeric expression>`
> [III] To cause the <alias name> database file, which is not indexed, to position its record pointer to the record number equal to the <numeric expression>.

> `SET RELATION [TO]`
> [III] To cancel any previously specified relation.

Commands

CLEAR

> `CLEAR`
> [II] To close all open files, select the PRIMARY work area, and release all active memory variables.

> `CLEAR ALL`
> [III] To close all open files, select work area number one, and release all active memory variables.

CLOSE

    CLOSE DATABASES
        [III] To close all open database and their associated index and format files, and select work area number one.

DISPLAY

    DISPLAY STATUS
        [III/II] To find out the current state of the working environment.

LIST

    LIST STATUS
        [III/II] To find out the current state of the working environment.

RESET

    RESET
        [II] To tell CP/M that a disk has been changed. Same as ^C from the keyboard.

SELECT

    SELECT <work area parameter>
        [III/II] To specify the currently selected work area.

Other

->

    <command> <alias name>-><field name>
        [III] To specify a field in the current record of a database file that is in use in a work area that is not currently selected. To specify a memory variable by using the prefix M-> when there is a field of the same name.

   •

    <command> <work area designator>.<field name>
        [II] To specify a field in the current record of a database file that is in use in the work area that is not currently selected. To specify a memory variable by using the prefix M. when there is a field of the same name.

ALGORITHMS

Closing Multiple Files

In dBASE III, CLOSE DATABASES will close all database files without releasing memory variables or closing ALTERNATE files. In dBASE II, the only way to close an unselected data file without releasing memvars is to execute a USE command in each work area:

```
SELECT SECONDARY
USE
SELECT PRIMARY
USE
```

More Files Per Area

Ever since dBASE was born, people have asked how to use more than the number of files allowed open at one time. Although this is a very common request in dBASE II, some dBASE III applications may also use this technique because of operating system limits (chapter 12). The trick here is in the phrase, "at one time," as demonstrated in this dBASE II example.

To have more than two files open in dBASE II, one of the currently open files *must* be closed when the third one is opened. Since the only advantage to keeping a file open is to keep the record pointer at a particular record, just STORE the record number to a memvar. Then when you want to go back there, USE the file and GO to the memvar. For example:

```
USE File1
*
SELECT SECONDARY
USE File2
LOCATE FOR <condition>
STORE # TO f2:rec:no
*
USE File3
LOCATE FOR <condition>
STORE # TO f3:rec:no
*
USE File2
GO f2:rec:no
*
USE File3
GO f3:rec:no
```

This does take more time than it would if the files were kept open, and it takes more code to implement. Nevertheless, it is still easily accomplished once the method is understood. Note that the code shown is only an example and does not contain the required error trapping for times when the LOCATE command fails to find a match.

CHAPTER TWENTY

FOREIGN AND CLOSED FILES

Any file that is not a type used by dBASE is considered a foreign file to dBASE (see chapter 12 for dBASE files). Foreign files can be either *executable* or *non-executable*, and even non-executable files can contain executable, or " binary," code. dBASE itself is an example of an executable file, and considered in this context, it would be a foreign file. Command and database files are not foreign, and they provide examples of non-executable files: database files have binary code in their header, and command files do not. Of course, command files are executable within dBASE, but they are non-executable at a system level because their code is not in machine language (binary).

dBASE uses special options of the APPEND FROM and COPY TO commands to exchange data between database files and foreign files. In order for a foreign data or text file to be usable in a dBASE database file, it must have its data structured in one of two forms, either System Data Format or Delimited.

Files in *System Data Format*, also referred to as *SDF*, have fields with a consistent length from record to record and do not eliminate unused blank space. Each field is placed end to end with nothing separating, or "delimiting," them. Records are separated by a carriage-return/line-feed pair (0D, 0A hex).

Fields in *Delimited* files are separated by a comma. Because the length of fields is marked with this delimiter, unused leading or trailing blanks may be removed. Additionally, character type fields can be delimited with (surrounded by) quotation marks or any other character. The purpose in further delimiting character strings is so that they can contain commas without counting as additional fields. This optional delimiter around character fields must be a character that will *not* occur within the field. As with SDF files, records are separated by a carriage-return/line-feed pair.

Many software programs use binary information inside their data files in order to manipulate them efficiently. These include files created in programs such as Framework, Multiplan, and 1-2-3. They all use a binary header in their files in a way that is similar to how dBASE handles .DBF and some other files. In order for data from these foreign files to be usable in dBASE, their control information must be removed, and their data left in a form that is either SDF or delimited. If the software program provides a means to write its files' data out to a file in one of these formats (as does Framework), then that data can be easily read into a database file. However, if this feature is not provided in the software, then the files will have to be *converted* by an additional software utility program, which may exist commercially or may have to be written.

Occasionally, a data file will be constructed from a word processor such as WordStar, MultiMate, or Microsoft Word. The format of these files is usually SDF or delimited depending upon how they were entered. And, depending upon the word processor and the mode or features used, these files are usually free of control codes. If there are control codes in the file such as those used for page breaks or print formatting, they should be removed before the file is read into dBASE. The programs Fix.asm and Fix.a86 in appendix D strip unwanted control characters from files and replace them with a space (20 hex).

dBASE provides an option in the COPY command to write data from a database file out to a text file in either SDF or delimited form. Some software programs are able to read in these forms, and some are not.

Also, because of dBASE's widespread popularity, some software programs, such as Framework, provide a means to read in a dBASE II or dBASE III file directly without having to COPY TO an intermediate file first.

When the DELIMITED option is used with the COPY command, its syntax affects the resulting character fields. For example, given a character field with a length of five that contains the string "abc<space><space>", different results will be produced by different versions of dBASE:

Syntax:	II-2.3x:	II-2.4x:	III-1.00:
DELIMITED	,'abc ',	,'abc',	,"abc",
DELIMITED WITH "	,"abc ",	,"abc",	,"abc",
DELIMITED WITH '	,'abc ',	,'abc',	,'abc',
DELIMITED WITH ,	,abc,	,abc,	,,abc,,
DELIMITED WITH BLANK	N/A	N/A	abc

Figure 20-1

In all versions of dBASE II, the APPEND FROM...DELIMITED command has no WITH option. dBASE II doesn't care what character is used to surround character fields, it will bring in the data anyway. In dBASE III, however, if any character other than the double quotation mark is used to surround character fields, the WITH option of the APPEND FROM...DELIMITED command *must* be used.

A good way to tell whether the source file to be used in the APPEND FROM command will work is to use the same syntax options with the COPY TO command and see if the resulting file matches the format of the source file to be used. Identical syntax in each command will both read from and write to files of identical formats.

In dBASE III, memo fields will neither copy nor append with SDF or DELIMITED in the syntax. Date type fields copied with either option will result in a text file format of YYYYMMDD, which is also required when APPENDing. For example:

```
* dBASE III...
*
. LIST STRUCTURE
Structure for database : D:DELI.dbf
Number of data records :      4
Date of last update      : 09/08/84
Field  Field name  Type         Width    Dec
    1  CHARACTERS  Character        5
    2  DATES       Date             8
    3  BOOLEAN     Logical          1
    4  MEMOS       Memo            10
    5  NUMBERS     Numeric          7      2
** Total **                        32
*
. SET HEADING OFF
. LIST
      1  ONE    11/11/11 .T. Memo 1234.56
      2  TWO    02/02/02 .F. Memo 2222.22
      3  THREE  03/03/83 .T. Memo  333.00
      4  FOUR   04/14/84 .F. Memo   44.44
*
```

```
    . COPY TO D-1 SDF
           4 records copied
    . TYPE D-1.TXT
    ONE   19111111T1234.56
    TWO   19020202F2222.22
    THREE19830303T 333.00
    FOUR 19840414F  44.44
    *
    . COPY TO D-2 DELIMITED
           4 records copied
    . TYPE D-2.TXT
    "ONE",19111111,T,1234.56
    "TWO",19020202,F,2222.22
    "THREE",19830303,T,333.00
    "FOUR",19840414,F,44.44
    *
    . COPY TO D-3 DELIMITED WITH *
           4 records copied
    . TYPE D-3.TXT
    *ONE*,19111111,T,1234.56
    *TWO*,19020202,F,2222.22
    *THREE*,19830303,T,333.00
    *FOUR*,19840414,F,44.44
    *
    . COPY TO D-4 DELIMITED WITH BLANK
           4 records copied
    . TYPE D-4.TXT
    ONE 19111111 T 1234.56
    TWO 19020202 F 2222.22
    THREE 19830303 T 333.00
    FOUR 19840414 F 44.44
```

Notice that the DELIMITED WITH BLANK syntax in dBASE III produces a result without commas delimiting fields. In fact, it acts more like the SDF option, with two exceptions. One is that trailing blanks in character fields and leading blanks in numeric fields are truncated. The other is that a BLANK space separates, or delimits, the fields.

In the dBASE II COPY command, when the DELIMITED WITH option is used, both character *and* logical fields are surrounded with the additional delimiter. For example:

```
    * dBASE II, version 2.4x...
    *
    . LIST STRUCTURE
    STRUCTURE FOR FILE:  D:DELI     .DBF
    NUMBER OF RECORDS:   00004
    DATE OF LAST UPDATE: 09/08/84
    PRIMARY USE DATABASE
```

```
FLD        NAME       TYPE WIDTH   DEC
001     CHARACTERS    C    005
002     DATES         C    008
003     BOOLEAN       L    001
004     NUMBERS       N    007     002
** TOTAL **                00022
*
. LIST
00001   ONE    11/11/11 .T.  1234.56
00002   TWO    02/02/02 .F.  2222.22
00003   THREE  03/03/83 .T.   333.00
00004   FOUR   04/14/84 .F.    44.44
*
. COPY TO D-1 SDF
00004 RECORDS COPIED
* If we could type out D-1.TXT, it would look like:
ONE  11/11/11T1234.56
TWO  02/02/02F2222.22
THREE03/03/83T 333.00
FOUR 04/14/84F  44.44
*
. COPY TO D-2 DELIMITED
00004 RECORDS COPIED
* If we could type out D-2.TXT, it would look like:
'ONE','11/11/11','T',1234.56
'TWO','02/02/02','F',2222.22
'THREE','03/03/83','T', 333.00
'FOUR','04/14/84','F',  44.44
*
. COPY TO D-3 DELIMITED WITH *
00004 RECORDS COPIED
* If we could type out D-3.TXT, it would look like:
*ONE*,*11/11/11*,*T*,1234.56
*TWO*,*02/02/02*,*F*,2222.22
*THREE*,*03/03/83*,*T*, 333.00
*FOUR*,*04/14/84*,*F*,  44.44
```

In both dBASE III and II, when either SDF or DELIMITED is used in the syntax of the COPY or APPEND commands, a filename extension of .TXT is assumed if not specified otherwise.

Closed Files

Certain operations in dBASE require that the file they manipulate be closed at the time. The commands that operate only on closed files one at a time are:

```
COPY FILE        [III]
DELETE FILE      [II]
ERASE FILE       [III]
MODIFY COMMAND
```

```
MODIFY FILE    [III]
RENAME
TYPE           [III]
```

These commands can be used on files of *any* type, except MODIFY and TYPE which are used on text files only. In dBASE III, the copying, erasing, and renaming of files can be accomplished faster and with more flexibility and fewer keystrokes by RUNning the operating system's corresponding command from the dot prompt.

MODIFY COMMAND assumes a filename extension of .PRG in 16-bit systems, and .CMD in 8-bit systems unless specified otherwise. In dBASE II, DELETE FILE assumes a filename extension of .DBF unless specified otherwise. All other closed-file commands take the filename in the syntax literally.

Newly changed files do not reflect the changes in the directory until after the file has been closed. Commands that read the directory are:

```
DIR            [III]
DIRECTORY      [III]
DISPLAY FILES
LIST FILES
```

When used without the <file directory parameter>, these directory commands assume database files.

<file directory parameter>	::=	LIKE <filename skeleton>
		| <filename skeleton> [III]
<filename skeleton>	::=	{ <filename character> }
		{ <wildcard symbol> }
<filename character>	::=	Any character allowed by the operating system to be in a filename
<wildcard symbol>	::=	? | *
?	::=	Any <filename character>
*	::=	{ Any <filename character> }

<wildcard symbols> are used in the same way as they are with the operating system's directory command. Check your operating system documentation for details.

When used without the <drive designator>, these directory commands assume the current drive, and directory if applicable.

<drive designator>	::=	<drive>:
		| <drive>:<directory path> [III]
		| <directory path> [III]

In dBASE III, all commands that include a <filename> allow both a <drive> and <directory> in the syntax. In dBASE II, only <drive> is allowed.

VOCABULARY

Operators

None.

Functions

FILE()

> FILE(<filename>)
> [III/II] To determine whether a file exists on the disk. <filename> is a character expression.

SET parameters

ALTERNATE

> SET ALTERNATE <switch>
> [III/II] To start/stop sending screen output to a file.
>
> SET ALTERNATE TO
> [III/II] To close an open "alternate" file.
>
> SET ALTERNATE TO <text filename>
> [III/II] To create or overwrite a text file for recording what appears on the screen.

Commands

APPEND

> APPEND FROM <text filename> DELIMITED [<condition>]
> [II] To add records to a database file by bringing in data from a delimited ASCII text file.
>
> APPEND FROM <text filename> DELIMITED [WITH <delimiter>] ;
>   [<condition>]
> [III] To add records to a database file by bringing in data from a delimited ASCII text file.
>
> APPEND FROM <text filename> SDF [<condition>]
> [III/II] To add records to a database file by bringing in data from an undelimited ASCII text file in System Data Format.

CLOSE

> CLOSE ALTERNATE
> [III] To close an open alternate file.

COPY

> COPY FILE <source filename.ext> TO <destination filename.ext>
> [III] To copy a closed file of any type.

COPY TO <text filename> [FIELDS <field name> {,<field name>}] ;
        [<database parameter>] DELIMITED [WITH <delimiter>]
    [III/II] To create a delimited ASCII text file from [specified fields in] the currently selected database file.

COPY TO <text filename> [FIELDS <field name> {,<field name>}] ;
        [<database parameter>] SDF
    [III/II] To create an undelimited ASCII text file in System Data Format from [specified fields in] the currently selected database file.

DELETE

DELETE FILE <filename.ext>
    [III/II] To remove a file from the disk.

DIRECTORY

DIR <file directory parameter> [[ON] <drive designator>] ;
                              [TO PRINT]
    [III] To display any files [on another drive] [and output to the printer].

DIRECTORY <file directory parameter> [[ON] <drive designator>] ;
                              [TO PRINT]
    [III] To display a listing of any files [on another drive] [and output to the printer].

DISPLAY

DISPLAY FILES <file directory parameter> [ON <drive designator>]
    [III/II] To display any files [on another drive].

ERASE

ERASE <filename.ext>
    [III] To remove a file from the disk.

LIST

LIST FILES <file directory parameter> [ON <drive designator>]
    [III/II] To get a listing of any type of file [on another drive].

MODIFY

MODIFY COMMAND <text filename.ext>
    [III/II] To edit any standard ASCII text file.

MODIFY FILE <text filename>
    [III] To create or edit a text file with no filename extension.

RENAME

```
RENAME <old filename.ext> TO <new filename.ext>
    [III/II] To rename a file.
```

TYPE

```
TYPE <text filename.ext>
    [III] To view the contents of command and other text files.

TYPE <text filename.ext> TO PRINT
    [III] To print the contents of command and other text files.
```

Other Resources

None.

ALGORITHMS

dBASE Text Processing

Although dBASE is a database management system, it may be used to manipulate lines of text created with a word processor or with a text editor by treating each line of text as a separate record. The algorithm is that any text can be considered as individual lines followed by a carriage return, so each line will be considered a separate dBASE record. A temporary database file is required with the structure:

```
STRUCTURE FOR FILE:   C:Text.dbf
FLD        NAME       TYPE WIDTH
001     LINE          C    080
** TOTAL **                00081
```

Now, by APPENDing to the database file with the SDF option, each line of the text file can be manipulated in dBASE as a single character field in a single record. Though the line length used here is eighty, it can be be increased to accommodate longer lines of text. In dBASE II, this is the only way to display a command file from within dBASE without entering the interactive world of MODIFY COMMAND. For example, these few lines of code read in the text and then print it.

```
USE Text
APPEND FROM Letter.txt SDF
USE Text
SET PRINT ON
LIST OFF
SET PRINT OFF
USE
```

If the text file contains data that is formatted in columns, then the database file can be set up with one field corresponding to each column in a line. Each line will still be a separate record, but will be split up into separate fields within each record. For example, assume a text file that contains a list of disk files. This can be easily obtained in MS(PC)-DOS with the command:

```
DIR > Filename.ext
```

In DOS, the greater-than sign (>) directs output to a file or device instead of the screen. As as example, taking a directory of the dBASE files in the current directory places this output in a file:

```
Volume in drive D has no label
Directory of  D:\APG

DBASE    EXE    105472   6-14-84    5:59p
DBASE    OVL    147456   6-14-84    5:59p
DB241          <DIR>     8-12-84   11:36a
DB24           <DIR>     8-12-84   11:37a
DB23D          <DIR>     8-12-84   11:37a
       5 File(s)   3489792 bytes free
```

By entering the text file with a word processor, we can easily determine that the filename begins in column one, extension in column ten, size or <DIR> in column fourteen, date in column twenty- four, and time in column thirty-four. Based on this format, the database file is set up like this:

```
Field  Field name  Type        Width   Dec
    1  FILENAME    Character      9
    2  EXTENSION   Character      4
    3  SIZE        Character     10
    4  DATE        Character     10
    5  TIME        Character      6
** Total **                      40
```

After APPENDing SDF from the text file, a LIST of the database file looks like this:

```
Record#  FILENAME EXTENSION SIZE       DATE        TIME
     1
     2   Volume i n dr     ive D has  no label
     3   Director y of        D:\APG
     4
     5   DBASE    EXE        105472    6-14-84     5:59p
     6   DBASE    OVL        147456    6-14-84     5:59p
     7   DB241               <DIR>     8-12-84    11:36a
     8   DB24                <DIR>     8-12-84    11:37a
     9   DB23D               <DIR>     8-12-84    11:37a
    10        5  File(s)   348 9792 bytes   free
```

The portions of the file that do not conform to the columnar format are discarded by deleting their records. In this example, we delete record numbers one, two, three, four, and ten.

CHAPTER TWENTY-ONE

PRINTING AND FORM GENERATORS

Printing is very similar to output screen handling (chapter 18, "Output"). It, too, is a process of one-way communication by which the programmer speaks to the operator. The output commands for printing are the same ones used in outputting to the screen. They are classified according to the mode in which they work, *formatted* or *unformatted*:

1. Formatted mode

@...SAY

This command places its output at the printer location specified by the programmer, thus formatting the report. In addition, it has options which allow the programmer to modify the display of its data, thus formatting the individual data item.

2. Unformatted mode

General:

```
?
??
```

Specialized:

```
DIR        [III]
DIRECTORY  [III]
DISPLAY
LIST
REMARK     [II]
TEXT...ENDTEXT [not in II-2.3x]
TYPE       [III]
```

Form Generators:

```
LABEL      [III]
REPORT
```

These commands are dependent upon the current printer head position and begin their output at that location. REPORT issues a form-feed first unless told otherwise.

All output commands go to the screen unless specifically directed to the printer. Two different commands are used to accomplish this.

1. Formatted mode

```
SET DEVICE TO <device parameter>    [III]
SET FORMAT TO <device parameter>    [II]

<device parameter> ::= PRINT | SCREEN
```

2. Unformatted mode

From a program:

```
SET PRINT <switch>
```

<switch> ::= ON | OFF

From the dot prompt:

```
<^P> to toggle the printer on and off
<^PrtSc> also does this on the IBM PC
```

TO PRINT option in the syntax of these commands:

```
DIR        [III]
DIRECTORY  [III]
DISPLAY    [III]
LABEL      [III]
LIST       [III]
REPORT
TYPE       [III]
```

As with screen handling, the most control is available with the @...SAY command. The form generators are useful utilities, but are restricted to the particular forms for which they are designed. When a report requires a form not available with one of the built-in form generators, a command file must be written, usually using @...SAYs, to print the report.

In the formatted mode, output is to *either* the printer or screen, but not both. In the unformatted mode, output directed to the printer *also* appears on the screen unless the screen is disabled with SET CONSOLE OFF.

Formatted Output

The <coordinates> specified in the @...SAY command control where the output will appear on the printer. The syntax and range is:

```
@ <coordinates> SAY <expression>
```

<coordinates>	::=	<row>, <column>
<row>	::=	numeric expression, dBASE II range 0 - 65,535, dBASE III range currently unknown. Also called <line>.
<column>	::=	numeric expression, range 0 - <n>
<n>	::=	maximum number of columns available on a particular printer

The main difference in using @...SAY on the printer instead of the screen is that the printer head cannot go backwards as the cursor can on the screen. Therefore, whenever the <row> number is smaller than previously executed, a form-feed will be generated. Similarly, when the <column> number is smaller than previously executed, a line-feed will be generated. Of course, <column> can decrease *if* <row> increases without getting an additional line-feed.

Relative addressing refers to the use of a <numeric expression> that includes a reference to the previous or current printer head position. The printer head position reference is available in two ways:

1. III only: Functions PCOL() and PROW() return current printer head position.

```
@ PROW()  , PCOL()+2 SAY <expression>
@ PROW()+1, PCOL()   SAY <expression>
```

2. III/II: Memvar set up and maintained by programmer returns previous (prior to last output) printer head position.

```
STORE 10 TO row
STORE 10 TO col
@ row  , col-10 SAY <expression>
@ row+1, col    SAY <expression>
STORE row + 2 TO row
@ row  , col+5  SAY <expression>
```

Note that the dollar sign ($) used in dBASE II, version 2.4x, for relative addressing on the screen cannot be used accurately when outputting to the printer.

In addition to formatting the report, we can also format the individual picture of each data item when it's displayed. The @...SAY command offers the programmer a variety of options for displaying data in a format different than the format in which it exists. These are the same as for output screen handling and are described in chapter 18, "Output."

Printer Configuration

Many printers accept instructions from software to change their various settings. Some printers require that certain changes be set with switches or other hardware devices, and still others do not allow certain settings to be changed at all. If your printer supports changing settings from software, this can be accomplished by sending the control codes to the printer with the CHR() function.

Control codes specified with CHR() statements are sent to the printer with either the @...SAY or ?? commands. The double question mark is used because there is no reason to send a carriage-return/line-feed pair with the control codes. These examples are all for the Epson FX-80 printer:

```
* To use unformatted output commands in dBASE III and II...
SET PRINT ON
* Enable condensed mode...
?? CHR(15)
<unformatted output commands>
* Restore normal mode, and cancel output to the printer...
?? CHR(18)
SET PRINT OFF

* To use formatted output commands in dBASE III...
* Note that this may confuse the PCOL() function.
SET DEVICE TO PRINT
* Enable emphasized mode...
@ <coordinates> SAY CHR(27) + "E"
<formatted output commands>
* Restore normal mode, and return output to the screen...
@ <coordinates> SAY CHR(27) + "F"
SET DEVICE TO SCREEN

* To use formatted output commands in dBASE II...
SET FORMAT TO PRINT
* Enable proportional mode...
@ <coordinates> SAY CHR(27) + "P1"
<formatted output commands>
* Restore normal mode, and return output to the screen...
@ <coordinates> SAY CHR(27) + "P0"
SET FORMAT TO SCREEN
```

The Last Line

Many printers have a buffer in which they store each line until they receive a carriage return. dBASE sends its carriage- return/line-feed pair at the beginning of a line rather than at the end. So, the last line received by the printer may not be printed until a carriage-return, line-feed, or form-feed is received. REPORT and LABEL do this automatically in dBASE III.

It's a simple matter to send the printer a carriage-return in the form of a CHR(13) at the end of any printing job in which this occurs. For operations with SET PRINT ON, use either a single question mark by itself or "?? CHR(13)", and for operations with SET DEVICE (or FORMAT in II) TO PRINT, use "@ <coordinates> SAY CHR(13)". The EJECT command also sends a form-feed.

Form Generators

These are quick utilities that make it possible to generate forms of a specific format. There are two built-in form generators in dBASE III, REPORT form (.FRM) and LABEL form (.LBL). dBASE II has only the REPORT form.

New form files are created with:

```
CREATE LABEL      [III]
MODIFY LABEL      [III]
CREATE REPORT     [III]
```

```
MODIFY REPORT     [III]
REPORT            [II]
```

Existing form files are changed with:

```
CREATE LABEL      [III]
MODIFY LABEL      [III]
CREATE REPORT     [III]
MODIFY REPORT     [III]
MODIFY COMMAND    [II]
```

Existing forms are output with:

```
REPORT FORM <report filename>   [III/II]
LABEL FORM <label filename>     [III]
```

In dBASE III, both the CREATE <form> and MODIFY <form> are menu driven and easy to operate. In fact, CREATE and MODIFY are interchangeable in this context since they both operate identically on forms. Both report and label forms are saved in a file with a header that dBASE uses to organize the specifications.

In dBASE II, the creation of a report form with the REPORT command is prompted with error trapping, and the form's details are saved in a standard ASCII text file with no special header. This file can be modified with any text editor. To change it with MODIFY COMMAND, use the .FRM extension with the filename. Since the questions that prompted you through the original creation of the file are not contained in the file, you will find it helpful to have your printer on when you originally create the file. That way, you will have a hard copy of the questions to guide you through the changes since there is neither prompting nor error trapping. A word of caution though: if you make any errors in editing the .FRM file by this method, the REPORT FORM command will crash. If you escape a REPORT FORM either by hitting the <Esc> key or by getting a syntax error, it must be closed before you can edit it with MODIFY COMMAND. In dBASE II, REPORT files are closed only when the data file (.DBF) in USE is closed.

Specifications:	dBASE III	dBASE II
Maximum number of fields:	24	24
Maximum page heading size:	240	254
Maximum column heading size:	260	253
Maximum total of all headings:		
(Includes expressions in dBASE III.)	1,440	720
Minimum size of logical fields:	3	8

Report forms may be created to use more than one database file. This requires that all three of these conditions be met:

1. All files to be included in the report must be able to be open simultaneously, and must be open when creating the report.
2. The expressions used in the REPORT FORM file must contain the proper work area prefix when reference is made to a file in other than the currently selected area.

3. The REPORT generator only moves the record pointer in the file in the currently selected area. Files in unselected areas can be linked so that they will move in concert with the file in the currently selected area.

Complete details on using more than one database file are in chapter 19, "Multiple Files." The report and label form options are:

<report options>   ::=   TO PRINT
                        | TO PRINT NOEJECT [III]
                        | TO FILE <text filename> [III]
                        | HEADING <character expression> [III]
                        | PLAIN

<label options>   ::=   TO PRINT
                       | TO FILE <text filename> [III]
                       | SAMPLE [III]

TO PRINT   ::=   Sends output to the printer with an initial form-feed.
TO PRINT NOEJECT ::=   Sends output to the printer without an
                       initial form-feed. (Use SET EJECT in II.)
TO FILE   ::=   Sends output to a text file. (Use SET ALTERNATE in II.)
HEADING   ::=   Adds an additional heading to the top line.
                       (Use SET HEADING in II.)
PLAIN   ::=   Eliminates page numbers, date, and
                       heading(s). In III, prevents ejects
                       between pages (use POKEs in II).
SAMPLE   ::=   Outputs rows of asterisks (*) which equal the specified size
                       of a single label.

Page Ejects

The ASCII code for a form-feed is ^L, or CHR(12). This is what dBASE sends to the printer to eject a page, and the printer then advances the paper to the next *top of form* setting. Some printers have a fixed form length that cannot be changed, and others allow various form lengths. Among those printers that allow you to set the length of form, some can be set from the software with CHRs, and others require that changes be made with switches on the printer itself (check your printer manual).

In dBASE II, the output must be directed to the printer for it to receive a form-feed from the EJECT command. In dBASE III, the printer will receive the form-feed even when the output is directed to the screen.

SET EJECT OFF in dBASE II and the NOEJECT option in the REPORT syntax of dBASE III both prevent only the *initial* form-feed from being executed prior to the running of the report. These commands will not prevent form-feeds from occurring between pages *during* the report.

There are two different methods for eliminating the page ejects during a REPORT. In dBASE III, use the PLAIN option in the REPORT syntax. In dBASE II, execute a POKE sequence before issuing the REPORT command. dBASE II POKE sequences for this purpose are in Technical Support Note 11 in appendix F.

VOCABULARY

Operators

None.

Functions

CHR()

> `CHR(<numeric expression>)`
> [III/II] To enter characters for which there are no keys. To send control characters to the printer or screen.

PCOL()

> `PCOL()`
> [III] To use the current printer head postion for relative addressing with @...SAY.

PROW()

> `PROW()`
> [III] To use the current printer head postion for relative addressing with @...SAY.

SET parameters

DELETED

> `SET DELETED <switch>`
> [III/II] To include or exclude records that are marked for deletion from being seen by commands that reposition a database file's record pointer. In II, only commands that allow the <scope> parameter are affected.

DEVICE

> `SET DEVICE TO <device parameter>`
> [III] To direct formatted output from @...SAY to either the screen or printer.

EJECT

> `SET EJECT <switch>`
> [II] To enable/disable the initial form-feed just prior to printing report forms.

FORMAT

> `SET FORMAT TO <device parameter>`
> [II] To direct formatted output from @...SAY to either the screen or printer.

HEADING

SET HEADING TO
[II] To cancel a previously specified report form heading.

SET HEADING TO <character string>
[II] To specify a heading for dBASE report forms.

MARGIN

SET MARGIN TO <numeric expression>
[III/II] To specify the left margin for all output to the printer.

PRINT

SET PRINT <switch>
[III/II] To enable/disable command-line mode, or "unformatted," output to the printer.

Commands

?

? <expression> {,<expression>}
[III/II] To output data in command-line, or "unformatted," mode on the next line.

??

?? <expression> {,<expression>}
[III/II] To output data in command-line, or "unformatted," mode on the current line.

@

@ <row>,<column> SAY <expression>
[III/II] To display an <expression> on the screen or printer.

@ <row>,<column> SAY <expression> FUNCTION "{<function>}"
[III] To display an <expression> on the screen or printer modified by the <function{s}>.

@ <row>,<column> SAY <expression> PICTURE <picture template>
[III] To display an <expression> on the screen or printer modified by the <picture template>.

@ <row>,<column> SAY <expression> USING "{<using symbol>}"
[II] To display an <expression> on the screen or printer modified by the <using symbol{s}>.

CREATE

> CREATE LABEL
>> [III] To create a new label form.
>
> CREATE REPORT
>> [III] To create a new report form.

EJECT

> EJECT
>> [III/II] To send a form-feed to the printer.

LABEL

> LABEL FORM <label filename> [<database parameter>] [<label options>]
>> [III] To output an existing label form.

MODIFY

> MODIFY COMMAND <text filename.ext>
>> [III/II] To edit any standard ASCII text file.
>
> MODIFY LABEL
>> [III] To change an existing label form.
>
> MODIFY REPORT
>> [III] To change an existing report form.

REMARK

> REMARK <character string>
>> [II] To display an undelimited <character string>.

REPORT

> REPORT FORM <existing report filename> [<database parameter >] ;
>>   [<report options>]
>> [III/II] To output an existing report form.
>
> REPORT [FORM <new report filename>]
>> [II] To create a new report form.

TEXT...ENDTEXT

> TEXT
>> { <character string> <new line> }
> ENDTEXT
>> [III/II] To output multiple lines of text.

TYPE

```
TYPE <text filename.ext> TO PRINT
```
[III] To print the contents of command and other text files.

<keypress>

```
<^P>
```
[III/II] To turn the printer on and off from the keyboard.

```
<^PrtSc>
```
[III] To turn the printer on and off from the keyboard.

```
<^S>
```
[III/II] To momentarily pause command execution and screen scrolling from the keyboard. ^S or ^Q to restart.

Other Resources

None.

ALGORITHMS

Print Screen Function [II]

In all versions of dBASE II running under MS(PC)-DOS, there is a simple way to print whatever is on the screen from within a command file. These commands set up the ability to print the screen:

```
POKE 56728, 205, 5, 195
SET CALL TO 56728
```

Then, whenever you wish to transfer the contents of the screen to the printer, simply issue the CALL command. At the time of this writing, the assembly language interface is not fully implemented in dBASE III.

Page Counter

When writing command files that print reports, it is desirable to keep a page counter in order to place a heading and page number on each page. This is usually done within a loop that counts each printed line until a certain number is reached, at which time a conditional branch prints a new heading, increments the page counter, and starts the line counter over again. By decrementing the line counter inside the IF...ENDIF structure, we cause a form-feed to automatically be sent to the printer, making any use of the EJECT command redundant.

```
* Page counter algorithm for one file.
*
* Initialize counters to starting values.
* Start t:line high enough to take the branch for a
* new page just inside the DO loop...
```

```
        STORE 61 TO t:line
        STORE  5 TO t:col
        STORE  0 TO t:pagectr
        *
        * Look at each record in the file sequentially...
        GO TOP
        DO WHILE .NOT. EOF
           *
           * Branch for new page...
           IF t:line > 60
              STORE 1 TO t:line
              STORE t:pagectr + 1 TO t:pagectr
              *
              * This next line causes a form-feed to be sent to the printer
              * because it is now a lower value than the last one sent...
              @ t:line  ,t:col+66 SAY 'Page' + STR(t:pagectr,3)
              @ t:line+1,t:col+66 SAY DATE()
              @ t:line+4,t:col+25 SAY <heading>
           ENDIF
           *
           @ t:line, t:col SAY <data from this record>
           *
           * Next record, and increment the line counter...
           SKIP
           STORE t:line + 1 TO t:line
        ENDDO
        *
        * EOA
```

In cases where more than one file is supplying data for the report, a separate loop is set up for each file, and a page counter is used inside each loop. This dBASE II example assumes that two files are open, Customer in PRIMARY and Products in SECONDARY. Each customer can have from none to over a hundred products. The files are linked by the key field Cust:code, on which both files are indexed.

```
        * Page counter algorithm for more than one file.
        *
        * Initialize counters to starting values.
        * Start t:line high enough to take the branch for a
        * new heading just inside the DO loop...
        STORE 61 TO t:line
        STORE  5 TO t:col
        STORE  0 TO t:pagectr
        *
        * Look at each record in the file sequentially...
        DO WHILE .NOT. EOF
```

```
*
* Branch for new page...
IF t:line > 60
   STORE 1 TO t:line
   STORE t:pagectr + 1 TO t:pagectr
   *
   * This next line causes a form-feed to be sent to the
   * printer because it is now a lower value than the
   * last one sent . . .
   @ t:line   ,t:col+66 SAY 'Page' + STR(t:pagectr,3)
   @ t:line+1,t:col+66 SAY DATE()
   @ t:line+4,t:col+25 SAY <heading>
ENDIF
*
* Print data from customer file...
@ t:line, t:col   SAY Cust:code
@ t:line, t:col+5 SAY Cust:name
*
* Save the key from this file to a memvar
* in order to find it in the product file...
STORE Cust:code TO m:cust:cod
*
* Set up another loop for the product file...
SELECT SECONDARY
FIND &m:cust:cod
DO WHILE Cust:code = m:cust:cod .AND. .NOT. EOF
   *
   * Branch for new page...
   IF t:line > 60
      STORE 1 TO t:line
      STORE t:pagectr + 1 TO t:pagectr
      *
      @ t:line   ,71 SAY 'Page' + STR(t:pagectr,3)
      @ t:line+1,71 SAY DATE()
      @ t:line+4,30 SAY <heading>
   ENDIF
   *
   * Print data from product file...
   @ t:line, t:col + 11 SAY Prod:code
   @ t:line, t:col + 18 SAY Prod:name
   @ t:line, t:col + 50 SAY Die:number
   *
   * Next record, and increment the line counter...
   SKIP
   STORE t:line + 1 to t:line
ENDDO
*
* Back to the customer file...
SELECT PRIMARY
```

```
        *
        * Next record, and increment the line counter...
        SKIP
        STORE t:line + 1 TO t:line
ENDDO
*
* EOA
```

In dBASE III where procedure files are available, one of the duplicated IF. . .ENDIF structures could be placed in a procedure and called from both places, thus eliminating the duplication. In dBASE II, however, it is rarely worth the time it takes to open another command file for just these few lines of code which occur in only two places.

Column Formatting

In some reports where there is likely to be a lot of blank space between columns, it is desirable to connect the columns with a string of characters to clearly show the connection between the two. An example of when this may be used is in an index to a document, where the index subject might vary from a few characters to most of the line:

```
TIME . . . . . . . . . . . . . . . . . . . . . . . . 27
LATITUDE/LONGITUDE, RELATION OF TIME . . . . . . . 88
```

This dBASE II expression creates the topic column in the above format, taking care of the two cases where the original topic has an even or odd length, and still ensuring that the periods line up correctly:

```
$(($(TRIM(Topic)+' ',1,2*INT((LEN(TRIM(Topic))+1)/2)) +;
'. . . . . . . . . . . . . . . . . . . . . . . . . .'),1,50)
```

(LEN(TRIM(Topic))+1) is the length of Topic plus <1 space>. By dividing this by two, taking the integer part, and multiplying by two, we end up with a number which is the smallest even integer greater than or equal to the length of TRIM(Topic). Using this number as the length of the inner substring expression removes the blank space if the original topic length is odd, thus making the length even in either case. Then we concatenate the string of periods to this even length version of the original topic, and finally truncate the periods to fit the report column width, which in this case is 50. The length parameter in the outer substring function determines the column width. The actual syntax in a dBASE II report form file would look something like this:

```
m=8
n
n
n
50, $(($(TRIM(Topic)+' ',1,2*INT((LEN(TRIM(Top ic))+1)/2)) +;
'. . . . . . . . . . . . . . . . . . . . . . . . . .'),1,50)
<TOPIC;========================================
5,Page:nmbr
<PAGE;====
```

To use this in dBASE III, replace the substring function $() with SUBSTR().

CHAPTER TWENTY-ONE

388

Blank Zeros in Report Forms [II]

The following report is based on this file structure:

```
STRUCTURE FOR FILE:  C:Zero.dbf
NUMBER OF RECORDS:    00013
FLD        NAME       TYPE WIDTH    DEC
001        NAME       C    020
002        NUMBER     N    009      002
** TOTAL **           00030
```

A numeric value of zero will always display. The only way to prevent the display is to convert the zero quantity to a character type with an algorithm for blanking zero amounts. When this is done in a report form however, the converted character type cannot be totalled.

In dBASE II, we can make another column invisible by declaring a width of zero, and its total will wind up in the character column. dBASE III does not allow a width of zero to be entered. This method can also be used to provide a column that acts as a counter without individual ones appearing in the column.

Name	With zero	No zero	
ONE	8.16	8.16	
TWO	0.00		
THREE	128.32	128.32	
FOUR	0.00		
FIVE	0.00		
SIX	0.00		
SEVEN	65536.32	65536.32	
EIGHT	0.00		
NINE	0.01	0.01	
TEN	0.00		
ELEVEN	0.00		
TWELVE	123456.78	123456.78	
THIRTEEN	1313.13	1313.13	
** TOTAL **			
	190442.72	190442.720	13

The way to eliminate zero printing is to convert the number to a string and use the substring function to either select the whole string or just the first character. Since we want nothing printed when the value is zero, the value itself *almost* provides the correct string length, except that dBASE II returns a logical true (.T.), so we add one to prevent this. If the number is non-zero, we generate a positive number at least as big as the field width. Fortunately, dBASE doesn't mind getting a length parameter that is longer than the string.

Here is the setup for the above report form that prints what appears to be three fields. There are actually six.

```
OPTIONS
PAGE HEADING?
DOUBLE SPACE?
TOTALS?              y
SUB-TOTALS?          n
FIELD 1              20,Name
   heading           <Name;==============
FIELD 2              10,Number
   heading           >With zero;=========
   totals            y
FIELD 3              9,$(STR(Number,9,2),1,1+(Number*Number*100000000000))
   heading           >No zero;=========
FIELD 4              0,Number*1.0
   heading
   totals            y
FIELD 5              5,"" ''
   heading
FIELD 6              0,1
   heading
   totals            y
```

Fields one and two are straightforward.

Field three is the algorithm to blank zeros. It converts the *Number* to a string of suitable length and number of decimals, and then either takes only the leftmost character which is blank or the whole string which looks just like the original number.

To take care of negative numbers, we multiply *Number* by itself (neither dBASE II nor III have an ABSolute value function). To make sure that the result is at least as large as the string length, multiply it by a large number. We've gotten the best results by using a multiplier at least as large as the one shown (one hundred billion). Certain large numbers that are powers of two are discarded by the substring function, and smaller multipliers may cause distorted results when *Number* is 8.16, 32.32, 64.16, and other similar combinations.

If *Number* is zero, a length of one is calculated and dBASE takes only the leftmost character which is a blank. Because this report column is a character type, it cannot be totalled. However, field four takes care of this problem.

Field four is the actual Number with a report column width of zero and a yes answer to the question about totals. This will not print the individual numbers because the field width is zero, but the total will be printed, overlapping field three. That's very close to where the total should be, but since the REPORT generator puts one space between each field, we need to move the total one position to the left. Multiplying *Number* by 1.0 adds one more decimal place to the total which moves it to the left one space. If this is not acceptable on the final report, the extra zero must be covered up by hand.

Field five is just some spacing to make room for the next total. A column heading cannot be used because once a numeric field is assigned a report width of zero and then totalled, all further totals will not line up with their respective columns.

Field six is a way to add a count field to a REPORT without printing a column of ones. Again, by specifying a field width of zero, nothing is displayed in the body of the table, but the total is shown.

Enhanced Data Output

Printer control sequences can be added directly to character fields in the database file in order to control the appearance of their output. This is useful in enhancing the appearance of LIST, DISPLAY, and other output commands without writing command files or report forms.

The field lengths must be wide enough to accommodate both the printer codes *and* the data without truncating the data. It is essential that a temporary database file be created and used with this method because some printer codes cannot be seen and will cause trouble during data editing or display on the screen.

As an example, in a file with fields *Firstname* and *Lastname*, these commands will cause all the first names to print with an underline, and all last names to print in the enlarged mode. The codes are for an EPSON RX-80 printer.

```
REPLACE ALL Firstname WITH CHR(27) +'-'+ CHR(49) +;
                           TRIM(Firstname) +;
                           CHR(27) +'-'+ CHR(48)

REPLACE ALL Lastname  WITH CHR(27) +'W'+ CHR(49) +;
                           TRIM(Lastname) +;
                           CHR(27) +'W'+ CHR(48)
```

In this example, the fields must be at least six characters wider than the maximum length of their data. Note that CHR(26) is the dBASE II end-of-file marker, and will cause a great deal of trouble if inserted in a database file.

Work-Arounds

1. Some versions of dBASE running on some computers will trap certain characters that are output with the CHR() function. If you determine positively that this is happening to you, adding 128 to the desired CHR() argument may or may not help.

```
        * If this doesn't work...
        ?? CHR(21)
        *
        * This might...
        ?? CHR(21 + 128)
```

2. dBASE cannot send a CHR(0). Most printers offer an alternative code because this is true of many software packages. Always use the alternate code.

3. dBASE II, version 2.3D, has trouble with multiple REPORT forms. See Technical Support Note 27 in appendix F.

CHAPTER TWENTY-TWO

ASSEMBLY LANGUAGE INTERFACE

Assembly language is a low-level language that is designed to write fast, compact programs. By low level, we mean that each instruction usually commands the CPU to perform a single operation such as *ADD* which adds two values, or *MOV* which moves a byte from one location to another. Thus, the actions of the CPU are closely controlled. This also means that an assembly language programmer is concerned with many details at the hardware and operating system level that do not concern a programmer working in a high level language like dBASE. Writing assembly language programs can be tricky and we assume that the readers of this section understand how to do this.

Occasionally, you may wish to perform an operation that dBASE II does slowly or is unable to do at all. In these cases, you can often write an assembly language routine that will perform the desired action. Assembly language routines can be placed in memory and then executed, or " called," directly from within dBASE.

The following discussion applies to dBASE II only because, at the time of this writing, dBASE III does not implement a set of commands which allow you to CALL assembly language routines. For now, dBASE III relies on the RUN command which allows COM or EXE programs to be executed. This takes longer because the file must be opened and loaded into memory each time it is RUN.

dBASE II has one function and four commands to provide direct access to memory. These are identical in both 8-bit and 16-bit versions of dBASE II.

```
PEEK( )
POKE
LOAD
SET CALL TO
CALL [<memvar name>]
```

All numeric parameters are expressed as *decimal* values, and the LOAD command requires the loaded file to be in Intel *hex* format. An example of Intel hex format is Datetest.h86 under Algorithms below. The PEEK( ) function returns the decimal value of the byte at the specified address. The address can be represented by any numeric expression, including a variable which is easily incremented or changed. For example:

```
STORE 58000 TO x
STORE PEEK(x) TO value
? value
```

```
STORE PEEK( 128 ) TO value
STORE 128 TO location
? PEEK( location ), PEEK( location + 1 )
```

The POKE command sequentially writes the byte list into memory beginning at the specified address. Both the byte list and the address must be in decimal. This command can be used to load both data and executable code into memory.

```
STORE 10 TO mmonth
STORE 12 TO mday
STORE 83 TO myear
POKE 58000, mmonth, mday, myear
```

This stores the decimal value 10 at location 58000, 12 at 58001, and 83 at 58002.

```
* Subroutine..: LEADZERO.LIB (8-bit systems only)
* Description.: Replaces leading blanks with leading zeros.
SET CALL TO 42000
POKE 42000,  34, 37,164, 70, 35,126,254, 32
POKE 42008, 194, 33,164, 54, 48,  5,194, 20
POKE 42016, 164, 42, 37,164,201
STORE "   123" TO string
CALL string
? string
```

8-Bit Systems

If you are going to POKE or LOAD directly into memory, it is important not to overwrite dBASE itself. Below is a table which shows where the "top" of dBASE is in memory on 8-bit systems in a typical environment such as a Z-80 or 8085 CPU running under CP/M 2.2. It is generally safe to POKE above this area as long as you also stay below the operating system's reserved areas (see CP/M memory map, chapter 2). There are approximately eight to twelve kilobytes of usable space on a 64K system.

dBASE version (8-Bit)	Top of dBASE (Hex)	Top of dBASE (Decimal)
2.3, 2.3A, 2.3B	A400	41984
2.4	B000	45056
2.41	C000	49152

When dBASE executes the SORT command, it uses the space between the top of dBASE and the bottom of CP/M's BDOS as a sort buffer. This means that any data or programs you may have loaded into high memory will be overwritten during a SORT and will need to be re-initialized. One way to avoid this problem is to use the CP/M utility MOVCPM to create a "protected" space at the top of memory. MOVCPM allows you to position the operating system in memory. It can be used to create a protected memory area for assembly language routines above CP/M. For example, if you have a 64K system and use MOVCPM to create a 48K or 56K system, there will be space between the top of the operating system (56K) and the top of memory (64K). Assembly language programs can be placed in this zone and never be disturbed or overwritten.

The CALL [<memvar>] command causes processing to branch to the address specified in a previously executed SET CALL TO <address> command. When the memory address is reached, the register pair HL will point to the first byte of <memvar>. If the memory variable is a character string, HL will point to the length byte (see chapter 7 for a diagram of character type data). The length byte of a memory variable may not be changed. There are about 254 bytes of stack available for assembler PUSHs and POPs. To get back to dBASE II, the assembler command RET is used. dBASE II handles the saving of all the registers. However, it is recommended that the HL register pair be saved (SHLD) upon entering an assembly routine and restored (LHLD) before returning to dBASE II.

The LOAD <filename> command loads a file into memory. The file must be a file in Intel hex format. SET CALL TO must still be executed to establish the CALL address before the assembly routine can be CALLed. An alternative to LOADing the hex file into memory is to convert the assembly routine into a dBASE II decimal POKE sequence and then POKE the routine into memory. The command file Hex2poke.cmd in appendix D is designed to make this conversion from the Intel hex format to the dBASE II POKE sequence. The Bindec.bas utility in appendix D converts .COM files into decimal POKE sequences.

16-Bit Systems

The following information is for dBASE II, version 2.4, running under CP/M-86, MS-DOS, and PC-DOS:

The SET CALL TO command establishes the address at which dBASE II will begin executing a subroutine. On a 16-bit machine using an 8086 or 8088 CPU, memory addresses are divided into 64K blocks called *segments*. Each address has two components, the segment and the offset within the specified segment. When the SET CALL TO command is issued, the address specified is always within the default code segment. The CALL (or CALL <memvar>) command then branches to this address and begins executing code. When a RETurn is encountered, the subroutine returns to dBASE and continues to execute any dBASE commands after the CALL statement.

When using CALL <memvar>, the address of the operand (memvar) is placed into the BX register. This is handy for passing parameters between dBASE and your subroutine. Another way to pass parameters is to POKE them into memory before executing your subroutine and then PEEK them back later and store them as memory variables for use by dBASE.

Example of SET CALL TO <memvar>:

```
STORE "June" TO month
SET CALL TO 58000
CALL month
```

In a 16-bit environment, subroutines should be loaded above DE00H (56832D). There are several ways to load a subroutine into memory. A common way is to use the LOAD command. When writing the subroutine, be sure to ORG it at DE00H or above and assemble it with an assembler which yields a file in Intel hex format (the CP/M-86 assembler will do this). The dBASE command file which calls the subroutine should LOAD the hex file, SET CALL TO the ORG address, then CALL the subroutine. See the example Datetest under Algorithms below.

Another way to get the subroutine into memory is to use the POKE command. To use POKE, translate the subroutine into a series of decimal values equivalent to the object code. This can be done by creating an executable file, loading it with a debugger, such as DDT or DEBUG, and dumping the memory image to a file. This will yield a hex dump of the object file which can be converted into decimal values. This series of decimal values can then be POKEd into memory to load the subroutine. Make sure that you have a RETurn instruction (decimal 195) as the final byte so that the subroutine will return to dBASE upon its completion.

Another method to produce a decimal POKE sequence from a COM or EXE file is to use the Bindec.bas utility in appendix D.

CP/M-86. If you are using CP/M-86, save the stack pointer (SP) on the way into the subroutine and restore it before you execute a RETurn back to dBASE. The CP/M assembler, ASM86, will output a file in Intel hex format with a file extension H86. This file can be directly loaded from dBASE using the LOAD command.

```
LOAD Testfile.H86
```

MS-DOS and PC-DOS. The Microsoft and IBM assemblers do not output a file in Intel hex format. Seattle Computer Products does have an 8086/8088 assembler which will yield a file in Intel hex format. This is the assembler we have used to create hex files under MS-DOS which can be LOADed. Simply issue a RETurn statement (decimal 195) at the end of the subroutine to get back to dBASE. If you do not have the Seattle assembler and you wish to use the LOAD command, you can assemble the subroutine under CPM-86 with ASM86 to create the HEX file and then transfer this file to the DOS environment.

VOCABULARY

Operators

None.

Functions

PEEK()

```
PEEK(<decimal address>)
```
[III/II] To view the contents of a byte in memory.

SET parameters

CALL

```
SET CALL TO
```
[II] To cancel a previously specified address for the CALL command.

```
SET CALL TO <decimal address>
```
[II] To specify the starting address of a machine language subroutine to be executed with the CALL command.

Commands

CALL

```
CALL
```
[II] To run a machine language subroutine that has been placed in memory with LOAD or POKE.

CALL <memvar name>
   [II] To pass a parameter to a machine language subroutine in memory.

LOAD

LOAD <Intel hex-format filename>
   [II] To place a machine language file in memory.

POKE

POKE <decimal address>, <data byte> {,<data byte>}
   [III/II] To place a value directly into memory one byte at a time.

RUN

! <executable filename or operating system command>
   [III] To execute an external program or operating system command.

RUN <executable filename or operating system command>
   [III] To execute an external program or operating system command.

Other Resources

None.

ALGORITHMS

Datetest

This is a short assembly language routine that provides a fast way to test if a date is valid or not. If the date is valid, no action is taken and the routine returns to dBASE. If the date is not valid, the memory locations where the date is temporarily stored are set to zero. The routine is assembled with ASM86 which produces an .H86 file. The .H86 file is in Intel hex format and can be LOADed into memory. DATETEST.PRG is a dBASE program which demonstrates the use of DATETEST routine.

```
; Subroutine.: DATETEST.A86
; Author.....: Jay W. Hanson
; Date.......: 06/24/83, 09/06/83
; Notice.....: Copyright 1983
; Notes......: Date test subroutine for use in dBASE-II/86 2.4
;
;    Assemble with ASM86 under CP/M-86.
;    The DATETEST.H86 file can be LOADed from dBASE II.
;    POKE the decimal date values to be checked before calling:
;         POKE month at 57501
;         POKE day at 57502, and
;         POKE year at 57503
; SET CALL TO 57504
; Then CALL to execute this routine
;
```

```
        ORG     57501
MONTH   DB      0           ; MONTH PARAMETER.
DAY     DB      0           ; DAY
YEAR    DB      0           ; YEAR
        ORG     57504       ; 4 BYTES ABOVE 'TOP' OF
                            ; dBASE II 2.4 (57500d) THIS
                            ; KEEPS CODE ABOVE MM/DD/YY BUFFERS
START:
;
; CHECK FOR 0 <= YEAR <= 99.
;
        MOV     AL,BYTE PTR YEAR        ; YEAR TO AL REGISTER
        OR      AL,AL                   ; IS IT < 1 ?
        JZ      ERROR                   ; YES, ERROR
        CMP     AL,100                  ; IS IT >= 99 ?
        JGE     ERROR                   ; YES, ERROR
;
; CHECK FOR 1 <= MONTH <= 12.
;
        MOV     AH,0
        MOV     AL,BYTE PTR MONTH       ; MONTH TO AL REGISTER
        OR      AL,AL                   ; IS IT < 1 ?
        JZ      ERROR                   ; YES, ERROR
        CMP     AL,12                   ; IS IT >= 12 ?
        JGE     ERROR                   ; YES, ERROR
;
; TEST DAYS IN MONTH.
;
        MOV     BX,OFFSET DTABLE-1 ; POINT BX TO DAY-IN-MONTH TABLE
        ADD     BX,AX                   ; POINT TO NUMBER OF DAYS FOR MONTH
        MOV     AH,BYTE PTR [BX]   ;    ...FETCH VALUE
        MOV     AL,BYTE PTR DAY    ; PICK UP DAY
        OR      AL,AL             ; 0 < DAY <= [DTABLE-1+MONTH]
        JE      ERROR
        CMP     AH,28             ; FEBRUARY?
        JNE     NOTLEAP           ; JUMP IF NOT FEBRUARY.
        PUSH    AX
        MOV     AL,BYTE PTR YEAR  ;
        AND     AL,3              ; CHECK IF YEAR IS DIVISIBLE BY 4
        POP     AX
        JNE     NOTLEAP           ; JUMP IF NOT LEAP YEAR.
        INC     AH                ; LEAP YEAR; SET DAYS/MONTH TO 29
NOTLEAP:
        CMP     AL,AH             ; EXCEEDS DAYS/MONTH?
        JG      ERROR             ; IF SO, ERROR
        RET                       ; OTHERWISE, IT IS A GOOD DATE
```

```
;
; SET MONTH, DAY, AND YEAR TO NULLS IF ERROR IN DATE.
;
ERROR:  MOV     BYTE PTR MONTH,0    ; ZERO OUT MONTH
        MOV     WORD PTR DAY,0      ; ZERO OUT DAY AND YEAR
        RET                         ; RETURN TO dBASE II
;;;         Jan Feb Mar Apr May Jun Jul Aug Sep Oct Nov Dec
DTABLE  DB  31, 28, 31, 30, 31, 30, 31, 31, 30, 31, 30, 31
        END
```

This is a listing of the hex file generated from the above assembly language source file with ASM86. This file can be LOADed directly into memory from dBASE II with the LOAD command. The extension H86 must be included in the LOAD command, otherwise dBASE II will assume HEX as the default file extension.

DATETEST.H86

```
:040000030000E09D7C
:1BE09D810000002EA09FE00AC074373C647D33B4002EA09DE00AC074293C0C27
:1BE0B8817D25BBECE003D88A272EA09EE00AC0741680FC1C750C502EA09FE0C1
:1BE0D3812403587502FEC43AC47F01C32EC6069DE0002EC7069EE00000C31FE6
:0BE0EE811C1F1E1F1E1F1F1E1F1E1F58
:00000001FF
```

```
* Program.: DATETEST.PRG
* Author..: Jay W. Hanson
* Date....: 09/06/83
* Notice..: Copyright 1983
* Notes...: Demonstrates the use of DATETEST.H86
*           If the date is not valid the memory locations 57501,
*           57502, and 57503 will contain zeros.
*
SET TALK OFF
STORE 0 TO mmonth, mday, myear
*
LOAD DATETEST.H86
SET CALL TO 57504
*
ERASE
@ 10,10 SAY 'ENTER MONTH' GET mmonth PICTURE '99'
@ 12,10 SAY 'ENTER DAY'   GET mday   PICTURE '99'
@ 14,10 SAY 'ENTER YEAR'  GET myear  PICTURE '99'
READ
*
```

```
POKE 57501, mmonth, mday, myear
*
* ---Display the values before and after the CALL.
? PEEK( 57501 ), PEEK( 57502 ), PEEK( 57503 )
CALL
? PEEK( 57501 ), PEEK( 57502 ), PEEK( 57503 )
*
IF PEEK( 57501 ) = 0
    ? "INVALID DATE"
ENDIF
*
CLEAR
SET TALK ON
RETURN
* EOF: DATETEST.PRG
```

Changing User Areas

It is possible to change user areas in CP/M-86 from within dBASE II, thus allowing for sixteen separate directory areas for your databases. This routine is primarily useful for users of hard disk systems, as a copy of Dbaseovr.com must be present in each user area being used.

First, PIP Dbaseovr.com to the user areas you wish to access. The syntax for this is:

```
PIP DBASEOVR.COM[G<destination>]=DBASEOVR.COM
```

For example:

```
PIP DBASEOVR.COM[G7]=DBASEOVR.COM
```

moves a copy of the dBASE the overlay to user area number seven.

Next, set Dbase.cmd and Dbasemsg.txt to a system file. This allows a file to be accessed from any user area (if set to SYS attribute in user area zero). Do the following:

```
STAT DBASE.CMD SYS
STAT DBASEMSG.TXT SYS
```

Next, create the following program in dBASE.

```
* USER.PRG
* The memvar "usr" is passed-in.
POKE 56832, 137, 38, 25,222,177, 32,178,usr
POKE 56840, 205,224,139, 38, 25,222,195
SET CALL TO 56832
CALL
RETURN
* EOF: User.prg
```

Set User.prg to system attribute from the operating system level.

```
STAT USER.PRG SYS
```

To change user areas from within dBASE II, place the digit representing the target area in the memvar usr, and DO the program:

```
* Changes to user area 7.
. STORE 7 TO usr
. DO User
```

Here is the source code for the above sequence of POKE instructions.

```
ORG        56832
;
MOV   [DE25H],SP          ; Save stack pointer
MOV   CL,20H              ; Function to change user number
MOV   DL,{POKE USR}       ; DL holds user no., poked with "usr"
INT   EOH                 ; BDOS call is interrupt 224
MOV   SP,[DE25H]          ; Restore stack pointer
RET                       ; Return to dBASE
```

Related Algorithms

Appendix D contains useful assembly language subroutines in MS(PC)-DOS, CP/M-80, and CP/M-86.

CHAPTER TWENTY-THREE

MULTI-USER ENVIRONMENT

At the time of this writing, Ashton-Tate has not announced multi-user versions of dBASE III. Therefore, this chapter deals exclusively with dBASE II.

dBASE II Multi-User is a version that allows several users to share access to data files. This need is commonly found on computer networks such as Ethernet and Omninet, and with multi-user operating systems such as TurboDOS and MP/M. At the time of this writing, dBASE II Multi-User has been released for 3COM Ethernet only. Ashton-Tate is currently testing versions of dBASE II Multi-User for other multi-user operating systems.

dBASE II Multi-User contains two new functions and two new commands in addition to the standard dBASE II command set:

```
LOCK()
LOCKNDX()
UNLOCK
UNLOCK INDEX
```

These additions to the language provide the capability to selectively lock or unlock records and index files. Complete data files are locked by *convention*, which is explained below. When more than one user has access to write to a file, it is important that the file be temporarily protected from writing by other users at the same time. The LOCK() function provides a way by which we can achieve this protection. If no locking system is used, a collision results when two or more users simultaneously attempt to edit the same record. Such a collision produces unpredictable results, and the file is not updated properly.

The LOCK() function operates as a flag which returns a logical true (.T.) if the current record is available (not locked), and false (.F.) if the current record is not available (is already locked). Thus, the status of a record can be tested to determine if it is currently in use (locked) or available for use (unlocked). Unlike other functions in dBASE that simply return a value, LOCK() also locks the current record when a value of true is returned. If several users test for a LOCK() on the same record, only the user whose test is received first will get a true value.

When a record is locked, a 512-byte block (one disk sector) is actually locked. This means that more than one record is effectively locked out at a time. The actual number of records locked depends on the record size and whether the record being locked overlaps a sector boundary. When a locked record overlaps a sector boundary, both sectors (1012 bytes) are locked.

An entire file can be locked by using the convention of locking record number one in the file. This requires the agreement of all users to check record number one before writing to the file. If the file is indexed, record one is probably not the first record in the file, but the GO 1 command positions the record pointer to record number one whether the file is indexed or not.

The LOCKNDX() function is used to lock the master index file in USE. LOCKNDX() is similar to the LOCK() function in the way it operates. It is used to see if a master index file is available or locked, and to lock it if it is available. dBASE allows up to seven indexes to be USEd with a data file, but only the first index file specified, the master index, is locked with the LOCKNDX() function. The master index should be locked before changing any fields that are part of the <key expression> of the master index.

The UNLOCK command is used to release the LOCK() on a record. When UNLOCK is used, it simply releases the LOCK(), but does not write any changes to the disk. Normally, when a record is ready to be unlocked, the USE command is executed. This both unlocks the record and writes any changes to the disk.

The UNLOCK INDEX command releases the LOCKNDX(), but does not write any changes to the disk. Changes are written to the disk only when the file is closed. UNLOCK INDEX is the *only* command that unlocks the LOCKNDX(). The usual procedure is to issue the UNLOCK INDEX command and then the USE command. This unlocks the index, and then the file is closed and updated. If the USE command is issued without UNLOCK INDEX having been executed, the index will remain locked even if a QUIT is issued.

Whenever a user will be adding or changing data, or in any way writing to the data file, it should be locked. These commands all write to the file and are considered *active* commands:

```
APPEND
BROWSE
CHANGE
DELETE
EDIT
MODIFY STRUCTURE
PACK
READ (when the object of its @...GET is a database field)
RECALL
REPLACE
UPDATE
```

Note that the INSERT command is missing from the active command list. It is *not* implemented in dBASE II Multi-User.

When a user will be reading a file without changing it, whether to lock or leave unlocked is a policy that must be determined by the application. By locking the file during a read-only operation, the user is assured of reading the very latest data since no other user can change the data at the moment when it is being read. This is particularly important during the *passive* commands that rely on the contents of data to create other files:

```
COPY
INDEX
JOIN
REINDEX
SORT
TOTAL
```

If the application does not require the operator to have the very latest up-to-the-second data, or if it is absolutely certain that there are no write operations being performed by another user, then it is perfectly safe to leave the file unlocked during these *passive* commands:

```
@...SAY
CONTINUE
COUNT
DISPLAY
FIND
GO
GOTO
<numeric expression>
LIST
LOCATE
READ (when the object of its @...GET is a memvar)
REPORT
SKIP
SUM
```

Because locking restricts access by other users, files should not be locked unless absolutely necessary, and they should be unlocked as soon as possible.

In any multi-user system, just as with single-user systems, proper backup procedures should be followed on a regular basis. Backup procedures are covered in chapters 11 and 12.

VOCABULARY

OPERATORS

None.

Functions

LOCK()

> LOCK( )
> [II] To inquire whether a record is locked and, if not, to lock it.

LOCKNDX()

> LOCKNDX( )
> [II]To inquire whether an index file is locked and, if not, to lock it.

SET parameters

None.

Commands

UNLOCK

> UNLOCK
> [II] To unlock a record.

UNLOCK INDEX
    [II] To unlock an index file.

Other Resources

None.

ALGORITHMS

3COM Ethernet

3COM Ethernet allows a mass storage device to be divided into volumes ranging from 64K to 32 megabytes in size. Users have access to a volume based on one of three attributes, PRIVATE, PUBLIC, or SHARED. In setting up shared database software on a 3COM Ethernet system, it is important to place files on volumes with appropriate access attributes.

dBASE II Multi-User and command files should be placed on a PUBLIC volume. A PUBLIC volume is read-only for all users except the creator of the volume. This allows anyone to execute, but not modify, these files. Shared data files must be placed on a SHARED volume. A SHARED volume allows any user to both read and write to its files. When doing major maintenance to a shared data file, it is a good idea to change the SHARED volume to a PRIVATE volume before commencing maintenance. This is a precautionary measure which prevents other users from gaining access to the file while major modifications are in progress.

It is important that all users designate the *same* drive when linking to a SHARED volume containing data files. Ethernet examines the user's drive designator when checking for a LOCK(). If two users are using the same data file, and each user is linked to different drives, both users will be allowed to LOCK() and write to the same record simultaneously.

If it is expected that a shared data file will have records appended, space for these records must be *preallocated*. This means that space for the new records must be allocated before the records are actually added. Preallocation is accomplished in two ways, both of which involve appending a number of blank records. In one method, the blank records are simply used for entry until all records have data in them, then more blank records are appended. The other method involves deleting the newly appended blank records and packing the data file. PACKing the data file does not release any disk space back to the operating system. So, for example, if a file had 100 records and fifty additional blank records were appended, deleted, and the file packed, the end-of-file marker would be placed after record 100, yet the fifty additional blank records would still be present. dBASE would think the file had 100 records, but DOS would include the full 150 records as the physical size of the file. Fifty additional records can then be APPENDed to the file without actually changing its physical size.

Because the File Allocation Table (FAT) in DOS does not know about shared volumes, a data file must not be physically extended while in a shared volume, otherwise the FAT may be damaged. When it is necessary to physically extend a file, the volume should first be made PRIVATE. Records can then be APPENDed, DELETEd, and the file PACKed. The volume can then be made SHARED again, and additional records can safely be APPENDed.

It is possible to modify the structure of a shared data file without deallocating the preallocated records. These operations should be carried out after the volume is made PRIVATE. First use the DOS COPY command to make a backup copy of the data file. (The DOS COPY command will copy the preallocated records whereas the dBASE COPY command will not.) The second step is to modify the structure of the original data file. Next, append from the backup data file to the new structure. The resulting file will have the new structure and still contain the preallocated records. Check the original data file to make sure it is intact before deleting the backup file.

It is often useful to use the DOS utility CHKDSK to correct errors in the directory or FAT. Sectors can get lost if a data file has been accidentally extended on a SHARED volume or some inadvertent simultaneous writes have occurred. Using CHKDSK with the /F option will recover lost clusters on the disk. For example, CHKDSK D:/F will check the directory of the volume linked to D: and fix any errors it finds. It asks if you want to write any lost data to files. If you say yes, CHKDSK recovers each chain of lost clusters into a file on the root directory with the filename FILE<nnnn>.CHK, where <nnnn> is a sequential number beginning with 0000. The files can be displayed on the console or executed to see if any valuable information has been recovered, and if not, they can be deleted to recover additional disk space.

Related Algorithms

Preallocating Disk Space in chapter 19, "Adding Data."

CHAPTER TWENTY-FOUR

DEBUGGING, OPTIMIZING, AND BENCHMARKING

dBASE programming bugs can be grouped into three categories according to whether they are syntax, structure, or logic related.

Syntax Related Bugs

Punctuation is missing or incorrect. dBASE will usually detect these kinds of errors and display the proper error message. On occasion, missing or incorrect punctuation will go unnoticed by dBASE and cause unexpected results. The best safeguard against this is to construct your command lines carefully according to the syntax shown in the Vocabulary of each chapter in this section, and to follow the suggested program documentation standards in chapter 13. Punctuation marks are *period, comma, semicolon, colon, apostrophe, quotation mark, and square bracket delimiters.*

Spacing is missing or incorrect. dBASE requires that words in a command line be separated by at least one space. More than one space is permissible but not required. Space around the arithmetic, relational, and logical operators is optional (desirable for readability). Drive designators and path names are part of the filename word and must not be separated by spaces.

Command, memvar, field, file, or alias names are misspelled. Most of these errors will cause a syntax error. However, there are times when dBASE will allow a misspelling to slip through. These kinds of errors are hard to detect and usually require a meticulous look through the file to find them. Obtaining a variable cross-listing is sometimes helpful when tracking down problems with variable names. See Crossref.prg in appendix B. Using the same name for files, fields, and memvars compounds this problem and thus is not recommended.

Memory variables are not initialized. Most dBASE commands will produce a syntax error if the memory variables named in the command have not been previously initialized. The memvars may have been initialized, but then were released somewhere along the way, possibly in a subroutine.

Files are misplaced. It is not uncommon to have one command file call another that exists in a location the programmer neglected to specify, such as on another drive or in another directory. The same problem occurs when the program tries to USE a database file and either it or its index file is in another location.

Command file contains control characters. When all syntax apparently checks out, and dBASE still shows a syntax error, there is the possibility that a character is present in the command line and that it cannot be seen. This usually results from writing the command file with a word processor that inserts special signals, for example page breaks, in the file. MODIFY COMMAND strips out control characters by simply opening the file and saving it with a <Ctrl-W>. (See chapter 25 for limitations of MODIFY COMMAND.) Often, the easiest solution is simply to delete the offending command line and retype it (including the carriage-return/line-feed). See Fix.asm in appendix D.

Structure Related Bugs

Structured commands are not closed.   For example, failing to match each IF with ENDIF, DO WHILE with ENDDO, DO CASE with ENDCASE, or TEXT with ENDTEXT. Proper indenting of commands, and using comments after ending, or "closing," commands, helps in detecting which closing statements go with which opening statements. An extra closing statement, such as an extra ENDIF, may also cause problems.

Nesting of structures is not correct.   Overlapping structures are definitely not supported in dBASE, and will cause unpredictable results. An example is a DO WHILE inside an IF statement with its matching ENDDO outside the ENDIF statement.
This method is *not* correct:

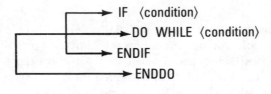

Figure 24-1

Either one of these methods *is* correct:

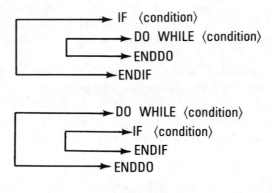

Figure 24-2

Logic Related Bugs

Intermediate steps are missing.   Neglecting to include necessary command line steps can alter the desired output or hinder program execution entirely. For example, executing a READ with more than 64 GETs in dBASE II without using either the CLEAR GETS or ERASE at some intermediate level causes program execution to freeze, and the operator ends up having to reset the system.

Sequence of steps is not correct. Some operations are order dependent—that is, one command must precede the other. For example, attempting to RENAME or DELETE a data file before it is closed with the USE, CLOSE, or CLEAR commands will generate the error, "File is currently open."

Looping criteria are incorrect. On occasion, a DO WHILE loop will repeat more or fewer times than the programmer intended. In this case, the looping condition is not specific enough. The programmer needs to determine whether the logical expression satisfactorily sets the upper and lower limits that the variables in the expression will take. For example, this DO WHILE structure, whose purpose is to output a list of duplicate entries, will loop forever in II and produce the "End of file encountered" error in III if the Name field of the last record equals the memvar mname.

```
USE Names
DO WHILE .NOT. EOF
    DO WHILE Name <> mname
        ? Name, Address
        SKIP
    ENDDO
    SKIP
ENDDO
```

The inner, or "nested," structure is simply lacking a test for end-of-file. This is the *correct* structure:

```
USE Names
DO WHILE .NOT. EOF
    DO WHILE Name <> mname .AND. (.NOT. EOF)
        ? Name, Address
        SKIP
    ENDDO
    SKIP
ENDDO
```

Note that these examples use the dBASE II function EOF rather than the dBASE III function EOF().

Another common looping error is not to include a command that has the potential to change the condition, such as the SKIP command in these examples.

Still another common problem is called a "fencepost" error. This is where the loop repeats one time too many or too few. Usually, this is a problem with a greater-than or less-than comparison, or with the conditional test being at the wrong end of the loop.

Branching conditions are not correct. This occurs by not formulating the intended logical expression correctly. The difficulty of formulating a correct Boolean condition can be simplified by using parentheses to force a desired pattern of evaluation. For example, these two statements are quite different:

```
IF isA .AND. .NOT. isB .OR. isC
    <commands 1>
ENDIF

IF isA .AND. .NOT. (isB .OR. isC)
    <commands 2>
ENDIF
```

In the first IF statement, <commands 1> will be executed if *isB* is false. In the second IF statement, <commands 2> will be executed only if both *isB* and *isC* are false.

When comparing character strings in the logical expression, failing to account for the state of SET EXACT will also cause unexpected results.

Debugging Techniques

There are two basic steps to follow in debugging dBASE programs: first, isolate the problem, and second, fix it.

Isolate.   Check operating system level assumptions. This top-down approach is often overlooked until the problem cannot be found elsewhere.

1.   Are you using the correct operating system version?

Some modifications of CP/M or DOS may affect the way dBASE functions.

2.   Is there enough memory available for dBASE to use certain commands?

Some commands in dBASE III require more than the minimum memory configuration.

3.   Is there enough space on the disk?

File corruption and loss of data can be prevented by maintaining adequate space on the disk for the intended dBASE operations.

4.   Are the correct files on the disk?

An older version of a command file or database file can give the wrong output. Some commands are not interchangeable between different versions of dBASE.

5.   Is the disk badly worn?

The integrity of the data is questionable on a disk that has been overused, although this will usually cause disk-read errors that produce blatant messages from the operating system.

Narrow the scope.   Determine what part of the dBASE program is giving the problem. The use of the SET parameters: TALK, ECHO, DEBUG, or STEP can help narrow the problem down to a specific area in the code.

Use these flags in a judicious manner as you proceed in the debugging process. Our suggestion is to first start with the SET TALK ON flag at the beginning of the program. If this does not reveal the problem or if the problem is narrowed down to a section of code, then use SET ECHO ON (with SET DEBUG ON if you want the output from ECHO to go to your printer) on a selected portion of the program. If the problem is extremely difficult to detect, then use the SET STEP ON flag on a very narrow portion of the code. At some point in this process you should be able to see what has been going wrong. The use of the debugging flags is illustrated in this example:

```
* Use this flag as a first attempt in debugging...
SET TALK ON
     * Use one of these flags inside the program
     * when the problem is more difficult to detect
     * or has been isolated to a particular
     * portion of code...
     SET ECHO ON
     * Use this flag if you want output from ECHO
     * to go to the printer instead of the screen...
     SET DEBUG ON
          * To narrow the problem to a specific line,
          * this flag can be used when necessary...
          SET STEP ON
          *
          * <<<--THE PROBLEM CODE IS IN THIS AREA-->>>
          *
          * Restore the STEP flag to its default state...
          SET STEP OFF
     * Restore the ECHO and DEBUG flags to their
     * default values...
     SET DEBUG OFF
     SET ECHO OFF
* Restore the TALK flag to its usual program mode...
SET TALK OFF
```

Remove selected portions of code.   Determine if the program will perform as expected without a chosen portion, or "module," of code. Remove a module by placing an asterisk (*) in front of each command line. This is called "commenting out" the code. The same purpose can also be accomplished by placing the module within an IF...ENDIF structure whose logical expression is always false:

```
* dBASE III...
IF .F.
   <code will never execute>
ENDIF

* dBASE II...
IF F
   <code will never execute>
ENDIF
```

Fix.   To fix the problem once you've isolated it, don't make several changes all at one time. Change a single item and observe the effect before changing another one. This is the best way to determine exactly what result is produced by which change.

1.   Correct syntax bugs.

Consult the dBASE manual or other syntax reference source to clear up any doubts, as well as to confirm assumptions about commands that you are certain should work.

Caution: *All* technical manuals, especially those in the fast-paced computer industry, can contain mistakes or be incomplete. If the command is written *exactly* as it appears in the manual and still produces a syntax error, check the syntax tables in appendix E. If you still get a syntax error, it could be a bug in dBASE itself. See Work-Arounds under Algorithms below.

2.   Correct structure bugs.

Obtain a program listing, or printout, and match all the DO WHILEs with ENDDOs, IFs with ENDIFs, and DO CASEs with ENDCASEs. Drawing a line on the listing from each structure's opening statement to its related closing statement can help you see that these statements are properly nested and that there are no unmatched statements.

3.   Correct logic bugs.

Make sure the logical expressions in the DO WHILE, IF, and CASE statements evaluate to the values intended, and that the proper looping or branching is occurring. There are at least three ways to check this:

a. Set the SET ECHO ON flag before running the program. This allows you to observe how often the program will loop with the DO WHILE commands and where the program is actually branching with the IF and DO CASE commands. The program displayed on the screen will scroll by very quickly on occasion, and you may want to press <Ctrl-S> to pause the computer at those times; press <Ctrl-S> or <Ctrl-Q> to restart.

b. Temporarily insert output commands (?, ??, or @...SAY) at selected places in the program to display the value of the expressions and/or variables you are using. This gives you a chance to see how the values are changing.

c. Determine in the interactive mode what the expressions in IF, CASE, and DO WHILE commands will evaluate to under known conditions. This can be done at the dot prompt by typing an output command followed by the logical expression. The result of this should be a logical true or false. This way, you can see whether the expressions will evaluate as you intend.

Review the purpose and specifications of the program.

a. Review program logic to see if it accomplishes the logic flow intended. You may have written the program correctly, but you may have used the wrong algorithms. Isolating a specific algorithm and running it alone will determine whether it is capable of accomplishing its purpose. Also, seeing how other programmers handle the same type of application will help you in deciding what algorithms to use (the appendixes contain subroutines and command files that may help).

b. Review data flow by determining if the data and database files are correctly processed in the program. Any number of possible mistakes can be made when handling the data in the program. These mistakes usually result from not understanding how dBASE actually works. Reviewing both the Fundamentals and the Implementation sections of this guide will help.

4.   Start with fresh materials.

Use different disks. Make a new working copy of dBASE system files from the master disk. Recopy data files used. Rebuild index files.

5. Experiment.

a. "Hack it out" interactively. If all the surrounding conditions are identical, all commands will function the same from the dot prompt as they will in a command file. Work with small modules of code interactively until the desired results are obtained, then add them to the command file.

b. Try other methods. Try new ways of accomplishing the same steps in the program. Read programs written by other programmers to see how they handle similar operations.

VOCABULARY

Operators

None.

Functions

TEST()

> TEST(<expression>)
> [II] To find out if the <expression> is valid, and if so, what type of data it contains.

TIME()

> TIME()
> [III] To get the operating system time.

TYPE()

> TYPE(<character expression>)
> [III] To find out if an expression contained within the <character expression> is valid, and if so, what type of data it contains.

> TYPE(<expression>)
> [II] To find out the data type of a valid <expression>.

SET parameters

DEBUG

> SET DEBUG <switch>
> [III/II] To send the output of ECHO and STEP to the printer in order to keep the screen display intact.

ECHO

> SET ECHO <switch>
>> [III/II] To enable/disable output of the command line just prior to execution.

STEP

> SET STEP <switch>
>> [III/II] To pause program execution after every command.

TALK

> SET TALK <switch>
>> [III/II] To enable/disable the display of interactive dBASE messages.

Commands

<keypress>

> <^S>
>> [III/II] To momentarily pause command execution and screen scrolling from the keyboard. ^S or ^Q to restart.

Other Resources

None.

ALGORITHMS

Optimizing Code

The way we think when working out an algorithm is not always the most efficient use of code, yet it facilitates our step-by-step creation and debugging of the appropriate algorithm. Once completely written *and* debugged, the code can be optimized to run as fast as possible. A good example is the elapsed time algorithm from the two benchmarking programs in appendix C. In order to think it through, it was written in this form:

```
hh  = INT( es / 3600 )
mm  = INT( es /   60 ) - (hr*60)
ss  =        es        - (mn*60) - (hr*3600)
et  = SUBSTR(STR(hh+100,3),2) +':'+ SUBSTR(STR(mm+100,3),2) +':'+ ;
      SUBSTR(STR(ss+100,3),2)
```

When proven results were obtained and the program had been thoroughly tested and debugged, it was rewritten to one line of code:

```
et = SUBSTR(STR( INT(es/3600)                        +100,3),2) +':'+;
     SUBSTR(STR( INT(es/  60) - ( INT(es/3600)*60 )  +100,3),2) +':'+;
     SUBSTR(STR(        es     - ( INT(es/  60)*60 )  +100,3),2)
```

Using the benchmark program to test both ways of coding its own algorithm revealed that the second form executes slightly faster than the first. However, merely condensing lines of code into fewer lines is not always an effective solution. Sometimes this can have the opposite effect and actually take longer to execute. When a function or operator is used repeatedly, it is usually faster to save it in a memvar and use the memvar instead of waiting for an evaluation to return a result every time. For example, when receiving an operator entry and then testing the result:

```
* Slower...
WAIT TO memvar
DO CASE
    CASE UPPER(memvar) = "A"
        <commands>
    CASE UPPER(memvar) = "B"
        <commands>
    CASE UPPER(memvar) = "C"
        <commands>
ENDCASE

* Faster...
WAIT TO memvar
STORE UPPER(memvar) TO memvar
DO CASE
    CASE memvar = "A"
        <commands>
    CASE memvar = "B"
        <commands>
    CASE memvar = "C"
        <commands>
ENDCASE
```

These are brief examples, and do not fully reflect real programming situations. The rule of thumb is:

- The more a function or operator must evaluate the same parameters, the more time will be saved by storing the evaluation once and using that memvar for multiple operations.

Benchmarking

A benchmark can be defined as a test to measure the performance of hardware, software, or both. We use the term here to refer to a test of the performance of dBASE commands running on a particular computer. We do not give specific times or results from our tests because they are affected by individual hardware configurations. We use these benchmarks primarily as a method of comparison. In other words, given more than one way to do something in dBASE, which one runs the fastest?

Most of the time, we want to time something that occurs in a time frame too small to measure. When this is the case, we place it in a loop and measure the time it takes for a number of repeated executions. The program Bnchmk_2.prg is designed to do this. At other times, we only want to know how long one line of code, such as indexing a file, will take. Bnchmk_1.prg is designed for this application. Both of these programs are written in dBASE III, and are in appendix C.

Work-Arounds

Rocks are hard, water's wet, and *all* programming languages have bugs. That's just a simple fact of programming life. It is as unrealistic to curse bugs as it is to deny their existence. The idea is to discover where they are, what they do, and how to work around them.

As you have seen throughout this book, every trouble spot has a relatively simple work-around, even if it reminds you of the man who goes to the doctor complaining that it hurts when he turns a certain way, and the doctor says, "So don't turn that way." Of course it's an inconvenience, but it need not become an obstacle. We are all able to choose how we experience bugs and what we do about them.

CHAPTER TWENTY-FIVE

THE INTERACTIVE MODE

The dot prompt is as interactive as one can get with dBASE. It is useful to the programmer for trying out bits of code and constructing the elements of an application. Once within a program, several commands enter the full-screen interactive mode, which puts the proverbial ball in the operator's court. Exactly how much freedom the operator has depends on which interactive command is used with which optional parameters.

These commands place the operator in full control with no limiting options:

```
ASSIST   [III]
BROWSE
CREATE
HELP
MODIFY
REPORT   [II]
SET <without parameters>   [III]
```

These database commands place the operator in control subject to limiting options in a format file:

```
APPEND
CHANGE   [III]
EDIT
INSERT
```

READ is the only interactive command that places the operator in control subject to limiting options in either a command or format file. The @...GET command and format files are covered in chapter 18, "Input."

The more freedom an interactive command offers, the more the operator is required to know about using the control keys to do such things as move the cursor, save or abandon the work, and move the record pointer. These control keys are well covered in the dBASE documentation, and are therefore omitted here. The best way to learn them is hands-on.

In dBASE III, all full-screen interactive commands (except ASSIST, HELP, MODIFY COMMAND, READ, and SET) have an *options menu* which is toggled on and off with the Control-Home keys (^Home), and a *cursor control menu* which is toggled with the F1 function key.

Modify Command

The one interactive command of most interest to the programmer is MODIFY COMMAND, often called MODI COMM. Some of the other names it has been called are not printable in this book. In dBASE II, MODI COMM still has its problems although they are fewer in 2.4 than in 2.3. In dBASE III, the bugs appear to be gone, but at the time of this writing, the command is limited to files under 5,000 bytes.

In both dBASE III and II, MODI COMM has limits that make it useful for quick changes to small command files only. A more fully featured word processor is highly recommended if you are doing any volume of code writing. As an example, being able to find a key command statement, or to move or copy blocks of code are very important tools for the prolific programmer, and are nonexistent in MODIFY COMMAND. dBASE III does add the ability to read in (^KR) and write out (^KW) an entire file.

In both dBASE III and II, MODI COMM converts TAB characters to single spaces. It also resets the eighth, or "high order," bit which means that any ASCII characters with a code value higher than 128 (decimal) are replaced with the corresponding character that has an ASCII code value of 128 less. For example, the character with an ASCII value of 197 becomes an uppercase "E" with an ASCII value of sixty-nine.

In dBASE II MODIFY COMMAND:

- Command lines can be only seventy-nine or fewer characters long, not counting the carriage-return/line-feed pair at the end of the command line. Longer lines are truncated to this length when the file is saved.
- The cursor can be backed up in a file only about 4,000 bytes. To back up more than this, exit with a Control-W (^W), and come back in.

In dBASE III MODIFY COMMAND:

- The file size cannot exceed 5,000 bytes. A warning message comes on at byte 4,981 when keying in or when a file larger than 4,981 bytes is read in with <Ctrl-KR>.
- While keying in, an automatic, or "soft," carriage return occurs after the sixty-seventh column. No semicolon needs to be placed at the end of the line because dBASE uses its own soft carriage return to know that the line is continued. However, we recommend using semicolons and hard carriage returns for both readability as well as portability with other word-processing programs.

dBASE III allows any word processing or text editing program to be *assigned* in the Config.sys file (chapter 12), so that executing MODIFY COMMAND causes the assigned program to come up instead. dBASE II must be exited in order to edit command files with an external editor. The process of moving back and forth from an external editor in dBASE II can be speeded up by running dBASE II from the system access command of the editor, if it has one. In WordStar, for example, this is the "R" (Run a program) option at the Opening Menu.

External programs must be used in a mode that does not insert control characters in the text for page breaks, line feeds, etc. In WordStar, for example, use the "N" (Non-document) option rather than the "D" (Document) option. Even when using an external editor, we recommend keeping command lines to seventy-nine characters or less because the program is more readable, will print out on regular eight and a half by eleven paper, and MODIFY COMMAND can be used for quick changes without truncating command lines.

External Memo

Some word processing programs ask for the name of the file being edited in order to save it to disk. When an external editor is assigned to edit memo fields, the file on which it is actually working is called *Dbasedit.tmp*. When the external program is exited, dBASE adds the contents of Dbasedit.tmp to the database-text file.

Function Keys

These are the default assignments of the function keys on the IBM PC. Other computers may have different default values, or the use of their function keys may not be implemented at all in dBASE.

```
* dBASE III...
*
Function key  F1  - help;
Function key  F2  - assist;
Function key  F3  - list;
Function key  F4  - dir;
Function key  F5  - display structure;
Function key  F6  - display status;
Function key  F7  - display memory;
Function key  F8  - display;
Function key  F9  - append;
Function key  F10 - edit;

* dBASE II...
*
FUNCTION KEY ASSIGNMENTS
KEY      ASSIGNMENT
F1       HELP;
F2       DISP;
F3       LIST;
F4       LIST FILES;
F5       LIST STRU;
F6       LIST STATUS;
F7       LIST MEMO;
F8       CREATE;
F9       APPEND;
F10      EDIT #;
```

VOCABULARY

Operators

None.

Functions

None.

SET parameters

CONFIRM

> SET CONFIRM <switch>
> [III/II] To enable/disable the feature that forces the operator to press return in order to exit each input field.

F

> SET F<function-key number> TO "<character string>"
> [II] To change the operation of the computer's function keys.

FUNCTION

> SET FUNCTION <numeric expression> TO <character expression>
> [III] To change the operation of the computer's function keys. <numeric expression> is the function-key number (from 2 to 10).

MENUS

> SET MENUS <switch>
> [III] To enable/disable the display of cursor control keys in full-screen commands.

SCOREBOARD

> SET SCOREBOARD <switch>
> [III] To toggle on/off the dBASE messages on line zero.

Commands

APPEND

> APPEND
> [III/II] To add records to a database file without command file control.

ASSIST

> ASSIST
> [III] To enter the menu-driven Assistant mode.

BROWSE

> BROWSE
> [III/II] To interactively review/edit several database records at a time.
>
> BROWSE FIELDS <field name> {,<field name>}
> [III/II] To interactively review/edit specified fields in several database records at a time.

BROWSE [FIELDS <field name> {,<field name>}] ;
        [LOCK <numeric expression>] [FREEZE <field name>] ;
        [NOFOLLOW]
[III] To interactively review/edit [specified fields in] several database records and to establish the working environment of the BROWSE mode.

CHANGE

CHANGE FIELD <field name> {,<field name>} [<database parameter>]
[II] To review/edit selected fields in database records. Rarely used due to the awkwardness of the prompted line mode.

CHANGE FIELDS <field name> {,<field name>} [<database parameter>]
[III] To review/edit selected fields in database records.

CHANGE [<database parameter>]
[III/II] To review/edit database records. Full-screen mode in III, command-line mode in II.

CREATE

CREATE LABEL
[III] To create a new label form.

CREATE REPORT
[III] To create a new report form.

CREATE [<database filename>]
[III/II] To begin a new database file in the interactive mode.

EDIT

EDIT
[III/II] To review/edit database records.

EDIT <numeric expression>
[III/II] To review/edit database records starting with a specified record number.

EDIT RECORD <numeric expression>
[III] To review/edit database records starting with a specified record number.

HELP

HELP
[III/II] To enter the HELP mode.

HELP <keyword>
[III/II] II = To display the HELP message for a particular command.
        III = To enter the HELP mode at the <keyword> page.

INSERT

INSERT [BEFORE]
[III/II] To insert a new record into an unindexed database file immediately following [or preceding] the current record, and place the operator in full-screen editing mode.

MODIFY

MODIFY COMMAND <command or procedure filename>
[III/II] To create or edit a command or procedure file.

MODIFY COMMAND <text filename.ext>
[III/II] To edit any standard ASCII text file.

MODIFY FILE <text filename>
[III] To create or edit a text file with no filename extension.

MODIFY LABEL
[III] To change an existing label form.

MODIFY REPORT
[III] To change an existing report form.

MODIFY STRUCTURE
[III/II] To modify a database structure interactively.

READ

READ
[III/II] To place the cursor in variables placed on the screen with @...GET.

READ NOUPDATE
[II] To put the cursor in non-key variables placed on the screen with @...GET whenever there is an open indexed database file.

REPORT

REPORT [FORM <new report filename>]
[II] To create a new report form.

SET

SET
[III] To enter the interactive SET-menu mode.

<keypress>

<^P>
[III/II] To turn the printer on and off from the keyboard.

<^PrtSc>

    [III] To turn the printer on and off from the keyboard.

<^R>

    [II] To repeat the previously issued command statement from the keyboard.

<^S>

    [III/II] To momentarily pause command execution and screen scrolling from the keyboard. ^S or ^Q to restart.

Other Resources

None.

ALGORITHMS

Command File Dot Prompt

There are a couple of ways to allow the operator to enter commands from the dot prompt while program control remains within a command file. One way is through the use of the macro (&):

```
* dBASE III...
*
STORE "Initialize" TO command
DO WHILE "" # command
   ACCEPT "DOT " TO command
   IF "" # command
      &command
   ENDIF
ENDDO

* dBASE II...
*
STORE "Initialize" TO command
DO WHILE " " # command
   ACCEPT "DOT " TO command
   IF " " # command
      &command
   ENDIF
ENDDO
```

To exit from this mode, the operator simply hits the <RETURN> key. Obviously, there is no error trapping, and if a command is improperly entered, it will produce a syntax error. If the operator enters CANCEL, EXIT [III], QUIT or RETURN, program control will transfer out of the command file. In dBASE II, control also returns to the real dot prompt when certain errors occur, such as FILE IS CURRENTLY OPEN.

There is a popular misconception that, in dBASE II, the TEST() function can be used to test the validity of a command. That is not true. TEST() in II and TYPE() in III can only be used to verify the validity of an expression, but not an entire command statement. At the time of this writing, dBASE does not have a facility to test the validity of a command. More control is obtained by placing a selection of commands in a DO CASE structure, and having the operator select a command from a menu. For example:

```
@ 5,5 SAY "A --> LIST Name, Address, City"
@ 6,5 SAY "B --> LIST Name, Telephone"
@ 7,5 SAY "C --> LIST Name, Sex, Age"
STORE "?" TO choice
DO WHILE .NOT. choice $ "ABC"
    STORE "?" TO choice
    @ 10,10 GET choice PICTURE "!"
    READ
    CLEAR GETS
ENDDO
*
DO CASE
    CASE choice = "A"
        LIST Name, Address, City
    CASE choice = "B"
        LIST Name, Telephone
    CASE choice = "C"
        LIST Name, Sex, Age
ENDCASE
```

On computers with function keys that are enabled in the version of dBASE being used, commands can be assigned to a function key for the operator to press.

Long Command Lines

During development, the repetitive interactive entering of long lines of code is made easier with the macro. The command statement is stored in a memvar and executed with the macro. For example:

```
STORE "USE Filename INDEX Ndx-1, Ndx-2, Ndx-3" TO u
&u
```

Different applications would each have a separate set of development macros which can be saved in a memory file and used when working on that application.

Work-Arounds

At the time of this writing, the only work-around for the limits of MODIFY COMMAND is to use another text editor or word processor. The programs in the appendix that were written by the authors were all written using WordStar. In dBASE III, MODI COMM's biggest limitation is size. Otherwise, it can be used with confidence if you don't want additional features such as global search and replace ability. In dBASE II, if you use MODI COMM occasionally, do not back up in the file more than a screenful or two; exit and come back in instead. Hit control keys individually for each move rather than holding them down. Handle with care: the more cautious you are, the less trouble you will have. Remember to always keep backups.

Related Algorithms

The second work-around in chapter 14, "Command File Handling."

APPENDIX A

dBASE III AND dBASE II ERROR MESSAGES

The dBASE III and dBASE II error messages are merged together in this alphabetical listing so as to provide a convenient way of describing them, since many of the explanations are the same for both versions. The dBASE II error messages in this listing can be distinguished from the dBASE III error messages in that dBASE II error messages *always* display in uppercase, and dBASE III error messages display in both upper- and lowercase. The only exception to this rule is the dBASE III "*** STACK OVERFLOW ***" error message.

Explanations for all the dBASE III error messages were not available at the time of this writing. You may request a more up-to-date listing of dBASE III error messages from the Software Support Center at Ashton-Tate.

`0% Sorted Records do not balance ...(PROGRAM ERROR)`

`ALIAS name already in use`

USE, when the database filename is already in USE as an alias name.

`Alias not found`

SELECT attempted to select a data area outside the A to J or one to ten range, or an alias that was not previously defined.

`ALTERNATE could not be opened`

`BAD DECIMAL WIDTH FIELD`

CREATE or MODIFY STRUCTURE when the decimal width is zero or greater than 254 in dBASE II version 2.3 (greater than 63 in version 2.42). In practice, the decimal width for a numeric field cannot be greater than 125 in dBASE II version 2.3 and 2.4 (and greater than 63 in version 2.42). A decimal width can be, at most, two less than the width of the field. A decimal width that is equal or one less than the field width will not allow the data to be entered.

BAD NAME FIELD

CREATE and MODIFY STRUCTURE if the field name is syntactically incorrect, has already been defined, has no characters, or has more than ten characters.
TOTAL if a field name is not in the source database.
UPDATE if a field name is syntactically incorrect.

BAD TYPE FIELD

CREATE or MODIFY STRUCTURE when the type is not character, numeric, or logical (C, N, or L).

BAD WIDTH FIELD

CREATE or MODIFY STRUCTURE when the field width is zero or greater than 255. Does not correctly test for logical which can only have a width of one, and numeric which cannot have a width greater than 127.

Beginning of file encountered

Attempt to position the record pointer above the top of the file.

*** BEYOND STRING
*** Execution error on SUBSTR() : start point out of range

The value of the <start> parameter in the substring function (SUBSTR() in III, $() in II) is greater than the length of the string. For example:

```
* ---In dBASE II:
STORE "now is the time" TO source
STORE $( source, 50, 10 ) TO another
*                        ↑_____This parameter exceeds the
*                                 length of the memory variable.
```

Cannot erase open file

ERASE or DELETE FILE if the file is currently open.

CANNOT INSERT - THERE ARE NO RECORDS IN DATABASE FILE

INSERT must be before or after an existing record. Cannot INSERT on an empty database. Cannot INSERT at the bottom, unless INSERT BEFORE is used. Use the APPEND command for these cases.

CANNOT OPEN FILE

LOAD or RESTORE could not open the specified input file.

Can't select requested database

SELECTing a work area outside the range of one through ten.

`** checksum error`

COMMAND FILE CANNOT BE FOUND

DO could not open the command file. A user will sometimes attempt to DO a command file that he knows exists, not realizing that inside that command file is another DO <command file> for a command file which does not exist.

Cyclic relation

SET RELATION INTO a work area that has a RELATION set which affects the currently selected work area.

DATA ITEM NOT FOUND

REPLACE had no replacement phrases or a field could not be found in the structure. Also occurs if the NOUPDATE clause is entered as two words instead of one.

Data type mismatch

SORT cannot sort on logical or memo data types.
REPLACE a field of one data type with a field or an expression of another data type.
SEEK, where <expression> is not the same data type as the master index key expression.
Attempt to compose an expression of differing data types.

DATABASE IN USE IS NOT INDEXED
Database is not indexed

FIND or SEEK attempted when an index was not open. FIND and SEEK are only permitted on indexed data files.

DIRECTORY IS FULL
Directory is full

An attempt is being made to open or create a file when the disk's directory is full.

DISK IS FULL

An error code was returned from the operating system when an attempt was made to write to the disk. On the 16-bit implementation of dBASE II, not all error codes returned from DOS were implemented. Therefore, the error message could appear when dBASE II overlooks simple syntax errors such as having a colon in the filename or forgetting to enter the filename in a REPORT FORM command.

Disk full when writing file — <filename>
Abort, Ignore or Delete old files (A,I, or D)?

Attempt to write to a disk that has no more room.

END OF FILE FOUND UNEXPECTEDLY
End of file encountered

   USE, APPEND FROM, UPDATE FROM attempted to open a data file with an incomplete structure. In dBASE II, the physical end-of-file was found before 522 bytes could be read.
   FIND or SEEK attempted to find on an index file that is out of balance or corrupted.
   REPORT, MODIFY REPORT attempted to open a report form file in dBASE III with an incomplete structure.
   SKIP attempted to skip past the end-of-file of a data file in dBASE III.
   In dBASE II, versions 2.3x and 2.4, when an attempt is made to index a file on more than 100 characters. Changed to TOO MANY CHARACTERS in 2.41 and 2.42.

End of file or ERROR on keyboard input

Excess header lines lost

***Execution error on + : concatenated string too large

   Attempt to concatenate characters where the total is greater than 254 characters.

***Execution error on LOG() :

   Function argument is zero or a negative number.

***Execution error on SORT :

***Execution error on SPACE() :

   Function argument is less than zero or greater than 254.

***Execution error on SQRT :

   Function argument is a negative number.

***Execution error on STR :

   Length parameter exceeds nineteen, or decimal parameter exceeds length minus one.

*** Execution error on SUBSTR() : start point out of range

   (See the error message, "*** BEYOND STRING").

expected ON or OFF

"FIELD" PHRASE NOT FOUND

CHANGE command had no "FIELD" phrase when needed.

FILE ALREADY EXISTS
File already exists

RENAME when the TO file is already on the disk.
CREATE when the data file to be created is already on the disk (dBASE III).

FILE DOES NOT EXIST
File does not exist

APPEND if FROM file cannot be opened.
DELETE FILE if file cannot be found.
ERASE (dBASE III) if file cannot be found.
RENAME if old file cannot be found.
USE when file cannot be opened.

FILE IS CURRENTLY OPEN
File is already open

DELETE FILE if file is currently open.
ERASE (dBASE III) if file is currently open.
RENAME if file is open elsewhere.
Attempt to open a file that has been opened in another work area.
Attempt to open the same index file in more than one work area.
Attempt to COPY or SORT a data file onto itself.
A command file calling itself.

File is not accessible

CREATE when filename contains invalid characters (such as \ = : + " < > ? * [ ] and |).
MODIFY COMMAND when the disk directory is full and there is no room for a new file or a backup (.BAK) file.
COPY when the target filename is omitted.

File too large---some data may be lost

Opening an existing file over 5,000 bytes with MODIFY COMMAND.

FOR and WHILE cannot both be specified

Attempt to use both FOR and WHILE in the same syntax.

FORMAT FILE CANNOT BE OPENED

SET FORMAT TO could not open the specified format file.

ILLEGAL DATA TYPE

SORT cannot sort logical type data.

ILLEGAL GOTO VALUE

GOTO (or any command that has a RECORD phrase) attempted to position the data file to record zero or record number 65536. There is no message on a GOTO value of 65537 in version 2.3D, from 65537 to 65546 in 2.3B, 65537 and 65538 in version 2.4, and 65537 to 65565 in version 2.41. Using a record number greater than those indicated will give the error message, "RECORD OUT OF RANGE."

ILLEGAL VARIABLE NAME

BROWSE, CHANGE, COPY, JOIN, RELEASE, REPLACE, SORT, and others where field names or memory variable names are syntactically incorrect. Only alphanumerics and colons are allowed in dBASE II variable and field names.

Improper data type in subsubtotal expression

REPORT FORM has logical or memo data type in a subtotal expression.

INDEX DOES NOT MATCH DATABASE
Index file does not match database

SET INDEX TO or USE was performed with an index that does not match the database. The fieldnames of the key expression stored in the index anchor node did not match those of the database file.

INDEX FILE CANNOT BE OPENED

SET INDEX TO or USE could not open an index file. The index file may not exist on the drive specified.

Index is too big (100 char maximum)

INDEX, when the index key expression has more than 100 characters. The dBASE II error message for this condition is "END OF FILE FOUND UNEXPECTEDLY" in versions 2.3x and 2.4. It is "TOO MANY CHARACTERS" in versions 2.41 and 2.42.

Insert impossible

Insufficient memory

Attempt to GET more variables than there are allowable GETS. The default is 128, and can be changed in the Config.db file from thirty-five to 1,023.

Attempt to RUN an external program, or bring up an external word processor in MODIFY COMMAND, when there is not enough memory in the computer. The amount of memory required is 256K for dBASE, 17K for the DOS file Command.com, plus whatever the external program requires.

Attempt to RUN an external program, or bring up an external word processor in MODIFY COMMAND, when Command.com is not on the A: drive or in the location specified by SET COMSPEC.

`Internal error - bucket overfilled`

Total characters used in all report parameters exceeds 1,440 bytes.

`Internal error - bucklen overfilled`

`Internal error - eval work area overflow`

`Internal error - illegal opcode`

`Internal error - Unknown scedit() code in dospc1:`

`Internal error - Unknown scedit() return code:`

`Internal error in CREATE REPORT state machine`

`*** Interrupted ***`

When the <Esc> key is pressed to abort a command or program.

`Invalid date (hit SPACE)`

Attempt to enter an invalid date in a date type variable

`Invalid function argument`

Function argument is the wrong data type or beyond the range allowed.

`JOIN ATTEMPTED TO GENERATE MORE THAN 65,534 RECORDS`

JOIN command tried to make an output file exceeding the record limit for a database.

`KEYS ARE NOT THE SAME LENGTH`

UPDATE if the key field in the USE data file is not the same length as in the FROM data file.

`---keyword not found`

Unrecognized word in the Config.db file.

Label contents must be CHARACTER type

LABEL FORM contains data types other than character.

Label contents: unknown scedit() return code:

Label file invalid

LABEL FORM when the specified file was not created with CREATE LABEL or MODIFY LABEL.

Line exceeds maximum of 254 characters

Attempt to execute a command statement over 254 bytes long either from the dot prompt, a command file, format file, or procedure.

MACRO IS NOT A CHARACTER STRING

When a macro references a memory variable that is not a character type. Usually the user is attempting a macro on a numeric memory variable. The memory variable has to be changed to a string, as in the following example:

```
* ---FINDing on a numeric key in dBASE II.
STORE STR(number,10) TO string
FIND &string

* ---In dBASE III, the SEEK command can be used with a
* ---numeric memory variable.
SEEK number
```

Memo file cannot be opened

USE when the .DBT data file containing the memo information is not on the same drive as the .DBF data file, or PATH has not been SET to the location of the .DBT file, or the .DBT file has been renamed.

Memory variable file invalid

RESTORE FROM a file not created with the SAVE TO command.

MORE THAN 5 FIELDS TO SUM

SUM is limited to five fields in dBASE II. dBASE III is limited to thirty-two fields.

MORE THAN 7 INDEX FILES SELECTED

SET INDEX TO or USE with more than seven index files. dBASE II cannot update more than seven indexes at one time.

NO DATABASE FILE IN USE, ENTER FILENAME:
No database is in USE, enter filename:

Any command that uses the currently selected data file when the file is not open. May seem mysterious when there is a data file in USE in a different work area.

NO EXPRESSION TO SUM

SUM command had no field or expression to sum.

NO FIND
No find

FIND or SEEK when the key expression is not in the index file.

NO "FOR" PHRASE

Missing FOR phrase in command line.

NO "FROM" PHRASE

UPDATE command had no input file.

No room for heading.

NON-NUMERIC EXPRESSION
Non-numeric expression

A dBASE II or dBASE III command (such as, the SUM command) was given a non-numeric expression, when expecting a numeric expression.

Not a Character expression

Attempt to use a date, logical, or numeric expression in a LABEL form.

NOT A dBASE II DATABASE
Not a dBASE database

An attempt to open a database that does not have a hexadecimal 02 as its first byte (dBASE III databases have a hexadecimal 83 if a memo field is present and hexadecimal 03 otherwise). This may indicate a corrupted header.

Not a Logical expression

Using a character, date, or numeric expression in a FOR or WHILE <condition>.

Not enough diskspace for sort

Not enough records to sort

Attempt to sort a data file with less than two records.

NUMERIC FIELD OVERFLOW
Numeric overflow (data was lost)

REPLACE when a numeric expression value is too large for a numeric field.
TOTAL (dBASE III) when the structure of the target database file is not large enough to hold the total.

"ON" PHRASE NOT FOUND

INDEX attempted without an "ON" phrase.

Operation with MEMO-type field invalid

A memo field cannot be used in expressions, such as in the expression portion of @...SAY commands.
INDEX ON, where a memo field is used in the key expression.

OUT OF MEMORY FOR MEMORY VARIABLES
Out of memory variable memory

(dBASE II). Attempt to store data to memory variables that exceeds the number of bytes in the memory buffer. The memory buffer is 1,536 bytes long. In all versions of dBASE II, logical variables occupy two bytes. In versions 2.3, 2.4, and 2.42, numeric variables occupy six, seven, and ten bytes respectively; and character variables occupy the length of the string plus one, two, and two respectively. The error message can also occur with memory fragmentation, that is, large gaps exist in the memory buffer that cannot be recovered. Because memory variables are stored on a first-fit basis, large gaps of unused space can occur with frequent STORE and RELEASE of memory variables or with frequent string manipulations. Memory variables intended to be used throughout the application should be initialized at the very beginning of the system and not RELEASEd at all. One way of recovering the memory fragmentation that may have occurred is to SAVE TO <memory file> and then RESTORE FROM <memory file>. This process compresses the memory variables and eliminates the large gaps between them.

(dBASE III). The default memory buffer size is 6,000 bytes long and can be increased in Config.db using the MVARSIZ parameter. Numeric variables occupy nine bytes, logical variables two, date variables nine, and character variables occupy the length of the string plus two.

Out of memory variable slots

An attempt to create more than 256 memory variables.

---out of range

Patch is invalid

   Invalid PATCH parameters in Config.db file.

RECORD LENGTH EXCEEDS MAXIMUM SIZE (OF 1000)

   CREATE or MODIFY STRUCTURE attempted to exceed the dBASE II record size limit.

RECORD NOT IN INDEX
Record is not in index

   GO (or any command with a RECORD phrase) positioning the record pointer to a record that is not in the index file. Usually caused by the index file not being in use when a record was added. Either REINDEX or create the index file again with the INDEX ON command.

Record not inserted

RECORD OUT OF RANGE
Record is out of range

   EDIT or GOTO a record number that is greater than the number of records in the database.
   Any command that has a RECORD clause with a record that is larger than the size of the database.
   When the record count in the data file is zero and the index file does not reflect an index to an empty data file.
   When the record count of the data file is different from that of the index file, and an attempt is made to access a record that is not in the index file.

Report file invalid.

   REPORT FORM when the specified file was not created with CREATE REPORT or MODIFY REPORT.

SAY/GET position is off the screen

   Coordinates of the @...SAY or @...GET command are out of range. The row position must be from zero to twenty-four, and column position must be from zero to seventy-nine when displaying to the screen.

SORTER INTERNAL ERROR, NOTIFY SCDP

   SORT when record counts between passes do not add up correctly. SCDP is the former development group for dBASE II. In this case notify the Software Support Center at Ashton-Tate.

SOURCE AND DESTINATION DATA TYPES ARE DIFFERENT

   Attempt to REPLACE a field of one data type with an expression of a different data type.

*** STACK OVERFLOW ***

String too large

Structure invalid

*** SYNTAX ERROR ***
Syntax error

An incorrect or incomplete construction of a command clause or expression.

Syntax error in contents

Syntax error in field expression.

A syntax error in the REPORT FORM file that escaped the error trapping of CREATE REPORT or MODIFY REPORT.

Syntax error in group expression

REPORT FORM contains a subtotal expression with mismatched data types.

Syntax error in subgroup expression

REPORT FORM contains a sub-subtotal expression with mismatched data types.

SYNTAX ERROR IN FORMAT SPECIFICATION

@...GET was issued for a field that could not be found.
Coordinates of the @ command are improperly formed.

SYNTAX ERROR, RE-ENTER
Syntax error, try again:

INPUT when a syntactically incorrect expression was entered.
REPORT when a syntactically incorrect expression was entered in the WIDTH,CONTENTS section of the report (dBASE II only).

** System error:

This message is not implemented in version 1.00.

"TO" PHRASE NOT FOUND

A required TO phrase could not be found in the command line.

This error will also occur if a previously undefined variable in the command line begins with the letter T, F, Y, or N. For example:

```
* ---The variable "total" was not previously defined.
STORE total + 1 TO newamount
```

TOO MANY CHARACTERS

APPEND, CHANGE, CREATE, EDIT, and INSERT commands when the input data is longer than the field length when dBASE II is installed with no full-screen operations, or when SCREEN is SET OFF. Attempt to index a file on a key expression of more than 100 characters (versions 2.41 and 2.42).

TOO MANY FILES ARE OPEN
Too many files are open

Any command that will cause the number of open files to exceed sixteen in dBASE II (thirteen in dBASE III if the DOS 2.x operating system was initialized with FILES=20). These include: data files, index files, form files, format files, alternate files, memory files, command files, procedure files, and temporary files when SORTing.

Too many indices

SET INDEX TO or USE with more than seven index files. dBASE III cannot update more than seven indexes at one time.

TOO MANY MEMORY VARIABLES

Any command creating memory variables, such as COUNT, STORE, or SUM attempting to make one more memory variable than the 64 memory variable limit.

Too many merge steps

Too many sort key fields.

Total label width exceeds maximum allowable size

---truncated

Command line truncated from Config.db file because the specified filename exceeds eight characters.

UNASSIGNED FILE NUMBER
Unassigned file #

Internal dBASE error. Improper use of the RESET command (in dBASE II) will sometimes cause it. A badly formatted or worn diskette is also known to cause it.
HELP without the Dbasemsg.txt file (dBASE II version 2.4x).

Unbalanced parenthesis

Must have matching parentheses in an expression.

Undetermined string

*** UNKNOWN COMMAND
*** Unrecognized command verb

When the first word in a command line is not a dBASE command verb.
(dBASE III). Using a macro (&) on a non-character variable at the beginning of a command line. When a macro is used on a non-character variable, the macro and variable name are left intact, that is, no macro substitution takes place. If this happens at the beginning of a command line, dBASE III is not be able to find a command that begins with a macro character.

Unknown function

Specifiying a function that is unrecognizable.

Unrecognized phrase/keyword in command

Specifying a conditional or assignment phrase beginning with an invalid keyword.

Unterminated string

A string expression without a terminating delimiter. The valid string delimiters are matching single quotes, double quotes, and left and right square brackets.

VARIABLE CANNOT BE FOUND
Variable not found

A command using a field name that could not be found in the structure of the currently selected data file, or in the area specified with a work area prefix.
A command using a memvar name that is not currently initialized.
(dBASE II) SUM on a database that does not contain a numeric field.

Warning – REPORT FORM EMPTY

"WITH" PHRASE NOT FOUND

REPLACE could not find a "WITH" phrase following a field name.

*** ZERO DIVIDE
Zero divide (result = 0)

Attempt to divide a number or numeric expression by zero.

APPENDIX B

SUBROUTINES

DATE ROUTINES

DATE-.PRG	Front-end program to utilize date routines
SETDATE.CMD	Sets the dBASE II system date
DATETEST.PRG	Verifies a date
CAL2JUL.PRG	Converts calendar to Julian
JUL2CAL.PRG	Converts julian to Calendar
WEEKDAY.PRG	Returns the day of week from calendar date
CHECKDAT.PRG	LISTs records when between two dates
JULIAN.PRG	Converts Gregorian date to a Julian Period day

GENERAL PURPOSE

AMT2WORD.PRG	Converts a dollar amount to word equivalent

MATH ROUTINES

MATH-.PRG	Front-end program to utilize math routines
SQROOT.PRG	Returns the SQUARE ROOT of a number
EXPONENT.PRG	Returns the EXPONENT of a number
NATLOG.PRG	Returns the NATURAL LOGARITHM of a number
TRIGDEMO.PRG	Demonstrates the use of TRIG.PRG
TRIG.PRG	Transcendental functions (SINE, COSINE, TANGENT, ARCSIN, ARCCOS, and ARCTAN)

DATE-.PRG

Description. Front-end program to utilize the DATETEST, WEEKDAY, JUL2CAL and CAL2JUL subroutines found in this section. This program shows how to pass the required memory variables to each subroutine and what to check for after each is executed.

```
* Program.: DATE-.PRG
* Author..: Luis A. Castro
* Date....: 01/19/84
* Notice..: Copyright 1984, Luis A. Castro, All Rights Reserved.
* Version.: dBASE II, version 2.4x
* Notes...: Front-end program to utilize DATETEST,
*           WEEKDAY, JUL2CAL, and CAL2JUL subroutines.
* Local...: select, mdate, row, string, is:error, julian
*
SET TALK OFF
SET BELL OFF
SET COLON OFF
SET RAW ON
ERASE
@ 2, 0 SAY "DEMONSTRATION of DATE ROUTINES"
@ 2,72 SAY DATE()
@ 3, 0 SAY "========================================="
@ 3,40 SAY "========================================="
STORE 11 TO row
STORE "X" TO select
DO WHILE select <> " "
   @ 10,0
   STORE " " TO select
   @ 5,0 SAY "1. CAL2JUL()  =  calendar to julian conversion"
   @ 6,0 SAY "2. JUL2CAL()  =  julian to calendar conversion"
   @ 7,0 SAY "3. DATETEST() =  verify a date"
   @ 8,0 SAY "4. WEEKDAY()  =  day of the week"
   @ 9,0 GET select PICTURE "!"
   READ
   IF select = " " .OR. .NOT. select $ "1234"
      LOOP
   ENDIF
   @ 9,0 SAY " "
   STORE "  /  /  " TO mdate
   STORE "0      " TO string
   * ---Enter date parameter.
   DO CASE
      CASE select $ "14"
         @ 10,0 SAY "ENTER DATE as MM/DD/YY ";
                GET mdate PICTURE "99/99/99"
      CASE select = "2"
         @ 10,0 SAY "ENTER JULIAN DATE as 999999 ";
                GET string PICTURE "999999"
      CASE select = "3"
         STORE "  /  /    " TO mdate
         @ 10,0 SAY "ENTER DATE as MM/DD/YY or MM/DD/YYYY ";
                GET mdate PICTURE "99/99/9999"
ENDCASE
READ
IF mdate = "  /  /  " .AND. "0" = TRIM(string)
   LOOP
ENDIF
STORE VAL(string) TO julian
@ row,0 SAY " "
*
* ---Execute a date routine.
DO CASE
   CASE select = "1"
```

```
    * ---CALENDAR TO JULIAN CONVERSION.
       ? "    CAL2JUL (",mdate,") ="
       * ---First, verify the date.
       DO Datetest
       * ---Now, get the julian date.
       IF is:error
          ?? " invalid date"
       ELSE
          DO Cal2jul
          ?? julian
       ENDIF
    CASE select = "2"
    * ---JULIAN TO CALENDAR CONVERSION.
       ? "    JUL2CAL (",TRIM(string),") =   "
       DO Jul2cal
       ?? mdate
    CASE select = "3"
    * ---VERIFY A DATE.
       ? "    DATETEST (",mdate,") =   "
       DO Datetest
       IF is:error
          ?? '"invalid"'
       ELSE
          ?? '"valid"'
       ENDIF
    CASE select = "4"
    * ---DAY OF THE WEEK.
       * ---First, verify the date.
       DO Datetest
       * ---Now, get the day of the week.
       ? "    WEEKDAY (",mdate,") =   "
       IF is:error
          ?? "invalid date"
       ELSE
          DO Weekday
          ?? week:num, " - " + week:day
       ENDIF
    ENDCASE
    STORE row + 1 TO row
ENDDO
SET BELL ON
SET TALK ON
SET COLON ON
SET RAW OFF
RELEASE select, mdate, row
RETURN
* EOF: DATE-.PRG
```

SETDATE.CMD

Description.   Sets the dBASE II system date with a verified date. This routine is only useful when using dBASE II on CP/M-80 or dBASE 2.3D on 16-bit computers, since dBASE II is not designed to load the computer's system date on these computers.

```
* Program.: SETDATE.CMD
* Author..: Luis A. Castro.
* Date....: 7/28/83, 11/20/83.
* Notice..: Copyright 1983 & 1984, Ashton-Tate, All Rights Reserved.
* Version.: dBASE II, version 2.3x, 2.4x
* Notes...: Sets the system date with a verified date.
*
SET TALK OFF
SET BELL OFF
IF $(DATE(),1,5)="00/00"
    *
    * ---The system date was not entered.
    ERASE
    @ 2, 0 SAY "S Y S T E M    D A T E"
    @ 3, 0 SAY "========================================="
    @ 3,40 SAY "========================================="
    *
    * ---Loop through until a valid date is entered.
    STORE F TO is:valid
    DO WHILE .NOT. is:valid
        STORE "  /  /  " TO mdate
        @ 5,0 SAY "Enter system date as MM/DD/YY ";
            GET mdate PICTURE "99/99/99"
        READ
        * ---Date verification routine.
        DO Datetest
    ENDDO
    *
    * ---The system date is set at this point.
    SET DATE TO &mdate
    RELEASE is:valid, mdate
ENDIF
SET BELL ON
SET TALK ON
RETURN
* EOF: SETDATE.CMD
```

DATETEST.PRG

Description.   Subroutine to verify a calendar date. This program will check for leap year and the special cases of years divisible by 100 and 400.

Input.   Assumes the date entered is in MM/DD/YY or MM/DD/YYYY format. Also assumes the date was entered with a "99/99/99" or "99/99/9999" picture clause.

Output.   Returns a error flag that is false if the date is correct and true otherwise.

```
* Program.: DATETEST.PRG
* Author..: Luis A. Castro
* Date....: 8/2/83, 11/20/83, 01/19/84
* Notice..: Copyright 1983 & 1984, Ashton-Tate, All Rights Reserved
* Version.: dBASE II, version 2.4x
* Notes...: Subroutine to verify a date.
* Local...: t:month, t:day, t:year
*
```

```
*    IN:    mdate-C-8         Calendar date, assumed to be in
*           or mdate-C-10.    MM/DD/YY or MM/DD/YYYY format.
*
*    OUT: is:error-L-1.       Validation flag
*
STORE T TO is:error
STORE TRIM(mdate) TO mdate
IF ( LEN(mdate) <> 8 .AND. LEN(mdate) <> 10 ) .OR.;
   " "$mdate .OR. "-"$mdate .OR. "."$mdate .OR. "+"$mdate
   * ---Must not contain special characters.
   RETURN
ENDIF
*
STORE VAL( $(mdate,1,2) ) TO t:month
STORE VAL( $(mdate,4,2) ) TO t:day
STORE VAL( $(mdate,7,LEN(mdate) - 6) ) TO t:year
*
DO CASE
   CASE t:month < 1 .OR. t:month > 12 .OR. t:day < 1 .OR.;
      t:day > VAL( $("003129313031303131303313031",;
      ( t:month - 13*INT(t:month/13) ) * 2 + 1, 2 ) )
      *
   CASE LEN(mdate)= 8 .AND. t:month=2 .AND.;
      t:day > 28 .AND. t:year/4 > INT(t:year/4)
      *
   CASE LEN(mdate)=10 .AND. t:month=2 .AND.;
      t:day > 28 .AND. ( (t:year/4 > INT(t:year/4) .AND.;
      t:year/100 = INT(t:year/100)) .OR.;
      t:year/400 > INT(t:year/400) )
      *
   OTHERWISE
      STORE F TO is:error
ENDCASE
*
RELEASE t:month, t:day, t:year
RETURN
* EOF: DATETEST.PRG
```

CAL2JUL.PRG

Description. Subroutine to provide calendar to julian conversion. Assumes the date to be valid and in MM/DD/YY format. The program will return the julian date to the memory variable "julian."

```
* Program.: CAL2JUL.PRG
* Author..: Anonymous, modified by Luis A. Castro.
* Date....: 1/12/83, 11/20/83, 01/19/84
* Notice..: Copyright 1983 & 1984, Ashton-Tate, All Rights Reserved
* Version.: dBASE II, version 2.4x
* Notes...: Calendar to julian date conversion.
* Local...: t:year, t:month, t:day
*
*    IN: mdate-C-8       Calendar date, assumes date is in
*                        MM/DD/YY format, and a valid date.
```

```
*    OUT: julian-N-6      Julian date
*
STORE VAL($(mdate,1,2)) TO t:month
STORE VAL($(mdate,4,2)) TO t:day
STORE VAL($(mdate,7,2) ) + 1900 TO t:year
STORE INT( 30.57 * t:month ) +;
      INT( 365.25 * t:year - 395.25 ) + t:day TO julian
*
* ---Adjust the julian date on leap year.
IF t:month > 2
   STORE julian - 1 TO julian
   IF INT( t:year / 4 ) * 4 <> t:year
      STORE julian - 1 TO julian
   ENDIF
ENDIF
*
RELEASE t:year, t:month, t:day
RETURN
* EOF: CAL2JUL.PRG
```

JUL2CAL.PRG

Description.   Subroutine to provide julian to calendar conversion. A julian date is expected. This program will return the date in MM/DD/YY format, and force leading zeroes where needed by use of the DATE() function.

```
* Program.: JUL2CAL.PRG
* Author..: Anonymous, modified by Luis A. Castro
* Date....: 1/12/83, 11/20/83, 01/19/84
* Notice..: Copyright 1983 & 1984, Ashton-Tate, All Rights Reserved
* Version.: dBASE II, version 2.4x
* Notes...: Julian to calendar date conversion.
* Local...: t:year, t:month, t:day, t:date, t:leapday
*
*    IN: julian-N-6      Julian date.
*   OUT: mdate-C-8       Calendar date in MM/DD/YY format.
*
STORE INT( julian / 365.26 ) + 1 TO t:year
STORE julian + INT( 395.25 - 365.25 * t:year ) TO t:day
STORE 1 TO t:leapday
*
* ---Calculate extra day for leap year.
IF INT(t:year/4) * 4 <> t:year
   STORE 2 TO t:leapday
ENDIF
*
* ---Calculate actual number of days.
IF t:day > ( 91 - t:leapday )
   STORE t:day + t:leapday TO t:day
ENDIF
*
```

```
* ---Calculate month, day, and year.
STORE INT( t:day / 30.57 ) TO t:month
STORE t:day - INT( 30.57 * t:month ) TO t:day
IF t:month > 12
   STORE 1 TO t:month
   STORE t:year + 1 TO t:year
ENDIF
STORE t:year - 1900 TO t:year
*
* ---Set-up the calendar date.
STORE STR(t:month,2)+"/"+STR(t:day,2)+"/"+STR(t:year,2) TO mdate
*
* ---Force leading zeroes.
STORE DATE() TO t:date
SET DATE TO &mdate
STORE DATE() TO mdate
SET DATE TO &t:date
*
RELEASE t:year,t:month,t:day,t:date,t:leapday
RETURN
* EOF: JUL2CAL.PRG
```

WEEKDAY.PRG

Description. WEEKDAY will return the day of the week as a character string in week:day (i.e., "SUNDAY", "MONDAY", ..., "SATURDAY") and as a number in week:num (i.e., 1, 2, ..., 7) for a given calendar date by using Reverend Zeller's theorem. Assumes the date is valid and in MM/DD/YY format. The week:day character string is trimmed before it is returned.

```
* Program.: WEEKDAY.PRG
* Author..: Bob Simpson, modified by Luis A. Castro
* Date....: 8/6/83, 11/20/83, 01/19/84
* Notice..: Copyright 1983 & 1984, Bob Simpson, All Rights Reserved
* Version.: dBASE II, version 2.4x
* Notes...: Gets the day of the week from a calendar date.
* Local...: t:date, t:month, t:day, t:century, t:yrcount
*
*    IN:    mdate-C-8      Calendar date, assumed to be in
*                          MM/DD/YY format, and a valid date.
*
*    OUT: week:num-N-1     Day of the week number value
*         week:day-C-9     Day of the week character value
*
STORE mdate TO t:date
* ---Format of MM/DD/YY will get MM/DD/YYYY for 20th century.
STORE $( t:date, 1, 5 ) + "/" +;
      STR( VAL( $( t:date, 7, 2 ) ) + 1900, 4 ) TO t:date
*
* ---Segments of julian date conversion code follows.
STORE VAL($(t:date,1,2)) TO t:month
STORE VAL($(t:date,4,2)) TO t:day
STORE VAL($(t:date,9,2)) TO t:yrcount
STORE 19 TO t:century
```

```
IF t:month > 2
    STORE t:month - 2 TO t:month
ELSE
    STORE t:month + 10 TO t:month
    STORE t:yrcount - 1 TO t:yrcount
ENDIF
*
* ---Reverend Zeller Theorem.
STORE INT( ( 13 * t:month - 1 ) / 5 ) + t:day + t:yrcount +;
      INT( t:yrcount / 4 ) + INT( t:century / 4 ) -;
      2 * t:century TO week:num
STORE INT( week:num - 7 * INT( week:num / 7 ) ) + 1 TO week:num
STORE TRIM( $( "SUNDAY    MONDAY    TUESDAY  WEDNESDAY" +;
                "THURSDAY FRIDAY    SATURDAY ",;
      ( week:num - 1 ) * 9 + 1, 9 ) ) TO week:day
*
RELEASE t:date, t:month, t:day, t:century, t:yrcount
RETURN
* EOF: WEEKDAY.PRG
```

CHECKDAT.PRG

Description.   This program demonstrates how to use JUL2CAL and CAL2JUL, so as to LIST records containing a date within the range of 30, 60, and 90 days from the current date. The datafile name and date field name are entered from the keyboard.

```
* Program.: CHECKDAT.PRG
* Author..: Luis A. Castro
* Date....: 10/24/83, 11/20/83, 01/19/84
* Notice..: Copyright 1983 & 1984, Ashton-Tate, All Rights Reserved.
* Version.: dBASE II, version 2.4x
* Notes...: Demonstrates how to use JUL2CAL and CAL2JUL,
*           so as to LIST accounts 30, 60, and 90 days old
*           on the date field of a datafile.
* Local...: day30, day60, day90, mdate, julian, mjulian,
*           isjulian, filename, field:name
*
SET TALK OFF
*
* ---Get system date and convert to julian date.
STORE DATE() TO mdate
DO Cal2jul
STORE julian TO mjulian
*
* ---Get 30-day-old calendar date into YY/MM/DD format.
STORE mjulian - 30 TO julian
DO Jul2cal
STORE $(mdate,7,2) + "/" + $(mdate,1,5) TO day30
*
* ---Get 60-day-old calendar date into YY/MM/DD format.
STORE mjulian - 60 TO julian
DO Jul2cal
STORE $(mdate,7,2) + "/" + $(mdate,1,5) TO day60
*
```

```
* ---Get 90-day-old calendar date into YY/MM/DD format.
STORE mjulian - 90 TO julian
DO Jul2cal
STORE $(mdate,7,2) + "/" + $(mdate,1,5) TO day90
*
ERASE
@ 2, 0 SAY "LIST accounts 30, 60, and 90 days old.
@ 2,72 SAY DATE()
@ 3, 0 SAY "======================================="
@ 3,40 SAY "======================================="
ACCEPT "Enter data filename " TO filename
ACCEPT "Enter date field:name " TO field:name
USE &filename
*
* ---Convert the field:name's MM/DD/YY format to YY/MM/DD.
? "Accounts 30 to 60 days old"
LIST FOR $(&field:name,7,2)+"/"+$(&field:name,1,5) <   day30 .AND.;
?
? "Accounts 60 to 90 days old"
LIST FOR $(&field:name,7,2)+"/"+$(&field:name,1,5) <   day60 .AND.;
         $(&field:name,7,2)+"/"+$(&field:name,1,5) >= day90
?
? "Accounts over 90 days old"
LIST FOR $(&field:name,7,2)+"/"+$(&field:name,1,5) < day90
USE
RELEASE day30, day60, day90, mdate, julian, mjulian,;
         isjulian, filename, field:name
SET TALK ON
RETURN
* EOF: CHECKDAT.PRG
```

JULIAN.PRG

Description.   Converts a Gregorian Calendar date to a Julian Period day. This algorithm is only accurate from 1/1/0000 to 12/31/3999 due to a problem with negative numbers. This command file is a subroutine to perform the calculation only. It expects to be passed a date whose format and content have already been verified by the calling file.

```
* Program..: JULIAN.PRG
* Author...: Merrill Anderson
* Date.....: January, 1984
* Notice...: Copyright 1983, 1984  Merrill Anderson. All rights reserved.
* Version..: dBASE II, version 2.4x
* Notes....: Converts a Gregorian Calendar date to a Julian Period day.
*
* Parameters passed:
*  Name        typ len  picture - description
* ----------- --- ---  ----------------------------------------
*  Input to program:
*  mdate        C   8   mm/dd/yyyy - Gregorian calendar date.
*
```

```
* Internal to program (optional output):
*   mm          N    2    Month of input date.
*   dd          N    2    Day of input date.
*   yr          N    4    Four digit year of input date.
*
* Output:
*   day         C    3    Day of week - three character abbr.
*   jd          N    7    Julian period day - total days
*                         (good from 0 to 3999 AD +\- ?).
*   mon         C    3    Month of year - three character abbr.
*   month       C    9    Month of year - full spelling.
*   weekday     C    9    Day of week - full spelling.
*
* If not done in a previous program...
SET TALK OFF
*
* Initialize local memvars...
STORE VAL($(mdate,1,2)) TO mm
STORE VAL($(mdate,4,2)) TO dd
STORE VAL($(mdate,7,4)) TO yr
STORE 1721060 TO base
*
* Calculate Julian Period Day...
STORE base + yr*365 + INT(yr/4) - INT(yr/100) + INT(yr/400) +;
  VAL($("0000310590901201511812122432733043334",mm*3-2,3)) +;
  dd - VAL($('110000000000',mm,1)) *;
  VAL($('10',1+INT(((yr/4)-INT(yr/4))+.75) *;
  INT(((yr/400)-INT(yr/400))+.9975),1)) to jd
*
* Calculate name of weekday...
        $(&field:name,7,2)+"/"+$(&field:name,1,5) >= day60
STORE $( "Monday   Tuesday  Wednesday" +;
  "Thursday Friday   Saturday Sunday   " ,;
  (INT(INT(((((jd/7.00)-INT(jd/7))*7)+.5))*9+1),9) TO weekday
STORE $(weekday,1,3) TO day
*
* Calculate name of month...
STORE $( "January  Febuary  March    April    May      " +;
  "June     July     August   SeptemberOctober  November " +;
  "December" ,mm*9-8,9) TO month
STORE $(month,1,3) TO mon
*
* Release local memvars and return to calling program...
RELEASE mm, dd, yy
RETURN
* EOF: Julian.prg
```

AMT2WORD.PRG

Description. AMT2WORD converts a dollar value to the word equivalent. Will not convert dollar amounts greater than 999,999.99 or less than 0.00.

Input. Expects two decimal places for the dollar value entered.

Output. The returned character string will vary in length depending on the dollar amount entered. The error flag will be true if there is an error in the conversion process.

```
* Program..: AMT2WORD.PRG
* Author...: Tom Rettig
* Date.....: August 26, 1983
* Notice...: Copyright 1983 by Ashton-Tate.  All rights reserved.
* Revised..: 1/11/84, 2/15/84
* dBASE....: II, version 2.4x
* Notes....: Converts a numeric dollar amount (to $999,999.99)
*            to words.
*
* Parameters passed:
*   name       type   length    description
*   ---------  ----   -------   --------------------------
* IN:
*   amt:full    N      3 - 9    Including 2 decimal places.
* OUT:
*   amt:word    C     23 - 86   Depending on the amount.
*   is:error    L      1        .T. if error in conversion.
*
* Expects: TALK (OFF)
*    Sets: EXACT (OFF)
*
* Initialize memory variables...
STORE "ONE   TWO   THREEFOUR FIVE SIX   SEVENEIGHTNINE TEN   ";
    TO t:unit
STORE "ELEVEN    TWELVE   THIRTEEN FOURTEEN FIFTEEN   " +;
    "SIXTEEN   SEVENTEENEIGHTEEN NINETEEN " TO t:teen
STORE "TEN    TWENTY THIRTY FORTY  FIFTY  SIXTY  SEVENTY" +;
    "EIGHTY NINETY" TO t:decade
STORE " " TO amt:word
STORE F TO is:error
*
* Convert decimal numbers to a string containing
* the cents amount...
STORE STR((amt:full-INT(amt:full))*100,2) TO t:cent:str
IF t:cent:str = " "
   STORE "0" + $(t:cent:str,2,1) TO t:cent:str
ENDIF
*
* Change the environment for upcoming branches...
SET EXACT ON
*
* Conditional branch...
DO CASE
   *
   * Branch for amounts too high or too low...
   CASE amt:full > 999999.99 .OR. amt:full < 0.00
      STORE T TO is:error
      RELEASE ALL LIKE t:*
      SET EXACT OFF
      RETURN
   *
   * Branch for zero dollars...
   CASE amt:full < 1.00
      STORE " NO " TO amt:word
*
* Branch for other conditions...
OTHERWISE
   *
   * Convert dollar amount to a character string...
   STORE STR(INT(amt:full),6) TO t:amt:str
   *
   * Branch for hundred thousands...
   IF $(t:amt:str,1,1) > "0"
      STORE $(t:amt:str,1,1) TO t:hunthous
      STORE amt:word +;
           TRIM($(t:unit,(VAL(t:hunthous)-1)*5+1,5)) +;
           " HUNDRED " TO amt:word
   ENDIF
   *
   * Branch for ten-thousands and thousands...
   IF $(t:amt:str,2,2) > "  "
      STORE $(t:amt:str,2,1) TO t:tenthous
      STORE $(t:amt:str,3,1) TO t:thousand
      *
      * Branch for combinations of ten-thousands
      * and thousands...
      DO CASE
```

```
            CASE $(t:amt:str,1,1) > "0" .AND.;
                VAL($(t:amt:str,2,2)) = 0
                STORE amt:word + "THOUSAND" TO amt:word
            CASE t:tenthous=" " .OR. t:tenthous="0"
                STORE amt:word +;
                    TRIM($(t:unit,(VAL(t:thousand)-1)*5+1,5));
                    + " THOUSAND" TO amt:word
            CASE t:thousand="0"
                STORE amt:word +;
                    TRIM($(t:decade,(VAL(t:tenthous)-1)*7+1,7));
                    + " THOUSAND" TO amt:word
            CASE t:tenthous="1"
                STORE amt:word +;
                    TRIM($(t:teen,(VAL(t:thousand)-1)*9+1,9));
                    + " THOUSAND" TO amt:word
            CASE t:tenthous>"1"
                STORE amt:word +;
                    TRIM($(t:decade,(VAL(t:tenthous)-1)*7+1,7));
                +"-"+ TRIM($(t:unit,(VAL(t:thousand)-1)*5+1,5));
                    + " THOUSAND" TO amt:word
        ENDCASE
        *
        * Branch for comma or space after thousands...
        IF VAL($(t:amt:str,4,3)) > 0
            STORE amt:word +", " TO amt:word
        ELSE
            STORE amt:word +" " TO amt:word
        ENDIF
    ENDIF
    *
    * Branch for hundreds...
    IF $(t:amt:str,4,1) > "0"
        STORE $(t:amt:str,4,1) TO t:hundred
        STORE amt:word +;
            TRIM($(t:unit,(VAL(t:hundred)-1)*5+1,5));
            + " HUNDRED " TO amt:word
    ENDIF
    *
    * Branch for tens and ones...
    IF VAL($(t:amt:str,5,2)) > 0
        STORE $(t:amt:str,5,1) TO t:tens
        STORE $(t:amt:str,6,1) TO t:ones
        *
        * Branch for combinations of tens and ones...
        DO CASE
            CASE t:tens=" " .OR. t:tens="0"
                STORE amt:word +;
                    TRIM($(t:unit,(VAL(t:ones)-1)*5+1,5));
                    + " " TO amt:word
            CASE t:ones="0"
                STORE amt:word +;
                    TRIM($(t:decade,(VAL(t:tens)-1)*7+1,7));
                    + " " TO amt:word
            CASE t:tens="1"
                STORE amt:word +;
                    TRIM($(t:teen,(VAL(t:ones)-1)*9+1,9));
                    + " " TO amt:word
            CASE t:tens>"1"
                STORE amt:word +;
                    TRIM($(t:decade,(VAL(t:tens)-1)*7+1,7));
                +"-"+ TRIM($(t:unit,(VAL(t:ones)-1).*5+1,5));
                    + " " TO amt:word
        ENDCASE
    ENDIF
ENDCASE
*
* Branch for one dollar or more and one cent or more,
* and put the word string together...
DO CASE
    CASE amt:word=" ONE" .AND. t:cent:str="01"
        STORE $(amt:word,2,LEN(TRIM(amt:word))+1) +;
            "DOLLAR and " + t:cent:str + " CENT" TO amt:word
    CASE amt:word=" ONE" .AND. (.NOT. t:cent:str="01")
        STORE $(amt:word,2,LEN(TRIM(amt:word))+1) +;
            "DOLLAR and " + t:cent:str + " CENTS" TO amt:word
    CASE (.NOT. amt:word=" ONE") .AND. t:cent:str="01"
        STORE $(amt:word,2,LEN(TRIM(amt:word))+1) +;
            "DOLLARS and " + t:cent:str + " CENT" TO amt:word
    OTHERWISE
        STORE $(amt:word,2,LEN(TRIM(amt:word))+1) +;
            "DOLLARS and " + t:cent:str + " CENTS" TO amt:word
ENDCASE
*
```

```
* Restore the environment and return to the calling program...
RELEASE ALL LIKE †:*
SET EXACT OFF
RETURN
* EOF: Amt2word.prg
```

MATH-.PRG

Description.   Front-end program to utilize the SQROOT, EXPONENT, and NATLOG subroutines found in this section.

```
* Program.: MATH-.PRG
* Author..: Luis A. Castro
* Date....: 01/19/84
* Notice..: Copyright 1984, Luis A. Castro, All Rights Reserved.
* Version.: dBASE II, version 2.4x
* Notes...: Front-end program to utilize the SQUARE ROOT,
*           EXPONENT, and NATURAL LOGARITHM subroutines.
* Local...: select, string, number, row
*
SET TALK OFF
SET BELL OFF
SET RAW ON
SET COLON OFF
ERASE
@ 2, 0 SAY "DEMONSTRATION of MATH ROUTINES"
@ 2,72 SAY DATE()
@ 3, 0 SAY "========================================="
@ 3,40 SAY "========================================="
STORE 10 TO row
STORE "X" TO select
DO WHILE select <> " "
   @ 9,0
   STORE " " TO select
   @ 5,0 SAY "1. SQROOT()   =   square root "
   @ 6,0 SAY "2. EXPONENT() =   exponent "
   @ 7,0 SAY "3. NATLOG()   =   natural logarithm "
   @ 8,0 GET select PICTURE "I"
   READ
   IF select = " " .OR. .NOT. select $ "123"
      LOOP
   ENDIF
   @ 8,0 SAY " "
   ACCEPT "ENTER A NUMBER " TO string
   IF string = " "
      LOOP
   ENDIF
   @ row,0 SAY " "
   STORE VAL(string) TO number
   * ---Execute a math routine.
   DO CASE
      CASE select = "1"
      * ---SQUARE ROOT.
         ? "   SQROOT (",string,") = "
         DO Sqroot
         ?? root
      CASE select = "2"
      * ---EXPONENT.
         ? "   EXPONENT (", string, ") = "
         DO Exponent
         ?? exponent
      CASE select = "3"
      * ---NATURAL LOGARITHM.
         ? "   NATLOG (", string, ") = "
         DO Natlog
         ?? natlog
   ENDCASE
   STORE row + 1 TO row
ENDDO
SET COLON ON
SET RAW OFF
SET BELL ON
SET TALK ON
RELEASE select, string, number, row
RETURN
* EOF: MATH-.PRG
```

SQROOT.PRG

Description.   SQROOT calculates the square root of a number. This program is an application of the Newton-Raphson method of square root approximation. It is the standard numerical method used for this approximation.

Input.   Expects the number parameter to be greater than or equal to zero.

Process.   The algorithm is as follows:

GIVEN THE SEQUENCE:
$$root(i+1) = (root(i) + number / root(i)) / 2$$

WHERE:
$$root(0) = number \text{ AND } number > 0$$

THEN:
$$\lim_{i \to \infty} root(i) = sqrt(number)$$

Output.   The returned value is rounded off to five decimal places.

```
* Program.: SQROOT.PRG
* Author..: Kelly Mc Tiernan
* Date....: 12/15/83
* Notice..: Copyright 1983, Kelly Mc Tiernan, All Rights Reserved
* Version.: dBASE II, version 2.4x
* Notes...: Calculates the square root of a number.
*
*     IN: number-N-10
*    OUT: root-N-10-5
*
STORE number TO root
DO CASE
   CASE number < 0
      ? "ERROR - CANNOT TAKE THE SQUARE ROOT "+;
        "OF A NUMBER < 0"
      CANCEL
   CASE number > 0
      STORE (0.5 * ( root + number / root )) TO root
      DO WHILE (root * root) > number
         STORE (0.5 * ( root + number / root )) TO root
      ENDDO
      * ---Round off to 5 decimal places.
      STORE INT( root * 100000 + .5 ) / 100000.00000 TO root
ENDCASE
RETURN
* EOF: SQROOT.PRG
```

EXPONENT.PRG

Description. EXPONENT calculates the exponent of a number. Uses Taylor Series Expansion to calculate e raised to the mantissa, and repeated multiplication by 2.7182818 for the characteristic. The reason for this is the limitation of a dBASE II numeric variable. This routine pushes dBASE II way beyond its numeric variable size limit.

Process. The algorithm is given below:

I. CALCULATION OF e RAISED TO THE CHARACTERISTIC

For number >= 1 we take INT(number) and use it for a counter, that is, $e * e * e \ldots$ n times will equal e raised to the n power.

Reasoning: $e^{x+y} = e^x * e^y$

Example: $e^{2.532} = e^2 * e^{.532}$

By saving this number, which may grow very large, we prevent expansion of our intermediate answer on both sides of the decimal point at the same time.

II. CALCULATION OF e RAISED TO THE MANTISSA

First we take INT(number*10000)/10000 to format number to the proper number of significant digits.

TAYLOR SERIES EXPANSION:
$$e^x = 1 + X + X^2/2! + X^3/3! + \ldots\ldots\ldots\ldots + X^N/N!$$

We add 1 to the mantissa, as this prevents excessively small intermediate results from being generated. We then divide the final intermediate result by e.

EXAMPLE: $e^{1.54} = e^1 * e^{.54}$

AND: $\dfrac{e^{1.54}}{e} = e^{.54}$

III. FINAL RESULT:

Obtained by multiplying the 2 intermediate results together. This is an application of the earlier "sum of the exponents" rule in reverse.

Output. The returned value is rounded to five decimal places.

```
* Program.: EXPONENT.PRG
* Author..: Kelly Mc Tiernan
* Date....: 12/18/83
* Notice..: Copyright 1983, Kelly Mc Tiernan, All Rights Reserved
* Version.: dBASE II, version 2.4x
* Notes...: Calculates the exponent of a number.
* Local...: first, factorial, interim, count, power, temp
*
```

```
*    IN: number-N-10
*   OUT: exponent-N-10-5
*
STORE number TO first
STORE 1 TO power, factorial, interim, exponent, temp
DO WHILE first >= 1
   STORE temp * 2.7182818 TO temp
   STORE first - 1 TO first
ENDDO
STORE (INT( first * 100000 ) / 100000) + 1 TO first
STORE 15 TO count
DO WHILE power < count
   STORE first * interim TO interim
   STORE factorial * power TO factorial
   STORE interim / factorial + exponent TO exponent
   STORE power + 1 TO power
ENDDO
STORE temp * ( exponent / 2.7182818 ) TO exponent
STORE INT(exponent) + INT( (exponent -;
     INT(exponent)) * 100000 + .5 ) / 100000.00000 TO exponent
RELEASE first, factorial, interim, count, power, temp
RETURN
* EOF: EXPONENT.PRG
```

NATLOG.PRG

Description.   NATLOG calculates the natural logarithm of a number. Uses repeated addition of log 2 while the number is greater than one, then uses Taylor Series Expansion to calculate the remainder of the logarithm. This routine is a partner routine to the exponent routine. Like the exponent program, it also pushes dBASE II's floating point capabilities.

Input.   Expects the number parameter to be greater than zero.

Process.   The algorithm is shown below:

I.   CALCULATION FOR LOG(N), N > 2 :

$$\log X * Y = \log X + \log Y$$

THUS:
$$N \leftarrow N / 2 ,$$
$$\log N = \log N + \log 2$$

WHERE:
  log 2 is approximately = 0.6931471

II. CALCULATION FOR LOG(N) , REMAINDER FROM N = N/2
TAYLOR SERIES EXPANSION FOR: -1 < X <= 1

$$\log (1+X) = X - X^2/2 + X^3/3 - \ldots\ldots\ldots\ldots\ldots + -X^N/N$$

OR:
$$\log X = SUM - (1-X)^N / N \text{ FOR } N = 1 \text{ TO INFINITY}$$

III. THIS IS ADDED TO THE RESULT OBTAINED IN I. BY THE RULE
GIVEN IN I. FOR log X/Y.

Output. The returned value is rounded to five decimal places.

```
* Program.: NATLOG.PRG
* Author..: Kelly Mc Tiernan
* Date....: 12/18/83
* Notice..: Copyright 1983, Kelly Mc Tiernan, All Rights Reserved
* Version.: dBASE II, version 2.4x
* Notes...: Calculates the natural logarithm of a number.
* Local...: first, interim, power
*
*    IN: number-N-10
*   OUT: natlog-N-10-5
*
STORE number TO first
STORE 0 TO natlog
DO CASE
   CASE first <= 0
      ? "ERROR - CANNOT TAKE THE NATURAL LOGARITHM "+;
        "OF A NUMBER <= 0"
      CANCEL
   CASE first > 2
      * ---Calculate integer portion.
      DO WHILE first > 2
         STORE first / 2 TO first
         STORE natlog + 0.6931471 TO natlog
      ENDDO
   CASE first < .5
      * ---Handle lower convergence.
      DO WHILE first < .5
         STORE first * 2 TO first
         STORE natlog - 0.69314718 TO natlog
      ENDDO
ENDCASE
* ---Handle upper convergence.
IF first > 1.1
   DO WHILE first > 1.1
      STORE first / 1.1 TO natlog
      STORE natlog + 0.09531018 TO natlog
   ENDDO
ENDIF
* ---Calculation the remainder.
```

```
STORE - ( first - 1 ) TO first
STORE 1 TO interim
STORE 0 TO power
DO WHILE power <= 25
    STORE power + 1 TO power
    STORE first * interim / 1 TO interim
    STORE natlog - interim / power TO natlog
ENDDO
STORE INT(natlog) + INT( (natlog -;
       INT(natlog)) * 100000 + .5 ) / 100000.00000 TO natlog
RELEASE first, interim, power
RETURN
* EOF: NATLOG.PRG
```

TRIGDEMO.PRG

Description. dBASE III program to demonstrate the use of the Trig procedure file. The functions in Trig include SINE, COSINE, and TANGENT as well as ARCSIN, ARCCOS, and ARCTAN. All angles are expressed in radians. Also included in Trig are the procedures Makdeg and Makrad, which handle degree to radian conversions, and a procedure called PI which sets an existing memory variable to the value of pi. The functions presented here are based on an article in *Microsystems* magazine by Robert Lurie[1], citing algorithms by J. F. Hart [2]. They are accurate to approximately twelve places, and the SET DECIMALS and SET FIXED commands in dBASE III are incorporated to enforce this limit.

1.   Robert Lurie "Improved Trigonometric Functions for CBASIC," *Microsystems* 4, No. 12 (December, 1983), 130-132.
2.   J. F. Hart et al. *Computer Approximations* (Kreiger Publishing Company, 1978).

Sample run: Trigonometric demonstration

Enter a value (in degrees)-> 60

In radians	1.047197551197
SINE is	0.866025403784
COSINE is	0.500000000000
TANGENT is	1.732050807569
Identity is	1.000000000000

Enter side one-> 40
Enter side two-> 50

ARCSINE is	0.927295218002 radians	53.130102354156 degrees
ARCCOSINE is	0.643501108793 radians	36.869897645844 degrees
ARCTANGENT is	0.674740942224 radians	38.659808254090 degrees

```
* Program.: TRIGDEMO.PRG
* Author..: Alastair Dallas
* Date....: 07/03/84
* Notice..: Copyright 1984, Ashton-Tate, All Rights Reserved
* Version.: dBASE III, version 1.00
* Notes...: Demonstrates the use of the Trig.prg procedure file.
*
SET TALK OFF
SET PROCEDURE TO Trig
SET DECIMALS TO 12
SET FIXED ON
*
CLEAR
@ 2, 0 SAY "TRIGONOMETRIC DEMONSTRATION"
@ 3, 0 SAY "========================================"
@ 3,40 SAY "========================================"
INPUT "Enter a value (in degrees)--> " TO value
?
DO Makrad WITH value
? "In radians   ", value
*
sin_val = value
DO Sine WITH sin_val
? "SINE is       ", sin_val
*
cos_val = value
DO Cosine WITH cos_val
? "COSINE is     ", cos_val
*
argument = value
DO Tangent WITH argument
? "TANGENT is    ", argument
*
* ---Identity computation.
* ---The computed value should be  1.000000000000
value = ( sin_val ^ 2 ) + ( cos_val ^ 2 )
? "Identity is  ", value
?
INPUT "Enter side one--> " TO side_one
INPUT "Enter side two--> " TO side_two
value = side_one / side_two
?
argument = value
DO Arcsin WITH argument
? "ARCSINE is   ", argument, " radians"
DO Makdeg WITH argument
?? argument, " degrees"
*
argument = value
DO Arccos WITH argument
? "ARCCOSINE is ", argument, " radians"
DO Makdeg WITH argument
?? argument, " degrees"
*
argument = value
DO Arctan WITH argument
? "ARCTANGENT is", argument, " radians"
```

```
DO Makdeg WITH argument
?? argument, " degrees"
?
SET FIXED OFF
CLOSE PROCEDURE
SET TALK ON
RETURN
* EOF: TRIGDEMO.PRG


* Program.: TRIG.PRG
* Author..: Alastair Dallas
* Date....: 07/03/84
* Notice..: Copyright 1984, Ashton-Tate, All Rights Reserved
* Version.: dBASE III, version 1.00
* Notes...: Transcendental functions for dBASE III.
*
* Assumes: SET DECIMALS TO 12
*          SET FIXED ON
*
PROCEDURE PI   { The value of PI to 15 places. }
PARAMETER value
   value = 3.14159265358979
RETURN
*
*
PROCEDURE Makdeg   { Convert radians to degrees. }
PARAMETER value
   value = value * (180/3.14159265358979)
RETURN
*
*
PROCEDURE Makrad   { Convert degrees to radians. }
PARAMETER value
   value = value * (3.14159265358979/180)
RETURN
*
*
PROCEDURE Sine   { Sine function }
PARAMETER argument
   * --- IN:  argument in radians
   * ---OUT:  argument = SINE( argument )
   DO Tan_half WITH argument
   argument = (argument + argument) / (argument * argument + 1.0)
RETURN
*
*
PROCEDURE Cosine   { Cosine function }
PARAMETER argument
   * --- IN:  argument in radians
   * ---OUT:  argument = COS( argument )
   DO Tan_half WITH argument
   argument = argument * argument
   argument = (1.0 - argument) / (1.0 + argument)
RETURN
*
*
```

```
PROCEDURE Tangent  { Tangent function }
PARAMETER argument
   * --- IN:  argument in radians
   * ---OUT:  argument = TAN( argument )
   DO Tan_half WITH argument
   argument = (argument + argument) / (1.0 - argument * argument)
RETURN
*
*
PROCEDURE Arcsin  { Arcsin function }
PARAMETER argument
   * --- IN:  argument = ratio of sides
   * ---OUT:  argument = ARCSIN( argument )
   value0 = argument
   value1 = 1
   DO CASE
      CASE value0 < 0.0
         value0 = -(value0)
         value1 = -1
      CASE value0 = 0
         value1 = 0
   ENDCASE
   DO CASE
      CASE value0 > 1.0
         ? "ILLEGAL ARCSIN ARGUMENT"
         CANCEL
      CASE value0 = 1.0
         argument = value1 * 0.5 * 3.14159265358979
      OTHERWISE
         argument = argument / SQRT( 1.0 - argument * argument )
         DO Arctan WITH argument
   ENDCASE
RETURN
*
*
PROCEDURE Arccos  { Arccos function }
PARAMETER argument
   * --- IN:  argument = ratio of sides
   * ---OUT:  argument = ARCCOS( argument )
   DO Arcsin WITH argument
   argument = 0.5 * 3.14159265358979 - argument
RETURN
*
*
PROCEDURE Arctan  { Arctangent function }
PARAMETER argument
   * --- IN:  argument = ratio of sides
   * ---OUT:  argument = angle in degrees
   value0 = argument
   IF value0 < 0.0
      value0 = -(value0)
   ENDIF
   DO CASE
      CASE value0 > 2.4142135623731
         value3 = 2
         value0 = -1.0 / value0
```

```
          CASE value0 > .41421356237310
              value3 = 1
              value0 = 1.0 - ( 2.0 / ( 1.0 + value0 ) )
          OTHERWISE
              value3 = 0
      ENDCASE
      value1 = 216.06230789724
      value2 = value0 * value0
      value4 = ( ( ( 12.888383034157 * value2 + 132.70239816398 ) *;
              value2 + 322.66207001325 ) * value2 + value1 ) * value0
      value5 = ( ( ( value2 + 38.501486508351 ) * value2 +;
              221.05088302842 ) * value2 + 394.68283931228 ) *;
              value2 + value1
      value0 = value4 / value5
      DO CASE
          CASE value3 = 1
              value0 = value0 + .78539816339745
          CASE value3 = 2
              value0 = value0 + 1.5707963267949
      ENDCASE
      IF argument < 0.0
          value0 = -(value0)
      ENDIF
      argument = value0
RETURN
*
*
PROCEDURE Tan_half  { Routine common to trig functions }
PARAMETER argument
   * --- IN:  argument in radians
   * ---OUT:  argument = scaled argument
   value0 = argument
   IF argument < 0.0
       argument = -(argument)
   ENDIF
   argument = argument / 6.2831853071795
   argument = ( argument - INT( argument ) ) * 8.0
   value2 = 0
   DO WHILE argument >= 1.0
       argument = 0.5 * argument
       value2 = value2 + 1
   ENDDO
   value1 = argument * argument
   value3 = ( value1 * .026247864594320 ) - 17.805646714386
   value4 = ( ( value3 * value1 ) + 1038.5171455198 ) * argument
   value5 = ( ( value1 - 181.2832834854 ) * value1 ) + 2644.5621951222
   argument = value4 / value5
   DO WHILE value2 > 0
       argument = (argument + argument) / (1.0 - (argument * argument))
       value2 = value2 - 1
   ENDDO
   IF value0 < 0.0
       argument = -(argument)
   ENDIF
RETURN
*
* EOF: TRIG.PRG
```

APPENDIX C
PROGRAMS

COMMAND SIMULATORS

S-UPDATE.PRG	Simulates the UPDATE command
S-JOIN.PRG	Simulates the JOIN command
S-TOTAL.PRG	Simulates the TOTAL command
QUIT_TO.PRG	Simulates the QUIT TO command under DOS

GENERAL PURPOSE

LABELS.PRG	Prints multi-column mailing labels
NDX-SIZE.PRG	Calculates the size of an index file
PARSENAM.CMD	Separates first and last names from a field
CHGCASE.CMD	Changes uppercase character fields to first letter capitals
SOFT-CUT.PRG	Segments a sentence at word boundaries
STD-DEV.PRG	Computes standard deviation
RANDOM.PRG	Creates a database with random char records
HEX2DEC.PRG	Converts hexadecimal to decimal.
DEC2HEX.PRG	Converts decimal to hexadecimal.

SYSTEM DEVELOPMENT

PRINTDOC.PRG	Prints system documentation
CROSSREF.PRG	Generates cross reference table of variables
PASSWORD.PRG	Accepts password into an application system
BACK_UP.PRG	Backs up before exit from application
BNCHMK_1.PRG	Benchmarks a single dBASE III command
BNCHMK_2.PRG	Benchmarks several dBASE III commands

PROGRAM GENERATORS

MENUGEN.PRG	Generates MAIN MENU and sub-menu programs
FORMGEN.PRG	Generates a report command file
NAMEGEN2.PRG	Generates STORE and REPLACE statements in dBASE II
NAMEGEN3.PRG	Generates STORE and REPLACE statements in dBASE III

S-UPDATE.PRG

Description. This program simulates the UPDATE command. The records of the FROM file are sequentially passed until the end-of-file. Each matching record in the FROM file is updated to the master file. If there is no match, a new record is added to the master file with the FROM file information. This program assumes the master file is indexed.

```
* Program.: S-UPDATE.PRG
* Author..: Luis A. Castro
* Date....: 01/11/83, 01/17/84, 06/24/84
* Notice..: Copyright 1983 & 1984, Luis A. Castro, All Rights Reserved
* Version.: dBASE II, version 2.4x
* Notes...: Simulates the UPDATE command.
*
SET TALK OFF
*
* ---The parameters may be initialized with STORE statements
* ---or entered from the keyboard with ACCEPT statements
* ---(i.e. the STORE verbs could be changed to ACCEPT verbs).
STORE "MASTER" TO masterfile
STORE "FROM" TO fromfile
STORE "Lastname+Firstname" TO key:expr
*
* ---Initialize macro to REPLACE or ADD to masterfile.
* ---Assumes Name field is replaced and Amount field is added.
STORE "Name WITH P.Name, "+;
      "Amount WITH Amount + P.Amount" TO Mreplace
*
SELECT PRIMARY
USE &fromfile
SELECT SECONDARY
* ---Assumes the master file and index file have the same name.
USE &masterfile INDEX &masterfile
SELECT PRIMARY
DO WHILE .NOT. EOF
   STORE &key:expr TO mkey
   SELECT SECONDARY
   FIND &mkey
   IF # = 0
      * ---No matching record.
      * ---So, add a blank record to masterfile.
      APPEND BLANK
   ENDIF
   * ---Update information to masterfile from fromfile.
   REPLACE &Mreplace
   SELECT PRIMARY
   SKIP
ENDDO
CLEAR
SET TALK ON
RETURN
* EOF: S-UPDATE.PRG
```

S-JOIN.PRG

Description. This program simulates the JOIN command. This is a "simple" join, that is, the JOINing criteria is the key of each file and there are no duplicate keys. This type of join executes very quickly, since FINDs can be used instead of LOCATEs. The program appends *firstfile* to *joinfile*, and rewinds *joinfile*. It then adds the *secondfile* fields to *joinfile* for records that match the key field.

```
* Program.: S-JOIN.PRG
* Author..: Luis A. Castro
* Date....: 01/11/83, 01/17/84, 06/24/84
* Notice..: Copyright 1983 & 1984, Luis A. Castro, All Rights Reserved
* Version.: dBASE II, version 2.4x
* Notes...: A command file that simulates the JOIN command.
*
SET TALK OFF
*
* ---The parameters may be initialized with STORE statements
* ---or entered from the keyboard with ACCEPT statements
* ---(i.e. the STORE verbs could be changed to ACCEPT verbs).
STORE "FIRST" TO firstfile
STORE "SECOND" TO secondfile
STORE "JOIN-TO" TO joinfile
STORE "Lastname+Firstname" TO key:expr
*
* ---Initialize macro to REPLACE to joinfile from secondfile.
* ---Assumes only Name and Amount fields need replacing.
STORE "Name WITH S.Name, Amount WITH S.Amount" TO Mreplace
*
* ---Joinfile has all the desired fields to be JOINed.
* ---It is created before the program is executed,
* ---and contains no records.
SELECT PRIMARY
USE &joinfile
APPEND FROM &firstfile
GO TOP
SELECT SECONDARY
* ---Assumes the second file and index file have the same name.
USE &secondfile INDEX &secondfile
SELECT PRIMARY
DO WHILE .NOT. EOF
    STORE &key:expr TO mkey
    SELECT SECONDARY
    FIND &mkey
    IF # <> 0
        * ---A matching record.
        SELECT PRIMARY
        * ---REPLACE to joinfile from secondfile.
        REPLACE &Mreplace
    ENDIF
    SELECT PRIMARY
    SKIP
ENDDO
CLEAR
SET TALK ON
RETURN
* EOF: S-JOIN.PRG
```

S-TOTAL.PRG

Description. This program simulates the TOTAL command. The TOTAL file is created with the COPY STRUCTURE TO command. The masterfile must be pre-sorted or indexed.

```
* Program.: S-TOTAL.PRG
* Author..: Luis A. Castro
* Date....: 01/11/83, 01/17/84, 06/24/84
* Notice..: Copyright 1983 & 1984, Ashton-Tate, All Rights Reserved
* Version.: dBASE II, version 2.4x
* Notes...: A command file that simulates the TOTAL command.
*
SET TALK OFF
*
* ---The parameters may be initialized with STORE statements
* ---or entered from the keyboard with ACCEPT statements
* ---(i.e. the STORE verbs could be changed to ACCEPT verbs).
STORE "MASTER" TO masterfile
STORE "TOTAL" TO totalfile
STORE "Lastname" TO key:field
STORE "Cost" TO field:01
STORE "Quantity" TO field:02
*
SELECT PRIMARY
USE &masterfile
* ---Create the total file.
COPY STRUCTURE TO &totalfile;
    FIELD &key:field, &field:01, &field:02
SELECT SECONDARY
USE &totalfile
SELECT PRIMARY
DO WHILE .NOT. EOF
   STORE &key:field TO mkey
   STORE 0 TO mfield:01, mfield:02
   *
   * ---Total numeric fields with duplicate key fields.
   DO WHILE &key:field = mkey .AND. .NOT. EOF
      STORE &field:01 + mfield:01 TO mfield:01
      STORE &field:02 + mfield:02 TO mfield:02
      SKIP
   ENDDO
   SELECT SECONDARY
   * ---Enter result into the total file.
   APPEND BLANK
   REPLACE &key:field WITH mkey,;
           &field:01 WITH mfield:01,;
           &field:02 WITH mfield:02
   SELECT PRIMARY
```

```
ENDDO
CLEAR
SET TALK ON
RETURN
* EOF: S-TOTAL.PRG
```

QUIT_TO.PRG

Description. Replaces the QUIT TO option missing in 16-bit versions of dBASE II running under MS(PC)-DOS. The following steps must be followed in order for this to work:

1. Rename dBASE.COM to dBASEII.COM.
2. Create two identical text files, dBASE.BAT and dBASE.QTO, each containing just one line: "dBASEII %1".
3. To use dBASE II, enter "dBASE" or "dBASE [program]" from the DOS system prompt.
4. To QUIT TO a file or files, enter "DO QUIT_TO" from the dBASE dot prompt or command file.
5. If QUITting TO more than one file, enter the filenames delimited with commas. Do not use quote marks around the filenames as you would with the real QUIT TO command.
6. To QUIT back TO dBASE, specify "dBASEII" at the QUIT_TO.PRG prompt. An endless loop will result if you tell it to QUIT TO the batch file (dBASE) instead of the software (dBASEII).

```
* Program..: QUIT_TO.PRG
* Author...: Tom Rettig
* Date.....: November 4, 1983
* Revised..: January 25, 1984 removed redundant code.
* Notice...: Copyright 1984 by Ashton-Tate.  All rights reserved.
* Version..: dBASE II, version 2.4.
* Notes....: Replaces the QUIT TO option missing in 16-bit
*            versions of dBASE II running under MS(PC)-DOS.
*
* Establish working environment, and prompt for the filename(s)...
SET TALK OFF
CLEAR
STORE " " TO program
ACCEPT "QUIT TO <file1> [,<file2>,<file3>,<etc.>] -->" TO program
*
* Open the batch file, and write the standard first line...
SET ALTERNATE TO dBASE.bat
SET ALTERNATE ON
SET CONSOLE OFF
? "dBASEII %1"
*
* Starting with the second line, write the user entries...
DO WHILE @(",",program) > 0
   ? $(program,1,@(",",program)-1)
   STORE $(program,@(",",program)+1) TO program
ENDDO
IF program > " "
   ? "&program"
ENDIF
*
```

```
* Write the standard last line which copies the "holding" batch
* file (dBASE.QTO) over the existing one so that a fresh batch
* file is used every time a new entry is made into dBASE...
? "copy dBASE.QTO dBASE.BAT/v"
*
* Close the batch file and quit out of dBASE II...
* (Execution resumes at the second line in the batch file.)
SET ALTERNATE OFF
SET ALTERNATE TO
QUIT
* EOF: Quit_to.prg
```

LABELS.PRG

Description.   This program prints mailing labels in multi-column format up to four labels across. Makes extensive use of macros, and uses about one-third of available memory for memory variables in dBASE II. If concerned with having enough memory, you may want to use the CLEAR command before running the program.

Input.   Uses a data file with the following structure:

field:name	type	length
NAME	C	\<number>
COMPANY	C	\<number>
ADDRESS	C	\<number>
CITY	C	\<number>
STATE	C	\<number>
ZIP	C	\<number>

Process.   Prints mailing labels more than one across (up to four) without printing a blank line when the Company field is blank. The pseudo-code for the program is as follows:

> [Initial flags]
> [Initial memory variables]
> [Initial macros]
> [Enter parameters]
> [Open Names data file]
> **DO WHILE**\<there are more records>
>   [Load output lines]
>   [Print contents of output lines]
>   **SKIP**
> **ENDDO**

Output.   When selecting three labels across, the labels will print as follows:

```
LUIS CASTRO             JAY HANSON             TOM RETTIG
80 ETIWANDA AVE.        UNIVERSE INC.          ENTERPRISE LTD.
NORTHRIDGE, CA 90356    535 CULVER BLVD.       13 COAST HWY
                        TASH CITY, CA 90501    MALIBU, CA 90265
```

```
* Program.: LABELS.PRG
* Author..: Luis A. Castro
* Date....: 9/15/82, 12/14/83
* Notice..: Copyright 1982 & 1983, Luis A. Castro, All Rights Reserved
* Version.: dBASE II, version 2.4x
* Notes...: Prints multi-column mailing labels.
*
SET TALK OFF
SET BELL OFF
SET COLON OFF
* ---Initialize memory variables.
STORE $(STR(0,133),1,132) TO blank,line1,line2,line3,line4
STORE 1 TO uptotal
STORE " " TO select
STORE 30 TO upwidth
STORE "Y" TO printer
* ---Initialize macros.
STORE [TRIM(City)+", "+TRIM(State)+"  "+TRIM(Zip)] TO Macro
STORE [line1+$(blank,1,upcount*upwidth-LEN(line1))] TO Mline1
STORE [line2+$(blank,1,upcount*upwidth-LEN(line2))] TO Mline2
STORE [line3+$(blank,1,upcount*upwidth-LEN(line3))] TO Mline3
STORE [line4+$(blank,1,upcount*upwidth-LEN(line4))] TO Mline4
* ---Display heading and enter parameters.
ERASE
@ 2, 0 SAY "P R I N T    M A I L I N G    L A B E L S"
@ 2,72 SAY DATE()
@ 3, 0 SAY "========================================="
@ 3,40 SAY "========================================="
@ 5, 0 SAY "Enter number of labels to go across ";
        GET uptotal PICTURE "9"
READ
* ---Test for uptotal values.
DO CASE
   CASE uptotal = 0
        RETURN
   CASE uptotal > 4
        STORE 4 TO uptotal
ENDCASE
* ---Output to the screen or printer.
@ 7,0 SAY "Output to the printer? [Y/N] " GET printer PICTURE "!"
READ
@ 8,0 SAY "Press <RETURN> to begin printing " GET select
READ
IF printer = "Y"
   SET CONSOLE OFF
   SET PRINT ON
ELSE
   ERASE
ENDIF
* ---Open the datafile and begin printing labels.
USE Names
DO WHILE .NOT. EOF
   *
```

```
* ---Store first column to output lines.
STORE TRIM(Name) TO line1
IF Company = " "
    STORE TRIM(Address) TO line2
    STORE &Macro TO line3
    STORE " " TO line4
ELSE
    STORE TRIM(Company) TO line2
    STORE TRIM(Address) TO line3
        STORE &Macro TO line4
    ENDIF
    *
    * ---Store rest of columns to output lines.
    IF uptotal > 1
        SKIP
    ENDIF
    STORE 1 TO upcount
    DO WHILE .NOT. EOF .AND. upcount < uptotal
        STORE &Mline1+TRIM(Name) TO line1
        IF Company = " "
            STORE &Mline2+TRIM(Address) TO line2
            STORE &Mline3+&Macro TO line3
        ELSE
            STORE &Mline2+TRIM(Company) TO line2
            STORE &Mline3+TRIM(Address) TO line3
            STORE &Mline4+&Macro TO line4
        ENDIF
        STORE upcount+1 TO upcount
        IF upcount < uptotal
            SKIP
        ENDIF
    ENDDO while .not.eof.and.upcount<uptotal
    *
    * ---Print the contents of memvars line1,...,line4.
    ? line1
    ? line2
    ? line3
    ? line4
    ?
    ?
    *
    SKIP
ENDDO while .not. eof
*
IF printer = "Y"
    SET PRINT OFF
    SET CONSOLE ON
ENDIF
?
? "THAT'S ALL FOLKS..."
SET COLON ON
SET BELL ON
SET TALK ON
CLEAR
RETURN
* EOF: LABELS.PRG
```

NDX-SIZE.PRG

Description. Calculates the approximate minimum and maximum sizes of index files. Index files are dynamic structures (see chapter 7) and, therefore, the sizes can only be approximated.

```
* Program..: NDX-SIZE.PRG
* Author...: Tom Rettig & Luis A. Castro
* Date.....: 8/7/83, 1/17/84, 6/24/84, 9/9/84
* Notice...: Copyright 1983 & 1984, Ashton-Tate.  All rights reserved.
* Version..: dBASE III, version 1.00; and dBASE II, versions 2.3x & 2.4x.
* Notes....: Calculates the approximate size of index files for
*            the version of dBASE in which it is running.
*
*            Newly created index files will usually be close
*            to the largest size calculated by this algorithm.
*
SET TALK OFF
?
?
DO WHILE 1 = 1
   ACCEPT "Enter total width of <key expression> --> " TO string
   STORE VAL(string) TO width
   DO CASE
      CASE width < 1
         SET TALK ON
         RETURN
      CASE width > 100
         ? "Total width cannot exceed 100 characters -- try again."
         LOOP
   ENDCASE
   ACCEPT "Enter total number of records in file --> " TO string
   STORE VAL(string) TO records
   *
   * ---Branch for version of dBASE, and calculate the minimum size.
   IF TYPE('0') = 'C'
      * ---dBASE II.
      STORE INT( records / INT( 509/(width+4) ) +1 ) * 512 TO indexsize
   ELSE
      * ---dBASE III.
      STORE INT( records / INT( 509/(width+8) ) +1 ) * 512 TO indexsize
   ENDIF
   *
   * ---Print the results.
   ? "Smallest approximate size will be:", indexsize*1, "BYTES."
   ? " Largest approximate size will be:", indexsize*2, "BYTES."
   ?
ENDDO
* EOF: Ndx-size.prg
```

PARSENAME.CMD

Description.   Separates one character field containing full names into two fields, one with the first name and one with the last. Add two fields to your .DBF file called First:name and Last:name to receive the parsed names. Leave plenty of room, you can always shorten them later.

```
* Program..: PARSENAM.CMD
* Author...: Tom Rettig
* Date.....: May 5, 1983
* Notice...: Copyright 1983 by Ashton-Tate.  All rights reserved.
* Version..: dBASE II, versions 2.3x, 2.4x
* Notes....: For separating one character field containing full
*            names into two fields, one with the first name and
*            one with the last.
*
SET TALK OFF
ERASE
@ 1,0 SAY '========================================='+;
        '========================================='
@ 2,0 SAY '||'
@ 2,28 SAY 'P A R S I N G   N A M E S'
@ 2,78 SAY '||'
@ 3,0 SAY '========================================='+;
        '========================================='
USE Anyfile
DO WHILE .NOT. EOF
    *
    * Separate the full name at the first space...
    STORE LEN(Char:field) TO length
    STORE @(' ',Char:field) TO location
    STORE $(Char:field,1,location-1) TO mfirstname
    STORE $(Char:field,location+1,length) TO mlastname
    *
    * Display the separation...
    STORE T TO isagain
    DO WHILE isagain
        STORE '?' TO correct
        @ 10,15 SAY #
        @ 10,23 SAY ' FULL NAME :'+Char:field
        @ 12,35
        @ 12,23 SAY 'FIRST NAME :'+mfirstname
        @ 13,35
        @ 13,23 SAY ' LAST NAME :'+mlastname
        @ 16,30 SAY 'Is this correct? ' GET correct PICTURE '!'
        READ
        *
        * If the display is correct, place in the file's newly created name
        * fields, skip to the next record, and repeat...
        IF correct='Y'
        REPLACE First:name WITH mfirstname, Last:name WITH mlastname
        SKIP
        STORE F TO isagain
    ELSE
        *
```

```
         * If the display is not correct, separate at the next space and
         * loop to display again...
         STORE @(' ',TRIM(mlastname)) TO location
         IF location<>0 .AND. mlastname>' '
             STORE mfirstname+' '+$(mlastname,1,location-1) TO mfirstname
             STORE $(mlastname,location+1,length) TO mlastname
             LOOP
         ELSE
             *
             * When all the options have been tried, the operator can make
             * the entry manually and loop to display...
             STORE $(STR(0,length+1),1,length) TO mfirstname,mlastname
             @ 10,23 SAY ' FULL NAME :'+Char:field+':'
             @ 12,17 SAY 'ENTER FIRST NAME ' GET mfirstname
             @ 13,17 SAY ' ENTER LAST NAME ' GET mlastname
             READ
             LOOP
         ENDIF
     ENDIF
   ENDDO
   @ 10,35
ENDDO
@ 10,0
@ 12,0
@ 12,11 SAY '********** P A R S I N G   I S   C O M P L E T E **********'
@ 13,0
@ 16,0
USE Anyfile
RELEASE ALL
SET TALK ON
RETURN
*
* EOF: Parsenam.cmd
```

CHGCASE.CMD

Description. Changes character fields from all uppercase to lowercase with the first letter capitalized. Substitute "Char:field" with the field name in your data file. To change back to upper case, issue the command: REPLACE ALL Char:field WITH !(Char:field).

```
* Program..: CHGCASE.CMD
* Author...: Tom Rettig
* Date.....: May 12, 1983
* Notice...: Copyright 1983 by Ashton-Tate.  All rights reserved.
* Version..: dBASE II, versions 2.3x, 2.4x
* Notes....: For changing character fields from all uppercase
*            to lowercase with the first letter capitalized.
*
ERASE
SET TALK OFF
SET COLON OFF
```

```
@ 1, 0 SAY "============================================"+;
            "============================================"
@ 2, 0 SAY "||"
@ 2,19 SAY "C H A N G I N G   T O   L O W E R   C A S E"
@ 2,78 SAY "||"
@ 3, 0 SAY "============================================"+;
            "============================================"
*
* Prompt user for current version of dBASE II.
STORE "?" TO version
DO WHILE version <> "3" .AND. version <> "4"
    @ 5,22 SAY "SELECT THE VERSION OF YOUR dBASE II:"
    @ 7,28 SAY "TYPE <3> FOR VERSION 2.3"
    @ 8,28 SAY "TYPE <4> FOR VERSION 2.4"
    @ 11,34 SAY "Version = 2." GET version
    READ
ENDDO
@ 5,10
@ 7,20
@ 8,20
@ 11,20
*
* Version 2.3 does not have a RANK function like 2.4 does,
* so create two strings in order to use a location number
* instead of an ASCII number.
IF version="3"
    STORE "ABCDEFGHIJKLMNOPQRSTUVWXYZ" TO ucase
    STORE "abcdefghijklmnopqrstuvwxyz" TO lcase
ENDIF
*
USE Anyfile
STORE (80-LEN(Char:field))/2 TO col
DO WHILE .NOT. EOF
*
* Display the record number and uppercase field, and
* blank the previous lowercase field if there was one.
@ 10,col SAY Char:field
@ 11,col-8 SAY #
@ 12,col
*
* Initialize the memory variables.
STORE " " TO new:char
STORE F TO isreplace
STORE 0 TO count
*
* Loop to work on each character one at a time
* for the length of the field.
DO WHILE count < LEN(TRIM(Char:field))
    STORE count+1 TO count
    STORE $(Char:field,count,1) TO char
    *
    * Determine identity of character according to version.
    IF version="3"
        *
        * Find location number in uppercase string.
        STORE @(char,ucase) to location
        *
```

```
            * If this character is in the uppercase string, and the
            * previous character was also, then replace this character
            * with the matching one from the lowercase string.
            IF location <> 0 .AND. isreplace
                STORE new:char+$(lcase,location,1) TO new:char
            ELSE
                * If this character is not in the uppercase string,
                * or if the previous character was not there,
                * do not replace.
                STORE new:char+char TO new:char
            ENDIF
            *
        ELSE
            * If this character is an uppercase letter,
            * and the previous character was also, then
            * replace with a lowercase letter.
            IF char >= "A" .AND. char <= "Z" .AND. isreplace
                STORE new:char+CHR( RANK(char)+32 ) TO new:char
            ELSE
                * If this character is not an uppercase letter,
                * or if the previous character was not alphabetical,
                * do not replace.
                STORE new:char + char TO new:char
            ENDIF
        ENDIF
        *
        * Set the logical memvar to replace the next character only if
        * this character is alphabetical (either upper or lower case).
        STORE .NOT. ( (char > "Z" .AND. char < "a");
                .OR. char < "A"  .OR. char > "z" ) TO isreplace
        *
        * Display the new field as replacements are made.
        * (removing this command will speed up the operation slightly)
        @ 12,col-1 SAY new:char
    ENDDO
    REPLACE Char:field WITH $(new:char,2,LEN(TRIM(Char:field))+1)
    SKIP
ENDDO
@ 10,0
@ 11,0
@ 12,0
@ 12,12 SAY "********** C H A N G E   I S   C O M P L E T E **********"
USE Anyfile
RELEASE ALL
SET COLON ON
SET TALK ON
RETURN
* EOF: Chgcase.cmd
```

SOFT-CUT.PRG

Description. This program demonstrates the algorithm to use in breaking a sentence at word boundaries.

Input. Input for a sample run could be the following:

```
    Enter first word :LUIS CASTRO
    Enter sentence of words :NOW IS THE TIME FOR ALL good men TO
    COME TO THE AID OF THEIR COUNTRY.
    Enter desired column width :20
```

Output. The output of the program would be:

> LUIS CASTRO NOW IS THE TIME FOR
>   ALL good men TO
>   COME TO THE AID OF
>   THEIR COUNTRY.

```
* Program.: SOFT-CUT.PRG
* Author..: Kevin Jay Shepherd & Luis A. Castro
* Date....: 06/26/84
* Notice..: Copyright 1984, Ashton-Tate, All Rights Reserved
* Version.: dBASE II, version 2.4x
* Notes...: Segments a sentence at word boundaries.
*
SET TALK OFF
ERASE
@ 2, 0 SAY "SEGMENT A SENTENCE AT WORD BOUNDARIES"
@ 2,72 SAY DATE()
@ 3, 0 SAY "========================================"
@ 3,40 SAY "========================================"
ACCEPT "Enter first word " TO firstword
ACCEPT "Enter the sentence " TO sentence
IF firstword = " " .OR. sentence = " "
    SET TALK ON
    RETURN
ENDIF
INPUT "Enter desired column width " TO maxwidth
IF maxwidth < 10
    SET TALK ON
    RETURN
ENDIF
*
* ---Initialize memory variables.
STORE 1 TO startpos
STORE maxwidth TO maxpos, backpos
STORE "  " TO spacing
* ---Initialize the left margin spaces for
* ---the second and any subsequent lines.
STORE $( STR( 0, LEN( firstword ) + 1 ),;
      1, LEN( firstword ) ) + spacing TO indent
* ---Initialize the first macro string.
STORE [? firstword + spacing + ] +;
      [$( sentence, startpos, maxpos - 1 )] TO Macro
STORE F TO finished
?
* ---Now, segment the character string at word boundaries.
```

```
DO WHILE .NOT. finished .AND. backpos >= startpos
   IF $( sentence, backpos, 1 ) = " "
      &Macro
      * ---Re-initialize macro string to indent with blanks.
      STORE [? indent + ] +;
            [$( sentence, startpos, maxpos - 1 )] TO Macro
      * ---Reset the pointers to the next segment.
      STORE maxwidth TO maxpos
      STORE backpos + 1 TO startpos
      STORE backpos + maxwidth TO backpos
      IF backpos > LEN( TRIM( sentence ) )
         * ---The end of the sentence has been encountered.
         * ---Reset back pointer to the length of the sentence.
         STORE LEN( TRIM( sentence ) ) TO backpos
         STORE T TO finished
      ENDIF
   ELSE
      STORE maxpos - 1 TO maxpos
      STORE backpos - 1 TO backpos
   ENDIF
ENDDO
* ---Print the last segment.
IF backpos < startpos
   * ---A word in the sentence was longer than the width.
   ? "THE FOLLOWING WORD IS TOO LONG FOR THE SELECTED WIDTH:"
   ? $( sentence, startpos )
   CANCEL
ELSE
   * ---Print the last portion of the sentence.
   ? indent + $( sentence, startpos )
ENDIF
*
CLEAR
SET TALK ON
RETURN
* EOF: SOFT-CUT.PRG
```

STD-DEV.PRG

Description. This program computes the standard deviation of the records of a numeric field in a data file. It uses the SQROOT subroutine found in Appendix B to compute the square root.

Input. In the example run given below, STD-DEV uses the following values in the Numbers data file:

```
    . USE Numbers
    . LIST Quantity
    00001      87
    00002      53
    00003      35
    00004      42
    00005       9
    00006      48
    00007      51
    00008      60
    00009      39
    00010      44
```

Output. With the above data, the results will be:

```
    Enter data file name :Numbers
    Enter numeric field name :Quantity

    . . . . . . . . . .
    RESULTS:
    ========
    NUMBER of items     =       10
    SUM of values       =    468.00000
    MEAN (average)      =     46.80000
    VARIANCE            =    389.73333
    STANDARD DEVIATION  =     19.74166
```

```
* Program.: STD-DEV.PRG
* Author..: Luis A. Castro
* Date....: 06/26/84
* Notice..: Copyright 1984, Luis A. Castro, All Rights Reserved
* Version.: dBASE II, version 2.4x
* Notes...: Computes the standard deviation of the records
*           of a numeric field in a datafile.
*
SET TALK OFF
ERASE
@  2, 0 SAY "COMPUTE STANDARD DEVIATION"
@  2,72 SAY DATE()
@  3, 0 SAY "========================================="
@  3,40 SAY "========================================="
ACCEPT "Enter datafile name " TO filename
ACCEPT "Enter numeric field name " TO field:name
STORE !( TRIM(filename) ) + "." TO filename
STORE $(filename,1,@(".",filename)-1) TO filename
IF filename = " " .OR. field:name = " "
    SET TALK ON
    RETURN
ENDIF
?
USE &filename
```

```
IF 0 <= TEST( &field:name )
* ---The field must be numeric and it must exist.
    ? "INVALID FIELD NAME or FIELD TYPE"
    SET TALK ON
    RETURN
ENDIF
*
STORE 0 TO items, sum, sumsquare, mean, variance, std:dev
DO WHILE .NOT. EOF
* ---Compute the sum of values and sum of values squared.
    STORE sum + &field:name TO sum
    STORE sumsquare + ( &field:name * &field:name ) TO sumsquare
    STORE items + 1 TO items
    ?? "."
    SKIP
ENDDO
IF items < 2
    ? "MUST HAVE TWO OR MORE ITEMS TO COMPUTE STANDARD DEVIATION"
    SET TALK ON
    RETURN
ENDIF
*
* ---Compute mean, variance, and standard deviation.
STORE sum / items TO mean
STORE ( sumsquare - ( sum * sum ) / items ) /;
    ( items - 1 ) TO variance
IF variance <> 0
* ---Must have a positive number for the square root.
    STORE variance TO number
    * ---Get the square root of the number.
    DO Sqroot
    STORE root TO std:dev
ENDIF
*
* ---Output results.
? "RESULTS:"
? "========"
? "NUMBER of items    = " + STR( items, 5 )
? "SUM of values      = " + STR( sum, 11, 5 )
? "MEAN (average)     = " + STR( mean, 11, 5 )
? "VARIANCE           = " + STR( variance, 11, 5 )
? "STANDARD DEVIATION = " + STR( std:dev, 11, 5 )
CLEAR
RETURN
* EOF: STD-DEV.PRG
```

RANDOM.PRG

Description. RANDOM.PRG builds a data file of 100 records with a character field of random values. The program assumes the data file is empty. The middle section of the program, with the heading "RANDOM NUMBER GENERATOR", has a simple random number generator. Approximately 10,000 random numbers can be generated.

```
* Program.: RANDOM.PRG
* Author..: Luis A. Castro & Kelly Mc Tiernan
* Date....: 06/25/84
* Notice..: Copyright 1984, Luis A. Castro & Kelly Mc Tiernan,
*           All Rights Reserved
* Version.: dBASE II, version 2.4x
* Notes...: Builds a datafile with random characters.
*           Assumes the datafile is empty.
*
SET TALK OFF
ERASE
@ 2, 0 SAY "R A N D O M    C H A R A C T E R    B U I L D E R"
@ 2,72 SAY DATE()
@ 3, 0 SAY "========================================="
@ 3,40 SAY "========================================="
ACCEPT "Enter datafile name " TO filename
ACCEPT "Enter field name " TO field:name
INPUT  "Enter seed value [0..999999] " TO seed
INPUT  "Enter number of chars in string [1..9] " TO char:total
IF seed < 1 .OR. seed > 999999 .OR.;
   char:total < 1 .OR. char:total > 9
   SET TALK ON
   ? "ERROR - INCORRECT PARAMETER VALUE(S)"
   RETURN
ENDIF
?
?
STORE 1 TO rec:count
STORE 100 TO rec:total
USE &filename
DO WHILE rec:count <= rec:total
   STORE " " TO chars
   STORE 1 TO char:count
   DO WHILE char:count <= char:total
      *
      * ---RANDOM NUMBER GENERATOR.
      STORE seed * 309.0 + .203125 TO seed
      STORE seed / 1.000000 - INT( seed ) TO seed
      STORE INT(seed*1000000) / 1000000.000000 TO seed, random
      *
      STORE chars + CHR( INT( random * 26 ) + 65 ) TO chars
      STORE char:count + 1 TO char:count
   ENDDO
   ?? $(chars+"          ",2,9)
   APPEND BLANK
   REPLACE &field:name WITH $(chars,2)
   STORE rec:count + 1 TO rec:count
ENDDO
? "Finished..."
CLEAR
SET TALK ON
RETURN
* EOF: RANDOM.PRG
```

HEX2DEC.PRG

Description. Converts hexadecimal numbers (1-FFFF) to decimal. A note of caution: some entry errors are possible and will produce meaningless results. This command file is designed to be a programmer's utility, and therefore is written to perform fast rather than to error-trap every possible mistake an operator can make. For example, it is possible to enter "DEAR" instead of "DEAF" and get a decimal equivalent of 56991 instead of 57007.

```
* Program..: HEX2DEC.PRG
* Author...: Tom Rettig
* Date.....: September 24, 1983
* Notice...: Copyright 1983, Ashton-Tate, All Rights Reserved
* Version..: dBASE II, versions 2.3x, 2.4x
* Notes....: For converting hexadecimal numbers (1-FFFF) to decimal.
*
SET TALK OFF
SET EXACT ON
STORE "123456789ABCDEF" TO hexstr
DO WHILE T
   ACCEPT "Hexadecimal -->" TO hex
   STORE !(hex) TO hex
   *
   DO CASE
      CASE hex = " "
         RELEASE hex,hexstr,decresult,decstr
         SET EXACT OFF
         SET TALK ON
         RETURN
      CASE LEN(hex) = 1 .AND. VAL(hex) >= 0
         STORE @(hex,hexstr) TO decresult
      CASE LEN(hex) = 2 .AND. VAL(hex) >= 0
         STORE (@( $(hex,1,1) ,hexstr) * 16) +;
               @( $(hex,2,1) ,hexstr) TO decresult
      CASE LEN(hex) = 3 .AND. VAL(hex) >= 0
         STORE (@( $(hex,1,1) ,hexstr) * 256) +;
               (@( $(hex,2,1) ,hexstr) *  16) +;
               @( $(hex,3,1) ,hexstr) TO decresult
      CASE LEN(hex) = 4 .AND. VAL(hex) >= 0
         STORE (@( $(hex,1,1) ,hexstr) * 4096) +;
               (@( $(hex,2,1) ,hexstr) *  256) +;
               (@( $(hex,3,1) ,hexstr) *   16) +;
               @( $(hex,4,1) ,hexstr) TO decresult
      OTHERWISE
         STORE 0 TO decresult
   ENDCASE
   *
   IF decresult > 0
      STORE STR(decresult,5) TO decstr
      DO WHILE $(decstr,1,1) = " "
         STORE $(decstr,2) TO decstr
      ENDDO
      ? "Decimal  =  -->:" + decstr
      ?
   ELSE
```

```
        ? "Hex number must be between 1-FFFF."
        ?
    ENDIF
    *
ENDDO
* EOF: Hex2dec.prg
```

DEC2HEX.PRG

Description. Converts decimal integers (1-65535) to hex. A note of caution: some entry errors are possible and will produce meaningless results. This command file is designed to be a programmer's utility, and therefore is written to perform fast rather than to error-trap every possible mistake an operator can make.

```
* Program..: DEC2HEX.PRG
* Author...: Tom Rettig
* Date.....: September 24, 1983
* Notice...: Copyright 1983, Ashton-Tate, All Rights Reserved
* Version..: dBASE II, versions 2.3x, 2.4x
* Notes....: For converting decimal integers (1-65535) to hex.
*
SET TALK OFF
SET EXACT ON
STORE "0123456789ABCDEF" TO hexstr
DO WHILE T
    STORE "     " TO decstr
    ACCEPT "Decimal integer -->" TO decstr
    STORE VAL(decstr) TO dec
    *
    DO CASE
        CASE decstr = "      "
            RELEASE dec,decstr,hexstr,hexresult
            SET EXACT OFF
            SET TALK ON
            RETURN
        CASE dec > 0 .AND. dec < 16
            STORE $(hexstr,INT(dec)+1,1) TO hexresult
        CASE dec > 15 .AND. dec < 256
            STORE $(hexstr,INT(dec/16)+1,1)+;
                $(hexstr,(dec/16.0000-INT(dec/16))*16+1,1) TO hexresult
        CASE dec > 255 .AND. dec < 4096
            STORE $(hexstr,INT(dec/256)+1,1)+;
                $(hexstr,(dec/256.0000-INT(dec/256))*16+1,1)+;
                $(hexstr,(dec/ 16.0000-INT(dec/ 16))*16+1,1) TO hexresult
        CASE dec > 4095 .AND. dec < 65536
            STORE $(hexstr,INT(dec/4096)+1,1)+;
                $(hexstr,(dec/4096.0000-INT(dec/4096))*16+1,1)+;
                $(hexstr,(dec/ 256.0000-INT(dec/ 256))*16+1,1)+;
                $(hexstr,(dec/  16.0000-INT(dec/  16))*16+1,1) TO hexresult
        OTHERWISE
            STORE " " TO hexresult
    ENDCASE
    *
```

```
    IF hexresult > " "
       ? "Hexadecimal  =  -->:" + hexresult
       ?
    ELSE
       ? "Decimal number must be 1-65535."
       ?
    ENDIF
    *
ENDDO
* EOF: Dec2hex.prg
```

PRINTDOC.PRG

Description.   Prints system documentation to a text file. This program generates the listing of data file and index file structures, memory file contents, and a database data dictionary. See chapter 10 for more information. Before this program can be used, a data file with the name, PRINTDOC.DBF, and with the field, PRINTLINE-C-254, must be created.

```
* Program.: PRINTDOC.PRG
* Author..: Luis A. Castro
* Date....: 06/26/84
* Notice..: Copyright 1984, Luis A. Castro, All Rights Reserved
* Version.: dBASE II, version 2.4x
* Notes...: Prints system documentation.  Uses PRINTDOC.DBF
*           with the field: PRINTLINE-C-254
*
SET TALK OFF
SET BELL OFF
SET COLON OFF
* ---Initialize the default output text file.
STORE "PRINTDOC.TXT" TO outfile
SET ALTERNATE TO &outfile

DO WHILE T

ERASE
@  1, 0 SAY "========================================="
@  1,40 SAY "========================================="
@  2, 0 SAY "||"
@  2,21 SAY "P R I N T   D O C U M E N T A T I O N"
@  2,78 SAY "||"
@  3, 0 SAY "========================================="
@  3,40 SAY "========================================="
@  5,25 SAY " 0. exit"
@  6,25 SAY " 1. data/index file structures"
@  7,25 SAY " 2. memory file structures"
@  8,25 SAY " 3. database data dictionary"
@  9,25 SAY " 4. change output file name"
*
STORE "Current output file :" + outfile TO filename
@ 15, (80 - LEN( filename )) / 2 SAY filename
*
STORE  5 TO selectnum
DO WHILE selectnum < 0 .OR. selectnum >  4
```

```
    STORE " " TO select
    @ 12,33 SAY " select : : "
    @ 12,42 GET select PICTURE "#"
    READ
    STORE VAL(select) TO selectnum
ENDDO

DO CASE

CASE selectnum= 0
    SET COLON ON
    SET BELL ON
    SET TALK ON
    CLEAR
    RETURN
CASE selectnum= 1
*   DO data/index file structures
    ERASE
    @ 2, 0 SAY "DATA/INDEX FILE STRUCTURES"
    @ 2,72 SAY DATE()
    @ 3, 0 SAY "========================================="
    @ 3,40 SAY "========================================="
    ACCEPT "Enter datafile name " TO filename
    STORE !( TRIM( filename ) ) + "." TO filename
    STORE $( filename, 1, @(".",filename) - 1 ) TO filename
    DO CASE
        CASE filename = " "
            LOOP
        CASE .NOT. FILE( filename + ".DBF" )
            ? "FILE DOES NOT EXIST"
            WAIT
            LOOP
    ENDCASE
    ACCEPT "Enter INDEX files [separated by commas] " TO indexline
    STORE indexline + " ,*" TO indexline
    ?
    * ---List the datafile structure.
    USE &filename
    SET ALTERNATE ON
    LIST STRUCTURE
    SET ALTERNATE OFF
    USE
    * ---Get index files.
    IF indexline <> " "
        SET ALTERNATE ON
        ?
        ? "Indexes:"
        SET ALTERNATE OFF
        USE Printdoc.dbf
        COPY STRUCTURE TO Printndx.$$$
        USE Printndx.$$$
        * ---Get one index file at a time.
        DO WHILE $( indexline, 1, 1 ) <> "*"
            *
            DO WHILE $( indexline, 1 ) = " "
                * ---Strip leading blanks.
                STORE $( indexline, 2 ) TO indexline
            ENDDO
```

```
          * ---Get index file name.
          STORE @(",",indexline) TO pos
          STORE TRIM( $( indexline, 1, pos - 1 ) ) TO token
          STORE $( indexline, pos + 1 ) TO indexline
          STORE !( TRIM( token ) ) + "." TO token
          STORE $( token, 1, @(".",token) - 1 ) TO token
          SET ALTERNATE ON
          ? "   " + token + " = "
          SET ALTERNATE OFF
          STORE token + ".NDX" TO token
          IF .NOT. FILE( token )
             ? "FILE DOES NOT EXIST - ",token
             LOOP
          ENDIF
          * ---Get index key expression.
          * ---This method will NOT always work, because
          * ---dBASE II does not accept some control chars.
          * ---You may have to edit the expression, afterward.
          APPEND FROM &token SDF FOR # < 2
          GO TOP
          STORE $( Printline, 11, 100 ) TO key:expr
          STORE $( key:expr, 1, 1 ) TO char
          STORE 1 TO pos
          STORE " " TO expression
          DO WHILE RANK( char ) <> 0 .AND. pos < 100
             STORE expression + char TO expression
             STORE pos + 1 TO pos
             STORE $( key:expr, pos, 1 ) TO char
          ENDDO
          SET ALTERNATE ON
          ?? expression
          SET ALTERNATE OFF
          DELETE ALL
          PACK
       ENDDO
       USE
       DELETE FILE Printndx.$$$
    ENDIF
    SET ALTERNATE ON
    ?
    ? "Linkages:
    ? "   <-->>"
    ?
    ? ".PA"
    ?
    SET ALTERNATE OFF
    RELEASE ALL EXCEPT outfile
    *
CASE selectnum= 2
*  DO memory file structures
    ERASE
    @ 2, 0 SAY "MEMORY FILE STRUCTURES"
    @ 2,72 SAY DATE()
    @ 3, 0 SAY "========================================="
    @ 3,40 SAY "========================================="
    ACCEPT "Enter MEMORY file name " TO filename
    STORE !( TRIM( filename ) ) + "." TO filename
    STORE $( filename, 1, @(".",filename) - 1 ) TO filename
```

```
    DO CASE
        CASE filename = " "
            LOOP
        CASE .NOT. FILE( filename + ".MEM" )
            ? "FILE DOES NOT EXIST"
            WAIT
            LOOP
    ENDCASE
    SAVE TO Printmem.mem
    RELEASE ALL EXCEPT filename
    RESTORE FROM &filename ADDITIVE
    ?
    * ---List the memory variables.
    SET ALTERNATE ON
    ? filename + ".MEM"
    ? $( "------------", 1, LEN( filename ) + 4 )
    LIST MEMORY
    ?
    ? ".PA"
    ?
    SET ALTERNATE OFF
    RELEASE ALL
    RESTORE FROM Printmem.mem
    RELEASE ALL EXCEPT outfile
CASE selectnum= 3
*   DO database data dictionary
    ERASE
    @ 2, 0 SAY "DATABASE DATA DICTIONARY"
    @ 2,72 SAY DATE()
    @ 3, 0 SAY "========================================="
    @ 3,40 SAY "========================================="
    @ 5, 0 SAY "Enter datafile list [separated by commas]"
    ACCEPT TO line
    IF line = " "
        LOOP
    ENDIF
    ?
    STORE line + ",*" TO line
    * ---Get field names.
    USE Printdoc.dbf
    COPY STRUCTURE TO Printdat.$$$
    USE Printdat.$$$
    INDEX ON $(Printline,1,10) TO Printndx.$$$
    * ---Get filenames.
    DO WHILE $(line,1,1) <> "*"
        *
        DO WHILE $(line,1) = " " .AND. LEN(line) > 1
            * ---Strip leading blanks.
            STORE $(line,2) TO line
        ENDDO
        * ---Get one file name.
        STORE TRIM( $( line, 1, @(",",line) - 1 ) ) TO token
        STORE $( line, @(",",line) + 1 ) TO line
        STORE !( TRIM( token ) ) + "." TO token
        STORE $( token, 1, @(".",token) - 1 ) TO token
```

```
        IF .NOT. FILE( token + ".DBF" )
           ? "FILE DOES NOT EXIST"
           LOOP
        ENDIF
        SELECT SECONDARY
        USE &token
        COPY STRUCTURE EXTENDED TO Printdbf.$$$
        USE Printdbf.$$$
        DO WHILE .NOT. EOF
           STORE Field:name TO mkey
           SELECT PRIMARY
           FIND &mkey
           IF # <> 0
              STORE LEN( TRIM( Printline ) ) - 15 TO value
              STORE ( value - 10 * INT( value / 10 ) ) TO modula
              STORE $( STR(0,11), 1, 10 - modula ) TO string
              REPLACE Printline WITH TRIM(Printline)+string+token
           ELSE
              APPEND BLANK
              REPLACE Printline WITH S.Field:name+"        "+token
           ENDIF
           SELECT SECONDARY
           ?? "."
           SKIP
        ENDDO
     ENDDO
     USE
     SELECT PRIMARY
     ?
     SET ALTERNATE ON
     ? "DATABASE DATA DICTIONARY"
     ? "========================="
     ?
     ? "FIELD NAME        DATA FILE OCCURRENCES"
     ? "----------        ------------------------------------"
     GO TOP
     DO WHILE .NOT. EOF
        ? TRIM(Printline)
        SKIP
     ENDDO
     ?
     ? ".PA"
     ?
     SET ALTERNATE OFF
     USE
     DELETE FILE Printdat.$$$
     DELETE FILE Printdbf.$$$
     DELETE FILE Printndx.$$$
     RELEASE ALL EXCEPT outfile
CASE selectnum= 4
*  DO change output file name
     ERASE
     @ 2, 0 SAY "CHANGE OUTPUT FILE NAME"
     @ 2,72 SAY DATE()
     @ 3, 0 SAY "========================================="
     @ 3,40 SAY "========================================="
```

```
    ACCEPT "Enter new file name " TO newfile
    STORE !( TRIM( newfile ) ) + "." TO newfile
    STORE $( newfile, 1, @(".",newfile) ) + "TXT" TO newfile
    DO CASE
        CASE newfile = outfile
            STORE " " TO select
            @ 6,0 SAY "TEXT FILE IS ALREADY OPEN.   " +;
                      "Restart it? [Y/N] ";
                  GET select PICTURE "!"
            READ
        CASE FILE( newfile )
            STORE " " TO select
            @ 6,0 SAY "TEXT FILE ALREADY EXISTS.   " +;
                      "Delete it? [Y/N] ";
                  GET select PICTURE "!"
            READ
        CASE newfile <> " .TXT"
            STORE "Y" TO select
    ENDCASE
    IF select = "Y"
        STORE newfile TO outfile
        SET ALTERNATE TO &outfile
    ENDIF
ENDCASE

ENDDO T
* EOF: PRINTDOC.PRG
```

CROSSREF.PRG

Description.   CROSSREF prints a cross-reference table of variables to a text file. Before this program can be used, the following data files must be created:

Crossnul.dbf –	GET:line-C-80
Crossget.dbf –	GET:line-C-80
Crossput.dbf –	PUT:token-C-10,
	PUT:file-C-8,
	PUT:line-C-250

```
* Program.: CROSSREF.PRG
* Author..: Roy M. Moore, modified by Luis A. Castro
* Date....: 11/1/83, 08/26/84
* Notice..: Copyright 1983, Roy M. Moore, All Rights Reserved.
* Version.: dBASE II, version 2.4x
* Notes...: Creates a reference table of variables for up to
*           30 command files.
*
CLEAR
SET TALK OFF
SET RAW ON
STORE "PRG" TO extension
*
```

```
ERASE
@ 2, 0 SAY "GENERATE CROSS-REFERENCE TABLE"
@ 2,72 SAY DATE()
@ 3, 0 SAY "========================================"
@ 3,40 SAY "========================================"
ACCEPT "Enter output filename " TO outfile
? "Enter command filename(s) [separated by commas] "
ACCEPT TO mfiles
STORE "N" TO listit
@ 9, 0 SAY "Print command files? [Y/N] ";
        GET listit PICTURE "!"
READ
*
* ---Separate list of files.
STORE '11' TO item
DO WHILE ',' $ mfiles
    STORE $( mfiles, 1, @(',',mfiles) - 1 ) TO filename&item
    STORE $( mfiles, @(',',mfiles) + 1 ) TO mfiles
    STORE STR( VAL( item ) + 1, 2 ) TO item
ENDDO
STORE mfiles TO filename&item
STORE item TO item:max
*
* ---Check to see if command file(s) exist.
DO WHILE item >= "11"
    STORE !( TRIM( filename&item ) ) + "." TO filename&item
    STORE $( filename&item, 1,;
        @(".",filename&item) - 1 ) TO filename&item
    IF .NOT. FILE( filename&item + "." + extension )
        ? "&filename&item" + " DOES NOT EXIST"
        CLEAR
        RETURN
    ENDIF
    STORE STR( VAL( item ) - 1, 2 ) TO item
ENDDO
*
* ---The following is a list of the dBASE II "reserved" words.
* ---Feel free to add or delete what you wish.
*
STORE ",*,AND,USE,WAIT,TO,SET,SKIP,NOT,OR,?," +;
    "ACCEPT,ALL,APPEND,READ,ON,SAY,BELL,BLANK,WHILE," +;
    "BOTTOM,WITH,CASE,CHR,CLEAR," TO tokens1
STORE tokens1 +;
    "COMMAND,CONFIRM,CONSOLE,CONTINUE,COPY,COUNT,CREATE," +;
    "DATE,DELETE,DELIMITED,DISPLAY,DO,EDIT,EJECT,ELSE," +;
    "ENDCASE,ENDDO," TO tokens1
*
STORE ",ENDIF,ENDTEXT,EOF,ERASE,ESCAPE,EXCEPT,EXTENDED," +;
    "FIELD,FILE,FILES,FIND,FOR,ADD,,FORM,FORMAT,FROM,GET," +;
    "GETS,GO,GOTO,HEADING,IF,INDEX," TO tokens2
STORE tokens2 +;
    "INPUT,INSERT,INT,INTENSITY,JOIN,LEN,LIKE,LINKAGE," +;
    "LIST,LOAD,LOCATE,LOOP,MARGIN,MEMORY,MODIFY,NOTE,OFF," +;
    "OTHERWISE," TO tokens2
*
```

```
STORE ",PACK,PEEK,PICTURE,POKE,PRIMARY,PRINT,QUIT,RAW," +;
   "BEFORE,RECALL,RECORD,RELEASE,REMARK,RENAME,REPLACE," +;
   "REPORT,RESET,RESTORE,RETURN," TO tokens3
STORE tokens3 +;
   "SAVE,SCREEN,SDF,SECONDARY,SELECT,SORT,STATUS,"+;
   "STORE,STR,STRUCTURE,SUM,TALK,TEST,TEXT,TOP,TOTAL," +;
   "TRIM,TYPE," TO tokens3
*
STORE ",ALTERNATE,UPDATE,VAL,CALL,DESCENDING,ADDITIVE,"+;
      "ASCENDING,EXACT,CANCEL,CHANGE,COLON," TO tokens4
*
* ---Setup the CROSSREF files.
SELECT PRIMARY
USE Crossget
COPY STRUCTURE TO Crossget.$$$
USE Crossget.$$$
*
SELECT SECONDARY
USE Crossput
COPY STRUCTURE TO Crossput.$$$
USE Crossput.$$$
INDEX ON PUT:token + PUT:file TO Crossput
*
SELECT PRIMARY
SET ALTERNATE TO &outfile
*
* ---Now, let's start generating the cross-reference table.
@ 10,0 SAY " "
STORE item:max TO item
*
DO WHILE item >= "11"
*
STORE filename&item + "." + extension TO mfile
?
? "Appending command file " + mfile + "... "
APPEND FROM &mfile SDF
GO TOP
IF listit = "Y"
   ? "Printing command file to " + outfile + "..."
   SET ALTERNATE ON
   SET CONSOLE OFF
   ?
   ? "Filename: " + filename&item
   ?
   LIST
   ?
   ? ".PA"
   SET CONSOLE ON
   SET ALTERNATE OFF
   GO TOP
ENDIF
*
* ---Process the command lines.
?
? "Getting the variable names... "
?
```

```
DO WHILE .NOT. EOF
   *
   STORE TRIM( GET:line ) TO workline
   IF workline = " " .AND. LEN( workline ) = 1
      * ---It must be a blank line.
      SKIP
      LOOP
   ENDIF
   *
   * ---Strip leading control characters and blanks.
   STORE 1 TO ptr
   STORE LEN( workline ) TO line:len
   DO WHILE RANK( $(workline,ptr,1) ) < 33 .AND. ptr < line:len
      STORE ptr + 1 TO ptr
   ENDDO
   STORE $( workline, ptr ) TO workline
   *
   * ---Ignore comment lines.
   IF workline = "*"
      SKIP
      LOOP
   ENDIF
   *
   STORE !( workline ) + " " TO workline
   STORE STR( #, 5 ) TO linenumber
   *
   * ---NOTE: This section of dBASE II code can be
   * ---rewritten in assembly code for faster execution.
   *
   * ---Parse a single command line, until end-of-string.
   STORE 1 TO ptr, lastptr
   STORE LEN( workline ) TO line:len
   *
   DO WHILE lastptr <= line:len
   *
   * ---Skip everything but string delimiters ( " ' [ )
   * ---and alpha characters.
   STORE lastptr TO ptr
   STORE RANK( $( workline, ptr, 1 ) ) TO num
   DO WHILE num <> 34 .AND. num <> 39 .AND. num <> 91 .AND.;
            ( num < 65 .OR. num > 90 ) .AND. ptr <= line:len
      STORE ptr + 1 TO ptr
      IF ptr <= line:len
         STORE RANK( $( workline, ptr, 1 ) ) TO num
      ENDIF
   ENDDO
   STORE ptr TO startptr, lastptr
   IF ptr > line:len
      LOOP
   ENDIF
   * ---Locate a token in the line.
   DO CASE
      CASE num > 64 .AND. num < 91
      * ---Alpha characters.
         DO WHILE ptr <= line:len .AND.;
            ((num>64 .AND. num<91) .OR. (num>47 .AND. num<59))
            STORE ptr + 1 TO ptr
```

```
                IF ptr <= line:len
                    STORE RANK( $( workline, ptr, 1 ) ) TO num
                ENDIF
            ENDDO
        CASE num = 34 .OR. num = 39 .OR. num = 91
        * ---Literal string.
            IF num = 91
                STORE 93 TO num
            ENDIF
            STORE @( CHR(num), $( workline, ptr + 1 ) ) TO pos
            IF pos = 0
                * ---Could not find matching string delimiter.
                STORE line:len + 1 TO ptr, lastptr
                LOOP
            ENDIF
            STORE ptr + pos + 1 TO ptr, lastptr
            LOOP
ENDCASE
STORE ptr TO lastptr
*
* ---END-OF-NOTE: Rewrite in assembly code up to this point.
*
STORE $( workline, startptr, lastptr - startptr ) TO token
STORE "," + token + "," TO token1
*
* ---If reserved word then get next token.
* ---DO CASE is used instead of IF...ENDIF to reduce
* ---the amount of code executed if a match is found.
DO CASE
    CASE token1 $ tokens1
        LOOP
    CASE token1 $ tokens2
        LOOP
    CASE token1 $ tokens3
        LOOP
    CASE token1 $ tokens4
        LOOP
ENDCASE
?? token + ","
*
* ---Check to see if token is already in the CROSSPUT table:
STORE $( token + "          ", 1, 10 ) +;
      $( filename&item + "          ", 1, 8 ) TO key:value
SELECT SECONDARY
FIND "&key:value"
*
IF # = 0
    * ---Token is not in the reference table.
    * ---Create a record for the new token.
    APPEND BLANK
    REPLACE PUT:token WITH token,;
            PUT:file  WITH filename&item,;
            PUT:line  WITH linenumber
ELSE
    * ---Token is already in the reference table.
    * ---Just add the command line number.
        REPLACE PUT:line WITH TRIM( PUT:line ) + linenumber
ENDIF
```

```
        *
    ENDDO
    SELECT PRIMARY
    SKIP
ENDDO
*
* ---Initialize for the next command file.
STORE STR( VAL( item ) - 1, 2 ) TO item
USE Crossget
COPY STRUCTURE TO Crossget.$$$
USE Crossget.$$$
*
ENDDO
*
* ---Print cross-reference table from CROSSPUT.$$$
?
? "Printing cross-reference table... "
SET CONSOLE OFF
SET ALTERNATE ON
?
? "VARIABLE     FILENAME   OCCURRENCES"
? "==========  ========  ====================="
*
SELECT SECONDARY
GO TOP
* ---The constant "work:width" should be a multiple of five.
STORE 50 TO work:width
STORE " " TO last:token
DO WHILE .NOT. EOF
    IF PUT:token <> last:token
        ? PUT:token + "   "
        ?? PUT:file + "   "
    ELSE
        ? $( STR( 0, 13 ), 1, 12 ) + PUT:file + "   "
    ENDIF
    ?? $( PUT:line, 1, work:width )
    *
    * ---Print the occurrence lines that follow.
    STORE work:width + 1 TO work:count
    DO WHILE work:count < 250
        IF LEN( TRIM ( $( PUT:line, work:count ) ) ) > 1
            ? $( STR( 0, 23 ), 1, 22 ) +;
                $( PUT:line, work:count, work:width )
        ENDIF
        STORE work:count + work:width TO work:count
    ENDDO
    *
    STORE PUT:token TO last:token
    SKIP
ENDDO
?
SET ALTERNATE OFF
SET ALTERNATE TO
SET CONSOLE ON
CLEAR
```

```
DELETE FILE Crossget.$$$
DELETE FILE Crossput.$$$
DELETE FILE Crossput.ndx
?
? "Finished..."
*
SET RAW OFF
SET TALK ON
RETURN
* EOF: CROSSREF.PRG
```

PASSWORD.PRG

Description. Password and entry program into an application system. It is called by the main menu before entering the loop of the menu.

```
* Program..: PASSWORD.PRG
* Author...: Tom Rettig
* Date.....: June 4, 1984
* Notice...: Copyright 1984, Tom Rettig & Associates. All rights reserved.
* Version..: dBASE II, version 2.4x
* Notes....: Password and entry program into an application system.
*
*    Called by...: Main menu before entering the loop of the menu.
*
*    Files used..: IN_const.mem -- holds the system constants.
*
* Establish working environment...
ERASE
SET DELETED ON
SET TALK OFF
RESTORE FROM IN_const
*
* Get the password...
SET COLON OFF
STORE T TO t:enter
DO WHILE t:enter
   IF pw:tries >= 3
      ?? CHR(7)
      SET COLOR TO sc:brt:blk
      @ 18,27 SAY "* * * W A R N I N G * * *"
      @ 20,17 SAY "THIS UNAUTHORIZED INTRUSION HAS BEEN RECORDED."
      @ 22,17 SAY "NO FURTHER ACCESS TO THE FILES WILL BE ALLOWED."
      ?? CHR(7)
      *
      * Once an attempt to enter has failed, the system will remain
      * inaccessible until the memvar pw:tries is changed back to
      * zero in the constant memory file...
      SAVE TO IN_const
      ?? CHR(7)
      QUIT
   ENDIF
   STORE $(blank,1,12) TO t:password
   @  6,20 SAY "Please enter your password -->"
```

```
        SET COLOR TO sc:invis
        @  6,50 GET t:password
        READ NOUPDATE
        CLEAR GETS
        SET COLOR TO sc:brt
        SET EXACT ON
        *
        * Note that the password itself is not listed as a literal to
        * prevent someone from just reading this command file to obtain
        * it.  Instead, it is a series of substring functions which
        * operates on a memvar called "a" restored from the constant file.
        * The memvar contains the string: "NOPQRSTUVWXYZ ABCDEFGHIJKLM"
        *
        IF !(t:password) # $(a,18,1)+$(a,16,1)+$(a,15,1)+$(a,06,1)+;
                           $(a,19,1)+$(a,14,1)+$(a,23,1)+$(a,23,1)
           @ 12,15 SAY "NOT A VALID PASSWORD -- PLEASE ENTER AGAIN."
           STORE pw:tries+1 TO pw:tries
           LOOP
        ENDIF
        SET EXACT OFF
        @  6,15
        @  6,25 SAY "HI.  Nice to see you today!"
        STORE F TO t:enter
        STORE 0 TO pw:tries
ENDDO
SET COLON ON
*
* Restore environment and move on to the main menu...
RELEASE ALL LIKE t:*
RETURN
*
* EOF: Password.prg
```

BACK_UP.PRG

Description.   Backs up changed files before exit from the application is allowed. This algorithm assumes that the files to be backed up are on the default drive of a hard disk, and that the backups will go to drive B:. Maximum file sizes are known, and are not calculated herein.

```
* Program..: BACK_UP.PRG
* Author...: Tom Rettig
* Date.....: May 28, 1984
* Notice...: Copyright 1984, Tom Rettig & Associates. All rights reserved.
* Version..: dBASE II, version 2.4x
* Notes....: For backing up changed files before exit from the
*            application is allowed.
*
*   Called by..: Main menu.
*       Calls..: IN_rotat.mem      Holds the designating letters
*                                  of the last disks used.
*
* Initialize target drive designator (default drive is source)...
STORE 'B:' TO t:drive
*
```

```
* Get the last rotation used...
RESTORE FROM IN_rotat ADDITIVE
*
*
ERASE
SET COLOR TO sc:dim
@  1, 0 SAY "B A C K U P   C H A N G E D   F I L E S"
@  1,72 SAY mdate
@  2, 0 SAY "======================================"+;
           "======================================"
@ 21, 0 SAY "======================================"+;
           "======================================"
SET COLOR TO sc:brt
*
STORE F TO t:is:mastr, t:is:loop
DO WHILE T
   STORE 0 TO t:count
   *
   * Count the changed files, and display number...
   IF bu:custm
      STORE t:count + 1 TO t:count
   ENDIF
   IF bu:invtm
      STORE t:count + 1 TO t:count
   ENDIF
   IF bu:prodm
      STORE t:count + 1 TO t:count
   ENDIF
   IF bu:po

   STORE t:count + 1 TO t:count
ENDIF
*
* Branch to exit if no (more) files to copy...
IF t:count = 0
   * Save the rotation flags...
   SAVE TO IN_rotat ALL LIKE ro:*
   RELEASE ALL LIKE ro:*
   IF .NOT. t:is:loop
      @ 10,25 SAY "There are NO files to backup."
   ELSE
      @ 10,25 SAY " Backup process is complete. "
   ENDIF
   @ 23, 9 SAY "Press any key to QUIT, "+;
               "or RETURN to return to the Main Menu..."
   STORE '?' TO t:select
   @ 23,71 GET t:select
   READ NOUPDATE
   CLEAR GETS
   *
   * Branch to quit or return...
   IF t:select = '?'
      RELEASE ALL LIKE ro:*
      RELEASE ALL LIKE  t:*
      RETURN
   ELSE
      * This is the only exit point from the application system...
      RELEASE ALL LIKE  t:*
```

```
        SAVE TO IN_const
        ERASE
        QUIT
    ENDIF
ENDIF [t:count = 0]
*
* Display number of files to be copied...
IF t:count = 1
    @ 10,25 SAY " There is 1 file to back up. "
ELSE
    @ 10,25 SAY "There are " +STR(t:count,1)+ " files to back up."
ENDIF
*
* Branch for first time in the loop...
IF .NOT. t:is:loop
    STORE T TO t:is:loop
ENDIF
*
*
*
* Branch to backup MASTER files: IN_invtm, IN_custm, and IN_prodm...
IF bu:invtm .OR. bu:custm .OR. bu:prodm
    *
    * Branch for prompt on the first loop only...
    IF .NOT. t:is:mastr
        STORE T TO t:is:mastr
        @ 15,23 SAY "Place MASTER disk '" + ro:mastr + ;
                "' in drive " + t:drive
    @ 23,13 SAY "Press any key when ready, or RETURN to abort backup..."
    STORE '?' TO t:select
    @ 23,67 GET t:select
    READ NOUPDATE
    CLEAR GETS
    @ 15,23
    @ 23,13
    *
    * Branch to abort...
    IF t:select = '?'
        SAVE TO IN_rotat ALL LIKE ro:*
        RELEASE ALL LIKE ro:*
        RELEASE ALL LIKE t:*
        RETURN
    ENDIF
ENDIF
*
* Back them up...
IF bu:invtm
    @ 15,24 SAY "Copying INVENTORY MASTER file..."
    USE IN_invtm
    COPY TO &t:drive.IN_invtm
    USE
    STORE F TO bu:invtm
    IF bu:custm .OR. bu:prodm
        @ 15,24
        LOOP
    ENDIF
ENDIF
*
```

```
IF bu:custm
   @ 15,24 SAY "Copying CUSTOMER MASTER file..."
   USE IN_custm
   COPY TO &t:drive.IN_custm
   USE
   STORE F TO bu:custm
   IF bu:prodm
      @ 15,24
      LOOP
   ENDIF
ENDIF
*
IF bu:prodm
   @ 15,24 SAY "Copying PRODUCT MASTER file... "
   USE IN_prodm
   COPY TO &t:drive.IN_prodm
   USE
   STORE F TO bu:prodm
ENDIF
*
* Increment the rotation counter...
STORE $('ABC',(@(ro:mastr,'ABC')+1)-3*INT((@(ro:mastr,'ABC')+1)/4),1);
      TO ro:mastr
*
   * Decrement the file counter, and redisplay number to be copied...
   STORE t:count - 1 TO t:count
   DO CASE
      CASE t:count = 1
         @ 10,25 SAY " There is 1 file to back up. "
      CASE t:count > 1
         @ 10,25 SAY "There are " +STR(t:count,1)+ " files to back up."
      CASE t:count < 1
         @ 10,25 SAY "There are NO files to back up."
   ENDCASE
   *
   @ 15,24 SAY "*********** DONE ************* "
   @ 23,11 SAY "Remove the MASTER disk, "+;
               "and press any key to continue..."
   SET CONSOLE OFF
   WAIT
   SET CONSOLE ON
   @ 15,24
   @ 23,11
   LOOP
ENDIF
*
*
IF bu:po
   @ 15,19 SAY "Place PURCHASE ORDER disk '" + ro:po +;
               "' in drive " + t:drive
   @ 23,13 SAY "Press any key when ready, or RETURN to abort backup..."
   STORE '?' TO t:select
   @ 23,67 GET t:select
   READ NOUPDATE
   CLEAR GETS
   *
```

```
        * Branch to abort...
        IF t:select = '?'
            SAVE TO IN_rotat ALL LIKE ro:*
            RELEASE ALL LIKE ro:*
            RELEASE ALL LIKE t:*
            RETURN
        ENDIF
        *
        * Back it up...
        @ 15,19
        @ 15,25 SAY "Copying PURCHASE ORDER file..."
        @ 23,13
        USE IN_po
        COPY TO &t:drive.IN_po
        *
        * Close the file...
        USE
        *
        * Increment the rotation counter...
        STORE $('ABC',(@(ro:po,'ABC')+1)-3*INT((@(ro:po,'ABC')+1)/4),1);
              TO ro:po
        *
        STORE F TO bu:po
        *
        * Decrement the file counter, and redisplay number to be copied...
        STORE t:count - 1 TO t:count
        DO CASE
            CASE t:count - 1
                @ 10,25 SAY " There is 1 file to back up. "
            CASE t:count > 1
                @ 10,25 SAY "There are " +STR(t:count,1)+ " files to back up."
            CASE t:count < 1
                @ 10,25 SAY "There are NO files to back up."
        ENDCASE
        *
        @ 15,24 SAY "************ DONE *************"
        @ 23, 7 SAY "Remove the PURCHASE ORDER disk, "+;
                    "and press any key to continue..."
        SET CONSOLE OFF
        WAIT
        SET CONSOLE ON
        @ 15,24
        @ 23, 7
        LOOP
    ENDIF
    *
ENDDO
*
* EOF: Back_up.prg
```

BNCHMK_1.PRG

Description. Measures the execution time of various dBASE commands. This measures the elapsed time of a single dBASE command, such as indexing a database file. The operator is prompted to enter the command to be timed. Commands that release or clear all memory variables may not be timed since the timing algorithm relies on the existence of four memvars: t1, t2, n1, and n2.

```
* Program..: BNCHMK_1.PRG
* Author...: Tom Rettig
* Date.....: May 21, 1984
* Notice...: Copyright 1984 by Ashton-Tate.  All rights reserved.
* Version..: dBASE III, version 1.00, 14 Jun 1984
* Notes....: For measuring the execution time of a single dBASE
*            command.
*
SET TALK OFF
DO WHILE .T.
   n1 = 1
   n2 = 0
   ?
   ? 'Enter a command to execute, or RETURN to exit:'
   ACCEPT '--> ' TO command
   IF '' = command
      SET TALK ON
      RETURN
   ENDIF
   ?
   ?
   ?
   ?
   *
   * Toggle switch algorithm...
   SET BELL OFF
   @ 22, 0 SAY "Talk is set "
   @ 23, 0 SAY "Press SPACE to change, or RETURN to continue."
   SET COLOR TO 15/0
   @ 22,12 SAY "OFF"
   toggle = ' '
   is_on  = .F.
   DO WHILE .NOT. toggle $ '?'
      STORE '?' TO toggle
      SET COLOR TO 0/0
      @ 22,15 GET toggle
      READ
      CLEAR GETS
      SET COLOR TO 15/0
      DO CASE
         CASE toggle = ' ' .AND. is_on
            @ 22,12 SAY "OFF"
            is_on    = .F.
         CASE toggle = ' ' .AND. (.NOT. is_on)
            @ 22,12 SAY "ON "
            is_on    = .T.
      ENDCASE
   ENDDO
```

```
@ 23,0
IF is_on
    SET TALK ON
ENDIF
SET BELL ON
SET COLOR TO 7/0
*
*
WAIT 'Press any key to START, <Ctrl-Break> to cancel...'
@ 23,0
?
? CHR(7) + 'Time started...'
*
* Get start time...
t1 = TIME()
*
* Timing loop...
DO WHILE n2 < n1
    *------------------Start of timed command--------------------

    &command

    *------------------End of timed command--------------------
    n2 = n2+1
ENDDO
*
* Get end time...
t2 = TIME()
*
? CHR(7) + '***DONE***'
?
? '          hh:mm:ss'
? '  Start:', t1
? ' Finish:', t2
? '          --------'
*
* Elapsed time algorithm:
IF is_on
    SET TALK OFF
ENDIF
*
* Convert start and end times to numeric seconds; es = elapsed seconds...
es = ( VAL(t2)*3600 + VAL(SUBSTR(t2,4))*60 + VAL(SUBSTR(t2,7)) ) -;
     ( VAL(t1)*3600 + VAL(SUBSTR(t1,4))*60 + VAL(SUBSTR(t1,7)) )
*
* Convert elapsed seconds to 'hh:mm:ss', and add leading zeros...
et = SUBSTR(STR( INT(es/3600)                    +100,3),2) +':'+;
     SUBSTR(STR( INT(es/  60) - ( INT(es/3600)*60 ) +100,3),2) +':'+;
     SUBSTR(STR(       es     - ( INT(es/  60)*60 ) +100,3),2)
*
* Based on the algorithm:
* hh  = INT( es / 3600 )
* mm  = INT( es /   60 ) - (hr*60)
* ss  =          es       - (mn*60) - (hr*3600)
* et  = SUBSTR(STR(hh+100,3),2) +':'+ SUBSTR(STR(mm+100,3),2) +':'+ ;
*       SUBSTR(STR(ss+100,3),2)
*
```

```
   *
   ? 'Elapsed:', et
   ?
ENDDO [WHILE .T.]
*
* EOF: Bnchmk_1.prg
```

BNCHMK_2.PRG

Description.   Measures the execution time of various dBASE commands. This measures several iterations
of a command or group of commands. Place the commands in the timing structure within the command
file, and initialize any memvars they might require in the memvar initialization structure provided. Measure
the elapsed time of the empty loop before adding commands to be timed. This will give you the "offset," or
time required by your equipment, for the timing loop alone. Number of executions must be the same for
both the offset and the test timings. Subtract the offset time from the test time for the highest accuracy.
Commands that release or clear all memory variables may not be timed since the timing algorithm relies on
the existence of four memvars: t1, t2, n1, and n2.

```
* Program..: BNCHMK_2.PRG
* Author...: Tom Rettig
* Date.....: May 21, 1984
* Notice...: Copyright 1984 by Ashton-Tate.  All rights reserved.
* Version..: dBASE III, version 1.00, 14 Jun 1984
* Notes....: For measuring the execution time of various dBASE
*            commands.
*
SET TALK OFF
DO WHILE .T.
   STORE 0 TO n1, n2
   ?
   INPUT  'Enter number of executions, RETURN to exit  --> ' TO n1
   *
   IF n1 = 0
      SET TALK ON
      RETURN
   ENDIF
   ?
   ?
   ?
   ?
   *
   * Toggle switch algorithm for setting TALK during the timing...
   SET BELL OFF
   @ 22, 0 SAY "Talk is set "
   @ 23, 0 SAY "Press SPACE to change, or RETURN to continue."
   SET COLOR TO 15/0
   @ 22,12 SAY "OFF"
   toggle = ' '
   is_on  = .F.
   DO WHILE .NOT. toggle $ '?'
      STORE '?' TO toggle
      SET COLOR TO 0/0
      @ 22,15 GET toggle
      READ
```

```
    CLEAR GETS
    SET COLOR TO 15/0
    DO CASE
       CASE toggle = ' ' .AND. is_on
          @ 22,12 SAY "OFF"
          is_on    = .F.
       CASE toggle = ' ' .AND. (.NOT. is_on)
          @ 22,12 SAY "ON "
          is_on    = .T.
    ENDCASE
ENDDO
@ 23,0
IF is_on
   SET TALK ON
ENDIF
SET BELL ON
SET COLOR TO 7/0
*
*---------------Initialize memvars used in timing loop---------


*---------------End initialization of memvars------------------
*
WAIT 'Press any key to START, <Ctrl-Break> to cancel...'
@ 23,0
?
? CHR(7) + 'Time started...'
*
* Get start time...
t1 = TIME()
*
* Timing loop...
DO WHILE n2 < n1
    *----------------Start of timed commands--------------------


    *----------------End of timed commands----------------------
    n2 = n2+1
ENDDO
*
* Get end time...
t2 = TIME()
*
? CHR(7) + '***DONE***'
?
? '              hh:mm:ss'
? '   Start:', t1
? '  Finish:', t2
? '          --------'
*
* Elapsed time algorithm:
IF is_on
   SET TALK OFF
ENDIF
```

```
    *
    * Convert start and end times to numeric seconds; es = elapsed seconds...
    es = ( VAL(t2)*3600 + VAL(SUBSTR(t2,4))*60 + VAL(SUBSTR(t2,7)) ) -;
         ( VAL(t1)*3600 + VAL(SUBSTR(t1,4))*60 + VAL(SUBSTR(t1,7)) )
    *
    * Convert elapsed seconds to 'hh:mm:ss', and add leading zeros...
    et = SUBSTR(STR( INT(es/3600)                         +100,3),2) +':'+;
         SUBSTR(STR( INT(es/  60) - ( INT(es/3600)*60 ) +100,3),2) +':'+;
         SUBSTR(STR(       es      - ( INT(es/  60)*60 ) +100,3),2)
    *
    * Based on the algorithm:
    * hh  = INT( es / 3600 )
    * mm  = INT( es /   60 ) - (hr*60)
    * ss  =        es        - (mn*60) ,- (hr*3600)
    * et  = SUBSTR(STR(hh+100,3),2) +':'+ SUBSTR(STR(mm+100,3),2) +':'+ ;
    *        SUBSTR(STR(ss+100,3),2)
    *
    *
    ? 'Elapsed:', et
    ?
ENDDO [WHILE .T.]
*
* EOF: Bnchmk_2.prg
```

MENUGEN.PRG

Description. This program is designed to generate main menu and submenu command files.

Input. MENUGEN requires the input of an output file name, menu heading, submenu file names, and main menu options. The input sequence in pseudo-code is:

```
* Input MENUGEN parameters.
[Enter output file name]
[Enter menu heading and expand the heading]
[Enter submenu file names and main menu descriptions]
```

Process. MENUGEN will generate the main menu and submenu command files to text files by using the SET ALTERNATE TO command. The pseudo-code is:

```
* Generate main menu and submenu programs.
[Generate main menu program header]
[Generate initial flags]
[Generate main menu display]
[Generate DO CASE for main menu options]
[Generate submenu programs]
```

Output. The main menu and submenu displays will look like the one below:

```
=================================================
||              S A M P L E    M E N U            ||
=================================================
||                                               ||
||                                               ||
||          0. exit                              ||
||          1. view records                      ||
||          2. add     "                         ||
||          3. edit    "                          ||
||          4. report                            ||
||                                               ||
||                                               ||
================== select : : ====================


V I E W    R E C O R D S                    12/31/84
=================================================

        Strike any key to continue...
```

```
* Program.: MENUGEN.PRG
* Author..: Luis A. Castro
* Date....: 2/7/83, 7/6/83, 3/30/84
* Notice..: Copyright 1983 & 1984, Luis A. Castro, All Rights Reserved
* Version.: dBASE II, version 2.4x
* Notes...: Generates main menu and submenu command files.
* Local...: choice, extension, outfile, heading, pos,
*           word, item, totalopts, yourname, select,
*           option, col:hdg, expanded, counter, length,
*           col:opts, prompt
*
CLEAR
SET TALK OFF
STORE ".PRG" TO extension
STORE "Your Name" TO yourname
*
* ---Loop through until (S)ave is selected.
STORE " " TO choice
DO WHILE choice <> "S"
    ERASE
    @ 2, 0 SAY "M E N U    G E N E R A T O R"
    @ 2,72 SAY DATE()
    @ 3, 0 SAY "========================================="
    @ 3,40 SAY "========================================="
    * ---Get program name.
```

```
ACCEPT "Enter PROGRAM name " TO outfile
STORE !( TRIM(outfile) ) + "." TO outfile
STORE $( outfile, 1, @(".",outfile) - 1 ) TO outfile
DO CASE
    CASE outfile = " "
        ERASE
        CLEAR
        SET TALK ON
        RETURN
    CASE FILE( outfile + extension )
        STORE "N" TO select
        SET BELL OFF
        @  6,0 SAY "COMMAND FILE ALREADY EXISTS.     "+;
                    "Delete it? [Y/N] ";
                GET select PICTURE "!"
        READ
        SET BELL ON
        @ $,0 SAY "C"
        IF select <> "Y"
            CLEAR
            SET TALK ON
            RETURN
        ENDIF
ENDCASE
STORE outfile + extension TO outfile
*
* ---Get MENU heading.
ACCEPT "Enter MENU heading " TO heading
IF heading = " "
    CLEAR
    SET TALK ON
    RETURN
ENDIF
STORE TRIM( !(heading) ) TO heading
STORE " " TO expanded
*
* ---E X P A N D   h e a d i n g.
*
* -Will NOT correctly expand the heading if more
* -than one space separates the words.
SET EXACT ON
DO WHILE heading <> " "
    STORE @(" ",heading) TO pos
    IF pos > 0
        STORE $(heading,1,pos-1) TO word
        STORE $( heading, pos+1, LEN(heading) - pos ) TO heading
    ELSE
        STORE heading TO word
        STORE " " TO heading
    ENDIF
    STORE 1 TO counter
    DO WHILE counter <= LEN(word)
        STORE expanded + $( word, counter, 1 ) + " " TO expanded
        STORE counter + 1 TO counter
    ENDDO
    STORE expanded + "    " TO expanded
ENDDO
```

```
STORE TRIM( expanded ) TO expanded
STORE $( expanded, 2, LEN( expanded ) ) TO expanded
STORE ( 80 - LEN( expanded ) ) / 2 TO col:hdg
SET EXACT OFF
*
* ---Enter MENU options.
?
? "Enter PROGRAM,DESCRIPTION options:"
? "   0:exit"
STORE "exit" to option10
STORE " " TO program10
STORE 8 TO length
*
* ---Loop through until a carriage return or
* ---more than 14 options are entered.
STORE "11" TO item
STORE "X" TO option&item
STORE " " TO program&item
DO WHILE option&item <> " " .AND. VAL( item ) - 10 <= 14
    STORE STR( VAL( item ) - 10, 2 ) TO prompt
    ACCEPT "  &prompt" TO option&item
    STORE TRIM ( option&item ) TO option&item
    IF " " <> option&item
        STORE @(",",option&item) TO pos
        DO CASE
            CASE pos=0 .OR. (pos=1 .AND. LEN(option&item) > 1)
            * ---A blank program name is assumed.
            CASE pos=1 .OR. pos>9 .OR. pos=LEN(option&item)
            * ---Line was begun with a comma, or program
            * ---name is greater than 8 characters, or
            * ---there is no menu description.
                ? "INVALID ENTRY"
              LOOP
            OTHERWISE
            * ---Get program name.
                STORE TRIM($(option&item,1,pos-1)) TO program&item
        ENDCASE
        STORE $( option&item, pos + 1 ) TO option&item
        IF length < LEN( option&item ) + 4
            STORE LEN( option&item ) + 4 TO length
        ENDIF
        STORE STR( VAL( item ) + 1, 2 ) TO item
        STORE "X" TO option&item
        STORE " " TO program&item
    ENDIF
ENDDO
STORE VAL(item)-11 TO totalopts
IF option11=" "
    CLEAR
    SET TALK ON
    RETURN
ENDIF
STORE ( 80 - length ) / 2 TO col:opts
*
```

```
* ---Redisplay menu frame and heading.
ERASE
@ 1, 0 SAY "========================================="
@ 1,40 SAY "========================================="
@ 2, 0 SAY "||"
@ 2,col:hdg SAY expanded
@ 2,78 SAY "||"
@ 3, 0 SAY "========================================="
@ 3,40 SAY "========================================="
STORE 4 TO counter
DO WHILE counter <= totalopts + 7
    @  counter,0   SAY "||"
    @  counter,78 SAY "||"
    STORE counter+1 TO counter
ENDDO
@ counter, 0 SAY "========================================="
@ counter,40 SAY "========================================="
*
* Display menu options, centered on the screen.
STORE "10" TO item
DO WHILE VAL( item ) - 10 <= totalopts
    @ VAL( item ) - 5, col:opts SAY ;
        STR( VAL( item ) - 10, 2 )+ ". " + option&item +;
        " [" + program&item + "]"
    STORE STR( VAL( item ) + 1, 2 ) TO item
ENDDO
SET BELL OFF
STORE " " TO choice
DO WHILE .NOT. (choice $ "ERS")
    STORE " " TO choice
    @ 22,0   SAY "COMMAND: (E)xit, (R)edo, (S)ave ";
            GET choice PICTURE "!"
    READ
ENDDO
SET BELL ON
IF choice="E"
    CLEAR
    SET TALK ON
    RETURN
ENDIF
ENDDO while choice <> "S"
*
* ---Generate MENU file.
SET RAW ON
ERASE
SET ALTERNATE TO &outfile
SET ALTERNATE ON
? [* Program.: ] + outfile
? [* Author..: ] + yourname
? [* Date....: ] + DATE()
? [* Notice..: Copyright 19] + $( DATE(), 7, 2 ) +;
                [, All Rights Reserved]
? [* Notes...: ]
? [* Local...: select, selectnum]
? [*]
```

```
? [SET TALK OFF]
? [SET BELL OFF]
? [SET COLON OFF]
?
? [DO WHILE T]
?
? [ERASE]
? [@  1, 0 SAY "======================================="]
? [@  1,40 SAY "======================================="]
? [@  2, 0 SAY "||"]
? [@  2,] + STR( col:hdg, 2 ) + [ SAY "] + expanded + ["]
? [@  2,78 SAY "||"]
? [@  3, 0 SAY "======================================="]
? [@  3,40 SAY "======================================="]
*
STORE 4 TO counter
DO WHILE counter <= totalopts + 7
    ? [@ ] + STR( counter, 2 ) + [, 0 SAY "||"]
    ? [@ ] + STR( counter, 2 ) + [,78 SAY "||"]
    STORE counter+1 TO counter
ENDDO
? [@ ] + STR(counter,2) +;
  [, 0 SAY "======================================="]
? [@ ] + STR(counter,2) +;

  [,40 SAY "======================================="]
*
STORE "10" TO item
DO WHILE VAL(item)-10 <= totalopts
    ? [@ ]+STR(VAL(item)-5,2)+[,]+STR(col:opts,2)+[ SAY ]+;
      ["]+STR(VAL(item)-10,2)+[. ] + option&item + ["]
    STORE STR(VAL(item)+1,2) TO item
ENDDO
? [STORE ] + STR( totalopts + 1, 2 ) + [ TO selectnum]
? [DO WHILE selectnum < 0 .OR. selectnum > ]+STR(totalopts,2)
IF totalopts < 10
    ? [    STORE " " TO select]
    ? [    @ ]+STR(totalopts+8,2)+[,33 SAY " select : : "]
    ? [    @ ]+STR(totalopts+8,2)+[,42 GET select PICTURE "#"]
ELSE
    ? [    STORE "  " TO select]
    ? [    @ ]+STR(totalopts+8,2)+[,33 SAY " select :   : "]
    ? [    @ ]+STR(totalopts+8,2)+[,42 GET select PICTURE "##"]
ENDIF
? [    READ]
? [    STORE VAL(select) TO selectnum]
? [ENDDO]
?
? [DO CASE]
? [    CASE selectnum= 0]
? [        SET COLON ON]
? [        SET BELL ON]
? [        SET TALK ON]
? [        CLEAR]
? [        RETURN]
STORE "11" TO item
```

```
DO WHILE VAL( item ) - 10 <= totalopts
    ? [    CASE selectnum=] + STR( VAL( item ) - 10, 2 )
    ? [    *   DO ] + option&item
    IF program&item <> " "
        ? [        DO ] + program&item
    ENDIF
    STORE STR(VAL(item)+1,2) TO item
ENDDO
? [ENDCASE]
?
? [ENDDO T]
? [* EOF: ] + outfile
?
SET ALTERNATE OFF
SET ALTERNATE TO
*
* ---Generate SUB-MENU programs.
*
STORE "11" TO item
DO WHILE VAL( item ) - 10 <= totalopts
    STORE !( program&item ) + extension TO subfile
    IF program&item = " " .OR. FILE ( subfile )
        STORE STR( VAL( item ) + 1, 2 ) TO item
        LOOP
    ENDIF
    STORE !( option&item ) TO heading
    STORE " " TO expanded
    *
    * ---E X P A N D   h e a d i n g .
    *
    * ---Will NOT correctly expand the heading if more
    * ---than one space separates the words.
    SET EXACT ON
    DO WHILE heading <> " "
        STORE @(" ",heading) TO pos
        IF pos > 0
            STORE $( heading, 1, pos - 1 ) TO word
            STORE $(heading,pos+1,LEN(heading)-pos) TO heading
        ELSE
            STORE heading TO word
            STORE " " TO heading
        ENDIF
        STORE 1 TO counter
        DO WHILE counter <= LEN( word )
            STORE expanded + $( word, counter, 1 ) + " " TO expanded
            STORE counter + 1 TO counter
        ENDDO
        STORE expanded + "   " TO expanded
    ENDDO
    STORE TRIM( expanded ) TO expanded
    STORE $( expanded, 2, LEN( expanded ) ) TO expanded
    SET EXACT OFF
    *
```

```
     * ---Generate SUB-MENU file.
     SET RAW ON
     ERASE
     SET ALTERNATE TO &subfile
     SET ALTERNATE ON
     ? [* Program.: ] + subfile
     ? [* Author..: ] + yourname
     ? [* Date....: ] + DATE()
     ? [* Notice..: Copyright 19] + $( DATE(), 7, 2 ) +;
                    [, All Rights Reserved]
     ? [* Notes...: ]
     ? [*]
     ? [ERASE]
     ? [@  2, 0 SAY "] + expanded + ["]
     ? [@  2,72 SAY DATE()]
     ? [@  3, 0 SAY "========================================="]
     ? [@  3,40 SAY "========================================="]
     ? [STORE " " TO select]
     ? [@ 5,0 SAY "Strike any key to continue... ";]
     ? [        GET select PICTURE "!"]
     ? [READ]
     ? [*]
     ? [RETURN]
     ? [* EOF: ] + subfile
     ?
     SET RAW OFF
     SET ALTERNATE OFF
     SET ALTERNATE TO
     STORE STR( VAL( item ) + 1, 2 ) TO item
ENDDO
*
ERASE
STORE $( outfile, 1, @(".",outfile) - 1 ) TO outfile
? [TO START "] + outfile + [" MAIN MENU, TYPE THE FOLLOWING:]
? [.]
? [. DO ]+outfile
? [.]
? [.]
CLEAR
SET TALK ON
SET RAW OFF
RETURN
* EOF: MENUGEN.PRG
```

FORMGEN.PRG

Description.   This program generates a command file which prints reports similar to the REPORT FORM command.

Input.   FORMGEN requires the input of a data file and output file name, report options, and column descriptors. The sequence in pseudo-code is:

```
* Input FORMGEN parameters.
[Enter data file name]
[Enter output file name]
[Enter report options]
[Enter column descriptors]
```

Process.   FORMGEN will generate the report program to a text file by using the SET ALTERNATE TO command. The pseudo-code is:

```
* Generate report command file.
[Generate report program header]
[Generate initial flags and memory variables]
IF <totals and/or subtotals>
    [Generate initial accumulators]
ENDIF
[Generate open data file]
[Generate DO WHILE .NOT. EOF]
    [Generate column headings]
    IF <totals and/or subtotals>
        [Generate control break code]
    ENDIF
    [Generate detail lines]
    [Generate updating of total and/or subtotal code]
[Generate ENDDO]
[Generate final totals and/or subtotals]
```

Output.   The generated program will display reports similar to the one shown below.

PAGE NO. 1

THIS IS THE NAMES REPORT

CUSTOMER	HOME ADDRESS	AMOUNT DUE
LUIS CASTRO	80 ETIWANDA AVE. #29	4858.35
JAY HANSON	535 CULVER BLVD.	2447.55
TOM RETTIG	13 COAST HIGHWAY	9863.25

```
* Program.: FORMGEN.PRG
* Author..: Luis A. Castro & Roy M. Moore
* Date....: 7/11/83
* Notice..: Copyright 1983, Ashton-Tate, All Rights Reserved
* Version.: dBASE II, version 2.4x
* Notes...: Generates a command file which prints reports
*           similar to the REPORT FORM command.
*           Includes subtotaling and totaling.
* Local...: equals, y:n, extension, datafile, formfile,
*           lmargin, pagelen, pagewidth, pagehdg, string,
*           issubtotal, totstack, substack, subfield,
*           Mcontents, Mwidth, option, item, prompt,
*           yourname, totalopts, stackcount, heading,
*           width, istotal, col
*
CLEAR
SET TALK OFF
STORE ".PRG" TO extension
STORE "Your Name" TO yourname
STORE "N" TO y:n
STORE "=========================================" +;
      "=========================================" TO equals
* ---Macros to determine WIDTH & CONTENTS of values entered.
STORE [VAL($(option&item,1,@(",",option&item)-1))] TO Mwidth
STORE [option&item,@(",",option&item)+1,] +;
      [LEN(option&item)-@(",",option&item)] TO Mcontents
*
* ---Open datafile name.
ERASE
@ 2, 0 SAY "REPORT  FORM  program  generator"
@ 2,72 SAY DATE()
@ 3, 0 SAY "========================================="
@ 3,40 SAY "========================================="
ACCEPT "Enter DATABASE filename " TO datafile
STORE !( TRIM(datafile) ) + "." TO datafile
STORE $( datafile, 1, @(".",datafile) - 1 ) TO datafile
DO CASE
   CASE datafile = " "
        ERASE
        CLEAR
        SET TALK ON
        RETURN
   CASE .NOT. FILE( datafile + ".DBF" )
        ? "FILE DOES NOT EXIST"
        CLEAR
        SET TALK ON
        RETURN
ENDCASE
USE &datafile
*
* ---Get REPORT FORM filename.
ACCEPT "Enter REPORT FORM filename " TO formfile
STORE !( TRIM( formfile ) ) + "." TO formfile
STORE $( formfile, 1, @(".",formfile) - 1 ) TO formfile
```

```
DO CASE
    CASE formfile = " "
        ERASE
        CLEAR
        SET TALK ON
        RETURN
    CASE FILE( formfile + extension )
        * ---Command file already exists.
        SET BELL OFF
        STORE "N" TO select
        @ 7,0 SAY "COMMAND FILE ALREADY EXISTS.   " +;
                  "Delete it? (Y/N) ";
              GET select PICTURE "!"
        READ
        SET BELL ON
        @ 7,0 SAY "C"
        IF select <> "Y"
            CLEAR
            SET TALK ON
            RETURN
        ENDIF
ENDCASE
STORE formfile + extension TO formfile
*
* ---Enter REPORT FORM parameters.
?
? "ENTER OPTIONS:"
ACCEPT "    Left Margin...<1>." TO lmargin
ACCEPT "    Lines/Page...<56>." TO pagelen
ACCEPT "    Page Width...<80>." TO pagewidth
* ---Set to default values if null entries.
IF VAL(lmargin) = 0
    STORE "1" TO lmargin
ENDIF
IF VAL(pagelen) = 0
    STORE "56" TO pagelen
ENDIF
IF VAL(pagewidth) = 0
    STORE "80" TO pagewidth
ENDIF
?
ACCEPT "Enter Page Heading." TO pagehdg
ACCEPT "Are Totals Required? (Y/N) " TO string
STORE @( string, "Yy" ) > 0 TO istotal
ACCEPT "Subtotals in Report? (Y/N) " TO string
STORE @( string, "Yy" ) > 0 TO issubtotal
*
* ---Set up environment for totaling.
STORE " " TO totstack,substack
IF issubtotal
    STORE 1 TO counter
    STORE " " TO subfield
    DO WHILE subfield = " " .AND. counter <= 3
        ACCEPT "Enter subtotal field" TO subfield
        STORE !(subfield) TO subfield
        IF 0 = TEST(&subfield)
        * ---If subfield not in the datafile.
            STORE " " TO subfield
```

```
        ENDIF
        STORE counter + 1 TO counter
    ENDDO
    IF counter > 3
        CLEAR
        SET TALK ON
        RETURN
    ENDIF
ENDIF
?
* ---Enter REPORT FORM Width,Contents.
? "ENTER COLUMN DESCRIPTORS:"
*
* ---Loop through until a carriage return
* ---or more than 12 options are entered.
STORE "11" TO item
STORE "X" TO option&item
DO WHILE option&item <> " " .AND. VAL( item ) <= 22
    STORE STR( VAL(item)-10, 2 ) + ". Width,Contents." TO prompt
    ACCEPT "&prompt" TO option&item
    STORE $(&Mcontents) TO string
    IF @(",",option&item) > 3 .OR. @(",",option&item) = 0 .OR.;
        option&item = " " .OR. 0 = TEST(&string)
        * ---Syntax error in input, or exit.
        * ---The TEST() function will return 0,
        * ---if the contents cannot be parsed.
        LOOP
    ENDIF
    IF TYPE(&string)="L"
        * ---Logicals are not accepted.
        LOOP
    ENDIF
    ACCEPT "     Heading........" TO heading&item
    IF LEN(heading&item) > &Mwidth
        STORE $(heading&item,1,&Mwidth) TO heading&item
    ENDIF
    * ---See if field entered is numeric, so as to inquire
    * ---about totaling and/or subtotaling for this field.
    * ---The TEST() function will always return a negative
    * ---number on numeric fields or numeric memory variables.
    IF 0 > TEST(&string) .AND. istotal
        ACCEPT "     Totals? (Y/N)" TO y:n
        IF !(y:n) = "Y"
            STORE totstack + "&item" TO totstack
        ENDIF
    ENDIF
    IF 0 > TEST(&string) .AND. issubtotal
        ACCEPT "     Subtotals? (Y/N)" TO y:n
        IF !(y:n) = "Y"
            STORE substack + "&item" TO substack
        ENDIF
    ENDIF
    ?
    STORE STR( VAL( item ) + 1, 2 ) TO item
    STORE "X" TO option&item
ENDDO
```

```
STORE VAL( item ) - 1 TO totalopts
IF option11=" "
    CLEAR
    SET TALK ON
    RETURN
ENDIF
*
* ---Create a temporary structure file to
* ---determine field LEN and DEC for numerics.
COPY STRUCTURE EXTENDED TO &datafile..$$$
USE &datafile..$$$
*
* ---Generate REPORT FORM file.
ERASE
SET RAW ON
SET ALTERNATE TO &formfile
SET ALTERNATE ON
? [* Program.: ] + formfile
? [* Author..: ] + yourname
? [* Date....: ] + DATE()
? [* Notice..: Copyright 19] + $( DATE(), 7, 2 ) +;
               [, All Rights Reserved]
? [* Local...: pagenum, line, pagehdg, col:hdg, condition,]
? [*          lastrec]
? [*]
? [SET TALK OFF]
? [SET BELL OFF]
? [SET MARGIN TO ] + lmargin
? [STORE 1 TO pagenum]
? [STORE 254 TO line]
? [STORE "] + pagehdg + [" TO pagehdg]
? [STORE ( ] + pagewidth + [ - LEN( pagehdg ) ) / 2 TO col:hdg]
STORE "11" TO item
IF istotal .AND. LEN(totstack) <> 1
    ? [*]
    ? [* ---Initialize accumulators.]
    STORE $( totstack, 2, LEN( totstack ) ) TO totstack
    STORE "11" TO item
    STORE    1  TO stackcount
    DO WHILE stackcount < LEN( totstack )
        IF item = $( totstack, stackcount, 2 )
            ? [STORE 0 TO total&item]
            STORE stackcount + 2 TO stackcount
        ENDIF
        STORE STR( VAL( item ) + 1, 2 ) TO item
    ENDDO
ENDIF
IF issubtotal .AND. LEN(substack) <> 1
    STORE $( substack, 2, LEN( substack ) ) TO substack
    STORE "11" TO item
    STORE 1 TO stackcount
    DO WHILE stackcount < LEN( substack )
        IF item = $( substack, stackcount, 2 )
            ? [STORE 0 TO subtot&item]
            STORE stackcount + 2 TO stackcount
        ENDIF
        STORE STR( VAL( item ) + 1, 2 ) TO item
    ENDDO
ENDIF
```

```
? [*]
? [* ---Open the datafile and print the report.]
? [USE ] + datafile
? [ERASE]
? [@ 2, 0 SAY pagehdg]
? [@ 2,72 SAY DATE()]
? [@ 3, 0 SAY "========================================"]
? [@ 3,40 SAY "========================================"]
? [STORE " " TO select]
? '@ 5,0 SAY "Output to the screen or printer? [S/P] ";'
? [        GET select PICTURE "!"]
? [READ]
? [DO CASE]
? [    CASE select = "S"]
? [        ERASE]
? [        STORE 22 TO pagelen]
? [    CASE select = "P"]
? [        SET FORMAT TO PRINT]
? [        STORE ] + pagelen + [ TO pagelen]
? [    OTHERWISE]
? [        ERASE]
? [        SET BELL ON]
? [        SET TALK ON]
? [        RETURN]
? [ENDCASE]
? [* ---Enter FOR <expression> for the report, such as,]
? [* ---STORE "STATE = 'CA'" TO condition]
? [STORE " " TO condition]
? [DO WHILE .NOT. EOF]
? [    IF line > pagelen]
? [        IF select = "S"]
? [            ERASE]
? [        ELSE]
? [            EJECT]
? [        ENDIF]
? [        @ 0,0 SAY "PAGE NO."]
? [        @ 0,9 SAY STR(pagenum,3)]
? [        @ 2,col:hdg SAY pagehdg]
? [        *]
? [        * ---Generate column headings.]
* ---Provide for proper column spacing.
STORE STR( totalopts, 2 ) TO colcount
DO WHILE VAL( colcount ) >= 11
    STORE "11" TO item
    STORE 0 TO col&colcount
    DO WHILE VAL( colcount ) > VAL( item )
        STORE col&colcount + &Mwidth + 1 TO col&colcount
        STORE STR( VAL( item ) + 1, 2 ) TO item
    ENDDO
    STORE col&colcount + ((VAL(colcount)-11)*2) TO col&colcount
    STORE STR( VAL( colcount ) - 1, 2 ) TO colcount
ENDDO
* ---Generate headings.
STORE "11" TO item
DO WHILE VAL(item) <= totalopts
    ? [        @ 4,] + STR(col&item,3) + [ SAY "]+heading&item+["]
    STORE STR( VAL( item ) + 1, 2 ) TO item
ENDDO
```

```
* ---Generate underlining.
STORE "11" TO item
DO WHILE VAL( item ) <= totalopts
    ? [        @ 5,] + STR(col&item,3) + [ SAY "] +;
      $(equals,1,&Mwidth) + ["]
    STORE STR( VAL( item ) + 1, 2 ) TO item
ENDDO
? [        STORE pagenum + 1 TO pagenum]
? [        STORE 7 TO line]
? [    ENDIF]
? [    * ---Test to see if the condition exists.]
? [    IF condition <> " "]
? [        IF .NOT. ( ] + "&" + [condition )]
? [            SKIP]
? [            LOOP]
? [        ENDIF]
? [    ENDIF]
*
* ---Control break for subtotals.
IF issubtotal .AND. LEN(substack) <> 1
    ? [    IF 0=TEST(lastrec)]
    ? [        * ---Field has not been initialized.]
    ? [        STORE ] + subfield + [ TO lastrec]
    ? [    ENDIF]
    ? [    *]
    ? [    * ---Print subtotals and reset accumulators]
    ? [    * ---upon control break.]
    ? [    IF lastrec <> ] + subfield
    STORE "11" TO item
    STORE   1  TO stackcount
    ? [        STORE line + 1 TO line]
    LOCATE FOR Field:name = subfield
    IF Field:type = "N"
        ? [        @ line,2 SAY "** SUBTOTAL FOR "] +;
          [+STR(lastrec,] + STR(Field:len,3) +;
          [,] + STR(Field:dec,2) + [)+" **"]
    ELSE
        ? [        @ line,2 SAY ] +;
          ["** SUBTOTAL FOR "+TRIM(lastrec)+" **"]
    ENDIF
    ? [        STORE line + 1 TO line]
    DO WHILE stackcount < LEN(substack)
        IF item = $( substack, stackcount, 2 )
            LOCATE FOR Field:name = $(&Mcontents)
            IF .NOT. EOF
                * ---Is a single field.
                ? [        @ line,] + STR(col&item,3) +;
                  [ SAY STR(subtot&item,] +;
                  STR(&Mwidth,3) + [,] + STR(Field:dec,1) + [)]
            ELSE
                * ---Is an expression.
                * ---Hard code DEC to 2.
                ? [        @ line,] + STR(col&item,3) + [ SAY ] +;
                  [STR(subtot&item,] + STR(&Mwidth,3) + [,2)]
            ENDIF
            ? [        STORE 0 TO subtot&item]
            STORE stackcount + 2 TO stackcount
        ENDIF
```

```
          STORE STR( VAL( item ) + 1, 2 ) TO item
     ENDDO
     ? [          STORE line + 2 TO line]
     ? [          STORE ] + subfield + [ TO lastrec]
     ? [     ENDIF]
ENDIF
*
* ---Detail line section.
? [    *]
? [    * ---Print detail line.]
STORE "11" TO item
DO WHILE VAL(item) <= totalopts
     STORE $(&Mcontents) TO string
     STORE &Mwidth TO width
     LOCATE FOR Field:name = string
     IF .NOT. EOF
        * ---The contents is a Field name.
        IF Field:type="C"
           * ---The field is a character type.
           ? [     @ line,] + STR(col&item,3) + [ SAY ] +;
           [$(] + string + [,1,] + STR(width,3) + [)]
        ELSE
           * ---The field is a numeric type.
           ? [     @ line,] + STR(col&item,3) + [ SAY ] +;
           [$(STR(] + string + [,] + STR(width,3) +;
           [,] + STR(Field:dec,2) + [),1,] + STR(width,3) + [)]
        ENDIF
     ELSE
        * ---The contents is an expression.
        USE &datafile
        IF 0 > TEST(&string)
           * ---The expression is a numeric type.
           * ---Hard code the LEN and DEC to 10,2.
           ? [     @ line,] + STR(col&item,3) + [ SAY ] +;
           [$(STR(] + string + [,10,2),1,] + STR(width,3) + [)]
        ELSE
           * ---The expression is a character type.
           ? [     @ line,] + STR(col&item,3) + [ SAY ] +;
           [$(] + string + [,1,] + STR(width,3) + [)]
        ENDIF
        * ---Reopen the STRUCTURE EXTENDED datafile.
        USE &datafile..$$$
     ENDIF
     STORE STR( VAL( item ) + 1, 2 ) TO item
ENDDO
*
* ---Accumulate totals and/or subtotals.
? [    STORE line + 1 TO line]
IF istotal .AND. LEN(totstack) <> 1
     ? [    *]
     ? [    * ---Accumulate totals and/or subtotals.]
     STORE "11" TO item
     STORE 1 TO stackcount
     DO WHILE stackcount < LEN(totstack)
        IF item=$(totstack,stackcount,2)
           ? [    STORE total&item+] + $(&Mcontents) +;
           [ TO total&item]
```

```
            STORE stackcount + 2 TO stackcount
        ENDIF
        STORE STR( VAL(item) + 1, 2 ) TO item
    ENDDO
ENDIF
IF issubtotal .AND. LEN(substack) <> 1
    STORE "11" TO item
    STORE 1 TO stackcount
    DO WHILE stackcount < LEN(substack)
        IF item = $( substack, stackcount, 2 )
            ? [    STORE subtot&item+] + $(&Mcontents) +;
            [ TO subtot&item]
            STORE stackcount + 2 TO stackcount
        ENDIF
        STORE STR( VAL(item) + 1, 2 ) TO item
    ENDDO
ENDIF
? [    SKIP]
? [ENDDO]
*
* ---Final subtotal and totals.
IF issubtotal .AND. LEN(substack) <> 1
    ? [*]
    ? [* ---Print last subtotal record after end-of-file.]
    ? [STORE line + 1 TO line]
    LOCATE FOR Field:name = subfield
    IF Field:type = "N"
        ? [@ line,2 SAY "** SUBTOTAL FOR "] + [+STR(lastrec,] +;
        STR(Field:len,3) + [,] + STR(Field:dec,2) + [)+" **"]
    ELSE
        ? [@ line,2 SAY "** SUBTOTAL FOR "+TRIM(lastrec)+" **"]
    ENDIF
    ? [STORE line + 1 TO line]
    STORE "11" TO item
    STORE    1  TO stackcount
    DO WHILE stackcount < LEN(substack)
        IF item = $( substack, stackcount, 2 )
            STORE $(&Mcontents) TO string
            LOCATE FOR Field:name = string
            IF .NOT. EOF
                * ---Is a single field.
                ? [@ line,] + STR(col&item,3) +;
                [ SAY STR(subtot&item,],&Mwidth,[,] +;
                STR(Field:dec,1) + [)]
            ELSE
                * ---Is an expression.
                * ---Hard code DEC to 2.
                ? [@ line,] + STR(col&item,3) + [ SAY ] +;
                [STR(subtot&item,],&Mwidth,[,2)]
            ENDIF
            STORE stackcount + 2 TO stackcount
        ENDIF
        STORE STR( VAL( item ) + 1, 2 ) TO item
    ENDDO
ENDIF
```

```
IF istotal .AND. LEN(totstack) <> 1
   ? [*]
   ? [* ---Print final totals.]
   STORE "11" TO item
   STORE 1 TO stackcount
   ? [STORE line + 2 TO line]
   ? [@ line,2 SAY "*** FINAL TOTALS ***"]
   ? [STORE line + 1 TO line]
   DO WHILE stackcount < LEN(totstack)
      IF item = $( totstack, stackcount, 2 )
         STORE $(&Mcontents) TO string
         LOCATE FOR Field:name = string
         IF .NOT. EOF
            * ---Is a single field.
            ? [@ line,] + STR(col&item,3) +;
              [ SAY STR(total&item,],&Mwidth,[,] +;
              STR(Field:dec,1) + [)]
         ELSE
            * ---Is an expression.
            * ---Hard code DEC to 2.
            ? [@ line,] + STR(col&item,3) +;
              [ SAY STR(total&item,],&Mwidth,[,2)]
         ENDIF
         STORE stackcount + 2 TO stackcount
      ENDIF
      STORE STR( VAL( item ) + 1, 2 ) TO item
   ENDDO
ENDIF
*
? [@ line + 1, 0 SAY " "]
? [SET FORMAT TO SCREEN]
? [RELEASE ALL]
? [SET TALK ON]
? [SET BELL ON]
? [RETURN]
? [* EOF: ] + formfile
?
SET ALTERNATE OFF
SET ALTERNATE TO
USE
DELETE FILE &datafile..$$$
CLEAR
SET RAW OFF
SET TALK ON
RETURN
* EOF: FORMGEN.PRG
```

NAMEGEN2.PRG
NAMEGEN3.PRG

Description.   For generating memory variable names from data file field names, and writing the memory variable initialization routines and the STORE and REPLACE code. NAMEGEN2.PRG runs in dBASE II and NAMEGEN3.PRG runs in dBASE III.

```
* Program..: NAMEGEN2.PRG
* Author...: Tom Rettig
* Date.....: March 28, 1984
* Notice...: Copyright 1984, Tom Rettig & Associates. All rights reserved.
* Version..: dBASE II, version 2.4x
* Notes....: For generating memory variable names from datafile
*            field names, and writing the memory variable
*            initialization routines and the STORE and REPLACE code.
*
*            Saves the output in a text file with the same name as
*            the database file and a .TXT extension.
*
* Establish working environment, and prompt for data file name...
SET TALK OFF
CLEAR
ACCEPT "Enter [drive:]<data file name> with no extension -->" TO datafile
STORE !(TRIM(datafile)) + ".DBF" TO datafile
*
* Open the file if it exists, otherwise exit...
IF FILE("&datafile")
   USE &datafile
ELSE
   ? datafile + " does not exist where I'm looking for it."
   SET TALK ON
   RETURN
ENDIF
*
* Copy to a structure extended file to access the fieldnames...
COPY TO Temp STRUCTURE EXTENDED
USE Temp
*
* Convert field names to lower case...
ERASE
@ 1, 0 SAY "========================================"+;
           "========================================"
@ 2, 0 SAY "||"
@ 2,19 SAY "C H A N G I N G   T O   L O W E R   C A S E"
@ 2,78 SAY "||"
@ 3, 0 SAY "========================================"+;
           "========================================"
*
DO WHILE .NOT. EOF
   *
   * Display the record number and uppercase field, and
   * blank the previous lowercase field if there was one.
   @ 10,20 SAY Field:name
   @ 11,20 SAY #
   *
   * Initialize the memory variables.
   STORE " " TO new:char
   STORE 0 TO counter
   *
   * Loop to work on each character one at a time
   * for the length of the field.
   DO WHILE counter < LEN(TRIM(Field:name))
      STORE counter+1 TO counter
      STORE $(Field:name,counter,1) TO char
      *
```

```
            * If this character is an uppercase letter,
            * replace with a lowercase letter.
            IF char >= "A" .AND. char <= "Z"
                STORE new:char+CHR( RANK(char)+32 ) TO new:char
            ELSE
                * If this character is not an uppercase letter,
                * do not replace.
                STORE new:char + char TO new:char
            ENDIF
            *
        ENDDO
        REPLACE Field:name WITH $(new:char,2,LEN(TRIM(Field:name))+1)
        SKIP
    ENDDO
    @ 10,0
    @ 11,0
    @ 12,12 SAY "********** C H A N G E   I S   C O M P L E T E **********"
    *
    * Index and reopen the structure file, and erase the screen...
    INDEX ON Field:type + Field:name TO Temp
    USE Temp INDEX Temp
    ERASE
    *
    * Initialize a text file to receive the output...
    STORE $(datafile,1,@(".",datafile)-1) TO textfile
    SET ALTERNATE TO &textfile
    SET ALTERNATE ON
    *
    * Output the initialization statements...
    STORE '00000000000000000000' TO zeros
    DO WHILE .NOT. EOF
        DO CASE
            CASE Field:type = 'C'
                ? 'STORE $(blank,1,' + STR(Field:len,3) + ' )' +;
                  ' TO m:' + $(Field:name,1,8)
            CASE Field:type = 'N' .AND. Field:dec = 0
                ? 'STORE ' + $(zeros,1,Field:len-Field:dec) +;
                  ' TO m:' + $(Field:name,1,8)
            CASE Field:type = 'N' .AND. Field:dec > 0
                ? 'STORE ' + $(zeros,1,Field:len-Field:dec-1) + '.' +;
                  $(zeros,1,Field:dec) + ' TO m:' + $(Field:name,1,8)
            CASE Field:type = 'L'

                ? 'STORE F TO m:' + $(Field:name,1,8)
        ENDCASE
        SKIP
    ENDDO
    *
    * Output the STORE statements...
    ?
    GO TOP
    DO WHILE .NOT. EOF
        ? 'STORE ' + !($(Field:name,1,1)) + $(Field:name,2,9) +;
          ' TO m:' + $(Field:name,1,8)
        SKIP
    ENDDO
    *
```

```
* Output the REPLACE statements...
?
GO TOP
DO WHILE .NOT. EOF
    ? 'REPLACE ' + !($(Field:name,1,1)) + $(Field:name,2,9) +;
      ' WITH m:' + $(Field:name,1,8)
    SKIP
ENDDO
*
* Close the text file...
SET ALTERNATE OFF
SET ALTERNATE TO
*
* Restore the environment, and exit...
SET TALK ON
RETURN
* EOF: Namegen2.prg
```

```
* Program..: NAMEGEN3.PRG
* Author...: Tom Rettig
* Date.....: August 30, 1984
* Notice...: Copyright 1984, Tom Rettig & Associates. All rights reserved.
* Version..: dBASE III, version 1.00
* Notes....: For generating memory variable names from data file
*            field names, and writing the memory variable
*            initialization routines and the STORE and REPLACE code.
*
*            Saves the output in a text file with the same name as
*            the database file and a .TXT extension.
*
* Establish working environment, and prompt for data file name...
SET TALK OFF
CLEAR ALL
ACCEPT "Enter [drive:]<data file name> with no extension -->" TO datafile
STORE UPPER(TRIM(datafile)) + ".DBF" TO datafile
*
* Open the file if it exists, otherwise exit...
IF FILE(datafile)
   USE &datafile
ELSE
   ? datafile + " does not exist where I'm looking for it."
   SET TALK ON
   RETURN
ENDIF
*
* Copy to a structure extended file to access the fieldnames...
COPY TO Temp STRUCTURE EXTENDED
USE Temp
*
* Convert field names to lower case...
REPLACE ALL Field_name WITH LOWER(Field_name)
*
* Index and reopen the structure file, and erase the screen...
INDEX ON Field_type + Field_name TO Temp
USE Temp INDEX Temp
CLEAR
*
* Initialize a text file to receive the output...
STORE SUBSTR(datafile,1,AT(".",datafile)-1) TO textfile
SET ALTERNATE TO &textfile
SET ALTERNATE ON
*
* Output the initialization statements...
STORE '00000000000000000000' TO zeros
DO WHILE .NOT. EOF()
   DO CASE
      CASE Field_type = 'C'
         ?  'm_' + SUBSTR(Field_name,1,8) + ' = SPACE(' + ;
                   STR(Field_len,3) + ')'
      CASE Field_type = 'N' .AND. Field_dec = 0
         ?  'm_' + SUBSTR(Field_name,1,8) ' = ' + ;
                   SUBSTR(zeros,1,Field_len-Field_dec)
      CASE Field_type = 'N' .AND. Field_dec > 0
```

```
           ? 'm_' + SUBSTR(Field_name,1,8) + ' = ' + ;
                   SUBSTR(zeros,1,Field_len-Field_dec-1) + '.' +;
                   SUBSTR(zeros,1,Field_dec)
        CASE Field_type = 'L'
           ? 'm_' + SUBSTR(Field_name,1,8) + ' = .F.'
        CASE Field_type = 'D'
           ? 'm_' + SUBSTR(Field_name,1,8) + ' = CTOD("  /  /  ")'
     ENDCASE
     SKIP
ENDDO
*
* Output the STORE statements...
?
GO TOP
DO WHILE .NOT. EOF()
    ? 'm_' + SUBSTR(Field_name,1,8) + ' = ' + ;
      UPPER(SUBSTR(Field_name,1,1)) + SUBSTR(Field_name,2,9)
    SKIP
ENDDO
*
* Output the REPLACE statements...
?
GO TOP
DO WHILE .NOT. EOF()
    ? 'REPLACE ' + UPPER(SUBSTR(Field_name,1,1)) + SUBSTR(Field_name,2,9) +;
     ' WITH m_' + SUBSTR(Field_name,1,8)
    SKIP
ENDDO
*
* Close the text file...
SET ALTERNATE OFF
SET ALTERNATE TO
*
* Restore the environment, and exit...
CLOSE DATABASES
SET TALK ON
RETURN
* EOF_ Namegen3.prg
```

APPENDIX D

ASSEMBLY LANGUAGE SUBROUTINES

ASSEMBLY CODE INTERFACE UTILITIES

HEX2POKE.CMD	INTEL hex file into dBASE II POKE sequence
HEX2POKE.PRG	INTEL hex file into dBASE II POKE sequence
BINDEC.BAS	Creates a POKE sequence from a binary file

CP/M-80 UTILITIES

SMALL-.CMD	Front-end to DWAIT, INKEY, LEADZERO, & LEFTJUST
DWAIT.ASM	Waits for console input or time-out delay
INKEY.ASM	Inkey function on CP/M 2.2
LEADZERO.ASM	Replaces leading blanks with leading zeroes
LEFTJUST.ASM	Left-justifies a string
FIX.ASM	Replaces a file's control chars with spaces
DISKSTAT.ASM	Returns the amount of space left on the disk

CP/M-86 UTILITIES

FIX.A86	Replaces a file's control characters with spaces
DISKSTAT.PRG	Returns the amount of space left on the disk
DISKSTAT.A86	Disk drive status assembly listing

DOS 2.0 UTILITIES

DOS-.PRG	Front-end to DOS utilities
DOS-COPY.PRG	Copies programs between directories on MS-DOS 2.0x
DOS-DATE.PRG	Gets IBM PC system date
DOS-PATH.PRG	Changes directories on MS-DOS 2.0x
DOS-STAT.PRG	Returns disk space remaining on a disk
DOS-TIME.PRG	Gets IBM PC system time
PC_DATE.PRG	Sets the IBM PC system date
FIX-DOS.ASM	Replaces a file's control characters with spaces
TIMEWAIT.ASM	Displays system time at specified location in menu

HEX2POKE.CMD

Description. Converts a HEX file into a dBASE II POKE sequence. The file this program generates has a LIB extension and can be added to a dBASE II command file using an editor or word-processor. The dBASE II datafile, HEX2POKE.DBF, must be created with the structure:

```
HDUMMY1     C     001
HLENGTH     C     002
HADDRESS    C     004
HDUMMY2     C     002
H11         C     002
H12         C     002
H13         C     002
<...............>
H20         C     002
H21         C     002
H22         C     002
<...............>
H26         C     002
```

Input. The input HEX file will look like the following:

```
:10A410002233A44E545D13237EFE20C225A40DC218
:10A4200017A4CA2FA47E36201213230DC225A42AF6
:05A4300033A4C9000087
:0000000000
```

Output. The output generated for the above HEX file is given below:

```
* Subroutine.: LEFTJUST.LIB
* Author.....: Luis A. Castro
* Created on.: 06/26/84
*
SET CALL TO 42000
* -------------0---1---2---3---4---5---6---7
POKE 42000,   34, 51,164, 78, 84, 93, 19, 35,;
            126,254, 32,194, 37,164, 13,194
POKE 42016,   23,164,202, 47,164,126, 54, 32,;
             18, 19, 35, 13,194, 37,164, 42
POKE 42032,   51,164,201,  0,  0
*
RETURN
* EOF: LEFTJUST.LIB

* Program.: HEX2POKE.CMD
* Author..: Luis A. Castro
* Date....: 09/14/82, 07/12/83, 01/17/84
* Notice..: Copyright 1982, 1983, & 1984, Ashton-Tate, All Rights Reserved
* Version.: dBASE II, version 2.4x
```

```
* Notes...: Creates a dBASE II POKE sequence from a HEX file.
* Local...: hexvalues, Mhexlen, Mhexaddr, filename,
*            address, linelen, decimals, item
*
SET TALK OFF
SET RAW ON
STORE "123456789ABCDEF" TO hexvalues
* ---Macros to convert hex values to decimal values.
STORE [@($(Hlength,1,1),hexvalues)*16 +;
    @($(Hlength,2,1),hexvalues)] TO Mhexlen
STORE [@($(Haddress,1,1),hexvalues)*4096+;
    @($(Haddress,2,1),hexvalues)*256+;
    @($(Haddress,3,1),hexvalues)*16+;
    @($(Haddress,4,1),hexvalues)] TO Mhexaddr
*
ERASE
@ 2, 0 SAY "H E X - T O - P O K E    C O N V E R T E R"
@ 2,72 SAY DATE()
@ 3, 0 SAY "========================================"
@ 3,40 SAY "========================================"
ACCEPT "Enter hex file....." TO filename
STORE !( TRIM(filename) ) + "." TO filename
STORE $( filename, 1, @(".",filename) - 1 ) TO filename
DO CASE
    CASE filename = " "
        SET TALK ON
        SET RAW OFF
        RETURN
    CASE .NOT. FILE(filename+".HEX")
        ? "FILE DOES NOT EXIST"
        SET TALK ON
        SET RAW OFF
        RETURN
ENDCASE
?
? "Copying structure to HEX2POKE.$$$...."
USE Hex2poke
COPY STRUCTURE TO Hex2poke.$$$
USE Hex2poke.$$$
? "Appending from &filename..HEX... "
APPEND FROM &filename..HEX SDF
GO TOP
*
* ---Generate the POKE sequence.
ERASE
SET ALTERNATE TO &filename..LIB
SET ALTERNATE ON
? [* Subroutine.: ]+filename+[.LIB]
? [* Author.....: Your Name]
? [* Created on.: ]+DATE()
? [*]
STORE &Mhexaddr TO address
? [SET CALL TO ]+STR(address,5)
? [* -----------0---1---2---3---4---5---6---7]
DO WHILE .NOT. EOF
    STORE &Mhexlen TO linelen
    STORE &Mhexaddr TO address
IF linelen <> 0
```

```
        STORE " " TO decimals
        STORE "11" TO item
        DO WHILE VAL(item)-10 <= linelen
            STORE decimals+","+STR(@($(H&item,1,1),hexvalues)*16;
                + @($(H&item,2,1),hexvalues),3) TO decimals
            STORE STR(VAL(item)+1,2) TO item
        ENDDO
        IF LEN(decimals)-2 <= 32
            ? [POKE ] + STR(address,5) + [,] + $(decimals,3)
        ELSE
            ? [POKE ]+STR(address,5)+[,] + $(decimals,3,32)+[;]
            ? [                 ]+$(decimals,35)
        ENDIF
    ENDIF
    IF ( # - 4 * INT( # / 4 ) ) = 0
        ? [* -----------0---1---2---3---4---5---6---7]
    ENDIF
    SKIP
ENDDO
? [*]
? [RETURN]
? [* EOF: ] + filename + [.LIB]
?
SET ALTERNATE OFF
SET ALTERNATE TO
CLEAR
DELETE FILE Hex2poke.$$$
SET RAW OFF
SET TALK ON
RETURN
* EOF: HEX2POKE.CMD
```

HEX2POKE.PRG

Description. Converts a HEX file into a dBASE II POKE sequence. The file this program generates has a LIB extension and can be added to a dBASE II command file using an editor or word-processor. The dBASE II datafile, HEX2POKE.DBF, must be created with the structure:

```
        HDUMMY1      C      001
        HLENGTH      C      002
        HADDRESS     C      004
        HDUMMY2      C      002
        H11          C      002
        H12          C      002
        H13          C      002
        <...............>
        H20          C      002
        H21          C      002
        <...............>
        H30          C      002
        H31          C      002
```

Input. The input HEX file will look like the following:

```
:10A410002233A44E545D13237EFE20C225A40DC218
:10A4200017A4CA2FA47E36201213230DC225A42AF6
:05A4300033A4C9000087
:0000000000
```

Output. The output is similar to the one generated by HEX2POKE.CMD.

```
* Program.: HEX2POKE.PRG
* Author..: Luis A. Castro
* Date....: 01/17/84
* Notice..: Copyright 1984, Ashton-Tate, All Rights Reserved
* Version.: dBASE II, version 2.4x
* Notes...: Creates a dBASE II POKE sequence from a HEX file.
* Local...: hexvalues, Mhexlen, Mhexaddr, filename,
*           address, linelen, decimals, item
*
SET TALK OFF
SET RAW ON
STORE "123456789ABCDEF" TO hexvalues
* ---Macros to convert hex values to decimal values.
STORE [@($(Hlength,1,1),hexvalues)*16 +;
   @($(Hlength,2,1),hexvalues)] TO Mhexlen
STORE [@($(Haddress,1,1),hexvalues)*4096+;
   @($(Haddress,2,1),hexvalues)*256+;
   @($(Haddress,3,1),hexvalues)*16+;
   @($(Haddress,4,1),hexvalues)] TO Mhexaddr
*
ERASE
@ 2, 0 SAY "H E X - T O - P O K E   C O N V E R T E R"
@ 2,72 SAY DATE()
@ 3, 0 SAY "========================================="
@ 3,40 SAY "========================================="
ACCEPT "Enter hex file....." TO filename
STORE !( TRIM(filename) ) + "." TO filename
STORE $( filename, 1, @(".",filename) - 1 ) TO filename
DO CASE
    CASE filename = " "
        SET TALK ON
        SET RAW OFF
        RETURN
    CASE .NOT. FILE(filename+".HEX")
        ? "FILE DOES NOT EXIST"
        SET TALK ON
        SET RAW OFF
        RETURN
ENDCASE
?
? "Copying structure to HEX2POKE.$$$...."
USE Hex2poke
COPY STRUCTURE TO Hex2poke.$$$
USE Hex2poke.$$$
? "Appending from &filename..HEX... "
APPEND FROM &filename..HEX SDF
GO TOP
*
```

```
* ---Generate the POKE sequence.
ERASE
SET ALTERNATE TO &filename..LIB
SET ALTERNATE ON
? [* Subroutine.: ]+filename+[.LIB]
? [* Author.....: Your Name]
? [* Created on.: ]+DATE()
? [*]
STORE &Mhexaddr TO address
? [SET CALL TO ]+STR(address,5)
? [* -----------0---1---2---3---4---5---6---7---8---9]
DO WHILE .NOT. EOF
    STORE &Mhexlen TO linelen
    STORE &Mhexaddr TO address
    IF linelen <> 0
        STORE " " TO decimals
        STORE "11" TO item
        DO WHILE VAL(item)-10 <= linelen
            STORE decimals+","+STR(@($(H&item,1,1),hexvalues)*16;
                + @($(H&item,2,1),hexvalues),3) TO decimals
            STORE STR(VAL(item)+1,2) TO item
        ENDDO
        DO CASE
            CASE LEN(decimals)-2 <= 40
                ? [POKE ] + STR(address,5) + [,] + $(decimals,3)
            CASE LEN(decimals)-2 <= 80
                ? [POKE ]+STR(address,5)+[,] + $(decimals,3,40)+[;]
                ? [                ]+$(decimals,43)
            OTHERWISE
            * ---LEN(decimals)-2 > 80
                ? [POKE ]+STR(address,5)+[,] + $(decimals,3,40)+[;]
                ? [                ]+$(decimals,43,40)+[;]
                ? [                ]+$(decimals,83)
        ENDCASE
    ENDIF
    IF ( # - 4*INT(#/4) ) = 0
        ? [* -----------0---1---2---3---4---5---6---7---8---9]
    ENDIF
    SKIP
ENDDO
? [*]
? [RETURN]
? [* EOF: ] + filename + [.LIB]
?
SET ALTERNATE OFF
SET ALTERNATE TO
CLEAR
DELETE FILE Hex2poke.$$$
SET RAW OFF
SET TALK ON
RETURN
* EOF: HEX2POKE.PRG
```

BINDEC.BAS

Description.   Creates a POKE sequence from a binary file.

```
100 'Program.: BINDEC.BAS
101 'Author..: Steve Manes, modified by Luis A. Castro
102 'Date....: August 1, 1983
103 'Notice..: Copyright 1983, Steve Manes, All Rights Reserved
104 'Notes...: Converts a binary file to a dBASE II decimal
105 '          POKE sequence.
107 '
200 DEFINT A-Z
250 '
300 'Get input and output filenames.
305 CLS
310 LOCATE 2, 1 :PRINT "Binary to hexadecimal file conversion"
320 LOCATE 5, 1 :INPUT "Source filename (with EXT.) - ",FILEIN$
330 LOCATE 6, 1 :INPUT "Output filename (.DTX)      - ",FILEOUT$
340 IF FILEIN$="" OR FILEOUT$="" THEN SYSTEM
345 PRINT
350 '
355 'Open input file.
360 OPEN "R", #1, FILEIN$, 1
370 FIELD #1, 1 AS ONEBYTE$
380 COUNT = 0
400 IF INSTR( "EXE,exe", RIGHT$(FILEIN$,3) ) <> 0 THEN ELSE 500
410     'Get file offset from EXE file header and initialize pointer.
415     'Get offset to program data.
420     'COUNT will equal the input file byte offset.
425     GET #1, 9
430     LOW.ORDER.BYTE = ASC( ONEBYTE$ )
435     GET #1, 10
440     HIGH.ORDER.BYTE = ASC( ONEBYTE$ )
445     COUNT = INT( (LOW.ORDER.BYTE * 16) + (HIGH.ORDER.BYTE * 4096) ) + 1
450     GOTO 700
500 'ELSE
510 IF INSTR( "COM,com", RIGHT$(FILEIN$,3) ) <> 0 THEN ELSE 600
520     'COM files have no program header.
530     'Initialize pointer to first byte.
540     COUNT = 1
550     GOTO 700
600 'ELSE
620     PRINT
630     PRINT "Can only convert COM or EXE type files."
640     CLOSE 1
650     END
700 'ENDIF
710 '
```

```
720  'Force .DTX extension to filename and open output file.
730  POSITION = INSTR( FILEOUT$, "." )
740  IF POSITION > 0 THEN FILEOUT$ = LEFT$( FILEOUT$, POSITION - 1 )
750  FILEOUT$ = FILEOUT$ + ".DTX"
810  OPEN "R", #2, FILEOUT$, 80
820  FIELD #2, 80 AS RESULT$
830  '
900  FALSE = 0
905  TRUE = NOT FALSE
910  CHARCOUNT = 0             'Number of chars in current string.
930  DECSTRING$ = ""           'ASCII decimal string.
940  RECNUM = 1                'Output file record number.
950  '
1030 TOTAL.BYTES = LOF(1)
2000 WHILE COUNT <= TOTAL.BYTES
2010    GET #1, COUNT
2020    BYTE = ASC( ONEBYTE$ )    'ASCII value of input byte.
2120    BYTE$ = HEX$( BYTE )    'Format leading zero.
2130    IF BYTE < 16 THEN BYTE$ = "0" + BYTE$
2210    BYTE$ = BYTE$ + "   "
2320    DEC$ = MID$( STR$( BYTE ), 2 )          'Strip leading blank in STR$
2330    DEC$ = STRING$(3-LEN(DEC$),"0")+DEC$+",+" "  'Format decimal byte
2340    DECSTRING$ = DECSTRING$ + DEC$          'Add it to DECSTRING$
2350    CHARCOUNT = CHARCOUNT + 1             'Increment character counter
2360    IF (CHARCOUNT MOD 16) = 0 THEN GOSUB 7000  'DUMP_STRING
2370    COUNT = COUNT + 1            'Increment input byte counter
2400 WEND
2410 '
3000 'Remove last comma in DECSTRING$.
3020 POSITION = ( CHARCOUNT MOD 16 )
3050 IF POSITION<>0 THEN DECSTRING$ = MID$(DECSTRING$,1,LEN(DECSTRING$)-2)
3100 DECSTRING$ = DECSTRING$ + STRING$( 80 - LEN(DECSTRING$), 26 )   'pad.
3200 GOSUB 7000   'DUMP_STRING
3210 LSET RESULT$ = STRING$( 80, 26 )     'A little extra padding.
3220 PUT #2, RECNUM
3230 CLOSE 1, 2
3250 LOCATE 22, 1 :PRINT "... done "
4000 SYSTEM
4010 '
4020 '
7000 'Subroutine: FORMAT_STRINGS_AND_PRINT_ON_SCREEN
7050 '+------------------------------------------------+
7110    DECSTRING$ = MID$( DECSTRING$, 1, LEN(DECSTRING$) - 2 )
7120    ROW = (RECNUM MOD 16) + 5
7130    LOCATE ROW + 1, 1  :PRINT STRING$( 80, " " );
7150    LOCATE ROW, 1        :PRINT DECSTRING$;
7220    DECSTRING$ = DECSTRING$ + CHR$(13) + CHR$(10)  'Add CR/LF.
7230    LSET RESULT$ = DECSTRING$
7240    PUT #2, RECNUM    'Write decimal string to .DTX file
7320    DECSTRING$ = ""
7330    RECNUM = RECNUM + 1       'Increment output record number.
7340 RETURN
7400 '
9000 'EOF: BINDEC.BAS
```

SMALL-.CMD

Description. Front-end program to utilize dWAIT, INKEY, LEADZERO, and LEFTJUST CP/M-80 assembly routines.

```
* Program.: SMALL-.CMD
* Author..: Luis A. Castro
* Date....: 01/20/84
* Notice..: Copyright 1984, Luis A. Castro, All Rights Reserved.
* Version.: dBASE II, version 2.4
* Notes...: Front-end program to utilize dWAIT, INKEY,
*           LEADZERO, and LEFTJUST CP/M-80 assembly subroutines.
* Local...: row, col, string, select, inchar
*
SET TALK OFF
SET BELL OFF
SET COLON OFF
SET RAW ON
ERASE
@ 2, 0 SAY "DEMONSTRATION of SMALL ASSEMBLY SUBROUTINES"
@ 2,72 SAY DATE()
@ 3, 0 SAY "========================================="
@ 3,40 SAY "========================================="
STORE "X" TO select
DO WHILE select <> " "
   @ 10,0
   STORE " " TO select
   @ 5,0 SAY "1. dWAIT    =  console input or time-out"
   @ 6,0 SAY "2. INKEY()  =  inkey function"
   @ 7,0 SAY "3. LEADZERO =  leading blanks with zeroes"
   @ 8,0 SAY "4. LEFTJUST =  left justify a string"
   @ 9,0 GET select PICTURE "!"
   READ
   IF select = " " .OR. .NOT. select $ "1234"
      LOOP
   ENDIF
   @ 9,0 SAY " "
   * ---Execute a routine.
   DO CASE
      CASE select = "1"
      * ---dWAIT.  console key or time-out delay.
         * ------------0---1---2---3---4---5---6---7
         POKE 42000,  33, 39,164, 53,194, 26,164, 44
         POKE 42008,  53,200, 14,  6, 30,255,205,  5
         POKE 42016,   0,254,  0,202, 16,164,201,  0
         POKE 42024, 100
         * ------------0---1---2---3---4---5---6---7
```

```
* ---The last value in the above poke sequence, 100,
* ---is the time-out limit, yielding a delay of 0.035n
* ---seconds (at 4MHz).  The largest value that can be
* ---used is 255, or about 9 seconds.
*
STORE " " TO string
@ 10,0 SAY "Enter a number [1..3] " GET string
READ
IF string < "1" .OR. string > "3"
    @ 12,0 SAY "Number is not [1..3] -- DELAY IN EFFECT"
    * ---Enable dWAIT.
    SET CALL TO 42000
    CALL
ENDIF
CASE select = "2"
* ---INKEY()
    * ------------0---1---2---3---4---5---6---7
    POKE 41984,  42,  6,  0, 34, 57,164, 33, 20,;
                164, 34,  6,  0,201, 42, 57,164
    POKE 42000,  34,  6,  0,201,245,121,254,  3,;
                202, 51,164,254,  6,194, 55,164
    POKE 42016, 123,254,255,202, 51,164,254,254,;
                202, 51,164,254,253,202, 51,164
    POKE 42032, 195, 55,164, 14,  0,241,201,241,;
                195,  0,  0,229, 14,  6, 30,255
    POKE 42048, 205, 56,164,225, 35,119,201
    * ------------0---1---2---3---4---5---6---7
    * ---Initialize INKEY().
    SET CALL TO 41984
    CALL
    @ 10,0 SAY "Strike any key to STOP"
    * ---Enable INKEY().
    SET CALL TO 42043
    * ---Do something until a character is pressed.
    STORE CHR( 0 ) to inchar
    STORE 11 TO row
    DO WHILE inchar = CHR( 0 ) .AND. row < 14
        STORE 0 TO col
        DO WHILE inchar = CHR( 0 ) .AND. col < 50
            @ row,col SAY "."
            STORE row + 1 TO row
            * ---Read first character from CP/M buffer.
            * ---CHR( 0 ) is returned if none is available.
            CALL inchar
        ENDDO
        STORE col + 1 TO col
    ENDDO
    * ---Restore dBASE II's input routines.
    * ---This closing operation MUST NOT BE FORGOTTEN.
    SET CALL TO 41997
    CALL
CASE select = "3"
* ---LEADZERO.
    * ------------0---1---2---3---4---5---6---7
    POKE 42000,  34, 37,164, 70, 35,126,254, 32
    POKE 42008, 194, 33,164, 54, 48,  5,194, 20
    POKE 42016, 164, 42, 37,164,201
    * ------------0---1---2---3---4---5---6---7
```

```
              SET CALL TO 42000
              ACCEPT "Enter a string with leading blanks " TO string
              IF TRIM(string) <> " "
                 ? "BEFORE: >" + string + "<"

                 CALL string
                 ? "AFTER:  >" + string + "<"
              ENDIF
           CASE select = "4"
           * ---LEFTJUST.
              * ------------0---1---2---3---4---5---6---7
              POKE 42000,   34, 51,164, 78, 84, 93, 19, 35,;
                           126,254, 32,194, 37,164, 13,194
              POKE 42016,   23,164,202, 47,164,126, 54, 32,;
                            18, 19, 35, 13,194, 37,164, 42
              POKE 42032,   51,164,201,  0,  0
              * ------------0---1---2---3---4---5---6---7
              SET CALL TO 42000
              ACCEPT "Enter a string with leading blanks " TO string
              IF TRIM(string) <> " "
                 ? "BEFORE: >" + string + "<"
                 CALL string
                 ? "AFTER:  >" + string + "<"
              ENDIF
        ENDCASE
        @ 11,0
        @ 12,0
        @ 13,0
 ENDDO
 SET BELL ON
 SET TALK ON
 SET COLON ON
 SET RAW OFF
 RELEASE row, col, string, select, inchar
 RETURN
 * EOF: SMALL-.CMD
```

DWAIT.ASM

Description.   Wait for console key or time-out delay. Often some advisory message needs to be displayed on the console, usually for minor error reporting. The message needs to be displayed long enough for the operator to read it and comprehend its meaning. Either of two techniques is typically employed, the most common being to wait for a user response to "PRESS ANY KEY TO CONTINUE." This, although perhaps necessary for more serious errors, often is unpleasant for the operator who must press a key for the program to proceed. The second method is to program a time delay loop, allowing enough time for the message to be digested. This is also undesirable, as there is nothing to do but wait. The approach this program follows is to combine these two tactics, giving the user a default time-out that can also be aborted at any time in the delay by pressing any key.

```
; Subroutine.: dWAIT.ASM
; Author.....: Raymond Weisling
; Date.......: 5/28/83, 6/10/83
; Notice.....: Copyright 1983, Raymond Weisling, All Rights Reserved.
```

```
; Notes......: Wait for console key or time-out delay.
;
            ORG     42000       ; dBASE II FREE AREA
LOOP:       LXI     H,COUNT     ; COUNTER ADDRESS
            DCR     M           ; REDUCE COUNTER BY ONE
            JNZ     CHECK       ; IF NOT ZERO, CHECK CONSOLE FOR KEY
            INR     L           ; POINT TO USER DELAY VALUE
            DCR     M           ; REDUCE DELAY BY ONE EVERY 35 MSEC
            RZ                  ; RETURN IF ZERO
CHECK:      MVI     C,6         ; CONSOLE I/O FUNCTION
            MVI     E,0FFH      ; SET CONSOLE INPUT REQUEST FLAG
            CALL    5           ; BDOS ADDRESS, READ CONSOLE STATUS
            CPI     0           ; TEST RESULT RETURNED
            JZ      LOOP        ; LOOP AGAIN IF NO KEY WAS HIT,
            RET                 ; ELSE QUIT IMMEDIATELY
COUNT       DB      0
USER        DB      0           ; FILLED BY dBASE II POKE, LAST BYTE
            END
```

INKEY.ASM

Description. An inkey function for use in dBASE II. After loading, the routine must be enabled by calling entry point 0A400H (41984). Calling this entry point disables dBASE II's normal keyboard input routines and enables the inkey routine. To use the inkey routine the user must define a string variable with a minimum of one character. Next, the call address is set to 0A43BH (42043) and the entry point is called with the previously defined string as a parameter. The first character of the string parameter is used to return the character if one is present or zero if no character is waiting to be read. **Once enabled, this routine is the only way to read the keyboard, so it must be used with caution**. To disable the inkey routine and re-enable the normal dBASE II keyboard input, the call address must be set to 0A40DH (41997) and that entry point called.

```
; Subroutine.: INKEY.ASM
; Author.....: Dave Green
; Date.......: 10/27/83, 11/3/83.
; Notice.....: Copyright 1983, Dave Green, All Rights Reserved
; Notes......: INKEY function for use in dBASE II.
;
;
        ORG     0A400H              ; DEFINE LOAD ADDRESS
;
; SETUP SECTION.
; MUST RUN THIS SECTION BEFORE THE OTHER SECTIONS CAN BE USED.
;
SETUP:  LHLD    0006H              ; GET DOS ENTRY POINT ADDRESS
        SHLD    ENTRY+1            ; MOVE IT TO JUMP INSTRUCTION
                                   ; IN CODE
        LXI     H,CMDTEST          ; GET COMMAND TEST ADDRESS
        SHLD    0006H              ; REPLACE NORMAL DOS ENTRY POINT
        RET
;
; RESTORE SECTION.
; MUST RUN THIS SECTION TO RESTORE THE NORMAL INPUT
; KEYBOARD INPUT FOR dBASE II.
;
```

```
RESTORE:
        LHLD    ENTRY+1         ; GET ORIGINAL DOS ENTRY POINT
        SHLD    0006H           ; PUT IT BACK
        RET
;
; THE NORMAL CALL 0005H IS DIVERTED TO THIS ROUTINE,
; WHICH INTERCEPTS DIRECT CONSOLE I/O COMMANDS.
; OTHER DOS COMMANDS ARE UNAFFECTED.
;
CMDTEST:
        PUSH    PSW             ; SAVE STATE
        MOV     A,C             ; MOVE COMMAND TO REGISTER A
        CPI     03H             ; RAW CONSOLE INPUT COMMAND
                                ; ISSUED?
        JZ      INTERCEPT       ; YES, INTERCEPT IT
        CPI     06H             ; DIRECT CONSOLE I/O COMMAND
                                ; ISSUED?
        JNZ     DOS             ; NO, PASS COMMAND TO DOS
        MOV     A,E
        CPI     0FFH            ; INPUT/STATUS REQUEST?
        JZ      INTERCEPT       ; YES, INTERCEPT IT
        CPI     0FEH            ; STATUS REQUEST?
        JZ      INTERCEPT       ; YES, INTERCEPT IT
        CPI     0FDH            ; INPUT REQUEST?
        JZ      INTERCEPT       ; YES, INTERCEPT IT
        JMP     DOS             ; COMMAND IS OUTPUT,
                                ; PASS IT TO DOS
;
INTERCEPT:
        MVI     C,0H            ; COMMAND IS CONSOLE INPUT, SO RETURN
                                ; BINARY 0.  IN OTHER WORDS, FOOL dBASE
                                ; INTO BELIEVING THERE IS NOTHING IN THE
                                ; BUFFER TO READ.
        POP     PSW
        RET
;
DOS:    POP     PSW             ; COMMAND IS NOT CONSOLE INPUT, PASS IT
                                ; TO DOS
ENTRY:  JMP     0000H           ; ADDRESS OF JUMP SET BY SETUP ROUTINE
;
;
; INKEY SECTION.
; THIS IS THE ROUTINE dBASE WILL ACTUALLY USE TO GET A CHARACTER.
;
INKEY:  PUSH    H               ; SAVE ADDRESS OF STRING PARAMETER
        MVI     C,06H           ; SETUP DIRECT CONSOLE I/O COMMAND
        MVI     E,0FFH
        CALL    ENTRY           ; CALL DOS ENTRY POINT DIRECTLY,
                                ; BY-PASSING 05H
        POP     H               ; GET ADDRESS OF STRING PARAMETER
        INX     H               ; POINT TO FIRST CHAR OF STRING
        MOV     M,A             ; MOVE CHAR (0 IF NO CHAR)
                                ; TO STRING PARAMETER
        RET
        END
```

LEADZERO.ASM

Description. Assembly subroutine to replace a character string's leading blanks with leading zeroes.

```
; Subroutine.: LEADZERO.ASM
; Author.....: Luis A. Castro
; Date.......: 1982
; Notice.....: Copyright 1982, Ashton-Tate, All Rights Reserved
; Notes......: Replace leading blanks with leading zeroes.
;
;
        ORG     42000   ; LOAD IN dBASE FREE AREA
        SHLD    SAVEHL  ; SAVE HL REGISTERS
        MOV     B,M     ; STORE LENGTH OF STRING TO COUNTER
;
LOOP:
        INX     H       ; SKIP TO NEXT CHARACTER
        MOV     A,M     ; FETCH CHARACTER
        CPI     ' '     ; IS IT A SPACE?
        JNZ     DONE    ; YES, DONE
        MVI     M,'0'   ; REPLACE SPACE WITH ZERO
        DCR     B       ; DECREMENT COUNTER
        JNZ     LOOP    ; REPEAT UNTIL DONE
DONE:
        LHLD    SAVEHL  ; RESTORE HL REGISTERS
        RET
;
SAVEHL  DB      0,0
        END
```

LEFTJUST.ASM

Description. Assembly subroutine to left-justify a character string.

```
; Subroutine.: LEFTJUST.ASM
; Author.....: Luis A. Castro
; Date.......: 06/15/83
; Notice.....: Copyright 1983, Ashton-Tate, All Rights Reserved
; Notes......: Left justify a character string.
;
        ORG     42000   ; LOAD IN dBASE II's FREE AREA
        SHLD    SAVEHL  ; SAVE HL REGISTER PAIR
        MOV     C,M     ; STORE LENGTH OF STRING TO COUNTER
        MOV     D,H     ; LOAD DE REGISTER PAIR
        MOV     E,L     ; WITH HL REGISTER PAIR
        INX     D       ; INCREMENT TO FIRST CHAR OF STRING
                        ; ON DE PAIR
;
LOOP:   INX     H       ; NEXT CHARACTER
        MOV     A,M     ; FETCH CHARACTER
        CPI     ' '     ; IS IT A SPACE?
        JNZ     JUST    ; IF NOT A SPACE, THEN JUSTIFY
```

```
            DCR     C         ; DECREMENT COUNTER
            JNZ     LOOP      ; REPEAT IF NOT END OF STRING
            JZ      DONE      ; END OF STRING REACHED, EXIT
;
JUST:       MOV     A,M       ; FETCH CHARACTER
            MVI     M,' '     ; REPLACE MEMORY WITH SPACE
            STAX    D         ; STORE CHARACTER IN ACCUMULATOR
                              ; TO NEXT AVAILABLE CHARACTER ON
                              ; LEFT OF STRING
            INX     D         ; INCREMENT BOTH POINTERS
            INX     H
            DCR     C         ; DECREMENT COUNTER
            JNZ     JUST      ; REPEAT UNTIL END OF STRING
;
DONE:       LHLD    SAVEHL    ; RESTORE HL PAIR
            RET
;
SAVEHL      DB      0,0
            END
```

FIX.ASM

Description. This program expects an ASCII filename on command line and writes back to the same filename and drive an output file with all characters less than 20H replaced by 20H except the 1AH EOF marks at real EOF. The output file has type of .FIX. A flag is set if CR and LF are also to be replaced. The program also prompts for the number of bytes from start of file at which to start processing.

```
; Subroutine.: FIX.ASM
; Author.....: Bob Doolittle
; Date.......: 08/12/84
; Notice.....: Copyright 1984, Ashton-Tate, All Rights Reserved.
; Notes......: CP/M 80 version.
;
            ORG     100H
;
;BDOS equates
;
SYSTEM      EQU     0                       ;System entry point
BDOS        EQU     5                       ;BDOS entry point
TBUF        EQU     80H                     ;Default buffer
FCB         EQU     5CH                     ;Default FCB
CFS         EQU     35                      ;Compute file size
CONIN       EQU     1                       ;Console in
CONOUT      EQU     2                       ;Console out
PSTR        EQU     9                       ;Print string
OPEN        EQU     15                      ;Open file
CLOSE       EQU     16                      ;Close file
READ        EQU     20                      ;Read sequential
WRITE       EQU     21                      ;Write sequential
MAKE        EQU     22                      ;Make file
DELETE      EQU     19                      ;Delete file
READR       EQU     33                      ;Read random
;
;ASCII equates
```

```
;
CR          EQU     13
LF          EQU     10
;
START:      XRA     A               ;Initialize CRLF flag to destroy CRLF
            STA     FLG
            LDA     FCB+1
            CPI     20H             ;Was input file on command line
            JNZ     ST2             ;Yes
            LXI     D,MES1          ;No, print message and abort
            MVI     C,PSTR
            CALL    BDOS
            JMP     EXIT
;
ST2:        LXI     D,MES4          ;Print CRLF message
            MVI     C,PSTR
            CALL    BDOS
            MVI     C,CONIN         ;Get response
            CALL    BDOS
            ANI     5FH             ;Make upper case
            CPI     'Y'
            JNZ     ST7
            MVI     A,1
            STA     FLG
ST7:        MVI     C,PSTR          ;Ask for # of bytes
            LXI     D,MES6
            CALL    BDOS
            LXI     D,CBUF          ;Get response
            MVI     C,10
            CALL    BDOS
            LXI     H,CBUF+2
            CALL    CONV            ;Convert to binary in HL
            CALL    DIV             ;Divide by 128
            SHLD    QUO             ;Save quotient and remainder
            CALL    CRLF
            CALL    CLEAR           ;Clear FCB+32-35, FCB+15 and FCB+12
            LXI     H,FCB
            LXI     D,FCB1
            MVI     C,9
MOVE:       MOV     A,M             ;Move file name & drive from FCB to FCB1
            STAX    D
            INX     H
            INX     D
            DCR     C
            JNZ     MOVE
            LXI     D,FCB
            MVI     C,OPEN          ;Open file
            CALL    BDOS
            INR     A               ;Was open successful?
            JNZ     ST3             ;Yes
            LXI     D,MES2          ;No, print message and abort
            MVI     C,PSTR
            CALL    BDOS
            JMP     EXIT
ST3:        LXI     D,MES5          ;Working message
            MVI     C,PSTR
            CALL    BDOS
            LXI     D,FCB
```

```
              MVI      C,CFS              ;Compute file size
              CALL     BDOS
              LHLD     FCB+33             ;Get last record+1
              SHLD     REC                ;Save locally
              DCX      H                  ;Last record number
              SHLD     FCB+33             ;Store it back
              MVI      C,READR
              LXI      D,FCB
              CALL     BDOS               ;Read last record
              LXI      H,TBUF-1
              MVI      C,0                ;Initialize counter
LOP:          INX      H                  ;Scan to 1st EOF mark and keep count
              INR      C
              MOV      A,M                ;Get byte
              CPI      1AH                ;Is it EOF?
              JNZ      LOP                ;No, keep looping
              PUSH     B                  ;Save count to EOF in last record
              CALL     CLEAR              ;Clear again
              LXI      D,FCB1
              MVI      C,DELETE           ;Delete any possible previous out file
              CALL     BDOS
              LXI      D,FCB
              MVI      C,OPEN             ;Re-open the input file
              CALL     BDOS
              LXI      D,FCB1
              MVI      C,MAKE             ;Make output file
              CALL     BDOS
;
FIRS:         LXI      D,FCB              ;Scan off quotient records
              MVI      C,READ
              CALL     BDOS
              ORA      A
              JZ       FST1               ;Read OK
              LXI      D,MES3
              MVI      C,PSTR
              CALL     BDOS
              POP      B                  ;Balance stack
              JMP      EXIT
;
FST1:         LHLD     REC                ;Bump record count down
              DCX      H
              SHLD     REC
              LHLD     QUO                ;Get DIV result
              MOV      A,H
              ORA      A                  ;Have we read sector with remainder ?
              JZ       FST2               ;Yes
              DCR      H                  ;No
              SHLD     QUO
              LXI      D,FCB1             ;Write sector
              MVI      C,WRITE
              CALL     BDOS
              JMP      FIRS
FST2:         MVI      A,80H
              ADD      L
              MOV      L,A                ;HL now has filter start address
```

```
FST3:   CALL    FILTER
        INX     H
        MOV     A,H
        ORA     A
        JZ      FST3            ;Filter to end of sector
        LXI     D,FCB1
        MVI     C,WRITE         ;Write to output file
        CALL    BDOS
LOOP:   LXI     D,FCB
        MVI     C,READ          ;Read a record to default buffer
        CALL    BDOS
        ORA     A               ;Was read successful?
        JZ      LO4             ;Yes
ERR:    LXI     D,MES3
        MVI     C,PSTR          ;No, print message and abort
        CALL    BDOS
        POP     B               ;Balance stack
        JMP     EXIT
;
LO4:    LHLD    REC             ;Get record count
        DCX     H               ;Decrement record count
        SHLD    REC             ;Save it
        MOV     A,H
        ORA     L               ;Are we at last record?
        JNZ     GOAH            ;No
        POP     B               ;Yes, get back count
        LXI     H,TBUF
;
LO1:    DCR     C               ;Are we at EOF
        JZ      LO2             ;Yes
        CALL    FILTER
        INX     H
        JMP     LO1             ;Loop
;
LO2:    LXI     D,FCB1
        MVI     C,WRITE         ;Write last record
        CALL    BDOS
        LXI     D,FCB1
        MVI     C,CLOSE         ;Close output file
        CALL    BDOS
EXIT:   JMP     SYSTEM          ;Finished
;
GOAH:   LXI     H,TBUF
        MVI     C,80H           ;Initialize record count
GO1:    CALL    FILTER          ;Scan the record
        INX     H
        DCR     C               ;End of record?
        JNZ     GO1             ;No
        LXI     D,FCB1
        MVI     C,WRITE         ;Write record to output file
        CALL    BDOS
        JMP     LOOP            ;Loop to read next record
;
FILTER: MOV     A,M
        ANI     7FH             ;Strip bit 7
        MOV     M,A
        CPI     20H             ;Is it < space
        RNC                     ;No
```

```
              MOV      B,A                  ;Save byte
              LDA      FLG                  ;Get CRLF flag
              ORA      A                    ;Are we killing CRLF ?
              JZ       FIL1                 ;Yes
              MOV      A,B                  ;No, get byte in A
              CPI      CR
              RZ                            ;Don't change
              CPI      LF
              RZ                            ;Don't change
FIL1:         MVI      M,20H                ;Replace anything < space by space
              RET
;
CONV:         LXI      D,0                  ;Convert # pointed to by HL to binary in HL
              XCHG                          ;Conversion stops when # < '0' is found
CONV1:        LDAX     D
              SUI      '0'
              RM
              CPI      10
              CMC
              RC
              INX      D
              DAD      H
              PUSH     H
              DAD      H
              DAD      H
              POP      B
              DAD      B
              MOV      C,A
              MVI      B,0
              DAD      B
              JMP      CONV1
;
DIV:          MVI      B,0FFH               ;Divide by 128
              LXI      D,-128               ;Quotient in H, remainder in L
DIV1:         DAD      D
              INR      B
              MOV      A,H
              ORA      A
              JP       DIV1
              LXI      D,128
              DAD      D
              MOV      H,B
              RET
;
CLEAR:        XRA      A                    ;Zero key fields in FCB
              LXI      H,FCB+32
              MOV      M,A
              INX      H
              MOV      M,A
              INX      H
              MOV      M,A
              INX      H
              MOV      M,A
              STA      FCB+15
              STA      FCB+12
              RET
```

```
CRLF:   MVI     E,CR
        MVI     C,CONOUT
        CALL    BDOS
        MVI     E,LF
        MVI     C,CONOUT
        CALL    BDOS
        RET
MES1:   DB      CR,LF,'     USAGE: FIX [d:]<filename.typ>'
        DB      CR,LF,'where d is an optional drive designator'
        DB      CR,LF,'and filename.typ is the file name and type'
        DB      CR,LF,'of the file to be processed. The output'
        DB      CR,LF,'file will be named filename.FIX.$'
MES2:   DB      CR,LF,'Cannot find file on specified drive.$'
MES3:   DB      CR,LF,'Read past EOF.$'
MES4:   DB      CR,LF,'Do you want to preserve CRLF''s (Y or N) ? $'
MES5:   DB      CR,LF,'Working...$'
MES6:   DB      CR,LF,'What is the size of the header (in bytes)? $'
CBUF:   DB      10,0
        DB      0,0,0,0,0,0,0,0,0,0,0,0,0
REC     DS      2                       ;Storage for record count
QUO:    DS      2                       ;Storage for quotient and remainder
FLG:    DB      0                       ;CRLF flag
FCB1:   DB      0,'        FIX'
        REPT    24
        DB      0
        ENDM
```

DISKSTAT.ASM

Description.   A disk drive status routine. This routine returns the amount of storage on a disk to a dBASE II memory variable. The memory variable must be initialized to ten characters, with the first character containing the drive letter. An "E" for error will be returned if the memory variable is not passed correctly. Otherwise, the memory variable will contain the amount of storage (in bytes) remaining on the disk. The order and syntax of the following example is extremely important!

```
.  SET CALL TO 42000
.  LOAD Diskstat
.  STORE "B000000000" TO value
.  CALL value
```

The memory variable "value" now contains the amount of storage remaining on drive B. To compute the number of Kilobytes on the drive, the formula is:

```
.  ? VAL( value ) / 1024
```

```
; Subroutine.: DISKSTAT.ASM
; Author.....: Kelly Mc Tiernan
; Date.......: 1983
; Notice.....: Copyright 1983, Kelly Mc Tiernan, All Rights Reserved
; Notes......: CP/M-80 disk drive status routine.
;
```

```
BDOS      EQU       00005H
FDPB      EQU       1FH
FALV      EQU       1BH
FDSK      EQU       19H
FCHG      EQU       0EH
;
          ORG       42000
;
START:    SHLD      SAVEHL              ; SAVE HL REG PAIR
          MVI       C,FDSK             ; DETERMINE CURRENT DISK
          PUSH      H                  ; SAVE HL
          CALL      BDOS               ;
          STA       SAVDSK             ; AND SAVE TO RESTORE
          POP       H                  ; GET IT BACK
          INX       H                  ; POINT TO FIRST BYTE OF VARIABLE
          MOV       A,M                ; GET IT
          ORA       A                  ; CLEAR CARRY
          SBI       41H                ; CONVERT ASCII A,B,C TO 0,1,2,..
          CPI       10H                ; LEGAL DRIVE NAME?
          JNC       KEEPDR             ; NO, KEEP CURRENT DRIVE
          MOV       E,A                ; GET DRIVE TO SELECT
          MVI       C,FCHG             ; SELECT FUNCTION
          CALL      BDOS               ;
;
KEEPDR:   LXI       H,0000H            ; TO SAVE SP
          DAD       SP                 ; GET SP
          SHLD      SAVESP             ; SAVE IT
          MVI       A,01H              ; TO INIT. SIG. DIGIT POINTER
          LXI       H,ANSWER           ; WHERE IT GOES
          MOV       M,A                ; INITIALIZE
          MVI       C,FDPB             ; GET DPB ADDRESS
          CALL      BDOS               ; HL HAS ADDRESS
          SHLD      DPBADR             ; SAVE BASE ADDRESS
          LXI       B,0005H            ; OFFSET TO DSM
          DAD       B                  ;
          MOV       E,M                ; GET FIRST BYTE
          INX       H                  ; FOR NEXT BYTE
          MOV       D,M                ; GET IT
          XCHG                         ; GET WHERE IT CAN BE USED
          MVI       B,03H              ; COUNT FOR SHIFT
DIV8:     ORA       A                  ; CLEAR CARRY FOR DIVISION
          MOV       A,H                ; GET FIRST BYTE
          RAR                          ; DIVIDE BY 2
          MOV       H,A                ; RESTORE HIGH BYTE
          MOV       A,L                ; GET LOW BYTE
          RAR                          ; DIVIDE BY 2 (SHIFT IN HB CARRY)
          MOV       L,A                ; RESTORE IT
          DCR       B                  ; FOR COUNT
          JNZ       DIV8               ; CONTINUE 3 TIMES (2*2*2=8)
          INX       H                  ; +1=ALV LENGTH
          SHLD      ALVLNG             ; SAVE LENGTH OF ALV
;
; NOW CALCULATE BLOCK SIZE FOR DRIVE
;
          LHLD      DPBADR             ; GET BACK BLOCK ADDRESS
          INX       H                  ; VECTOR INTO DPB FOR BSH
          INX       H                  ;
```

```
            MOV     E,M             ; GET IT
            MVI     D,00H           ; ZERO HB
            DCX     D               ; FOR VECTOR INTO TABLE
            DCX     D               ;
            DCX     D               ;
            MOV     A,E             ; GET IT
            ORA     A               ; CLEAR CARRY
            RAL                     ; MULTIPLY BY 2
            MOV     E,A             ; GET BACK VECTOR
            LXI     H,TABLE         ; BASE ADDRESS
            DAD     D               ; ADD IN VECTOR
            MOV     E,M             ; GET LB (STORED LB,HB)
            INX     H               ; NEXT BYTE
            MOV     D,M             ; DE NOW CONTAINS BLOCK SIZE
            XCHG                    ; GET IT TO WHERE WE CAN SAVE IT
            SHLD    BLS             ; SAVE IT
;
;
; NOW LET'S DETERMINE SPACE LEFT ON DISK
;
            MVI     C,FALV          ; LET'S GET ALV ADDRESS NOW
            CALL    BDOS            ; HL CONTAINS ADDRESS
            LDA     ALVLNG          ; GET LENGTH
            MOV     B,A             ; INTO COUNTER 1
            LXI     D,0000H         ; BIT COUNTER ZEROED
            DCX     H               ; SET FOR LOOP CONTROL
            SHLD    TEMP            ; SAVE HL
            DI                      ; DISABLE INTERRUPTS BEFORE SP
                                    ; CHANGE
            LHLD    BLS             ; GET BLOCK SIZE
            SPHL                    ; FOR ADDITION
            LXI     H,0000H         ; INITIALIZE
            SHLD    SIZE0           ;    "    "
            SHLD    SIZE1           ;    "    "
BITCNT:     LHLD    TEMP            ; RESTORE HL
            INX     H               ; POINT TO BYTE
            MVI     C,08H           ; COUNTER 2 FOR BITS/BYTE
            MOV     A,M             ; GET FIRST BYTE
            ORA     A               ; CLEAR CARRY
            SHLD    TEMP            ; SAVE HL POINTER
BIT1:       LHLD    SIZE0           ; GET LOW WORD TOTAL
            RAR                     ; ROTATE A TO COUNT ZERO BITS
            JC      BIT2            ; DON'T COUNT 1'S
            DAD     SP              ; IF UNALLOC. THEN ADD 1 BLOCK
                                    ; TO TTL.
            JNC     BIT2            ; IF NO CARRY FROM DAD H
            INX     D               ; ELSE ADD 1 TO HIGH WORD
BIT2:       SHLD    SIZE0           ; SAVE NEW LOW WORD FOR UNALLOC.
            DCR     C               ; COUNTER
            JNZ     BIT1            ; NEXT BIT
            DCR     B               ; COUNT FOR BYTES
            JNZ     BITCNT          ; DO NEXT BYTE
            XCHG                    ; GET HIGH WORD INTO HL
            SHLD    SIZE1           ; SAVE IT
            LHLD    SIZE0           ; FOR CORRECTION FACTOR
            LXI     SP,0E000H       ; ERROR OFFSET
            DAD     SP              ; TWO'S COMP. OF 2000H (SUBTRACT
                                    ; OFFSET)
```

```
            SHLD    SIZE0           ; SAVE RESULT
            JC      EX1             ; EXIT IF CARRY (LOW WORD >
                                    ; 2000H)
            LHLD    SIZE1           ; FOR BORROW
            DCX     H               ; SUBTRACT 1
            SHLD    SIZE1           ; SAVE RESULT
EX1:        LHLD    SAVESP          ; RESTORE STACK POINTER
            SPHL                    ;
            EI                      ; ENABLE INTERRUPTS
;
;
; NOW WE CONVERT TO A DECIMAL STRING
;
            LXI     H,ANSWER+1      ; TO INITIAIZE DATA AREA
            MVI     B,0AH           ; COUNTER
            MVI     A,00H           ; INITIALIZE TO 0
INIT1:      MOV     M,A             ;
            INX     H               ; NEXT BYTE
            DCR     B               ;
            JNZ     INIT1           ; REPEAT FOR 10 BYTES
            MVI     C,0AH           ; TOTAL # OF SIG DIGITS COUNTER
            LXI     H,SIZE0         ; POINTER TO LOWEST BYTE
            XCHG                    ; SAVE IT
            LXI     H,TBL2          ; POINT TO SUBTRACTION TABLE
            XCHG                    ; GET BACK DATA TABLE ADDRESS
MINUS:      ORA     A               ; CLEAR CARRY FOR LOW BYTE
            MVI     B,03H           ; COUNTER FOR SUBS
MIN0:       MOV     A,M             ; GET DATA
            XCHG                    ; GET SUB TABLE POINTER
            SBB     M               ; SUBTRACT DIGIT
            INX     H               ; POINT TO NEXT TABLE ENTRY
            XCHG                    ; GET BACK DATA POINTER
            MOV     M,A             ; PUT BACK RESULT
            INX     H               ; POINT TO NEXT DATA BYTE
            DCR     B               ; DONE WITH LOW 3 BYTES ?
            JNZ     MIN0            ; CHECK FOR NEG ON LAST BYTE SBB
LAST1:      MOV     A,M             ; GET MOST SIG BYTE
            XCHG                    ; GET TABLE POINTER
            SBB     M               ; SUBTRACT IT
            DI                      ; DISABLE INTERUPTS BEFORE CALL
            CP      AD1             ; ADD 1 TO SIG DIGIT IF IT WENT
            EI                      ; ENABLE INTERUPTS ON RETURN
            DCX     H               ; MOVE POINTER BACK TO BEGINNING
            DCX     H               ; OF TABLE
            DCX     H               ;
            XCHG                    ; GET BACK DATA POINTER
            MOV     M,A             ; PUT BACK RESULT
            DCX     H               ; MOVE POINTER BACK TO BEGINNING
            DCX     H               ; OF DATA
            DCX     H               ;
            DI                      ; DISABLE INTERUPTS
            CM      PUTBK           ; PUT BACK IF NEG AND MOVE ON
            EI                      ; ENABLE INTERUPTS
            DCR     C               ; ONLY TO OVERRIDE SBB M
            INR     C               ;
            JNZ     MINUS           ; NO, DO AGAIN
;
```

```
;
; NOW LETS CONVERT TO ASCII (ADD 30H) AND PASS BACK
; TO 10 DIGIT DBASE VARIABLE
;
         LXI    H,ANSWER+1        ; POINT TO ANSWER BUFFER
         MVI    B,0AH             ; FOR ALL 10 BYTES
FILL:    MVI    A,30H             ; TO CONVERT TO ASCII
         ADD    M                 ; UNPACKED BCD+30=ASCII
         MOV    M,A               ; PUT CORRECTED ANSWER BACK
         INX    H                 ; NEXT DIGIT
         DCR    B                 ; DONE ?
         JNZ    FILL              ;
         LHLD   SAVEHL            ; OLD HL POINTER (VERY OLD)
         MOV    A,M               ; LET'S DO A LITTLE ERROR
                                  ; CHECKING
         CPI    0AH               ;
         JNZ    ERROR             ; VARIABLE WRONG LENGTH
         INX    H                 ; NOW LET'S GIVE dBASE THE ANSWER
         XCHG                     ; I KINDA LIKE THIS INSTRUCTION
         LXI    H,ANSWER+1        ; SHOULD BE OBVIOUS BY NOW
         MVI    B,0AH             ; COUNTER TO MOVE BYTES
PASS:    MOV    A,M               ; GET BYTE
         INX    H                 ; FOR NEXT BYTE
         XCHG                     ; WHERE TO SEND
         MOV    M,A               ; SEND IT
         INX    H                 ; WHERE TO SEND NEXT ONE
         XCHG                     ; BACK TO SOURCE POINTER
         DCR    B                 ; COUNTER FOR BYTES PASSED
         JNZ    PASS              ; DO NEXT BYTE
         JMP    FINIS             ; NORMAL END OF ROUTINE
ERROR:   INX    H                 ; POINT TO FIRST BYTE
         MVI    A,'E'             ; ERROR CODE
         MOV    M,A               ; SEND ERROR CODE TO DBASE
FINIS:   LDA    SAVDSK            ; GET BACK DISK IN USE NO.
         MOV    E,A               ; PUT IN E FOR BDOS CALL
         MVI    C,FCHG            ; FUNCTION TO CHANGE DISK
         CALL   BDOS              ; BACK TO ORIGINAL DRIVE
         LHLD   SAVESP            ; RESTORE SP
         SPHL                     ;
         LHLD   SAVEHL            ; RESTORE HL
         RET
;
;
;    SUBROUTINES FOR CALCULATIONS
;
PUTBK:   ORA    A                 ; CLEAR CARRY
         MVI    B,04H             ; COUNTER FOR ADDS
PUT1:    MOV    A,M               ; GET DATA
         XCHG                     ; POINT TO SUB TABLE
         ADC    M                 ; ADD BACK IN AMMOUNT
         INX    H                 ; POINT TO NEXT SUB TABLE BYTE
         XCHG                     ; BACK TO DATA POINTER
         MOV    M,A               ; PUT BACK RESULT
         INX    H                 ; POINT TO NEXT DATA BYTE
         DCR    B
```

```
            JNZ     PUT1                ; NEXT BYTE
            DCX     H                   ; RESET DATA POINTER
            DCX     H                   ;
            DCX     H                   ;
            DCX     H                   ;
            PUSH    H                   ; SAVE HL
            LXI     H,ANSWER            ; POINT TO SIG DIGIT POINTER
            INR     M                   ; INCREMENT TO NEXT DIGIT
            POP     H                   ; RESTORE HL
            DCR     C                   ; COUNT FOR SIG DIGITS DONE
            RET                         ; RETURN TO CALLER
;
AD1:        PUSH    PSW                 ; SAVE REGISTERS
            PUSH    B                   ;
            PUSH    D                   ;
            PUSH    H                   ;
            LXI     H,ANSWER            ; ANSWER TABLE
            MOV     E,M                 ; GET POSITION
            MVI     D,00H               ; FOR VECTOR
            DAD     D                   ; VECTOR TO SIG DIGIT
            INR     M                   ; ADD 1 TO DIGIT
            POP     H                   ; RESTORE REGISTERS
            POP     D                   ;
            POP     B                   ;
            POP     PSW                 ;
            RET                         ;
;
SAVEHL: DS      2
SAVESP: DS      2
DPBADR: DS      2
ALVLNG: DS      2
BLS:    DS      2
TEMP:   DS      2
SAVDSK: DS      1
;
TABLE:  DB      00H
        DB      04H
        DB      00H
        DB      08H
        DB      00H
        DB      10H
        DB      00H
        DB      20H
        DB      00H
        DB      40H
;
SIZE0:  DS      2
SIZE1:  DS      2
;
;
ANSWER: DS      10H                     ; TOTAL SIG DIGITS+POINTER
;
```

```
TBL2:      DB        000H,0CAH,09AH,03BH
           DB        000H,0E1H,0F5H,005H
           DB        080H,096H,098H,000H
           DB        040H,042H,00FH,000H
           DB        0A0H,086H,001H,000H
           DB        010H,027H,000H,000H
           DB        0E8H,003H,000H,000H
           DB        064H,000H,000H,000H
           DB        00AH,000H,000H,000H
           DB        001H,000H,000H,000H
;
END
```

FIX.A86

Description. This program expects an ASCII filename on command line and writes back to the same filename and drive an output file with all characters less than 20H replaced by 20H except the 1AH EOF marks at real EOF. The output file has type of .FIX. A flag is set if CR and LF are also to be replaced. The program also prompts for the number of bytes from start of file at which to start processing.

```
; Subroutine.: FIX.A86
; Author.....: Bob Doolittle
; Date.......: 08/12/84
; Notice.....: Copyright 1984, Ashton-Tate, All Rights Reserved.
; Notes......: CP/M 86 version.
;
M          EQU       Byte Ptr 0[BX]
;
           ORG       100H
;
;BDOS equates
;
BDOS       EQU       224                 ;BDOS entry point
TBUF       EQU       80H                 ;Default buffer
FCB        EQU       5CH                 ;Default FCB
CFS        EQU       35                  ;Compute file size
CONIN      EQU       1                   ;Console in
CONOUT     EQU       2                   ;Console out
PSTR       EQU       9                   ;Print string
STRIN      EQU       10                  ;Console string input
OPEN       EQU       15                  ;Open file
CLOSE      EQU       16                  ;Close file
READ       EQU       20                  ;Read sequential
```

```
WRITE     EQU     21                      ;Write sequential
MAKE      EQU     22                      ;Make file
DELETE    EQU     19                      ;Delete file
READR     EQU     33                      ;Read random
;
;ASCII equates
;
CR        EQU     13
LF        EQU     10
;
START:    MOV     Byte Ptr FLG,0          ;Initialize CRLF flag to destroy CRLF
          MOV     AL,Byte Ptr .FCB+1
          CMP     AL,20H                  ;Was input file on command line
          JNZ     ST2                     ;Yes
          MOV     DX,(Offset MES1)        ;No, print message and abort
          MOV     CL,PSTR
          INT     BDOS
          JMP     EXIT
;
ST2:      MOV     DX,(Offset MES4)        ;Print CRLF message
          MOV     CL,PSTR
          INT     BDOS
          MOV     CL,CONIN                ;Get response
          INT     BDOS
          AND     AL,5FH                  ;Make upper case
          CMP     AL,'Y'
          JNZ     ST7
          MOV     AL,1
          MOV     Byte Ptr FLG,AL
ST7:      MOV     CL,PSTR                 ;Ask for # of bytes
          MOV     DX,(Offset MES6)
          INT     BDOS
          MOV     DX,(Offset CBUF)        ;Get response
          MOV     CL,STRIN
          INT     BDOS
          MOV     BX,(Offset CBUF)+2
          CALL    CONV                    ;Convert to binary in HL
          CALL    DIV                     ;Divide by 128
          MOV     Word Ptr QUO,BX         ;Save quotient and remainder
          CALL    CRLF
          CALL    CLEAR                   ;Clear FCB+32-35, FCB+15 and FCB+12
          MOV     BX,FCB
          MOV     DX,(Offset FCB1)
          MOV     CL,9
MOVE:     MOV     AL,M           ;Move file name and drive from FCB to FCB1
          MOV     SI,DX
          MOV     [SI],AL
          INC     BX
          INC     DX
          DEC     CL
          JNZ     MOVE
          MOV     DX,FCB
          MOV     CL,OPEN                 ;Open file
          INT     BDOS
          INC     AL                      ;Was open successful?
          JNZ     ST3                     ;Yes
          MOV     DX,(Offset MES2)        ;No, print message and abort
          MOV     CL,PSTR
```

```
          INT     BDOS
          JMP     EXIT
ST3:      MOV     DX,(Offset MES5)      ;Working message
          MOV     CL,PSTR
          INT     BDOS
          MOV     DX,FCB
          MOV     CL,CFS               ;Compute file size
          INT     BDOS
          MOV     BX,Word Ptr .FCB+33  ;Get last record+1
          MOV     Word Ptr REC,BX      ;Save locally
          DEC     BX                   ;Last record number
          MOV     Word Ptr .FCB+33,BX  ;Store it back
          MOV     CL,READR
          MOV     DX,FCB
          INT     BDOS                 ;Read last record
          MOV     BX,TBUF-1
          MOV     CL,0                 ;Initialize counter
LOP:      INC     BX                   ;Scan to 1st EOF mark and keep count
          INC     CL
          CMP     M,1AH                ;Is it EOF?
          JNZ     LOP                  ;No, keep looping
          PUSH    CX                   ;Save count to EOF in last record
          CALL    CLEAR                ;Clear again
          MOV     DX,(Offset FCB1)
          MOV     CL,DELETE            ;Delete any possible previous out file
          INT     BDOS
          MOV     DX,FCB
          MOV     CL,OPEN              ;Re-open the input file
          INT     BDOS
          MOV     DX,(Offset FCB1)
          MOV     CL,MAKE              ;Make output file
          INT     BDOS
;
FIRS:     MOV     DX,FCB               ;Scan off quotient # of records
          MOV     CL,READ
          INT     BDOS
          OR      AL,AL                ;Read OK ?
          JZ      FST1                 ;Yes
          MOV     DX,(Offset MES3)     ;No
          MOV     CL,PSTR
          INT     BDOS
          POP     CX                   ;Balance stack
          JMP     EXIT
;
FST1:     MOV     BX,Word Ptr REC      ;Bump record count down
          DEC     BX
          MOV     Word Ptr REC,BX
          MOV     BX,Word Ptr QUO      ;Get DIV result
          OR      BH,BH                ;Have we read sector with remainder ?
          JZ      FST2                 ;Yes
          DEC     BH                   ;No
          MOV     Word Ptr QUO,BX      ;Dec and store sector counter
          MOV     DX,(Offset FCB1)     ;Write sector
          MOV     CL,WRITE
          INT     BDOS
          JMPS    FIRS                 ;Loop for more
```

```
FST2:    ADD     BL,80H              ;BL now has filter start address
FST3:    CALL    FILTER
         INC     BX
         OR      BH,BH
         JZ      FST3                ;Filter to end of sector
         MOV     DX,(Offset FCB1)
         MOV     CL,WRITE            ;Write to output file
         INT     BDOS
LOOP:    MOV     DX,FCB
         MOV     CL,READ             ;Read a record to default buffer
         INT     BDOS
         OR      AL,AL               ;Was read successful?
         JZ      LO4                 ;Yes
ERR:     MOV     DX,(Offset MES3)
         MOV     CL,PSTR             ;No, print message and abort
         INT     BDOS
         POP     CX                  ;Balance stack
         JMPS    EXIT
;
LO4:     DEC     Word Ptr REC        ;Decrement record count
         JNZ     GOAH                ;If not at last record
         POP     CX                  ;Yes, get back count
         MOV     BX,TBUF
;
LO1:     DEC     CL                  ;Are we at EOF
         JZ      LO2                 ;Yes
         CALL    FILTER
         INC     BX
         JMPS    LO1                 ;Loop
;
LO2:     MOV     DX,(Offset FCB1)
         MOV     CL,WRITE            ;Write last record
         INT     BDOS
         MOV     DX,(Offset FCB1)
         MOV     CL,CLOSE            ;Close output file
         INT     BDOS
EXIT:    MOV     CL,0                ;Finished
         MOV     DL,0
         INT     BDOS
;
GOAH:    MOV     BX,TBUF
         MOV     CX,80H              ;Initialize record count
GO1:     CALL    FILTER              ;Scan the record
         INC     BX
         LOOP    GO1                 ;Loop to end of record
         MOV     DX,(Offset FCB1)
         MOV     CL,WRITE            ;Write record to output file
         INT     BDOS
         JMPS    LOOP                ;Loop to read next record
;
FILTER:  AND     M,7FH               ;Strip bit 7
         CMP     M,20H               ;Is it < space
         JNAE    L_1
         RET                         ;No
L_1:     TEST    Byte Ptr FLG,0FFH   ;Are we killing CRLF ?
         JZ      FIL1                ;Yes
         MOV     AL,M
```

```
            CMP     AL,CR
            JNZ     L_2
            RET                         ;Don't change
L_2:        CMP     AL,LF
            JNZ     FIL1
            RET                         ;Don't change
FIL1:       MOV     M,20H               ;Replace anything < space by space
            RET
;
CONV:       MOV     DX,0                ;Convert # pointed to by HL to binary in HL
            XCHG    BX,DX               ;Conversion stops when # < '0' is found
            MOV     SI,DX               ;Binary returned in BX
            MOV     AH,0
CONV1:      MOV     AL,[SI]
            SUB     AL,'0'
            JNS     L_4
            RET
L_4:        CMP     AL,10
            CMC
            JNB     L_5
            RET
L_5:        INC     SI
            SHL     BX,1
            MOV     CX,BX
            SHL     BX,1
            SHL     BX,1
            ADD     BX,CX
            ADD     BX,AX
            JMPS    CONV1
;
DIV:        MOV     AX,BX               ;Divide BX by 128
            MOV     CL,128
            DIV     CL
            MOV     BH,AL               ;Quotient in BH, remainder in BL
            MOV     BL,AH
            RET
;
CLEAR:      XOR     AL,AL               ;Zero key fields in FCB
            MOV     BX,FCB+32
            MOV     M,AL
            INC     BX
            MOV     M,AL
            INC     BX
            MOV     M,AL
            INC     BX
            MOV     M,AL
            MOV     Byte Ptr .FCB+15,AL
            MOV     Byte Ptr .FCB+12,AL
            RET
;
CRLF:       MOV     DL,CR
            MOV     CL,CONOUT
            INT     BDOS
            MOV     DL,LF
            MOV     CL,CONOUT
            INT     BDOS
            RET
L_6         EQU     $
```

```
          DSEG
          ORG     Offset L_6
MES1      DB      CR,LF,'     USAGE: FIX [d:]<filename.typ>'
          DB      CR,LF,'where d is an optional drive designator'
          DB      CR,LF,'and filename.typ is the file name and type'
          DB      CR,LF,'of the file to be processed. The output'
          DB      CR,LF,'file will be named filename.FIX.$'
MES2      DB      CR,LF,'Cannot find file on specified drive.$'
MES3      DB      CR,LF,'Read past EOF.$'
MES4      DB      CR,LF,'Do you want to preserve CRLF''s (Y or N) ? $'
MES5      DB      CR,LF,'Working...$'
MES6      DB      CR,LF,'What is the size of the header (in bytes)? $'
CBUF      DB      10,0
          DB      0,0,0,0,0,0,0,0,0,0,0,0
REC       RS      2                       ;Storage for record count
QUO       RS      2                       ;Storage for quotient and remainder
FLG       DB      0                       ;CRLF flag
FCB1      DB      0,'          FIX'
          DB      0,0,0,0,0,0,0,0,0,0,0,0,0,0,0,0,0,0,0,0,0,0,0,0,0,0,0,0,0
```

DISKSTAT.PRG

Description. A disk drive status routine for CP/M-86. This routine returns the amount of storage on a disk to a dBASE II memory variable. It is important that the memory variable, t:storage, be initialized to ten characters with the first character containing the drive letter. An "E" for error will be returned if the memory variable is not passed correctly. Otherwise, the memory variable will contain the amount of storage (in bytes) remaining on the disk.

```
* Program.: DISKSTAT.PRG
* Author..: Kelly Mc Tiernan
* Date....: 1983
* Notice..: Copyright 1983, Kelly Mc Tiernan, All Rights Reserved.
* Version.: dBASE II, version 2.4
* Notes...: Disk drive status routine.
*
*    IN: drive-C-1        Disk drive letter
*   OUT: storage-N-10     Number of bytes remaining on disk
*        is:error-L-1     Validation flag
*
STORE T TO is:error
* ---Parameter checking.
STORE !(drive) TO drive
IF LEN(drive) > 1 .OR. drive < "A" .OR. drive > "P"
   RETURN
ENDIF
* -----------0---1---2---3---4---5---6---7---8---9
POKE 56832,  6, 30, 83,177, 25,205,224, 46,162,203,;
         222, 91, 83,138, 87,  1,128,234, 65,128,;
         250, 16,119,  4,177, 14,205
POKE 56859,224,177, 31,205,224, 38,139,119,  2,129,;
         230,255,  0,131,238,  3,209,230, 38,139,;
          71,  5,187,189,222,  3,243
POKE 56886, 30,  7,191,199,222,252,165,177,  3,211,;
         232,  5,  2,  0,171,177, 27,205,224, 46,;
         139, 14,201,222, 75,184,  0
* -----------0---1---2---3---4---5---6---7---8---9
```

```
POKE 56913,   0, 81, 89, 67, 73,227, 26, 38,128, 63,;
           255,117,  3,233,243,255, 81,185,  0,  1,;
           209,233,116,234, 38,133, 15
POKE 56940,117,247, 64,233,243,255, 45,  2,  0, 46,;
           139, 14,199,222,247,225,190,204,222, 30,;
             7, 91, 83,139,251, 71,139
POKE 56967,216,185,  9,  0,176,  0, 43, 28, 70, 70,;
            27, 20,114,  7,254,192, 78, 78,233,241,;
           255, 78, 78,  3, 28, 70, 70
POKE 56994, 19, 20,  4, 48,170, 70, 70,226,224,138,;
           195,  4, 48,170, 46,138, 22,203,222,177,;
            14,205,224, 91, 31,  7,195
* -----------0---1---2---3---4---5---6---7---8---9
POKE 57021,  0,  4,  0,  8,  0, 16,  0, 32,  0, 64
POKE 57036,  0,202,154, 54,  0,225,245,  5,128,150,;
           152,  0, 64, 66, 15,  0,160,134,  1,  0,;
            16, 39,  0,  0,232,  3,  0
POKE 57063,  0,100,  0,  0,  0, 10,  0,  0,  0
* -----------0---1---2---3---4---5---6---7---8---9
STORE !(drive)+"000000000" TO t:storage
SET CALL TO  56832
CALL t:storage
STORE ( t:storage = "E" ) TO !s:error
IF .NOT. !s:error
   STORE VAL(t:storage) TO storage
ENDIF
RELEASE t:storage
RETURN
* EOF: DISKSTAT.PRG




; Subroutine.: DISKSTAT.A86
; Author.....: Kelly Mc Tiernan
; Date.......: 1983
; Notice.....: Copyright 1983, Kelly Mc Tiernan, All Rights Reserved
; Notes......: CP/M 86 DISK DRIVE STATUS ROUTINE
;
;
         ORG     0DE00H                  ; TOP OF DBASE
;
;
BDOS    EQU     0E0H        ; BDOS CALL = INTERUPT 224
GETALV  EQU     1BH         ; GET ALLOCATION VECTOR ADDRESS
GETDPB  EQU     1FH         ; GET DISK PARAMETER BLOCK ADDRESS
BSHOFF  EQU     02H         ; OFFSET , DPB , TO BSH (BLOCK SIZE)
DSMOFF  EQU     05H         ; DPB TO DSM (MAXIMUM BLOCK NUMBER)
SELDSK  EQU     0EH         ; SELECT DISK FUNCTION NUMBER
GETDSK  EQU     19H         ; GET CURRENT DISK FUNCTION
DSKBYT  EQU     01H         ; OFFSET TO DISK SELECTOR BYTE (MEMVAR)
;
START:  PUSH    ES                      ; SAVE SEGMENT REGISTERS
        PUSH    DS                      ;
        PUSH    BX                      ; SAVE MEMVAR ADDRESS
        MOV     CL,GETDSK               ; GET CURRENT DISK NUMBER
        INT     BDOS                    ;
```

```
        MOV     BYTE PTR SAVDSK,AL ; SAVE IT FOR RETURN ROUTINE
        POP     BX                 ; RESTORE POINTER
        PUSH    BX                 ; BUT KEEP IT ON STACK
        MOV     DL,DSKBYT[BX]      ; GET SELECTED DISK BYTE
        SUB     DL,41H             ; CONVERT LETTER TO NUMBER
        CMP     DL,10H             ; LEGITIMATE DISK SELECTOR
        JA      KEEPDR             ; KEEP DEFAULT IF NOT LEGAL
        MOV     CL,SELDSK          ; SELECT DISK FUNCTION
        INT     BDOS               ;
KEEPDR: MOV     CL,GETDPB          ; LET'S GET DPB ADDRESS
        INT     BDOS               ; GO FETCH IT
        MOV     SI,ES:BSHOFF[BX]   ; GET BSH FOR VECTOR
                                   ; CALCULATION
        AND     SI,00FFH           ; CLEAR HIGH BYTE (JUST JUNK)
        SUB     SI,03              ; SET UP VECTOR
        SHL     SI,1               ; MULTIPLY BY 2 TO VECTOR
                                   ; INTO TABLE
        MOV     AX,ES:DSMOFF[BX]   ; GET DSM FOR LATER USE
        MOV     BX,OFFSET BLKTBL   ; GET BASE ADDRESS OF LOOKUP
                                   ; TABLE
        ADD     SI,BX              ; CALCULATE VECTOR
        PUSH    DS                 ; GET DESTINATION SEGMENT
        POP     ES                 ;
        MOV     DI,OFFSET BLKSIZ   ; GET DESTINATION ADDRESS
        CLD                        ; CLEAR DIRECTION FLAG
                                   ; (MOVE DOWN)
        MOVSW                      ; MOVE BLOCKSIZE FROM TABLE
        MOV     CL,03H             ; COUNT FOR SHIFT AX = AX/8
        SHR     AX,CL              ; ALV LENGTH = DSM / 8 + 1 + 1
                                   ; (FOR OUR COUNT)
        ADD     AX,02              ;
        STOSW                      ; SAVE ALV LENGTH (DI UPDATED
                                   ; BY MOVSW)
        MOV     CL,GETALV          ; NOW GET ALV ADDRESS
        INT     BDOS               ;
        MOV     CX,WORD PTR ALVLNG ; GET BACK ALV LENGTH FOR
                                   ; COUNTER
        DEC     BX                 ; PREP FOR COUNTER ROUTINE
        MOV     AX,0000H           ; ZERO THIS, IT'S OUR BIT
                                   ; COUNTER
        PUSH    CX                 ; SET UP FOR ENTRY TO COUNTR
COUNTR: POP     CX                 ; GET BACK COUNT OF BYTES
CNT0:   INC     BX                 ; NEXT (OR FIRST) BYTE
        DEC     CX                 ; COUNT BYTES
        JCXZ    DNECNT             ; EXIT ON ALL BYTES ALV
                                   ; PROCESSED
        CMP     ES:BYTE PTR[BX],0FFH ; CHECK FOR 8 BLOCKS FULL
        JNZ     INCNTR             ; IF NOT THEN COUNT 0'S
                                   ; (FREE BLOCKS)
        JMP     CNT0               ; DO NEXT BYTE
INCNTR: PUSH    CX                 ; SAVE OUTSIDE LOOP COUNTER
        MOV     CX,100H            ; FOR TESTING BITS AND COUNTER
CNT1:   SHR     CX,1               ; FOR BIT TO TEST
        JZ      COUNTR             ; SHR=0 THEN ALL BITS TESTED
        TEST    ES:[BX],CX         ; TEST BIT FOR SET
        JNZ     CNT1               ; NOT A 0 BIT, DON'T COUNT
        INC     AX                 ; AX IS OUR BIT COUNTER
        JMP     CNT1               ; DO NEXT BIT
```

```
DNECNT: SUB     AX,02H              ; 4 BLOCK ERROR ON IBM PC
        MOV     CX,WORD PTR BLKSIZ  ; GET BACK BLOCK SIZE
        MUL     CX                  ; CALCULATE SPACE LEFT
        MOV     SI,OFFSET CONTBL    ; GET SUB TABLE FOR HTA
                                    ; DECIMAL CONV.
        PUSH    DS                  ; SET UP ES FOR MOVE
        POP     ES                  ; (HTA = HEX TO ASCII)
        POP     BX                  ; GET BACK MEMVAR ADDRESS
        PUSH    BX                  ; LEAVE A COPY ON STACK (TO
                                    ; RESTORE)
        MOV     DI,BX               ; GET IT TO DESTINATION
                                    ; REGISTER
        INC     DI                  ; POINT TO FIRST BYTE
        MOV     BX,AX               ; GET LOW WORD OUT OF AX
                                    ; ( NEEDED )
        MOV     CX,09H              ; TOTAL ANSWER BYTES TO
                                    ; CALCULATE
ANSWER: MOV     AL,00               ; ZERO SIG DIGIT COUNTER
ANS0:   SUB     BX,[SI]             ; SUBTRACT LOW WORD
        INC     SI                  ; POINT TO HIGH WORD
        INC     SI                  ;
        SBB     DX,[SI]             ; SUBTRACT HIGH WORD
        JB      NXTBYT              ; PUTBACK AND DO NEXT
                                    ; SIGNIFICANT DIGIT IF >
        INC     AL                  ; OTHERWISE COUNT FOR
                                    ; SIGNIFICANT DIGIT
        DEC     SI                  ; POINT BACK TO LOW WORD
        DEC     SI                  ;
        JMP     ANS0                ; AND DO AGAIN
NXTBYT: DEC     SI                  ; POINT TO LOW WORD
        DEC     SI                  ;
        ADD     BX,[SI]             ; PUT BACK
        INC     SI                  ; HIGH WORD
        INC     SI                  ;
        ADC     DX,[SI]             ; PUT IT BACK
        ADD     AL,30H              ; CONVERT TO ASCII
        STOSB                       ; PLACE INTO ANSWER
        INC     SI                  ; POINT TO NEXT SIGNIFICANT
                                    ; DIGIT SUB IN TABLE
        INC     SI                  ;
        LOOP    ANSWER              ; EXIT ON DONE
DONE:   MOV     AL,BL               ; GET LAST BYTE
        ADD     AL,30H              ; CONVERT TO ASCII
        STOSB                       ; AND SAVE IT
        MOV     DL,BYTE PTR SAVDSK  ; GET BACK CURRENT DRIVE
        MOV     CL,SELDSK           ; SELECT DISK FUNCTION
        INT     BDOS                ;
        POP     BX                  ; RESTORE POINTER
        POP     DS                  ; RESTORE SEGMENTS
        POP     ES                  ;
        RET                         ; RETURN TO DBASE
;
BLKTBL  DB      00H,04H,00H,08H,00H,10H,00H,20H,00H,40H
BLKSIZ  RW      1
ALVLNG  RW      1
SAVDSK  RB      1
;
```

```
CONTBL   DW       0CA00H
         DW       0369AH
         DW       0E100H
         DW       005F5H
         DW       09680H
         DW       00098H
         DW       04240H
         DW       0000FH
         DW       086A0H
         DW       00001H
         DW       02710H
         DW       00000H
         DW       003E8H
         DW       00000H
         DW       00064H
         DW       00000H
         DW       0000AH
         DW       00000H
END
```

DOS-.PRG

Description.   Front-end program to utilize the DOS subroutines: DOS-STAT, DOS-COPY, DOS-PATH, DOS-TIME, and DOS-DATE.

```
* Program.: DOS-.PRG
* Author..: Luis A. Castro
* Date....: 01/22/84
* Notice..: Copyright 1984, Luis A. Castro, All Rights Reserved.
* Version.: dBASE II, version 2.4
* Notes...: Front-end program to utilize the DOS subroutines:
*           DOS-STAT, DOS-COPY, DOS-PATH, DOS-TIME, DOS-DATE.
* Local...: string, select
*
SET TALK OFF
SET BELL OFF
SET COLON OFF
ERASE
@ 2, 0 SAY "D O S    Assembly   Subroutines   Demonstration"
@ 2,72 SAY DATE()
@ 3, 0 SAY "========================================="
@ 3,40 SAY "========================================="
STORE "X" TO select
DO WHILE select <> " "
   @ 11,0
   STORE " " TO select
   @  5,0 SAY "1. DOS-STAT =   disk space remaining"
   @  6,0 SAY "2. DOS-COPY =   copy utility"
   @  7,0 SAY "3. DOS-PATH =   directory functions"
   @  8,0 SAY "4. DOS-TIME =   system time"
   @  9,0 SAY "5. DOS-DATE =   system date"
   @ 10,0 GET select PICTURE "I"
   READ
   IF select = " " .OR. .NOT. select $ "12345"
      LOOP
   ENDIF
```

```
@ 12,0
@ 13,0
@ 14,0
@ 10,0 SAY " "
* ---Execute a routine.
DO CASE
    CASE select = "1"
        * ---DOS-STAT =   disk space remaining.
        STORE " " TO drive
        @ 11,0 SAY "Enter a drive letter " GET drive PICTURE "!"
        READ
        IF drive <> " "
            @ 11,0 SAY "E"
            DO Dos-stat
            IF is:error
                ? "UNSUCCESSFUL"
            ELSE
                ? "DISK SPACE REMAINING = ",storage," BYTES "
                ?? storage/1024," KILOBYTES"
            ENDIF
            RELEASE storage
        ENDIF
        RELEASE drive,is:error
    CASE select = "2"
    * ---DOS-COPY =   copy utility
        ? "Enter <source> <destination> of COPY "
        ACCEPT TO string
        STORE !(TRIM(string)) TO string
        DO CASE
            CASE string = " "
            CASE @(" ",string) > 0 .AND.;
                @(" ",string) < LEN(string)
                STORE $(string,1,@(" ",string)-1) TO source
                STORE $(string,@(" ",string)+1) TO dest
                DO Dos-copy
                IF is:error
                    ? "FILE I/O ERROR"
                ELSE
                    ? "COPY COMPLETED"
                ENDIF
                RELEASE source,dest,is:error
        ENDCASE
    CASE select = "3"
    * ---DOS-PATH = directory functions.

        ? "Enter <[MD,RD,CD]> <pathname>"
        ACCEPT TO string
        STORE !(string) TO string
        DO CASE
            CASE string = " "
            CASE @(" ",string) > 1 .AND.;
                @(" ",string) < LEN(string)
                STORE $(string,1,@(" ",string)-1) TO command
                STORE $(string,@(" ",string)+1) TO path
                DO Dos-path
                IF is:error
                    ? "UN-SUCCESSFUL"
```

```
                ELSE
                    ? "SUCCESSFUL"
                ENDIF
                RELEASE command,path,is:error
            ENDCASE
        CASE select = "4"
        * ---DOS-TIME = system time.
            DO Dos-time
            ?
            ? "MILITARY TIME: ",time:dos
            ? " [AM/PM] TIME: ",time:ampm
            RELEASE time:dos,time:ampm
        CASE select = "5"
        * --- DOS-DATE = system date.
            DO Dos-date
            ?
            ? "Current date is ",date:dos
            RELEASE date:dos
    ENDCASE
    @ 11,0
ENDDO
SET BELL ON
SET TALK ON
SET COLON ON
RELEASE string, select
RETURN
* EOF: DOS-.PRG
```

DOS-COPY.PRG

Description.   Performs a DOS 2.0 copy function. Full path names may be specified for copying between directories.

```
* Program.: DOS-COPY.PRG
* Author..: Kelly Mc Tiernan
* Date....: 12/12/83
* Notice..: Copyright 1983, Kelly Mc Tiernan, All Rights Reserved.
* Version.: dBASE II, version 2.4
* Notes...: Performs a DOS 2.0 COPY function.
*
*    IN: source-C-63      Pathname of source
*        dest-C-63        Pathname of destination
*   OUT: is:error-L-1     Validation flag
*
STORE F TO is:error
* ---Parameter check.
STORE !(source) TO source
STORE !(dest) TO dest
IF LEN(source) > 63 .OR. LEN(dest) > 63
    * ---DOS 2.0 does not allow paths over 63 chars.
    RETURN
ENDIF
```

```
* ---POKE the pathnames into memory.
STORE 1 TO t:counter
STORE 57088 TO t:address
DO WHILE t:counter <= LEN(source)
   POKE t:address, RANK($(source,t:counter,1))
   STORE t:address+1 TO t:address
   STORE t:counter+1 TO t:counter
ENDDO
POKE t:address,00
STORE 1 TO t:counter
STORE 56962 TO t:address
DO WHILE t:counter <= LEN(dest)
   POKE t:address, RANK($(dest,t:counter,1))
   STORE t:address+1 TO t:address
   STORE t:counter+1 TO t:counter
ENDDO
POKE t:address,00
* -----------0---1---2---3---4---5---6---7---8---9
POKE 56832,          80, 83, 81, 82,156,137, 38,126
POKE 56840,222,180, 60,186,130,222,185, 32, 00,205,;
          33,114, 77,163, 00,224,180, 61,176, 00
POKE 56860,186, 00,223,205, 33,114, 63,137,195,185,;
          16, 00,180, 63,205, 33,114, 52, 09,192
POKE 56880,116, 22,185, 16, 00,180, 64,186, 00,223,;
         135, 30, 00,224,205, 33,114, 32,135, 30
* -----------0---1---2---3---4---5---6---7---8---9
POKE 56900, 00,224,235,221,180, 62,205, 33,114, 20,;
         135, 30, 00,224,180, 62,205, 33,114, 10
POKE 56920,139, 38,126,222,157, 90, 89, 91, 88,195,;
         180, 62,205, 33,135, 30, 00,224,180, 62
POKE 56940,205, 33,139, 38,126,222,157, 90, 89, 91,;
          88, 67,198, 07, 69, 00, 75,195
* -----------0---1---2---3---4---5---6---7---8---9
SET CALL TO 56832
STORE " " TO t:flag
CALL t:flag
* ---FILE I/O ERROR.
STORE ( t:flag = "E" ) TO ls:error
RELEASE t:flag,t:counter,t:address
RETURN
* EOF: DOS-COPY.PRG
```

```
; Subroutine.: DOS-COPY.A86
; Author.....: Kelly Mc Tiernan
; Date.......: 12/12/83
; Notice.....: Copyright 1983, All Rights Reserved.
; Notes......: MS-DOS 2.0X COPY function.
;
;
        ORG    DE00H          ; 56832 DECIMAL=TOP OF DBASE
;
START:  PUSH   AX             ; SAVE MACHINE STATE.
        PUSH   BX             ; PROBLEMS WILL ARISE IF
        PUSH   CX             ; THESE ARE NOT SAVED.
```

```
        PUSH    DX
        PUSHF               ; SAVE FLAGS
        MOV     [SAVSTK],SP ; SAVE STACK POINTER
;
        MOV     AH,3CH      ; CREATE DESTINATION FILE
        MOV     DX,[DEST]   ; ASCIIZ (zero-terminated)
                            ; PATHNAME
        MOV     CX,0020H    ; FILE ATTRIBUTE
        INT     21H         ; DOS FUNCTION CALL
        JC      ERROR       ; ERROR HANDLING ROUTINE
        MOV     [SAVHNDLE],AX ; SAVE NEW FILE HANDLE
;
        MOV     AH,3DH      ; OPEN FILE (SOURCE FILE)
        MOV     AL,00       ; READ ONLY
        MOV     DX,SRCE     ; ASCIIZ PATHNAME
        INT     21H         ; FUNCTION CALL
        JC      ERROR
        MOV     BX,AX       ; GET NEW HANDLE WHERE WE CAN
                            ; USE IT
;
RDWRTE: MOV     CX,0010H    ; BYTES TO R/W (BUFFER)
        MOV     AH,3FH      ; READ SOURCE FILE
        INT     21H         ; READ IT
        JC      ERROR       ; CARRY=FILE ERROR, ALL TREATED
                            ; THE SAME WAY
        OR      AX,AX       ; CHECK FOR ZERO=EOF
        JZ      DONE        ; IF SO GO CLOSE FILES
        MOV     CX,0010H    ; BYTES TO WRITE ( =READ )
                            ; THIS IS A 16-BYTE BUFFER.
                            ; IT CAN BE INCREASED TO ?KELLY?
                            ;
        MOV     AH,40H      ; WRITE FUNCTION
        MOV     DX,SRCE     ; OLD ASCIIZ SOURCE PATH=BUFFER
        XCHG    [SAVHNDLE],BX ; GET DESTINATION FILE HANDLE
        INT     21H         ; WRITE TO FILE
        JC      ERROR
;
        XCHG    [SAVHNDLE],BX ; GET BACK SOURCE HANDLE
        JMP     RDWRTE      ; DO NEXT READ/WRITE
;
DONE:   MOV     AH,3EH      ; CLOSE FILES
        INT     21H         ; FIRST FILE
        JC      ERROR
;
        XCHG    [SAVHNDLE],BX ; NEXT FILE HANDLE
        MOV     AH,3EH
        INT     21H
        JC      ERROR
;
        MOV     SP,[SAVSTK] ; RESTORE MACHINE STATE
        POPF                ; RESTORE FLAGS
        POP     DX
        POP     CX
        POP     BX
        POP     AX
        RET                 ; RETURN TO DBASE
;
```

```
ERROR:  MOV     AH,3EH           ; FIRST TRY TO CLOSE FILES
        INT     21H
        XCHG    [SAVHNDLE],BX
        MOV     AH,3EH
        INT     21H
;
        MOV     SP,[SAVSTK]      ; RESTORE MACHINE STATE
        POPF                     ; RESTORE FLAGS
        POP     DX
        POP     CX
        POP     BX
        POP     AX
;
        INC     BX               ; POINT TO FIRST CHAR. OF "ERROR"
        MOV     BYTE PTR[BX],'E'; 'E' IS ERROR CODE TO DBASE PRG.
        DEC     BX               ; RESTORE POINTER
        RET                      ; RETURN TO DBASE
;
SAVSTK    RS    02
SAVHNDLE  RS    01
SRCE      RS    64               ; SOURCE FILE POKED FROM DBASE
DEST      RS    64               ; DESTINATION FILE POKED
;                                ; FROM DBASE
END.
```

DOS-DATE.PRG

Description. Loads the IBM PC system date. Based on the following 8086 assembly routine:

```
        MOV     AH,2AH           ; DOS FUNCTION CALL IN AH
        INT     21H              ; INTERRUPT TYPE 21
        MOV     [F00D],DX        ; MOVE MONTH & DAY FROM DX
        MOV     [F00F],CX        ; MOVE YEAR FROM CX
        RET                      ; RETURN TO dBASE II
```

```
* Program.: DOS-DATE.PRG
* Author..: "Anonymous", Luis A. Castro
* Date....: 07/01/83, 10/31/83, 01/20/84
* Notice..: Copyright 1983, Ashton-Tate, All Rights Reserved.
* Notes...: Loads the IBM-PC system date.
*
*   OUT: date:dos-C-8    Date in MM/DD/YY format.
*
SET CALL TO 61440
POKE 61440, 180,42,205,33,137,22,13,240,137,14,15,240,195
CALL
* ---Get the month, day, and year.
```

```
STORE STR(PEEK(61454),2) + "/" +;
      STR(PEEK(61453),2) + "/" +;
      STR(PEEK(61456)*256+PEEK(61455)-1900,2) TO date:dos
*
* ---You may also want to set the dBASE II system date
* ---with the command: SET DATE TO &date:dos
*
RETURN
* EOF: DOS-DATE.PRG
```

DOS-PATH.PRG

Description.   Accessing DOS 2.0 directories from within dBASE II. The following guidelines need to be considered:

1.   Make sure your PATH is initially set to your directory containing **DBASE.COM** and related overlays, **traced from the root directory!** (\\). That is:

    A>PATH=\DBASE <cr>

2.   The functions implemented are RD=remove directory, MD=make directory, and CD=change directory. You may enter them in either lower-or uppercase. The error flag is set if no match is found in "command."

3.   If an illegal operation is attempted, that is, remove a directory containing files, or change to a directory not already in existence, an **OPERATION ERROR** is detected in the assembly routine and the error flag is set.

4.   You must have a copy of this routine in each directory before changing to it in order to trace backward in your directory structure after a CD function call.

```
* Program.: DOS-PATH.PRG
* Author..: Kelly Mc Tiernan
* Date....: 01/22/84
* Notice..: Copyright 1984, Kelly Mc Tiernan, All Rights Reserved.
* Version.: dBASE II, version 2.4
* Notes...: Accessing DOS 2.0 directories from within dBASE II.
*
*    IN: path-C-63       Parameter containing DOS 2.0 pathname.
*        command-C-2     Parameter containing DOS 2.0 directory
*                        command [MD,RD,CD].
*   OUT: is:error-L-1    Validation flag.
*
STORE T TO is:error
* ---Parameter checking.
STORE !(path) TO path
STORE !(command) TO command
IF LEN(path) > 63
   * ---DOS 2.0 does not allow paths over 63 chars.
   RETURN
ENDIF
```

```
SET CALL TO 56832
* ----------0---1---2---3---4---5---6---7---8---9
POKE 56832,          83,156,137, 38, 61,222,138, 15
POKE 56840,181, 00, 67,186, 63,222,137,215,137,222,;
          252,243,164,198, 05, 00,180, 00,205, 33
* ---This byte receives a parameter------^
POKE 56860,114, 07,139, 38, 61,222,157, 91,195, 75,;
          138, 15,181, 00, 67, 73,198, 07, 69, 67
POKE 56880,137,223,176, 32,243,170,139, 38, 61,222,;
          157, 91,195
* ----------0---1---2---3---4---5---6---7---8---9
DO CASE
   CASE command="MD"
   * ---Make directory.
      POKE 56857, 57
   CASE command="RD"
   * ---Remove directory.
      POKE 56857, 58
   CASE command="CD"
   * ---Change directory.
      POKE 56857, 59
   OTHERWISE
      * ---Not a directory command.
      RETURN
ENDCASE
* ---Execute the routine.
CALL path
IF $(path,1,2) <> "E "
   * ---NO OPERATION ERROR.
   STORE F TO is:error
ENDIF
RETURN
* EOF: DOS-PATH.PRG
```

```
; Subroutine.: DOS-PATH.A86
; Author.....: Kelly Mc Tiernan
; Date.......: 01/22/84
; Notice.....: Copyright 1984, All Rights Reserved.
; Notes......: Accessing DOS 2.0 directories.
;
        ORG     DE00H              ;56832 DECIMAL=TOP OF DBASE
;
START:  MOV     [SAVSTK],SP        ; SAVE STACK POINTER
        PUSH    BX                 ; SAVE VAR POINTER
        PUSHF                      ; SAVE FLAGS
;
        MOV     CL,[BX]            ; GET VAR SIZE
        MOV     CH,00              ; ZERO HIGH BYTE FOR CX COUNTER
        INC     BX                 ; POINT TO FIRST BYTE OF CHAR
                                   ; STRING
        MOV     DX,BUFFER          ; WHERE TO PUT PATH NAME
        MOV     DI,DX              ; GET POINTER FOR STRING MOVE
        MOV     SI,BX              ; SOURCE STRING=DBASE VAR "PATH"
```

```
          CLD                        ; DIRECTION = UP
          REP:MOVSB                  ; MOVE STRING TO BUFFER
          MOV     BYTE PTR[DI],00    ; STRING MUST BE TERMINATED WITH
                                     ; 00
          MOV     AH,00              ; DIRECTORY FUNCTIONS POKED FROM
                                     ; DBASE, MD=57, RD=58, CD=59
          INT     21                 ; MS-DOS FUNCTION CALL
          JC      ERROR              ; FUNCTION ERROR, HANDLE AS
                                     ; GENERAL
;
          MOV     SP,[SAVSTK]        ; RESTORE STACK POINTER
          POPF                       ; RESTORE FLAGS
          POP     BX                 ; RESTORE VAR POINTER
          RET                        ; RETURN TO DBASE
;
ERROR:    DEC     BX                 ; POINT TO LENGTH BYTE AGAIN
          MOV     CL,[BX]            ; AND GET INTO COUNTER AGAIN
          MOV     CH,00
          INC     BX                 ; POINT TO FIRST CHAR. IN VAR
          DEC     CX                 ; COUNT=COUNT-1
          MOV     BYTE PTR[BX],'E'   ; 'E' IS ERROR CODE TO DBASE PRG.
          INC     BX                 ; POINT TO NEXT BYTE OF STRING
          MOV     DI,BX              ; DESTINATION FOR SPACE FILL
          MOV     AL,20H             ; ASCII SPACE
          REP:STOSB                  ; FILL FOR COUNT=CX (1 LESS
                                     ; STRING LENGTH)
;
          MOV     SP,LSAVSTK]        ; RESTORE STACK POINTER
          POPF                       ; RESTORE FLAGS
          POP     BX                 ; RESTORE VAR POINTER
          RET                        ; RETURN TO DBASE
;
;
SAVSTK    RS      02
BUFFER    DB      00                 ; NO STORAGE RESERVED
          END.
```

DOS-STAT.PRG

Description. An MS-DOS 2.0 disk drive status routine. This routine returns the amount of storage on a disk to a dBASE II memory variable. The memory variable must be initialized to ten characters, with the first character containing the drive letter. An "E" for error will be returned if the memory variable is not passed correctly. Otherwise, the memory variable will contain the amount of storage (in bytes) remaining on the disk.

```
* Program.: DOS-STAT.PRG
* Author..: Kelly Mc Tiernan
* Date....: 12/12/83
* Notice..: Copyright 1983, Kelly Mc Tiernan, All Rights Reserved.
* Version.: dBASE II, version 2.4
* Notes...: Disk drive status routine.
*
*     IN: drive-C-1        Disk drive letter
*    OUT: storage-N-10     Number of bytes remaining on disk
*         is:error-L-1     Validation flag
```

```
*
STORE T TO is:error
* ---Parameter checking.
STORE !(drive) TO drive
IF LEN(drive) > 1 .OR. drive < "A" .OR. drive > "P"
    RETURN
ENDIF
* -----------0---1---2---3---4---5---6---7---8---9
POKE 56832,           6, 83,138, 87,  1,128,234, 64,;
         128,250, 17,118,  2,178,  0,180, 54,205
POKE 56850, 33, 61,255,255,116, 77,190,  0,  0,247,;
         225,185,  0,  0,135,214,247,227,135,209
POKE 56870,150,247,227,  3,200,135,209,150, 11,201,;
         117, 51,190,108,222, 30,  7, 95, 87, 71
* -----------0---1---2---3---4---5---6---7---8---9
POKE 56890,139,216,185,  9,  0,176, 48, 43, 28, 70,;
          70, 27, 20,114,  7,254,192, 78, 78,233
POKE 56910,241,255, 78, 78,  3, 28, 70, 70, 19, 20,;
         170, 70, 70,226,226,138,195,  4, 48,170
POKE 56930, 91,  7,195, 91,198, 71,  1, 69,  7,195,;
           0,202,154, 54,  0,225,245,  5,128,150
* -----------0---1---2---3---4---5---6---7---8---9
POKE 56950,152,  0, 64, 66, 15,  0,160,134,  1,  0,;
          16, 39,  0,  0,232,  3,  0,  0,100,  0
POKE 56970,  0,  0, 10,  0,  0,  0,  0
* -----------0---1---2---3---4---5---6---7---8---9
STORE !(drive)+"000000000" TO t:storage
SET CALL TO  56832
CALL t:storage
STORE ( t:storage = "E" ) TO is:error
IF .NOT. is:error
    STORE VAL(t:storage) TO storage
ENDIF
RELEASE t:storage
RETURN
* EOF: DOS-STAT.PRG
```

```
; Subroutine.: DOS-STAT.A86
; Author.....: Kelly Mc Tiernan
; Date.......: 01/23/84
; Notice.....: Copyright 1984, All Rights Reserved.
; Notes......: MS-DOS 2.0x disk drive status routine
;
;
        ORG     0DE00H              ; TOP OF DBASE.COM
;
DOS     EQU     21H                 ; MS DOS FUNCTION CALL
CURDSK  EQU     19H                 ; GET CURRENT DISK FUNCTION
SELDSK  EQU     0EH                 ; SELECT DISK FUNCTION
DSKBYT  EQU     01H                 ; OFFSET TO DISK SELECTOR BYTE
;
```

```
START:    PUSH     ES                  ; SAVE EXTRA SEGMENT
          PUSH     BX                  ; SAVE VAR POINTER
          MOV      DL,DSKBYT[BX]       ; GET DISK SELECTOR BYTE
          SUB      DL,40H              ; CONVERT TO HEX 01,02 ..
          CMP      DL,11H              ; CHECK FOR LEGAL DRIVE SPEC.
          JBE      DSKOK               ; SKIP NEXT, = SET TO DEFAULT
                                       ; DRIVE
          MOV      DL,00H              ; SET DRIVE SPEC. TO DEFAULT
DSKOK:    MOV      AH,36H              ; GET DISK FREE SPACE FUNCTION
          INT      DOS                 ; CALL DOS TO GET IT
          CMP      AX,0FFFFH           ; MEANS ILLEGAL DRIVE
          JZ       ERROR               ; QUIT HERE ON ERROR
          MOV      SI,0000H            ; ZERO OUT OUR TEMP REG. (32
                                       ; BIT *)
          MUL      CX                  ; AVAIL. CLUSTERS * SECTORS /
                                       ; CLUSTER
          MOV      CX,0000H            ; ZERO OUT FOR LATTER USE
          XCHG     DX,SI               ; SAVE CARRY OVER = HIGH WORD
                                       ; 1ST MUL
          MUL      BX                  ; LOW WORD * BYTES PER CLUSTER
          XCHG     DX,CX               ; SAVE CARRY OVER, THIS MUL,
                                       ; IN CX
          XCHG     AX,SI               ; GET BACK HIGH WORD
          MUL      BX                  ; HIGH WORD * BYTES PER CLUSTER
          ADD      CX,AX               ; ADD CARRY OVER FROM LAST MUL
          XCHG     DX,CX               ; PUT HIGH WORD IN DX ( NORMAL
                                       ; PLACE )
          XCHG     AX,SI               ; LOW WORD IN PROPER PLACE
          OR       CX,CX               ; CHECK FOR OVERFLOW ( IF CX<>0 )
          JNZ      ERROR               ; EXIT TO ERROR IF NUMBER TO
                                       ; LARGE
          MOV      SI,OFFSET CONTBL    ; GET SUB TABLE FOR HEX TO ASCII
                                       ; CONV.
          PUSH     DS                  ; MAKE ES=DS JUST IN CASE
          POP      ES                  ;
          POP      DI                  ; OLD BX POINTER INTO DI
          PUSH     DI                  ; SAVE COPY ON STACK
          INC      DI                  ; POINT TO FIRST BYTE OF STRING
          MOV      BX,AX               ; GET LOW WORD OUT OF AX, WE NEED
                                       ; IT
          MOV      CX,09H              ; TOTAL ANSWER BYTES TO CALCULATE
ANSWER:   MOV      AL,30H              ; ZERO SIG DIGIT COUNTER
ANS0:     SUB      BX,[SI]             ; SUBTRACT LOW WORD
          INC      SI                  ; POINT TO HIGH WORD
          INC      SI                  ;
          SBB      DX,[SI]             ; SUBTRACT HIGH WORD
          JB       NXTBYT              ; PUT BACK AND DO NEXT SIG
                                       ; DIGIT IF >
          INC      AL                  ; OTHERWISE COUNT IT AND DO
                                       ; NEXT ONE
          DEC      SI                  ; POINT BACK TO LOW WORD
          DEC      SI                  ;
          JMP      ANS0                ; DO AGAIN, UNTIL SUB>NUMBER
NXTBYT:   DEC      SI                  ; POINT TO LOW WORD
          DEC      SI                  ;
          ADD      BX,[SI]             ; PUT BACK
          INC      SI                  ; POINT TO HIGH WORD
```

```
          INC     SI          ;
          ADC     DX,[SI]     ; AND PUT BACK
          STOSB               ; PLACE BYTE INTO ANSWER
          INC     SI          ; POINT TO NEXT CONTBL NUMBER
          INC     SI          ;
          LOOP    ANSWER      ; DO NEXT BYTE AND EXIT ON DONE
DONE:     MOV     AL,BL       ; GET LAST BYTE
          ADD     AL,30H      ; CONVERT TO ASCII
          STOSB               ; PLACE IT IN ANSWER STRING
          POP     BX          ; RESTORE REGISTERS
          POP     ES          ;
          RET                 ; RETURN TO DBASE
ERROR:    POP     BX          ; GET BACK VAR POINTER
          MOV     BYTE PTR DSKBYT[BX],'E'
                              ; E IS ERROR CODE
                              ;
          POP     ES          ; RESTORE ES
          RET                 ; AND RETURN TO DBASE
;
;
CONTBL    DW      0CA00H
          DW      0369AH
          DW      0E100H
          DW      005F5H
          DW      09680H
          DW      00098H
          DW      04240H
          DW      0000FH
          DW      086A0H
          DW      00001H
          DW      02710H
          DW      00000H
          DW      003E8H
          DW      00000H
          DW      00064H
          DW      00000H
          DW      0000AH
          DW      00000H
END
```

DOS-TIME.PRG

Description. Loads the IBM PC system time. Based on the following 8086 assembly routine:

```
          MOV     AH,2CH      ; DOS FUNCTION CALL IN AH
          INT     21H         ; INTERRUPT TYPE 21
          MOV     [F00D],DX   ; MOVE SECONDS FROM DX
          MOV     [F00F],CX   ; MOVE HOUR & MINUTES FROM CX
          RET                 ; RETURN TO dBASE II
```

```
* Program.: DOS-TIME.PRG
* Author..: Anonymous, Luis A. Castro, Robert Goldin
* Date....: 07/01/83, 10/31/83, 01/20/84
* Notice..: Copyright 1983 & 1984, Ashton-Tate, All Rights Reserved.
* Version.: dBASE II, version 2.4
```

```
* Notes...: Loads the IBM-PC system time.
* Local...: t:hour, t:min, t:sec
*
*   OUT: time:dos-C-8       Time in 24-hour format: [hh:mm:ss]
*        time:ampm-C-8      Time in AM/PM format: [hh:mm AM/PM]
*
SET CALL TO 61440
POKE 61440,180,44,205,33,137,22,13,240,137,14,15,240,195
CALL
*
* ---Get the time values from memory.
STORE STR(PEEK(61456),2) TO t:hour
STORE STR(PEEK(61455),2) TO t:min
STORE STR(PEEK(61454),2) TO t:sec
*
* ---Replace leading blanks with leading zeros.
IF $(t:hour,1,1) = " "
    STORE "0" + $(t:hour,2,1) TO t:hour
ENDIF
IF $(t:min,1,1) = " "
    STORE "0" + $(t:min,2,1) TO t:min
ENDIF
IF $(t:sec,1,1) = " "
    STORE "0" + $(t:sec,2,1) TO t:sec
ENDIF
*
* ---Concatenate the three variables for 24-hour format.
STORE t:hour + ":" + t:min + ":" + t:sec   TO time:dos
*
* ---AM/PM Format Conversion.
DO CASE
    CASE t:hour = "00"
        STORE "12:" + t:min + " AM" TO time:ampm
    CASE t:hour < "12"
        STORE STR(VAL(t:hour),2)+":"+t:min+" AM" TO time:ampm
    CASE t:hour = "12"
        STORE "12:" + t:min + " PM" TO time:ampm
    CASE t:hour > "12"
        STORE STR(VAL(t:hour)-12,2)+":"+t:min+" PM" TO time:ampm
ENDCASE
RELEASE t:hour, t:min, t:sec
RETURN
* EOF: DOS-TIME.PRG
```

PC_DATE.PRG

Description. Sets the IBM PC DOS system date from the dBASE II system DATE(). Based on the following 8086 assembly routine:

```
        MOV        CX,[FOOF]        ; MOVE YEAR INTO CX
        MOV        DX,[FOOD]        ; MOVE MONTH & DAY INTO CL
        MOV        AH,2BH           ; DOS FUNCTION CALL IN AH
        INT        21H              ; INTERRUPT TYPE 21
        MOV        [FO21],AL        ; AL = 0 IF SET, FF IF NOT
        RET                         ; RETURN TO dBASE II
```

```
* Program.: PC_DATE.PRG
* Author..: Tom Rettig
* Date....: 12/29/83
* Notice..: Copyright 1983, Ashton-Tate, All Rights Reserved.
* Version.: dBASE II, version 2.4
* Notes...: Sets the IBM-PC DOS system date from the dBASE II
*           system DATE().
*
*   OUT: is:set    True if DOS took the date.
*                  False if not a valid DOS date.
*
* ---Parse the dBASE system date into memory variables.
STORE VAL( $( DATE(), 1, 2 ) ) TO t:month
STORE VAL( $( DATE(), 4, 2 ) ) TO t:day
* ---The year is stored in two bytes, high order and low order.
STORE INT( 1900 / 256 ) TO t:year:hi
STORE VAL( $( DATE(), 7, 2 ) ) +;
      1900 - INT( 1900 / 256 ) * 256 TO t:year:low
*
* ---Place the parsed date into memory where the
* ---assembly routine can get to it.
POKE 61453, t:day, t:month, t:year:low, t:year:hi
*
* ---Place the assembly routine into memory, and run it.
POKE 61457, 139, 14, 15,240,139, 22, 13,240
POKE 61465, 180, 43,205, 33,162, 33,240,195
SET CALL TO 61457
CALL
*
* ---Check to see if DOS accepted the date.
STORE PEEK( 61473 ) = 0 TO is:set
*
RELEASE t:day, t:month, t:year:hi, t:year:low
RETURN
* EOF: PC_DATE.PRG
```

FIX-DOS.ASM

Description. This program expects an ASCII filename on command line and writes back to same filename and drive an output file with all characters less than 20H replaced by 20H except the 1AH EOF marks at real EOF. The output file has type of .FIX. A flag is set if CR and LF are also to be replaced. The program also prompts for the number of bytes from start of file at which to start processing.

```
;   Subroutine.: FIX.ASM
;   Author.....: Bob Doolittle
;   Date.......: 08/12/84
;   Notice.....: Copyright 1984, Ashton-Tate, All Rights Reserved.
;   Notes......: PC/MS-DOS version.
;
M           EQU     Byte Ptr 0[BX]
;
CSEG        SEGMENT
            ASSUME  CS:CSEG,DS:CSEG

            ORG     100H
;
;BDOS equates
;
BDOS        EQU     21H                 ;BDOS entry point
TBUF        EQU     80H                 ;Default buffer
FCB         EQU     5CH                 ;Default FCB
CFS         EQU     35                  ;Compute file size
CONIN       EQU     1                   ;Console in
CONOUT      EQU     2                   ;Console out
PSTR        EQU     9                   ;Print string
STRIN       EQU     10                  ;String input function
OPEN        EQU     15                  ;Open file
CLOSE       EQU     16                  ;Close file
READ        EQU     20                  ;Read sequential
WRITE       EQU     21                  ;Write sequential
MAKE        EQU     22                  ;Make file
DELETE      EQU     19                  ;Delete file
READR       EQU     33                  ;Read random
;
;ASCII equates
;
CR          EQU     13
LF          EQU     10
;
START:      MOV     Byte Ptr FLG,0      ;Initialize CRLF flag to destroy CRLF
            MOV     BX,FCB+1
            MOV     AL,Byte Ptr [BX]
            CMP     AL,20H              ;Was input file on command line
            JNZ     ST2                 ;Yes
            MOV     DX,(Offset MES1)    ;No, print message and abort
            MOV     AH,PSTR
            INT     BDOS
            JMP     EXIT
;
ST2:        MOV     DX,(Offset MES4)    ;Print CRLF message
            MOV     AH,PSTR
            INT     BDOS
            MOV     AH,CONIN            ;Get response
            INT     BDOS
            AND     AL,5FH              ;Make upper case
            CMP     AL,'Y'
            JNZ     ST7
            MOV     AL,1
            MOV     Byte Ptr FLG,AL
ST7:        MOV     AH,PSTR             ;Ask for # of bytes
```

```
            MOV     DX,(Offset MES6)
            INT     BDOS
            MOV     DX,(Offset CBUF)    ;Get response
            MOV     AH,STRIN
            INT     BDOS
            MOV     BX,(Offset CBUF)+2
            CALL    CONV                ;Convert to binary in HL
            CALL    DIV                 ;Divide by 128
            MOV     Word Ptr QUO,BX     ;Save quotient and remainder
            CALL    CRLF
            CALL    CLEAR               ;Clear FCB+32-35, FCB+15 and FCB+12
            MOV     BX,FCB
            MOV     DX,(Offset FCB1)
            MOV     CL,9
MOVE:       MOV     AL,M                ;Move file name and drive from FCB to FCB1
            MOV     SI,DX
            MOV     [SI],AL
            INC     BX
            INC     DX
            DEC     CL
            JNZ     MOVE
            MOV     DX,FCB
            MOV     AH,OPEN             ;Open file
            INT     BDOS
            INC     AL                  ;Was open successful?
            JNZ     ST3                 ;Yes
            MOV     DX,(Offset MES2)    ;No, print message and abort
            MOV     AH,PSTR
            INT     BDOS
            JMP     EXIT
ST3:        MOV     DX,(Offset MES5)    ;Working message
            MOV     AH,PSTR
            INT     BDOS
            MOV     DX,FCB
            MOV     AH,CFS              ;Compute file size
            INT     BDOS
            MOV     BX,FCB+33
            MOV     AX,Word Ptr [BX]
            MOV     REC,AX
            DEC     Word Ptr [BX]
            MOV     AH,READR
            MOV     DX,FCB
            INT     BDOS                ;Read last record
            MOV     BX,TBUF-1
            MOV     CL,0                ;Initialize counter
LOP:        INC     BX                  ;Scan to 1st EOF mark and keep count
            INC     CL
            CMP     M,1AH               ;Is it EOF?
            JNZ     LOP                 ;No, keep looping
            PUSH    CX                  ;Save count to EOF in last record
            CALL    CLEAR               ;Clear again
            MOV     DX,(Offset FCB1)
            MOV     AH,DELETE           ;Delete any possible previous out file
            INT     BDOS
            MOV     DX,FCB
            MOV     AH,OPEN             ;Re-open the input file
            INT     BDOS
            MOV     DX,(Offset FCB1)
```

```
            MOV     AH,MAKE              ;Make output file
            INT     BDOS
;
FIRS:       MOV     DX,FCB              ;Scan off quotient records
            MOV     AH,READ
            INT     BDOS
            OR      AL,AL
            JZ      FST1               ;Read OK
            MOV     DX,(Offset MES3)
            MOV     AH,PSTR
            INT     BDOS
            POP     CX                 ;Balance stack
            JMP     EXIT
;
FST1:       MOV     BX,Word Ptr REC    ;Bump record count down
            DEC     BX
            MOV     Word Ptr REC,BX
            MOV     BX,Word Ptr QUO    ;Get DIV result
            OR      BH,BH              ;Have we read sector with remainder ?
            JZ      FST2               ;Yes
            DEC     BH                 ;No
            MOV     Word Ptr QUO,BX
            MOV     DX,(Offset FCB1)   ;Write sector
            MOV     AH,WRITE
            INT     BDOS
            JMP     SHORT FIRS
FST2:       ADD     BL,80H             ;BX now has filter start address
FST3:       CALL    FILTER
            INC     BX
            OR      BH,BH
            JZ      FST3               ;Filter to end of sector
            MOV     DX,(Offset FCB1)
            MOV     AH,WRITE           ;Write to output file
            INT     BDOS
LOOP:       MOV     DX,FCB
            MOV     AH,READ            ;Read a record to default buffer
            INT     BDOS
            OR      AL,AL              ;Was read successful?
            JZ      L04                ;Yes
ERR:        MOV     DX,(Offset MES3)
            MOV     AH,PSTR            ;No, print message and abort
            INT     BDOS
            POP     CX                 ;Balance stack
            JMP     SHORT EXIT
;
L04:        DEC     Word Ptr REC       ;Decrement record count
            JNZ     GOAH               ;Not at last record
            POP     CX                 ;Get back count
            MOV     BX,TBUF
;
L01:        DEC     CL                 ;Are we at EOF
            JZ      L02                ;Yes
            CALL    FILTER
            INC     BX
            JMP     SHORT L01          ;Loop
;
```

```
LO2:     MOV     DX,(Offset FCB1)
         MOV     AH,WRITE            ;Write last record
         INT     BDOS
         MOV     DX,(Offset FCB1)
         MOV     AH,CLOSE            ;Close output file
         INT     BDOS
EXIT:    MOV     AH,0               ;Finished
         INT     BDOS
;
GOAH:    MOV     BX,TBUF
         MOV     CX,80H             ;Initialize record count
GO1:     CALL    FILTER             ;Scan the record
         INC     BX
         LOOP    GO1
         MOV     DX,(Offset FCB1)
         MOV     AH,WRITE           ;Write record to output file
         INT     BDOS
         JMP     SHORT LOOP         ;Loop to read next record
;
FILTER:  AND     M,7FH              ;Strip bit 7
         CMP     M,20H              ;Is it < space ?
         JNAE    L_1
         RET                        ;No
L_1:     TEST    Byte Ptr FLG,0FFH  ;Are we killing CRLF ?
         JZ      FIL1               ;Yes
         MOV     AL,M
         CMP     AL,CR
         JNZ     L_2
         RET                        ;Don't change
L_2:     CMP     AL,LF
         JNZ     FIL1
         RET                        ;Don't change
FIL1:    MOV     M,20H              ;Replace anything < space by space
         RET
;
CONV:    MOV     DX,0               ;Convert # pointed to by HL to binary in HL
         XCHG    BX,DX              ;Conversion stops when # < '0' is found
         MOV     SI,DX                    ;Result returned in BX
         MOV     AH,0
CONV1:   MOV     AL,[SI]
         SUB     AL,'0'
         JNS     L_4
         RET
L_4:     CMP     AL,10
         CMC
         JNB     L_5
         RET
L_5:     INC     SI
         SHL     BX,1
         MOV     CX,BX
         SHL     BX,1
         SHL     BX,1
         ADD     BX,CX
         ADD     BX,AX
         JMP     SHORT CONV1
;
DIV:     MOV     AX,BX              ;Divide BX by 128
         MOV     CL,128
```

```
          DIV       CL
          MOV       BH,AL                 ;Quotient in BH, remainder in BL
          MOV       BL,AH
          RET
;
CLEAR:    XOR       AL,AL                 ;Zero key fields in FCB
          MOV       BX,FCB+32
          MOV       M,AL
          INC       BX
          MOV       M,AL
          INC       BX
          MOV       M,AL
          INC       BX
          MOV       M,AL
          MOV       BX,FCB+15
          MOV       Byte Ptr [BX],AL
          MOV       BX,FCB+12
          MOV       Byte Ptr [BX],AL
          RET
;
CRLF:     MOV       DL,CR
          MOV       AH,CONOUT
          INT       BDOS
          MOV       DL,LF
          MOV       AH,CONOUT
          INT       BDOS
          RET
MES1      DB        CR,LF,'    USAGE: FIX [d:]<filename.typ>'
          DB        CR,LF,'where d is an optional drive designator'
          DB        CR,LF,'and filename.typ is the file name and type'
          DB        CR,LF,'of the file to be processed. The output'
          DB        CR,LF,'file will be named filename.FIX.$'
MES2      DB        CR,LF,'Cannot find file on specified drive.$'
MES3      DB        CR,LF,'Read past EOF.$'
MES4      DB        CR,LF,'Do you want to preserve CRLFs (Y or N) ? $'
MES5      DB        CR,LF,'Working...$'
MES6      DB        CR,LF,'What is the size of the header (in bytes)? $'
CBUF      DB        10,0
          DB        0,0,0,0,0,0,0,0,0,0,0,0
REC       DW        0                     ;Storage for record count
QUO       DW        0                     ;Storage for quotient and remainder
FLG       DB        0                     ;CRLF flag
FCB1      DB        0,'         FIX'
          DB        0,0,0,0,0,0,0,0,0,0,0,0,0,0,0,0,0,0,0,0,0,0,0,0

CSEG      ENDS
          END       START
```

TIMEWAIT.ASM

Description.   TIMEWAIT is essentially two functions, neither of which is available in dBASE II. One is a current time display, and the other is a data entry loop which is entered conditionally upon sensing keyboard input. It is ideal for displaying the time in a menu while waiting for a menu selection to be entered. It can then record the times of entry and return (which could be used to determine the elapsed time of subroutines or data entry). It can be used to lock out certain data and command files from access after a particular time.

TIMEWAIT was developed for use on the IBM PC with the monochrome board and monitor, and it may not run on other systems or even on the PC with a color card and monitor. The source code printed here will need to be compiled into an EXE file with the IBM MACRO-Assembler in order to convert it to POKE sequences with BINDEC.BAS.

TIMEWAIT prints the current system time at locations specified in an entry character variable (ROW,COLUMN). Format for X,Y is identical to dBASE convention in the "@ <row>, <column>" command. Two character variables *must* be pre-initialized before calling this routine and in the following order:

```
STORE "00:00:00" TO memvar1
STORE "x,y" TO memvar2
```

Caution: No error checking is done for the correct initialization of these variables! When keyboard entry is detected, the time display is erased and keyboard entry will commence at the same X,Y coordinates and the contents will be written to memvar2. Keyboard entry will cease when a carriage return is detected or string length exceeds the pre-initialized length of memvar2. The time when keyboard entry commenced will reside in memvar1.

```
; Program.: TIMEWAIT.ASM
; Author..: Steve Manes
; Date....: 1983
; Notice..: Copyright 1983, Steve Manes, All Rights Reserved
; Version.: dBASE II, version 2.4
; Notes...: Prints current system time at specified location
;           while waiting for a keypress input.
;
;   CALLing convention from dBASE II:  CALL memvar2
;
CSEG     SEGMENT 'CODE'
         ASSUME CS:CSEG
                 mov si,bx          ; we need BX so save variable address in SI

                 mov ch,45          ; turn off cursor
                 mov cl,13
                 mov ah,1
                 int 10h

;-----------------------------------------------------------------;
; Convert screen coordinates to binary. Hold X,Y address word in DI  ;
;-----------------------------------------------------------------;
                 sub cx,cx          ; clear the register
                 mov ch,2           ; through the loop twice
                 mov dl,10          ; multiplier
```

```
convert_XY:
                sub ax,ax              ; clear the register
                inc bx                 ; next digit
                mov al,byte ptr [bx]   ; read 1st digit
                and al,0Fh             ;  and convert to binary
                inc bx                 ; next digit
                mov dh,byte ptr [bx]
                cmp dh,'0'             ; is it a digit?
                jb next_nmbr

                mul dl                 ; two digit #. Mult hi-digit by 10
                and dh,0Fh             ; convert low digit to binary
                add al,dh              ; add high and low digits to AL
                inc bx

next_nmbr:      dec ch                 ; decrement loop counter
                cmp ch,0               ; have X and Y been converted?
                je load_Y              ; no, X loaded; Y not converted yet.

load_X:         mov cl,al              ; store X temporarily in CL
                jmp convert_XY

load_Y:         sub bx,bx              ; clear the register
                mov bl,al              ; load Y value
                mov bh,cl              ; load X value
                mov di,bx              ; store coordinates in DI

                jmp main_prog          ;  and move on

print_time      PROC    NEAR
                push si                ; save string pointer
                mov bx,0               ; "zero" display page
                mov cx,1               ; display one character
                mov dx,di              ; get X,Y coordinates
                sub si,9               ; back up to preceding TIME variable
                mov bp,8               ; loop counter
write:          mov ah,2               ; locate cursor
                int 10h
                mov al,byte ptr [si]   ; write character
                mov ah,10
                int 10h
                inc dl                 ; increment cursor column
                inc si                 ; next character in string
                dec bp                 ; decrement counter
                cmp bp,0               ; all eight characters displayed?
                ja write               ; no, finish writing time
                pop si                 ; restore original string pointer
                ret
print_time      ENDP

make_ascii      PROC    NEAR
                div dl                 ; divide AX value by 10
                add al,'0'             ; convert remainder to ASCII
                add ah,'0'             ; convert quotient to ASCII
                dec bx                 ; back up string pointer
                mov byte ptr [bx],ah   ; write low digit to string
                dec bx
```

```
                    mov byte ptr [bx],al        ; write high digit to string
                    dec bx
                    ret
make_ascii          ENDP

main_prog:

                    mov bx,si                   ; X,Y variable contents address -1
                    sub bx,1                    ; move to end of previous TIME
                                                ;   variable.
                    mov ah,2Ch                  ; get current time from BIOS
                    int 21h

                    mov dl,10                   ; divisor
                    sub ax,ax                   ; clear the register
                    mov al,dh                   ; load seconds and convert to ASCII
                    call make_ascii
                    sub ax,ax
                    mov al,cl                   ;load minutes
                    call make_ascii
                    sub ax,ax
                    mov al,ch                   ; load hours
                    call make_ascii

                    call print_time             ; write current time to screen
                    mov ah,0Bh                  ; see if key has been pressed
                    int 21h
                    cmp al,0FFh                 ; is character available?
                    je keybd_entry              ; yes, get input
                    jmp main_prog               ; no, keep writing time
```

```
;-------------------------------------------------------------------------;
; This routine will write the keyboard entry to the original screen       ;
; coordinate variable. Entry will stop when carriage return is detected   ;
; or the length of the entry string equals the original length of the     ;
; screen coordinate variable.                                             ;
;-------------------------------------------------------------------------;
```

```
keybd_entry:                                    ; erase screen at time variable
                    mov bp,8                    ; loop counter
                    mov cx,1                    ; character count
                    mov bx,0                    ; "zero" display page
                    mov dx,di                   ; get original X,Y coordinates
erase:              mov ah,2                    ; locate cursor
                    int 10h
                    mov al,' '                  ; print ASCII space
                    mov ah,10
                    int 10h
                    inc dl                      ; next column
                    dec bp                      ; decrement loop counter
                    cmp bp,0                    ; all 8 characters blanked?
                    ja erase                    ; no, blank the next character

                    mov dx,di                   ; cursor back to original X,Y
                    mov ah,2
                    int 10h
                    mov ch,12                   ; turn cursor back on
                    mov cl,13
                    mov ah,1
                    int 10h
```

```
              mov bx,si                 ; null the CALLing variable
              mov cl,byte ptr [bx]      ; get length byte
Init:         inc bx                    ; next character
              mov byte ptr [bx],' '     ; ASCII space character
              dec cl
              cmp cl,0                  ; are all characters blanked?
              ja init                   ; no, blank the next character

              mov bx,si                 ; variable contents address -1
              mov cl,byte ptr [bx]      ; load length byte to loop limiter
key1:         inc bx
              mov ah,1                  ; keyboard input function
              int 21h
              cmp al,0Dh                ; carriage return?
              je dB_return              ; yes, exit program
              mov byte ptr [bx],al      ; no, write it to string
              dec cl                    ; decrement loop counter
              cmp cl,0                  ; limit reached?
              je dB_return              ; yes, exit program
              jmp key1                  ;   and continue reading input.

dB_return:
              ret                       ; should be an intra-segment RET

CSEG    ENDS
        END
;-------------------------------------------------------------------;
```

APPENDIX E
TABLES

OPERATORS
SET PARAMETERS
COMMANDS
OTHER RESOURCES
METAVARIABLES
ASCII CHART

OPERATORS

+

```
III/II ::=  <command> +<numeric expression>
```

–

```
III/II ::=  <command> – <numeric expression>
```

^

```
III    ::=  <command> <numeric expression 1> ^ <numeric expression 2>
```

* *

```
III    ::=  <command> <numeric expression 1> ** <numeric expression 2>
```

*

```
III/II ::=  <command> <numeric expression 1> * <numeric expression 2>
```

/

```
III/II ::=  <command> <numeric expression 1> / <numeric expression 2>
```

+

```
III/II ::=   <command> <numeric expression 1> + <numeric expression 2>
III/II ::=   <command> <character expression 1> + <character expression 2>
III    ::=   <command> <date> + <numeric expression>
```

−

```
III/II ::=   <command> <numeric expression 1> − <numeric expression 2>
III/II ::=   <command> <character expression 1> − <character expression 2>
III    ::=   <command> <date> − <numeric expression>
III    ::=   <command> <date 1> − <date 2>
```

=

```
III/II ::=   <command> <expression 1> = <expression 2>
```

#

```
III/II ::=   <command> <expression 1> # <expression 2>
```

<>

```
III/II ::=   <command> <expression 1> <> <expression 2>
```

<

```
III/II ::=   <command> <expression 1> < <expression 2>
```

<=

```
III/II ::=   <command> <expression 1> <= <expression 2>
```

>

```
III/II ::=   <command> <expression 1> > <expression 2>
```

>=

```
III/II ::=   <command> <expression 1> >= <expression 2>
```

$

```
III/II ::=   <command> <character expression 1> $ <character expression 2>
```

.NOT.

```
III/II ::=   <command> .NOT. <logical expression>
```

.AND.

III/II ::=   <command> <logical expression 1> .AND. <logical expression 2>

.OR.

III/II ::=   <command> <logical expression 1> .OR. <logical expression 2>

SET Parameters

ALTERNATE

```
III/II ::=    SET ALTERNATE <switch>
III/II ::=    SET ALTERNATE TO
III/II ::=    SET ALTERNATE TO <text filename>
```

BELL

```
III/II ::=    SET BELL <switch>
```

CALL

```
II     ::=    SET CALL TO
II     ::=    SET CALL TO <decimal address>
```

CARRY

```
III/II ::=    SET CARRY <switch>
```

COLON

```
II     ::=    SET COLON <switch>
```

COLOR

```
III    ::=    SET COLOR TO <command-line mode values> ;
                          [,<full-screen mode values>] ;
                          [,<border value>]
II     ::=    SET COLOR TO <background> <delimiter> <foreground>
```

CONFIRM

```
III/II ::=    SET CONFIRM <switch>
```

CONSOLE

```
III/II ::=    SET CONSOLE <switch>
```

DATE

```
II     ::=  SET DATE TO <nn/nn/nn>
```

DEBUG

```
III/II ::=  SET DEBUG <switch>
```

DECIMALS

```
III    ::=  SET DECIMALS TO <numeric expression>
III    ::=  SET DECIMALS [TO]
```

DEFAULT

```
III/II ::=  SET DEFAULT TO <drive letter>
```

DELETED

```
III/II ::=  SET DELETED <switch>
```

DELIMITERS

```
III    ::=  SET DELIMITERS <switch>
III    ::=  SET DELIMITERS TO <character expression>
III    ::=  SET DELIMITERS TO DEFAULT
```

DEVICE

```
III    ::=  SET DEVICE TO <device parameter>
```

ECHO

```
III/II ::=  SET ECHO <switch>
```

EJECT

```
II     ::=  SET EJECT <switch>
```

ESCAPE

```
III/II ::=  SET ESCAPE <switch>
```

EXACT

```
III/II ::=  SET EXACT <switch>
```

FILTER

```
III    ::=  SET FILTER TO <logical expression>
III    ::=  SET FILTER [TO]
```

FIXED

```
III    ::=  SET FIXED <switch>
```

FORMAT

```
III/II ::=  SET FORMAT TO <format filename>
III/II ::=  SET FORMAT TO
II     ::=  SET FORMAT TO <device parameter>
```

FUNCTION

```
III    ::=  SET FUNCTION <numeric expression > TO <character expression>
II     ::=  SET F<function-key number> TO "<character string>"
```

HEADING

```
II     ::=  SET HEADING TO
II     ::=  SET HEADING TO <character string>
```

HEADINGS

```
III    ::=  SET HEADINGS <switch>
```

HELP

```
III    ::=  SET HELP <switch>
```

INDEX

```
III/II ::=  SET INDEX TO
III/II ::=  SET INDEX TO <index filename> {,<index filename>}
```

INTENSITY

```
III/II ::=  SET INTENSITY <switch>
```

LINKAGE

```
II     ::=  SET LINKAGE <switch>
```

MARGIN

```
III/II ::=  SET MARGIN TO <numeric expression>
```

MENUS

III   ::= SET MENUS <switch>

PATH

III   ::= SET PATH TO <path> {,<path>}
III   ::= SET PATH [TO]

PRINT

III/II ::= SET PRINT <switch>

PROCEDURE

III   ::= SET PROCEDURE TO <procedure filename>
III   ::= SET PROCEDURE [TO]

RAW

II   ::= SET RAW <switch>

RELATION

III   ::= SET RELATION INTO <alias name>
III   ::= SET RELATION INTO <alias name> TO <key expression>
III   ::= SET RELATION INTO <alias name> TO <numeric expression>
III   ::= SET RELATION [TO]

SAFETY

III   ::= SET SAFETY <switch>

SCOREBOARD

III   ::= SET SCOREBOARD <switch>

SCREEN

II   ::= SET SCREEN <switch>

STEP

III/II ::= SET STEP <switch>

TALK

III/II ::= SET TALK <switch>

UNIQUE

```
III    ::=  SET UNIQUE <switch>
```

COMMANDS

`*`

```
III/II ::=  * <comment>
```

`=`

```
III    ::=  <memvar name> = <expression>
```

`?`

```
III/II ::=  ? <expression> {,<expression>}
```

`??`

```
III/II ::=  ?? <expression> {,<expression>}
```

`@`

```
III/II ::=  @ <row>,<column>
III/II ::=  @ <row>,<column> GET <variable>
III/II ::=  @ <row>,<column> GET <variable> PICTURE "<picture template>"
III    ::=  @ <row>,<column> GET <variable> FUNCTION "{<function>}"
III    ::=  @ <row>,<column> GET <date/numeric variable> RANGE <n1>,<n2>
III/II ::=  @ <row>,<column> SAY <expression>
III    ::=  @ <row>,<column> SAY <expression> FUNCTION "{<function>}"
III    ::=  @ <row>,<column> SAY <expression> PICTURE <picture template>
II     ::=  @ <row>,<column> SAY <expression> USING "{<using symbol>}"
```

ACCEPT

```
III/II ::=  ACCEPT <prompt> TO <memvar name>
```

APPEND

```
III/II ::=  APPEND
III/II ::=  APPEND BLANK
III/II ::=  APPEND FROM <database filename> [<condition>]
III/II ::=  APPEND FROM <text filename> SDF [<condition>]
III    ::=  APPEND FROM <text filename> DELIMITED [WITH <delimiter>] ;
                                        [<condition>]
II     ::=  APPEND FROM <text filename> DELIMITED [<condition>]
```

ASSIST

```
III    ::=  ASSIST
```

AVERAGE

```
III    ::=  AVERAGE <numeric expression list> [<database parameter>]
III    ::=  AVERAGE <numeric expression list> [<database parameter>] ;
               TO <memvar name list>
III    ::=  AVERAGE [<database parameter>]
III    ::=  AVERAGE [<database parameter>] TO <memvar name list>
```

BROWSE

```
III/II ::=  BROWSE
III/II ::=  BROWSE FIELDS <field name> {,<field name>}
III    ::=  BROWSE [FIELDS <field name> {,<field name>}] ;
               [LOCK <numeric expression>] [FREEZE <field name>] ;
               [NOFOLLOW]
```

CALL

```
III/II ::=  CALL
III/II ::=  CALL <memvar name>
```

CANCEL

```
III/II ::=  CANCEL
```

CHANGE

```
III/II ::=  CHANGE [<database parameter>]
III    ::=  CHANGE FIELDS <field name> {,<field name>} ;
               [<database parameter>]
II     ::=  CHANGE FIELD <field name> {,<field name>} ;
               [<database parameter>]
```

CLEAR

```
III/II ::=  CLEAR GETS
III    ::=  @ <row>,<column> CLEAR
III    ::=  CLEAR
III    ::=  CLEAR ALL
III    ::=  CLEAR MEMORY
II     ::=  CLEAR
```

CLOSE

```
III      ::=  CLOSE ALTERNATE
III      ::=  CLOSE DATABASES
III      ::=  CLOSE FORMAT
III      ::=  CLOSE INDEXES
III      ::=  CLOSE PROCEDURE
```

CONTINUE

```
III/II ::=  CONTINUE
```

COPY

```
III      ::=  COPY FILE <source filename.ext>;
                    TO <destination filename.ext>
III/II ::=  COPY STRUCTURE TO <database filename>
III/II ::=  COPY STRUCTURE TO <database filename> ;
                         FIELDS <field name> {,<field name>}
III/II ::=  COPY TO <database filename> ;
                 FIELDS <field name> {,<field name>} ;
                 [<database parameter>]
III/II ::=  COPY TO <database filename> [<database parameter>]
III/II ::=  COPY TO <structure-extended filename> ;
                 [FIELDS <field name> {,<field name>}] ;
                 STRUCTURE EXTENDED
III/II ::=  COPY TO <text filename> ;
                 [FIELDS <field name> {,<field name>}] ;
                 [<database parameter>] DELIMITED [WITH <delimiter>]
III/II ::=  COPY TO <text filename> ;
                 [FIELDS <field name> {,<field name>}] ;
                 [<database parameter>] SDF
```

COUNT

```
III/II ::=  COUNT [<database parameter>]
III/II ::=  COUNT [<database parameter>] TO <memvar name>
```

CREATE

```
III      ::=  CREATE LABEL
III      ::=  CREATE REPORT
III/II ::=  CREATE [<database filename>]
III/II ::=  CREATE [<database filename>] ;
                 FROM <structure-extended filename>
```

DELETE

```
III/II ::=  DELETE
III/II ::=  DELETE FILE <filename.ext>
```

DIRECTORY

```
III    ::=  DIR <file directory parameter>;
               [[ON] <drive designator>] [TO PRINT]
III    ::=  DIR [[ON] <drive designator>] [TO PRINT]
III    ::=  DIRECTORY <file directory parameter> ;
               [[ON] <drive designator>] [TO PRINT]
III    ::=  DIRECTORY [[ON] <drive designator>] [TO PRINT]
```

DISPLAY

```
III/II ::=  DISPLAY FILES <file directory parameter> ;
                      [ON <drive designator>]
III/II ::=  DISPLAY FILES [ON <drive designator>]
III/II ::=  DISPLAY MEMORY
III/II ::=  DISPLAY STATUS
III/II ::=  DISPLAY STRUCTURE
III/II ::=  DISPLAY [OFF] [<database parameter>] ;
               [<expression> {,<expression>}]
```

DO

```
III/II ::=  DO <command filename>
III    ::=  DO <procedure name>
III    ::=  DO <subroutine> WITH <expression> {,<expression>}
```

DO CASE...ENDCASE

```
III/II ::=  DO CASE
             { CASE <logical expression>
                 <commands> }
            ENDCASE
III/II ::=  DO CASE
             { CASE <logical expression>
                 <commands> }
               OTHERWISE
                 <commands>
            ENDCASE
```

DO WHILE...ENDDO

```
III/II ::=  DO WHILE <logical expression>
               <commands>
            ENDDO
```

EDIT

```
III/II ::=   EDIT
III/II ::=   EDIT <numeric expression>
III    ::=   EDIT RECORD <numeric expression>
```

EJECT

```
III/II ::=   EJECT
```

ERASE

```
III    ::=   ERASE <filename.ext>
II     ::=   @ <row>,<column> ERASE
II     ::=   ERASE
```

EXIT

```
III    ::=   EXIT
```

FIND

```
III/II ::=   FIND <character string>
III/II ::=   FIND "<character string>"
II     ::=   FIND &<character memvar name>
II     ::=   FIND "&<character memvar name>"
II     ::=   FIND <number>
```

GO

```
III/II ::=   <numeric expression>
III/II ::=   GO <database position>
III/II ::=   GO <numeric expression>
III/II ::=   GOTO <database position>
III/II ::=   GOTO <numeric expression>
```

HELP

```
III/II ::=   HELP
III/II ::=   HELP <keyword>
```

IF...ENDIF

```
III/II ::= IF <logical expression>
              <commands>
           ENDIF
III/II ::= IF <logical expression>
              <commands>
           ELSE
              <commands>
           ENDIF
```

INDEX

```
III/II ::= INDEX ON <key expression> TO <index filename>
II     ::= INDEX
```

INPUT

```
III/II ::= INPUT <prompt> TO <memvar name>
```

INSERT

```
III/II ::= INSERT BLANK [BEFORE]
III/II ::= INSERT [BEFORE]
```

JOIN

```
III    ::= JOIN WITH <alias name> TO <new filename> ;
              FOR <logical expression>
III    ::= JOIN WITH <alias name> TO <new filename> ;
              FOR <logical expression> FIELDS <field name list>
II     ::= JOIN TO <new filename> FOR <logical expression>
II     ::= JOIN TO <new filename> FOR <logical expression> ;
              FIELDS <field name list>
```

LABEL

```
III    ::= LABEL FORM <label filename> [<database parameter>] ;
              [<label options>]
```

LIST

```
III/II ::=  LIST FILES [ON <drive designator>]
III/II ::=  LIST FILES <file directory parameter> ;
                       [ON <drive designator>]
III/II ::=  LIST MEMORY
III/II ::=  LIST STATUS
III/II ::=  LIST STRUCTURE
III/II ::=  LIST [OFF] [<database parameter>] ;
                 [<expression> {,<expression>}]
```

LOAD

```
II     ::=  LOAD <Intel hex-format filename>
```

LOCATE

```
III/II ::=  LOCATE <database parameter>
```

LOOP

```
III/II ::=  DO WHILE <logical expression>
                 <commands-1>
                 LOOP
                 <commands-2>
            ENDDO
```

MODIFY

```
III/II ::=  MODIFY COMMAND <command or procedure filename>
III/II ::=  MODIFY COMMAND <text filename.ext>
III/II ::=  MODIFY STRUCTURE
III    ::=  MODIFY FILE <text filename>
III    ::=  MODIFY LABEL
III    ::=  MODIFY REPORT
```

NOTE

```
III/II ::=  NOTE <comment>
```

PACK

```
III/II ::=  PACK
```

PARAMETERS

```
III    ::=  PARAMETERS <memvar name> {,<memvar name>}
```

POKE

III/II ::= POKE <decimal address>, <data byte> {,<data byte>}

PRIVATE

III   ::= PRIVATE <memvar name> {,<memvar name>}
III   ::= PRIVATE ALL
III   ::= PRIVATE ALL EXCEPT <memvar name skeleton>
III   ::= PRIVATE ALL LIKE <memvar name skeleton>

PROCEDURE

III   ::= PROCEDURE <procedure name>

PUBLIC

III   ::= PUBLIC <memvar name> {,<memvar name>}

QUIT

III/II ::= QUIT
II   ::= QUIT TO <quit parameter> {,<quit parameter>}

READ

III/II ::= READ
II   ::= READ NOUPDATE

RECALL

III/II ::= RECALL [<database parameter>]

REINDEX

III/II ::= REINDEX

RELEASE

III/II ::= RELEASE <memvar name> {,<memvar name>}
III/II ::= RELEASE ALL
III/II ::= RELEASE ALL EXCEPT <memvar name skeleton>
III/II ::= RELEASE ALL LIKE <memvar name skeleton>

REMARK

II   ::= REMARK <character string>

RENAME

III/II ::= RENAME <old filename.ext> TO <new filename.ext>

REPLACE

III/II ::= REPLACE <field name> WITH <expression> ;
                {,<field name> WITH <expression> }
III/II ::= REPLACE <field name> WITH <expression> ;
                {,<field name> WITH <expression> } ;
                  [<database parameter>]

REPORT

III/II ::= REPORT FORM <existing report filename> ;
                    [<database parameter>] [<report options>]
II   ::= REPORT [FORM <new report filename>]

RESET

II   ::= RESET

RESTORE FROM

III/II ::= RESTORE FROM <memvar file name>
III/II ::= RESTORE FROM <memvar file name> ADDITIVE

RETURN

III/II ::= RETURN
III   ::= RETURN TO MASTER

RUN

III   ::= RUN <executable filename or operating system command>
III   ::= ! <executable filename or operating system command>

SAVE TO

III/II ::= SAVE TO <memvar file name> ALL EXCEPT <memvar name skeleton>
III/II ::= SAVE TO <memvar file name> ALL LIKE <memvar name skeleton>
III/II ::= SAVE TO <memvar filename>

SEEK

III   ::= SEEK <expression>

SELECT

```
III/II ::=  SELECT <work area parameter>
```

SET

```
III/II ::=  SET <set parameter> <switch>
III/II ::=  SET <set parameter> TO <set object>
III    ::=  SET
```

SKIP

```
III/II ::=  SKIP
III/II ::=  SKIP <numeric expression>
```

SORT

```
III    ::=  SORT TO <new filename> ON <field name> ;
                [<sort parameter>]{ ,<field name> [<sort parameter>] } ;
                [<database parameter>]
II     ::=  SORT ON <field name> TO <new filename> ;
                [<sort parameter>]
```

STORE

```
III/II ::=  STORE <expression> TO <memvar name> {,<memvar name>}
```

SUM

```
III/II ::=  SUM <numeric expression list> [<database parameter>]
III/II ::=  SUM <numeric expression list> [<database parameter>];
                TO <memvar name list>
III    ::=  SUM [<database parameter>]
III    ::=  SUM [<database parameter>] TO <memvar name list>
```

TEXT...ENDTEXT

```
III/II ::=  TEXT
            { <character string> <new line> }
            ENDTEXT
```

TOTAL

```
III/II ::=  TOTAL ON <key field name> TO <new filename> ;
                [<database parameter>]
III/II ::=  TOTAL ON <key field name> TO <new filename> ;
                [<database parameter>] FIELDS <field name list>
```

TYPE

```
III    ::=   TYPE <text filename.ext>
III    ::=   TYPE <text filename.ext> TO PRINT
```

UNLOCK

```
II     ::=   UNLOCK
II     ::=   UNLOCK INDEX
```

UPDATE

```
III/II ::=   UPDATE FROM <database filename> ON <key field name> ;
                 REPLACE <field name> WITH <expression> ;
                 { ,<field name> WITH <expression> } [RANDOM]
III/II ::=   UPDATE FROM <database filename> ON <key field name> ;
                 [RANDOM]
II     ::=   UPDATE FROM <database filename> ON <key field name> ;
                 ADD <field name list> [RANDOM]
II     ::=   UPDATE FROM <database filename> ON <key field name> ;
                 REPLACE <field name list> [RANDOM]
```

USE

```
III/II ::=   USE <database filename>
III/II ::=   USE <database filename> ALIAS <alias name>
III/II ::=   USE <database filename> INDEX <index filename> ;
                             {,<index filename>}
III/II ::=   USE <database filename> INDEX <index filename> ;
                             {,<index filename>} ;
                 ALIAS <alias name>
```

WAIT

```
III/II ::=   WAIT
III/II ::=   WAIT TO <memvar name>
III    ::=   WAIT <prompt>
III    ::=   WAIT <prompt> TO <memvar name>
```

ZAP

```
III    ::=   ZAP
```

\<keypress\>

```
III/II ::=   <Escape>
III/II ::=   <^P>
III/II ::=   <^S>
III    ::=   <^PrtSc>
II     ::=   <^R>
```

OTHER RESOURCES

&

```
III/II ::=   &<character memvar name>
II     ::=   FIND &<character memvar name>
II     ::=   FIND "&<character memvar name>"
```

,

```
III/II ::=   <command> <item> { , <item> }
```

;

```
III/II ::=   <command line> { ; <new line> <command line> }
```

->

```
III    ::=   <command> <alias name>-><field name>
```

.

```
II     ::=   <command> <work area designator>.<field name>
```

.

```
III/II ::=   <command> &<memvar name>.<character string>
```

()

```
III/II ::=   <command> ( <expression 1> <operator> <expression 2> )
```

" "

```
III/II ::=   "<character string>"
```

' '

```
III/II ::=   '<character string>'
```

[ ]

III/II ::= [<character string>]

;

II   ::= <command> "<text 1> ; <text 2>"

METAVARIABLES

```
<coordinates, screen> ::= <row>, <column>
               <row> ::= Numeric expression, range 0 - 23
                         Also called <line>
            <column> ::= Numeric expression, range 0 - 79
```

```
<coordinates, printer> ::= <row>, <column>
               <row> ::= numeric expression, dBASE II range
                         0 - 65,535, dBASE III range unknown.
                         Also called <line>.
            <column> ::= numeric expression, range 0 - <n>
                 <n> ::= maximum number of columns available
                         on a particular printer
```

```
<database parameter> ::=  <scope> | <condition>
             <scope> ::= ALL | NEXT <n> | RECORD <x>
               ALL ::= The entire database, all records.
          NEXT <n> ::= The next <n> records starting with
                       the current record.
        RECORD <x> ::= The specified record, one only.
               <n> ::= In III, any positive numeric
                       expression.  In II, must be a literal
                       or macro-memvar.  The command will stop
                       when it reaches the current record
                       number + <n> or the end of file,
                       whichever comes first.
               <x> ::= A positive numeric expression between
                       one and the maximum number of records
                       that are in the database file.
         <condition> ::= FOR <logical expression>
                       | WHILE <logical expression>
               FOR ::= Looks at every record from the top
                       of the file to the bottom.  Acts on
                       those records for which the logical
                       expression evaluates to true.  As with
                       all sequential  access, this is
                       considerably slower if the file is indexed.
```

```
           WHILE ::= Looks at, and acts on, the current
                     record and each successive record until
                     the condition is no longer true.  File
                     must be indexed or sorted on a
                     component of the <logical expression>
                     in order for every record meeting the
                     condition to be grouped together where
                     they all can be acted upon.
```

```
     <database position> ::= TOP    | BOTTOM
```

```
     <device parameter> ::= PRINT | SCREEN
```

```
<file directory parameter> ::= LIKE <filename skeleton>
                             | <filename skeleton>    [III]
       <filename skeleton> ::= { <filename character> }
                               { <wildcard symbol> }
      <filename character> ::= Any character allowed by
                               the operating system to be in a filename.
        <wildcard symbol> ::= ? | *
                         ? ::= Any <filename character>
                         * ::= { Any <filename character> }
```

```
       <key expression> ::= <dBASE III expression>
                          | <dBASE II expression>
  <dBASE III expression> ::= Character type to 100 characters
                           | Numeric to largest accurate number
                           | Date type, one date
   <dBASE II expression> ::= Character type to 100 characters
                           | Numeric to largest accurate number
```

```
       <label options> ::= TO PRINT
                         | TO FILE <text filename>       [III]
                         | SAMPLE                        [III]
            TO PRINT ::= Sends output to the printer with an initial
                         form-feed.
             TO FILE ::= Sends output to a text file.  (Use SET
                         ALTERNATE in II.)
              SAMPLE ::= Outputs rows of asterisks (*) which equal
                         the specified size of a single label.
```

```
         <report options> ::= TO PRINT
                              | TO PRINT NOEJECT              [III]
                              | TO FILE <text filename>       [III]
                              | HEADING <character expression> [III]
                              | PLAIN
                  TO PRINT ::= Sends output to the printer with an
                               initial form-feed.
          TO PRINT NOEJECT ::= Sends output to the printer without an
                               initial form-feed. (Use SET EJECT in II.)
                   TO FILE ::= Sends output to a text file.  (Use SET
                               ALTERNATE in II.)
                   HEADING ::= Adds an additional heading to the top
                               line.  (Use SET HEADING in II.)
                     PLAIN ::= Eliminates page numbers, date, and
                               heading(s).  In III, prevents ejects
                               between pages (use POKEs in II).
```

```
         <sort parameter> ::= <dBASE II parameter> | /{<dBASE III parameter>}
    <dBASE II parameter> ::= ASCENDING | DESCENDING
   <dBASE III parameter> ::= A | D | C
                        A ::= Ascending order
                        D ::= Descending order
                        C ::= Case independent (ignores differences
                              between uppercase and lowercase letters)
```

```
                 <switch> ::=  ON | OFF
```

```
    <work area parameter> ::= <dBASE III work area name>
                            | <dBASE II work area name>
 <dBASE III work area name> ::= A | B | C | D | E | F | G | H | I | J
                              | 1 | 2 | 3 | 4 | 5 | 6 | 7 | 8 | 9 | 10
                              | <alias name>
              <alias name> ::= <name specified in ALIAS
                               option of USE command>
                             | <filename of open database
                               file if ALIAS not specified>
 <dBASE II work area name> ::= PRIMARY | SECONDARY
```

```
       <work area prefix> ::= <dBASE III prefix>
                            | <dBASE II prefix>
        <dBASE III prefix> ::= A | B | C | D | E | F | G | H | I | J
                              | <alias name>
         <dBASE II prefix> ::= P | S
   <dBASE III concatenator> ::= ->
    <dBASE II concatenator> ::= .
        <dBASE III example> ::= @ <coordinates> SAY B->Fieldname
         <dBASE II example> ::= @ <coordinates> SAY S.Fieldname
```

ASCII CODE TABLE

CONTROL CHARACTERS

BINARY	HEX	DECIMAL	SYMBOL	CODE	DESCRIPTION
0000000	00	0	NUL	^@	Null
0000001	01	1	SOH	^A	Start of Heading
0000010	02	2	STX	^B	Start of Text
0000011	03	3	ETX	^C	End of Text
0000100	04	4	EOT	^D	End of Transmission
0000101	05	5	ENQ	^E	Enquiry
0000110	06	6	ACK	^F	Acknowledge
0000111	07	7	BEL	^G	Bell
0001000	08	8	BS	^H	Backspace
0001001	09	9	SH	^I	Horizontal Tabulation
0001010	0A	10	LF	^J	Line Feed
0001011	0B	11	VT	^K	Vertical Tabulation
0001100	0C	12	FF	^L	Form Feed
0001101	0D	13	CR	^M	Carriage Return
0001110	0E	14	SO	^N	Shift Out
0001111	0F	15	SI	^O	Shift In
0010000	10	16	DLE	^P	Data Link Escape
0010001	11	17	DC1	^Q	Device Control 1
0010010	12	18	DC2	^R	Device Control 2
0010011	13	19	DC3	^S	Device Control 3
0010100	14	20	DC4	^T	Device Control 4
0010101	15	21	NAK	^U	Negative Acknowledge
0010110	16	22	SYN	^V	Synchronous Idle
0010111	17	23	ETB	^W	End of Transmission Block
0011000	18	24	CAN	^X	Cancel
0011001	19	25	EM	^Y	End of Medium
0011010	1A	26	SUB	^Z	Substitute
0011011	1B	27	ESC	^[	Escape
0011100	1C	28	FS	^\	File Separator
0011101	1D	29	GS	^]	Group Separator
0011110	1E	30	RS	^^	Record Separator
0011111	1F	31	US	^_	Unit Separator

ASCII CODE TABLE

PRINTABLE CHARACTERS

BINARY	HEX	DECIMAL	SYMBOL	BINARY	HEX	DECIMAL	SYMBOL
0100000	20	32	SPACE	1010000	50	80	P
0100001	21	33	!	1010001	51	81	Q
0100010	22	34	"	1010010	52	82	R
0100011	23	35	#	1010011	53	83	S
0100100	24	36	$	1010100	54	84	T
0100101	25	37	%	1010101	55	85	U
0100110	26	38	&	1010110	56	86	V
0100111	27	39	'	1010111	57	87	W
0101000	28	40	(	1011000	58	88	X
0101001	29	41	)	1011001	59	89	Y
0101010	2A	42	*	1011010	5A	90	Z
0101011	2B	43	+	1011011	5B	91	[
0101100	2C	44	,	1011100	5C	92	\
0101101	2D	45	-	1011101	5D	93	]
0101110	2E	46	.	1011110	5E	94	^
0101111	2F	47	/	1011111	5F	95	_
0110000	30	48	0	1100000	60	96	`
0110001	31	49	1	1100001	61	97	a
0110010	32	50	2	1100010	62	98	b
0110011	33	51	3	1100011	63	99	c
0110100	34	52	4	1100100	64	100	d
0110101	35	53	5	1100101	65	101	e
0110110	36	54	6	1100110	66	102	f
0110111	37	55	7	1100111	67	103	g
0111000	38	56	8	1101000	68	104	h
0111001	39	57	9	1101001	69	105	i
0111010	3A	58	:	1101010	6A	106	j
0111011	3B	59	;	1101011	6B	107	k
0111100	3C	60	<	1101100	6C	108	l
0111101	3D	61	=	1101101	6D	109	m
0111110	3E	62	>	1101110	6E	110	n
0111111	3F	63	?	1101111	6F	111	o
1000000	40	64	@	1110000	70	112	p
1000001	41	65	A	1110001	71	113	q
1000010	42	66	B	1110010	72	114	r
1000011	43	67	C	1110011	73	115	s
1000100	44	68	D	1110100	74	116	t
1000101	45	69	E	1110101	75	117	u
1000110	46	70	F	1110110	76	118	v
1000111	47	71	G	1110111	77	119	w
1001000	48	72	H	1111000	78	120	x
1001001	49	73	I	1111001	79	121	y
1001010	4A	74	J	1111010	7A	122	z
1001011	4B	75	K	1111011	7B	123	{
1001100	4C	76	L	1111100	7C	124		
1001101	4D	77	M	1111101	7D	125	}
1001110	4E	78	N	1111110	7E	126	~
1001111	4F	79	O	1111111	7F	127	DEL

Non-printable characters (ASCII code 128 through 255) are graphic characters which vary from machine to machine and thus are not shown here.

APPENDIX F

TECHNICAL SUPPORT AND REFERENCE NOTES

TECHNICAL REFERENCE NOTES

TECHNICAL SUPPORT NOTES

dBASE II 2.3B, 2.4
Technical Reference Note # 2
Copyright 1983, Ashton-Tate, All Rights Reserved

@ <coordinates> [SAY <exp> [USING <format>]]   **10 March 1983**
[GET <variable> [PICTURE <format>]]

The items listed below describe the anomalies to the @...SAY...GET command in dBASE II. Possible work-arounds are also discussed.

1. Logical variables are not displayed properly in @...SAY commands. In many cases, the contents of other memory variables will be displayed. [2.3]

Work-arounds
- Display the logical variable by using an IF statement:

```
IF logical
    @ x,y SAY ".T."
ELSE
    @ x,y SAY ".F."
ENDIF
```

- Display the logical variable by using the ? command:

```
? logical
```

2. When using an @...SAY...USING statement with an "##/##" format to display a string variable, the "##/##" will be displayed instead of the variable. [2.3, 2.4]

Work-around
- Use the "XX/XX" clause instead of the "##/##"

3. The @...SAY with or without the USING or PICTURE clause will not properly display numeric variables larger than nine places. An overflow condition will be displayed in the form of leading asterisks ("****") and some trailing digits. A larger format value for the USING or PICTURE will not correct the problem either. [2.3]

Work-around
- Convert the numeric variable to a character string and print the character string:

```
@ row,col SAY STR( number, 14, 2 )
```

or

```
STORE STR( number, 14, 2 ) TO string
@ row,col SAY string
```

4. When using the substring ("$") function in an @...SAY command, if the third parameter in the substring function is a numeric variable, the output will not display correctly. For example, the following segment of code will display an incomplete portion of the contents of the memory variable "source." [2.3, 2.4]

```
* ---The following code will not give the desired results.
STORE "this is a string" TO source
STORE 3 TO length
@ row,col SAY $( source, 1, length)
```

Work-around
- STORE the substring to a memory variable and display the memory variable:

```
* ---This will work.
STORE $( source, 3, 8 ) TO string
@ row,col SAY string
```

5. When using an @...SAY...USING statement with an "xxxx" format to display a string variable, the "x"s are displayed instead of the value in the variable. [2.3, 2.4]

Work-around
● Use uppercase "X"s instead of lowercase.

6. When using an @...SAY...USING statement with an "AAAA" format to display a string variable, the "A"s are displayed instead of the value in the variable. [2.3, 2.4]

7. When using an @...SAY...USING statement with an "XXXX" format to display a numeric variable, the "X"s are displayed instead of the value in the variable. [2.3]

Work-around
● Use "9"s instead of "X"s.

8. After 64 @...SAY...GETs or @...GETs the cursor will go wild (usually, to the far right of the screen) and the system will hang. [2.3, 2.4]

Work-around
● Use CLEAR GETS or ERASE before the 64th GET to clear the GET table.

9. READing a numeric variable with an @...GET...PICTURE clause with a format beginning with a period will not work correctly. For example, in the following segment of code, if one enters a value of "123," the memory variable "number" will receive a value of "123.000" instead of the desired value of "0.123." [2.3, 2.4]

```
* ---The following code will not give the desired results.
@ row,col GET number PICTURE ".999"
READ
```

Work-around
● Begin the numeric PICTURE clause with the character nine, such as,

```
* ---This will work.
@ row,col GET number PICTURE "9.999"
READ
```

10. The TRIM function does not work in @...SAY commands. For example, the following segment of code will print the trailing blanks of the "source." [2.3, 2.4]

```
* ---The following code will not give the desired results.
STORE "hello   " TO source
@ row,col SAY TRIM( source )
```

Work-around
● STORE the TRIM of the memory variable to another memory variable and display the variable, such as,

```
* ---This will work.
STORE "hello   " TO source
STORE TRIM( source ) TO string
@ row,col SAY string
```

dBASE II version 2.3B, 2.4
Technical Reference Note # 9
Copyright 1983, Ashton-Tate, All Rights Reserved

Notes on using multiple indexes.
17 March 1983
Revised: 14 February 1984

There are some known difficulties in using multiple indexes on a data file. Listed below are the difficulties and some known solutions.

1. dBASE II will only update the master index, when PACKing a database with more than one index open. [2.3]

2. dBASE II will take a very long time to update records when performing READs and REPLACEs on multiple indexes. The reason is that dBASE will sequentially scan through the second (and subsequent) indexes to locate the record number so as to update the key. It does not traverse the index tree, since it assumes the key has been modified. Some ways of getting around this slow updating process are listed below. These methods assume the PRIMARY area has the data file with the multiple indexes and the SECONDARY area has either no data file in USE or a data file with only one index in USE. The Names data file has two fields (Name and Address); where Index1 is indexed on the Name and Index2 is indexed on the Address. [2.3, 2.4]

• If there is no data file in the SECONDARY or the data file in the SECONDARY is in USE with only one index, then perform the GETs and READ to memory variables in the SECONDARY, and the REPLACEs in the PRIMARY. The reason for this is that dBASE II will perform the sequential scan through the second index on the READ statement as well as on the REPLACE. By performing the READ in the SECONDARY, one eliminates one sequential scan. See below.

```
USE Names INDEX Index1,Index2
STORE Name TO mname
SELECT SECONDARY
@ 5,0 SAY "Edit name" GET mname
READ
CLEAR GETS
SELECT PRIMARY
REPLACE Name WITH mname
```

• If there is no data file in the SECONDARY, then set up a workfile in the SECONDARY with the identical structure and do any adding or updating to the workfile, but only REPLACEs and APPENDs to the PRIMARY. See below.

```
* ---Initialization.
USE Names INDEX Index1,Index2
COPY STRUCTURE TO Workfile
SELECT SECONDARY
USE Workfile
APPEND BLANK
* ---If updating, then do the following:
SELECT SECONDARY
REPLACE Name WITH P.Name
@ 5,0 SAY "Edit name" GET Name
READ
CLEAR GETS
SELECT PRIMARY
REPLACE Name WITH S.Name
* ---If adding records, then do the following:
SELECT SECONDARY
DELETE ALL
APPEND BLANK
@ 5,0 SAY "Enter new name" GET Name
READ
CLEAR GETS
SELECT PRIMARY
* Deleted records will not be APPENDed.
APPEND FROM Workfile
```

- Close the indexes alternatively as one is doing the adding or updating of records. See below.

```
* ---If adding records.
USE Names INDEX Index1,Index2
APPEND BLANK
STORE # TO recordnum
* Index1 is indexed on Name.
SET INDEX TO Index1
GO recordnum
@ 5,0 SAY "Enter name" GET Name
READ
CLEAR GETS
* Index2 is indexed on Address.
SET INDEX TO Index2
GO recordnum
@ 6,0 SAY "Enter address" GET Address
READ
CLEAR GETS
SET INDEX TO Index1,Index2
* ---If updating records.
USE Names INDEX Index1,Index2
FIND &mkey
STORE # TO recordnum
SET INDEX TO Index1
GO recordnum
```

```
@ 5,0 SAY "Edit name" GET Name
READ
CLEAR GETS
SET INDEX TO Index2
GO recordnum
@ 6,0 SAY "Edit address" GET Address
READ
CLEAR GETS
SET INDEX TO Index1,Index2
```

- Open the data file both in PRIMARY and SECONDARY with one index in each, do the READs in one area, and do REPLACEs to the other area. This method is tricky (and you may corrupt your data file if you're not careful how you implement it). *This method only works on version 2.3, since 2.3 allows the same data file to be opened in both areas.* [2.3]

```
USE Names INDEX Index1
SELECT SECONDARY
USE Names INDEX Index2
SELECT PRIMARY
@ 5,0 SAY "Edit name" GET Name
@ 6,0 SAY "Edit address" GET Address
READ
CLEAR GETS
SELECT SECONDARY
REPLACE Name WITH P.Name, Address WITH P.Address
```

---

dBASE II version 2.3, 2.4
Technical Reference Note # 11
Copyright 1983, Ashton-Tate, All Rights Reserved

Known difficulties using MODIFY COMMAND   **28 March 1983**
                                                              Revised: 14 February 1984

MODIFY COMMAND does not always function properly, and will sometimes give unexpected results. Listed below are the difficulties we have experienced with the command. We suggest you always maintain backup copies of your command files when making changes. These problems are being addressed in the next release of dBASE II. Instead of the MODIFY COMMAND, you may want to use a word processor such as Screen Editor (SED) available from Ashton-Tate.

1. Extraneous data is occasionally appended to the end of the command file.

- The extraneous data can be deleted by using MODIFY COMMAND's cursor commands for deleting lines or individual characters.
- A "RETURN" statement may be inserted just before the extraneous material in order to prevent dBASE II from attempting to read it.

2. In responding to the command MODIFY COMMAND <filename>, dBASE II will occasionally load the ".BAK" file instead of the ".PRG" file. Consequently, the modifications you believe you are making to the ".PRG" file will actually be recorded in the ".BAK" version of that file. When you later execute the command file and dBASE II runs the ".PRG" file, it will appear as though dBASE did not save the modifications you made to the file. [2.3]

- We recommend that you include the extension ".PRG" in the MODIFY COMMAND syntax (e.g., "MODIFY COMMAND Menu.prg"). This will prevent dBASE II from loading the wrong file.

3. When you attempt to enlarge a command file stored on a disk that is almost filled to capacity, dBASE II will sometimes corrupt the disk's contents. For this reason, avoid using the command when your disk is nearly full. Instead, copy the file to another disk with plenty of free disk space.

4. On rare occasions, dBASE II will write command line instructions into the data fields of an open database.
- We recommend closing all databases and associated indexes prior to using MODIFY COMMAND.

---

dBASE II 2.3B, 2.4
Technical Reference Note # 12
Copyright 1983, Ashton-Tate, All Rights Reserved

SET ALTERNATE TO [<file>] 13 May 1983

This command is used to assign all output to a disk textfile. The command SET ALTERNATE TO <file> with a filename will open the ALTERNATE file. However, on 2.3B the SET ALTERNATE without a filename will generate a null directory entry (see below). This command is used in conjunction with the SET ALTERNATE ON/OFF flag. The SET ALTERNATE ON will enable the echoing process, and the SET ALTERNATE OFF will turn it off.

1. The SET ALTERNATE TO without a filename will generate a null directory entry. This is the command to close the ALTERNATE file, but it cannot be used. [2.3]

Work-around
- Use the CLEAR or QUIT command to close the ALTERNATE file, or open another ALTERNATE file.

2. @...SAY commands do not send output to the ALTERNATE file (that is, not with just the SET ALTERNATE ON command). You will have to use the SET FORMAT TO PRINT command in addition to the SET ALTERNATE ON. [2.3, 2.4]

Work-around
- Use the SET FORMAT TO PRINT command in addition to the SET ALTERNATE ON in the following way:

```
SET ALTERNATE TO <filename>
SET ALTERNATE ON
```

```
SET FORMAT TO PRINT
* ---Disable the printer (limited to CP/M 2.2).
POKE PEEK( 2 ) * 256 + 15, 201
*
*     Statements using the @...SAY commands go here.
*
* ---Enable the printer (limited to CP/M 2.2).
POKE PEEK( 2 ) * 256 + 15, 195
SET FORMAT TO SCREEN
SET ALTERNATE OFF
```

3. Issuing the command DISPLAY FILE LIKE *.* will upset the output to an ALTERNATE file. [2.3]

Work-around

● This problem is corrected in version 2.4.

4. If output to an ALTERNATE file is done from a command file, that command file must not contain blank lines, as they will append garbage to the ALTERNATE file. [2.3]

Work-around
● Blank lines should be deleted from the command file.

---

dBASE II version 2.3, 2.4
Technical Reference Note # 13
Copyright 1983, Ashton-Tate, All Rights Reserved

Known difficulties using index files in dBASE II.   **6 May 1983**
                                                                  Revised: 8 March 1984

1. Negative SKIPs on an indexed data file does not work because dBASE II loses its place in the index. An example of this is when performing a LIST after a SKIP <-number>. The records will not list in sequence. If this disordered condition exists when a REPLACE command is executed, a duplicate index entry may be added to the index file. [2.3]

2. INSERTing a record on an indexed data file will create three index entries at the current index pointer position. Therefore, it is not possible to INSERT with an index open on version 2.3.

3. The following sequence of commands will create two index entries at the current index pointer position. There is no work-around. You will not be able to use these two commands in sequence. [2.3]

```
DISPLAY RECORD <number>
REPLACE <field> WITH <value>
```

4. The index expression cannot exceed 100 characters. However, the FIND command cannot find on a key expression of 99 and 100 characters. [2.3]

● Key expressions of 98 and fewer characters will work.

5. An index file will become unbalanced when the key field is consistently modified. Two error messages indicating the index has become unbalanced are RECORD NOT IN INDEX and END-OF-FILE FOUND UNEXPECTEDLY. [2.3, 2.4]

- The index file will need to be recreated with the INDEX ON <expression> TO <index filename> command. Or, in version 2.4 with the REINDEX command. Such as,

```
* ---On version 2.3
USE <file>
INDEX ON <exp> TO <indexfile>

* ---On version 2.4
USE <file> INDEX <indexfile>
REINDEX
```

- A batch method of updating records where the key field is expected to be modified is given below.

```
* ---Update.cmd
USE Mainfile INDEX Mainname
COPY STRUCTURE TO Main.$$$
SELECT SECONDARY
USE Main.$$$
STORE T TO is:more
DO WHILE is:more
    SELECT PRIMARY
    ACCEPT "Enter key" TO mkey
    IF mkey = " "
        STORE F TO is:more
        LOOP
    ENDIF
    FIND &mkey
    IF # = 0
        ? "NO FIND"
        LOOP
    ENDIF
    DELETE
    SELECT SECONDARY
    APPEND BLANK
    REPLACE Name WITH P.Name, Address WITH P.Address
    @ 5,0 SAY "Name...." GET Name
    @ 6,0 SAY "Address." GET Address
    READ
    CLEAR GETS
ENDDO
```

```
SELECT SECONDARY
USE
SELECT PRIMARY
APPEND FROM Main.$$$
USE
* EOF: Update.cmd
```

6. The index file will not get updated correctly when PACKing a large data file that has many deleted records.[2.3]

• PACK the data file with no indexes open, then rebuild the indexes with the INDEX ON <expression> TO <index filename> command. Such as,

```
* ---Using the PACK command.
USE <file>
PACK
INDEX ON <exp> TO <indexfile>
* ---Using the COPY command to pack.
USE <origfile>
COPY STRUCTURE TO <tempfile>
USE
DELETE FILE <origfile>
RENAME <tempfile> TO <origfile>
USE <origfile>
INDEX ON <exp> TO <indexfile>
```

7. Logical fields are not indexed correctly. There is no work-around. [2.3, 2.4]
8. Cannot index on the concatenation of two numeric fields. The numeric fields will be summed instead of concatenated. [2.3, 2.4]

• The fields will have to be converted to STRings when creating the index. Such as,

```
INDEX ON STR(part:no,5)+STR(subpart,3) TO indexname
```

9. Using INSERT BLANK on an indexed database places the operator into the INSERTed record in full-screen mode. Use APPEND BLANK when dealing with an open index. [2.3, 2.41]

---

dBASE II 2.3B, 2.4
Technical Support Note # 10.1
Copyright 1982, Ashton-Tate, All Rights Reserved

Disabling the semicolon function.   **2 June 1983**

The semicolon has two uses in dBASE II. The one familiar to most users is in its use as a continuation symbol for command lines. The other use is for the centering of strings. This function was designed for the

REPORT FORM command but extends to the other display commands such as ?, LIST, and DISPLAY. An undesirable side effect of the centering function is that the semicolon itself cannot be displayed.

To allow users the ability to output the semicolon character, the following POKE statement was developed. It will disable the semicolon's ability to center strings. However, it will not affect its function as a continuation symbol for command lines.

1. It can be temporarily POKEd while in dBASE II.

   To disable the semicolon function:

   ```
   POKE 3353,255        (version 2.3, 8-bit)
   POKE 4803,255        (version 2.3D, 16-bit)
   ```

   To restore the semicolon function:

   ```
   POKE 3353,59         (version 2.3, 8-bit)
   POKE 4803,59         (version 2.3D, 16-bit)
   ```

2. On dBASE II version 2.4 the SET RAW ON command will automatically disable the semicolon function.

---

dBASE II version 2.3, 2.4, 2.41
Technical Support Note # 11.4
Copyright 1983, Ashton-Tate, All Rights Reserved

Disabling page ejects.
2 June 1983
Revised: 26 July 1984

The page eject routine is executed (1) whenever an EJECT command is used or (2) whenever the row coordinate in an @ <row>,<col> SAY command being sent to the printer decreases in value.

When sending a page eject to the printer, dBASE II does the following:

1. Send a formfeed character (ASCII 12) to the LST: device.
2. Zero-out the dBASE II line counter for the printer.

Many programmers have requested the disabling of this routine so as to print duplicate reports on a single page. The POKE instruction that follows is designed to meet this request. It will disable page eject, but will still zero-out the line counter. However, this is not the recommended way to program your applications (see item 2).

1. It can be temporarily POKEd while in dBASE II.

   To disable the sending of the formfeed:

```
        POKE 14888,0,0            (version 2.3b, Osborne only)
        POKE 15025,0,0            (version 2.4, Osborne only)
        POKE 15001,0,0            (version 2.4, Apple only)
        POKE 15021,0,0            (version 2.3b, 8-bit)
        POKE 15170,0,0            (version 2.4, 8-bit)
        POKE 15325,0,0            (version 2.41, 8-bit)
        POKE 19329,144,144,144    (version 2.3D, 16-bit)
        POKE 20100,144,144,144    (version 2.4, CPM-86)
        POKE 20034,144,144,144    (version 2.4, MS-DOS)
        POKE 19984,144,144,144    (version 2.41, MS-DOS)
```

To restore the sending of the formfeed:

```
        POKE 14888,205,5          (version 2.3b, Osborne only)
        POKE 15025,205,5          (version 2.4, Osborne only)
        POKE 15001,205,5          (version 2.4, Apple only)
        POKE 15021,205,5          (version 2.3b, 8-bit)
        POKE 15170,205,5          (version 2.4, 8-bit)
        POKE 15325,205,5          (version 2.41, 8-bit)
        POKE 19329,232,197,183    (version 2.3D, 16-bit)
        POKE 20100,232,203,180    (version 2.4, CPM-86)
        POKE 20034,232, 13,181    (version 2.4, MS-DOS)
        POKE 19984,232, 63,181    (version 2.41, MS-DOS)
```

2. Normally, one would not need to use the above POKE instruction. The command file given
    below is a model of how most multi-page reports should be constructed.

```
        USE Filename
        SET FORMAT TO PRINT
        STORE 51 TO row
        DO WHILE .NOT. EOF
           IF row >= 50
              @ 1,0 SAY "REPORT HEADING"
              STORE 4 TO row
           ENDIF
           @ row,   0 SAY Field1
           @ row,  40 SAY Field2
           @ row+1, 0 SAY Field3
           @ row+2,40 SAY Field4
           STORE row+4 TO row
           SKIP
        ENDDO
        RELEASE row
        SET FORMAT TO SCREEN
        RETURN
```

dBASE II 2.3B, 2.4
Technical Support Note # 16
Copyright 1983, Ashton-Tate, All Rights Reserved

Changing the record count of a dBASE II header. 9 March 1983

What follows are some known methods for correcting a faulty record count in a dBASE II data file. *Method 1.* This method does *not* work in all instances. Enter dBASE and type the following:

```
. USE <sickfile>
. APPEND
```

At this point, the screen will clear and dBASE will display the proper format for appending new records to the use file. Check the displayed record number. If it appears correct, enter a new record and then exit APPEND. This should correct the record count exhibited in the data file header. (You may then delete the new record.) If it is incorrect, then exit APPEND; this method will not work.

```
. CLEAR
. QUIT
```

Method 2. Use the COPY command and make a new copy of the file under a different filename. Since the COPY command keeps an internal counter, it will restore the correct record count to the header of the new file after completing the copy.
Enter dBASE II and type the following:

```
. USE <sickfile>
. COPY TO <newfile>
```

Method 3. With this method you will need to create and run a BASIC program. This program will work with Microsoft BASIC or PC-DOS BASIC. You can write this program in dBASE with MODIFY COMMAND (see below).

```
100 'Program.: FIXHEAD.BAS
102 'Author..: Luis A. Castro
103 'Date....: March 9, 1983
104 'Notes...: To run this program, type the following:
106 '
112 '    A>MBASIC FIXHEAD    (MicroSoft BASIC)
114 '    A>BASICA FIXHEAD    (IBM PC BASIC)
116 '
200 PRINT "Changing record count on header of DBF file"
210 PRINT
220 INPUT "Enter filename   ", FILENAME$
230 OPEN "R", #1, FILENAME$, 3
240 FIELD #1, 1 AS DUMMY$, 2 AS OLDNUMBER$
250 GET #1, 1
260 PRINT "Number of records "; CVI( OLDNUMBER$ )
270 INPUT "         Change to  ", NEWNUMBER%
```

```
280 LSET OLDNUMBER$ = MKI$( NEWNUMBER% )
290 PUT #1, 1
300 SYSTEM
```

Method 4. Can use DDT or DEBUG to patch the two bytes in the data file header containing the record count. This method assumes the entire data file will fit into memory at one time and you should not use this method otherwise. The new record count value must be converted to hexadecimal before it can be patched in.

IF DDT IS AVAILABLE:

```
A>DDT Filename.DBF        (user input is in boldface)
  <DDT version information>
NEXT PC
yyyy xxxx
-S101
0101 ll  aa    (where aa is low-order byte of new value)
0102 hh  bb    (where bb is high-order byte of new value)
0103 xx  .

-<control-C>
A>SAVE pp Filename.DBF   (where pp is the number of pages)
```

IF DEBUG IS AVAILABLE:

```
A>DEBUG Filename.DBF       (user input is in boldface)
-E 101
xxxx:0101  ll.aa <space> hh.bb <RETURN>
      (where aa is the low-order and bb is the high-order
       byte of the new record count value)
-W
-Q

A>
```

---

dBASE II version 2.3B, 2.4
Technical Support Note # 20.1
Copyright 1983, Ashton-Tate, All Rights Reserved

Using dBASE II under the MP/M operating system.   **16 March 1983**
                                                                        Revised: 14 February 1984

dBASE II, under MP/M, is not able to share data files and update them with the proper record locking or file locking required. dBASE II was designed for single-user systems and does not implement record lock or file lock. Therefore, when attempts are made to use data files in a shared mode, the results are unpredictable. The patches and notes that follow are not intended to allow dBASE II to run as a multi-user system, but to allow dBASE II to run with reasonable performance on a multi-user environment as a *single-user system*.

1. The patch that follows is the true close patch. It forces dBASE II to close the data file when the user closes the file in dBASE II. The error message, "FILE IS CURRENTLY OPEN," will occur frequently if this patch is not made. This patch assumes that both the debugger tool (DDT, RDT, or MONITOR) and DBASE.COM are on the same disk drive. [only for 2.3]

IF CP/M IS AVAILABLE, TYPE THE FOLLOWING:

```
A>DDT DBASE.COM        (user input is in boldface)
  <DDT header>
NEXT PC
4800 0100
-S3D4F
3D4F 01 00
3D50 C3 .
-<control-C>
A>SAVE 71 DBASE.COM
```

IF ONLY MP/M IS AVAILABLE:

```
0I>RDT DBASE.COM       (user input is in boldface)
   <RDT header>
NEXT PC
4800 0100
-S3D4F
3D4F 01 00
3D50 C3 .
-IDBASE.COM
-W008E
-<control-C>
0I>
```

IF ONLY TURBODOS IS AVAILABLE:

```
0A}MONITOR      (user input is in boldface)

* L DBASE.COM
0100-47FF
* E 3D4F
3D4F  01= 00
3D50  C3= <ESCAPE>
* S DBASE.COM
0100-47FF
* Q
0A}
```

On version 2.4, the above one-byte patch is automatically inserted from the INSTALL program. The user will run INSTALL, select the appropriate terminal option he or she is using, then type "Y" at the following prompt:

```
CHANGE MACRO, DATE, ETC. (Y/N)?
```

One of the prompts that follow will allow the user to select the operating system. Select "B" for MP/M II, and the true close patch will be made. The prompt will appear as follows:

```
ENTER OPERATING SYSTEM
     A - CP/M 2.2
     B - MP/M II SYSTEM
```

2. On occasion MP/M will print a close checksum error on the screen and terminate dBASE II. Checksum verification under MP/M is designed to "insure that the activity of one user does not adversely affect other users on the system." These checksum errors under MP/M are caused by restrictions to the way FCBs are handled, and are not implemented on CP/M systems. To ensure upward compatibility from CP/M, MP/M is provided with compatibility attribute flags that can be set to ignore these checksum errors. For more information on these compatibility attribute flags and how to properly enable them, you will want to refer to:

MP/M II Operating System
PROGRAMMER'S GUIDE
MP/M II V2.1 Compatibility Attributes
Addendum #1 to the First Printing - 1981
MP/M is a trademark of Digital Research
Compiled February 4, 1982

On MP/M you will want to SET compatibility attribute F3 to ON for all dBASE II files.

3. On some hardware configurations using MP/M the SORT and INDEX command's will fail when using "large" data files. An alternate way of sorting is by using the COPY command with an index file (that is, if the index was created successfully). The proper way to do this is listed below.

```
USE <oldfile>
INDEX ON <keyfield> TO <indexfile>
USE <oldfile> INDEX <indexfile>
COPY TO <sortedfile>
```

4. The QUIT TO command does not work and there is no work around.

5. We suggest the user close and reopen his or her data files before *and* after any complex sequence of commands to insure the proper updating of the files. You may use the CLEAR command to close the data files or the USE command with no filename. If two data files are in use, remember to SELECT each of the workareas (SELECT SECONDARY and SELECT PRIMARY) when performing the USE with no filename.

---

dBASE II 2.3D
Technical Support Note # 27
Copyright 1983, RSP Inc., All Rights Reserved

REPORT FORM patch for IBM PC with   **14 March 1983**
MS-DOS and CP/M-86.

   This patch fixes a problem after a number of complicated REPORT FORM commands. A large range of manifestations is likely with different programs. It is assumed a copy of your system disk is on drive A and a copy of our dBASE II system disk is on drive B.

   Notes from Wayne: There is one too many PUSH instructions. The PUSH is in all 8080 releases of dBASE but does not cause a problem (yet), because the main overlay always resets the stack pointer. This bug took over eight hours to find.

```
A>DEBUG DBASERPG.OVR        (User input is in boldface)

-E544 90

-U544

XXXX:0544 90          NOP
XXXX:0545 87DA        XCHG       BX,DX

-W

-Q

A>
```

---

dBASE II version 2.3, 2.4
Technical Support Note # 36
Copyright 1983, Ashton-Tate, All Rights Reserved

Recreating a corrupted dBASE II header.   **31 May 1983**

   To "recreate" a corrupted dBASE II data file header, follow the steps listed below. This method will only work with a dBASE II header that contains 31 or fewer fields. You will also need to run a BASIC program.

   Step 1 Use the CREATE command in dBASE II to construct a new dBASE II header.

   Step 2 Run the BASIC program listed below. This program will work with Microsoft BASIC or PC-DOS BASICA. You can write this program in dBASE II with the MODIFY COMMAND.

```
100 'Program.: NEWHEAD.BAS
101 'Author..: Luis A. Castro
102 'Date....: May 31, 1983
103 'Notes...: The headers involved must have 31 or fewer fields.
120 '          Run the program from CP/M or DOS as follows:
130 '
140 '     A>MBASIC NEWHEAD/S:520     (MicroSoft BASIC)
150 '     A>BASICA NEWHEAD/S:520     (IBM PC BASIC)
160 '
200 PRINT "Inserting a new dBASE II header" : PRINT
210 INPUT "Enter new header FILENAME.EXT ", FILE.NEW$
220 OPEN "R", #1, FILE.NEW$, 520
230 FIELD #1, 1 AS NEWCODE$, 2 AS NEWRECS$, 5 AS NEWDATE.SIZE$
240 FIELD #1, 8 AS D$, 240 AS NEW1$, 240 AS NEW2$, 32 AS NEW3$
250 GET #1, 1
260 INPUT "Enter receiving FILENAME.EXT  ", FILE.OLD$
270 OPEN "R", #2, FILE.OLD$, 520
280 FIELD #2, 1 AS OLDCODE$, 2 AS OLDRECS$, 5 AS OLDDATE.SIZE$
290 FIELD #2, 8 AS D$, 240 AS OLD1$, 240 AS OLD2$, 32 AS OLD3$
300 PRINT "Number of records "; CVI( OLDRECS$ )
310 INPUT "         Change to  ", NEWRECS%
315 LSET OLDCODE$ = NEWCODE$
320 LSET OLDRECS$ = MKI$( NEWRECS% )
330 LSET OLDDATE.SIZE$ = NEWDATE.SIZE$
350 LSET OLD1$ = NEW1$
360 LSET OLD2$ = NEW2$
370 LSET OLD3$ = NEW3$
380 PUT #2, 1
390 SYSTEM
```

dBASE II 2.4 (16-bit)
Technical Support Note #72.3
Copyright 1983, Ashton-Tate, All Rights Reserved

Patch for dBASE II version 2.4   **2 February 1984**
to support the International Character Set.

Microsoft has modified MS-DOS to support the International Character Set. Some MS-DOS versions contain an undocumented feature that allows filenames to contain any of the international characters. Following is a patch to dBASE II, version 2.4, to support this feature. After the patch has been made, dBASE II will sign on as "Ver 2.4A".

This patch assumes DEBUG.COM and DBASE.COM are on drive A.

NOTE: <S> = space bar; user input is in boldface.

```
A> DEBUG DBASE.COM
-E53F8  <CR>
19D3:53F8  0A.90  <S>  C5.90  <CR>
-E7C16  <CR>
19D3:7C16  20.41  <CR>
-W  <CR>
Writing 7E00 bytes
-Q  <CR>
```

The following is a patch to the dBASE II DEMONSTRATOR:

```
A> DEBUG DBASE.COM
-E53E0  <CR>
19D3:53E0  0A.90  <S>  C5.90  <CR>
-E7C00  <CR>
19D3:7C00  20.41  <CR>
-W  <CR>
Writing 7E00 bytes
-Q  <CR>
A>
```

The following is a patch to Friday!:

```
A> DEBUG FRIDAY.COM
-E53F8  <CR>
19D3:53F8  0A.90  <S>  C5.90  <CR>

-W  <CR>
Writing 7C00 bytes
-Q  <CR>*
```

The above patch will also work on RunTime by patching DBRUN.COM.

---

dBASE II 2.4 (16-bit)
Technical Support Note #74.1
Copyright 1984, Ashton-Tate, All Rights Reserved

Patch to correct dBASE II from cutting off the   **2 February 1984**
last few lines of a command procedure.

dBASE II version 2.4 under MS-DOS will not read the last 512 byte block of a text file such as a .PRG file when the last block contains less than 128 bytes. Consequently, certain errors will arise. Some that have been reported are listed below:

●   Syntax errors at the end of the command file.

- The error message "COMMAND FILE CANNOT BE FOUND" displays when attempting to DO a command file.
- Command execution stops unexpectedly and returns to the dot prompt.
- The RunTime version does not "crunch" command files completely.

The following patch will correct this problem under MSDOS for DBASE.COM *only*. It will not correct the problem in DBRUN.COM. This patch assumes both DEBUG.COM and DBASE.COM are on drive A.

NOTE: <S> = space bar; user input is in boldface.

```
A> DEBUG DBASE.COM
- E5662  <CR>
1028:5662  OA.E9  <S>  CO.3D <S>  75.21 <CR>

- E77A2  <CR>
1028:77A2  00.3C  <S>  00.03  <S>  00.74 <S>  00.04  <S>
           00.08  <S>  00.CO  <S>

1028:77A8  00.75  <S>  00.03  <S>  00.E 9 <S>  00.B9  <S>
           00.DE  <S>  00.E9  <S>

1028:77AE  00.D4  <S>  00.DE  <CR>

- W  <CR>
Writing 7EOO bytes
- Q  <CR>

A>
```

CURRICULUM FOR EDUCATORS

This curriculum was written to complement the *Advanced Programmer's Guide*. It is intended as a module to implement in a classroom. No particular learning sequence is implied by the order of the curriculum; it simply follows the lines of the book. The learning sequence is best determined by an experienced educator who can structure the course according to the skills and goals of the group.

As with any subject matter which requires that the student analyze and learn a vocabulary, student skills become synonymous with study skills. We stress, for the sanity of both the student and teacher, the use of dictionaries and other references applying what was *just* studied to a practical application. After the student uses the new skill a couple of times it is no longer "new." Going on to the next item becomes an adventure into "what else can be done."

Mark Kevitt
Training and Curriculum Development Manager
Ashton-Tate
August, 1984

FUNDAMENTALS

Computerized Data Management (Chapter 1)

Completion Objective The student will be able to identify the need for computerization of information management systems.

Subject Detailed:

1. Data vs. information defined.
2. Function of a computer system defined.
3. Basic components of information residing in a computer system: data, programs, instruction set, binary representation of data, and ASCII.

Purpose(s) The benefits gained through using computers in managingdata is furthered by this basic examination of the fundamentals.

Basic Computer Literacy—Hardware (Chapter 1)

Completion Objective The student will be able to identify the principle elements of a computer system, and relate programs and data to the functionality of the principal elements.

Subject Detailed:

1. Definition and relationships of principal elements:
   a. Central Processing Unit (CPU)
   b. Main Memory (RAM)
   c. Secondary Storage (disk drives, magnetic tape, etc.)
   d. Input/Output Devices (terminals, printers, etc.)
2. Functional relationship between principal elements and data or programs with the integration of:
   a. Registers
   b. Arithmetic and Logic Unit
   c. Control Unit
   d. Organization of data on disks
3. Explanation of factors influencing computing speed.

Purpose(s) By understanding these hardware fundamentals, analysis of the needs of an organization with respect to the required hardware to implement the data processing is facilitated.

Basic Computer Literacy—Operating System (Chapter 2)

Completion Objective The student will be able to:

1. Identify the basic purpose and functions of operating systems.
2. Use the functional parts and utilities which compose the most popular microcomputer operating systems.

Subject Detailed:

1. Definition of operating systems.
2. Functional parts of DOS and CP/M.
3. The relationship between the operating system and dBASE.

Purpose(s) Having the basic knowledge on operating systems further aids in the resolution of a company's hardware and software requirements for data processing.

Basic Computer Literacy—Languages (Chapter 3)

Completion Objective The student will be able to:

1. Choose a language appropriate for an application.
2. Delineate the steps in generating a running application with compiled language.
3. Explain the strengths of interpreted languages, pseudo compilers, and procedural vs. nonprocedural languages.

Subject Detailed Explain and illustrate:

1. Languages versus applications.
2. Composition of machine language.
3. Use of assembly language.

4. High level languages, compiled languages, interpreted languages, and pseudo compilers.
5. Procedural versus nonprocedural languages.

Purpose(s) By having the fundamental knowledge about languages,the development time is reduced and functionality of the intended application is greatly enhanced.

Basic Computer Literacy—Programming (Chapters 4, 5)

Completion Objective The student will know how to approach programming an application in a structured manner:

1. Defining the problem.
2. Designing a solution.
3. Coding.
4. Documentation.
5. Software testing.
6. Debugging.

Subject Detailed:

1. Programming defined.
2. Problem definition and typical questions, such as purpose, inputs, outputs, and operations.
3. Designing a solution: modularity, relationship between variables and constants in the problem, top down approach, stepwise refinement, simplicity, research existing algorithms. selection of the best data structures, and use of control structures (sequencing, branching, repetition, subprograms).
4. Coding: pseudo-code first, top-down design, using library routines, short and independent modules, use procedures in dBASE III.
5. Documentation: definition of purpose and what constitutes "good" documentation, establishing and maintaining a change log, preambles in each section, internal comments, variable names and field names which have meaning, position using indentations for meaning.
6. Testing and debugging: debugging defined, examples emphasizing testing, testing procedures outlined, common types of errors, such as syntax, logic, misunderstanding program design, explained.

Purpose(s) Having the basic knowledge of programming reduces error, speeds development, and allows the student to achieve completion of an application either through managing programmers or learning the language and personally writing the application.

dBASE Data Fundamentals (Chapters 6, 7)

Completion Objective The student will be able to use dBASE's data types (character, numeric,logical, date, and memo fields) to construct different data structures.
Subject Detailed:

1. Data type defined.
2. Character data type defined and common operations illustrated: concatenating strings, splitting up strings, testing strings for equality, and finding substrings.

3. Numeric data type defined, dBASE II and III limits, arithmetic procedures and mathematical functions.
4. Implementation of logical data type, Boolean operators, relational operators, arithmetic operators.
5. Definition of purpose and dBASE III handling of date data type and memo fields.
6. Definition and relationship of relational to structured data types.
7. The use and definition of dBASE's two structured data types (data file-static and index file-dynamic).
8. Internal structure of dBASE's two structured data types.
9. Use of dBASE data files to construct trees and networks.

Purpose(s) By being able to use dBASE to construct the appropriate data structures, the student improves the workability of dBASE for his or her application.

Fundamentals: Multi-user

Completion Objective The student will be able to use unique features found in multi-user database systems.
Subject Detailed:

1. File lockout and record lockout are defined and illustrated.
2. Purpose in executing multi-user features in program execution.

Purpose(s) This knowledge increases the range of utility for a dBASE application.

SYSTEM DESIGN

Systems Design (Chapter 8)

Completion Objective The student will be able to define and use the methods and tools of a systems analyst.
Subject Detailed:

1. System defined and examples given.
2. System analysis defined and broken into component parts: process analysis final outcome analysis.
3. Tools in final outcome analysis.
4. Management information systems (MIS) defined and broken into component parts: planning, administration, and operations.
5. Software for MIS by component part.
6. Accounting information systems defined and detailed: transaction network, three primary accounting reports and accounting cycle.
7. Operational business information model.

Purpose(s) Mastery of the concepts and tools of the systems analyst aids in the alignment of an organization's objectives and goals with its information.

Database Design (Chapter 9)

Completion Objective The student will be able to properly design a database.
Subject Detailed:

1. Data file design: removing all repeating fields, correct for partial dependence, correct for transitive dependence.
2. Linkage of data files: tree and network linkages, cyclical linkages, naturally inherent and business rule linkages, adjustment to compensation for machine performances.
3. Future changes: hidden keys, addition of dependent fields, and high-usage of secondary key.

Purpose(s) To minimize future database restructuring, application program rewriting, and redundant data. This leads to increased data integrity and faster data searching times.

System Documentation (Chapter 10)

Completion Objective The student will be able to write system documentation which can serve as complete specifications to the programmer, a teaching aid to the user, or as a document between the user and developer.
Subject Detailed Definition and explanation of the following with relationship to complete documentation:

1. Startup
2. System Limitations
3. Log of Changes
4. Data Structures
5. Program Logic
6. Reports

Purpose(s) To achieve a maximum amount of recorded pre-plannning which can be used for the substance of a contract, specifications for the programmer, or as a teaching document for the user.

System Security, Recovery, and Backup (Chapter 11)

Completion Objective The student will be able to deter unauthorized viewing or editing of data, and recover data affected by power pollutants or equipment malfunctions.
Subject Detailed Definition and explanation of:

1. Security systems including: user logon sequence, access level structure, user log.
2. Implementation (Program Control) limited access to menu options, separate menus per class of users.
3. System crashes defined
      a. Power pollutants such as blackouts and brownouts, voltage transients, electrical noise.
      b. Equipment malfunctions such as disk damage, parity errors.
4. Crash Recovery
      a. dBASE data file structures affected.
      b. Recovery procedures, "never update in-place" rule, date-and-time field for time-stamping.

c. System backup.
d. Catastrophe.

Purpose(s) Learning system security and recovery in order to protect data.

IMPLEMENTATION

Implementation: Preliminaries (Chapter 12)

Completion Objective The student will be able to use the implementation section to its fullest and will implement two basic ground rules for preventive programming: making backup copies and closing files. The student will be able to identify the necessary or optional files in order to run dBASE or execute a feature. The student will understand command syntax of both dBASE II and dBASE III. The student will be able to describe the correct installation procedure for each version of dBASE. The student will know how to set the correct operating system configurations and will understand the use of buffers. The student will know about the large number of add-on software available for dBASE.

Subject Detailed Define and explain:

1. Organization of Implementation Section and purpose in its construction
2. Backup and close files
3. Necessary Files and Optional Files: dBASE III version 1.00, dBASE II version 2.4x, and dBASE II version 2.3x.
4. Filenames syntax.
5. Installation requirements and procedures.
6. Operating System Configurations. To increase speed for dBASE II, mandatory for dBASE III: system parameters in Config.sys for DOS to change the number of buffers and files and how to speed up dBASE III search for any editor.
7. dBASE Buffer Structure.
8. Use of optional dBASE III Configuration File called Config.db.
9. Add-On Software.

Purpose(s) By addressing these preliminary issues, a programmer is able to use dBASE to begin programming. This includes whatever version or configuration is appropriate for the intended application.

Implementation: Program Documentation (Chapter 13)

Completion Objective The student or programmer will be able to write standardized code that is fully documented for ease of reading and debugging.

Subject Detailed Documentation standards defined, illustrated, and justified:

1. Filenames: categories of database system, separator, unique function, dot, extension.
2. Alias Names: dBASE II—two work areas of Primary and Secondary; dBASE III—ten work areas designated by alias.
3. Field Names: descriptive vs. cryptic, logic fields, reserved words, and capitalization.
4. Memory Variable (Memvar) Names: lower case, descriptive vs. cryptic; adding "m" descriptive to take advantage of RELEASE ALL LIKE, RELEASE ALL EXCEPT, and SAVE ALL LIKE; distinguishing between numeric memvar and character memvar.

5. Program Documentation: dBASE comment commands, * and NOTE; headers to command files; footers to command files; indentation in command files; capitalization for dBASE reserved words.
6. dBASE Language use of four-letter abbreviations.
7. Algorithms: recording details for documentation, including the structure of a file to generate a memvar listing; end structure comments noting structural ending statements in lengthy conditional structures.

Purpose(s) By learning and following these program documentation standards, the student or programmer has adequate later references noted in order to quickly debug, clarify design, or implement future modifications.

Command File Handling (Chapter 14)

Completion Objective The student will be able to:

1. Write command files using dBASE's four programming structures.
2. Define the constituents of a command line.
3. Correctly use dBASE III's procedure file.
4. Demonstrate "parameter passing."
5. Write programs which use multiple command files or procedures.
6. Set up a subroutine library.
7. Know about dBASE RunTime.

Subject Detailed:

1. What dBASE III structured programming commands are.
2. Command file definition.
3. Command line definition and comparison to an English sentence.
4. dBASE's method of "parsing" a command line defined.
5. Basic programming structures defined and illustrated.
6. Nesting defined and diagrammed.
7. dBASE III's "procedure" file defined.
8. Data exchange among command files defined and illustrated.
9. Programming vocabulary delineated and defined.
10. dBASE III algorithms to demonstrate the use of subroutines.
11. Recursion is defined, and the proper way to use multiple command files in a program is illustrated.
12. How to set up a routine library.
13. RunTime explained.
14. Work-arounds for dBASE II versions 2.3x, 2.4.

Purpose(s) As a result of learning how to handle command files, the student has the foundation for writing programs.

Implementation: Working Environment (Chapter 15)

Completion Objective The student will be able to set the conditions of the working environment in order to achieve the characteristics desired of the operations.

Subject Detailed:

1. Definition of Working Environment.
2. Environmental changes basic rules defined.
3. Set parameters, type, and default listings given.
4. Set parameters given by process affected.
5. Set parameters defined as well as delineated.
6. Algorithms to demonstrate the management of the working environment.

Purpose(s) By knowing how to manipulate the working environment, the students enhance their ability to make dBASE execute their desired application.

Implementation: Data Handling (Chapter 16)

Completion Objective The student will be able to use the power inherent in the use of operators, functions, and expressions to store, evaluate, and output data.

Subject Detailed Definitions and examples of:

1. Data types: direct vs. indirect handling
2. Operators which function for each data type: numeric, character, date, relational, and logical.
3. Functions to evaluate data and return results: character processes, database processes, date processes, numeric processes, output processes, system processes, validation processes.
4. Definition and examples of expressions.
5. Examination of general data functions: TEST(), TYPE().
6. In-depth analysis of each data type including the appropriate functions and algorithms.

Purpose(s) This analysis constitutes one of the most important language level blocks of information. A thorough understanding enables the student to construct multiple ways of data handling.

Implementation: Memory Variables (Chapter 17)

Completion Objective The student will be able to use memory variables for the storage of temporary or "working" data.

Subject Detailed:

1. Definition and purpose of memory variables.
2. Command summary for memory variable implementation.
3. Specifications and characteristics of memory variables.
4. Use of the Macro and appropriate algorithms.
5. The effects of redundancy.
6. Implementing permanent memory variables.
7. Memory management with memory variables.

Purpose(s) Students can use memory variables to:

1. Hold frequently used constants.
2. Save communications from the operator.
3. Serve as a "buffer" area for data entry.

4.   Save results of expressions and functions.
5.   Serve as a scratch pad for numeric equations and counters.

Implementation: Screen Handling (Chapter 18)

Completion Objective The student will be able to construct appropriate screens for the operator.
Subject Detailed:

1.   Purpose of screen handling as a distinct topic.
2.   How to build screens for easier use.
3.   Screen conventions.
4.   Example screens: main menu, data entry, report menu.
5.   In-depth analysis of output and input screen programming with dBASE including commands, functions, set parameters, and algorithms.

Purpose(s) The correct construction of screens is the point of ultimate human interface with the computer. The usability of the program by the operator must be fully considered and planned for by the programmer. Mastery of screen handling enables the student to accomplish the correct construction of screens.

Implementation: Data File Handling (Chapter 19)

Completion Objective The student will be able to manipulate database files and their contents.
Subject Detailed:

1.   Opening and closing a data file defined with potential problems, dBASE manipulation thereof, and appropriate commands explained. Algorithms: Periodic File Saving. The effects of subroutines on open data files.
2.   Adding data to a database file defined and commands given for adding from another file, the keyboard, and memvars.
3.   The purpose in preallocating disk space.
4.   Ordering the file by its data defined by its revision of the natural order and the two commands: INDEX and SORT. SET parameters, commands, and algorithms to do routine maintenance; case independent order; true data order; descending date order; set reverse on; ordering by mixed data types; index file size; and related work-arounds.
5.   Moving around in the file is defined in two categorical divisions of sequential and random with emphasis placed upon the power inherent in the scope and condition of the appropriate commands. Utilization of commands to move by data or by record are explained and illustrated. Command and function summary with algorithms illustrating:

     FOR vs. WHILE
     Eliminate separating blanks
     Binary locate
     Check for duplicates

6.   Changing the data in the file is defined as a variation on adding data with locating being the first step. An examination is done of each mode and the command and set parameters.

7. Displaying the data in the file is examined as a command definition basis with the appropriate SET parameters. The algorithms given are for interactive display, multiple screens, and work-arounds.

8. Copying the data to another file is defined with emphasis on the process. Functions, set parameters and appropriate commands are accompanied by algorithms to obtain faster copy and work-arounds.

9. Working with multiple files and multiple disks is explained for both dBASE II and III. Set parameters and commands are accompanied by algorithms to close multiple files and use more files per area.

10. Work-arounds are found in all appropriate areas.

Purpose(s) The correct implementation of database file handling permits the execution of well-designed programs in dBASE. The clean coding of data and their files constitutes the heart of the database system.

Implementation: Foreign and Closed Files (Chapter 20)

Completion Objective The student will be able to identify foreign files, delineate which are executable vs. non-executable and know how to use foreign files in dBASE.

Subject Detailed:

1. Foreign files broken into the categories of executable vs. non-executable.
2. How dBASE exchanges data with foreign files.
3. System Data Format and Delimited files.
4. Methods of working with formats and the associated dBASE commands.
5. dBASE requirements of working with closed files.
6. All dBASE commands associated in working with foreign files are defined relative to that association.
7. Algorithm: "dBASE Text Processing"

Purpose(s) In knowing how to manipulate foreign files within dBASE, the student gains further flexibility in construction and functionality of applications programs.

Printing and Form Generators (Chapter 21)

Completion Objective The student will be able to produce printed output from a dBASE application, when and how desired.

Subject Detailed:

1. Definition and explanation of formatted versus unformatted modes.
2. Changing printer configurations for those printers addressable from the software, with examples for the Epson FX-80.
3. Built-in form generators for dBASE II, III.
4. Forcing last line buffers to print.
5. Controlling page ejects in the report form generator for dBASE II and III.
6. Vocabulary of commands and functions controlling printing and form generators.
7. Algorithms: print screen function, page counter, column formatting, blank zeros in report forms (II), and enhanced data output.
8. Work-arounds to anomalies.

Purpose(s) The enhanced ability of the student to implement printing and form generation with dBASE II and III adds to the quality of hard-copy output.

Assembly Language Interface (Chapter 22)

Completion Objective The student will be able to execute assembly language routines from within a dBASE program.
Subject Detailed:

1. Definition of Assembly Language and the purpose for using it with a dBASE program.
2. dBASE II's four commands and one function to access memory directly, defined and examples provided.
3. How to avoid overwriting dBASE when directly storing to memory.
4. Working in CP/M-86, PC-DOS, and MS-DOS environments.
5. Assembly Language interface environment defined.
6. Algorithms given to test a date.

Purpose(s) By knowing how to interface assembly language routines into a dBASE command file, the student is able to perform operations not available in dBASE.

Implementation: Multi-User Environment (Chapter 23)

Completion Objective The student will be able to use two new functions and two new commands in dBASE II to lock and unlock data files for simultaneous use under a multi-user environment.
Subject Detailed:

1. Definitions and uses of: LOCK (), LOCKNDX(), UNLOCK, and UNLOCK INDEX.
2. dBASE's implementation of the above commands and functions.
3. "Active commands," defined for writing to the file, vs. "passive commands."
4. Algorithms on: 3Com Ethernet and dBASE Multi-User.

Purpose(s) These skills expand the use of dBASE for the student into the multi-user environment.

Debugging, Optimizing and Benchmarking (Chapter 24)

Completion Objective The student will be able to fully implement a structured approach to locating and correcting bugs and benchmarking and optimizing code.
Subject Detailed:

1. dBASE programming bugs categorized, defined, and illustrated.
2. Debugging Techniques systematized into the two areas of isolating and fixing with steps to sequentially follow in each.
3. Vocabulary defined.
4. Algorithms for optimizing code and benchmarking.

Purpose(s) The advantages of using a structured approach to debugging are innumerable, beginning with one's sanity. Once the program is debugged, the ability to benchmark and optimize execution will add the polish of a professional programmer.

Implementation: The Interactive Mode (Chapter 25)

Completion Objective The student will be able identify the interactive commands broken down into commands with full control vs. commands with limiting options. The student will know how to best use the interactive command MODIFY COMMAND.

Subject Detailed:

1. Full control commands itemized vs. limiting option commands.
2. MODIFY COMMAND capabilities detailed.
3. Interactive Mode commands defined.
4. Algorithms: "Command File Dot Prompt"

Purpose(s) The ability either to use dBASE interactively or to allow an operator of an applications program to do so is the knowledge to be gained from this chapter. It is a primary level of knowledge necessary for every user.

GLOSSARY

ALGORITHM

A prescribed set of specific actions or rules for the solution of a problem in a finite number of steps.

ANOMALY

A deviation from the model. Something that does not operate entirely as intended under a certain set of conditions. Marked by irregular or abnormal performance. In programming, a bug can be considered an anomaly.

ARGUMENT

A value supplied to a command, function, or subroutine. Used interchangeably with *parameter*.

ARRAY

A group of items arranged in a meaningful pattern, such as a table. A data structure in which each item can be identified by its unique position in the arrangement.

ASCII

Acronym for American Standard Code for Information Interchange, the system by which letters, punctuation, spaces, control codes, etc. are encoded into numerical values for interpretation by the computer.

BASIC

Acronym for Beginner's All-purpose Symbolic Instruction Code, a widely-known programming language available on microcomputers.

BATCH

A sequence of commands that perform a given task and that can be put into operation with a single command.

BAUD

The rate of information transfer between two terminals and/or peripherals. Often, but incorrectly, used as a synonym for "bits per second." It actually refers to the number of times the signal changes per second. This is equivalent to the bits per second rate in many, but not all, cases. A character-per-second value is usually reached by dividing a bits-per-second value by 10.

BCD

Acronym for Binary Coded Decimal, a method for representing decimal numbers (0-9) as 4-bit, 6-bit, or 8-bit (one byte) symbols. An example, is 7 = 0111.

BDOS

Acronym for Basic Disk Operating System. In CP/M, the BDOS is part of the operating system which provides a standard interface allowing application programs to access the operating system service routines. The operating system interfaces directly with the hardware and provides low level routines to perform such functions as sending a character to the screen, accepting a character from the keyboard, or opening a disk file. These routines can be called by application programs via the BDOS.

BENCHMARK

A program used to test and compare different hardware and software systems.

BINARY

The fundamental language of the computer itself. Letters and numbers are represented by groups of ones and zeros, and these in turn represent the off-and-on flow of electricity through the circuitry of the microprocessor. A condition in which there are two possible alternatives.

BIOS

Acronym for Basic Input/Output System, the section of the operating system that is responsible for interfacing to the hardware environment.

BIT

BIT stands for BInary digiT. It represents the smallest unit of information in a digital computer. It can have a value of either 1 or 0 and represents a switch.

BOOLEAN

For George Boole, English mathematician, 1815-1864. Boole developed mathematical tools to express logical concepts. Boolean algebra is a system of logic functions and operators which permit computations and operations on binary (True/False, On/Off) values.

BOOT

Short for "bootstrap," this refers to the initial commands necessary to load the remainder of the operating system. Thus, the system is "booted" or "pulled up by its own bootstraps."

BUFFER

A storage area of memory that holds data during transfer from one device to another. Buffers often compensate for differing rates of flow between terminals and/or peripherals.

BUG

An error in either the software or hardware of a computer system. One story goes that an early IBM mainframe went down, and the problem was discovered to be an insect caught in the circuitry.

BYTE

A unit of storage. One byte is equivalent to one character, or 8 bits, of storage.

CANCEL

To nullify a command already given, or to abort a function in progress.

CARRIAGE RETURN

Synonymous with the return lever of a typewriter, this key returns the cursor to the left margin and also provides the ENTER function. A carriage return is often used with a line feed to move the cursor to the begining of the next line.

CENTRAL PROCESSING UNIT (CPU)

The main functional unit of a microcomputer. It consists of a chip which executes program instructions and its surrounding circuitry, together often referred to as the system or "mother" board. This chip, actually a microprocessor in itself, performs all the primary handling of the data and for that reason is often called "the computer itself."

CHIP

A tiny, thin square of semiconducting material, such as silicon, carefully etched to produce an integrated circuit. This miniaturization of electronic circuitry gives us the capacity of an early mainframe in the desktop computer.

CLOCK

An internal piece of hardware that produces a regular continuous pulse. The clock is used to synchronize computer functions.

CLOCK SPEED

The number of pulses per second produced by the computer's clock, usually measured in MHz (megahertz), or millions of cycles per second.

COBOL

Acronym for COmmon Business Oriented Language: The most commonly used high-level language for business programming.

CODE

The set of symbols that represents instructions to the computer. "To code" is synonymous with "to program," and "code" is used as a noun in the same way as "program."

COMMAND

1. An instruction or request for the computer to perform a particular operation.
2. The verb that begins an instruction to dBASE and always appears as the first word in a command line. Specifically called the command *verb*.
3. The entire instruction to dBASE on one command line, including the command verb and all of its parameters. Specifically called the command *statement*.

COMPILER

A program which translates a high-level language, such as COBOL or Fortran, into a form which is executable by the computer. A compiler completes this translation process before the program is executed. Compare INTERPRETER.

COMPUTER

An electronic device that is capable of recording data, manipulating it as prescribed in a written program, and displaying the results.

CONCATENATE

To attach, or "add," one character string to another.

CONSOLE

The portion of the computer hardware that is used to interface with the operator. Specifically refers to the display portion of the console when used as a SET parameter in dBASE.

CONSTANT

A data item whose value cannot be changed during execution of the program. A constant may be either a *literal* or a *variable*.

COPY

To make a duplicate of. This operation can occur between disk and memory, disk and disk, file and file, etc.

CORE

The internal memory of the computer. The core capacity, or memory of the computer itself (this does not include disk storage) is determined by the amount of semiconductor memory available.

CP/M

Control Program for Microcomputers, an operating system for microcomputers developed by Digital Research, Inc.

CPS

Characters Per Second, the standard measure of printer speed.

CPU

See Central Processing Unit.

CRT

Cathode Ray Tube. This television-like screen, together with the keyboard, make up the terminal of the computer.

CURSOR

A special marker or indicator on the display screen designed to direct your attention to where the next letter or number will appear. The cursor travels along with the flow of communication between operator and computer.

CYCLE

Synonymous with one pulse of the computer's internal clock. The CPU's speed is determined by this independently-generated time frame. For example, a function could be said to take ten cycles (or ten pulses of the clock).

DDT

Dynamic Debugging Tool. This is a CP/M utility designed to run, test, modify, and debug machine language programs.

DEBUG

To find and correct all the errors in a program or in the hardware. Also the name of a DOS debugging utility similar to DDT above.

DECREMENT

To decrease a value. A decrease of one is implied if no number is specified.

DENSITY

The amount of information a disk can hold in relation to its surface area. Density is dependent upon a disk's formatting. The formatting characteristics are determined by how many tracks per inch and how many sectors per track are available for storage. A single density 8-inch floppy disk can hold 241K. A double density disk of the same size can hold roughly twice that amount, and a quad density disk can hold about four times that amount.

DEVICE

Any part of the computer that can send or receive information. For example, a keyboard is an input device, a CRT is an output device and a disk drive is both, or an I/O device.

DIGITAL

Refers to communicating data via an electronic signal according to its presence or absence. Numbers and words are expressed using combinations of 0 and 1, or on and off. For comparison, analog computers express different quantities by using a signal of varying intensity.

DIRECTORY

A summary of all the files on a disk, analogous to a table of contents.

DISK

A flat, circular disk of magnetic material, on which data is recorded by a disk drive. See FLOPPY DISK, HARD DISK.

DISK DRIVE

A peripheral device that reads information from and writes information to a disk.

DOCUMENTATION

The literature accompanying a program or computer that explains its purpose, capabilities, and operation. It guides the operator in successfully using the product.

DOS

Disk Operating System. DOS is often used as a shortened form of PC-DOS or MS-DOS, an operating system designed for the Intel 8086 family of microprocessors by Microsoft, Inc.

DOT-MATRIX PRINTER

A printer that creates images by printing a series of dots very close together so that the characters appear solid.

DRIVER

A portion of the computer's operating system which handles the input and output (I/O) to peripheral devices. The driver is otherwise known as a device handler.

DS

Abbreviation for double sided, in reference to a floppy disk format.

DSDD

Double sided double density, in reference to a floppy disk format. (SSDD = single sided double density)

DUMP

To output information to a screen or printer.

EBCDIC

Stands for Extended Binary Coded Decimal Information Code. The code or format used to represent alphanumeric and special characters on IBM mainframe computers. Microcomputers use the ASCII representation for alphanumerics.

ED

A line editor that comes with CP/M.

EDLIN

A line editor which comes with MS DOS similar to ED.

ENCRYPTION

The act of replacing recognizable symbols with unrecognizable symbols.

END OF FILE (EOF)

The end of a quantity of data, signified by special markers. The standard value to mark the end of an ASCII text file is the symbol ^Z (decimal 26).

ENDLESS LOOP

See *LOOP, ENDLESS.*

EXECUTE

The carrying out of command instructions by the computer. Used interchangeably with *run*.

EXPRESSION

A meaningful combination of operators, constants, and variables used in a program to perform a desired operation.

FETCH

To obtain a value, usually from RAM, ROM or mass storage, and place it into a CPU register or some other location.

FIFO

Acronym for First In, First Out. FIFO defines the order in which data in a queue is processed. The most recent element to arrive is placed at the end of the queue, and the element that has been waiting the longest is processed first. This is in contrast to LIFO.

FILE

A collection of related data. The information within a dBASE file is stored as individual records.

FILE CONTROL BLOCK (FCB)

A block of data which contains information necessary to define a disk file. The FCB contains information such as the filename, the file size, and which drive the file is located on. The FCB is held in memory when the file is in use.

FIRMWARE

A program that has been permanently recorded onto a chip. Frequently used programs are often stored this way and cannot be accidentally erased or lost.

FLAG

A variable within a program used to indicate some difference, error, or deviation in the data.

FLOPPY DISK

A flexible disk of magnetic material, protected by a cardboard envelope used to store data and programs. Floppies are most commonly either 8, 5 1/4, or 3 1/2 inches in diameter.

FOREGROUND

In a multi-user or multi-tasking computer system, those programs that take priority over others that are executing simultaneously. Programs of lesser priority run in the background.

FORTRAN

Stands for FORmula TRANslation, an older but still popular high-level programming language, used in scientific and technical applications.

FUNCTION

A built-in subroutine that performs common data handling operations. An input is evaluated and a result is returned.

HANDSHAKING

When one device (e.g. computer) is sending data to a second device (e.g. printer) faster than the second device can process it, the second device must send a signal to let the first device know when it is ready to receive more data. Otherwise, some data will be lost. Handshaking is the process of one device querying another to see if it is ready to receive data before sending. The transmitting device will not send until the receiving device sends a signal saying that it is ready.

HARD DISK

A rigid metal disk coated with magnetic material, which has a far greater storage capacity than a floppy disk. Hard disks are often permanently installed in their case. Some hard disks are removable, but the read/write heads are enclosed with the disks in a special container which prevents dust or other contamination from contacting the disk.

HARDWARE

The mechanical and electrical or "hard" part of a computer system. This is in contrast to software, the programs that are executed by the hardware.

HEAD

The electromagnetic device, residing within the disk drive, that both reads and writes information on a floppy or hard disk.

HEX

Short for hexadecimal.

HEXADECIMAL

Another name for base 16. In a hexadecimal digit, there are 16 possible values: the numbers 0-9 and letters A-F. Hexadecimal is a convenient and compact way to represent binary information.

HOME

The upper left corner of the CRT, where the first character printed appears.

HOUSEKEEPING

Those functions necessary to the operation of a computer but not directly related to the current program in progress. Examples of housekeeping include opening and closing files, clearing memory, verification functions, and so on.

HZ

Short for Hertz, one cycle per second.

I/O

Short for Input/Output.

INCREMENT

To increase a value. By one is implied if no number is specified.

INITIALIZE

To set up in preparation for operation. For example, one initializes a disk by formatting it.

INPUT

Data coming into the CPU or RAM of the computer from the terminal, drives, and so forth.

INSTRUCTION

A program step, or command, that tells the computer exactly what to do for a particular operation.

INTEGRATED SOFTWARE

Programs that interrelate, eliminating the need for entering data twice for two different operations. Framework is an example of an integrated program. It contains a spreadsheet, word processor, database, and graphics package in a single program.

INTEL HEX FORMAT

A standard format for storing binary information on disk or tape.

INTERFACE

The connection or boundary between any two parts of a computer system, including any of its devices, the software, or the human operator. Two components must by properly interfaced before they can interact.

INTERPRETER

A type of translator which converts a program into machine language. An interpreter accomplishes the translation process while the program is running. dBASE is an example of an interpreter. Compare COMPILER.

INTERRUPT

To stop the operation in progress for new instructions.

ITERATION

The act of repeating, such as executing the same set of commands in a loop.

KEYBOARD

A device the operator uses to input information, analogous to a typewriter.

KHZ

Short for KiloHertz, or 1,000 cycles per second.

KILOBYTE

1024 bytes, two raised to the tenth power. Since each byte represents one character, one kilobyte produces about 150 written words. The RAM of most microcomputers varies from 48K to 512K. Abbreviation: "K."

LANGUAGE

A set of symbols that a programmer uses to encode instructions to the computer. A low level language requires less interpretation by the computer but is more difficult to program in than a higher level language. Higher level languages more closely approximate human communication. Languages must be translated into a form that is understood by a computer. This translation is usually accomplished by a compiler or interpreter. Different languages were designed for different purposes, for example, FORTRAN for technical uses, COBOL for business, and BASIC for more general purposes.

LIFO

Acronym for Last in, First Out. This is the order in which a stack of information is handled by a program. The element that was most recently stored on the stack (last in) is the first to be processed (first out).

LITERAL

The actual value or content of a data item. A literal is also a *constant* because it cannot be changed during program execution.

LOOP

The repetition of a series of commands. For example, a loop can perform the same set of instructions on every specified record, until all records have been processed.

LOOP, ENDLESS

See ENDLESS LOOP.

MACHINE CODE

The native language understood by the computer consisting of binary information, 0's and 1's. Machine code can be executed directly by the CPU.

MACRO

A single word that represents an entire subroutine in assembly language. Large groups of frequently used commands can easily be programmed by entry of the correct symbol or "macro." dBASE also allows the construction of macros.

MAIN MEMORY

The electronic storage area of the computer itself, exclusive of disks or any other external memory. Programs and data to be processed are first loaded into the main memory, or RAM, from the disk. Main memory is volatile and will not retain data if power is removed.

MASS STORAGE

Memory that is external to the computer and non-volatile, such as floppy disks, hard disks, magnetic tape, etc.

MEDIA

Any material data are written to and read from, including paper tape, punch cards, or the magnetic surfaces of hard and floppy disks.

MEGABYTE

1,000 kilobytes or 1,048,576 bytes. Abbreviation: MB. See KILOBYTE.

MEMORY

Any storage area for data and programs, internal or external to the computer.

METAVARIABLE

From METAlanguage VARIABLE. Metalanguage is a language that is used to describe another language, which in this case is dBASE. A metalanguage variable is a description of an element in the command line syntax that is to be supplied when actually running the code. Symbols, words, and

conventions were formalized in the metalanguage called *Bakus-Naur Form*, which specifies that the angle brackets <> be used to delimit metavariables. A metavariable example is <command filename>.

MHZ

Short for MegaHertz, or 1,000,000 cycles per second.

MICROCOMPUTER

The smallest computer, compared to minicomputers and mainframe computers, made possible by the development of single-chip microprocessors.

MICROPROCESSOR

An integrated circuit which contains many of the elements of a computer. A microprocessor is sometimes called "a computer on a chip," also known as a CPU. Microprocessors are also found in non-computer devices such as printers and terminals. A device that contains a microprocessor is often referred to as "smart" as in "smart terminal."

MICROSECOND

One millionth of a second.

MILLISECOND

One thousandth of a second.

MNEMONIC

A code or symbol that facilitates remembering its operation or purpose. Pronounced "neh-mah-nick." For example, RET is a mnemonic for RETurn.

MODE

An environmental state of conditions under which operations occur. Full-screen mode and interactive mode are examples.

MODEM

An acronym for MOdulator DEModulator. A device which converts signals generated by the computer into a form which can be transmitted over telephone lines or optical cables.

MODULE

A set of related commands within a routine.

MONITOR

The display screen in a computer system.

MULTI-TASKING

A multi-tasking system allows two or more tasks or programs to execute simultaneously. Concurrent CP/M is an example of such a system.

MULTI-USER

A multi-user system allows two or more users to share the resources of a computer and its peripherals.

NULL STRING

A character string with a length of zero. Formed by placing two string delimiters next to each other with nothing in between. For example, STORE "" TO <null variable>. Not allowed in dBASE II.

NULL VARIABLE

A character type variable with a length of zero. A variable containing a null string. Not allowed in dBASE II.

OBJECT CODE

Usually object code is synonymous with machine code. However, in some cases, object code may refer to a form of compact intermediate code which is close to machine code but still requires some translation (interpretation) before it can be executed by the computer.

OEM

An acronym for Original Equipment Manufacturer. This is a company which purchases components, and sometimes software, to add to their products before they are sold.

OPERATING SYSTEM

Software which manages the resources of the computer system. The operating system provides a uniform interface between application programs and the hardware. It also provides a set of utilities to perform frequent tasks such as formatting and copying disks, editing files, and debugging programs.

OPERATOR

1. A symbol representing an operation, such as addition, to be performed on two parameters, or "operands." 2. The person operating the computer.

ORG

Abbreviation for ORiGin. In Assembly Language programs, the ORG defines the starting address of the code.

OUTPUT

Information sent from a computer to a peripheral device such as a printer, disk drive, or terminal.

PARAMETER

A value supplied to a command, function, or subroutine. Used interchangeably with *argument*.

PERIPHERAL

An external device which is attached to the computer such as a disk drive, printer, terminal, or modem.

PRINTER

A device which prints alphanumeric and graphical data that has been output from a computer. There are many different types of printers but they are all designed to produce images on paper.

PROCEDURE

A complete program or subroutine contained within a *procedure file*. Handled by dBASE essentially the same as a command file.

PROCEDURE FILE

A collection of up to thirty-two individual *procedures* in one file.

PROGRAM

A sequence of instructions that is ultimately executed by the CPU. Also called software.

RAM

An Acronym for Random Access Memory. This is the main memory in a computer composed of semiconductor material. It is also called Read/Write memory, meaning that the data can be easily read or altered. RAM is volatile and will lose its data if the power is removed.

READ

To retrieve information from a storage device such as a disk or tape, or from memory.

RECORD

A record is a body of related information composed of fields.

RECURSION

A method of repeating a routine whereby the routine calls itself. The process of a routine (R1) which, while executing, either calls itself or calls another routine (R2) which then either calls R1 or still another routine (R3), which calls R1 or R2, and so on.

ROM

An acronym for Read Only Memory. ROM is a type of memory which is non-volatile. The contents of a ROM is permenantly recorded and may be read by the CPU whenever needed.

ROUTINE

A set of commands that perform a particular operation.

RUN

To operate or execute a program.

SECTOR

The smallest unit of storage on a disk that may be read. A sector is usually between 128 and 512 bytes in size.

SET PARAMETER

An argument of the SET command. Used to establish a surrounding, or "working," environment that will influence the operation of some commands.

SOFTWARE

A series of instructions which is executed by the computer. A program.

SORT

To place information in a predetermined sequence such as alphabetically or in numeric order.

SOURCE CODE

Computer instructions written by a human, usually in a high level language such as BASIC, dBASE, or Pascal. Source code is translated to machine code which is executed by the computer.

STACK

A data structure used to save temporary information during program execution. A stack is usually a sequential set of memory locations where data is stored on a LIFO basis. The last data "pushed" (stored) on the stack is the first data to be "popped" (retrieved) off the stack.

STRING

Alphanumeric data or character type data. Any combination of letters, numbers, or special characters (*,&,%,$, etc.). Numbers represented as strings cannot be used in calculations unless they are first converted into numeric type data.

SUBROUTINE

A routine that is designed to carry out a specific operation or action when called by another routine. A subroutine is subordinate to the master, or "main," program which calls it. The main routine temporarily passes control to the subroutine which then executes and returns control to the main routine. Examples are a subroutine which computes the sine of an angle, or a subroutine which sorts a list of names by zip code and prints a mailing list.

SUBSTRING

A portion, or "subset," of a string. For example, *alpha* is a substring of *alphabet*.

SYSTEM

A series of related parts or components which work together. A computer system contains elements such as a CPU, a terminal, a printer, an operating system, and application software.

THROUGHPUT

The overall speed with which a computer system can process information or accomplish a task.

TPI

An acronym for Tracks Per Inch. Refers to how many recording tracks per inch are available. The greater this number the greater the storage capacity of the disk. An IBM PC floppy disk has forty-eight tracks per inch.

TRACK

A circular path on the disk. Tracks form a series of concentric rings on the disk surface where each ring is a separate track.

TRANSIENT PROGRAM

A program that is not part of the operating system. An application program.

TRUNCATE

To abruptly cut off before the existing end. To shorten.

USER FRIENDLY

An implementation that contributes to the quality of a person's experience in using it. User friendly implies that something is easy to understand and use, especially for beginning, or "novice," users.

UTILITY

A program used to perform common tasks such as formatting disks, sorting information, copying files, or debugging programs.

VARIABLE

A data item with a label, or "name," that can be used by referring to the variable name instead of the *literal* value. The value of a variable may be changed during program execution if the program allows. dBASE has two variable types: database field and memory. For example, in the expression STORE "JOHN" TO NAME, NAME is a variable which has been assigned the literal value of JOHN.

VOCABULARY

A collection of words or phrases that compose a language.

WINCHESTER DISK

A high-capacity fixed disk in a sealed unit. The Winchester technology was developed by IBM in the 1970s. A hard disk.

ASHTON-TATE ■™
PUBLISHING GROUP

8901 South La Cienega Boulevard,
Inglewood, CA 90301, (213) 642-4637

ORDER FORM

FORM OF PAYMENT:

☐ Check ☐ MasterCard ☐ VISA

TITLE	Quantity	Price Each	Total Price	TITLE	Quantity	Price Each	Total Price
Advanced Programmer's Guide Featuring dBASE III and dBASE II		28.95		Framework: On-the-Job Applications		19.95	
Application Junction (1985 version)		29.95		Get Connected: A Guide to Telecommunications		24.95	
BASIC Booster Library for the Apple® Macintosh		29.95*		IBM PC Public Domain Software, Volume I		24.95	
BASIC Booster Library for the IBM® PC		29.95*		Introduction to UNIX™ System V		17.95	
Data Management for Professionals		15.95		MacBASIC Programming		24.95	
dBASE II® for Every Business		19.95		MACPACK: Creative Activities with MacPaint and MacWrite		15.95	
dBASE II for the First-Time User		19.95		Personal Computing and C		19.95	
dBASE II Guide for Small Business		24.95		Personal Financial Management		29.95*	
dBASE II Progammer's Companion		29.95*		Soft Words, Hard Words: A Common-Sense Guide to Creative Documentation		14.95	
dBASE III™ for Every Business		19.95		Special Effects Library for the Apple IIc and Apple IIe		29.95*	
dBASE III™ for Sales Professionals		29.95*		Special Effects Library for the Commodore 64™		29.95*	
dBASE III Trail Guide		29.95*		System Design Guide Featuring dBASE II		18.50	
Everyman's Database Primer Featuring dBASEII		19.95		The Illustrated dBASE II Book		16.95	
Everyman's Database Primer Featuring dBASE III		19.95		The Reference Encyclopedia for the IBM Personal Computer		69.95	
Exploring Pascal: A Compiler for Beginners		39.95*		Through the MicroMaze: A Visual Guide from Ashton-Tate		9.95	
Framework: A Developer's Handbook		24.95		Through the MicroMaze: A Visual Guide to Getting Organized		9.95	
Framework:™ An Introduction		15.95		Up and Running: Adventures of Software Entrepreneurs		15.95	
Framework: An Introduction to Programming		24.95		User's Guide to dBASE II		15.95	
Framework: A Programmer's Reference		24.95					

*Book/disk package.

Name: _____

Company: _____

Address: _____

City: _____ State: _____ Zip: _____

Phone: ( ) _____

SHIPPING CHARGES
(U.S. Domestic)

Books are mailed book rate and take 3-4 weeks to arrive.

Up to $20 . . . $2.00
$20.01 to $30 . . . $3.00
$30.01 to $40 . . . $4.00
$40.01 to $50 . . . $5.00
$50.01 to $60 . . . $6.00
Over $60 . . . $7.00

MERCHANDISE TOTAL	
SHIPPING CHARGE (See Chart)	
SUBTOTAL	
CA SALES TAX 6½% (Residents Only)	
ORDER TOTAL	

Thank You For Your Order

SURVEY

Thank you for purchasing an Ashton-Tate book.

Our readers are important to us. Please take a few moments to provide us with some information, so we can better serve you.

Once we receive your reader card, your name will be kept on file for information regarding program disks to accompany the book.

Name: _____

Company Name: _____

Address: _____

City/State: _____ Zip:_____

Country: _____ Date:_____

1) How did you first learn about this publication?
21-1 ( ) Someone who saw or bought it
-2 ( ) Software dealer or salesperson
-3 ( ) Hardware dealer or salesperson
-4 ( ) Advertising
-5 ( ) Published review
-6 ( ) Computer store display
-7 ( ) Computer show
-8 ( ) Book store
-9 ( ) Directly from Ashton-Tate

2) Where did you purchase this publication?
22-1 ( ) Directly from Ashton-Tate™
-2 ( ) From my dBASE II® Dealer
-3 ( ) Computer show
-4 ( ) Book store

3) Have you purchased other Ashton-Tate books and publications?
23-1 ( ) Yes 23-2 ( ) No
If Yes, please check which ones:
23- 3 ( ) *dBASE II for the First-Time User*
- 4 ( ) *Data Management for Professionals*
- 5 ( ) *System Design Guide*
- 6 ( ) *dNEWS™*
- 7 ( ) *Through the MicroMaze*
- 8 ( ) *Everyman's Database Primer*
- 9 ( ) *Reference Encyclopedia for the IBM® Personal Computer*
-10 ( ) *IBM PC Public Domain Software, Vol. I*

4) What type of software programs are you using now?
24- 1 ( ) Accounting
- 2 ( ) Spreadsheet
- 3 ( ) Word Processing
- 4 ( ) Other (Please specify) _____

_____

5) What type of software programs are you interested in?
25- 1 ( ) Academic/Scientific
- 2 ( ) Agriculture
- 3 ( ) Building
- 4 ( ) Business
- 5 ( ) Financial
- 6 ( ) Health Care
- 7 ( ) Home/Hobby
- 8 ( ) Insurance
- 9 ( ) Membership/Registry
-10 ( ) Professional
-11 ( ) Real Property
-12 ( ) Software Utilities
-13 ( ) Spreadsheet
-14 ( ) Integrated

6) Whom are you purchasing the book for?
27-1 ( ) Business
-2 ( ) Self

7a) Who will be the actual reader?
28-1 ( ) I will be
-2 ( ) Someone else will be

Title: _____

7b) What make and model computer do you use?
28-3 _____

8) Do you expect to purchase other software programs during the next 12 months? If so, what type?
29-1 ( ) Accounting
-2 ( ) Sales
-3 ( ) Inventory
-4 ( ) Other (Please specify)_____

_____

9) What subjects would you like to see discussed?
30-1 _____
_____
_____

10) How can we improve this book?
31-1 _____
_____
_____
_____

11) What is your primary business?
A. Computer Industry
32-1 ( ) Manufacturing
-2 ( ) Systems house
-3 ( ) DP supply house
-4 ( ) Software
-5 ( ) Retailing
-6 ( ) Other _____
B. Non-Computer Business
33-1 ( ) Manufacturing
-2 ( ) Retail trade
-3 ( ) Wholesale trade
-4 ( ) Financial, banking
-5 ( ) Real estate, insurance
-6 ( ) Engineering
-7 ( ) Government
-8 ( ) Education

34-1 ( ) Military
-2 ( ) Health services
-3 ( ) Legal services
-4 ( ) Transportation
-5 ( ) Utilities
-6 ( ) Communications
-7 ( ) Arts, music, film
-8 ( ) Other

12) What is your position and title? Please check one in each list
POSITION
35- 1 ( ) Data processing
- 2 ( ) Engineering
- 3 ( ) Marketing/Advertising
- 4 ( ) Sales
- 5 ( ) Financial
- 6 ( ) Legal
- 7 ( ) Administration
- 8 ( ) Research
- 9 ( ) Operations/production
-10 ( ) Distribution
-11 ( ) Education
-12 ( ) Other _____
TITLE
35-13 ( ) Owner
-14 ( ) Chairperson
-15 ( ) President
-16 ( ) Vice President
-17 ( ) Director
-18 ( ) Manager
-19 ( ) Dept. head
-20 ( ) Independent contractor
-21 ( ) Scientist
-22 ( ) Programmer
-23 ( ) Assistant
-24 ( ) Other _____

13) How many employees are in your company?
36-1 ( ) Less than 10
-2 ( ) 10 to 25
-3 ( ) 26 to 100
-4 ( ) 101 to 300
-5 ( ) 301 to 1,000
-6 ( ) over 1,000

14) I would like to remain on your mailing list.
37-1 ( ) Yes 37-2 ( ) No

38-1 I'd like to purchase additional copies of the current edition of this book at $28.95 plus $1.50 handling.
☐ My check is enclosed
My MasterCard/Visa card number is:

_____

Expiration date _____

Signature _____

BUSINESS REPLY MAIL

FIRST CLASS   PERMIT NO. 959   CULVER CITY, CA

POSTAGE WILL BE PAID BY ADDRESSEE

ASHTON · TATE ▪ ™

10150 WEST JEFFERSON BOULEVARD
CULVER CITY, CALIFORNIA 90230